from the

MODERN REPERTOIRE

Series Two

EDITED BY ERIC BENTLEY

From the
MODERN REPERTOIRE
Series Two

INDIANA UNIVERSITY PRESS

FOR NATANYA NEUMANN

Contents

Illustrations

Preface

This second series is perfectly continuous with the first. There is nothing to retract in the Preface to the earlier volume where the principles behind the whole enterprise are stated. Here are ten more plays: that is all. Only two have ever been published in America before, and even they have never before been anthologized. All seven translations have here their first American publication; three plays were specially translated for inclusion in this volume. All the translators—Maurice Edwards, David Magarshack, Jacques Barzun, Beatrice Gottlieb, William Becker, Winifred Smith, and Charles Laughton—are workers of high quality. All have written with the stage in view, and the last-named of them is after all a master of the actor's art. Only one of the ten playwrights in this book was also in the first series. This is Bertolt Brecht; and the reason is that his collected works, announced so long ago under my editorship, will appear piecemeal, from one series to the next, so long as there is no other way to get them into print. The publication of a radio play in the present volume marks a new departure and I felt that the reader would be glad to have Mr. MacNeice's notes on radio-writing, too; nevertheless, the play appears here for its intrinsic merits and not as "representing" another medium. There is another new departure: the inclusion of American authors. They were not excluded from the first on principle; indeed, T. S. Eliot might be considered American. But America really enters our scene with the publication of *him* and *The King and the Duke*: much is to be learned from both as to the legitimate resources and methods of an American theatre inspired by poets, not browbeaten by boobs, an American theatre emptied of morons and peopled with men of good will.

[E. B.]

Plans for the Future

Of Series One, it was necessary to write in the Preface: "if it is well-received, other volumes will follow." The same can now be said of Series Two. Among plays under consideration for Series Three (excluding those already listed in Series One, page xiv) are:

Jean Anouilh, *Medea* (tr. needed)
Guillaume Apollinaire, *The Breasts of Tiresias* (tr. Richard Grenier)
Bertolt Brecht, *The Exception and the Rule* (tr. Eric Bentley)
————, *Mother Courage* (tr. Desmond Vesey and Eric Bentley)
————, *Puntila* (tr. Gerhard Nellhaus and Richard Grenier)
Paul Claudel, *The Satin Slipper* (as shortened and adapted to the stage by Barrault)
Georges Courteline, *The Bureaucrats* (tr. Jacques Barzun)
Fernand Crommelynck, *The Magnificent Cuckold* (tr. needed)
Eduardo De Filippo, *Millionaire Naples* (tr. Dorothy Bourne)
————, *Filumena Marturano* (tr. Dorothy Bourne)
Georges Feydeau, *Keep an Eye on Emily!* (tr. needed)
Nicolai Gogol, *The Gamblers* (new tr. needed)
Sacha Guitry, *Deburau* (tr. Granville Barker)
Robert Hivnor, *The Ticklish Acrobat*
Theodore Hoffman, *Rich But Happy*
Alfred Jarry, *King Ubu* (new tr. needed)
Leon Katz, (after James Joyce) *Finnegan's Wake*
————, (after Kafka and Gide) *The Trial*
Alexander Ostrovsky, *The Diary of a Scoundrel* (ad. Rodney Ackland)
Jules Romains, *Doctor Knock* (tr. Granville Barker)
————, *Donogoo* (tr. Gilbert Seldes)
Stephen Spender, *To the Island*
Giovanni Verga, *Cavalleria Rusticana* (tr. Eric Bentley)
Robert Penn Warren, *Cass Mastern's Wedding Ring*
William Carlos Williams, *Tituba's Children*
Carl Zuckmayer, *Captain of Koepenick* (new tr. needed)

Series Four will be a somewhat different venture. It will be subtitled "The Theory of Theatre." The chief theories of modern theatre will be presented at length and in the words of their chief exponents—from, say, Zola's Preface to *Thérèse Raquin* to Brecht's *Little Organum for the Theatre*.

The leisure needed for the preparation of this volume was most generously procured for me first by a Guggenheim Fellowship and then by a Rockefeller Foundation grant-in-aid.

[E. B.]

Jest, Satire, Irony and Deeper Significance

A COMEDY IN THREE ACTS

BY CHRISTIAN DIETRICH GRABBE

Translated by MAURICE EDWARDS

CHARACTERS

BARON VON HALDUNGEN
LIDDY, *his niece*
SIR WERNTHAL, *her fiance*
COUNT MURDAX
MR. MOLLFELS
RATPOISON, *a poet*
VILLAGE SCHOOLMASTER
TOBIAS, *a farmer*
LITTLE GOTTLIEB, *his son*
GRETCHEN, *maidservant of the judge's wife*
KONRAD, *a blacksmith*
FOUR NATURAL SCIENTISTS
THE DEVIL
HIS GRANDMOTHER
EMPEROR NERO, *her servant*
GRABBE, *author of the comedy*
THIRTEEN APPRENTICE TAILORS
OTHER SECONDARY CHARACTERS

The scene is laid in and near the BARON'S *village.*

ACT ONE

SCENE ONE

SCHOOLMASTER'S *Room.*

SCHOOLMASTER, *sits at the table and pours one glass after another out of a large bottle.* — *Utile cum dulci,* Schnapps with sugar! — Today's going to be a tough grind. I have to take up the first declension with those farm boys. A bumpkin and the first declension! About as bad, it seems to me, as a crow trying on a starched dickie! *He looks out the window.* Confound it all, here comes bow-legged Tobias with that simpleton son of his! Hang it all, where can I hide the Schnapps? — Quick, quick, I'll bury it down my stomach! *He souses down the bottle with great rapidity.* Ah, of such a mouthful, Pestalozzi himself need not have been ashamed! Empty bottle out the window!

Enter TOBIAS *and* LITTLE GOTTLIEB.

TOBIAS. Hope you slept well, Professor.

SCHOOLMASTER. Thanks, old pal, thanks! — All's well with the family?

TOBIAS. Oh, so so! The wife's healthy, but my best pig's on his last legs! He moans and groans like an old man.

SCHOOLMASTER. A pity, a pity — as much for the pig as for the old man.

TOBIAS. Well, what's new on the political horizon, Professor? What do the latest papers say? Have the Greeks won? Have they driven out the arch-enemy?

SCHOOLMASTER. The aspects are not unfavorable. The Hamburg Non-Partisan knocked off 30,000 Turks again, and the Nuremberg Correspondent continues untiringly to rape Greek virgins of the noblest families; while it is also being whispered about, and this from the most dependable sources, that Ypsilanti's split army won a great battle on the 25th of next month.

TOBIAS, *mouth agape.* On the 25th of next — ?

SCHOOLMASTER. Don't look so surprised, Tobias! The couriers are fast nowadays! Improved post roads, improved post roads!

TOBIAS. So help me God! Such a post road — where the courier runs ahead of the news by one month — I'd sure like to see that once before I die!

SCHOOLMASTER. Frankly, around here something like that is rare. But certainly in your own experience, Tobias, you must have observed that a good horse on a good road cuts down the running time from one hour to half an hour; now if you can imagine an even better horse and an even finer road, then you naturally reach the point where the horse does the stretch in a quarter of an hour, in ten minutes, in one minute, in nothing, in nothing at all, and finally in less than nothing at all! Do you get it?

TOBIAS. I get it, but the Devil get me if I understand it!

SCHOOLMASTER. Since you already got it, it doesn't much matter whether you also understand it. Still, as Cicero said to Caesar —— Oh, oh, what's that you're pulling out of your pocket?

TOBIAS. Well, that's just why I came with Little Gottlieb to call on you. My wife sends you her compliments, and begs you to be kind enough to accept this sausage.

SCHOOLMASTER. Be kind enough? *He grabs the sausage and gobbles it down.*

TOBIAS. You see, our Little Gottlieb has the worms, and so his mother thinks that some day he might become a scholar. Isn't that right, Little Gottlieb? Don't you want to become a scholar?

LITTLE GOTTLIEB. Yes, I have worms.

SCHOOLMASTER. My good fellow, you may rest assured I know how to assess the very promising talents of your most hopeful son.

TOBIAS. Now my wife and I would like you to take the boy into your home, and, with all due, respect, make a minister of him. It would make us so proud to see him, with all due respect, standing in the pulpit! And to show how much we appreciate all this, every Saint Martin's Day we want to send you nine fat geese and a kegful of Schnapps.

SCHOOLMASTER. A kegful? And filled to the brim?

TOBIAS. Burping full, Professor!

SCHOOLMASTER. Every inch a Schnapps! Your son belongs to the intelligentsia! I shall not only initiate him into the deepest mysteries of dogmatics, of homiletics, and the other related sciences of theology, but shall also see to it that he is instructed in the plastic, idyllic, and mephytic major sciences of our country preachers, as well as in porkchopping, cattle-slaughtering, and dungloading. And, in order to show you how close to my heart I hold Little Gottlieb and his welfare, I shall take him up to the castle with me this very day. There I shall present him as a genius to the young Baroness and her uncle who just arrived yesterday; and perhaps he will be thought worthy of an extraspecial subsidization for his studies.

TOBIAS. Now do that, Professor! But I beg you, don't stuff the boy with learning. I got a pair of oxen that pull with their heads, so I know what hard work headwork is! Good morning to you!

SCHOOLMASTER, *to* LITTLE GOTTLIEB. Now come here, you little fool, and pay attention! I'm going to tell you what you've got to do up at the castle in order to look like a genius: either you must never open your mouth—then they'll think, confound it, he must have a lot to keep quiet about, for he doesn't say a word; — or you must say something absolutely non-sensical — then they'll think, confound it, he must have said something very profound, for we, who otherwise understand everything, don't understand this; — or you must eat spiders and swallow flies, — then they'll think, confound it all, there's a big man for you (or, rather, a big boy), for he abhors neither flies nor cobwebs. So tell me, stupid, which do you want to do?

LITTLE GOTTLIEB. I want to keep my mouth shut.

SCHOOLMASTER. Well shut up then, and as far as I'm concerned, with your hand glued to your mouth, for that looks even more allegorical and poetical. However, all that notwithstanding, I can't let you off without another very necessary prerequisite: you must occasionally show a genius-like absentmindedness. Which you do more or less like this, Little Gottlieb: you stick a dead cat into your watchpocket before leaving the house; later on you take a walk with a beautiful lady and together with her in the evening dusk you gaze at the stars; all of a sudden you pull out the dead cat and hold it up to your nose as if you wanted to blow into it; and then the lady, pale as death, shrieks: "Holy cats, a dead cat!" You, however, answer distractedly: "Oh, Lord, I thought it was a constellation!" — Something like that gives you a reputation for originality, you abortion! *He gives him a box on the ear.*

LITTLE GOTTLIEB. Ow! Ow! Ow!

SCHOOLMASTER. Don't be alarmed, my little one! *Utile cum dulci,* an *ear,* because it is useful; a *box* of candy because it is sweet; thus a *box* on the *ear.* It is one of the niceties of my educational methods, I'll have you know, that with every interesting lesson, I give the pupil a tooth-rattling slap in the face. Then always later on, whenever he recalls the slap, he will also remember the lesson which accompanied it. — So, *allons,* on to the castle! Dip the pen deep into the inkwell and make a thick, dark splash right smack over my nose and face! For my gracious masters should be able to perceive, even upon my countenance, the traces of my diligence! LITTLE GOTTLIEB *makes a thick splash across his face, and both leave.*

SCENE TWO

Bright, warm summer day. The DEVIL *sits on a hill and freezes.*

DEVIL. 'Tis cold — cold, 'tis warmer in Hell! — Just because the number seven appears most frequently in the Bible, satirical grandmother had me wear seven fur shirtsies, seven fur jacketkins, and seven fur capsies, — but still 'tis cold — cold — God get me but it's cold! — If I could only steal some wood or set a forest on fire — set a forest on fire! — Oh, by all ye angels, it *would* be something all right if the Devil had to freeze to death! — Steal wood, — burn forest, — burn — steal — *He freezes to death.*

A NATURAL SCIENTIST, *enters botanizing.* Truly, there are rare plant growths to be found in this region; Linnaeus, Jussieu — Lord Christ, what's this lying here on the ground? A dead man, and as one can clearly see, frozen! Now, that *is* peculiar. A miracle, if there really be such a thing as a miracle! We note down that today, the second of August, the sun stands flaming in heaven; it is the hottest day I've ever experienced; and this man here, against all laws and observations of learned men, dares to, manages to freeze himself to death! — No, it's impossible! absolutely impossible! I shall have to put on my glasses! *He puts on his glasses.* Extraordinary! Extraordinary! Here I've put on my glasses, and the fellow is nonetheless frozen. Highly extraordinary! I shall take him to my colleagues. *He grabs the* DEVIL *by the collar and drags him away.*

Room in the Castle

The DEVIL *lies on the table and four* NATURAL SCIENTISTS *stand about him.*

FIRST NATURAL SCIENTIST. You will concede, gentlemen, that this dead being here presents itself as a most complicated case.

SECOND NATURAL SCIENTIST. That depends upon your point of view! It is a shame, though, that his fur clothes are so labyrinthically knotted together the world circumnavigator Cook himself could not untangle them.

FIRST NATURAL SCIENTIST. You will concede that it is a man?

THIRD NATURAL SCIENTIST. Certainly! He has five fingers and no tail.

FOURTH NATURAL SCIENTIST. The only question to be resolved then is: what kind of a man is he?

FIRST NATURAL SCIENTIST. Right! But here one cannot proceed cautiously enough; and, although it is a bright day, I should suggest that in addition a strong light be put on.

THIRD NATURAL SCIENTIST. Quite right, dear colleague!

They strike a light and set it on the table near the DEVIL.

FIRST NATURAL SCIENTIST, *after all four have examined the* DEVIL *with the most exacting attention.* Gentlemen, I think I now feel clear as to the identity of this puzzling cadaver, and I hope I do not err. Note this turned-up nose, these thick, big-mouthed lips — note, I say, this inimitable trait of god-like coarseness spread over the entire countenance, and you will no longer doubt that you see lying before you one of our present-day reviewers, indeed a genuine specimen.

SECOND NATURAL SCIENTIST. Dear colleague, I cannot fully agree with your otherwise unusually ingenuous opinion. Not to mention that our present-day reviewers, especially the theatrical critics, are more simple than they are coarse; and so I perceive on this dead face not a single one of those characteristics you have just enumerated for us. I maintain, on the contrary, something positively maidenlike there; the bushy, overhanging eyebrows indicate that delicate, female timidity which tries to conceal even its own glances; and the nose which you call turned-up, seems rather out of politeness to have been tilted back, in order to leave an extra-large open expanse upon which the languishing lover may lavish his kisses; — enough, if all does not deceive me, then this frozen person is, indeed, a parson's daughter.

THIRD NATURAL SCIENTIST. I must confess, sir, that your hypothesis strikes me as somewhat bold. I conjecture it to be the Devil.

FIRST *and* SECOND NATURAL SCIENTISTS. But that is *ab initio* impossible, for the Devil does not fit into our system.

FOURTH NATURAL SCIENTIST. Esteemed colleagues, let us not wrangle! Now I shall give you *my* opinion, to which I wager you will immediately accede. Observe the monstrous ugliness screaming out at us from every feature of this face, and you cannot help but concede that, were there no German female writers, such a gargoyle would be inconceivable.

THE THREE OTHER NATURAL SCIENTISTS. Yes, it is a German woman writer; we yield to your cogent arguments.

FOURTH NATURAL SCIENTIST. I thank you, my colleagues! — But what is this? Observe how, since we set the burning light before its nose, the corpse begins to stir? Now the fingers palpitate — now she shakes her head — she opens her eyes — she's alive!

DEVIL, *raising himself upright on the table.* Where — am I? —Ugh, I'm still freezing! *To the* NATURAL SCIENTISTS. Please, gentlemen, close both those windows there; — I can't stand drafts.

FIRST NATURAL SCIENTIST, *while he closes the windows.* You must have weak lungs.

DEVIL, *while he climbs down off the table.* Not always! Not when I'm sitting in a well-heated oven.

SECOND NATURAL SCIENTIST. What? You sit in well-heated ovens?

DEVIL. I make a habit of doing so every now and then.

THIRD NATURAL SCIENTIST. A most curious habit! *Writes it down.*

FOURTH NATURAL SCIENTIST. You're a writer, Madam, are you not?

DEVIL. A writer? What do you mean? Such women are plagued by the Devil, but God preserve the Devil that they be the Devil themselves!

ALL FOUR SCIENTISTS. What? So then you *are* the Devil? The Devil? *They start to run off.*

DEVIL, *aside.* Ha, for once now I can lie to my heart's content. *Aloud.* Gentlemen! Gentlemen! Where are you going? Be calm! Relax! Surely you're not running away from some mere play on my name, are you? *The* NATURAL SCIENTISTS *turn back.* They *call* me the Devil, but that's not who I really *am.*

FIRST NATURAL SCIENTIST. With whom then have we the honor of speaking?

DEVIL. With Theophilus Christian Devil, Vicar in the Duchy of ——'s Service, Honorary Member of a Society for the Advancement of Christianity among the Jews, and Knight of the Papal Order for Civil Distinguished-Service recently — in the Middle Ages — bestowed upon me by the Pope for keeping the rabble in constant fear of him.

FOURTH NATURAL SCIENTIST. Which means you must have reached a ripe old age by now.

DEVIL. You err; I am only eleven years old.

THIRD NATURAL SCIENTIST, *to the second.* The biggest bag of lies I've ever seen!

SECOND NATURAL SCIENTIST, *to the third.* And so accordingly will he please the women!

The DEVIL *has been getting closer and closer to the light and involuntarily stuck his finger into it.*

FIRST NATURAL SCIENTIST. Good Lord, Vicar, what are you doing? Why, you're putting your finger into the light!

DEVIL, *confused; withdrawing the finger.* I — I love it, I love to put my finger into the light.

THIRD NATURAL SCIENTIST. Peculiar passion! *Writes it down.*

The BARON, LIDDY, WERNTHAL, *and* RATPOISON *enter.*

FOURTH NATURAL SCIENTIST. Ah, the Baron and the rest of the company.

FIRST NATURAL SCIENTIST, *to the newcomers.* Let me herewith present you Vicar Theophilus Devil, who in the Middle Ages became a Knight of the Order for Civil Distinguished-Service, and who is not only accustomed to sitting in well-heated ovens, but also likes to stick his finger into the light.

RATPOISON. Why, Vicar, you come as though called upon to unite as a couple the fair Liddy with Sir Wernthal.

DEVIL, *embarrassed.* To couple? I? *Half outloud.* Holy cats, I don't know the service.

LIDDY. Don't curse so, Vicar! There are still a couple of months before the coupling!

WERNTHAL. Liddy, how can you so long deny me this hand which I so full of longing press to my lips?

LIDDY, *indignantly pulling away her hand.* Sir Wernthal, please! I don't relish such foolishness.

WERNTHAL. O my dearest lady, my devotion to you is so boundless that I —

BARON. A pinch of snuff, Sir Wernthal? WERNTHAL *takes it and sneezes.*

Meanwhile the DEVIL *has turned back to the light and once again holds his finger in it.*

THE FOUR SCIENTISTS, *who have followed by their glances each of his movements, call out.* Look, look, gentlemen, the Vicar has his finger in the light again!

DEVIL. Oh, there I go again — *He tears off his left arm with his right hand, and with it thrashes the* NATURAL SCIENTISTS *out of the room; whereupon he sets the arm back on and returns to the party.*

RATPOISON. Sir! Sir! How I marvel at you! You rip out your arm and set it back on again just like taking off and putting on a stocking! Truly, that would be audacious enough in poetry — how much more so in life!

DEVIL. You get yourself worked up over nothing! Simple sleight-of-hand! I studied theology in the University of _____, and one can hardly walk out those halls of learning without picking up a few such parlor tricks!

A SERVANT, *enters.* The Schoolmaster wishes to be admitted; he has with him a young genius whom he would like to present to this company.

BARON. Tell that old drunk of a schoolmaster he and that genius of his can go hang themselves!

LIDDY. Why, Uncle dear, don't spoil our fun. The Schoolmaster is the jolliest duck I know; and yet in the midst of all his tomfoolery, he still knows right well what he's doing. Very likely he's fished up some sort of terribly stupid village lout whom he will introduce to us as a great poet, and quite brazenly compare him to Homer and Ariosto.

BARON. All right, show him in. *Exit* SERVANT. But you, Vicar, you should be able to trip him up!

DEVIL. I'll get him to say his prayers, Baron!

WERNTHAL, *to* LIDDY. But you still are, and always will be —

BARON. A pinch of snuff, Sir Wernthal? WERNTHAL *takes it and sneezes.*

LIDDY. The Schoolmaster has apparently brought along some fresh herring again, Ratpoison.

RATPOISON. That confounded herring! *He exits fuming.*

BARON. What's this about herring, my malicious niece? Whatever it is, it seems to have annoyed Ratpoison considerably.

LIDDY. Patience, Uncle darling! You will find out any minute now, straight from the Schoolmaster's mouth.

SCHOOLMASTER *and* LITTLE GOTTLIEB *enter.*

SCHOOLMASTER, *with deep bows.* May I have the honor and the —

WERNTHAL. Good heavens, Professor, what's that frightful splash of ink doing all over your face?

SCHOOLMASTER, *appears astonished.* I — an inksplash — really? — Ah, your grace, now you can see for yourself with what diligence — with what zeal —

LIDDY. Don't work yourself up so, Professor! We know what something like that means where you're concerned, don't we? Yesterday, while the sun was setting, a big idea dawned upon you; and, as at that moment there was no white paper about, in the heat and hurry of passion, you simply had to write it down on your face!

SCHOOLMASTER. My dear young lady, that's not a bad guess —

LIDDY. Or else by chance you saw yourself in the mirror; and, your face striking you as too impossible, you blotted it out!

SCHOOLMASTER. You are becoming bitter, Miss, becoming bitter! Ink is the true lifeblood of a scholar, and woe to the scholar whose lifeblood sits in his face, for it looks very ugly and makes black spots.

BARON *and* WERNTHAL. A mad pedant.

LIDDY, *softly to the* SCHOOLMASTER. All joking aside! Did Old Mary get the money?

SCHOOLMASTER. Yes, gracious miss, and she wept for joy —

LIDDY. Quiet! Here's another Louis d'or for her. I shall visit her this evening.

DEVIL, *who gradually in the meantime has approached the light again, suddenly begins to weep and sob.*

BARON. Hey there, what's got into the Reverend all of a sudden? He's blubbering like a millwheel.

WERNTHAL. Upon my word, tears are running down his cheeks!

SCHOOLMASTER. A Vicar? — Little Gottlieb, make a nice bow!

LIDDY. What's bothering you, sir?

DEVIL. How can you ask! Something noble must have taken place here!

BARON. Noble?

SCHOOLMASTER. The Vicar's right; just this minute Miss Liddy gave me a Louis d'or for poor Old Mary.

DEVIL. You see now, gentlemen?

WERNTHAL. And on account of that you began to cry?

DEVIL, *drying his eyes.* Yes, it made me melancholy.

LIDDY. Now relax; it's not going to happen so soon again!

BARON. No, that's most singular for a Vicar.

WERNTHAL. What do you make of this, Professor?

SCHOOLMASTER. Your reverences seem most sentimental.

BARON. Sentimental? Where did you pick up that miserable word?

SCHOOLMASTER. In the *Journal for Elegant Society*.[1]

BARON. The *Journal for Elegant Society*? And where did you pick that up?

LIDDY. Now, Uncle dear, just remember the herring aesthetic Ratpoison ran away from.

SCHOOLMASTER. Yes, Baron, but there's a story that goes with it. I have a rather distant cousin in town, Mr. Pennysucker, who runs a not unprofitable business in packing wire, gems, copper plates, fish, and old trousers.

BARON. We can believe it.

SCHOOLMASTER. Every two weeks this man sends me a small package of half-spoiled herring for which I pay the ludicrously low price of fourteen groschen; each herring, however, he wraps up individually, and very carefully, in fresh proofsheets, usually of the most miserable poetic works and magazines; in this way I am kept rather well posted with the best products of our newer literature.

BARON. Hahaha! A herring literature!

SCHOOLMASTER. It is thus I receive the poetry of August Kuhn,[2] the Tales of Krug von Nidda,[3] the Jew's Harp or Lyre-Tones by Theodor Hell,[4] the Tragedies of a certain Mr. Houwald.[5]

WERNTHAL. By Jove, those are all famous writers for women, each one a ladies' favorite.

LIDDY. Sir Wernthal, if, as now seems to be the fashion, one calls the dullest writers, ladies' favorite, one deals us a really poor compliment.

BARON. Liddy, don't blame Wernthal! Think! Houwald, the tender, soulful Houwald! Wrapped around a herring! What an outrage!

SCHOOLMASTER. Not an outrage, Baron; rather an improvement! This good man likes upon occasion to be satirical, too! Thus for some time now he has been trying to write a parody on "Guilt,"[6] which, I feel, with all its faults, is much beyond your critics' comprehension; his mighty concoction is called, so I am led to believe, "The Flyflap"[7] and contains much triviality, but not a grain of salt; since, however, my wrapped herrings have taken pity upon it, it has become salty through and through, so that even Müllner,[8] were he to put it to his mouth, would exclaim: "I have never before tasted anything so salty!"

BARON. Bravissimo, Professor, you are my man! — But how on earth do you, stuck out there in the village, hit upon these sarcastic views on modern writing?

SCHOOLMASTER, *bowing before* LIDDY. Here stands my teacher; — when the

---

[1]The *Journal for Elegant Society* ("Zeitung für die elegante Welt") a widespread and influential magazine of belles-lettres (1801-52).

[2]August Kuhn (1784-1829), teacher, scholar, poet, novelist.

[3]Friedrich Albrecht Franz Krug von Nidda (1776-1843), soldier-writer.

[4]Theodor Hell (pseudonym of Karl Gottfried Theodor Winkler, 1775-1856), Dresden writer.

[5]Christoph Ernst, Freiherr von Houwald (1778-1845), tragedian.

[6]*Guilt* ("Die Schuld") one of the best known tragedies of fate by Amadeus Gottfried Adolf Müllner (1774-1829).

[7]*The Flyflap* ("Die Fliegenklatsche") referring to a satire by Houwald in which a "Fliegenklatsche" fatally figures.

[8]Müllner, see note 6.

young lady was sick last winter, I had to read her aloud, evenings, out of
the most recently published works; I profited no little from that experience, especially as she condemned most of them to the fire.

LIDDY. The Schoolmaster does me too great honor.

During this conversation the DEVIL *has slipped off to the side; grinning ma-*
liciously, he has broken a chair to pieces, stuck the single pieces into the
fireplace, taken out his chemical lighter, set the wood on fire, pulled out the
folding screen and hid himself behind it.

WERNTHAL, *who misses him first.* But where is our Reverend?

BARON. He seems to have slipped out. Probably he too is one of these new
scribblers.

SCHOOLMASTER. Yes, yes, indubitably they'll wrap him the same way around
a spoiled herring.

BARON, *angry.* Precisely how they should pack up the whole Leipzig pub-
lishing business! Young Jewboys, whose education consists of nothing
but eating pork, straddle the critical benches, and raise not only the most
miserable poetic quacks to the stars, but insult even honorable men with
their praises — LIDDY *turns away and talks with* WERNTHAL. *The* BARON
carries on all the stronger. Rimesters, so dumb that every time one of their
pieces appears before the public the asses jack its price, are called excellent
poets; — actors so boring, everyone naturally applauds with joy when they
finally retire, are called profound artists; — old hags with voices so sharp
they could cut a slice of bread are called true dramatic singers! — the
Tragic Muse has turned into a streetwalker whom every scoundred ravishes
and out of that union produces five-legged mooncalves so abominable I
pity the dog that waters them! The words, "soulful, inspired, sentimental,
marvellous" are becoming so monstrously misused that already I can see
the time when carved upon the gallows of our most infamous escaped jail-
breaker will stand the inscription: "This man was inspired, sentimental,
marvellous, and soulful." — O that finally a powerful genius might arise,
who, panzered from head to foot with godly strength, shall scale Parnas-
sus and drive the rabble back into the swamps from which it has crawled
forth!!

SCHOOLMASTER. This genius has arisen, Baron; he stands before you; it is
Little Gottlieb.

LIDDY, *who can't help here but laugh outloud.* Is that so?

SCHOOLMASTER. It *is*, Miss Liddy, it *is!* He threw his mother's crockery out
the window and smashed it to pieces.

LITTLE GOTTLIEB, *half crying.* I — I — I —

SCHOOLMASTER. Look, can you not see with what presence of mind he throws
himself into a picturesque pose? How he scratches behind his ears? The
exact stance of Hogarth's whining streeturchin! I have maintained from
the beginning that Little Gottlieb has a great potential talent for the
painterplay.

BARON. Professor, what do you mean by a "painterplay"?

SCHOOLMASTER. Painterplays are something new, Baron. A child who likes
to play with colors and little pictures is very happy to have invented

them; his personality is such that everything which he perceives is paintable; so that, for example, the personages which appear in his paintings are always simpletons; as, among others, the Knight Nanni, Van Dyck, Spinarosa, the Duchess of Sorrento,[9] etc.

BARON. Well, Sir Wernthal, what do you think of this explanation of painterplays?

WERNTHAL. I fear the Schoolmaster finds them more paintable than their creators would have liked.

LIDDY. I don't understand why, gentlemen, but it seems unusually close in this room.

WERNTHAL, *who already has had to wipe his forehead several times.* Yes, yes, I feel a growing heat. It almost seems as though the heat's been turned on.

BARON. What are you thinking of? It's the sun shining down the chimney.

LIDDY. Which of the two is right, Little Gottlieb?

LITTLE GOTTLIEB. Yes.

LIDDY. O dear, but he's a stupid yokel, Professor!

SCHOOLMASTER. A yokel-genius, like so many to be found today. He needs to be understood; he has depth! Nor shall his writings be wrapped round spoiled herrings!

LIDDY. That speaks in his favor; for at least it proves that as yet he has written nothing.

WERNTHAL, *to* BARON. Don't you see the smoke spreading all over the room? That couldn't possibly come from the sun!

BARON. I acknowledge my error — has any fire broken out nearby?

DEVIL, *singing out from the fireplace behind the folding screen to the melody of Goethe's Fisherman Song.*
"Ah, if only you knew how cosy it is
For the Devil in the fire — "   *He trills.*

BARON. Of all things, isn't that the voice of the Knight of the Papal Civil Service?

SCHOOLMASTER, *runs behind the folding screen and comes back horrified.* No, no, no! My hair's on end! The Vicar's sitting there in the middle of the blazing fireplace, swallowing glowing coals, and striking up his trills; may God have mercy upon us!

ALL. What!? *They tear away the folding screen; the* DEVIL *is seen getting up out of the fireplace.*

SCHOOLMASTER. Do you see now how he climbs out? *O tempora, o mores!*

BARON, *to the* DEVIL. Dammit, Sir, what kind of behavior is this? Are you mad? To squat in the fireplace? To eat coals —

DEVIL, *aside.* Now I must be coarse and show an unabashed front! *To* SCHOOLMASTER. You low-down snotrag of a stinking toad, how dare you maintain I was sitting in the fireplace?

SCHOOLMASTER. Sir —

DEVIL. Yes, now I am firmly convinced that the fifty bottomless barrels of

[9]Van Dyck and Knight Nanni are characters in *Country Life* ("Landleben"), a drama by Johann Friedrich Kind (1768-1843); the painter Spinarosa and the Duchess of Sorrento figure in Houwald's "Das Bild" (portrait, picture).

Danaid were fifty Schoolmasters, for everything else gets filled up eventually, but not such a drunken sot of a "How to box children's ears" specialist! How, I ask it once again, how could you, you drunken leech, see me sitting in the fireplace if you hadn't been blind tipsydrunk? I was only sitting in front of it, blowing the coals.

SCHOOLMASTER. What in blazes, Vicar —

DEVIL. What? You're still not ready to shut up, you —

LIDDY. Quiet! I've had enough of this insult and abuse.

BARON. Just tell us, how did you get the fire started?

DEVIL, *with obvious pleasure.* Why, with that lovely chair which was standing there in the corner!

BARON. So? With that lovely chair? — Liddy, what have you to say to *this?*

LIDDY. It was the best chair in the whole house!

DEVIL. Was it really? That's just what I thought! *He gloats.*

BARON. Should I have the rascal put in the doghouse?

WERNTHAL. I should have nothing against it.

LIDDY. Uncle, what *are* you thinking of? The man is just beginning to interest me! I beg you, let him have a room in the castle! I'll pay for whatever chairs he may break.

BARON. O you women! How quickly you fall in love with madness! *To* DEVIL. If you would like to stay with us, Sir, you will find a charming room at your disposal.

DEVIL. I accept your most agreeable offer and thank you from the bottom — *To himself.* What? Thanks? That were magnanimity! *Aloud.* I don't give a damn whether you offer me lodging or not! It is also highly imprudent, if not downright silly for you to take a total stranger into your house without further investigation! Moreover, where is that lowdown dog of a servant who is to show me the room? *He exits.*

BARON. There, niece, you have a guest who's brazen enough.

WERNTHAL. Why don't you say: blazing enough!

BARON. And I fear, my dear, you shan't be able to put up with him for even one hour.

LIDDY. Don't let that worry you.

BARON. He'll be sure to push his insolence to the extremest limits.

LIDDY. In that case I'll have him thrown out of the castle.

BARON. Ah, you *do* know how to help yourself when it's necessary! — Your arm! Let's have coffee in the garden.

LIDDY. I'll be along in a minute.

BARON and WERNTHAL off.

LIDDY, *to* SCHOOLMASTER. Here! — Here's something extra for your thirsty palate. — Now there, don't be ashamed; I know your old weakness. — But get that Louis d'or over to Mary as fast as you can.

SCHOOLMASTER. Immediately, your grace!

LIDDY. Adieu. *Goes off.*

SCHOOLMASTER. A divine girl! — And you, Little Gottlieb, and you? You've been misunderstood, you poor child! Still, console yourself, for it was the same with all the great minds: Solon, Plato, Cartouche,[10] Robespierre, Henry IV, and Caligula; these too all experienced this same sad fate! — Come! I want to lock you up for four days and give you nothing to eat; perhaps that will make you even more meditative than you already are. LITTLE GOTTLIEB *screams; the* SCHOOLMASTER *goes out with him.*

SCENE FOUR

Another room in the castle.

DEVIL, *enters.* Just you wait, Baron! So you've given me a room in your castle, — you'll soon rue the day! — Liddy wants to marry Wernthal, — so she gets a husband. — I'll put a stop to that or I'm not the Devil! — Still I don't understand what makes me so irritable! I feel so despondent, — so upset, so melancholy — God get me, but the horseshoe on my hoof must have got loose. *While he tears loose the cloths wrapped about the foot and takes a look at his hoof.* Oh, oh! Only too true! The shoeing is off, it's worn out! I can hardly touch the floor! Woe! Woe! Unfortunately there's nothing else to be done but conquer these trepidations of mine and call a blacksmith. *He re-wraps the bindings and calls.* Service!

SERVANT, *comes.* You called, sir?

DEVIL. Listen, my good man! — Is there a blacksmith in the village?

SERVANT. There are two here, your grace.

DEVIL. Then go, my son, and summon that one of the two who laughs the least!

SERVANT. Oh, then I'd better fetch Fat Konrad. He's become awfully sad again — ever since the old highway was repaired. *Goes off.*

DEVIL. I — o woe is me! Now how in the world am I going to let this blacksmith know I've a horse's hoof? Woe is me! O woe is me! — Ha, here he comes! Courage!

BLACKSMITH, *enters.* Your grace has commanded —

DEVIL. Are you the — the —

BLACKSMITH. I am the village smithy. — Where's the nag I'm supposed to shoe?

DEVIL, *heated.* Sir, I am no ... *Slaps his hand to his mouth.* Oh what an idiot am I! — Take a seat, Mr. Blacksmith, take a seat! — Have you a wife?

BLACKSMITH. Sure I have.

DEVIL. Must be a fine woman!

BLACKSMITH, *sighing.* Well now, everyone has his weak points!

DEVIL, *likewise sighing.* Yes, indeed!

BLACKSMITH, *standing up.* If you will be kind enough to tell me —

DEVIL. Ha, you're in a hurry, a great hurry! Father of a family? Y'wear

---

[10]Louis Dominique Cartouche (1693-1721), leader of a band of robbers and murderers, often glorified by poets and painters for his courage.

boots! Y'have feet! *Playing with the buttons on his vest.* Nor I — nor do I have a horse's hoof!

BLACKSMITH. Why, I'm sure of that — even without looking, your Grace.

DEVIL. Yes, that you'll be sure of even without looking, and with looking, Mr. Smithy! I don't have a horsehoof — none — at most only . . . *Softly, while, with tremendous effort and violent sneezing, he brings forth the words "noble, conscientious, Christ, etc."* Mr. Smith, you are a n-n-oble, con- consci- conscientious, cultivated man, a religious, diligent, ch- church-church-going Christian, — to you I can entrust . . . *While he tries to hide his right leg behind the left* . . . I have a hoof on my right foot!

BLACKSMITH, *with inquisitive glances.* How? What? A hoof? O my!

DEVIL. No, no, no! Not so much a hoof as a horse's foot — or, rather more exactly, a horse-like, — that is, a human-like — well, in short, a somewhat thick sole, which from a distance a near-sighted man might take for a horse's hoof.

BLACKSMITH, *stammering out of curiosity.* If — if your Grace would show me the — sole —

DEVIL. Right away, my dear Smith, right away! — But lock the door first! — So! — *After loosening the cloths from his horsehoof, he shows it to the* BLACKSMITH, *and, ashamed, hides his face in his handkerchief.* Now, if only you would be so kind as to fit your horshoe onto it!

BLACKSMITH, *taking the foot in his hand.* Listen, Mister, that's not the sole of a foot; it's a horse's hoof the like of which in all Christendom not another nag — not another soul, I meant to say — has to show!

DEVIL, *always with his face in the handkerchief, lisping.* Shoe it on! Shoe it on!

BLACKSMITH. Just by chance I've got here in my pocket a horseshoe as big as a chandelier. I'll shoe it on you in real style! *He shoes it on.* There, now it fits fast.

DEVIL, *glad.* Does it fit?

BLACKSMITH. That'll be one gulden.

DEVIL, *to himself.* One gulden? I should be a fool! *Aloud.* Cheapskate, have you any idea whom you have just fitted? I am Satan himself, I am . . .
The BLACKSMITH *runs out; the* DEVIL *calls out after him* . . .
five hundred thousand years old; and get this, I got your grandfather, and I hope I get you too; the minute you breathe a word about me I'll wring your neck! And I should pay you! — you ought to be hanged! Go hang yourself! *Coming back.* How the old sinner tore out of here when he heard my real name! — But I've got to hand it to him, he did me up right well! The horseshoe fits as if it were grown on! Ah, it's a real feeling of power that goes through me! *He dangles his horsehoof, swinging it back and forth several times.* Now I shall try to sleep for an hour or so in order to get completely back in shape, and then foul up that wedding with doubled zeal!
He sits down in an armchair and pulls a book out of his pocket.
Yes, it's a good thing I brought along that old, unfailing sleeping pill, Klopstock's *Messiah!* I need read only three verses of it, and I'm tired as

the deuce! *Opening the book.* Where did I leave off the last time? Ah, page 29. *He reads two verses and falls asleep.*

ACT TWO

SCENE ONE

Hall in the Castle.

DEVIL, *enters with wrapped-up horsehoof.* There's a giant of a scoundrel prowling about here whose long fingers seem to point uninterruptedly to the gallows upon which he will ultimately hang! Perhaps he will fit into my plan! — Quiet, there he is! I'll step off to the side and listen in on what he has to say.

COUNT MURDAX, *enters.* That Liddy's a gorgeous creature and just right for me. She has, as far as I can make out from the outside, a pair of tits fit for no king. I shall either marry her or murder her.

DEVIL, *stepping out, to himself.* An estimable man! *Aloud.* Count Oxhead, if I'm not mistaken?

COUNT. Count Murdax, if you don't want to be thrashed.

DEVIL. Your grace is infatuated with the young baroness?

COUNT, *groaning.* Beyond all limits!

DEVIL. Then I shall procure her for you.

COUNT. What?

DEVIL. But only under certain conditions.

COUNT. Stipulate whatever you wish!

DEVIL. First, you must make your oldest son study philosophy.

COUNT. Good.

DEVIL. Second, you must murder thirteen tailor's apprentices.

COUNT. Do you take me for a fool, you rat? What kind of crazy conditions are these? To murder thirteen tailor's apprentices! And why, of all people, tailor's apprentices?

DEVIL. They're the most innocent.

COUNT. That's true! — But still thirteen! What a mob! No, if necessary I'll lop off seven, but not a single head more!

DEVIL, *annoyed.* What's this, do you think you can bargain with me like a Jew? *Will go.*

COUNT. Listen, mister, I'll do away with nine — eleven — yes, even twelve; only spare me the thirteenth; twelve's a nice round number!

DEVIL. Good, I'll be satisfied if you would just break a couple of ribs on Number Thirteen.

COUNT. Well, if it's just a couple of ribs, I won't mind! — But — but —

DEVIL. What, still "butting"?

COUNT. Yes, look here! I'm wearing a new coat and a new white vest, and with this mass slaughter they'll be sure to get all messed up.

DEVIL. Is that all? You can simply put on a napkin!

COUNT. Well let the vulture grab me, but that's right! Sure, I'll put on a napkin.

DEVIL. And tomorrow I shall wait for you by the Pavilion in the woods at Schallbrunn; there you will drop the napkin, and take up the Baroness in your arms!

COUNT. Hohoho! I won't need a napkin for that! *Exits.*

DEVIL. "Success!" says Octavio Piccolomini![11] — Judging by my ability to read faces, I'm not going to have any more trouble with Sir Wernthal then, than I had yesterday noon, three thousand years ago, with pious Aeneas when I saw him run away from Dido. They both look exactly alike.

WERNTHAL, *enters, talking to himself.* Soon the wedding! My bride is clever, beautiful, and noble. — But I'm 12,000 Reichstaler in debt, and she's too shrewd to hand me over such a sum without question; — I wish she were on Bald Mountain and I had her purse in my pocket!

DEVIL, *stepping out, to himself.* Another estimable man! *Aloud.* Your Servant, Sir Wernthal! How are you?

WERNTHAL. Miserable, Vicar.

DEVIL. How much do you want for your bride?

WERNTHAL, *enraged.* Sir, you — !

DEVIL. I am just a passionate collector of illegitimate June bugs, young brides, and fat landlords, and wouldn't haggle much over the price.

WERNTHAL. So! A collector! Wouldn't haggle! — What do you offer me for Liddy? She's a capital beauty, all right.

DEVIL. For her beauty, I bid 2,000 Reichstaler in Convention mint.

WERNTHAL. She has a brain.

DEVIL. For that I deduct 5 groschen, 2 pfennig; in a girl that's a shortcoming.

WERNTHAL. She has a fine, soft hand.

DEVIL. Which makes for soft slaps; for that I'll pay you 7,000 Reichstaler in gold.

WERNTHAL. She is still chaste!

DEVIL, *making a sour face.* Ah, chastity here, chastity there; I can't offer you any more than 3 groschen, 1 pfennig in copper for that.

WERNTHAL. Sir, are you unaware that a pound of mutton costs over 4 groschen on the current exchange?

DEVIL. Pooh, ever since the dimmer street lighting and the introduction of the border tariff, mutton has become very expensive and chastity extraordinarily cheap. In Berlin, for example, one can get a portion of chastity in the evening for 2, 3, or when it's high, for 4 counterfeit silver groschen, not counting the rebate.

WERNTHAL. But Liddy has both feeling, imagination —

DEVIL. Feeling ruins the complexion; imagination makes blue circles under the eyes and spoils the blood. For the whole lot I offer you, in the name of irony, thruppence.

WERNTHAL. You have rather disgusting taste.

DEVIL. To be short and sweet, and so that once and for all you shut your

[11]From "Wallensteins Tod" (Schiller), Act II, Scene V, next-to-the-last verse.

mouth about the somewhat conventional, but for my money unbearable, peculiarities of the Baroness, I'll give you for the whole lot of them 11,000 Reichstaler in Dutch round ducats; and now I ask you, does not my bid seem acceptable?

WERNTHAL. How much does that amount to altogether?

DEVIL, *counting on his fingers.* For Beauty: 2000 Reichstaler in Convention mint; for Chastity: 3 groschen, 1 pfennig, in copper; for the soft hand: 7000 Reichstaler in gold; for Feeling and Imagination: thruppence, in the name of irony; so that you shut up about the conventional qualities: 11,000 Reichstaler in Dutch round ducats; — altogether that makes 20,000 Reichstaler, 3 groschen, 4 pfennig. From that, however, I deduct 5 groschen, 2 pfennig for her brain, — thus there remain 19,999 Reichstaler, 22 groschen, 2 pfennig.

WERNTHAL. Agreed, Mr. Bride and Junebug Collector! — When do I get the money?

DEVIL. Right away! — Promise this first, though: to lure Liddy into the Pavilion at Schallbrunn tomorrow morning; to delay the servants following her; and not to search afterwards for those who shall carry her off.

WERNTHAL. I pledge myself to all that, with the exception that I lure the Baroness to Schallbrunn, for if I did so they would surely suspect me. I advise you to let aesthetic Ratpoison suggest to Liddy a drive out there; he reads a great deal in the writings of the neoromantic school and is infatuated with pavilions in the woods.

DEVIL. I'll see if I can persuade him to do so. For this limiting condition, however, you must be satisfied if I settle half the account in Hungarian paper currency.

WERNTHAL. Why, sir, you are damned stingy!

DEVIL, *feeling flattered, smirks.* Oh, I beg you — why, you make me blush! Indeed, I like to be damned, like to be called stingy, in fact love it, but I'm still far from stingy enough! *Goes off with* WERNTHAL.

SCENE TWO

RATPOISON'S *Room*

RATPOISON, *sits at a table, trying to write a poem.* Ah, ideas! Plenty of rimes, but ideas! Ideas! Here I sit, drink coffee, chew pencils, write down this, cross out that, and can't find one idea, not a single idea! — Ha, now what should I make of that? — Wait a minute! Was that an idea which just struck me? — Magnificent! Divine! Precisely on the idea that I can't find any ideas, I shall compose a Sonnet; and, indeed, this idea about the absolute loss of ideas is the most brilliant idea which could have occurred to me! I write a poem, as it were, about something I am not able to write a poem about! How piquant! How original!

He paces before the mirror. Upon my word, I really do look like a genius! *He sits down at the table.* Now I shall begin!

He writes.

Sonnet

"I sat down at my table chewing pens,
    Just like — — "

Hmn, what in the world so sits that it looks like me when I chew a pen? Where can I find an appropriate image for that? I'll go to the window and see if I can't observe something similar outside! *He opens the window and looks out.* There's a boy sitting on the wall, and — Naw, it doesn't look like that! But across the way on the stone bench, an old beggar's sitting there, eating a piece of hard bread — No, that would be too commonplace, too ordinary! *He closes the window and walks about the room.* Hmn, hmn! No inspiration? Then I shall have to enumerate everything which chews. A cat chews, a polecat chews, a lion — Stop! A lion! — What does a lion chew? He chews either a sheep, or an ox, or a goat, or a horse — Stop! A horse! — Now what the mane is to a horse, the quill is to a pen; thus both look rather alike — *Shouting.* Eureka, there's the image! Bold, daring, new, Calderonian!

"I sat down at my table chewing pens,
    Just like

While he writes it down.

the lion, 'ere the grey of dawn
His rapid-running pen, a horse, does chew on — "

He reads these two lines over once again, outloud, and smacks his lips as though they tasted good. No, no! Never before has there been such a metaphor! I shudder before my own poetic powers! *Cosily sipping down a cup of coffee.* The horse a lion's pen! And then that adjective "rapid-running"! How apt! How apropos! For what pen runs more rapidly than a horse? Also the words "'ere the grey of dawn": that's first-rate Homer! Of course they don't really have anything to do with the rest of the poem; but they do constitute an independent image; they make for an epic poem in miniature! Oh, I must look into the mirror again! *Contemplating himself therein.* By Jove, a most brilliant face! True, the nose is quite immense; still, that's the price of genius! *Ex ungue leonem,* for by his nose, you shall know him!

DEVIL, *enters. Bon jour,* Mr. Ratpoison!

RATPOISON, *turns around, and while he is preparing to greet the* DEVIL, *notices the horsehoof from which the bindings have slipped down.* God almighty, the Devil! *He tries to rush past the* DEVIL *and gain the door.*

DEVIL, *sees his bare hoof and stamps it furiously on the floor.* Abominable carelessness! *To* RATPOISON. Don't be alarmed! I've read your poetry!

RATPOISON, *immediately cajoled.* You have? You have?

DEVIL. Yes, and it pleased me exceedingly.

RATPOISON, *completely confiding.* O you bestow upon me praise which I can hardly — You too write poetry?

DEVIL. I —

RATPOISON, *does not let a word out of his mouth.* You must write poetry!
Do try it! I am sure you will compose magnificent poems!

DEVIL, *aside.* Because I have praised his.

RATPOISON. I only beg you to write under another name. Not because you
need be ashamed of your poetry, as is the fashion, but rather to conceal
that which is characteristic of your name. Just as a person, for example,
who's very twisted and gloomy could be called *bright*,[12] so you could
entitle yourself Angel, Heaven, or Virtue.

DEVIL. You give advice worth following, Mr. Ratpoison! — I have, moreover,
already staged several works; such as, only recently, "The French Revolution," a Fourteen Year Tragedy, with a Prologue by Louis XV, and Choruses by Emigrants. The play has been very badly received, however,
especially by virtue of its fatal error: that it guillotined the critics. Besides,
I can't get it to play a second run either in Prussia, Austria, or England,
in spite of the fact that many of my friends there are working underground
on it. The censor is too rigid. Still, I have hopes that it will be revived again
in Spain with a few minor changes, which is why the Duke of Angoulême[13]
doesn't drink up all my Spanish bitters. — I am busy now with a farce
comedy currently running under the title: The Greek War for Freedom,
by the Author of the French Revolution, published by the Turkish
Emperor.

RATPOISON. I see I have been acquainted with your work for some time now,
Mr. Devil, without knowing you as its author. And I must admit there is
something undeniably colossal about it! But still you take far too many
liberties with time and place! And what about the verse! The verse!
Also the views and attitudes toward the world which you express in them
ought to —

DEVIL. And do you happen to know what the world is?

RATPOISON. What a question! The world is the essence of all existence, from
the smallest worm to the largest solar system.

DEVIL. So let me tell you, then, that this essence of the All, which you honor
with the name "world," is nothing more than a mediocre, indifferent
comedy. It has been smeared together during vacations by a beardless,
loud-mouthed angel who, if I'm not mistaken, is still in the twelfth grade,
and lives in the ordinary world which man finds incomprehensible. The
copy in which we are found is on the shelves of the Lending Library at
X, I believe. It is being read at this very moment by a beautiful lady
known to the author who will hand him her opinion at teatime this
evening, that is, over six trillion years from now.

RATPOISON. Sir, I'm going mad! —If the world is a comedy, then what in the
world is Hell which is likewise in the world?

---

[12]Here is a play on words impossible to duplicate in English. The original has
"hell" (bright, clear), which is at the same time a pun on Theodor Hell, one of the
authors satirized above (Act One, Scene Three).

[13]Louis Antoine de Bourbon, Duke of Angoulême (1775-1844), oldest son of
Count Artois, later King Charles X. An ardent defender of royalist ideas, in 1823
he suppressed the Spanish Revolution.

DEVIL. Hell is the ironical part of the play, and, as usually happens, turns out to be better than Heaven, which should be the purely amusing part.

RATPOISON. And is Hell really nothing more? How — then how are criminals punished?

DEVIL. We keep on laughing at a murderer until he finally laughs at himself for having taken the trouble to kill someone. The severest punishment for one of the damned, however, is simply this: he must read the "Evening News"[14] and the "Freethinker"[15] but is not allowed to spit on them.

RATPOISON. Lord in Heaven, Mr. Devil, I note that not only my poetry, but all world literature as well is known in Hell.

DEVIL. But of course! Not only the Bad comes to Hell, but also the Wretched, Deplorable, and Trivial; thus even the good Cicero sits there as well as the nasty Catiline. Since nowadays the newer literature is the most miserable of the Miserable, we prefer to occupy ourselves with it.

RATPOISON. Why, if literature is the chief business in Hell, — what kind of unusual small businesses might you have down there?

DEVIL. Well, during off-hours we usually make window panes or eyeglass lenses out of ghosts because they are invisible and for that reason also transparent. Thus recently, when my grandmother had a strange whim to look into Virtue, she set the philosophers Kant and Aristotle both upon her nose; but as she looked through them it became steadily darker, and she made herself a lorgnette out of two Pomeranian farmers instead. She could then see as plainly as she wished.

RATPOISON, *clapping his hands together over his head.* Fantastic! Fantastic! — Tell me, do you also know your way about Heaven?

DEVIL. Why not? Only the other day Zamiel out of "Der Freischütz"[16] came down to Hell. He pretended to be a cousin of mine, but because of the generosity he had shown his hunter friend Max I had to use force in leading him back to Heaven. True, he resisted terribly, but finally, after I punched an iron ring through his nose, he said in a hollow voice: "Time will tell," and followed me to the gates of Heaven. There Socrates received him with open arms, and led him at once to the barber to have his beard sheared off and hence look a little more civilized.

RATPOISON. Oh, since you are so well acquainted up in Heaven, I entreat you: do tell me what they are doing, those immortal heroes of virtue, those whom I have chosen as the guiding stars of my life and writing! Above all, what is that sublime exemplar of friendship up to, the divine Marquis Posa?

DEVIL. You mean the one in *Don Carlos?*

RATPOISON. Himself, the Maltese!

DEVIL. If you think he's in Heaven you're mistaken; he sits near me in Hell.

---

[14]"Die Abendzeitung," published in Dresden from 1817-1821 under the joint editorship of Theodor Hell and Friedrich Kind; from 1822-43, under Hell alone.
[15]"Der Freimütige," 1803-34. During the period 1808-29 edited by August von Kotzebue and August Kuhn with the sub-title, "Unterhaltungblatt für gebildete unbefangene Leser."
[16]Referring to von Weber's "Der Freischütz" which opened in Berlin, June 18, 1821.

RATPOISON. What?

DEVIL. Yes, yes, the Marquis Posa, finding himself all of a sudden in Hell, was just as surprised as Zamiel finding himself in Heaven. But we took away his resounding megaphone and made him take up the vocation for which he was most talented. He has since become a panderer and calls his alehouse: "At the Queen Elizabeth."

RATPOISON. Impossible! Impossible! Posa a tavernkeeper? I can't picture it!

DEVIL. Calm down! His present position seems to suit him well; he's getting fat and has a paunch already.

RATPOISON. A paunch? — But what about that other famous model of self-sacrifice — the noble and magnificent painter, Spinarosa[17] — surely he sits in the front ranks of the blessed, right next to Curtius and Regulus?

DEVIL. No, you're off again in your calculations! Spinarosa is employed in Posa's tavern as headwaiter; there he practices that self-sacrifice for which, heretofore, much as he wanted to, he could never quite free himself; only now, when he has to serve a guest a tankard of Merseburger, his eager, hall-open mouth shows but too clearly that sacrificing this mug costs him much more in self-control than did giving up the tedious and dull Camilla. Recently he even tried to steal a sip on the sly, but Posa dealt him such a club behind the ears it took him two weeks to forget it.

RATPOISON. God! How could anyone be so mistaken! Posa gives Spinarosa a box on the ear! I give up! — — And you call Camilla tedious! No, you can't be serious, your devilish majesty! O, I beg you, how does she fare, this ideal creature of love? This woman, who, even in the later, so-called best years of her life, even after the sixteenth birthday of the son she bore, never once forgot her lover, and indeed still sighed sweetly for him, as if she were only eighteen. O surely she, the sublime one, together with Thekla and Julia, now glides over the fields of eternal peace!

DEVIL. Yes, she reached Heaven and attached herself to the two girls. When Thekla once absentmindedly called her "Mother," however, it made her so furious she came down to us in Hell. Here she stood all alone, resuming the contemplations she had begun in Heaven as to whether or not she could really see, and maintained them uninterruptedly for three weeks. Finally, by chance, Falstaff passed by, thirsting strongly again for champagne and other sweets; and I don't know yet just how it happened, but he mistook Camilla for a glass of syrup, picked her up in his hand, and swilled her right down. Afterwards he complained to me that the syrup must have been very bad, because it had given him a terrible belly-ache.

RATPOISON. I despair and almost fear to question any further. — How are my favorite tragic heroes, Schiller's Wallenstein and Müllner's Hugo?[18]

DEVIL. They're both in Hell. When he died, Hugo thought Heaven would open up for him; but, like any dying person, he was easily mistaken. And though his brother snatched the revenging sword away from the Cherub, it was not that he might throw it away, but rather to per-

---

[17]Spinarosa, and Camilla, the daughter of the Duchess of Sorrento, are important characters in Houwald's tragedy, "Das Bild."

[18]Hugo, Count Orindur, is the hero of Müllner's tragedy, "Die Schuld."

sonally behead his murderer. And if in doing so he winked and smiled, he acted as one does with a young, unruly dog, coaxing him on with gesture and grimace, only to thrash him that much more soundly afterwards. — Now, as for Wallenstein, we found out after having examined him properly, that he was excellently qualified for a school principalship. So we immediately installed him in our Infernal Gymnasium at Z; and would have found him most satisfactory had he not had one shortcoming; every time he lifted his stick to discipline a worthless brat, he kept on yelling "there isn't room here to hit him," "well, here goes," "I'd still rather not do it," and so forth, for so long that by the time he finished the brat had stuck a large paper pigtail on him from behind.

RATPOISON. The Devil take . . . *Correcting himself with a bow.* Mr. Devil, you may take me, should I become breathless with astonishment and wonder! Still, carry on! What are the poets themselves up to? Schiller, Shakespeare, Calderon, Dante, Ariosto, Horace; how do they keep busy? what are they doing?

DEVIL. Shakespeare is writing commentaries on Franz Horn;[19] Dante has just thrown Ernst Schulze[20] out the window; Horace married Maria Stuart; Schiller sighs over Baron Auffenberg;[21] Ariosto bought a new umbrella; Calderon reads your poetry, sends you his hearty greetings, and advises you to visit Liddy at the Pavilion in the woods near Schallbrunn because this little house lies in a genuinely romantic region.

RATPOISON. O fortunate me! O most fortunate man that I am! I'll climb to the top of the roof! Calderon reads my poetry! Calderon sends me his greetings! I could consume a candle with joy! Greet the Señor de la Barca a thousand times more, — I am his most passionate admirer, — I will go to the Pavilion with Liddy even if I have to carry her there, — I —

DEVIL. Enough! My time is up! — If you should ever need me, you know, of course, that I live in Hell. It's a bit far from the village; but if you should wish to get there in a hurry, you must travel via Berlin, Dresden, Leipzig, or Paris where you go to the King's Wall, Fish Alley, Slipshod Row, or the Palais Royal, respectively; from these Tartarus is but five minutes away, and you will find only the best roads from there on. — Indeed, it will soon be evening! Sleep only so so! *He starts to leave.*

RATPOISON, *stopping him.* Apropos! Just one last word! May I not be let in on the secret as to why you have come up to earth?

DEVIL. Because they're housecleaning down in Hell!

RATPOISON. I thank you for your most obliging answer.

DEVIL. Sleep only so so! *Exits.*

---

[19]Franz Horn (1781-1837), writer, lectured on Shakespeare in Berlin.
[20]Ernst Schulze (1789-1817), author of *The Enchanted Rose* ("Die bezauberte Rose") lectured as Privatdozent in Göttingen on ancient languages and literatures.
[21]Joseph, Freiherr von Auffenberg (1798-1857), connected with the theater in Karlsruhe; later in life wrote a number of historical tragedies, largely imitations of Schiller.

SCENE THREE

A height before the village.

MOLLFELS, *enters.* See, there it lies, the home town! Listen: the vesper bells
in the grey church steeple are ringing! How pleasant, after four years
absence, they sound! — Even the ancient castle rests unchanged; proud
and stately it rises there out of the midst of its blooming summer garden,
and the first glimmer of the sunset glow makes purple plays of light in
its mighty windows! — O Liddy! O Liddy! How I do love thee! *Vexed.*
If only I weren't so damned ugly!

SCHOOLMASTER, *enters, unnoticed by* MOLLFELS. Here will I take my stand,
look down upon the plains of my schoolship, and indulge my patriotic
fantasies. How much everything could be improved! If the farmers were
forced to go to school until they learned something, even at the end of
the world, they'd still have to be kept after school with only bread and
water for a full six weeks. Moreover, what sort of practical application
could be made of that large oak forest over there? Ah, when will the
happy day of the Enlightenment dawn, the day when they will be cut
into schoolbenches; these benches systematically arranged and set up in
the fields; knowledge-hungry boys and young men drawn to them; and
me created director of it all? O, then with the help of a balloon, I would
make the evening sun my glowing lectern, — I would use the church
steeple as a pen, — that lake would be my inkwell, — and those mountains there would be a side of bacon which parents and patrons out of
gratitude would give me. *He sinks into deep contemplation.*

MOLLFELS, *steps forward and slaps him on the shoulder.* There you are, lost
in genuine pedagogical revery, Professor!

SCHOOLMASTER. Mr. Mollfels! — I'm delighted with this happy surprise!
How did you like Italy, the country where the stones speak? Any signs
of old age yet on the Venus de Medici? I hope the Pope's boots were
clean when you kissed his foot? Is —

MOLLFELS. I'll relate it all at my own leisure. Only tell me, is everything
here the same as before?

SCHOOLMASTER. Nothing important has occurred in your absence. Yesterday
the fire engine was dragged out to fight day-before-yesterday's fire; and
rich Bartholomew married Kathrine with whom he was so passionately
in love; he has since had a shirt made out of buckskin just like his
trousers, because his wife's fisticuffs hurt him so. As far as my own humble self is concerned, it's been with me as with Father Homer: I haven't
tasted roast pork in two years.

MOLLFELS. Why, what makes you come to the conclusion that old Homer
never tasted roast pork?

SCHOOLMASTER. Because he *described* it with such delicacy, Mr. Mollfels.

MOLLFELS. Then you must describe brandy very badly!

SCHOOLMASTER. No, not brandy, — virtue.

MOLLFELS. Still, there's no rule without an exception! But tell me: how are things up at the Castle? Is Miss Liddy still bright and gay?

SCHOOLMASTER. A chimney sweep has come to the castle; he calls himself a Vicar, and seems to have been predestined two weeks before his birth to the loss of his innocence. — The cheerfulness of the Baroness and her uncle's bad temper rest at status quo.

MOLLFELS. There! For the good news, a copy of the Memoirs of Jacob Casanova de Seingalt, Morocco bound, and for all that, out of bounds. I bought it from a Jew whom I couldn't get rid of any other way, and have no further use for it. *Exit.*

SCHOOLMASTER. The "Memoirs" of Jacob Casanova de Seingalt! The Napoleon of prostitution? This General of the most Victorious Underdogs? What should I, a haggard schoolmaster, make of these things? — But wait! I shall send it to the judge's wife as an exchange present for the pork and beans she sends over; she's an expert on everything and will therefore be most properly qualified to study Jacob Casanova de Seingalt.

TOBIAS, *enters.* Good evening, Professor!

SCHOOLMASTER. Good evening, Tobias! *Aside.* How the Devil can I shake this fellow off?

TOBIAS. Well, now, how's Little Gottlieb doing? Have you taken him up to the castle?

SCHOOLMASTER. Haven't you heard, Mr. Tobias, that about an hour ago a dentist who pulls teeth for nothing arrived at the inn?

TOBIAS. As if I care! See, I've got two good rows of teeth; they're so healthy I can whet my pitchfork on them.

SCHOOLMASTER. What does that mean? You can get them pulled now for nothing! You can't refuse something for nothing!

TOBIAS. Yes, that's right, too! You can't pass by a little profit! I'll go over there and let him rip out a couple of back molars! *He goes off.*

SCHOOLMASTER. O holy simplicity! Sweet innocence! Thou hast abandoned the Luxury of Cities and alighted upon the Hovel of the Peasant! Tobias lets his teeth be pulled because he can get it done for nothing. O! O! O! *Exits.*

SCENE FOUR

Room in the Castle. LIDDY *and the* BARON *enter.*

BARON. Let this be a warning, my child! I do not at all trust Sir Wernthal!

LIDDY. He has his shortcomings; that he possesses some manly qualities, however, was only recently demonstrated in his duel with Count Naubek.

BARON. In his duel? Oh yes, two young gentlemen did have a duel yesterday; it seems that one of them upon his honor assured the other that he had been pilloried several times already, and the other just did not want to believe him! — — Good night! I've said enough! *Exits.*

LIDDY. As a matter of fact, Uncle's warnings are beginning to take effect! Wernthal is not the man I took him for when we first met! — — Strange that against my will, a certain Mollfels strikes my fancy, — he had the ugliest face one could imagine, yet he was the most gifted and excellent man I've known.

SERVANT, *enters.* A Mr. Mollfels is waiting in the hall.

LIDDY, *astonished.* Who? — Mollfels? — What does he look like?

SERVANT. We have just pulled seven old women out of the castle pond. They jumped terror-stricken into the water upon seeing his face.

LIDDY, *to herself.* Without doubt, it is he! *Aloud.* Show him in! *The* SERVANT *exits.* It will cost me some pains to hide my amazement.

MOLLFELS, *enters.* Ha, there I perceive her again! *Aloud.* Madam, I come from Italy and hasten to greet you.

LIDDY. Welcome home, Mr. Mollfels, welcome! — Did Italy live up to your expectations? How did you like Rome?

MOLLFELS. Grey ruins look out of green shrubbery; loud steps resound down lonely streets; and whoever hears, in this seven-hilled city of the past, the last thunder of the distant horizon dying out over the ruins of the Capitol, feels truly quite moved. How different, were the lookout a churchtower in Berlin!

LIDDY. It seems to me that in Rome Death should be almost beautiful.

MOLLFELS. But certainly! Indeed, there one is almost ashamed to be alive!

LIDDY. Did you look up my brother in Florence?

MOLLFELS. Here are letters from him and his wife!

LIDDY. O hurry! *She opens the letters.*

MOLLFELS, *observes her during the reading.* What a charming woman! One can hear the music of her movements! The unquenchable flames of her eyes sparkle like two brilliant fireflies, and her bosom heaves over her heart like a lake over its springs! Happy the chosen one who can rest his weary head on such bliss! *Pacing up and down.* No, I'll be damned if I can stand this any longer! I have to find out if there's any hope for me, or whether I ought to hang myself from that oak tree! Ugly or not ugly, I am going to declare my love to her now, do or die! *He steps up to* LIDDY. Madam, do not let my proposal frighten you, for I myself know only too well that my figure is such as to make horses shy away from it, mistaking it as they do for an abandoned road crossing, — that my boots, even with my calves tucked in them, are as empty as a pair of hollowed-out tree trunks, — that my ears —

LIDDY. For heavens sake, Mr. Mollfels, are you delirious?

MOLLFELS. And my nose! Hohoho, my nose! All mankind shudders! As misshapen as the intestines of a tiger, red as a fox, flat as a story by Karoline Pichler,[22] and as short as a second.

LIDDY. As a second! — How long is your right arm?

MOLLFELS. A leap year long! Standing up straight I can button my shoes with it! When I say standing up straight, however, I don't mean to compare myself with a Prussian guardsman, but rather with a Leipzig militia

---

[22]Karoline Pichler (1769-1843), a minor Austrian novelist and story writer.

man. The Devil only knows where my back learned its excessive servility: I am bent in a permanent bow, tirelessly observing my own legs, which look not unlike two swollen Turkish sabres!

LIDDY. Leave those sabres out of the picture, and relieve at last my amazement and curiosity! What is this enthusiastic self-portrayal of yours supposed to lead up to?

MOLLFELS. To this: that I prostrate myself before you, that I worship you, that I love you!

LIDDY. Well, I must grant you this: you do know how to *begin* your declaration of love! At least you start off with descriptions of your person, though according to them I should sooner have surmised that, due to your legs, you were going to become a baker, than that you were declaring me your love.

MOLLFELS. O do not break my heart with my legs! No man can hate these two antipodes of horror, these two wreckers of friendship, these two panaceas against love, more grimly than I! Even were I to save the life of some noble man who had fallen into the morass, he'd strike me and run away should he even so much as glance at my legs! But for all that, madam, the power of passion makes me stammer out anew my declaration of love! It has done me some good in that I am now ashamed to eat beef and mustard, they being too common for a lover; — and that in my ecstasy, I've written an insipid tragedy whose content is so foolish I really shouldn't tell you about it.

Instead of Fate, I let it be governed by *ennui,* the divinity of the anti-fatalists. This divinity is honored by opening the scene with a reading from the dramatic works of Eduard Gehe.[23] Unexpectedly, the declaration resounds from out the temple that the goddess has decreed the downfall of the exalted Princess Salvavenia.[24] The people howl, the bells ring, the Princess wails as if she were already in Satan's claws, and everything is precipitated off the stage in wild confusion.

At this moment, Ossian enters and eats a sandwich. When he has finished, the scene changes to the audience chamber of the Emperor's palace. The Emperor wears a Napoleon coat and the lords stand about his majesty in grey leggings which they have unbuttoned in grief. Two stockings lie in one corner of the room. Very angry with each other, they want to poison each other. A plush jerkin hangs nearby, turning the pages of an encyclopedia and drinking a cup of tea. Then a revenge-seeking hypochondriacal broomstick with bloodthirsty mien slinks in —

LIDDY. Gracious heavens! stop it! I fear I shall lose my reason!

MOLLFELS. I only wanted to show you mine is already gone — out of love.

LIDDY. I hope you're not really serious about this love, for I am engaged to Sir Wernthal.

MOLLFELS. Alas, then let the earth consume me! I am an unhappy man! — Engaged? — Indeed, my tears are on the run! *Passing his hand over his forehead.* If — if I should have to do away with myself in this my

---

[23]Eduard Heinrich Gehe (1793-1845), author of a number of Schiller-like dramas (*Gustav Adolf, Dido, Anna Boleyn*), various opera librettos, and novellas.
[24]From the Latin: *salva venia* — with permission to say.

sorrow, then I shall have to shoot myself; for if I were to drown myself,
I would have to worry about getting a cold; and to stand before God's
Judgment Seat with the sniffles would be, on account of the sneezing,
partly disturbing, and, in part, unseemly. *He exits.*

LIDDY. That man could please a girl more than he thinks.

ACT THREE

SCENE ONE

Evening. SCHOOLMASTER's *Room, lighted by a lamp.*
SCHOOLMASTER *and* BLACKSMITH *in conversation.*

BLACKSMITH. Yes, Professor, he had a horsehoof and a tufted heel!

SCHOOLMASTER. It's the Devil, Konrad, it's the Devil! Any textbook of natural history will tell you the Devil has a horse's hoof!

BLACKSMITH. And he yelled out after me that he was Satan, and threatened
to wring my neck if I spread the news.

SCHOOLMASTER. Hoho, don't worry about that! I have other plans for him!
— What do you say we catch Old Harry, lock him up in a cage, wander
about the markets and fairs with him, set him up as a mermaid, or, to
make the posters even more attractive, as a "mer"-ry widow, and give
ourselves second billing as two professors of mermaidry?

BLACKSMITH. We might strike it rich!

SCHOOLMASTER. Or we could also present him to the public exactly as he
is, as the Devil. Then we'd make him dance, letting him jump to the
tune "How lovely lights our way the morning star!" and force him to let
us put your head into his mouth as if he were a trained lion, all to the
amazement of the onlookers.

BLACKSMITH. It would be hard to put my head into his mouth; he has a
rather small snout.

SCHOOLMASTER, *walking up and down the room in proud, stately strides.*
You pitiful, doubting Thomas! I've knocked far more difficult things
into the heads of my pupils.

BLACKSMITH. I haven't seen the least sign of it in my boy.

SCHOOLMASTER. Your boy! That stupid sack of potatoes! The wise Con-
fucious himself, though he never saw hops or malt, would have lost several wagonloads on him! — Confidentially, what was your wife thinking
about when she became pregnant? The kid's got a head like a horse.

BLACKSMITH. Oh that was due to that cursed stallion who broke loose during a shoeing. My wife was standing in the kitchen pouring vinegar
onto the salad when suddenly she looked up at the window and saw him
staring her in the face.

GRETCHEN, *enters.* Good evening, Professor! The judge's wife ordered me
to call you a shameless ox and to smash you on the head with Jacob
Casanova de Seingalt!

SCHOOLMASTER, *while picking up the individual volumes of the work.* Hmn, hmn! Has Madam no use then for these books, neither for instructional purposes nor for kitchen reading?

GRETCHEN. Ah, the Professor, how dumb he is! Such goods were not made for kitchen reading, as any Christian soul a mile away could tell. Madam is beside herself with anger.

SCHOOLMASTER. Hmn! Hmn! But there are only three volumes here, and I sent Madam four — what's happened to the fourth?

GRETCHEN. Well, right in the very heat of scolding, Madam stuck the fourth volume into her knitting bag.

SCHOOLMASTER. In the heat of scolding into her knitting bag? Why, why what puzzling inconsistency!

GRETCHEN. Adieu, Professor! *Off.*

SCHOOLMASTER. Smithy, smithy, now I've got it! This is how we're going to lure the Devil into our hands! Can you build a bird cage?

BLACKSMITH. I think so, yes.

SCHOOLMASTER. So run — run and make me one tonight that's as big as a man, with a door five feet high. And tomorrow evening I shall place it in the woods, lay the Memoirs of Jacob Casanova de Seingalt inside, and hide in the bushes. Now, with a fellow like the Devil, it is always to be presumed that he goes out poaching; when, while making the rounds, he nears the cage, I hope the Memoirs of Jacob Casanova de Seingalt — which, according to the judge's wife who stuck the fourth volume into her knitting bag, must be especially sinful — will lure him, due to the magnetic power with which Satan is drawn to Evil, irresistibly to the cage. Then I shall rush out, shut the door behind him, and whistle through my fingers.

BLACKSMITH, *while trying to make the* SCHOOLMASTER *an obliging compliment.* Why, Professor, you worked that out downright philo — filou — yeah, you spread it out broad as a whale!

SCHOOLMASTER, *giving him a friendly pat on the shoulder.* Philosophical is the word, my friend, philosophical! Etymologists trace it back to the phrase: "Phil is so fickle." One has only to elide the words; change the vowel "i" in "is" to "o"; drop the extra "s," which is, after all, a mere orthographical adjustment; substitute "ph" for the "f" in fickle, making for more consistent spelling anyway, since Phil is spelled with "ph"; and instead of that awkward "kle" ending, simplify it all to "al." And the word philosophical is most unphilosophically, but right philologically explained and deduced.[25]

BLACKSMITH, *as if he understood him.* Quite right, Professor! Deduced! That's the hitch, there's the rub! — Now "official" is something else again. Oh, oh, we smithies aren't so dumb, we smithies aren't so dumb! *Off.*

[25]Here the translator has had to take the liberty of trying to do in English what Grabbe did in German but, of necessity, with entirely different words. The original is a play on the similarity in sound, in German, of "philosophisch" and "viele Strohwisch."

SCHOOLMASTER, *while getting into a dressing gown.* My, it's late already — I'll just pour myself out a small glass of stomach tonic and then jump into bed. — What, who's knocking there? Come in!

RATPOISON *and* MOLLFELS *come into the room.*

RATPOISON. Sorry to disturb you at bedtime like this, Professor! — But do you know any remedy against shooting oneself? Mr. Mollfels is suffering from the idea!

SCHOOLMASTER. If I might suggest anything it would be to give him a dose of eight to twelve bottles of wine. They would at least postpone a little the evil deed.

RATPOISON. *Bene,* Professor! A dozen bottles of wine! Presto! Close the shutters! We're going to make a jolly night of it! Aren't we, Mollfels?

MOLLFELS. All right, in the name of hell, let it be! Torture is the foil of joy, and so I will torture myself! Here's the gold! Produce the wine, Professor. If, all this notwithstanding, I still persist in the idea of shooting myself, there'll be plenty of time tomorrow to catch up.

SCHOOLMASTER, *who has fallen into the liveliest activity.* Hurrah! Tweedledum and tweedledee! That was a manly speech, Mr. Mollfels; and "produce the wine" is my motto! *He rushes to the bedroom door.* Little Gottlieb, Little Gottlieb! Get up! Get up! Put on the lanterns and light up your pants! Get up! Get up! You must come along with me to the tavern and help carry back the wine.

LITTLE GOTTLIEB, *comes out from the bedroom half asleep, eyes blinded, in nothing but a long nightshirt, whining crankily.* Ugh — hrmph — ugh! The room's steaming! The Turks are drumming!

SCHOOLMASTER. You rascal, are you crazy? What's got into you? There! Rub some water over your eyes! Quick! Quick! Quick! Where are your pants? Your shirt? Here! Put on my coat! There! It fits you royally! Like a black velvet train! Now you look like the First Lady of the Theatre! Come, come, come! *Off with* LITTLE GOTTLIEB.

MOLLFELS. Ha! Ha! Ratpoison, you could easily insert this scene without any changes into one of your comedies.

RATPOISON. O my God, Mollfels, are you in your right mind? Such coarse low-comedy! Nowadays comedy must be fine, so refined it can no longer be seen; then should the audience nevertheless see it, it is overjoyed; not, to be sure, over the play, but over its own cleverness at having found something there where nothing was to be found. Moreover, the German is much too cultured and too rational to be able to tolerate real, strong, bold humor!

MOLLFELS. Yes, yes, he does not laugh until he is sure that afterwards he will be able to formally account for his having laughed.

RATPOISON. Believe me, if anyone really wrote a play that, even in its most unimportant parts, was based upon a profounder view of life, and dared carry out his ideas freely and originally, he would be misunderstood for that very reason by the vast majority of the public who cannot see the wood for the trees.

MOLLFELS. It sounds as though you must have written such a play, and that it flopped.

RATPOISON. Ah, don't say "flopped!" It sounds so hard! "Failed" sounds so much gentler.

MOLLFELS. May I make a suggestion? In the future write nothing but tragedies. If you lend them the necessary degree of banality, they cannot fail but earn the most thundering applause. The plot, especially, you must so fashion that it be charmingly flat and trivial; otherwise every nearsighted sheepshead should be able to see through it. You must not assume the least understanding or spirit of inquiry on the part of your reader; and if, through mishap, a striking scene should creep in, be careful to remark at the end of it what its purpose be, and in what connection it be taken with the rest. —And you must by all means spread everything sufficiently thick, for thickness is pleasing even if it be oozing mud. — Above all, though, always bear in mind the taste of the ladies, for they, though never recognized by a true poet as qualified judges, are now considered the highest court of appeal in the realm of art; whether they were there elected on account of their neuroses or their skill in shredding lint is still an undecided question. Much more decided a point is, Mr. Ratpoison, that if one possess strength enough to scorn one of these rules, he is decried as a blind, crazy, raw visionary who slops together beauty and paltriness. If at this moment Homer or Shakespeare were to appear with their works, judgments might be expected to follow in which the Iliad were called a senseless hodgepodge and Lear a bombastic pigsty; yes, some critics might perhaps drop Homer a well-meaning hint that he model himself after *The Enchanted Rose*[26] or order Shakespeare to diligently study the novels of Helmina von Chézy[27] and Fanny Tarnow[28] that he may learn human psychology from them.

RATPOISON, *who has coughed several times during* MOLLFELS'S *speech and expressed signs of disapproval.* My principles do not permit me to fully second your satirical attacks upon the rules. Rule seems to me much more indispensable; it is the trouser leg of genius. On what should the Artist depend, how should he find himself, if not by virtue of his relationship to the critics he —

MOLLFELS. The artist should rely upon his own genius. He should have a detached understanding of the calm, clear workings of his own mind, and as far as his relationship to the critics is concerned, it is the following: the critics put up the barriers, making them only as wide as their brains, hence very narrow; genius enters, finds them impossibly small, breaks them to pieces which he throws at the heads of the carping critics so that they howl out, loud and screamingly. When the common rabble hears this outcry, it says in the simplicity of its soul: they are criticizing!

RATPOISON. Hmn, according to this every badly reviewed poet will think you on his side.

MOLLFELS. I am so far from being on his side that I have already pointed

---

[26]"Die bezauberte Rose" (1818), a romantic tale in 3 cantos by Ernst Schulze.
[27]Helmina von Chézy (1783-1850), a dilettante writer of the romantic school.
[28]Fanny Tarnow (1779-1862), novels, translated Balzac, George Sand, together with von Chézy published the women's magazine, *Iduna.*

out to the government its cruelty towards the public in still delaying the execution of a dozen poets for their miserable works.

RATPOISON, *in uncomprehending unrest.* No! No! That would be too much! To execute them! Merciful heaven, what a gruesome idea! Heinrich Döring, Friedrich Gleich, Methusalem Müller, Karl Stein[29] — O my teeth chatter, my teeth chatter! *Heaving a sigh.* Ah, here comes the Schoolmaster with the wine!

SCHOOLMASTER *and* LITTLE GOTTLIEB *enter, each loaded down with bottles.*

SCHOOLMASTER, *sings.* Vivat Bacchus, let Bacchus live,
  Bacchus was a wonderful man!

To LITTLE GOTTLIEB. Sing, you silly dope, sing along!

LITTLE GOTTLIEB, *quacks.* Vivat Bacchus, let Bacchus live,
  Bacchus was a wonderful man!

MOLLFELS. Little Gottlieb, you croak so badly the stones wish they had ears they could stop up.

SCHOOLMASTER. Heh heh? Hasn't the child a most lovable voice? I have already put away in my desk twenty-two letters from the Sirens; they want him for an exclusive engagement; only I answer them each time that he is still too young.

RATPOISON. You long-nosed cudgel-master, stop blowing and set up the glasses.

SCHOOLMASTER, *setting them on the table.* There they are!

RATPOISON. Hurry, then, fill them up!

SCHOOLMASTER. Patience! Patience! Half a minute! *He runs to the bed, pulls off the bedsheets, and wraps them around his head.*

MOLLFELS. Zounds, what kind of a mad disguise is that?

SCHOOLMASTER. Mere precaution, Mr. Mollfels, mere precaution! Should I fall down, I prefer my head bandaged while I do my drinking!

MOLLFELS. O wise, experienced practitioner! As your humble pupil, I copy your precautionary measures!

RATPOISON. And I, too, do the same! *They tear loose two sheets and wrap them the same way around their heads.*

SCHOOLMASTER. Indeed, gentlemen, in these monstrous bedsheets our three heads look like the three unhappy flies which fell into the middle of the milkpail.

MOLLFELS. Professor, tell us a story out of your childhood.

RATPOISON. Yes, yes, out of your childhood. *They sit down around the table and fill their glasses.*

SCHOOLMASTER, *drinks.* Fuimus troes,[30] the golden years of indiscretion are gone! — Little Gottlieb, where are you? — Open your snout, you lout! A gulp of germanized champagne won't damage your patriotism any! — — Now, gentlemen, to proceed with this tale out of those *tempi passati* is a ticklish undertaking for a schoolmaster who must earn the respect of his pupils and for a husband whose wife plagues him with jealousy!

---

[29]Döring, Gleich, Müller, and Stein: minor writers, translators, publishers of the period.
[30]Virgil, *Aeneid*, Canto II, v. 325.

MOLLFELS. No prefaces! You have been in love! You shall have to tell us about your first love!

RATPOISON. Hu — how it thrills the dried-out pedagogical billy-goat to hear about his first love!

SCHOOLMASTER. O you beautiful, wild, never-to-return-again, vanished days when I — Touch glasses, gentlemen: long live Little Hannah Honeysweet!

MOLLFELS *and* RATPOISON. Here's to her!

SCHOOLMASTER. Forgive me, but I so immeasurably treasure this girl that to drink but a single glass to her health I find impossible! *He pours down six glasses in a row.*

RATPOISON *and* MOLLFELS. Bravo, Professor! We too know how to treasure your little Hannah! *They likewise pour down six glasses.*

SCHOOLMASTER. And now that we've all properly honored Little Hannah, I shall proceed with my narrative. The sweet child was an angel; but her father, the principal of the City School, was nothing but a shabby filou. He wore a wig which tied in the back and which dogs and cats lay in wait for from early morning until midnight, taking it, as they did, for a rat nest; and his worn-out leathery pants were once cited as a Phoenician mausoleum by one of our historians in a learned disputation on the oldest traces of German commerce with foreign nations.

RATPOISON *and* MOLLFELS. Hoho! A mausoleum! *They drink.*

SCHOOLMASTER, *to* LITTLE GOTTLIEB, *who stands idle in a corner.* You malicious, envious, cold-blooded, mischievous, treacherous young monkey, why do you stand there in the corner? Why don't you open your mouth? You certainly don't want to stay sober and mock our carousing, do you? Drain this bottle, *stante pede,* or I'll bite off your left thumb! LITTLE GOTTLIEB *grabs the bottle and downs it with great glee.*

Again to RATPOISON *and* MOLLFELS. Well, so this principal was a harpagon, and we students hated him as much as we loved his daughter. But since I was a wideawake lad, and he needed company to while away the time on long winter evenings when he never burned a light, I was quite in his favor, and had regularly to visit him at approaching dusk. There in the dark room I would sit with him and his daughter, he on my left, she on my right. Now while gossiping about his editions of Pliny, I would manage furtively to press her tiny, little hand; after feeling her response, I would go further, gradually wind my arm about her dainty neck, tug at her neckerchief, and tickle her neighboring bosom. One night, to my great distress, the old man sat in her place; I, unaware, of the change, began as usual to play with her. To be sure, Little Hannah's close-buttoned dress and big steel buttons did strike me as strange, but I, in my infatuated blindness, would not let myself be disturbed. The principal himself, whose wife had been dead for some time, probably enjoyed my tendernesses, for he didn't move a finger and remained still as a mouse; but finally, when I whispered in his ear: "Little Hannah, Little Hannah, how come so flat, shriveled up, and ugly tonight!" this insult to his beauty threw him into such a rage he lambasted me a blow on the face that not only yanked me out of my deceptive illusion but also left such a powerful imprint upon my cheek that the next day everybody wanted to know if that mark had been tattooed on my face.

MOLLFELS, *half tipsy.* Delightful, Professor, delightful! So you tickled the old Principal on the vest! O joy! O joy! O joy!

SCHOOLMASTER. Long live tickling!

MOLLFELS. Let it live! *They souse without restraint.*

SCHOOLMASTER. Jimminy Crickets, Mollfels, look at Ratpoison's heavy eyes!

RATPOISON, *grips the* SCHOOLMASTER, *in his drunkenness, by the vest.* Right? Isn't that right? Aren't my poems the dullest, tritest, most unworthy scrawling mess?

SCHOOLMASTER. They are just as good as the poetry of Elise von Hohen-hausen, born of Ox.[31]

RATPOISON. Crush me, pulverize me, Professor, step on me! I am a worm, an unworthy ninny! My verse contains no sap, my thought no sense! I am a worm, a mincing worm! Fling me into the swamp! Fling me into the swamp!

SCHOOLMASTER, *constantly drinking and gradually becoming as drunk as the rest.* Do not weep, Little Ratpoison; speak softly so that Nightwatchman doesn't hear! You're in heat! Your heart's overflowing! — Is't not so, Mollfels?

MOLLFELS, *embracing the* SCHOOLMASTER. Ah, my Liddy, my Liddy!

SCHOOLMASTER, *girlish.* Don't crumple my neckerchief, Karl dear! *Pointing to* LITTLE GOTTLIEB, *who has emptied his bottle and now comes tumbling out of the corner.* But hide yourself! Dearest friend, hide yourself! Here comes my father!

MOLLFELS. I should say you were a little drunk, Liddy!

SCHOOLMASTER. Unfortunately, dearest Karl, I've peered a little too deep into the glass!

RATPOISON, *falling on the floor.* "Nonsense, you win, and I must give in!"[32] *He falls asleep.*

LITTLE GOTTLIEB, *scrambles up on the* SCHOOLMASTER *and looks into his face.* You bad Schoolmaster, you! Thrashed me! Hit me! Scolded me! I'm drunk! I'll hit you back! I'll hit you back!

SCHOOLMASTER. O most honored Father! Forgive me! I can't help it: I must marry my Karl or I shall die! Be not so cruel, most magnanimous of fathers! On bended knee, I pray you, be not so cruel to your un-happy daughter! *Pardonnez-moi, Monsieur!*

MOLLFELS. Yes, Baron, pardon us, and hinder not our present and eternal joy!

    LITTLE GOTTLIEB *tumbles head over heels onto the floor.*

SCHOOLMASTER, *happy.* Victory, victory! He pardons us, he tumbles to the floor! Karl, Karl, in my arms! We may love each other!

---

[31]Elisabeth Philippine Amalie, Freifrau von Hohenhausen, geborne von Ochs (1789-1857), writer of poems and tales, translations of Byron and Scott, during 1822-24 a member of Berlin literary circles.

[32]Said by the dying Talbot in Schiller's "Jungfrau von Orleans," Act III, Scene VI.

MOLLFELS, *looks over* LITTLE GOTTLIEB. Now that I look a little more closely at your father, he seems to have become a hell of a lot smaller!

SCHOOLMASTER. He's had the measles, my beloved!

MOLLFELS. Ugh! Ugh!

SCHOOLMASTER. Good God, why do you sigh?

MOLLFELS. Woe, woe! I'm afraid I'm going to fall off the table!

SCHOOLMASTER. Frankly, I can give you no other advice than that you climb
up on it.

MOLLFELS *climbs up on the table so that he shouldn't fall off, and then falls
down.*

SCHOOLMASTER, *raises a horrible cry and claps his hands together over his
head.* O fate, fate, unrelenting fate! No human cunning can ward you
off; no mortal can escape you! Mollfels climbs *up* on the table, and, that
notwithstanding, he has to fall *down!* O fierce, marble-hearted monster!
He gnashes his teeth.

MOLLFELS. Will no one help me up? Professor! Liddy! Where are you two?

SCHOOLMASTER. *Zaïre, vous pleurez?*[33] That pains me, upon my honor, that
pains me! — *Venez, ma chère!* It's pitch-black outside! Let's go to
church and play the organ! *He takes* MOLLFELS *by the arm and waddles
out with him.*

SCENE TWO

A meadow, break of day.

COUNT MURDAX *is out taking a walk, thirteen* TAILOR APPRENTICES *meet him.
he puts on his napkin, and kills them all.*

SCENE THREE

A road in the village.

The four NATURAL SCIENTISTS *enter, bloody headed; each with a flintstone
in his hand.*

ALL FOUR TOGETHER. There, quite on purpose, we've cracked our heads
and racked our brains with these flintstones and still cannot determine
what kind of fellow that so-called finger-in-the-light-sticking Vicar is!
O! O! O!

ONE OF THEM. Do not despair, gentlemen! Science calls! Let us try once
more! Courage! Let's crack our heads and rack our brains again!

ALL FOUR. Once again: crack our heads, rack our brains! *They strike themselves on their heads with the flintstones — get nothing but sparks — and
go off cursing.*

SCHOOLMASTER *comes in with* MOLLFELS *and* RATPOISON.

SCHOOLMASTER. That was a mad night! To my astonishment, when I woke

---

[33]Voltaire's "Zaïre," Act IV, Scene II.

up I was lying at the foot of the church organ, right in front of the pedals.

MOLLFELS. And I was sitting, legs akimbo, on the sarcophagus of the Baronial family vault.

RATPOISON. I was lying under your desk, Professor; and Little Gottlieb was next to me, snoring like a Dachshund.

SCHOOLMASTER. It is now my humble suggestion that each of us partake of a light morning snack; it will dissipate the aftermath of drunkenness, or, to put it more elegantly, drive away the hangover.

RATPOISON. I am most upset that I cannot join you; I have a commission to perform for the Baroness, who, as you know, brooks no delay. *Off.*

SCHOOLMASTER. Ratpoison is a fool. If he knew the joy of eating a nice salted herring with straight rum at the corner tavern after an all-night drunk, he wouldn't give a damn about his commission!

MOLLFELS. I shall go with you, Professor! Come! I have a mighty appetite! *Both off.*

SCENE FOUR

Room in the Castle. RATPOISON *and* LIDDY *enter.*

RATPOISON. No, Madam, do not refuse me my request: consent to a walk in the woods. Schallbrunn is one of the most fascinating places on earth; like a shepherd hut out of Guarini's *Pastor Fido*,[34] it lies in the green solitude of the forest; like two liquified nightingales, two murmuring brooks twitter through the stillness of these surroundings; and, as a poeticizing Count[35] so feelingly expressed it, pilgrims bloom there and murmur sweet prayers in the woods!

LIDDY. Nicely declaimed, Mr. Ratpoison! — How far is it to Schallbrunn?

RATPOISON. Not quite a mile, and the way alternates charmingly between arbored heights and grassy valleys.

LIDDY. Be prepared then: the carriage should be ready within the hour, and we can drive to the Pavilion with my Uncle. *She goes out with* RATPOISON.

SCENE FIVE

Bushy woods. Evening.

The SCHOOLMASTER *enters with a giant bird cage on his back.*

SCHOOLMASTER. The sun has gone down; the tired world has put on its starry nightcap; one half the earth now seems dead; behind curtains

---

[34]Referring to "Il pastor fido," the pastoral play by Giovanni Battista Guarini (1538-1612).

[35]Meaning Otto Heinrich Graf von Loeben, called Isidorus Orientalis (1786-1825), a pseudoromantic poet and novelist. This is probably a take-off on his pastoral-chivalric novel "Arkadion" (1811-12) or his poems of a "contemplative pilgrim."

bad dreams terrify unprotected sleep; magic begins its dread service of the pale Hecate; murder slinks about its hideous business in giant robberstrides, roused by its howling nightwatcher, the wolf; the blacksmith has put together a cage for me; here in the bushy thicket I will set it up; the axe blows of the woodstealing Devil echo in the distance, and I shall have greatly deceived myself if the magical effect of three volumes of Jacob Casanova de Seingalt, published by Wilhelm von Schutz, do not lure him here! Just to make sure, however, I shall intensify the effect with the posthumous writings of the late Althing,[36] and lay them on the Casanova like bad pepper on fat ham. *He sets the cage in the shrubbery, opens the door, places the Casanova and Althing's posthumous writings within, and then steps aside. Pause. The* DEVIL *comes in sniffing.*

SCHOOLMASTER. Ha, there he is already! How it tickles his nose!

DEVIL. I smell two things here: to the left, something abominably licentious, — to the right, something drunken, child-chastising.

SCHOOLMASTER. I'll be damned, — can that be some sort of allusion to me?

DEVIL, *while going toward the* CASANOVA. The lascivious draws me powerfully on . . . *Turning toward the* SCHOOLMASTER . . . but also the drunken baits me no less . . . *Standing still.* If only I knew which of the two were more immoral! *He sniffs harder.*

SCHOOLMASTER. O Lord, my conscience!

DEVIL. I have it! That drunken sot, the child-chastiser is the worser; and the abominable licentious one is, in comparison, innocence itself! *He hurries to the* SCHOOLMASTER.

SCHOOLMASTER, *as he eases away from him in a circle.* Holy Sacrament, now I'm in a fine mess! I never dreamt I could be more culpable than the *Memoirs* of Jacob Casanova de Seingalt and Althing's *Posthumous Writings!* It's nothing but simple calumniation by the malicious Mr. Mephistopheles! — Thank God, here's a piece of a church pew I must have stuck into my coatpocket last night! I'll hold it before his nose and shy him away with it! *He does so.*

DEVIL, *sneezes violently and recoils.* Phew! The drunken sot has bettered himself with a piece of church pew! Phew! — Nay, now I'd rather turn back to the licentious one, even though it be more moral! *He runs eagerly back into the cage, and just as he has the Casanova in his hand, the* SCHOOLMASTER *jumps up and slams the door behind him. Crying out.* O ye elements, they've locked me in, I'm caught! *Violently rattling the bars.* In vain! In vain! The bars are laid crisscross — in the shape of a cross: I cannot break them! *He looks at the* SCHOOLMASTER. O you rascally, swindling, mean — No, I meant to say: you sweet, most lovable, worthy man! Set me free! O set me free!

SCHOOLMASTER. Go whistle for it! With bacon, you catch mice; with Casanova and Althing, the Devil! *He picks up the cage, sets it on his back, and carries off the* DEVIL.

---

[36]Althing: pseudonym for Christian August Fischer (1771-1829), writer of obscene tales, and translator of Lesage's "Gil Blas."

COUNT MURDAX *enters with his accomplices.*

COUNT MURDAX, *clears his throat, spits, and begins his speech.* Comrade accomplices! Baroness Liddy is lounging over there in the woods in the Pavilion at Schallbrunn! Inasmuch as she will not amicably accept my suit, I have decided to take her, with your help, *par force! —* Have you brushed your hair over those gallow-physiognomies of yours so that I need not be ashamed of you?

THE ACCOMPLICES. Yes.

COUNT. Good.

They go off.

MOLLFELS, *comes on with three armed* SERVANTS. Suspicious hordes sneak through the forest, — Miss Liddy is at Schallbrunn. — I fear, I fear a conspiracy against her! *To the* SERVANTS. Load your pistols; perhaps there'll be an opportunity to leave your mark on a couple of scoundrels!

They load their pistols and go off.

SCENE SIX

Bare room in the pavilion at Schallbrunn. LIDDY, BARON, *and* RATPOISON *enter.*

LIDDY. Ratpoison, you have disappointed us terribly! — If it's romantic here, then — Ooh, Uncle dear, I'm frightened! Order the carriage and let's get away from this bandit hideout.

BARON. Why, child, you're trembling! This isn't at all like you!

LIDDY. I beseech you, order the carriage, order the carriage!

BARON. Hello there! Landlord! *The* LANDLORD *enters.* Have you fed my horses?

LANDLORD. I don't feed strange horses! *Exits.*

LIDDY. The old bear!

BARON, *rushing after him.* You miserable fool, now you *will* feed them!

LIDDY. Uncle, where are you going? — He doesn't hear me and goes storming down the steps! — And not even a light in this gloomy room! — Ratpoison, where are you?

RATPOISON, *with pinched voice.* I, gracious lady, I —

LIDDY. Heavens, what was that? What a racket on the floor!

RATPOISON, *teeth chattering.* It was only a mouse! Such dread I've never felt before! — At last! There comes Uncle with a light!

BARON, *rushes in violently, a light in his hand.* Show me your face, Ratpoison! *After lighting it up.* No, you know nothing about it! You're not in this!

LIDDY. By all ye Saints, what does this mean?

BARON. That landlord is a traitorous scoundrel! He lets a band of robbers into the house and refuses me my horses!

LIDDY. O Lord! We are lost!

BARON. And if they wanted only our money — but they are determined to have you Liddy, you!

RATPOISON. Oh, if that's all, Liddy, then save us! Need knows no command! If you grant the Captain a private audience, you can easily get rid of the probable resulting complications by a so-called trip to the country.

LIDDY. Shut up, you miserable versifier, shut up; and hide your miserable self over there behind that stove! *Ripping out a hatpin.* Before a single one of those scoundrels dare touch my hand, this hatpin shall penetrate my breast ten times! — — On your feet, dear Uncle! Barricade the door! In danger the weakest is often the strongest!

BARON. Heroic, courageous child! *They barricade the door.*

LIDDY. Shove the table in front of it!

BARON. It's too heavy for us.

LIDDY. Then I'll manage it alone!

BARON. Liddy, Liddy, its monstrous top will crush you! — In the name of the Lord, where do you get all that strength?

LIDDY. Take the sword and give me your hunting knife! — Ha, they're coming!

The COUNT *and his* ACCOMPLICES *storm the door and, after some shoving, break it down;* LIDDY *throws the hunting knife at one's head; the mob stops short a moment; shortly thereafter* MOLLFELS' *voice is heard; pistol shots ring out, the attackers scatter,* MOLLFELS *bursts in, and his* SERVANTS *follow with the captured* COUNT.

LIDDY. We're saved! *She faints in* MOLLFELS' *arms.*

MOLLFELS, *to the* BARON, *pointing to the* COUNT. There's the ringleader of this cursed attack ... *While two* SERVANTS *enter with* SIR WERNTHAL ... and we found that one nearby. Count Murdax maintains he sold the Baroness for about 20,000 Reichstaler to a landlord-and-bride collector; also, he very carefully stuffed all his pockets full of onions so that later he could wring tears of commiseration from his eyes. *The* SERVANTS *turn out* WERNTHAL's *pockets and a mess of onions tumble forth.*

LIDDY, *recovering.* You, Mollfels, you risked your life for me; if you wish my hand in return, it is yours.

MOLLFELS. Blissfully happy I sink before you —

LIDDY. Not so! A man like you need bend before no maiden! Joyfully I press this kiss upon those lips so often used to mock themselves!

BARON. Well done! I bless your union!

RATPOISON. And I shall prepare the prothalamium!

LIDDY, *smiling.* Ratpoison, you are a frightful coward!

RATPOISON. I am a poet, gracious lady!

BARON, *to* WERNTHAL *and the* COUNT. But you, you wretches, disgraces to the nobility, you shall be pitilessly punished, as you so well deserve! I'm going to have you two bound and tied together like the lowest of thieves, — have you carried through the town at high noon, — have you —

COUNT, *getting heated.* Zounds, this overtaxes my patience! You want me bound and dragged through the streets! Ho, is that the reward I get for so divinely playing my role? Do you think, Mr. Theatrebaron, that I didn't know you were the Actor W————y,[37] and that you dare do nothing against me? — Quick, Wernthal, let's climb down into the orchestra and get to the musicians; they are my most intimate friends and wouldn't touch a hair on our heads. *The* COUNT *and* WERNTHAL *clamber down into the orchestra.*

The SCHOOLMASTER *enters with the* DEVIL *in the cage and the cage on his back.*

SCHOOLMASTER. Congratulations, Baron, upon your and your niece's happy rescue from the clutches of Count Murdax.

BARON. Am I in my right mind, Professor? Isn't that the Vicar you're dragging along in that cage?

SCHOOLMASTER, *sets the cage on the table.* Ha, if the Devil's a man of God, then he might well be a Vicar or a Bishop, for this frosty chimney sweep is none other than Satan in person!

All present, even the COUNT *and* WERNTHAL *in the orchestra, call out, astonished*: What? Satan? A miracle!

SCHOOLMASTER. Yes, for the second time I've redeemed the oppressed earth from this creature, and like a sparrow in a cage I deliver him to mankind to be disposed of at its pleasure.

DEVIL. Baron, I entreat you to free me from this cage, to free me from the Schoolmaster! He teases me continuously, runs with me through thick and thin, tickles me with long nettles, and sprinkles sand on my head three times every minute —

SCHOOLMASTER. It's the Devil, Baron, the Devil. He deserves this. Everyone give me your attention! I shall now test him with my chief experiment! First, he shall have to eat this hymnal, and then give me his paw. *He holds the hymnal out to the* DEVIL. Eat! *The* DEVIL *bristles up, resists.* Eat, Hound of Heaven, eat! *The* DEVIL *resists all the more*

SERVANT, *enters.* A beautiful young lady, dressed like a Russian, has appeared in the hallway, no one knows how.

DEVIL, *shouting with joy.* O that's my grandmother! That's my grandmother! And she's wearing a Russian fur dress because she's afraid of catching cold!

RATPOISON. That's where you're wrong, Satan! The Servant's talking about a beautiful young lady, not about your grandmother!

DEVIL. You fool! As if my grandmother were old and ugly! Didn't you know that we immortals stay eternally young? Should I nevertheless become shrivelled and old, then my special grief would be due to the discovery of Rumford soup. *The* DEVIL'S GRANDMOTHER, *a woman in the bloom of youth and wearing a very stylish Russian winter suit, enter. and greets the party with a silent bow.*

THE DEVIL'S GRANDMOTHER. Professor, let my grandson out of that cage and demand what you will in return for this favor.

SCHOOLMASTER. Then I demand that he give me his paw, Your Serene Highness.

THE DEVIL'S GRANDMOTHER. Give him your paw! *The* DEVIL *gives his paw*

---

[37]Possibly referring to the actor Werdy, who played in Dresden for twenty years

to the SCHOOLMASTER, *whereupon the latter lets him out of the cage.* Well, my dear grandson, you can now make merry! They're all done cleaning up down in Hell! You can come right back home with me; already there is steaming hot coffee on the table, waiting to warm you up.

DEVIL. Wonderful, grandmother, wonderful! — But I like something to read with my coffee! — Professor, do you have on you any of Dr. Krug's[38] works, especially those touching upon the latest stand in the Greek affair?

SCHOOLMASTER. Why yes, they sent me some red herrings today; by means of these same herrings ... *While he pulls several packages out of his pocket* ... I can offer you *Tales* from Van der Velde,[39] the *Collected Works* of the drowned Luise Brachmann[40] and, if I'm not mistaken, even the *West-Ostlicher Divan* and *Wilhelm Meisters Wanderjahren* of Goethe.

DEVIL. Oi, what a pile of printed trash! — Grandmother, didn't you bring along a servant who could carry them for us?

THE DEVIL'S GRANDMOTHER. Certainly, I brought Emperor Nero; he's outside on the steps cleaning your riding boots.

DEVIL, *calls.* Nero! Nero!

THE ROMAN EMPEROR NERO, *enters in livery, the* DEVIL'S *riding boots in his hand.* Your Grace called?

DEVIL. Hand me those boots! *He pulls them on;* — *to* NERO. What's your friend Tiberius up to these days?

NERO. He's lying out in the bleaching field drying his wash.

DEVIL. The smart thing to do! — — Here, my good Nero, — take the Greek situation under your left arm, the poetic works of Luise Brachmann under your right, and carry them along after us.

NERO. Very good, your Grace!

DEVIL, *to the rest of them, laughing roguishly.* Au revoir! *He, his* GRAND-MOTHER, *and the* EMPEROR NERO *with books under his arm, all vanish.*

SCHOOLMASTER. What was that, Baron?

BARON. I'm asking *you*, Professor!

RATPOISON. I just got an idea for a naively mad ballad: "How Nero cleaned the Devil's riding boots!"

BARON. Are you not amazed, Liddy?

MOLLFELS. Liddy and I haven't been following it too carefully.

BARON. That I praise: it becomes lovers! *To an entering* SERVANT. Is our coach damaged?

SERVANT. It hasn't been touched.

BARON. Then go fetch the wine; you'll find a basketful of it in there. *The* SERVANT *off.* Let's revive ourselves with some punch.

---

[38]Wilhelm Traugott Krug (1770-1842), until 1834 Professor of Philosophy at Leipzig; Grabbe heard some of his lectures, and is here satirizing his polemical writings on current events.

[39]Franz Karl van der Velde (1779-1824), popular writer of his day — tales and historical novels.

[40]Luise Brachmann (1777-1822), stimulated and influenced by Novalis, poetess and story writer, committed suicide by throwing herself into the Saale near Halle.

SCHOOLMASTER, *just waking up*. Baron, how right you are!

The SERVANT *brings in the basket of wine.*

RATPOISON, *at the window*. But who's that down there coming through the woods with a lantern? It looks as though he's wending his way here!

SCHOOLMASTER, *likewise at the window*. O the Devil be hanged! Seems to me that fellow's coming here to help us drink up the punch! Why, it's that cursed Grabbe, or, as he really ought to be called, that pigmy crab, the author of this play! He's as dumb as a crowbar, insults every other writer even though he amounts to nothing himself, is knock-kneed, squints, and has the insipid face of a monkey! Shut the door on him, Baron, shut the door in his face!

GRABBE, *outside the door*. O you damned Schoolmaster! You big bag of lies!

SCHOOLMASTER. Shut the door on him, Baron, shut the door in his face!

LIDDY. Professor, professor, how embittered you are against the man who created you! *Knocking*. Come in!

GRABBE *enters with a burning lantern.*

Easy Money

A COMEDY FROM *THE TAMING OF THE SHREW*

BY A L E X A N D E R O S T R O V S K Y

Translated by DAVID MAGARSHACK

Reprinted from EASY MONEY AND TWO OTHER PLAYS
by permission of George Allen & Unwin, Ltd.

CHARACTERS

SAVVA GENNADITCH VASSILKÓV, *a provincial businessman, aged 35, speaks with a strong provincial accent, also dresses provincially*
IVAN PETROVICH TELYÁTEV (JOHNNIE), *a man about town, aged 40*
GRIGÓRY BORISSOVICH KUCHÚMOV, *aged 60, a very imposing gentleman, a retired civil servant of low rank, has many titled relations on his mother's side and by marriage*
YEGOR DIMITRICH GLÚMOV (GEORGE)
NADEZHDA ANTONOVNA CHEBOKSÁROVA, *an elderly lady of imposing manners*
LYDIA YURYEVNA CHEBOKSÁROVA, *her daughter, aged 24*
ANDREY, *Cheboksárova's footman*
GRIGÓRY, *Telyátev's footman*
NICHOLAS, *Kuchúmov's footman*
VASSILY, *Vassilkóv's valet*
MAID
A BOY *from the café*
PARK STROLLERS

ACT ONE

(IN PLACE OF A PROLOGUE)

The Sax Gardens, part of the Petrovsky Park in Moscow. To the right of the spectators—gates into the Park, to the left—a café. STROLLERS *pass over the stage, stop, read the notices on the gates, and walk on.* TELYÁTEV *and* VASSILKÓV *come out of the café.*

TELYÁTEV, *chewing something.* Yes, yes, old fellow, of course . . . *Aside.* I wish I could shake him off!

VASSILKÓV. What I mean is that, being such a pretty girl, everybody naturally finds her very attractive.

TELYÁTEV. You never said a truer word in your life, old fellow, or a more self-evident one. I must congratulate you on this remarkable discovery. It is, if you don't mind my saying so, as plain as the nose on your face. *Takes off hat and bows.* To say that Lydia is beautiful is the same as saying that twice two is four. Hasn't that occurred to you yet?

VASSILKÓV. What I wanted to say was that I liked her very much.

TELYÁTEV. Upon my word, old fellow, that sounds even dafter. Who doesn't like her? Good God, do you think I care a damn whether *you* like her or not? You're quite a stranger here, I suppose?

VASSILKÓV. Yes, I'm not from these parts.

TELYÁTEV. Now, I should have been surprised if you told me that she liked you. That would have been something to write home about! But that you like her is not such a sensation. I know fifteen men, all grown-up and highly presentable, who are head over ears in love with her and there are scores of schoolboys who are in the same boat. They simply swarm round her, crowds of them, with eyes popping out of their heads. Do you know what I should advise you? Just for a change try to get her to like you.

VASSILKÓV. But is it really so very difficult?

TELYÁTEV. Try it, old fellow, try it and see how far you get.

VASSILKÓV. How do I set about it? What qualities must I possess?

TELYÁTEV. Such as neither you nor I have got.

VASSILKÓV. For instance?

TELYÁTEV. To begin with, half a million or thereabouts.

VASSILKÓV. That's nothing.

TELYÁTEV. Nothing? Since when have millions begun to pop out of the ground like mushrooms? Of course, if you are a relation of the Rothschilds, it's a different matter, then we needn't waste any words on it.

VASSILKÓV. Neither the one nor the other, I'm sorry to say, but we live in a time when people with a lot of brains . . .

TELYÁTEV. Ah, there you are, old fellow, with brains and a lot of them, too! This means that you have to have brains in the first place, but brainy chaps are as rare among us as millionaires, and I suppose a damn

sight rarer than that. But we'd better quit talking about brains, for i
any of my friends should happen to overhear us, they'd laugh their head
off. To hell with brains, then. Who are we to talk of brains, if the
good Lord hasn't given us any?

VASSILKÓV. No, sir. I, for one, refuse to renounce my claim to brains so
easily. But what else ought a man to possess to make a good impression
on her?

TELYÁTEV. The handsome uniform of a Guards officer not below the rank
of a colonel at least and the manners of a perfect gentleman, which I'm
very much afraid it is quite impossible for you to acquire.

VASSILKÓV. That's very strange. Is there nothing else, no other qualities o
mind and heart, by which one could win the affection of that girl?

TELYÁTEV. But how do you expect her to find out these precious qualitie
of mind and heart of yours? Will you write a book on astronomy and
read it to her?

VASSILKÓV. I'm sorry, I'm very sorry indeed that she is so unapproachable.

TELYÁTEV. Why be so very sorry about that?

VASSILKÓV. I'll be quite frank with you. Because I'm engaged in a certair
line of business where I simply must have such a wife, I mean, one a
beautiful as Lydia and as well bred as she.

TELYÁTEV. There is no must about it, old fellow. You'd better tell me
something else. Are you very rich or what?

VASSILKÓV. Not yet.

TELYÁTEV. That means that you hope to get rich.

VASSILKÓV. At the present day . . .

TELYÁTEV. Leave the present day out of it.

VASSILKÓV. But why should I? I firmly believe that at the present day it is
very easy to get rich.

TELYÁTEV. Well, that depends, old fellow, that depends . . . . Tell me
have you anything in the nature of a dead cert at the moment? Don't
be afraid, I shan't rob you.

VASSILKÓV. I'm quite sure *you* won't rob me. The only certain source o
income I possess is an estate and some woods to the total value of some
fifty thousand.

TELYÁTEV. That's not bad, not bad at all. In Moscow with fifty thousand
you could easily raise another hundred thousand on credit, which means
that you have a sure one hundred and fifty thousand. On so much
money you can live a long time very pleasantly.

VASSILKÓV. But you have to pay it back one day, you know.

TELYÁTEV. Why trouble your head about that, old fellow? Why be so over
conscientious? Do you like to have something to worry about? Can't you
live without a worry in your head? Let your creditors worry, let them
rack their brains how to get their money back. Why should you inter
fere in somebody else's business? It's our business to borrow, theirs to
lend and get their money back.

VASSILKÓV. I'm afraid I don't know anything about that. I've never had
anything to do with that kind of financial operation. My business trans
actions are based on different principles.

TELYÁTEV. You're still young, the time will come when you'll be glad to adopt our principles.

VASSILKÓV. I doubt it. However, I should like you to introduce me to Lydia and her mother. Although I don't seem to stand much of a chance with her, hope springs eternal, you know. Ever since I saw her for the first time about a week ago, I can't get her out of my head. I even found out where they lived and took an apartment in the same house to make sure that I should see her more often. I admit that for a steady businessman of my age it's rather ridiculous to fall in love, but, I'm afraid, I can't do anything about it. Where love is concerned, sir, I am only a boy. Please, introduce me to her, I beg of you.

TELYÁTEV. Why not? It'll be a pleasure, I assure you.

VASSILKÓV, *pressing his hand firmly.* Thank you, sir. If I can be of any assistance to you in anything . . .

TELYÁTEV. A bottle of champagne every now and then, old fellow, that's all. I don't take any other bribes. So it's a deal?

VASSILKÓV. Any time you like, sir. *Grips his hand.* You don't know how grateful I am to you!

TELYÁTEV. Please, please, my hand! Good God, what an iron grip you have!

VASSILKÓV, *looking round without releasing his hand.* Isn't it them?

TELYÁTEV. It's them. It's them.

VASSILKÓV. I'll go nearer and have a good look at her. You know, I'm such a sentimental bloke! You probably think me funny . . .

TELYÁTEV. But don't take my hand away with you, old fellow, please, leave me my hand!

VASSILKÓV. I beg your pardon, sir. I hope to find you here again.

TELYÁTEV. To be sure, old fellow.

VASSILKÓV *hurries off,* GLÚMOV *comes in.*

GLÚMOV. Who was the funny old boy with you just now?

TELYÁTEV. That's what the good God has sent to plague me with for my sins.

GLÚMOV. What do you get out of it?

TELYÁTEV. Stands me drinks. One bottle of champagne after another.

GLÚMOV. That's not too bad.

TELYÁTEV. I'll lead him on and on and one fine morning I'll probably touch him for a thousand or so.

GLÚMOV. That's even better, if, that is, he really does give you something.

TELYÁTEV. I think he will. You see, he needs me.

GLÚMOV. Cut it out, old man, do me a favour! Who on earth can possibly need you for anything?

TELYÁTEV. You'd better listen to me.

GLÚMOV. All right, I'm listening.

TELYÁTEV. I met him for the first time here in the park about a week ago. I was walking along that path when I suddenly saw a man standing there with his mouth gaping, his eyes wide open and his hat on the back of his head. I must say, old fellow, I couldn't help wondering what had caught the old boy's fancy. There was no elephant about or any

cockfighting. I got nearer and what do you think he was staring at?
Have a guess, old fellow.

GLÚMOV. Search me. What kind of a wonder can one see in a public park?

TELYÁTEV. He was staring at sweet Lydia!

GLÚMOV. He certainly knows a good thing when he sees one.

TELYÁTEV. Lydia and her mamma were in their carriage, round them was
the usual crowd of young fellows, both of them were talking to some
one, I don't know to whom, and there he was, some distance away
simply devouring Lydia with his eyes. As soon as their carriage moved
on, he made a rush after it, knocking over half a dozen people in his
path, including myself. He apologized, of course, and that's how we got
acquainted.

GLÚMOV. Let me congratulate you, old man.

TELYÁTEV. And today, just think of it, he saw me talking to Lydia and her
mum and he almost took me by the scruff of the neck, fairly dragged me
in here and began treating me to champagne, one bottle, then another.
We had quite a little celebration. And it was only a few minutes ago
that he confessed to me that he was in love with Lydia and wanted to
marry her. You see, old fellow, his business—and what his business may
be I'm damned if I know—requires that he should marry just such a girl
as Lydia and no other. Well, of course, he implored me to introduce
him to her.

GLÚMOV. The old idiot! What infernal cheek! Arrives here from Kamchatka
or some other such remote hole and makes straight for one of Moscow's
loveliest girls. For his business, you see, absolutely demands that he
should marry her! His business, if you please, demands it! My business
demands that I should marry an heiress, but I'm damned if I can get
one to marry me. But he . . . What kind of a bird does he think he is?
What is his business, by the way?

TELYÁTEV. Allah alone knows that, old fellow.

GLÚMOV. Tell me what his speech and manners are like and I'll tell you at
once what his business is.

TELYÁTEV. I bet you anything, you won't. He is a man of good birth, but
speaks like a Volga boatman.

GLÚMOV. He's the owner of a steamship line, he runs his steamers on the
Volga.

TELYÁTEV. When he settled the bill for the drinks, he took out a wallet,
you'll hardly believe me, old fellow, so big . . . *Shows with his hands how
big* . . . about a foot at least. And you should have seen what was in that
wallet! All sorts of shares, balance sheets in foreign languages, greasy
letters written on greyish paper by a peasant's hand.

GLÚMOV. Is he rich?

TELYÁTEV. Hardly, old fellow, hardly rich. He says he owns a small estate
and some woods worth altogether fifty thousand.

GLÚMOV. Hm . . . Nothing sensational. Sorry, but he is not the managing
director of a steamship line after all.

TELYÁTEV. He is not rich, or else he's damned stingy. As soon as he'd paid
for the drinks, he entered it in a notebook!

GLÚMOV. Is he a clerk by any chance? What's his character like? What kind of man is he?

TELYÁTEV. A very ingenuous chap, as coy as a boarding school girl.

GLÚMOV. Ingenuous? He isn't a cardsharper, is he?

TELYÁTEV. Can't say, old fellow, impossible to tell. But he drinks like a fish: empties one glass after another, unflustered and unhurried, as if it were ginger pop. We had a bottle each and his face didn't even colour or his voice crack.

GLÚMOV. Must be a native of Siberia. Yes, quite certainly a native of Siberia.

TELYÁTEV. Smokes expensive cigars, speaks excellent French, though with a slight accent.

GLÚMOV. I've got it! He is a representative of some London firm. No doubt about it!

TELYÁTEV. Have it your own way, old fellow. I give it up.

GLÚMOV. Well, whoever he is, let's have some fun with him. We haven't had a good laugh for a long time and we all seem to be going about like poodles with our tongues hanging out.

TELYÁTEV. The joke may be on us, you know.

GLÚMOV. Not at all. We're going to be the villains in this melodrama, at least I am. This is what we'll do: you'll introduce the old boy to Lydia and I'll tell her mother that he owns goldmines. We'll have good sport watching her spread out the net for him.

TELYÁTEV. But when they find out that it's all a practical joke and that all he owns is some silly little estate in some God-forsaken hole . . . .

GLÚMOV. What do we care? We'll say that he told us about his goldmines himself, that he boasted to us about them.

TELYÁTEV. But, really, old fellow, it seems a poor kind of a joke to me!

GLÚMOV. Are you sorry for him or what? Don't be such an ass. We'll say he doesn't gather gold ingots in his mines, but only blackberries in his woods.

VASSILKÓV *comes up.*

TELYÁTEV. Well, old fellow, have you gazed your fill on your beauty?

VASSILKÓV. To my entire satisfaction!

TELYÁTEV. Let me introduce to you a pal of mine, George Glùmov—Savva Vassilkóv.

VASSILKÓV, *clasps* GLÚMOV's *hand in his iron grip.* How do you do? Very pleased to meet you, sir.

GLÚMOV, *disengaging his hand and shaking it.* But I am not pleased at all to have my hand crushed, old man.

VASSILKÓV. I'm sorry, it's a bad provincial habit of mine.

GLÚMOV. Is your name really Savva, sir? Is it the same as Sabbatai?

VASSILKÓV, *very courteously.* No, sir. It's quite a different name.

GLÚMOV. Is it the same as Sebastian?

VASSILKÓV. No, sir. Sebastian is really a Greek name, meaning, worthy of honour, but Savva is an Arab name.

TELYÁTEV. Do you know Greek, old fellow?

VASSILKÓV. A little.

TELYÁTEV. And Tartar?

VASSILKÓV. I can follow a conversation in Tartar if spoken in the Kazar dialect, but in the Crimea I could hardly make myself understood.

GLÚMOV, *aside.* Damn it, can't make him out at all.

TELYÁTEV. Is it long since you left the Crimea, old fellow?

VASSILKÓV. Ten days or so. I stopped there on my way back from England

GLÚMOV, *aside.* The damn liar!

TELYÁTEV. Do you usually go to the Crimea via England?

VASSILKÓV. No, I was in England and I came back via the Suez Canal. was interested in the construction works and the different engineering plants in the Canal zone.

GLÚMOV, *aside.* Maybe he isn't such a liar, after all. *To* VASSILKÓV: We've just been talking of matches, sir. I don't mean those you burn your fingers on, but those which, according to popular belief, are made in heaven.

VASSILKÓV. I heartily approve of the subject, sir.

GLÚMOV. I'd like to marry Lydia Cheboksárova myself, old man.

VASSILKÓV. Many folks would like to do the same, I daresay, she's such a picture!

GLÚMOV. But the many are fools, old man. They hardly know themselve why they want to marry her. They admire her beauty and they want to have it for their own exclusive enjoyment, they want to put it away like frozen capital. No, sir, beauty is not frozen capital. It ought to yield interest. Only a fool can marry Lydia without some ulterior motive The man who should marry her ought to be either a cardsharper or one who is out to make a brilliant career for himself. The cardsharper could use her to attract custom, inexperienced youths with money to waste and the man who wants to get on in the Civil Service could use her a a bait for his superiors and as a means to quick promotion.

VASSILKÓV. I don't agree with you, sir.

GLÚMOV. That's the only sensible view to take, old man. It's the modern view on life, completely up-to-date.

VASSILKÓV. I still don't agree.

GLÚMOV. All this mawkish talk about virtue being its own reward is damn silly. And why, sir? Because it's so unpractical. Please, don't forget that today we live in a practical age.

VASSILKÓV. No, sir. I should very much like to contest your point of view

GLÚMOV. By all means, old man, if you must.

VASSILKÓV. Honesty is even now a paying proposition, sir. In a practical age it is not only better, but also more profitable to be honest. I'm afraid you don't quite know what a practical age means or you seem rather apt to run away with the idea that dishonesty and deceit is good business. Quite the contrary is the truth, sir. In an age of romance and sentiment deceit has a much better chance of succeeding and is much more easily hidden. To stoop to conquer an innocent maiden with her head full of romantic ideas, to deceive a poet whose eyes are in a fine frenzy rolling, to impose on an incurable dreamer or to play tricks on your superior in the Civil Service who is steeped in elegiac poetry, is much easier than to get the better of a hard-headed, practical business-man. No, sir, in the present age honesty is definitely the best policy.

TELYÁTEV. Lydia and her mamma are coming this way.

VASSILKÓV, *catches hold of* TELYÁTEV's *hand*. Introduce me, I implore you!

TELYÁTEV. Ouch! *Snatching his hand away*. With the greatest of pleasure, old fellow.

MRS. CHEBOKSÁROVA *and* LYDIA *come up*.

TELYÁTEV, *to* MRS. CHEBOKSÁROVA. May I introduce you to a millionaire?

MRS. CHEBOKSÁROVA. I daresay you'll overcharge me even for pulling my leg, you naughty man.

TELYÁTEV. Not at all, my dear lady, I assure you. No interest on the trans-action whatever.

MRS. CHEBOKSÁROVA. In that case, do! Only you're such a shameless liar that I don't believe a word you say.

TELYÁTEV. Really, my dear lady, you make me blush. Savva Vassilkóv!

MRS. CHEBOKSÁROVA. Wait, wait! What an extraordinary name!

TELYÁTEV. Never mind the name. All millionaires have such names. VASSIL-KÓV *comes up*. Let me introduce you to my friend Mr. Savva Vassilkóv.

MRS. CHEBOKSÁROVA. I'm so pleased to meet you.

VASSILKÓV. Me too, ma'am. I'm afraid I don't know anybody in Moscow.

TELYÁTEV. He's a stout fellow. He speaks Greek. *Walks up to* LYDIA.

MRS. CHEBOKSÁROVA. From your name I should say you were born in Greece.

VASSILKÓV. No, ma'am. I am a native of Russia. I was born near the Volga.

MRS. CHEBOKSÁROVA. Where do you live?

VASSILKÓV. In the country, ma'am, but most of the time I'm travelling about.

MRS. CHEBOKSÁROVA, *to* GLÚMOV. Be a darling, George, find me my footman.

GLÚMOV *comes up*.

VASSILKÓV. Allow me, ma'am. I'll get him for you immediately. What's his name?

MRS. CHEBOKSÁROVA. Andrey.

VASSILKÓV. I shan't be a minute, ma'am.

MRS. CHEBOKSÁROVA. Thank you so much. Get my shawl from him, will you? I'm beginning to feel chilly. *Speaks softly to* GLÚMOV.

TELYÁTEV, *to* LYDIA. I am always well armed against chills.

LYDIA. A pity! You are such a nice man and I could easily fall in love with you, were you not such a disgusting rake.

TELYÁTEV. A rake! Well, perhaps you're right. I'm not particularly fond of the blameless life. Virtuous men, as a rule, are very jealous, and no one can accuse me of jealousy. Shall I prove it to you?

LYDIA. Do.

TELYÁTEV. With pleasure. I'm going to introduce you to a rival of mine who is sure to take my place in your heart.

LYDIA. That may not be as difficult as you think.

VASSILKÓV, *carrying shawl, almost runs up to* MRS. CHEBOKSÁROVA, *followed by* ANDREY.

VASSILKÓV. Here he is! I found him! *Gives shawl to* MRS. CHEBOKSÁROVA.

MRS. CHEBOKSÁROVA. You gave me such a fright! *Puts on shawl.* Thank you. Andrey, see that our carriage waits for us outside the theatre.

ANDREY. Very good, ma'am. *Goes out.*

TELYÁTEV, *to* VASSILKÓV. My dear Savva . . .

LYDIA. What a name! Is he a foreigner?

TELYÁTEV. He's a native of Magpie Mountain.

LYDIA. Where's that? I never heard of it. I'm sure there's no such place on the map.

TELYÁTEV. It's only been discovered recently. VASSILKÓV *comes up.* Let me introduce you to my friend, Savva Vassilkóv. LYDIA *bows.* He was in London, Constantinople, Never-never-land and Kazan. He tells me that he's seen many beautiful girls, but that he's never met such a beautiful creature as you, dear Lydia.

VASSILKÓV, *blushing to the roots of his hair.* How do you do?

LYDIA. Do you know Mrs. Churil-Plenkov in Kazan?

VASSILKÓV, *stammers.* Very well, indeed.

LYDIA. Is it true that she has separated from her husband?

VASSILKÓV, *unable to overcome his shyness, with unexpected explosive emphasis.* God forbid!

LYDIA, *looking curiously at him.* Do you happen to know Podvorotnikov?

VASSILKÓV, *quickly, with the same explosive energy.* He's one of my best pals, ma'am!

LYDIA *exchanges glances with* TELYÁTEV. *A short, awkward silence.* VASSILKÓV *effaces himself, completely covered with confusion.*

LYDIA. What a funny man!

TELYÁTEV. He's a bit odd. He was a prisoner of war in Central Asia for a very long time, poor fellow. *They speak apart.*

GLÚMOV, *to* MRS. CHEBOKSÁROVA. He owns goldmines, the richest in the world. I understand that every hundredweight of sand yields him over ten pounds of pure gold.

MRS. CHEBOKSÁROVA, *looking at* VASSILKÓV. Really?

GLÚMOV. He says so himself. That's why he is such a wild-looking man. He spends most of his time in the wilderness with the natives.

MRS. CHEBOKSÁROVA, *looks fondly at* VASSILKÓV. You don't say so? I should never have guessed it, to look at him.

GLÚMOV. How are you to guess a gold prospector from his looks? Do you expect him to wear an overcoat made of gold? Isn't it enough that his pockets are lined with gold? You should see the tips he gives to the waiters!

MRS. CHEBOKSÁROVA. What a pity he's throwing his money about like that.

GLÚMOV. Who should he be saving it up for? He hasn't a soul in the whole world. What he wants is a good wife and, particularly, a clever mother-in-law.

MRS. CHEBOKSÁROVA, *looks more fondly at* VASSILKÓV. He's quite a handsome man!

GLÚMOV. Yes, among the aborigines he passes for an Apollo.

MRS. CHEBOKSÁROVA, *to* LYDIA. Let's take our last stroll round the gardens, my dear. Gentlemen, I've been ordered by my doctor to take a stroll in the park every evening. Who wants to join us?

VASSILKÓV. I should like to very much, ma'am, if you don't mind.

MRS. CHEBOKSÁROVA, *smiling pleasantly.* Not at all. I should be delighted.

  MRS. CHEBOKSÁROVA, LYDIA *and* VASSIILKÓV *walk off.*

GLÚMOV. Well, the hunt's up.

TELYÁTEV. Did you spin the jolly old yarn, old fellow?

GLÚMOV. Catch me missing such a chance!

TELYÁTEV. So that's why she was looking so sweetly at him!

GLÚMOV. Let mamma and her darling daughter run after him and let him die of love! We shall work them into a state of absolute frenzy with each other and then knock the ground from under their feet.

TELYÁTEV. Only don't make a slip, old fellow. I shouldn't be in the least surprised if he did marry fair Lydia and carry her off to Magpie Mountain. He simply gives me the jim-jams, old fellow, it's like being crushed by some jolly old avalanche.

      KUCHÚMOV *comes up.*

KUCHÚMOV, *in the distance, singing to himself. Ma in Ispania, ma in Ispania . . . mille e tre . . .*[1] *Walks up haughtily, holding his head high.*

TELYÁTEV. How d'ye do, Prince?

KUCHÚMOV. How are you, my dear old chap? What a beefsteak I had today, gentlemen! Mmmm . . . it simply melted in the mouth. *Mille e tre . . .*

GLÚMOV. At the Club or at a tea-shop?

KUCHÚMOV. Don't talk tommy rot! A rich businessman gave a special dinner in my honour. I was very useful to him, let me tell you, and he wants me to pull some more wires for him. I promised to do my best, of course. It's a mere bagatelle for me, you know!

GLÚMOV. Promises are two a penny.

KUCHÚMOV. What a scorching tongue you have! *Shakes a finger at him.* You'd better be careful or we'll make it too hot for you in Moscow. I've only to say the word . . .

GLÚMOV. Why don't you? I might with luck find myself among intelligent people for a change.

KUCHÚMOV. All right, all right! *Waving him away.* One can't say a word to you.

TELYÁTEV. If you can't get the better of a fellow, you'd better not start on him, that's *my* rule.

KUCHÚMOV. *Mille e tre . . .* Yes, yes, of course . . . I forgot to tell you. Listen to this, gentlemen. I had a bit of good luck yesterday. I won eleven thousand off a chap.

TELYÁTEV. Did you or did someone else win it, old fellow?

GLÚMOV, *excitedly.* Where and when, tell me quickly.

KUCHÚMOV. At the Club.

TELYÁTEV. And did you get the money?

---

[1] From Leporello's aria in Mozart's *Don Giovanni.*

KUCHÚMOV. I got it all right.

TELYÁTEV. Spill the jolly old beans, old fellow.

GLÚMOV. It's a miracle, if true.

KUCHÚMOV, *angrily*. No miracle at all! Do you think me incapable of winning such a packet? I called at the Club yesterday, walked through the rooms a few times, glanced at the menu, ordered some oysters . . .

GLÚMOV. Oysters this month?

KUCHÚMOV. Did I say oysters? I meant sturgeon, of course. Well, a chappie walks up to me . . .

TELYÁTEV. A stranger?

KUCHÚMOV. A complete stranger, didn't know him from Adam. Says to me, would Your Highness like a game of baccarat? Why not, said I, why not? I had plenty of cash on me, why not take a risk, I thought to myself, all I could lose was only a thousand or so. Well, we sat down to it, started with low stakes at first, one rouble, and, gentlemen, I was in luck! What they call, a fool's luck. He kept on asking for new packs of cards, but it didn't help him any, he had to give it up in the end as a bad job. We cast up the accounts, twelve thousand and five hundred! He took out the money . . .

GLÚMOV. But you just said eleven thousand!

KUCHÚMOV. Did I? Well, you see, I have such an atrocious memory. I suppose it must have been somewhere between the two figures.

TELYÁTEV. Who can afford to lose twelve thousand at one go, old fellow? Such people are worth cultivating.

KUCHÚMOV. They tell me he's only just arrived in Moscow.

GLÚMOV. But I was at the Club yesterday and didn't hear a thing.

KUCHÚMOV. I arrived very early. There was hardly a soul there and the whole thing only took about half an hour.

GLÚMOV. You owe us a dinner today.

TELYÁTEV. Vassilkóv has invited us to dinner. You'd better stand us a few glasses of brandy, Prince. It's getting chilly and I'd like to get something warm inside me.

KUCHÚMOV. But I can't trust you. Even a couple of glasses will run me into some money and you'll drink up the whole bottle.

TELYÁTEV. Not at all, old fellow! Just a glass or two, I assure you.

KUCHÚMOV. If that's all you want, I don't mind. You'd better have dinner at my place next Sunday. I've some fresh sturgeon, got it alive from Nizhny, a brace of woodcocks, and a Burgundy you've never had the like . . .

TELYÁTEV, *takes him by the arm*. Come on, come on, old fellow. My teeth are beginning to chatter. If I'm not careful I'll catch a chill. *They all go out.*

MRS. CHEBOKSÁROVA, LYDIA, VASSILKÓV *and* ANDREY *come up.*

MRS. CHEBOKSÁROVA, *to* ANDREY. Fetch the carriage, please.

ANDREY. Verry good, ma'am. *Goes out and returns presently.*

MRS. CHEBOKSÁROVA *to* VASSILKÓV. Thank you very much for your company. We must go home now. Do come to see us.

VASSILKÓV. When will it be convenient for me to call, ma'am?

MRS. CHEBOKSÁROVA. Any time you like. We are at home every day between two and four in the afternoon, but why not come to dinner, without any ceremony? In the evenings we usually go out for a drive.

VASSILKÓV. I shall consider it a great privilege to call on you at the earliest opportunity, ma'am. *To* LYDIA. I'm a plain, outspoken businessman, Miss Lydia. Permit me to express my admiration for your incomparable beauty!

LYDIA. Thank you, sir. *Moves away and, seeing that her mother is still talking to* VASSILKÓV, *signals to her impatiently.*

MRS. CHEBOKSÁROVA. So we'll be expecting you, Mr. Vassilkóv.

VASSILKÓV. I shall not disappoint you, ma'am. If I may, I shall avail myself of your kind invitation tomorrow. I don't live far from you.

MRS. CHEBOKSÁROVA. Indeed?

VASSILKÓV. In the same house, ma'am, only in a different wing.

On leaving MRS. CHEBOKSÁROVA *turns round and looks at* VASSILKÓV *a few times.* VASSILKÓV, *hat in hand, remains rooted to the spot for a long time, staring after them.*

VASSILKÓV. How nice she is to me! It's wonderful! She's either a very good-natured woman or a very perspicacious one to have seen through my uncouth exterior and discovered how essentially good I am at heart. But how easily I get bowled over by a pretty face! That's what comes of devoting all my leisure hours to pure and applied mathematics. Dry figures dry up your heart and at the first chance it turns against you and makes an ass of the mathematician. This is how my heart has revenged itself on me. I've fallen in love suddenly, like a boy of sixteen, and am about to make a damned ass of myself. It's a good thing I'm so sure of myself where money is concerned and, however madly I may be in love with a girl, I shall never spend beyond my income. This respect for my bank account has saved my bacon more than once. *Falls into a reverie.* Lydia! Lydia! What have you done to me! My heart misses a beat every time I think of you. But what if you should have no heart, what if all you should care for is money! With no experience of women I am an easy prey for an unscrupulous and designing girl. She can make me her plaything, her helpless slave. What a blessing it is that I have such a keen sense of business and a holy dread of living beyond my means.

KUCHÚMOV, TELYÁTEV *and* GLÚMOV *come up.*

TELYÁTEV. Well, how do you feel now, old fellow? Better? Accept my congratulations!

VASSILKÓV. I don't know how to thank you, sir. But depend on it, I don't easily forget a kindness.

TELYÁTEV. If you should happen to forget it, I shall jolly well remind you of it. You owe me a bottle of bubbly, old fellow. Let's have dinner and you can pay your debt. *To* KUCHÚMOV. Let me introduce you to our new friend, Prince. Savva Vassilkóv!

KUCHÚMOV. How do you do? Are you a newcomer to Moscow?

VASSILKÓV. Yes, Your Highness.

TELYÁTEV. He's no Highness, old fellow. Just Grisha Kuchúmov. We call him Prince because we're so fond of him.

KUCHÚMOV. Yes, sir, our society is very exclusive. It's very difficult for a stranger to get into it. You have to possess a lot of . . . er . . .

TELYÁTEV. Don't talk such utter rot, old fellow.

GLÚMOV. If our society had really been so exclusive, you and I would never have got into it.

TELYÁTEV. What about it, gentlemen? Let's have a drink straight from the wood right here!

VASSILKÓV. If you desire it, gentlemen. Waiter, a bottle of champagne!

GLÚMOV. And four glasses!

KUCHÚMOV. Yes, I'll do you the honour of joining you in a glass.

GLÚMOV. And from here straight to the Club for a game of cards. *To* KUCHÚMOV. I'd like to see some of your twelve thousand!

KUCHÚMOV. Be careful not to add to them yourself.

TELYÁTEV, *to his* FOOTMAN, *standing at the gates of the park.* Grigory! Help me on with my coat, my dear fellow, will you? Do you know where to find my carriage?

GRIGORY. Yes, sir. It's right here near the gates, sir.

KUCHÚMOV, *to his* FOOTMAN. Nicholas! NICHOLAS *comes up.* Don't stand there gaping at me, man! Stand by the gates and help me into the carriage.

> BOY *from café brings out champagne and glasses.*

VASSILKÓV. Help yourselves, gentlemen. Please, do me the honour.

> *All lift their glasses.*

TELYÁTEV, *to* VASSILKÓV. Good luck, old fellow. I don't think you'll get her, but I wish you good hunting.

GLÚMOV. Of course, he won't get her. He'll come the hell of a cropper.

KUCHÚMOV. What are you talking about?

GLÚMOV. He wants to marry Lydia.

KUCHÚMOV. Wants what? I shan't allow it!

GLÚMOV. He won't ask your permission.

VASSILKÓV. Gentlemen, I bet you three thousand that I shall marry Lydia.

KUCHÚMOV. I never bet.

GLÚMOV. I'd gladly take you on, but I haven't a bean in the world.

TELYÁTEV. And I, old fellow, am afraid to lose.

VASSILKÓV. Gentlemen, you've got the wind up! Then why laugh at me? What about it? It's my last offer. Here's the three thousand. *Takes out the money, but all shake their heads.* The wine has loosened my tongue. I am in love with Lydia, gentlemen, and I'm going to marry her, come what may! I'm not in the habit of wasting words. You'll see, it will be all as I say. Now, let's to dinner!

ACT TWO

A richly furnished room with oil paintings, carpets, curtains. A door at either side and one in the middle. VASSILKÓV *is pacing the room,* TELYÁTEV *enters from door to left.*

TELYÁTEV. I thought you'd left a long time ago. Why don't you go and join the ladies? Is your courage giving out, old fellow?

VASSILKÓV. One of my chief troubles is that I don't know how to carry on a conversation.

TELYÁTEV. What's there to know? The only thing you must remember is never, especially after dinner, start any discussion on a scientific subject. Keep the ball rolling by saying any darned silly thing that comes into your head so long as it is bright, witty and slightly scandalous, but all you talk about is trigonal pyramids and cubic feet.

VASSILKÓV. I've just been thinking out a very jolly story which I'm sure will raise a laugh.

TELYÁTEV. Marvellous, old fellow. Go right in and tell it to them or you'll forget it.

VASSILKÓV. And where are you off to in such a hurry?

TELYÁTEV. Lydia has expressed a wish for some flowers, and I'm going to a florist's to get them for her.

VASSILKÓV. So you are my most dangerous rival, after all!

TELYÁTEV. Don't give it a thought, old fellow. A man who has for the past twenty years never missed a single ballet is no damn good as a husband. Don't be afraid of me, buck up and go tell them your story!

VASSILKÓV *goes out through door to left;* GLÚMOV *enters by same door.*

GLÚMOV. Is *he* still here? What a pertinacious ass! It's high time he was sent packing. He's been given plenty of rope, why doesn't he hang himself? We've had enough fun with him here. What a pity we did not accept his bet.

TELYÁTEV. Even now I should think twice before taking it on.

GLÚMOV. I admit he fleeced us all right that night at the Club. But what do you think about Kuchúmov? What a beauty! Boasts that he's won twelve thousand the day before and can't cough up even six hundred. Meets a man for the first time and already owes him money . . . Where are you off to?

TELYÁTEV. To Petrovka.

GLÚMOV. I'll come with you.

They go out. KUCHÚMOV *and* MRS. CHEBOKSÁROVA *come in.*

KUCHÚMOV, *hums. Muta d'accento e di pensier.*[2]

MRS. CHEBOKSÁROVA. For some time now I've been getting nothing but bad news.

---

[2] From the Duke's aria in Verdi's *Rigoletto: Muta d'accento e di pensier.*

KUCHÚMOV. Humm . . . Yes . . . It's very unpleasant! . . . *e di pensier* . . .

MRS. CHEBOKSÁROVA. Not a day passes without a piece of really terrible news.

KUCHÚMOV. What is he doing there, your husband, I mean? How could he permit things to . . . to come to such a pass? I can't make him out at all. Seems to be one of us, a man of intelligence.

MRS. CHEBOKSÁROVA. But what can he do? You read his letter: bad harvest, drought, all the timber burnt in the sawmill which has been running at an ever mounting loss for years. He writes that he must have thirty thousand immediately or he'll have to sell the estate, which is already in the receiver's hands and is to be sold by public auction.

KUCHÚMOV. What is he worrying about, the imbecile? Hasn't he plenty of friends? Take me, for instance. Tell him to write to me personally. *Muta d'accento* . . .

MRS. CHEBOKSÁROVA. Ah, my dear Grigory, I always knew that you would not let us down!

KUCHÚMOV. What nonsense, my dear. . . . As an old friend of the family I'm always ready to oblige. . . . It's of no account to me. . . .

MRS. CHEBOKSÁROVA. My dear Grigory . . . Heaven help me . . . I must be frank with you, let the others still think we're rich. I have a daughter, she's twenty-four. . . . Think of it, my dear friend!

KUCHÚMOV. Of course, of course . . .

MRS. CHEBOKSÁROVA. We have no one to support us. At present we still get things on credit, but even that's only a drop in the ocean. Winter will soon be upon us: theatres, balls, concerts. Only a mother knows how much money all that eats up. Lydia is only interested in getting everything she wants. She has no idea of the value of money and she doesn't care how much she spends. When she goes shopping, she'll ransack the shops, order everything to be sent home without asking the price of anything and leave me to pay the bills.

KUCHÚMOV. And what about finding a suitable husband for her?

MRS. CHEBOKSÁROVA. It's so difficult to please her.

KUCHÚMOV. When I was young, such a girl would have been abducted long ago. Even today, if only I were a widower . . .

MRS. CHEBOKSÁROVA. You're always joking, but what is a mother to do? After so many happy and untroubled years, suddenly such a blow . . . Last winter I took her out everywhere, spared nothing for her, spent everything to the last penny, even the money that was specially put aside for her trousseau, and all for nothing. And now I have been waiting and waiting for money from my husband and instead I get this dreadful letter. I really don't know how we're going to live. How am I to break the news to Lydia? It will kill her.

KUCHÚMOV. But, of course, if you want anything, then please don't be ashamed to . . . er . . . I mean, let me be a father to Lydia while your husband is away. I've known her since childhood and, believe me, I love her more than a daughter . . . I love her . . . yes.

MRS. CHEBOKSÁROVA. I don't know how much you love her, but there is no sacrifice too great that I would not make for her.

UCHÚMOV. It's the same with me, it's the same with me, my dear lady. By the way, what's this Vassilkóv doing at your house? You ought to be more careful about people.

MRS. CHEBOKSÁROVA. Why shouldn't he be here?

UCHÚMOV. I don't like him. Who is he? Where did he come from? No one knows.

MRS. CHEBOKSÁROVA. I don't know, either. All I know is that he's a gentleman and his manners are unobjectionable.

UCHÚMOV. What does that matter?

MRS. CHEBOKSÁROVA. He speaks excellent French.

UCHÚMOV. Yes, yes, but that doesn't mean a thing, either.

MRS. CHEBOKSÁROVA. People say that he's engaged in some business of importance.

UCHÚMOV. Is that all you know about him? Not very much, my dear lady, not very much.

MRS. CHEBOKSÁROVA. I don't think he's a fool.

UCHÚMOV. Let me be the judge of that, ma'am. How did he get here at all?

MRS. CHEBOKSÁROVA. I don't really remember. Somebody introduced him. Telyátev, I think. All sorts of people come to see us.

UCHÚMOV. Is he thinking of marrying Lydia or what?

MRS. CHEBOKSÁROVA. I don't know. He may.

UCHÚMOV. Is he a man of property?

MRS. CHEBOKSÁROVA. To tell you the truth I'm so little interested in him that it never occurred to me to find out.

UCHÚMOV. He talks too much: "at the present day, at the present day..."

MRS. CHEBOKSÁROVA. Everybody seems to talk like that nowadays.

UCHÚMOV. But he should realize that one gets bored with that kind of talk. If you must talk, go where people want to listen to you. But is the present day so much better than the past? Where are the palaces of our princes and our counts? Who owns them today? The Petrovs and the Ivanovs. What's happened to our brass bands, I ask you? In the past there would be brass bands playing by the ponds at sunset and later there would be a display of fireworks and even ambassadors would come to watch. . . . That was the time of Russia's glory. But now . . . these newcomers . . . such gentry should be sent about their business.

MRS. CHEBOKSÁROVA. But why? On the contrary, I want to be very nice to him. In our present position anybody might come in useful.

UCHÚMOV. You'd hardly find *him* of any earthly use. You'd better put your trust in us old men. Of course, I can't marry Lydia. I have a wife, alas, alack! But, you know, old men are liable to have all sorts of fancies. If an old man wants something badly, nothing is too expensive for him, he'd gladly give all he has. I have no children. You could do anything you like with me. I could become Lydia's father by adoption or . . . just her good friend. An old man would gladly give everything

for . . . er . . . a caress. I can't take all my hundreds of thousands t·
the grave with me, can I? Well, good-bye. I must be off to my club.

MRS. CHEBOKSÁROVA. Will you come to see us again soon? *She sees him o*
to the door.

KUCHÚMOV. Yes, of course. I lost a bet to your daughter and I must bu
her a box of chocolates. You see, that's the sort of man I am. Ho·
blooded, like some scalliwag of twenty, by gad! *Goes out.*

MRS. CHEBOKSÁROVA. It isn't a box of chocolates we want.

MRS. CHEBOKSÁROVA *remains standing at the door, lost in thought.* VASSILKÓ
comes in and picks up his hat.

MRS. CHEBOKSÁROVA. Are you going already?

VASSILKÓV. It's time I went home.

MRS. CHEBOKSÁROVA. Why are you in such a hurry? *Sits down on couch.*

VASSILKÓV. Can I do anything for you?

MRS. CHEBOKSÁROVA. Take a seat, please. VASSILKÓV *sits down.* I should lik·
to have a talk with you. We have known each other for some time, bu
I don't seem to know anything about you. We've hardly exchanged mor
than a few words. I suppose the company of old women bores you.

VASSILKÓV. Not at all, ma'am. What would you like to know about me?

MRS. CHEBOKSÁROVA. I should like at least to know enough to be able t·
answer any questions I'm asked about you. We have so many visitor
and no one seems to know you.

VASSILKÓV. I am so little known here because I spent all my time in th
provinces.

MRS. CHEBOKSÁROVA. Where were you educated?

VASSILKÓV. At a provincial high school, but I specialized in my particula·
line without any help.

MRS. CHEBOKSÁROVA. That's very nice. Are your parents still living?

VASSILKÓV. Only my mother who has lived in the country all her life.

MRS. CHEBOKSÁROVA. Then you're almost alone in the world. Are you
civil servant?

VASSILKÓV. No, I'm engaged in private business undertakings mostly wit
small people, builders, contractors, foremen . . .

MRS. CHEBOKSÁROVA. Ah, that's very nice. Yes, yes. I remember now. It
rather the rage at present, I believe . . . even some very rich people . .
to get closer to the poorer classes. When engaged in this business ·
yours you, of course, wear a red silk—or is it velvet?—caftan. Last yea·
I saw a millionaire in a train and—would you believe it?—he wore
simple . . . What do you call it?

VASSILKÓV. Sheepskin?

MRS. CHEBOKSÁROVA. Yes, sheepskin and a beaver hat!

VASSILKÓV. No, I don't wear any fancy dress.

MRS. CHEBOKSÁROVA. But you must have a big fortune to spend your tim·
like that?

VASSILKÓV. To begin with, my business in itself is rather profitable . . .

MRS. CHEBOKSÁROVA. You mean, it's so picturesque, don't you? They sin·

songs, dance in a ring and, I suppose, you probably have your own private oarsmen to take you out boating on the Volga.

ASSILKÓV. I'm afraid I've never come across anything like that, ma'am, but you're quite right, without some capital it is impossible to start my kind of business.

MRS. CHEBOKSÁROVA. Of course not. I thought so. One can guess at once that you are a man of means. *Pause.* Why are you always having arguments with Lydia? It rouses her temper. She's a girl of character.

ASSILKÓV. That she is a girl of character is very good. I admire people of mettle. In a woman it is a mark of particular distinction. But it is a pity Miss Lydia has no notion of things which everybody nowadays knows about.

MRS. CHEBOKSÁROVA. But why should she, my dear Savva, have any notion of things which are known to everybody? She's had a higher education. We have a large French library. Ask her something about mythology, please, do! You know, she is so well read in French literature! She knows lots of things which girls of her age haven't a notion of. The cleverest man about town couldn't say anything that would in the least surprise or embarrass her.

ASSILKÓV. Such an education is merely of a self-defensive kind, ma'am. It is useful in a way, but not in our present age. Of course, I have no right to lecture anyone, but I shouldn't have tried to convince Miss Lydia if I hadn't . . .

MRS. CHEBOKSÁROVA. If you hadn't what?

ASSILKÓV. If I hadn't thought that I might be of some help to her. If she'd only change her present ideas, she'd get quite a different view about life and people. She'd be more likely to value a man's inner qualities.

MRS. CHEBOKSÁROVA. Yes . . . inner qualities. . . . You're quite right.

ASSILKÓV. Then I could hope to deserve her friendship. But, as it is, I cannot be amusing and I do not want to appear ridiculous.

MRS. CHEBOKSÁROVA. Of course not. She's still very young, you know, she'll change her views a hundred times. I must confess I love to hear you talk and I often repeat the things you say to my daughter when we are alone.

ASSILKÓV. Thank you. To tell you the truth, I was beginning to think that the best thing to do would be to give up trying to change Miss Lydia. I don't like to go on making a fool of myself.

MRS. CHEBOKSÁROVA. Now this is really unworthy of you.

ASSILKÓV. I don't see why I should humiliate myself; after all, it isn't I who need her, it's she who needs me.

MRS. CHEBOKSÁROVA. Young man, please, regard me as your ally, one who is ready to give you all the support you want. *Mysteriously.* All the support, mind you, because I am convinced that you are not only an honest, but also an honourable man.

LYDIA *comes in and stops at the door.*

ASSILKÓV, *gets up and kisses* MRS. CHEBOKSÁROVA's *hand.* Good-bye, ma'am.

MRS. CHEBOKSÁROVA. Good-bye, my dear boy.

VASSILKÓV *bows to* LYDIA *and goes out.*

LYDIA. What were you talking to him about, mother? Tell me, please
He's a horrid man. He's mad!

MRS. CHEBOKSÁROVA. My dear, I know what I'm doing. Our presen
position doesn't permit us to be very choosy.

LYDIA. What position? What's wrong with our position? I'm not goin
. to put up with him any longer whatever our position may be. H
doesn't know our life, our interests. He doesn't belong!

MRS. CHEBOKSÁROVA. But, my dear, he very often talks very sensibly.

LYDIA. But who gave him the right to lecture people? What kind of
preacher does he think he is? You must admit, mother, that a drawin
room is not a lecture hall, or a technological institute, or an enginee
ing laboratory.

MRS. CHEBOKSÁROVA. You are so merciless to him, Lydia.

LYDIA. But, mother, I'm sick of listening to him! He always talks o
economic laws! Who cares about economic laws? The only laws for yo
and me, mother, are the laws of the world of fashion. If everybod
wears a certain style of dress, then I, too, shall wear such a dres
I'd rather die than wear anything else. We have no time to think o
any laws, all we have time for is to go to a shop and buy. No, mothe
he is crazy!

MRS. CHEBOKSÁROVA. But I think, my dear, that he is simply trying to b
original. There are many men like that. He's not particularly wel
educated, you know, perhaps not even clever, and certainly not witty
but he has to talk to be noticed at all. So he's trying to be origina
But he probably thinks and behaves like any other decent man.

LYDIA. You may be right, mother, but I am nevertheless sick of th
sight of him.

MRS. CHEBOKSÁROVA. He's a man of means, darling. One has to hav
patience with such people. Don't we put up with the rest of them
Half of the men who come to see you are frightful boasters an
shameless liars.

LYDIA. What do I care whether they are liars or not? The importan
thing is that they are amusing and he is a bore. That's what I shal
never forgive him.

MRS. CHEBOKSÁROVA. There is another reason, darling, why we shoul
be so patient with him and I would ask you . . .

LYDIA. What other reason? Tell me what that other reason is, mother

MRS. CHEBOKSÁROVA. I know you're a sensible girl and I hope you'll b
brave enough to listen to me calmly.

LYDIA, *frightened.* What is it, mother? What is it?

MRS. CHEBOKSÁROVA. I got a letter from your father . . .

LYDIA. What's the matter with him? Is he ill? Is he dying?

MRS. CHEBOKSÁROVA. No.

LYDIA. What do you mean? I don't understand you, mother.

MRS. CHEBOKSÁROVA. I wrote to your father to ask him to send us money

We owe such a lot to all sorts of people and we want a lot more for the winter season. I got his reply today . . .

LYDIA. What does he say?

MRS. CHEBOKSÁROVA, *inhaling smelling salts.* He says that he has no money, that he wants thirty thousand himself, or our estate will be sold by auction, and the estate is our last hope.

LYDIA. That's a great pity, mother, but you will agree that you needn't have told me anything about it, that you should have spared me this news, that you had no business to tell me that we were ruined.

MRS. CHEBOKSÁROVA. But you were bound to learn of it sooner or later, dear.

LYDIA. But why, mother? Why should I have had to hear of it at all? *Almost in tears.* You'll have to find some way of getting us out of this mess, you must get some money one way or another, for we can't leave Moscow and go to the country, can we? And we can't live in Moscow like paupers. Somehow or other, you simply must arrange everything so that our life goes on as before. I must get married this winter. I must find a rich husband. You are a mother. You ought to know how important that is. Can't you think of something, haven't you already thought of something to make it possible for us to live through the winter without degrading ourselves? It is your business to think of some way out, it is your duty, mother! Why should you tell me something which I oughtn't to know? You rob me of my peace of mind, you deprive me of my poise which is the best ornament a girl can have, you make me look harassed and ugly. If you must worry, mother, you should worry by yourself. If you must weep you should weep in your room where I can't see you. Would you feel less miserable, if I wept with you. Please, tell me, mother, would you really be happier, if I were unhappy?

MRS. CHEBOKSÁROVA. Of course not, child. Of course, I shouldn't be happier if you were unhappy.

LYDIA. Very well, then, mother, why should I be unhappy at all, why should I cry, why should I be robbed of my peace of mind and my poise? People age from worry. Worry brings wrinkles to one's face. I already feel that I've grown older by ten years. I've never known the meaning of want and I don't intend to know it. All I know is that I like to go shopping: I know the best underwear, silks, carpets, furs, furniture. I know that when I want something I go to the best shop in town, get it and pay for it, if I have any money, or tell the shop-assistants to send it, if I haven't any. But I never knew and I don't consider it necessary to know where money comes from or how much money I need for the winter or for the whole year. I never knew whether an article was dear or cheap and I always thought that bargain-hunting was mean and degrading. I hate the very thought of it, it makes me feel so cheap. I remember that once, on returning from a shop, the thought occurred to me: haven't I paid rather a lot for my dress? There was nobody with me at the time, I was in the carriage by myself, and yet I felt so ashamed that I blushed crimson and hardly knew where to hide myself. I recalled seeing an old woman in the shop, a horrible, fat old woman, who was bargaining for a piece of cloth. She'd hold it in her hand, then put it down, then pick it up again: she couldn't bring herself to pay such a lot of money for it and yet she was afraid to let it out of her hands. She was all the time whispering to two other ugly old women, while the shop assistants were smirking behind her back. Please, mother, why do you torture me like that?

MRS. CHEBOKSÁROVA. I realize, darling, that I ought not perhaps to have told you of our position, but what else could I do? If we are to stay in Moscow, we shall have to cut down our expenses, we shall have to sell our silver, some at least of our pictures, and our jewelry.

LYDIA. No, no, mother! We can't do that! The whole of Moscow will learn that we're bankrupt, they'll come to us with sour faces, feigning sympathy, they'll heap stupid advice on us, they'll shake their heads, they'll make all kinds of commiserating noises in their throats, and everything they do will be so artificial and insincere, so insulting! I tell you, mother, they will not even take pains to disguise their glee. *Covers face with hands.* No! No.!

MRS. CHEBOKSÁROVA. But what are we to do, dear?

LYDIA. What are we to do? We mustn't demean ourselves. Let's do up our apartment again, let's buy a new carriage, let's get new liveries for the servants, and the dearer the better.

MRS. CHEBOKSÁROVA. But how are we to pay for it all?

LYDIA. He will pay for everything.

MRS. CHEBOKSÁROVA. Who?

LYDIA. My husband.

MRS. CHEBOKSÁROVA. But who is your husband? Who is he?

LYDIA. I don't know. Anyone will do.

MRS. CHEBOKSÁROVA. Has anyone proposed to you?

LYDIA. No one has proposed to me, mother, no one dared propose to me. All the men who wanted to marry me got nothing but icy contempt from me. For I was myself looking for a handsome man with a big fortune, but all I want now is a man with a fortune, and there are many such men.

MRS. CHEBOKSÁROVA. I hope you're not disappointed in your expectations, dear.

LYDIA. Has beauty lost its price? No, mother, you needn't worry. There are not so many beautiful girls about, but there are thousands of rich fools.

Enter ANDREY.

ANDREY. Mr. Telyátev, ma'am.

LYDIA. Here's the first one.

MRS. CHEBOKSÁROVA, *to* ANDREY. Show him in, please.

ANDREY *goes out.*

LYDIA. Leave us alone, mother. Don't interfere with us at all. He'll pay for everything.

MRS. CHEBOKSÁROVA. But if . . . ?

YDIA. But if? Well, didn't you tell me yourself that Vassilkóv has a big fortune? You'll have to send for him. He owns goldmines, he is a fool—the gold will be ours.

MRS. CHEBOKSÁROVA. I'd better send for him now. I'd like to speak to him first. He'll have to be prepared. *Goes out.*

Enter TELYÁTEV *with a bouquet.*

YDIA. How quick you are and how you spoil me! Tell me why do you go to such trouble to please me?

TELYÁTEV. Does this surprise you, old girl? When didn't I carry out your commands?

YDIA. But why do you spoil me so?

TELYÁTEV. Well, you see, old girl, I'm made that way. It's my business to be nice to pretty girls. I have nothing else to do.

YDIA. Then it's just a way of amusing yourself, is it? But, my dear man, don't you realize that you might turn my head by your attentions?

TELYÁTEV. I plead guilty to that crime.

YDIA. It is either no crime at all or a very great crime. It depends on whether your actions are sincere or not.

TELYÁTEV. Of course, they are sincere.

YDIA. But your constant efforts to please me, your never-ending flattery, don't you think that all this is really a kind of bait with which you hope to catch me? You make me believe that you're so devoted to me that I can hardly remain indifferent to such devotion.

TELYÁTEV. Oh, I say, old girl, all the better, you know, all the better! You don't expect me to like your indifference, do you? It's about time my feelings found an echo in your heart, old girl.

YDIA. It's easy for you to talk like that, for your feelings are nothing but neatly turned phrases. You've had so much experience in your life that you remain complete master of every situation. But just think of an inexperienced young girl like myself whose feelings for a man awaken for the first time in her life! Don't you agree that her position is extremely difficult, if not dangerous?

TELYÁTEV. Quite possible, old girl. I can't tell you anything about it, I've never been a girl myself.

YDIA. Once a young girl is foolish enough to betray her true feelings for a man, she runs the risk of either becoming his plaything or making herself ridiculous, neither of which is pleasant. Don't you agree?

TELYÁTEV. You're quite right, old girl, quite right.

DIA. So, pray, if you don't mean anything, don't try to turn my head. Be sincere with me, I implore you. Don't tell me anything you don't mean. Don't make love to me if you don't like me!

TELYÁTEV. But who put that horrible idea into your head, old girl? Good heavens! I always say what I mean.

DIA. Really?

TELYÁTEV. Of course. As a matter of fact, I say even less to you than I really and truly feel.

DIA. But why don't you?

TELYÁTEV. I daren't, old girl. I'm afraid you might give me the cold shoulder, you know. Do you want me to try?

LYDIA. Yes, do!

TELYÁTEV. I can hardly believe it, old girl. Is it a dream, or what? What a lucky day for me! What date is it?

LYDIA. Why is it such a lucky day for you?

TELYÁTEV. But, really, old girl, how could I expect this from you? You're nice to me, you condescend to come down from your unscaleable heights, you actually do not disdain to come down to earth for me. Before, you were always like the goddess Diana, contemning the low tribe of men, with the moon in your hair and a quiver at your side. But now you've become a simple, friendly, even artless shepherdess, one of those they put into the ballet, who dance so charmingly, with their aprons fluttering . . . *He imitates a ballerina dancing as a shepherdess.*

LYDIA. Does this really make you happy?

TELYÁTEV. What do you think I am, old girl, a jolly old bronze horseman?

LYDIA. How easy it is to make you happy! I'm very glad I am able to make you so happy.

TELYÁTEV. You are glad to make me happy? My dear girl, are you really the Lydia I knew or some other heavenly creature?

LYDIA. Why are you so surprised? Don't you deserve happiness?

TELYÁTEV. I don't know if I deserve it, but I do know that I'm about to go raving mad with happiness.

LYDIA. Do go raving mad!

TELYÁTEV. I'm liable to do all sorts of foolish things, old girl.

LYDIA. Do do all sorts of foolish things!

TELYÁTEV. You're either making fun of me, which is not fair, you know, or else . . .

LYDIA. Go on, finish the sentence!

TELYÁTEV. Or else you're in love with me!

LYDIA. Unhappily, I am.

TELYÁTEV. But why unhappily, old girl? What's there to be unhappy about? It's happiness, heavenly bliss. Darling, you couldn't have done anything better! *He embraces her lightly.*

LYDIA. Johnnie, are you mine?

TELYÁTEV. I am yours, darling, I am your slave for ever!

LYDIA, *raising her eyes at him.* Really and truly?

TELYÁTEV. Yes, darling, for ever, for my whole life and even longer, that's possible.

LYDIA. Oh, I'm so happy, Johnnie!

TELYÁTEV. It's I who am so happy, old girl. *Kisses her.*

LYDIA. Oh, God, how wonderful! Mummy!

TELYÁTEV. Why mummy, old girl? What's mummy got to do with it? Three is a jolly old crowd, you know.

---

[3]In the text " 'The Bronze Horseman' or the 'Stone Guest,' " a poem and a play by Alexander **Pushkin**.

ʏᴅɪᴀ. I know, Johnnie. We don't want her really, but I'm so happy.

ᴇʟʏᴀ́ᴛᴇᴠ. All the better, darling.

ʏᴅɪᴀ. I am so happy, Johnnie, that I simply must share my happiness with her.

ᴇʟʏᴀ́ᴛᴇᴠ. I'm against sharing anything with anyone! There'll be more left for the two of us, old girl.

ʏᴅɪᴀ. Yes, you're quite right, darling, we mustn't share our happiness with anyone, for there's so little happiness in the world as it is. But all the same, Johnnie, we'll have to tell her.

ʟʏᴀ́ᴛᴇᴠ. I don't quite get you, old girl. What have we to tell her?

ᴅɪᴀ. That we love each other, Johnnie, and that we want to be inseparable for the rest of our lives.

ʟʏᴀ́ᴛᴇᴠ. So that's it, old girl? The jolly old marriage lines, wedding bells and confetti? Pardon me, but I really didn't bargain for that!

ᴅɪᴀ. What do you mean, Johnnie? What didn't you bargain for? Tell me.

ʟʏᴀ́ᴛᴇᴠ. I am ready to be your lover, your slave, everything, in fact, but if it's wedding bells you want, then I'm very sorry and all that, you know.

ᴅɪᴀ. How dared you make love to me?

ʟʏᴀ́ᴛᴇᴠ. I dared do nothing of the sort, old girl. The only thing I did was not to prevent you from loving me. I should never dream of preventing anyone from loving me, old girl.

ᴅɪᴀ. You are not worthy of my love, sir!

ʟʏᴀ́ᴛᴇᴠ. Quite true, old girl, quite true. I am not worthy of your love, but is one only to fall in love with a girl whom one is worthy to love? What kind of a jolly old ass would I have been to refuse your love and read you a moral lesson instead! Pardon me, old girl, but if you want someone to teach you morals, you'd better turn to someone else. I am not a moralist, either by inclination or on principle. In my opinion, old girl, the less morals a woman has, the better it is for everybody all round.

ᴅɪᴀ. You are a monster!

ʟʏᴀ́ᴛᴇᴠ. You're absolutely right, old girl. You ought therefore to be jolly grateful to me for having refused to marry you.

ᴅɪᴀ. I hate you! *Goes out.*

ʟʏᴀ́ᴛᴇᴠ. Gosh, that was a narrow squeak! A jolly lucky thing I got out of it unscathed. I'm afraid I shall have to stop fooling round. If I'm not damn careful some young lady will make a fool of me and, before I realize it, I'm a husband! Flesh is weak, one must run from sin as from the devil. *Goes to the door. Enter* ᴠᴀssɪʟᴋᴏ́ᴠ. Good luck, old fellow! *Goes out.*

Enter ᴍʀs. ᴄʜᴇʙᴏᴋsᴀ́ʀᴏᴠᴀ.

s. ᴄʜᴇʙᴏᴋsᴀ́ʀᴏᴠᴀ. I'm so glad to see you again, so glad. Your company has become absolutely indispensable to me. Please, sit down beside me.

ssɪʟᴋᴏ́ᴠ. You sent for me, ma'am?

s. ᴄʜᴇʙᴏᴋsᴀ́ʀᴏᴠᴀ. I'm so sorry if I have troubled you. I want advice

badly. I'm such a helpless creature. I know only one serious man an
that's you.

VASSILKÓV. Thank you. What can I do for you?

MRS. CHEBOKSÁROVA. I had a talk with Lydia. We want to change ou
mode of life, we are tired of all this constant hullabaloo. We've d
cided to receive no one but you. We're very rich, of course, but eve
a lot of money doesn't justify a life of senseless pleasure.

VASSILKÓV. I quite agree.

MRS. CHEBOKSÁROVA. Lydia wants to finish her education and she can
do that without a guide. We decided to turn to you.

VASSILKÓV. I should be very pleased to be of service to you, but wha
could I teach Lydia? Spherical trigonometry?

MRS. CHEBOKSÁROVA. Yes, yes, why not? You must admit that to teach
young girl is quite a pleasant occupation.

VASSILKÓV. Quite. But what does Lydia want to know spherical trigonon
etry for?

MRS. CHEBOKSÁROVA. She's a very queer girl, but she has a heart of gol
She is a very good girl really. *Mysteriously.* You know she really hat
the sight of those empty-headed young men.

VASSILKÓV. That's news to me, ma'am.

MRS. CHEBOKSÁROVA. As for me, I have hated the sight of them for
long time. You are so different. Any mother could entrust her daught
to you without any fear. Forgive me, my dear Savva, for my franknes
but I should be so happy if Lydia learnt to like you.

VASSILKÓV. Thank you.

MRS. CHEBOKSÁROVA. If I could, I should force her to like you, only
see her happy.

VASSILKÓV. Is there no other way than using force?

MRS. CHEBOKSÁROVA. I don't know. You'd better try to find out for you
self. You are in love with my daughter, aren't you? Wait, let me loc
into your eyes. Don't say anything, I can see for myself. But why a
you so shy? Shall I speak to her for you? Or else you'll start yo
arguments again and end up, God forbid, by quarrelling.

VASSILKÓV. No, let me talk to her myself, but I shall have to prepa
myself, think things over first.

MRS. CHEBOKSÁROVA. What's there to think over or to prepare yourself fo

Enter LYDIA.

MRS. CHEBOKSÁROVA. Darling, Savva has asked me for your hand. I'd
happy if you accepted him, but I don't want to force you to do an
thing against your own will.

LYDIA. In a matter of such importance, mother, I must obviously decide f
myself. Had I been in love, I should have listened to the promptings
my heart rather than to you, but I'm absolutely indifferent to any
my admirers. You know, mother, that I have refused many men who'
asked for my hand, but I feel that it's high time I got married a
I'm ready to do whatever you want.

VASSILKÓV. Which means that you don't love me?

LYDIA. No, I don't love you. Why should I deceive you? We can talk over later. Mother, you've undertaken to arrange my life for me. Remember, I shall hold you responsible for my future happiness.

MRS. CHEBOKSÁROVA. My dear Savva, she has accepted you!

VASSILKÓV. I am very sorry.

LYDIA. Sorry? Why? Because I don't love you?

VASSILKÓV. No, that I was in such a hurry.

LYDIA. You can still refuse to marry me but you can't love me very much if you do it so lightheartedly. Don't be angry with me, rather be grateful to me for being so frank with you. I could easily have pretended to be in love with you—pretence costs nothing—but I don't want to. All brides say that they are terribly in love with their husbands, but don't believe them: real love comes later. Don't be vain, take me for your wife. Why should I love you? You aren't handsome, you have such a funny name, and even your surname is so common. All this may not amount to much, but it takes time to get used even to small things. Why should you be angry with me? Because you are in love with me? Thank you very much, but try to win my love and we shall be happy together.

VASSILKÓV. I don't want sacrifices from anyone.

LYDIA. It seems to me you don't know what you want.

VASSILKÓV. Not at all. I know perfectly well what I want. I could marry a girl who did not love me. You are quite right, love may come with time. But I want that you should respect me, for without respect marriage is impossible.

LYDIA. That's understood. I shouldn't have agreed to marry you if I didn't respect you.

VASSILKÓV. You were frank with me and I'll be frank with you. You told me that you didn't love me and I tell you that I fell in love with you perhaps long before you deserved it. You, too, must be worthy of my love. Otherwise, I'm afraid, it might easily turn to hate.

LYDIA. Really!

VASSILKÓV. You can refuse to marry me. There is still time.

LYDIA. Why should I? *Laughs.* Let's play a comedy with each other, try to be worthy of each other's love.

VASSILKÓV. I don't want to play a comedy. I want our future to be bright and happy.

LYDIA. Not at all, you want nothing but a comedy. You propose to me, I accept you. What else do you want? You say you love me, you should therefore be infinitely happy, and not start an argument about my duties to you. We ought each to know our own duties. Only the poor, who have nothing to live on, argue about how to live.

MRS. CHEBOKSÁROVA. I can see, my dears, that you really are in love with each other and that your arguments are, so to speak, only literary.

VASSILKÓV. Allow me as your fiancé to present you with these. *He gives her a box with ear-rings and a brooch.* I bought them today by chance and, it seems, they have come in very useful.

MRS. CHEBOKSÁROVA, *gasps.* But they must have cost a fortune!

VASSILKÓV. Only three thousand, ma'am.

LYDIA. It seems to me there's quite a good chance that I might fall i
love with you!

She extends her hand to VASSILKÓV *who kisses it politely.*

ACT THREE

Same drawing room as in Act Two, only more richly furnished. To th
right of the spectators—a door to VASSILKÓV'S *study, to the left—a door*
LYDIA'S *room, in the middle—entrance door.* VASSILKÓV *comes out of h*
study with briefcase and newspapers. He glances quickly through the new
papers and rings. Enter VASSILY.

VASSILKÓV. The Kazan estate of the Cheboksárovas with its sawmill an
forest is to be sold in a few days. What a pity! The sawmill ought to b
very profitable and there's plenty of good timber in the forest. Go
Yermolayev and tell him to meet me at the Stock Exchange in abo
an hour. Let him wait for me there. I'm going to authorize him
buy the estate in my name. Tell him that he should in any case ma
all the necessary arrangements for leaving immediately for Kazan.

VASSILY. Very good, sir.

VASSILKÓV. I wish you'd dress yourself more decently, Vassily.

VASSILY. It don't make no difference to me, sir. In them boots, jack
and velvet cap I looks exac'ly like the English factory 'ands I see
when I was with you in England. I likes that very much, sir. No o
can't mistake *me* for no bloomin' butler.

VASSILKÓV. Very well. It's your business, Vassily, please yourself.

VASSILY. Thank you, sir. *Goes out.*

VASSILKÓV *takes out a bill and checks it carefully.* MRS. CHEBOKSÁRO
comes out of LYDIA'S *room.*

MRS. CHEBOKSÁROVA. You're a real bear, Savva. Only just got married a
already you don't seem to care for anything but your business.

VASSILKÓV. One thing doesn't interfere with another, mumsie.

MRS. CHEBOKSÁROVA. What do you mean, mumsie?

VASSILKÓV. I like the word. It's a nice pet name and a very apt one, t

MRS. CHEBOKSÁROVA. Oh, all right. *Comes up to him.* Are you happ
Savva? Tell me, are you really happy, my son? *Takes him lovingly*
the ear.

VASSILKÓV, *kissing her hand.* Yes, I am happy. I am completely happ
I can frankly say now that I have had a few days of real happiness
my life. Do you know, mumsie . . .

MRS. CHEBOKSÁROVA. Again mumsie!

VASSILKÓV. I am sorry.

MRS. CHEBOKSÁROVA. I knew Lydia would make you happy. I should ne
have let my darling marry you otherwise.

VASSILKÓV. I should have been happier if . . . if . . .

MRS. CHEBOKSÁROVA. If what? *Sits down.* Aren't you satisfied, you ungrateful wretch?

VASSILKÓV. I should have been absolutely satisfied if my ideal of life were an interminable succession of visits all over Moscow varied with a concert or a theatre in the evening. I should be perfectly satisfied if I were not ashamed of such a life and if I could afford it.

MRS. CHEBOKSÁROVA. But if all decent people live like that there is nothing to be ashamed of. Besides, it doesn't really cost such an awful lot.

VASSILKÓV. Doesn't it? According to my reckoning I've already spent a small fortune. I don't know and I don't want to know how much Lydia is spending herself. What she does with her money is not my business.

MRS. CHEBOKSÁROVA. And quite right, too.

VASSILKÓV. She has her money and I have mine. But I'm beginning to be worried how much more it's going to cost me this year.

MRS. CHEBOKSÁROVA. What nonsense, dear! Just go on living as you do. Such expenses will hardly embarrass you.

VASSILKÓV. Hardly embarrass me? But only six months of such a life will cost me about twenty-five thousand.

MRS. CHEBOKSÁROVA. Is that such a lot? Are you really so mean? You look so sorry for yourself, I can hardly believe my eyes.

VASSILKÓV. It doesn't matter at all whether I look sorry for myself or not. What matters is where am I to get all that money?

MRS. CHEBOKSÁROVA. That's not my business. You ought to know all about that.

VASSILKÓV. To live on such a scale I must be worth a million at least.

MRS. CHEBOKSÁROVA. We shouldn't mind if you were worth two.

VASSILKÓV. But I'm not worth two or even one. I've just a moderate income.

MRS. CHEBOKSÁROVA. I hope at any rate that you're worth half a million. Even that isn't so bad.

VASSILKÓV. You know perfectly well that all I have is my estate, a little ready money and what my business brings me in. I cannot afford to spend more than seven or eight thousand a year.

MRS. CHEBOKSÁROVA. But what about your goldmines?

VASSILKÓV. Which goldmines? What are you talking about?

MRS. CHEBOKSÁROVA. Your goldmines.

VASSILKÓV. I have no goldmines. I haven't even a coppermine.

MRS. CHEBOKSÁROVA, *gets up.* Then why have you played such a cruel joke on us?

VASSILKÓV. I played no joke on you.

MRS. CHEBOKSÁROVA. But you assured us you had a fortune.

VASSILKÓV. But I have and not such a small one at that.

MRS. CHEBOKSÁROVA. Don't talk such nonsense! You don't seem to know what you're talking about. You don't understand the simplest things which even children understand.

VASSILKÓV. What do you mean? How is my fortune not a fortune? Wha
is it then in your opinion?

MRS. CHEBOKSÁROVA. What is it? I'll tell you. It's penury, poverty, that':
what it is. What you are pleased to call a fortune may satisfy th
needs of a bachelor: it may suffice him for glove money. But how d
you expect to keep my poor darling on it?

VASSILKÓV. I intend to make her happy and I'll do my utmost to mak
her happy.

MRS. CHEBOKSÁROVA. Without a real fortune? This is ridiculous!

VASSILKÓV. I have enough, I'm telling you, and I'm doing my best to ge
more.

MRS. CHEBOKSÁROVA. How much is enough? She wants a really big for
tune to make her happy and it's impossible to get a big fortune wit
your kind of business. You have to have special Government conces
sions for that, railway concessions and so on. And these you will neve
be able to get. One can also obtain a big fortune by inheritance o
if one is very lucky, by winning it at cards.

VASSILKÓV. You forgot to mention something else: you can also get a bi
fortune by robbing a bank. Would you like me to do that?

MRS. CHEBOKSÁROVA. Do you really think so? How little you know me!
can see I'll have to do something myself to convince you of the erro
of your ways.

VASSILKÓV. Which errors? Let me give you a good tip: mind your ow
business! *Takes his hat.*

MRS. CHEBOKSÁROVA. Are you going out?

VASSILKÓV. Yes. Good-bye. *Goes out.*

MRS. CHEBOKSÁROVA. What a worry this son-in-law of mine is! Still, wh
else would have married Lydia if they'd known that she hasn't
penny in the world? I'll have to do my best for him. What else
there to do?

Enter ANDREY.

ANDREY. Mr. Kuchúmov, ma'am.

MRS. CHEBOKSÁROVA. Just in time! *To* ANDREY. Show him in. ANDREY go
out. I'll tackle him at once.

Enter KUCHÚMOV.

KUCHÚMOV, *hums. Pace e gioia son con voi!*[4]

MRS. CHEBOKSÁROVA. I'm so glad to see you. Please, be seated.

KUCHÚMOV, *sitting down. Pace e gioia* . . . And where is our dear nymph

MRS. CHEBOKSÁROVA. She's flown off on visits. She'll be back soon.

KUCHÚMOV. And the satyr who snatched her away from us?

MRS. CHEBOKSÁROVA. He's gone off on business. He's always preoccupie
with his business.

KUCHÚMOV. A tight-fisted fellow! Still, what has he to worry about? It
we who're kept on tenterhooks with our mouths watering at the sig
of the sour grapes, like the fox in the fable.

MRS. CHEBOKSÁROVA. How you do talk! At your age, too!

---

[4]From Rossini's opera, *The Barber of Seville.*

KUCHÚMOV. My heart is still young, dear lady. I'm of a volcanic nature!

MRS. CHEBOKSÁROVA. Incidentally, have you received a letter from my husband?

KUCHÚMOV. Yes, I have. Don't worry, I'll send him the money tomorrow. It's a bagatelle: only thirty thousand. You can safely dismiss it from your thoughts.

MRS. CHEBOKSÁROVA. I have another favour to ask you, my dear Grigory.

KUCHÚMOV. What's that? What's that?

MRS. CHEBOKSÁROVA. Could you get a better job for a friend of mine, something big, a trusteeship or the management of a large estate?

KUCHÚMOV. It depends who it is for.

MRS. CHEBOKSÁROVA, *shrugging her shoulders.* It's for my son-in-law.

KUCHÚMOV. I see! So it's as bad as that, is it? I knew it all the time.

MRS. CHEBOKSÁROVA. Yes, my dearest friend, it seems we've made a little mistake.

KUCHÚMOV. What right had he to marry your daughter in that case? He swore he'd buy her the keys of heaven, and now he can't even support her. A man of straw, after all! Do you know he must be a cadger by nature, must have some lawyer's blood in him. What does he want a job for? To take bribes. How do you expect me to recommend him then? He'll probably disgrace me, the rotter!

MRS. CHEBOKSÁROVA. But, please, have pity on me. He's my son-in-law.

KUCHÚMOV. You told me yourself a minute ago that you were mistaken in him. But he didn't deceive me, no, ma'am! I never trusted that ugly face of his.

MRS. CHEBOKSÁROVA. Please, don't talk like that. Don't you like to be the benefactor of a man who is married to such a pretty wife?

KUCHÚMOV. Who told you I didn't? On the contrary, my dear lady, I'd be glad to help him.

MRS. CHEBOKSÁROVA. You probably think that women can't show their gratitude. No, my dear Grigory, if they want to . . .

KUCHÚMOV. Of course, of course. I'm off at once. Only tell me how, what and where?

Enter LYDIA.

KUCHÚMOV. In the presence of such beauty, I am dumb.

LYDIA. I'm sorry to hear that. Please, don't go dumb, you talk so nicely. *Sits down in an armchair.* I'm so fagged out. I've been rushing about like mad all over Moscow.

MRS. CHEBOKSÁROVA. You're quite right, Lydia. Mr. Kuchúmov not only talks well, he also acts well. He's sending thirty thousand to your father tomorrow to save our estate and he's also doing us a personal favour. We should be very grateful to him. *Looks significantly at her daughter.*

ANDREY *comes in.*

ANDREY. Mr. Glúmov, ma'am.

MRS. CHEBOKSÁROVA. Show him into my sitting room. *Goes out, followed by* ANDREY.

LYDIA. Really, Mr. Kuchúmov, what's come over you? Since when have you become a benefactor of humanity? To help others means to deprive oneself of something. What on earth could induce you to do that?

KUCHÚMOV. And is it you, my dear, who ask me that?

LYDIA. Why shouldn't it be me?

KUCHÚMOV. Why, don't you know that I'm ready to sacrifice not only my wealth but my life for you?

LYDIA. It's hardly likely that I'd require so big a sacrifice, but is it really true that you're sending money to my father?

KUCHÚMOV. Tomorrow, tomorrow, my dear.

LYDIA. That is really noble of you. It's impossible not to value such friendship.

KUCHÚMOV. It's much more than friendship, my dear Lydia. Shall I tell you what? I'm going to buy that estate from your father and make you a present of it.

LYDIA. Fine! Please, buy it as a present for me. I like presents so much.

KUCHÚMOV. Tomorrow I'm going to write to your father and tell him that I've decided to buy his estate. I'll send him thirty thousand as a deposit. Money is no object with me. All I care for, my dear, is your goodwill, just your goodwill.

LYDIA. How can I show my goodwill to you? You are already practically a member of our family.

KUCHÚMOV. Hear, hear! A member of your family . . .

LYDIA. However, what member of my family can you be? You're a little too old to be my brother. Would you like to be my pappie for the time being?

KUCHÚMOV, *kneels at her feet and kisses her hand.* Yes, your pappie, your pappie . . .

LYDIA. Don't be too naughty, pappie.

KUCHÚMOV. I want to be naughty, I want to be naughty! *Kisses her hand again.*

GLÚMOV *appears in the doorway and withdraws quickly.*

LYDIA, *gets up from armchair.* You ought to be ashamed of yourself to behave like that. You're not a baby.

KUCHÚMOV *gets up.* ANDREY *enters.*

ANDREY. Mr. Telyátev, ma'am.

LYDIA. Ask him to come in.

ANDREY *goes out.*

KUCHÚMOV. *Addio, mia carina!* I'm off on your business.

LYDIA. On what business is that?

KUCHÚMOV. I'll tell you later. *Goes out.*

TELYÁTEV *comes in.*

TELYÁTEV. Pronounce my death sentence, old girl, but be quick about it. If you decide to be cross with me, I'll retire to a primeval forest and end my miserable life there. But I'd rather you knocked me on the head now and then forgave me. I can't live without you, Lydia. I'm beginning to suffer from spleen like an Englishman and I'll end up by shooting myself.

LYDIA. Why should I be angry with you?

TELYÁTEV. Your words are daggers, old girl.

LYDIA. How are you worse than anybody else? There are many men who are worse than you.

TELYÁTEV. Take pity on me. Do you enjoy torturing me? Tell me straight that I am a cad.

LYDIA. I should hate to contradict you. You're much to blame. You're very much to blame. You are the cause of my marrying a man I don't love.

TELYÁTEV. You don't love him? That's fine.

LYDIA. It seems he doesn't love me, either.

TELYÁTEV. He doesn't love you! Wonderful!

LYDIA. What's wonderful about that?

TELYÁTEV. I don't know how you feel about it, old girl, but to me, a sinful bachelor, such a situation is heaven. Don't we, poor, homeless fellows, wander about the whole world in search of just such situations?

LYDIA. You're immoral to the very marrow of your bones.

TELYÁTEV. If you want to call me names, old girl, I don't object.

LYDIA. Why call you names? Because you love me? Why should I abuse someone who loves me? Or because you refused to marry me although you loved me? But that's an old story already. You can't do anything about it now.

TELYÁTEV. I can't marry you, that's true enough. But I can love you, can't I?

LYDIA. I can't very well forbid you that. It flatters a woman's vanity. The more admirers, the merrier.

TELYÁTEV. What do you want many admirers for? Be satisfied with one for the time being.

LYDIA. You don't seem to know life at all. One admirer is dangerous, people will start gossiping at once, but many admirers kill suspicion, for how are they to tell which is her lover?

TELYÁTEV. Let *me* be your lover, old girl. You can have four others as decoys for prying eyes.

LYDIA, *laughing*. You're such a silly idiot that one can't be angry with you.

TELYÁTEV. The clouds have cleared away. Can I now start saying sweet nothings to you?

LYDIA. Do. I like listening to you. You're a darling really, aren't you?

TELYÁTEV. Of course I'm a darling, old girl. How wonderful you look! You've certainly changed for the better, such a change always . . .

LYDIA. No, perhaps you'd better spare me. I've been a married woman such a short time that I'm not used to your talk yet.

TELYÁTEV. What a pity you're not used to it. Do get used to it quickly and save me from boredom. Let's start again. Do you intend to take a lover soon? It's an old Italian custom, you know, for a married woman to have a *cavalier servente*.

LYDIA. But the question is, surely, is it done here?

TELYÁTEV. It's high time we introduced this admirable custom. One ought never to be ashamed of importing anything that's worthy of imitation.

LYDIA. And what will the husbands say?

TELYÁTEV. They'll get used to it with time. Of course, at first many of us cavaliers will get a beating, even a very bad beating, especially from our shopkeepers and tradesmen, and some may even be dragged to the courts, but with time the custom is sure to take root. The first in the field will have to run the risk of a beating, so as to pave the way for the others. No reform is possible without a certain amount of sacrifice. Somebody will have to sacrifice himself for the good cause.

LYDIA. Sounds lovely, but, I'm afraid, it will take a long time before we adopt this custom.

TELYÁTEV. It's already on the way, old girl. A few of us have already sacrificed ourselves. One I saw walking about with a peach of a black eye, another had had even worse luck, poor fellow.

LYDIA. All right, when this admirable custom does take root . . .

TELYÁTEV. Then you'll give me a chance, won't you, old girl?

LYDIA. If you prove worthy. You're such a windbag.

TELYÁTEV. Why a windbag?

LYDIA. Because there's nothing but wind in your head, darling.

TELYÁTEV. Not at all, old girl. I'll tell you why. Because I have no one to whom I could be constant. Command me and I'll be as constant as a telegraph pole.

LYDIA. I'll give you a trial.

TELYÁTEV. You will? Shall I kneel at your feet?

LYDIA. No, don't do that. Spare me the ceremony, I can do very well without it.

TELYÁTEV. Just as you say, old girl. However, I feel I must show my devotion in some more tangible way.

LYDIA, *giving him her hand.* You may kiss my hand.

   GLÚMOV *enters and remains in the background.*

TELYÁTEV, *without noticing* GLÚMOV. Won't you take your glove off first? What kind of a kiss is that? The electricity with which my whole being is charged won't reach your heart through the glove. Kid is a very bad conductor, old girl. *Kisses her wrist above glove.*

LYDIA. That'll do. You can't be allowed to take any liberties. Give you an inch and you'll take an ell.

TELYÁTEV. Only half an inch, old girl. This . . . *Seeing* GLÚMOV. Hullo, George. I didn't notice you.

GLÚMOV. Don't mind me, carry on.

LYDIA. What do you mean? What's there to carry on? Do you want to suggest that there's something between us? I've only let Johnnie, who is an old friend of mine, kiss my hand. I'd gladly let you do the same. *Extends her hand to* GLÚMOV.

GLÚMOV. Thank you very much, but I'm not in the habit of kissing anybody's hand. I only kiss the hand of my mother or my mistress.

LYDIA. In that case you'll never kiss my hand.

GLÚMOV. Who knows? All sorts of things can happen in life. If Mahomet doesn't go to the mountain . . .

LYDIA. Let's go, Johnnie. *Offers her arm to* TELYÁTEV. He's a very rude man. *To* GLÚMOV. Are you waiting for my husband? He'll be back soon.

GLÚMOV. Yes, madam, I am waiting for your husband. I've a lot to tell him.

LYDIA. Do me a great favour, tell him something funny. He's grown particularly morose lately. No one in the world can make people laugh as much as you: you're so excruciatingly funny yourself. TELYÁTEV *and* LYDIA *go out.*

GLÚMOV. I'll make all of you laugh all right. Bravo, my dear Lydia, bravo! I came intending to make love to you, but I find that two others have preceded me. All that remains now is to get them all at each other's throats with the husband to make up the quartet. Vassily!

VASSILY *enters.*

VASSILY. Did you call, sir?

GLÚMOV. Yes. When is Mr. Kuchúmov usually here?

VASSILY. He's always to be fahnd 'ere at two o'clock, sir. Master ain't at 'ome as a rule then.

GLÚMOV. Where is he?

VASSILY. In conference at 'is hoffice, with a great many other rich people, talkin' business, sir.

GLÚMOV. What sort of business?

VASSILY. As 'ow to get more money for theirselves, sir.

GLÚMOV. Is your master rich?

VASSILY. Course 'e is, sir.

GLÚMOV. I suppose to you anyone who has a hundred-rouble note is a rich man.

VASSILY. Maybe not only an 'undred or a thousand but more'n that, sir.

GLÚMOV. That's nothing, my man, nothing.

VASSILY. Maybe it's nothin' to you, sir, but we 'ave only to look for more and we'll find it. I didn't ought to be talkin' to you, sir. Master don't approve of it and you mayn't understand nothin' of it, neither. 'E's a scholar, 'e is, sir, and 'e ain't lyin' on 'is back all the bloomin' day, neither. Many a night he ain't slep' not a wink, sir, workin' all the time, burnin' the midnight oil, in a manner o' speakin'. You don't understand much what I'm talkin' abaht, do you? I was on me way to London to join me master, but ten miles from there I 'ad to go back with 'im, came back in a train with a hengine, sir. But it's a bloomin' waste o' time talkin' to you at all, sir. *Goes out.*

GLÚMOV. What the hell is he talking about? Kuchúmov is here every day at two. I'll make a note of that.

Enter VASSILKÓV, LYDIA, TELYÁTEV *and* MRS. CHEBOKSÁROVA.

GLÚMOV, *to* VASSILKÓV. Good morning.

VASSILKÓV. How are you?

GLÚMOV. What are you looking so worried about?

VASSILKÓV. I'm very busy. I don't go about all day long chasing dogs in the street as you do. Gentlemen, make yourselves at home, be nice to the ladies, but you must excuse me. I haven't much time. I've important business to attend to.

TELYÁTEV *and* GLÚMOV. Carry on. Don't mind us.

VASSILKÓV. I shall be free at lunch. If you like to stay to lunch, do so, if not, be off. Good-bye. *Goes into his study.*

MRS. CHEBOKSÁROVA. How very polite, I must say.

TELYÁTEV. We don't mind, he's a good fellow.

GLÚMOV. Let's go. I don't like to lunch in private houses: they've always something homely for you, either it is some rhubarb wine[5] in a large decanter in the middle of the table or some homemade brandy or a cup without a handle or pasties tasting of tallow. Of course, at your house everything is first-class, but I still prefer to have lunch either at an hotel or at the club.

TELYÁTEV. Let's go to the English Club. They're serving a special lunch there today.

GLÚMOV. All right. *They bow and go out.*

MRS. CHEBOKSÁROVA. Darling, your husband is either a miser or he hasn't any money at all.

LYDIA, *frightened.* What do you mean, mother?

MRS. CHEBOKSÁROVA. He told me himself a little while ago that he can't afford to live as we do and that he'll have to cut down expenses. What shall we do if he finds out that we borrowed right and left before your marriage and that he'll have to pay the bills?

LYDIA. And what about the goldmines?

MRS. CHEBOKSÁROVA. It's a story invented by Glúmov.

LYDIA. Mother, I'm done for. Like a butterfly I can't live without gold dust. I'll die, I'll just die, mother.

MRS. CHEBOKSÁROVA. I still believe, dear, that he has plenty of money, but he's stingy. If you could be nicer to him . . . Do try to overcome your aversion for him, dear.

LYDIA, *thoughtfully.* Be nicer to him? Nicer, did you say, mother? Oh, if it is really necessary I shall be so nice to him that he'll die of sheer happiness and leave me a rich widow. It would be nice to find out what each caress of mine is worth in gold. I may as well start straight away.

MRS. CHEBOKSÁROVA. Don't talk like that, Lydia, you make me frightened.

LYDIA. There's nothing more frightening than poverty, mother.

MRS. CHEBOKSÁROVA. You're wrong, Lydia. Vice is more terrible than poverty.

LYDIA. Vice? What is vice? To be afraid of vice when everybody is vicious is both stupid and unprofitable. The greatest vice in the world, mother, is poverty. Never, never shall I be poor. A woman must have courage to make use of her beauty. Till now I did not bother to attract him. I was reserved, frigid, I kept myself aloof, but now I'll see what I can do when I fling shame to the winds.

MRS. CHEBOKSÁROVA. Stop raving, Lydia. I'm terrified to hear you talk like that.

LYDIA. You're old, mother, and poverty has lost its sting for you, but I am young and I want to live. Life to me means glitter, men's adulation, dazzle and splendour.

MRS. CHEBOKSÁROVA. I refuse to listen to you.

---

[5]In the text "kvass," a Russian soft drink made out of bread.

LYDIA. Who is richer, mother, Telyátev or Kuchúmov? I must know for I hold them both in the hollow of my hand.

MRS. CHEBOKSÁROVA. Both of them are rich, dear, and both fling their money about, but Kuchúmov is richer and more good-natured.

LYDIA. That's all I want to know. Where are the bills from the shops? Give them to me!

MRS. CHEBOKSÁROVA, *produces the bills from pocket.* Here they are, all of them. *Goes out.*

LYDIA *grasps the bills in her hand and goes with determined step towards the door of her husband's study.* VASSILKÓV *comes out at the same time and they meet half way.*

LYDIA. I wanted to see you.

VASSILKÓV. And I wanted to see you.

LYDIA. That's excellent then. We met half way. Where shall we go, to your study or to my room? *Pointing to her room.* There, darling? Tell me, please.

VASSILKÓV. Let's for the time being stay where we are: half way. I want to have a serious talk to you before lunch. You must forgive me, Lydia, for leaving you so much to yourself.

LYDIA. The less I see of you, the more I want you, darling. *Embraces him.*

VASSILKÓV. What's the matter with you? What's come over you? Why this sudden change?

LYDIA. But, darling, am I a doll or what? Am I not a woman? What did I marry you for? Why should I be ashamed to show my love for you? I'm not a little girl. I'm a grown-up woman of twenty-four. I don't know how other women feel about it, but to me my husband is everything. Do you understand, darling, everything! I kept too long aloof from you. I can see now that I was wrong.

VASSILKÓV. *Quite* wrong, my dear.

LYDIA. When I feel like strangling you in my arms, I shall strangle you. I warn you in time, darling, in case you'd like to prevent me.

VASSILKÓV. Why should I?

LYDIA. I don't know what's come over me so suddenly. I didn't care for you before, but now I feel such a violent attraction to you. Can you feel my heart pounding, darling? I love you so much! *Cries.*

VASSILKÓV. But why are you crying?

LYDIA. Because I'm so happy.

VASSILKÓV. It's me who should be crying. I expected to possess only a beautiful body and I found a loving, devoted heart. Do love me, Lydia, I think I am worthy of your love.

LYDIA. I'd love you anyway, my strong, wild man.

VASSILKÓV. Yes, I am a wild man, but with a tender heart and cultivated tastes. Let me hold your lovely hand, darling. *Takes* LYDIA's *hand.* How lovely it is! What a pity I'm not a painter!

LYDIA. Everything I have is yours, darling, not only my hand. *Clings to him.*

VASSILKÓV, *kisses her hand.* Give me both your hands. LYDIA *hides bills in her pocket.* What are you hiding there?

LYDIA. Don't ask me, darling, please don't.

VASSILKÓV. Why implore me so much? If you have a secret, you can keep it. I am not interested in other people's secrets.

LYDIA. How can I have any secrets from you, darling? Aren't we one, body and soul? I'll tell you my terrible secret. I have in my pocket the bills for my trousseau which mother should have paid. But she is in financial difficulties now. Father can't send her any money, he seems to have invested it all in some business deal. I wanted to settle them out of my own pocket, but I don't know if I can raise enough money just now. That's all there is to it, darling. You see, it isn't really important.

VASSILKÓV. Show me your bills.

LYDIA, *gives him the bills.* Here they are, darling. Do you really want to see them?

VASSILKÓV. Yes. I'm going to pay for your trousseau because you've made me so happy. If I had married a poor girl, I should have had to pay for her trousseau and she might not have loved me as much as you do.

LYDIA. No, no. I will settle everything myself. I must repay mother for all she's done for me.

VASSILKÓV. Keep your money for your own needs, darling.

MRS. CHEBOKSÁROVA *enters.* VASSILKÓV *sits down at the table and begins to add up the bills.*

LYDIA, *softly to* MRS. CHEBOKSÁROVA. He'll pay for everything. *Lies down on couch and takes book. Aloud.* Mother, do be very quiet. Savva is busy. *Softly to* MRS. CHEBOKSÁROVA *who sits down at the head of the couch.* He's entirely in my hands.

VASSILKÓV, *stops in his adding up.* Lydia, there's a bill here for the new wallpaper and curtains which are hardly part of your trousseau.

LYDIA. But, darling, we had to have everything new for the wedding. We had such crowds of people. But for the wedding we shouldn't have bothered about it.

MRS. CHEBOKSÁROVA. The old ones would have been good for another winter.

VASSILKÓV. All right, all right. *Goes on adding up figures.*

LYDIA, *softly to* MRS. CHEBOKSÁROVA. Yes, I'm telling you he's going to pay for everything, absolutely for every damn thing.

A fashionably dressed MAID *enters and gives* LYDIA *a bill.* LYDIA *motions her to give it to her husband.* MAID *hands bill to* VASSILKÓV, *who glances at it, nods to his wife and goes on counting. The* MAID *comes in again and hands another bill to* LYDIA *who gets up and throws it negligently on the table. The* MAID *goes out and* ANDREY *comes in with two more bills and the same scene is repeated.* ANDREY *goes out.* VASSILY *comes in with a large bundle of bills and gives it to* VASSILKÓV.

VASSILY. There are 'undreds of 'em, sir. All from the French shops.

VASSILKÓV. Give them to your mistress.

VASSILY *hands them to* LYDIA *who drops them on the floor.*

VASSILY, *picking them up.* Why throw 'em on the floor, ma'am. Them's kind of documents, them's got to be paid.

LYDIA. Go away! I can't stand the sight of you!

ASSILY *puts the bills carefully together, places them on the table in front f* VASSILKÓV *and goes out.*

ASSILKÓV, *gets up and paces room.* I've finished. The bills come altogether to thirty-two thousand five hundred and forty-seven roubles and ninety-eight copecks. This is rather a large sum for me, but, as I've given you my word, I'm going to pay the lot. I'll borrow the money today, but to balance our budget we'll have to cut down expenses drastically for a long time. There is a small, one-storied house opposite. It has only three windows looking out onto the street. I've already been to see it and I think that it will do very nicely for us. We're going to dismiss our servants. I'll keep Vassily and you'll have one maid only, an inexpensive one. We'll dismiss the chef and engage a cook. We'll also sell our horses.

YDIA, *laughs.* How can we manage without horses? Aren't horses made to take us from one place to another? How are we going to go out? Are we going to fly in a balloon?

ASSILKÓV. When it's dry, we shall use our feet, and when it's wet or slushy, we shall hire a cab.

YDIA. So that's what your love really amounts to!

ASSILKÓV. I don't want to go bankrupt because I love you.

YDIA. You'd better hurry up and pay the bills. The shopkeepers are waiting, they at least are respectable people. It's not nice to keep them waiting. They must be paid.

ASSILKÓV. Why not pay them yourself? You have money of your own, haven't you?

YDIA. I shan't pay.

ASSILKÓV. They can summons you, you know.

YDIA. But I have no money! Oh, God!

RS. CHEBOKSÁROVA, *excitedly.* Why do you torture us? We deserve better treatment. We've made a mistake. You're a poor man, but we're doing our best to rectify our mistake. Of course, a boor like you cannot be expected to appreciate the delicacy of our feelings. Take my husband, for example. He had a very important and responsible position in the Civil Service. Lots of money passed through his hands, and—do you know?— he cared so much for me and my daughter that whenever a large sum was required to keep up our social position or simply to meet some whim of ours, he . . . he never bothered to make any distinction between his money and public money. Do you see? He didn't hesitate to sacrifice his career on the altar of his home and family! Eventually, he had to stand his trial and was forced to leave Moscow for the provinces.

ASSILKÓV. And serves him jolly well right!

RS. CHEBOKSÁROVA. If you can't appreciate what he did for us, try at least to appreciate our present position. You are poor, but we shan't let you remain poor. We have good connections. We are looking for and we shall find a lucrative trusteeship or some other good job for you. All you'll have to do is to follow my husband's example and be as exemplary a family man as he. *Goes up to* VASSILKÓV, *puts hand on his shoulder and whispers.* Don't be squeamish, you understand? *Points to his pocket.*

Leave it to me to see to it that those in authority look the other way
Just help yourself to what's going.

VASSILKÓV. Go to the devil with your infernal advice! No poverty and no
beautiful woman will ever make a thief of me. If you dare speak to me
again of thieving, I'll throw you out of my house. Lydia, stop crying
I'll pay your bills, but for the last time and on condition that tomorrow
we move to that small house with the three windows. There's a small
room for your mother there. We're going to live modestly. We shall do
no entertaining and you will receive no visitors. *Begins to check the
bills again.*

LYDIA, *leaning aaginst her mother's shoulder.* We must accept his offer
Softly to her mother. We'll get all the money we want and we'll live as
before. *Aloud to husband.* I agree, darling. I can't very well oppose
you when I ought really to be grateful to you. *Softly to her mother*
Watch me pull the wool over his eyes. *Aloud to her husband.* All right
darling, we shan't receive anyone.

VASSILKÓV, *going over his accounts again.* I knew I could depend on you.

LYDIA. But what about old Kuchúmov, darling? He's almost a member of
the family.

VASSILKÓV, *counting.* All right, we'll make an exception for Kuchúmov.

        LYDIA *presses her mother's hand convulsively.*

MRS. CHEBOKSÁROVA, *softly.* What's in your mind?

LYDIA, *softly.* No one has ever humiliated me as much as he. I'm no longer
a woman, I'm a serpent. I'm going to sting him till he howls with pain

VASSILKÓV, *immersed in his calculations.* You're a frightful spendthrift, dar
ling.

LYDIA, *goes over to him and embraces him.* Please, forgive me, dearest. I'm
a mad, spoilt woman, but I'll do my best to reform. I want you to teach
me a lesson, angel, don't spare me.

VASSILKÓV. Then it's peace?

LYDIA. Yes, darling, peace for ever and ever.

VASSILKÓV. That's fine, darling. At least we understand each other perfectly
now. You know that I am thrifty to a fault and I know that you are
spoilt and improvident, but that you love me and that you'll do your
best to make me happy. A plain businessman like me could hardly have
hoped for such happiness from a spoilt society woman like you, and
that's why this happiness is so dear to me, Lydia, my angel. *He embraces
his wife.*

ACT FOUR

A very modestly furnished room, which also serves as VASSILKÓV's *study;*
each side windows, at the back to the right of the spectators a door leading
into the hall, to the left a door leading to the inner rooms; between the

ɔors *a tiled stove; the furniture is poor: a writing desk, an old piano.*
ᴀssɪʟᴋóv *sits at desk and arranges papers,* ᴠᴀssɪʟʏ *stands in front of him.*
ᴀssɪʟᴋóv. Well, Vassily, it seems your mistress is getting used to the new
house and to you.

ᴀssɪʟʏ. I ain't sure abaht 'er gettin' used to the 'ahse, sir. When you're
aht, sir, they ain't 'alf carryin' on, 'er and 'er ma, burstin' aht laughin'
as if enjoyin' some joke agin somebody. As for me, sir, I ain't 'alf surprised I ain't long gawne and drownded meself, it's so fed up I am, sir,
with everythin' 'ere.

ᴀssɪʟᴋóv. Why, what's wrong?

ᴀssɪʟʏ. It's the missus and 'er ma, sir. They will hinsist, sir, that I be
wearin' them tails and white shirt an' collar of an evenin' and that carst
orf blue liverie with them brass buttons and fancy trahsers in daytime,
sir. But I keeps on refusin', for I ain't no bloomin' butler, sir, nor no
blinkin' footman, neither. I am your valet, sir, been kind of hassistant
to you, if I may say so, sir, travellin' together all rahnd the world, in a
manner of speakin'. Why, sir, we almost drownded together in the sime
boat like for the good of yer business.

ᴀssɪʟᴋóv, *gets up.* Of course, of course, Vassily.

ᴀssɪʟʏ. And she nearly devahred me alive for them fruit, sir.

ᴀssɪʟᴋóv. Which fruit?

ᴀssɪʟʏ. In a manner of speakin', sir. There weren't more'n this much of
it, sir. *Shows on finger how little there was of it.*

ᴀssɪʟᴋóv. Of what?

ᴀssɪʟʏ. Of a piece o' radish, sir. I ain't 'alf fond o' radishes, sir. There
weren't more'n that, sir. I was sittin' in the hall, havin' a good time
like, sir, eatin' me bit o' radish.

ᴀssɪʟᴋóv. Well, Vassily, I don't think you ought to, you know.

ᴀssɪʟʏ. But we workin' folk, sir, ain't 'alf fond of a tasty bit o' radish!

ᴀssɪʟᴋóv. Don't forget, Vassily, what I told you: while I am away you are
not to let anyone into the house except Mr. Kuchúmov.

ᴀssɪʟʏ. Very good, sir. You can rely on me, sir.

ᴠᴀssɪʟᴋóv *and* ᴠᴀssɪʟʏ *go out. Enter* ʟʏᴅɪᴀ.

ᴅɪᴀ. Where's that repulsive, doddering old fathead? For three days I've
been imprisoned in this ghastly hole. I can't go near the windows even
for fear of being spotted by some of my old friends who are no doubt
driving past the house purposely to catch sight of me. Glúmov, I suppose, has his verses all written. Dearest Kuchúmov, my darling pappie,
please get me out of this hovel! Mummy and I could go back to our old
apartment and have a nicer time than ever before. If only I could have
some music to distract me. There's great comfort in a waltz! Say what
you will, but Johann Strauss is the greatest connoisseur of a woman's
heart. *Opens piano and plays a few bars.* What a rotten piano! He got
it on purpose to humiliate me. Wait, my precious one, I'll lead you such
a dance! *Listens to the sound of a carriage outside.* I wish I could go up
to the window, but how can a society girl even show herself at such a
crazy peep-hole. Is it Kuchúmov? He usually comes at two. It's him!

It's him! He's at the door now. Yes, I can recognize his steps. I wonde
what's going to happen now?

Behind the scenes KUCHÚMOV's *voice is heard asking:* "Is your mistress ;
home?" *and* VASSILY's *voice answering:* "Yes, sir." KUCHÚMOV *comes in.*

LYDIA. At last, dear pappie. Aren't you ashamed of yourself to have bee
away so long?

KUCHÚMOV, *kisses* LYDIA's *hand and looks round the room angrily.* What
all this? What's all this? Where has he dragged you to? What furnitur
It's like a low-class village inn. What does it all mean, I ask you? M
angel, don't be angry with me for talking to you like that. In suc
rooms one can't help being rude. How did it all happen? How did yo
allow yourself to be placed in such a humiliating situation? You a
dragging the name of the Cheboksárovas in the mud, madam!

LYDIA. Don't blame me, pity me rather.

KUCHÚMOV. It's impossible to pity you, madam. You are disgracing yo
family. What would your poor father say if he knew of your humi
ation?

LYDIA. But what am I to do?

KUCHÚMOV. You must run away, madam, run away at once.

LYDIA. But where? Mother has no money. He paid all our debts.

KUCHÚMOV. That was only his duty. For the possession of such a treasu
as you, for the happiness which you bestowed on this . . . this sea-lio
he is in duty bound to carry out your slightest whim.

LYDIA. He doesn't seem to regard me as such a treasure or to value tl
happiness I gave him.

KUCHÚMOV. If he doesn't, all the better. You ought to know your ow
worth. Go back to your old apartment with your mother. Ther
nothing wrong about that. To live in this hencoop is a disgrace.

LYDIA. But, pappie, what are we to live on? Mother hasn't a bean, neith
have I. We can't even hope to get anything on credit.

KUCHÚMOV. Credit! What do you want credit for? You ought to be ashame
of yourself to talk like that. You should have come to me. You a
ashamed to ask me for money, but you aren't ashamed to live in such
hovel. You, our queen of fairies, seem to have forgotten how to co
mand. You have only to wave a wand and this hovel will be transform
into a palace.

LYDIA. Which wand, pappie?

KUCHÚMOV. You, as a fairy princess, ought to know that better than
mortal men. Fairy princesses and lovely women have many magic wan
they can wave.

LYDIA, *throwing her arms round his neck.* Do you mean that, pappie?

KUCHÚMOV. Yes, yes . . . *He has a sudden attack of giddiness and sits dou
quickly on a chair.* Will forty thousand be enough for a start?

LYDIA. I don't know, pappie.

KUCHÚMOV. You don't want much for the time being. You'll go back
your old apartment. It is beautifully decorated and it isn't taken y
You have plenty of fine dresses and things. Forty thousand should
quite enough for a start. Listen, my dear, if you refuse, I shall throw

out of the window of my carriage or lose it at cards at my club. I'll get rid of it in one way or another if you won't take it.

YDIA. Then let me have it, pappie.

UCHÚMOV, *searches his pockets.* Good heavens, such a thing happens only to me. I put the money in my wallet to give it to you, but I must have left my wallet at home. Forgive me, child. *Kisses her hand.* I'll be certain to bring it tomorrow for your house-warming party. I hope you'll move today. I'll order a special pie at the best pastrycook's in Moscow and I'll buy a gold salt-cellar, a very large one, five pounds in weight, at the best jeweller's in Moscow and place the money there. I wish I could change it all for gold coins, but I could hardly get so much gold at the bank. I will, however, get about one hundred gold half-imperials and add it to the forty thousand for luck.

YDIA. Thank you, thank you, pappie! *Strokes his head.*

UCHÚMOV. What bliss! What bliss! What does money matter! If I possessed millions, life without such a pair of eyes as yours and without your caresses, my dear, would be pure misery!

Enter MRS. CHEBOKSÁROVA.

YDIA. Mother, darling, dear Grigory advises us to go back to our old apartment.

UCHÚMOV. Naturally, you can't stay here, my dear, you can't stay here.

RS. CHEBOKSÁROVA. Oh, dear Grigory, you can't imagine what I've been through! How I suffer! How I suffer! You know the kind of life I led when I was younger. I get a heart attack at the very memory of it. I would have taken Lydia to her father, but he doesn't want us to come. He doesn't mention having received any money from you, either.

UCHÚMOV. I don't suppose he's got it yet. *Counts on his fingers.* Tuesday, Wednesday, Thursday, Friday . . . He must have got it last night or this morning.

YDIA. We ought to go back immediately, mother.

RS. CHEBOKSÁROVA. We must think it over, Lydia. I can't help feeling that your husband is really very rich and that he is only pretending to be in difficulties.

DIA. Whether he is rich or poor, he has so humiliated me that everything between us is finished. Dear Grigory has done so much for us already and he doesn't want me to stay with my husband. We shall have money for all our expenses, pappie has promised me.

RS. CHEBOKSÁROVA. Pappie! Fie, Lydia, where did you learn to talk like that? A mother can't bear to listen to you.

DIA. How do you like that? Are you ashamed of me? Then, please, don't be ashamed of me any more. I've made up my mind, mother, that the only thing I shall be ashamed of in future is poverty. I shall be ashamed of nothing else . . . Think, mother! We are both women. We haven't the means to live decently and to live decently means to you to live in luxury, doesn't it? How can you therefore demand that I should be ashamed of anything? No, mother, whether you like it or not, you'll have to close an eye to certain things in future. Such is the fate of all

mothers who bring up their daughters in the lap of luxury and leav
them without a penny.

KUCHÚMOV. Benissimo! I can hardly believe that so young a woman posses
es so much commonsense.

LYDIA. Mother, pappie promises to give us forty thousand as soon as w
have moved out of here.

MRS. CHEBOKSÁROVA, *overjoyed.* Really? *To* KUCHÚMOV. You are a ver
very generous man. But, nevertheless, dear, don't you think we'd bette
sleep on it?

LYDIA. Why sleep on it? All we can expect here is humiliation, but the
is happiness!

MRS. CHEBOKSÁROVA. Come to my room, dear. Let's discuss this thing proj
erly. The chief thing that we simply mustn't forget is that we have
keep up appearances.

LYDIA. You can rely on me for that, mother.

KUCHÚMOV. I am not a little schoolboy, I know how to enjoy happine
without trumpeting it abroad, I know how to hold my tongue.

VASSILY'S *voice is heard behind the scenes:* "No, sir. Master's orders we
not to admit no one." GLÚMOV'S *voice:* "Don't be a fool, man!" KUCHÚMO
LYDIA *and* MRS. CHEBOKSÁROVA *go out.* KUCHÚMOV'S *hat remains on tabl
Enter* GLÚMOV *and* VASSILY.

GLÚMOV. What are you talking about, you old idiot? Did he give yc
orders not to admit me? That's impossible.

VASSILY. I ain't no idiot, sir. I shan't let no one call me an idiot, sir.
ain't my fault if I been told to admit no one.

GLÚMOV. Who told you not to admit me, your master or your mistress?

VASSILY. Never mind that, sir. Orders is orders and I ain't making no e
ception for nobody. But if you hinsist on knowin' I don't mind telli
you: it's master who told me not to let you in and mistress don't wa
to see you, neither.

GLÚMOV. You're a born fool, your folly is quite incurable, but you probab
know the reason why your master ordered you not to admit me. What
it? Even an ass like you ought to know it. So out with it, and to hel
your memory here's a silver rouble for you; it's more than your inform
tion is worth.

VASSILY. Thank'ee, sir. *Takes coin and puts it in his pocket.* Wot'll I te
ye like? You know 'ow it is 'ere, sir. If you come, somebody else'll com
and another and another. There won't be no end of visitors, sir. O
glass of vodka for you, that's gone, then two more are gone, then fou
six, eight, ten, and all that costs an 'eap o' money, sir. And master,
says our business's gettin' not 'alf slack like. You'd feel the sime w
yerself, sir. Why should we feed all them good-for-nothin' wastrels, si
It's all gone dahn the drain like and nobody the better for it. Of cours
if missus's friends were all respectable businessmen, it wouldn't 'alf mal
a difference, but with all them rough customers, sir . . .

GLÚMOV. That'll do. Give me a piece of paper and get out of here. I wa
to write a note for your master and then I'll go.

ᵥASSILY. The piper's on the table, sir. Only don't wiste much of it, it's very hexpensive. I'll be leavin' you now, sir. *Goes out.*

ᴳLÚMOV, *takes pen and paper.* What shall I say? *Notices* KUCHÚMOV's *hat.* Hullo! Whose may this be? *Examines hat and whistles significantly.* It's Kuchúmov's, by gad! The dear princeling is already here, is he? Excellent! Vassilkóv has already got his letter. Telyátev, too. They'll meet here together, the whole bunch. What a party! What a situation! Let me say a few words, so that they'll not suspect me. *Writes and reads aloud.* "My dear Savva, I looked in for a moment to talk a certain business over with you. I am very sorry you were out. I'll look in a little earlier tomorrow. Yours, Glúmov." That's right. Written clearly, in large characters. Let me place it here, in the middle of his desk, so that he'll see it at once.

ᴛELYÁTEV's *voice is heard behind the scenes*: "You can't keep me out, old ᵉellow me lad." *Enter* TELYÁTEV *and* VASSILY.

ᴛELYÁTEV, *to* GLÚMOV. Have you seen Lydia?

ᴳLÚMOV. I have not. What do I want to see her for? I came in to see Savva, but missed him and left him a note. Good-bye, if you want Vassilkóv, you'd better go to the Stock Exchange. He knocks about there all day long.

ᴛELYÁTEV. So much the better.

ᴳLÚMOV. It seems he has taken up a new kind of business, buying and selling silk.

ᴛELYÁTEV. An excellent line, old fellow.

ᴳLÚMOV. On a lucky day, he may make as much as five roubles.

ᵥASSILY. That ain't true, sir.

ᴳLÚMOV. There's a typical businessman for you. Comes to Moscow and throws his money about as if he owned all the goldmines in the world, but after six weeks all his money is gone, he either joins the army or is sent home by the police by foot convoy, or else his dear daddy arrives, finds him in a pub, takes hold of him by the hair and drags him home four hundred miles. *Looks at his watch.* However, it's time I went. Been talking too long. *Goes out quickly.*

ᴛELYÁTEV, *sits down at desk with his hat in left hand.* Well, old fellow me lad, so you still insist that I am not to be admitted to this house!

ᵥASSILY. Yes, sir.

ᴛELYÁTEV. Are you quite sure it isn't your own bright idea?

ᵥASSILY. No, sir. Strewth, it ain't. I durstn't do no such thing, sir.

ᴛELYÁTEV. And aren't you sorry for me, old fellow me lad?

ᵥASSILY. I ain't 'alf sorry for you, sir. You ain't like the rest of 'em, sir.

ᴛELYÁTEV. Better, eh?

ᵥASSILY. Much better, sir.

ᴛELYÁTEV. Sit down, old fellow me lad, sit down. VASSILY *sits down with hands on his knees.* Let's have a jolly old palaver, old fellow me lad.

ᵥASSILY. If it's talkin' you want, sir, I don't mind obligin' you.

ᴛELYÁTEV. That's fine. I understand you've been in London, but have you ever been in Morocco?

ᵥASSILY. Never 'eard of no such country, sir. Wot would I be wantin' in

Morocco, sir? I've 'ad enough wanderin' rahnd the world, sir. All wants to know is 'ave they enough bread in their bellies and warm clothin' to their backs for a cold day like?

TELYÁTEV. I can't tell you whether they have enough to eat there, but they don't want any warm clothes because it's jolly hot there all the year round.

VASSILY. Wot I says, sir, is let everybody mind 'is own business, so long as we 'ere 'ave good hexpectations.

TELYÁTEV. But what kind of expectations?

VASSILY. Good hexpectations, sir. In ahr business we've 'ad plenty of trouble of one kind and another. We've known 'unger and cold, sir. Of course it's been like that since the flood, sir, but the good Lord feeds his sparrers, sir.

TELYÁTEV. I see you're quite a philosopher, old fellow me lad, but do you think it's wise to peer too deeply into every bally thing?

VASSILY. I don't mind talking abaht somethin' else, sir.

TELYÁTEV. That'll do, old fellow me lad. I'll have another chat with you another time. *Absentmindedly takes* KUCHÚMOV's *hat from desk and tries to put it on at the same time as his own.* What's this, old fellow me lad?

VASSILY. It can 'appen to heverybody, sir. We ain't 'alf sinners, all of us, sir.

TELYÁTEV. What sin are you muttering about?

VASSILY. Sometimes one can't 'elp pinchin' even an 'at that don't fit one's head, sir.

TELYÁTEV. You're talking through your hat, old fellow me lad.

VASSILY. You'd better try 'em on, sir. The one that fits is yourn.

TELYÁTEV. That's better, old fellow me lad. Now you're talking jolly old horse sense. *Tries on his own hat first.* This is mine. And whose is this? Well, well, well . . . if it isn't the good old princeling's! Is the old boy here?

VASSILY, *mysteriously.* 'E is 'ere, sir.

TELYÁTEV. Where is he?

VASSILY *silently and solemnly points to the door leading to the inner room.*

TELYÁTEV. Why is he admitted and not I?

VASSILY. 'Cause he's a relation, sir.

TELYÁTEV. He is as much a relation as yourself, old fellow me lad. You'll have to excuse me now. I'll stay here and you'd better go back to your cubbyhole in the hall.

VASSILY. Master anyways ain't usually at 'ome at this time, sir, otherwise . .

TELYÁTEV. That'll do, old fellow me lad. Don't wait for me to chuck you out of here.

VASSILY. I suppose, sir, you ain't 'alf goin' to, if you say so. *Goes out.*

TELYÁTEV, *takes out letter from pocket and reads*:

> "Do not, Telyátev, be conceited,
> Such miracles are not unknown,
> The princeling will not be defeated,
> At two Lydia will be his own."

And so it seems, he will not be defeated! He's a relation, and I'm held at bay by that precious ass of a philosopher. What am I to do? To give her up without a fight is hardly gentlemanly, besides, I'm damned if I will. Let's wait and see how she sees him off. I'd like to see their faces when they find me here in the role of avenging fate. What a situation for them! Maybe I'd better take the bull by the horns and see what's going on in there. It's not very nice, to be sure, but . . . Where the hell are they? *Goes up to a door and listens at the keyhole.* Nobody there. Let's investigate. *Opens door carefully, goes out and closes it as carefully.* VASSILKÓV *and* VASSILY *come in.*

VASSILKÓV, *hurriedly.* Did anyone call here while I was out?

VASSILY. Mr. Glúmov, sir. He left a note.

VASSILKÓV, *sternly.* And who else?

VASSILY. Mr. Kuchúmov, sir . . .

VASSILKÓV. All right, you can go. VASSILY *goes out.*

VASSILKÓV. Kuchúmov is so old that it's impossible even to suspect him; after all, my wife has some taste. *Stops in front of desk and sees* GLÚMOV's *note. Takes out letter from pocket and compares the two handwritings.* Not at all alike, and I thought it might be he. *Reads letter:*

> "To 'Change the husband does repair,
> For all his interests are there,
> His lovely wife at home he left,
> *She* is of interest bereft.
> Does she do naught or nowhere go?—
> 'Praps 'tis as well he does not know.
> Alas, poor husband!
>
> *He'll* meet some friends during the day,—
> At business, lunch, may be at play,
> They'll bargain, chatter, joke and laugh,
> Maybe a drink or two they'll quaff,
> Schemes they will plan and stories tell,—
> Maybe his *wife's* a friend as well!
> Alas, poor husband!

"Be at home at two o'clock for certain and you'll understand the meaning of these words." *Short pause.* What is it, a leg-pull or a calamity? If a leg-pull, then it is stupid and inexcusable to laugh at a man without regard to his feelings. If a calamity, then why does it break so soon and so unexpectedly? If I knew my wife, I shouldn't have been at a loss. I know how a simple girl or woman loves, but I'm hanged if I can tell what a society girl feels at heart. I don't know her at all. I can't penetrate her mind. I am a stranger to her and she is a stranger to me. She doesn't care what a man feels, all she is interested in is what he says. She wants fine speeches and I can't make fine speeches. Damn fine speeches! How easily we adopt some stranger's way of speaking and how slow we are to change our way of thinking. Everybody seems to be making speeches now as they do in the English Parliament, but they still think as they used to think in the days when no English Parliament was even thought of. And as for doing anything . . . They just do nothing . . . What the hell can this letter mean? I'll show it to Lydia. But if . . . if . . . my God! What am I to do then? How am I to behave? It's silly to try to prepare oneself for such an eventuality, it's silly to play-act. What my stupid provincial heart tells me, I'll do. *Opens box with pistols, examines them, and replaces in box, which remains open. Goes to door which opens from inside.* TELYÁTEV, *walking backwards, comes in.* Telyátev, real friends don't behave like that!

TELYÁTEV. Hullo, old fellow. *Softly.* Wait a minute, they'll be coming out presently.

VASSILKÓV. Answer my questions, or I'll kill you on the spot!

TELYÁTEV. Sh . . . Quiet, I tell you. *Listens.* What do you want to know?

VASSILKÓV. Have you come to see my wife?

TELYÁTEV. Yes.

VASSILKÓV. Why?

TELYÁTEV. To spend a jolly hour or two, old fellow. A little flirtation, you know, doesn't do anyone any harm.

VASSILKÓV. Why should you pick on my wife to flirt with? Aren't there any others?

TELYÁTEV. Because, old fellow, I've got good taste.

VASSILKÓV. We are going to fight a duel!

TELYÁTEV. All right, old fellow, all right. Don't make such an infernal noise. I can hear voices.

VASSILKÓV. I don't care a damn whether you hear voices or not. The pistols are ready.

TELYÁTEV. Don't be a silly ass, old fellow. Cool down. Have a drink of cold water.

VASSILKÓV. Look here, Telyátev, I am a quiet, peaceful man, but there are times when . . . I can't tell you the hell I'm in now. I . . . You see, I'm nearly crying. Here are the pistols. Choose which you like.

TELYÁTEV. If you want to make me a present of them, let me have the two. Why separate them? But if you really want to fight, then why be in such a confounded hurry, old fellow? I am going to have a lovely dinner today. After a good dinner I always feel a bit heavy; I shouldn't mind being killed then.

VASSILKÓV. No, we're going to fight it out now, right here, without any seconds.

TELYÁTEV. No, sir. I also can be obstinate. I am not going to fight any duels. What an awful place you have here, old fellow. Everything, you know, must be done properly. Wait! Wait! You'd better tell me first why you moved to this frightful hole.

VASSILKÓV. I haven't enough money to live anywhere else.

TELYÁTEV. Why didn't you say so before, old fellow? Here. *Takes out wallet.* How much do you want? You'd better take the lot, I can get on very well without money in Moscow.

VASSILKÓV. Do you want to buy me off with your money? Do you want to buy my wife from me?

TELYÁTEV. Listen, old fellow. Better kill me, but don't insult me. I respect you more than you think or than you deserve.

VASSILKÓV. I'm sorry. I seem to have gone mad.

TELYÁTEV. I'm offering you the money simply because I'm good-natured or rather because of the general improvidence about money matters all round. When you have money, give it all to the first man you meet, when you haven't any, borrow it from the first man you meet.

VASSILKÓV. All right, let me have the money. How much have you got there?

TELYÁTEV. Count them later, old fellow. About five thousand, I think.

VASSILKÓV. I must count them now and give you a receipt.

TELYÁTEV. Don't bother, old fellow. I usually give receipts to people, I don't accept any from anybody. Even if I did, I'd lose them.

VASSILKÓV. Thanks. I'll pay you good interest on your loan.

TELYÁTEV. Pay me with champagne, old fellow. I take no other interest.

VASSILKÓV. Nevertheless, we'll have to fight, you know, because you are making love to my wife.

TELYÁTEV. It isn't worth while, old fellow, not worth while. Just consider: if your wife is an honest woman, all my love-making will be a waste of time, though, as far as I'm concerned, a jolly pleasant waste of time, but if she is not honest, she isn't worth endangering anyone's life for.

VASSILKÓV. What do you advise me to do then if she is unfaithful? *In despair.* What am I to do?

TELYÁTEV. Send her packing, old fellow. That's all.

VASSILKÓV. I was so happy. She pretended so well that she was in love with me. Think how much the love of such a beautiful woman means to a man like me, an awkward provincial businessman with no social pretensions of any kind—it's just heaven! And now I find that she's unfaithful to me. My whole world has suddenly collapsed about my ears. I can't bear the thought that she's deceiving me!

TELYÁTEV. All right, old fellow, shoot *her,* why shoot me?

VASSILKÓV. Because it was you who led her astray. She is a good woman by nature, but in your cesspool a woman is capable of losing everything, honour, conscience and shame! And you are the most dissolute man of them all. Take a pistol or I'll beat your brains out with a chair.

TELYÁTEV. To hell with you! I'm sick of the sight of you. Come on, let's shoot it out! *Makes for the desk with the pistols, but stops to listen at the door.* Listen to me, old fellow, before fighting it out, let's hide behind the stove.

VASSILKÓV. No! Let's fight at once!

TELYÁTEV, *takes him by the shoulders.* Quiet, quiet, you silly ass! *Drags him behind the stove.*

Enter KUCHÚMOV and LYDIA.

KUCHÚMOV, *sings.* In mia mano al fin tu sei.[6]

LYDIA. Good-bye, pappie!

---

[6]From Bellini's opera *Norma,* Act II.

KUCHÚMOV, *sings.* Kiss me, my darling, your kisses are so sweet . . . *Addio, mia carina! . . .*

LYDIA. With pleasure, pappie! *Kisses him.*

VASSILKÓV *and* TELYÁTEV *come out from behind the stove.*

LYDIA. Hell!!! *Runs off into a corner.*

KUCHÚMOV, *wagging a finger.* Gentlemen, gentlemen! I . . . Just as an old friend of the family, you know . . . *Honi soit qui mal y pense!*

VASSILKÓV, *pointing to the door.* Get out! I'll send my seconds to you tomorrow.

KUCHÚMOV. Don't do that, young man! I'm not going to fight any duels with you. My life is much too valuable to Moscow to put in jeopardy against yours, which, as far as I can see, is of no value to anybody.

VASSILKÓV. I'll kill him! *Goes to desk.*

KUCHÚMOV. Please, young man, please . . . This is no joke, young man. *Runs out.*

Enter MRS. CHEBOKSÁROVA.

MRS. CHEBOKSÁROVA. What's all this row about?

VASSILKÓV. Take your daughter away from me. I'm quits with you. I'm returning her to you as dissolute as she was when I took her from you. She complained that my name was too common for her own exalted one. It is my turn now to complain that she has disgraced my common but honest name. When she married me, she said that she did not love me. Having lived with her only one week, I can say that I have nothing but contempt for her. She married me a poor girl. I even had to pay for her trousseau and for her dresses. Let her consider that as payment for her caresses, which I was not the only one to enjoy!

LYDIA. What a tragedy!

MRS. CHEBOKSÁROVA. Don't be so excited, Savva. I'm sure it's only a misunderstanding. But even if married couples separate, it is usually done decently, without any scandal.

VASSILKÓV, *to* TELYÁTEV. Don't leave me, my friend. I have still some arrangements to make. Here's your money. Take it. I merely wanted to earn you good interest for the sake of our friendship. Take it! *Gives money back to* TELYÁTEV, *who shoves it negligently into a pocket.* LYDIA *looks keenly at the money.* I must make a few arrangements, write to my mother . . . I'm going to shoot myself! *Lowers head on chest.*

TELYÁTEV. Don't be an ass, old fellow. You are an ass, Savva, you know. I had a friend who was married twice and both his wives ran away from him. Do you think he ought to have shot himself twice? Look at me, Savva. Listen to me, I am a sensible chap, I can give you some really good advice. First of all, for heaven's sake don't try to shoot yourself in a room. It isn't done. Gentlemen usually shoot themselves in the Petrovsky park. Secondly, have dinner with me tonight. We'll discuss everything later.

VASSILKÓV, *to* MRS. CHEBOKSÁROVA. Take your daughter away from me at once. Take her away at once!

LYDIA. Don't you worry. I'll go sooner than you think. We intended to go back to our old apartment today, anyway. We've already taken it and we shan't even look from our big windows at this miserable hovel with its miserable owner. You played a comedy and we, too, played a comedy. We have more money than you, but we are women and women do not like to pay anything back. I pretended to love you, I pretended in spite of the disgust I sometimes felt for myself, but, you see, I had to make you pay my debts. I succeeded in making you pay them and I am satisfied. Have you realized what a fine actress I am? With such a talent no woman will ever know want. Shoot yourself! The sooner, the better. Telyátev, don't try to dissuade him! By shooting yourself you will make me a free woman again and I shan't make the same mistake a second time in the choice of a husband or a . . . you know what I mean, don't you? Good-bye! All I want is never to see you again. *To her mother.* Have you sent for a cab?

MRS. CHEBOKSÁROVA. I have. It's waiting.

MRS. CHEBOKSÁROVA *goes out, followed by* LYDIA.

VASSILKÓV. This is the end of everything for me.

TELYÁTEV. Don't talk tommy rot, old fellow. You have still plenty to live for.

VASSILKÓV. No, it's the end. If I were as heartless as she is, I'd rave and kick myself for being such a fool, but I would have got over it. If I had been unfaithful to her, I would have forgiven her. But I am a good-natured man. I believed in her, and she merely took an unfair advantage of my good nature. I shouldn't have minded it so much if she had only laughed at me or at my undistinguished origin, but she laughed at something which I consider the most precious part of me: my good heart, my love, the great happiness she herself had given me. It isn't my vanity that she hurt so much, it is the very essence of my whole being, my very soul. My soul is dead, all that is left is to kill my body. *Sits down, buries his face in his hands and cries.*

TELYÁTEV. Listen, old fellow, you'd better stop crying or you'll make me cry, too. Just think what I'd look like! Stop, Savva, for heaven's sake stop! Just let me take you in hand for a few hours. Let's have dinner. Leave it to me to make it a good one.

VASSILKÓV, *takes pistol and puts it in pocket.* What's that, old man? *He runs to window.* It's their carriage. They've gone. *Looks completely done in.* Take me anywhere you like. I don't care what happens to me.

ACT FIVE

A boudoir in the former CHEBOKSÁROVA *apartment, to the left of the spectators a door to the drawing room, in the middle entrance door, to the left a french window.* LYDIA *in morning dress lies on a settee.* MRS. CHEBOKSÁROVA *enters.*

MRS. CHEBOKSÁROVA. Hasn't he been yet?

LYDIA. Not yet.

MRS. CHEBOKSÁROVA. I have lost my head completely. What are we to do? A week ago Kuchúmov, instead of fulfilling his promise to bring the forty thousand when we moved in here, gave me only six hundred and thirteen roubles, and he pulled such a long face as though he were doing me a great favour. We're up to our neck in debt again. Don't forget that all our furniture has to be paid for. Our old furniture was sold by that scoundrel of a husband of yours.

LYDIA. Kuchúmov promised faithfully to bring it today. It isn't fair not to believe him when he did such a favour to father.

MRS. CHEBOKSÁROVA. But did he? I have my doubts about that. I got a letter from your father today. He tells me he got no money from anyone, that his estate has been sold and that he himself lives with a friend. He says that after the sale of the estate he was left with only very little money and that he intends to start a dairy business in partnership with some tartar or bashkir.

LYDIA. I see it now! Do you know who bought the estate?

MRS. CHEBOKSÁROVA. Who?

LYDIA. Kuchúmov. He promised to buy it and give it to me as a present.

MRS. CHEBOKSÁROVA. I don't think so, dear. Your father writes that at the auction a certain Yermolayev, an agent of Vassilkóv, made the largest bid. Isn't that him? *Points to window.*

LYDIA. Don't try to be funny, mother. How could he buy the estate? You saw yourself that he was borrowing money from Telyátev and promised him a high rate of interest for it, and people offer high rates of interest only if they want money badly. Besides, he is too stupid for such a deal. Don't let us even discuss him.

MRS. CHEBOKSÁROVA. All right. I won't.

LYDIA. I consider myself disgraced, mother, because I married him. I must wipe all memory of him from my mind. I should have returned all his presents if they were not so valuable. I ordered my jewels to be reset so that they shouldn't remind me of him.

MRS. CHEBOKSÁROVA. I'll go see if the carriage has arrived. I managed to get it on credit from a coachmaker and have even got our coat-of-arms painted on it. We'll have to hire the horses, but at least we shall have our own carriage. A hired carriage can always be recognized. *Goes out.*

LYDIA. Yes, experience is a great thing. I am still too credulous and credulity can lead to some irreparable mistake.

Enter ANDREY.

ANDREY. Mr. Kuchúmov, ma'am.

LYDIA. Show him in!

ANDREY *goes out.* KUCHÚMOV *comes in.*

KUCHÚMOV, *kneels and kisses* LYDIA's *hand. Il segreto per esser felice.*[7]

LYDIA. Don't be naughty. Sit down. I want to talk to you.

KUCHÚMOV. What frigidity! What icy chill in your voice, child.

LYDIA. I've had enough of your jokes! Listen to me. You forced me to leave my husband, we are running up big debts. I am ashamed to re-

---

[7]From Donizetti's opera, *Lucretia Borgia*, Act II, Sc. 5.

mind you of the money as though I were your mistress, but you promised it to us yourself.

KUCHÚMOV, *sits down*. You must either kill me or you must forgive me for being so absentminded. I was counting the money and putting it in my wallet to bring it to you, when suddenly my wife came into the room. I put it into a drawer, started talking to my wife and . . . it slipped my memory! I'll bring it in half an hour.

LYDIA. Who bought my father's estate, pappie?

KUCHÚMOV. I did, of course.

LYDIA. Father writes that an agent of Vassilkóv bought it.

KUCHÚMOV. That's quite true. I asked a certain Vassilkóv, a businessman I know, to effect the purchase for me. I stood godfather to his son. He must have got someone else to go to Kazan as his agent. What a funny letter he sent me! I'll bring it to you in less than ten minutes! *Gets up and looks round the room. Sings.* Io son ricco, tu sei bella.[8] Yes, this is nice, and that is not so bad. What a perfect taste you have, my dear. You want some greenery here. I'll send you a large palm and some tropical plants. Under the palm we shall exchange our intimate secrets. I'll send it to you today. *Sits down near* LYDIA.

LYDIA, *moving away*. When you bring us the money, I shall again call you pappie and, maybe, I shall even learn to love you.

KUCHÚMOV, *sings*. Io son ricco, tu sei bella! As you can scarcely have any doubts about my honesty, you needn't be so parsimonious with your love, darling.

LYDIA. Do you think so? I'm afraid I am in a very bad temper today, I am not in the mood for love. For some time now I've heard of nothing but riches, my husband owns goldmines, you own mountains of gold. Telyátev is almost a millionaire and, they say, even Glúmov has got very rich. All my admirers extol my beauty, all of them promise to heap riches on me, but neither my husband nor my admirers can oblige me even with pin-money. I have nothing to drive out in, I have to hire a hackney carriage drawn by a couple of dray-horses.

KUCHÚMOV. That's terrible! But in half an hour, my love, everything will be in order. It's my fault, I admit it. I alone am to blame.

LYDIA. I live apart from my husband and you come to see me every day at a certain hour. What will people say?

KUCHÚMOV. It's too late to stop people talking now, my child. The harm's done, however virtuously you've behaved. In my opinion, if you have to become the object of gossip, then why not give the gossips something real to talk about? To be slandered for nothing is the worst thing that can happen to anyone, my darling. I tell you, in half an hour . . . Of course, unless something unforeseen happens . . . There may not be so much money at my office, or something simply has to be paid immediately, then, of course, it may take a day or two . . . in any event, not more than a week and then you can have everything that your heart desires.

---

[8]From Donizetti's opera, *The Love Potion*, Act II, Sc. 1.

LYDIA, *gets up*. In a week? In ten minutes it must be here! Do you hear?
I shan't let you into the house if you don't bring me all the money in
ten minutes!

KUCHÚMOV. Ten minutes? Am I the god Mercury to fly so fast? I may be
detained by business.

LYDIA. No one is going to detain you: your money is in your drawer, the
letter from Vassilkóv, I suppose, is in another. Good-bye!

KUCHÚMOV. I'll clear myself in your eyes, but . . . *Points his finger accusingly
at her* . . . I shan't forgive such behaviour towards me for a long time. *Goes
out.*

LYDIA. This is where all my confidence is beginning to forsake me. A
shiver runs down my spine. Is Kuchúmov deceiving me or not? *In a
determined voice.* He is! So far he hasn't carried out even one of his
promises. What is there left for me to do? Despair and suicide or . . .
No, that's also suicide, only more slow and more painful . . .

Enter ANDREY.

ANDREY. Mr. Telyátev, ma'am.

LYDIA, *thoughtfully.* Show him in.

ANDREY *goes out.* TELYÁTEV *comes in.*

LYDIA. Where have you been all this time? Why didn't you come to see
me?

TELYÁTEV. A man who has no business is usually very busy. Why so serious,
old girl? *Looks at her closely and makes a clucking noise with his tongue.*
Tch-tch-tch . . .

LYDIA. What's the matter?

TELYÁTEV. A wrinkle, old girl. There, on your forehead. A little one, a
very little one, but definitely a wrinkle.

LYDIA, *in dismay.* It's not true!

TELYÁTEV. Look at yourself in the glass. Tch-tch-tch . . . At your age, too!
What a shame!

LYDIA, *in front of the glass.* Stop tch-tch-tch-ing! I'm sick of you!

TELYÁTEV. Don't think too much, old girl. Above everything else don't
overdo thinking. May the good God save and preserve you from thought.
Our women preserve their beauty so long because they never think at
all.

LYDIA. Oh, Johnnie, anyone else in my place would have gone grey by
now! How can I help thinking? Who else will do the thinking for me?

TELYÁTEV. Why, old girl, what do you want? Your position is assured: you
live alone, in a beautiful apartment, you are absolutely free to do what
you like, you are rich, as I heard you say yourself, you have crowds of
admirers, your husband has gone out of your life . . .

LYDIA, *happily.* Has he shot himself?

TELYÁTEV. No, he changed his mind.

LYDIA. What a pity! Can I trust you with a secret?

TELYÁTEV. Very much so, old girl.

LYDIA. You won't tell it to anyone?

TELYÁTEV. I can't promise you that, but I usually forget all about it, and
that's even better. Tell me a secret at one ear and it is sure to fly out

at the other immediately. In an hour I shan't for the life of me be able to remember what the secret was about.

YDIA. Our position is desperate. We have simply nothing to live on.

ELYÁTEV. There is hardly a family that hasn't got the same kind of secret.

YDIA. Listen to me! You are quite impossible. I left my husband only because . . . No, I'm too ashamed to tell it to you.

ELYÁTEV. Why be ashamed, old girl? Go on, tell me. I am a particular kind of a bloke, no woman is ever ashamed before me.

YDIA. All right, I shan't be ashamed before you, either. I left my husband because Kuchúmov promised to lend me forty thousand.

ELYÁTEV. What a funny old boy! Why didn't he promise you eighty thousand?

YDIA. Could he lend me eighty thousand?

ELYÁTEV. Of course. He could lend you two hundred thousand, that is to say, he could promise to lend it to you, but whether he'd ever give you the money is a different question. He rarely has as much as ten roubles in his pocket.

YDIA. You're slandering him. He bought my father's estate for a lot of money. I saw him give six hundred roubles to my mother myself.

ELYÁTEV. I can't tell you anything about the estate, but I know where he got the six hundred roubles from. For five days he was running all over Moscow trying to raise the money and after a lot of trouble he got it from some money-lenders who charged him two thousand for it for one month. I thought he was trying to get the money for your husband to whom he lost it ages ago at cards.

YDIA, *in despair.* You're killing me!

ELYÁTEV. Why? Kuchúmov is a very nice man. Don't be afraid for him. We all love him, but he is very forgetful. He did have a large fortune a long time ago and he very often forgets that he squandered it years ago. Mind you, there is no reason why he shouldn't forget it: he still gives wonderful receptions, balls and dinners, he still drives about in splendid carriages, only all that is his wife's and is held in trust for her nieces. He himself gets no more than ten roubles for his club expenses. On his birthday or during holidays he usually gets thirty roubles and sometimes even a hundred. That's when you ought to see him! He comes to the club, sits down at the head of the table, orders oysters and champagne, and how pernickety he is! He runs the waiters off their feet, he keeps five waiters fussing round him and, as for the chefs, it is a real black day for them!

YDIA, *going pale.* What am I to do? I owe so much money!

ELYÁTEV. Why be so alarmed about it? Who doesn't owe money today?

YDIA. Johnnie, you have a large fortune, have pity on me! Don't let me perish! TELYÁTEV *bows his head.* Please, help me to save the honour of my family. You are such a good sport, Johnnie. Please, save me! *Puts her hands on his shoulders and bows her head.*

ELYÁTEV. All this is very nice of you, old girl, and I'd be glad to help you, only I'm hardly myself today.

LYDIA, *looks into his eyes.* What's the matter? Are you getting married o
are you already married?

TELYÁTEV. I am neither married nor am I getting married, but tomorrow
expect to be taken to the debtors' jail.

LYDIA. That's impossible! Where's all your money? I saw you yoursel
lending money to my husband.

TELYÁTEV. Why shouldn't I? It wasn't my money.

LYDIA. But haven't you any money of your own?

TELYÁTEV. I can't remember the time when I had any money of my own
Yesterday I learnt that I owed about three hundred thousand. Ever
thing you have ever seen in my possession belongs to someone else: m
horses, my carriages, my apartment, my clothes. Nothing has been pai
for. At first I received bills, then summonses, then orders of execution
I must have borrowed huge sums from money-lenders. All my creditor
will do me the honour of paying me a visit tomorrow. It will be a wor
derful scene. My furniture, my carpets, mirrors and pictures were all o
hire and have already been removed. My carriage and horses have als
gone, and the tailor is coming early tomorrow morning to fetch m
clothes. I am quite sure that my creditors will be tickled to death.
shall receive them in my dressing gown, for that is the only thing in th
world that is mine, and I shall offer them a cigar each. They will loo
at my empty walls and will say: "Go on, have a good time, old fellow!" On
of them, who is angry with me because of an affair with his wife, ma
insist on being paid, which, of course, means that I shall have to spen
two months in jail, but he'll soon get fed up paying for my food. I
time they will let me out and I shall be free again and I shall hav
plenty of credit again, because I am a nice chap and because I hav
about eleven grandmothers and old aunts whose sole heir I am. Yo
can't imagine, old girl, how much money I had to spend on stampe
paper for bills of exchange alone! If I were to sell it by the hundrec
weight, I should get more money than my creditors will get from m
tomorrow.

LYDIA. And you are so unruffled?

TELYÁTEV. Why should I worry? My conscience is clear of blame as m
pockets are of money. All my creditors have got three times the mone
I owed them long ago. They are suing me merely as a matter of forn

LYDIA. But where am I to get money, a lot of money, heaps and heaps c
money? Can't I get it from anybody?

TELYÁTEV. Yes, of course.

LYDIA. From whom?

TELYÁTEV. From businessmen who are not in the habit of throwing it
the winds.

LYDIA. What a pity!

TELYÁTEV. It is a great pity, old girl. Even money seems to have got mor
sense now: it all goes to the businessmen, and not to us. Before mone
was not so hard to get, it was easy money. I, too, got easy money, mone
that came easily and went easily. Only recently I understood why you
money and my money was easy money. It was because we did not ear

it ourselves. Money which you earn by hard work is sensible money. It keeps still. You and I whistle for it, but it doesn't come. Such money, if granted the gift of speech, would say: "We know the kind of money you want, we shall have nothing to do with you." And, however much you begged, it wouldn't come to you. Which is really unfair, for we are all such charming people.

LYDIA. I'm going to become an actress.

BELYÁTEV. You need talent for that, old girl.

LYDIA. I'll go to the provinces.

BELYÁTEV. Hardly worth while, old girl. You won't meet any man there worth catching. What kind of a career is that?

LYDIA. But, Johnnie, please help me. I want money!

BELYÁTEV. Come here, I'll show you something. *He takes her to the window.* Do you see that little tumbledown house in the street, looking at the world with its three tiny windows? That's where there is lots of money.

LYDIA. My husband has lots of money?

BELYÁTEV. Yes, he has. He is not only richer than any of us, but he is so rich that it makes you dizzy only to think of it. Today the rich man is not he who has a lot of money, but he who knows how to make money. If your husband today has three hundred thousand in ready money, then you can bet your life that in about a year he'll have a million and in five years—five million.

LYDIA. It's impossible! I don't believe you. Go away! It's he who sent you to me.

BELYÁTEV. But, please, listen to me first. After you left him, we had dinner at the Troitzky restaurant. He sat there without looking at anyone, without eating or drinking. Then a few queer customers came up to him, whispered something in his ear, and he got a little livelier. Then they brought him a telegram, he read it and his eyes began to shine. "No," said he, "it's silly to shoot myself. Let's have a good time instead. Congratulate me." Well, of course, I congratulated him, we embraced and off we went to have a good time. I introduced him to a few of my old friends, they are not really old, you understand, they are, in fact, still very, very young and pretty, but I've known them for some time.

LYDIA, *at the window.* Look, whose carriage is that? What a lovely thing, how luxurious! Could it be the one mother has got?

BELYÁTEV. No, old girl, you're mistaken. That's the carriage your husband has given to one of my pretty friends. He also bought her the horses and hired a coachman you might exhibit at the Zoo. There she is, leaving his house, a pretty little blonde with cornflower-blue eyes.

LYDIA. Oh, I'm going to faint! That isn't a carriage, it's a dream! One could die of happiness merely to sit in it. What's happened to me? I seem to hate him now and even to be jealous. I could kill that blonde! Look at her, turning up that snub nose of hers!

BELYÁTEV. That isn't jealousy, old girl, it's envy.

LYDIA. Does he love her?

BELYÁTEV. Whom?

LYDIA. That blonde.

TELYÁTEV. Why should he? To love her and to give her money is a bit too much of a good thing. Would you like to hear what your husband told me about himself?

LYDIA. Yes, tell me. I'd like to know.

TELYÁTEV. He went abroad, spent some time studying the railway system, came back to Russia, got a small job of railway construction and set to work. He lived in barracks with his workers and Vassily. You've met Vassily, haven't you? A jolly fellow.

LYDIA. Really!

TELYÁTEV. After building his first stretch of railway, he undertook to build another, a much bigger one, and then another, bigger and bigger. And now when he got that telegram, he said to me, "Well, old chap, I shan't take less than a million for that!" And I said to him, "Of course not, old fellow!" It didn't matter to me either way, I wasn't going to lose anything.

LYDIA. I'm going to die!

TELYÁTEV. What's the matter?

LYDIA, *lies down on the settee.* Call mother, call her quickly!

TELYÁTEV, *opens door.* Mrs. Cheboksárova!

Enter MRS. CHEBOKSÁROVA.

LYDIA. Mother, for heaven's sake!

MRS. CHEBOKSÁROVA. What's the matter, Lydia? What's happened, my darling?

LYDIA. For heaven's sake, mother, go to my husband and tell him to come here at once. Tell him I'm dying!

MRS. CHEBOKSÁROVA, *looks closely at her daughter.* All right, dear, I can see that you are very ill. I'll go at once. *Goes out.*

ANDREY *comes in.*

ANDREY. Mr. Glúmov, ma'am.

LYDIA, *raising herself.* Shall I receive him or not? I don't know whether my husband will agree to take me back. A drowning man catches at a straw. *To* ANDREY. Show him in.

ANDREY *goes out.* GLÚMOV *comes in.*

GLÚMOV. Hullo, what's the matter?

LYDIA. I am a little out of sorts. And how are you? I hear you're rich.

GLÚMOV. Not yet, but I have hopes. I've got a very good job.

TELYÁTEV. You've all the qualifications for it, old fellow.

GLÚMOV. I was lucky, that's all. An old lady has been looking for a long time for . . . how shall I put it?—not a manager exactly, but a . . .

LYDIA. A confidential secretary?

GLÚMOV. Yes, madam, a confidential secretary. She wants an honest man to whom she can entrust . . .

TELYÁTEV. Herself and her fortune?

GLÚMOV. Almost. She owns houses, estates, companies and what not. She can't possibly look after it herself! She has quarrelled with all her heirs. I am trying to convert it all into money and I receive a big commission on all the deals.

ELYÁTEV. A noble, trusting woman. You must admit, old fellow, you can't find many more like her.

LÚMOV. Hardly. I suppose she is the only one left in the whole world: I know them all by heart.

ELYÁTEV. We were just talking of easy money and how difficult it is to find it now. But you are luckier than any of us: you have found it!

LÚMOV. But think, old man, how long and how persistently I looked for it!

YDIA. So you have plenty of money now, haven't you?

LÚMOV. Plenty is always relative. The Rothschilds would probably consider it little, but to me it is a lot.

YDIA. Lend me twenty thousand, please.

LÚMOV. No one lends money to young, pretty ladies, for it would be highly indelicate to remind them, should they forget about their debt, and to summons them for it, is even more indelicate. Either you politely refuse to give it to them or you make them a present of it.

YDIA. All right, I don't mind, make me a present of it.

LÚMOV. I'm afraid I can't give it to you. You remember you told me that I should never kiss your hand. I don't forget an insult.

YDIA. Kiss it.

LÚMOV. Now it's too late, or rather too early. Wait a year for me, then I'll come to kiss your hand. Tomorrow I'm leaving for Paris with my boss. She hasn't the faintest idea of money and I'm going to be her cashier. She is suffering from asthma and fatty degeneration of the heart. Here the doctors don't give her more than a year to live and in Paris with the travelling to the different spas and the help of the latest medical advice she is sure to die long before that. So you can see that I have no time to waste. For the next year I shall have to nurse a very sick woman, but afterwards I shall be able to enjoy the fruits of my labour and spend a lot of money, with your active participation, if you want.

YDIA. You are a really wicked man!

LÚMOV. Before you seemed to admire this trait in my character,—we seem to share it.

YDIA. Yes, when you didn't overstep the borderline, but now—good-bye!

LÚMOV. Good-bye. I leave in the pleasant hope that in about a year you'll change your mind, you'll learn to value me and we shall probably meet again like two kindred souls.

YDIA. That's enough. I don't want to hear any more.

LÚMOV. *Au revoir,* then.

TELYÁTEV. Good-bye, old fellow. Pleasant journey. Remember me to Paris: my poor ghost still wanders there at every street crossing.

LÚMOV. Good-bye, Telyátev. *Goes out.*

MRS. CHEBOKSÁROVA *comes in with medicine bottles, followed by a* MAID *with pillows.* MAID *puts pillows on couch and goes out.*

MRS. CHEBOKSÁROVA. You must lie down, Lydia. Please, don't exhaust yourself. I can see by your look that you are very ill. I told your husband of your sudden illness. He'll be here presently. Here are the smelling salts and the drops which did you so much good before.

LYDIA, *reclines on the pillows.* How did he receive you?

MRS. CHEBOKSÁROVA. Very politely, though I'm afraid rather coldly. H
asked whether you were seriously ill and I said, yes, very seriously. Wha
are you laughing at, Mr. Telyátev?

TELYÁTEV. I'm afraid, ma'am, I can't remain unaffected: I have either t
cry or to laugh.

MRS. CHEBOKSÁROVA. You don't know Lydia's nature or her constitution
She is such a nervous child. Even as a baby she was very nervous.

TELYÁTEV. Pardon me, ma'am, but I haven't the faintest idea of her const
tution. It is a mystery to me.

LYDIA. Johnnie, you are such a clown, you'll make me laugh.

MRS. CHEBOKSÁROVA. Really, Mr. Telyátev, you will make her laugh and h
may come in any moment.

TELYÁTEV. Shall I hide somewhere?

LYDIA, *languorously*. No, stay here, Johnnie. I like to see you. You giv
me such strength.

TELYÁTEV. If you wish, old girl, I shall not only stay here, but I shall r
main standing before you rooted to the ground. Look at me as muc
as you like, but in this comedy I crave only a walking on part.

Enter ANDREY.

ANDREY. Mr. Vassilkóv, ma'am.

LYDIA, *in a weak voice*. Show him in.

ANDREY *goes out.* MRS. CHEBOKSÁROVA *adjusts the pillows.* TELYÁTEV *pu
handkerchief to his eyes. Enter* VASSILKÓV.

VASSILKÓV, *after a general bow*. You sent for me?

LYDIA. I am dying.

VASSILKÓV. In that case you should have sent either for a doctor or a pries
I'm neither the one nor the other.

LYDIA. You abandoned me and mother.

VASSILKÓV. I did not abandon you, it's you who left me without even sayin
good-bye.

LYDIA. So you want us to part?

VASSILKÓV. Just as you like.

LYDIA. Do you want me to ask you to forgive me?

VASSILKÓV. By all means.

LYDIA. I am to blame only for having left you without realizing how littl
money I have. You are to blame for everything else.

VASSILKÓV. We are quits then: I was to blame and you left me. What el
is there to discuss? Good-bye!

LYDIA. No, no! Wait, please!

VASSILKÓV. What do you want?

LYDIA. You haven't paid anything for your share of the blame, but I ca
be made to pay cruelly for mine. I am in debt all round and I might b
put in prison together with all sorts of shopkeepers and tradesmen.

VASSILKÓV. Oh? So that's what you're afraid of? That's the sort of d
honour that you dread? Don't be afraid. Many an honest man finds h
way to the debtors' jail. From there it is possible to escape. It is righ
to dread the Moscow Pit, as the debtors' jail is called, but you shoul
dread more that bottomless pit which is called vice and in which t

good name, honour and decency of a woman perishes. You're afraid of the pit, but you're not afraid of that abyss from which there is no return to the straight and narrow road.

LYDIA. Who bade you preach to me?

VASSILKÓV. He who bids those who can see help the blind to find the way, who bids the wise to warn the foolish ones and who bids the learned to teach the ignorant.

LYDIA. You have no right to teach me.

VASSILKÓV. I have a right to teach you, the right of pity.

LYDIA. Are you talking of pity? You find your wife in such a hopeless predicament and you refuse to pay some miserable debts for her.

VASSILKÓV. I don't throw my money away, not for anything in the world!

MRS. CHEBOKSÁROVA. I can't understand your philosophy. All this sounds strange to me. Do you mean to say, sir, that to pay a wife's debt is throwing your money away?

VASSILKÓV. What kind of a wife is she to me? Besides, she told me herself that she had more money than I.

MRS. CHEBOKSÁROVA. She told you! What will a woman not say in anger? However much a wife may insult her husband, the wife is always more to be pitied than the husband. We are such weak, nervous creatures, every quarrel takes so much out of us. A quick-tempered woman may commit some foolishness rashly, but she is also quick to repent.

VASSILKÓV. But she doesn't say that she repents.

LYDIA. But I do repent. I'm sorry for what I've done.

VASSILKÓV. Isn't it a bit late?

MRS. CHEBOKSÁROVA. No, no! She may have been carried away, but she was not unfaithful. She will never be unfaithful.

VASSILKÓV. I know she has not been unfaithful to me. I paid your servants more than you paid them. But I don't know what saved her from being unfaithful: her honour or the fact that Kuchúmov could not raise the money. *To* LYDIA. What do you want?

LYDIA. I should like to live with you again.

VASSILKÓV. That's impossible. You change your mind so quickly that you may decide to leave me again tomorrow. I've had quite enough with one dishonour, I do not want another.

LYDIA. But you must save me.

VASSILKÓV. There is only one way of saving you: I shall offer you honest work and I shall pay you for it.

LYDIA. What kind of work and what pay?

VASSILKÓV. I offer you the job of my housekeeper. I'll pay you a thousand a year for it.

LYDIA, *gets up from couch.* Get out!!!

VASSILKÓV *goes out.*

TELYÁTEV, *removes handkerchief from eyes.* Now that you're well again, I can stop crying.

LYDIA. I'm not in the mood for your jokes now. Quickly, run and bring him back!

TELYÁTEV *runs out.*

MRS. CHEBOKSÁROVA. What an obstinate mule he is! What an awful man! A real gentleman would never have behaved like that. He'd rather kill his wife than make such a proposal to her.

VASSILKÓV and TELYÁTEV come back.

LYDIA. Please, forgive me. I didn't quite understand. Tell me what does "housekeeper" mean and what are a housekeeper's duties?

VASSILKÓV. With pleasure. I will explain it to you, but I must warn you that if you don't accept my offer, I shall never come back to you. A housekeeper is a woman who looks after a house. There is nothing humiliating about such work. These will be your duties: I have an old mother in the country who is an excellent housewife. You will be entirely at her beck and call: she'll teach you how to pickle mushrooms, how to make all sorts of household drinks, jams and so on, she'll give you the keys of the pantry and the cellar, and she will keep you under her eye. I need such a housekeeper, as I'm often away on business.

LYDIA. This is terrible, terrible!

VASSILKÓV. Shall I conclude?

LYDIA. Go on.

VASSILKÓV. When you have learnt how to run a house, I'll take you to our country town where you will be able to dazzle all our provincial ladies by your fine dresses and your exquisite manners. I shan't be niggardly with my allowance for you, but I shall never live beyond my income. As a businessman with ever expanding interests in every part of our vast country, I badly need such a wife as you. If, later on, you are nice to me, I'll take you to Petersburg. There we'll have our box at the opera to hear Patti, I shouldn't mind spending a thousand for it. I have very influential business connections in Petersburg, but I'm rather uncouth and raw in my manners. I want a wife who could receive and entertain important people, including a Cabinet minister or two. You have everything I need in a wife, but first you will have to unlearn certain habits which you've acquired from Telyátev and the rest.

TELYÁTEV. But I never dreamt that dear Lydia would get such a marvelous chance of rising from a kitchen maid to a Petersburg leader of fashion.

VASSILKÓV, *looking at his watch.* Do you accept my offer or not? But I warn you, that, to begin with, you will be my housekeeper and that for a very long time.

LYDIA. Please, take pity on me! Take pity on my pride! I am a lady, a lady born and bred, a lady from the crown of my head to the soles of my feet! Please, make some concession to me!

VASSILKÓV. I shall make no concessions whatever. Why should I have pity on your pride when you refused to have pity on my simplicity and good nature? Even in making you the offer of becoming my housekeeper I do it out of love.

LYDIA. At least don't call it housekeeper! It's such a horrid word!

VASSILKÓV. Not at all, I think it's an excellent word.

LYDIA. You must give me time to think it over.

VASSILKÓV. All right, you can **think it over.**

Enter ANDREY.

ANDREY. The broker's men are here to make an inventory of the furniture, ma'am.

LYDIA *and* MRS. CHEBOKSÁROVA. Good God!

LYDIA *buries her face in a pillow.*

TELYÁTEV. What's all the fuss about? Calm yourselves. The furniture of two of my friends was distrained by bailiffs yesterday, today it will be your furniture, tomorrow mine, the day after tomorrow Kuchúmov's. It's a kind of epidemic now.

LYDIA, *to her husband.* Save me from disgrace! I accept your offer! I agree to everything. What can I do? I wanted to shine like an inextinguishable star, but you want me to be a meteor which bursts into dazzling light for a moment and flickers out in some swamp. But I agree, I agree, only, please, I implore you, save me!

VASSILKÓV *goes out with* ANDREY, *who comes back.*

ANDREY. Mr. Kuchúmov, ma'am.

LYDIA. I think I'd better receive him.

TELYÁTEV. Yes, you should receive him.

LYDIA. Show him in.

ANDREY *goes out, enter* KUCHÚMOV, *followed a little later by* VASSILKÓV.

KUCHÚMOV, *humming. Io son ricco* . . . What's the matter?

LYDIA. Bailiffs are making an inventory of my furniture. Have you brought the forty thousand?

KUCHÚMOV. *Io son ricco* . . . No, fancy what bad luck! VASSILKOV *enters and stops at the door.* My valet, whom I loved like a son, stole all my money and ran off to America, I believe.

TELYÁTEV. I am very sorry for your valet. With the money he stole from you he could not only never reach America, he could hardly reach the next station.

KUCHÚMOV. Don't crack such silly jokes! I don't like it. I've dispatched telegrams all over the country. I suppose they'll catch him soon, return me the money and then, my child, I'll give it to you.

TELYÁTEV. But, surely, he didn't pinch everything, he must have left something behind.

KUCHÚMOV. Of course, he left something. I never leave my house without a thousand in my pocket.

VASSILKÓV. In that case you'd better pay me the six hundred roubles which you lost to me at cards.

KUCHÚMOV. Oh, you're here? Very nice, too. I wanted to pay you back a long time ago. A debt at cards is a matter of first importance to me. *Takes out wallet.* Goodness gracious! What's that? Where's the money? I must have put it in my left pocket. No? Oh, I see, I've put on another coat! However, you can get the money from Mrs. Cheboksárova.

VASSILKÓV. All right, I'll get it from her. Lydia, I have paid your debts. Now get ready to leave for the country.

LYDIA. As you please.

VASSILKÓV. I am leaving tomorrow. Be ready to leave with me.

LYDIA, *offers hand to her husband.* Thank you for granting me a whole day to weep. I have many things to cry over. I have to cry over the lost

dreams of my youth, over my mistake, over my humiliation. I have t
cry over something which I can never bring back. My goddess of carele:
joy has been thrown off her pedestal and in her place there stands th
rude idol of industry and commerce, whose name is income. Poor, tende
creatures! Pretty, happy-go-lucky girls! How my heart bleeds for you
Never again will you have husbands with perfect manners and very ba
heads for figures. Ethereal creatures, away with your dreams of unreali:
able happiness! Never again dream of men who can squander a fortun
with such inimitable grace, but marry men who can make a fortun
without a suspicion of grace and who are known as businessmen!

TELYÁTEV. Spare us, spare us, old girl, those who are good for nothing in
plore you!

KUCHÚMOV, *sings. Io son ricco . . .*

TELYÁTEV. No, old fellow, you are not rich. You should sing: *Noi siam
poveri,* we are poor.

LYDIA. This is the sacrifice I am making for you.

VASSILKÓV. I don't want any sacrifices from anybody.

LYDIA. I see that I've met my match in you. Very well, I'll make a clea
breast of it. I have accepted your offer because I consider it profitable.

VASSILKÓV. But remember, I shall never spend beyond my income!

LYDIA. I suppose I shall never be allowed to forget it.

VASSILKÓV. Only those to whom money comes easily can afford to live be
yond their income.

TELYÁTEV. It's gospel truth, old fellow, it's more than that: it's what I'v
been saying all along!

VASSILKÓV, *to* TELYÁTEV. Good-bye, old man. I am very sorry for you. T
morrow you won't have anything to eat and no roof over your head.

TELYÁTEV. Would you like to lend me some money? No, old fellow, don'
you lend me anything. It will only be a dead loss, for you won't see
penny of it. Moscow, Savva, is a city where the Telyátevs and th
Kuchúmovs will never go under. Even if we haven't a penny, we shal
always have honour and credit. For a long time to come every sho,
keeper in town will be honoured to dine and wine us at his expens
The tailors, it is true, do not show much respect for us, but even an ol
overcoat and an old hat can be worn with such distinction that peop!
will move aside to let you pass. Good-bye, old fellow, don't be sorry fo
us. Virtue shines through even the meanest rags! *Embraces* KUCHÚMO\

LYDIA *goes up shyly to* VASSILKÓV, *puts her hand on his shoulder and burie
her head on his chest.*

The Epidemic

BY OCTAVE MIRBEAU

Translated by JACQUES BARZUN

CHARACTERS

THE MAYOR
THE LEADER OF THE OPPOSITION
THE LEADER OF THE MAJORITY
DOCTOR TRICEPS
THE VERY OLD MEMBER
FOUR MEMBERS OF THE COUNCIL
THE USHER

Place: *The meeting room of the City Council in a large seaport. On the walls, which are paneled in dark wood, the portraits of all the Presidents of the Republic from Thiers to Loubet. All around the room, on wooden brackets, various busts symbolizing the Republic and suggesting different political interpretations of its meaning. In the middle, a monumental fireplace, above the mantel of which is the shield of the city and the tricolor flag. Large doors to right and left. In the center, a long table covered with green baize. Each* COUNCILLOR'S *place is marked by a blotter, inkstand and paper.*

As the curtain rises, the MAYOR *is seen near the mantelpiece, talking to a group of* COUNCILLORS. *Others are scattered in small knots around the room. Two are seated at the table writing. The* SECRETARY, *with a pen between his teeth, is sorting out papers.*

MAYOR. I think, gentlemen, we can begin.

LEADER OF OPPOSITION, *drawing his watch.* A quarter to eleven. And I always lunch at half past. The meeting was called for nine o'clock. It's outrageous.

MAYOR. But the day after Christmas! People are bound to be a little unpunctual! Nobody's fault, least of all mine.

LEADER OF OPPOSITION. Some are still not here.

MAYOR. But we have a quorum.

LEADER OF OPPOSITION. Then let's get down to business.

Enter DR. TRICEPS, *left.*

MAYOR. Ah! Here is Dr. Triceps.

DOCTOR. All my apologies, Mr. Mayor. All my apologies, gentlemen. I have been detained by a delicate operation. Since early morning I have been reassembling the sensibility of my cook, which had become extravasated into her waffle iron. Do I make myself clear?

MAYOR. Do you mean it?

DOCTOR. Yes indeed. It was no trifle, I assure you!

MAYOR. Her waffle iron! What risks people run! *To the* COUNCILLORS. With your permission, gentlemen, we will get on to our business.

DOCTOR. By all means. Once again my apologies, apologies. *They all take their places noisily.*

MAYOR. The meeting will please come to order. *Leafing through papers.* I have here excuses from our absent colleagues. Hardly any of importance. Do you want to hear them?

FIRST COUNCILLOR. No point, no point.

MAYOR, *absent-mindedly riffling.* Colds, bronchitis, lumbago. Wives at the maternity ward. Anyhow, no one can say our members contribute to the lowering of the birthrate. *To the* SECRETARY. Add these to the minutes.

SECOND COUNCILLOR. Isn't that too much——?

MAYOR. It's the rule. *In a graver voice.* But I am bound to mention our colleague Isidore T. Barbaroux, who was arrested last night . . .

FIRST COUNCILLOR. Again? It's the third time!

MAYOR. . . . and whose absence today, if not justified, is at least explained by this— er— judicial— er— formality. Please note, gentlemen, that I do not incriminate him, but merely report . . .

DOCTOR. And what is the so-called reason for this arrest?

MAYOR. The same as before. If my information is correct—and I rather think it is—the reason is purely commercial. Our honorable colleague was taken into custody for selling bad meat to the troops—or allegedly bad meat. We do not have to pass on the incident, which is, I repeat, purely commercial. We must not pre-judge the case.

DOCTOR. May I speak?

MAYOR. Besides, the crime of a single man . . . *Murmurings* . . . if it *is* a crime— does not reflect on our corporate entity.

VOICES. Hear, hear!

DOCTOR. Without going fully into the heart of the matter, let me make a point. I am convinced that whenever our colleague Barbaroux has been prosecuted, it is not his meat that has been condemned but his opinions. Do you understand? *Laughter and shouts of approval.* I mean it!

MAYOR. That may be saying too much, Doctor.

DOCTOR. Not at all! As a man of science, I know what I am talking about. I am familiar with the subject and I say that it is anti-scientific to pre- tend that decaying animal food—

FIRST COUNCILLOR. Have you ever eaten any?

DOCTOR. Unquestionably. And yet you see that I am as healthy as ever. *Slapping his chest.* The frame is sound.

A VOICE. Three cheers!

DOCTOR. But let me be perfectly clear about this. I not only do not think that spoiled meat is harmful; I believe it possesses uncommonly stimulat- ing properties for the human stomach. Do you understand? Consider game! Why should a favorable factor in pheasants become noxious in beef? It's absurd! Ripeness is all, and every rotting thing is equal be fore the law.

SECOND COUNCILLOR. Of course!

LEADER OF OPPOSITION. Is this a political allusion?

SEVERAL COUNCILLORS. Oh, drop it!

DOCTOR. The facts of the case irresistibly suggest to me that the indictment of our colleague Barbaroux is part of a political game. I shall not say anything now of its interference with the principle of free enterprise. I shall come back to that at the proper time and discuss its economic, social, therapeutic and biological significance. But I want my basic point to be entered on the record.

MAYOR, *canvassing his* COUNCIL *with a glance.* The Council has no objec tion. We all feel that the views of our eminent colleague are for all of us a source of light and leading. Into the record.

DOCTOR. I thank the Mayor for his generous words. They compensate me for many an injustice suffered in the exercise of my profession. *The Doctor's colleagues on each side shake his hand. A few bravos. The emo tion is pervasive.* May I add that our colleague Barbaroux has always proved a most loyal butcher in his dealings with civilians, and if it be true that he has sold inferior or spoiled meats, it has always been to soldiers whose stomachs have apparently become surprisingly— er— in tolerant— or else to the poor, which doesn't count.

MAYOR. Do you want that in the record as well?

DOCTOR. Well. *Querying the* MAYOR. What do you think?

MAYOR. Well— er—.

DOCTOR. We'll see later. *To the* SECRETARY. I'll give you a revised draft of the whole at the end of the meeting.

SECRETARY. Oh, good!

MAYOR. The incident is closed. *Rising as if for a great speech.* And now, gentlemen, we shall take up the urgent and, I may say, very grave question for which I have called this special secret session.

> *Surprise and alarm. A sleeping member wakes.*

SECOND COUNCILLOR. What is it all about?

VOICES. Quiet! Let him speak!

MAYOR. Gentlemen, I have some news, unpleasant and unfortunate news, to impart to you. *Attention grows.* But do not be unduly alarmed. When I say unfortunate, it is only in order to make my words—

LEADER OF MAJORITY. Your eloquent words—

MAYOR. —to make my words suit the expectations which the usual feelings of sensitive persons—

LEADER OF MAJORITY. Hear! hear!

MAYOR. —or indeed those of my watchful opponents—

LEADER OF MAJORITY. —Just so!

MAYOR. —who, as rivals, do not, if I may say so, hesitate to encroach upon my prerogatives, in short—

LEADER OF OPPOSITION. —Speak so we can understand you!

MAYOR. —Then please do not interrupt. *He vainly tries to catch the thread of his discourse.* Gentlemen, there is nothing in what I have to tell you that is disturbing, nothing that should alarm you. The fact in itself is not unusual. It is not really news, news of the sort which—in a word, gentlemen, it is rather a recurrent nuisance . . .

LEADER OF MAJORITY. Good! good!

MAYOR. It's an annual event, a sort of counterpart—

LEADER OF OPPOSITION. To the point! And no more of these underhand political digs. We aren't here to play politics.

MAYOR. It is not a matter of politics.

LEADER OF MAJORITY, *with finality.* It's not a matter of politics.

LEADER OF OPPOSITION. Then what *is* it? Why the mystery, this beating around the bush?

LEADER OF MAJORITY. I don't know what it's about, but I tell you—

LEADER OF OPPOSITION. If you don't know, then shut up.

LEADER OF MAJORITY. I will if I choose. I don't take orders from you.

MAYOR. Gentlemen, gentlemen, please!

LEADER OF MAJORITY. We aren't in your saloon here, with all the women and pimps of the town!

MAYOR. Gentlemen!

LEADER OF OPPOSITION. Just try and come into my saloon, as you call it! I dare you to! Saloon! The best café in town, the handsomest, Louis Fourteenth decoration throughout! Just come, once!

LEADER OF MAJORITY. I certainly will, with a couple of cops to close it down! *They rise and threaten each other from opposite sides of the table*. I don't understand how such places are allowed—it's a crime against public decency.

MAYOR. Gentlemen, please sit down!

LEADER OF OPPOSITION. And what about the wormy flour you trade in, and the dried mud you sell as coffee, and your so-called "Russian Tea," which is nothing more than last year's carrot tops!

LEADER OF MAJORITY. Who, me?

LEADER OF OPPOSITION. Yes, you! You and your "homemade" cookies which date back to the French Revolution!

VOICES. That's enough now!

LEADER OF OPPOSITION. A saloon! My place is a first-class place of entertainment with the finest cinematograph machine!

MAYOR. Gentlemen, I beg of you!

VOICES. That's enough! Sit down! Out with them!

Slow calming down.

MAYOR, *soothing, fatherly*. Gentlemen, I implore you, in the name of patriotism! I appeal to your feelings of amity and brotherly love. I call upon your devotion to our great city, upon your true inward municipal self. *Louder*. No! The matter I bring before you is not a matter of politics. It is our fair city which is at stake, the interests of our city, the salvation of our city, the city you love, the city that you represent and that you govern. Gentlemen! *With a catch in his voice*. Within this city there has broken loose an epidemic of typhoid fever!

The COUNCILLORS *pale; they gaze at each other in silence.*

LEADER OF MAJORITY, *petrified*. An epidemic, *within* the city?

LEADER OF OPPOSITION, *terrified*. *OUR* city?

MAYOR. You see right enough that it is not a matter of politics.

LEADER OF MAJORITY *and* OPPOSITION, *together*. In this city, an epidemic. In the city!

MAYOR. When I say in the city, that isn't altogether accurate . . . Thank heaven, the epidemic is not *inside* the city. It is . . .

LEADER OF OPPOSITION. Well, where is it actually? Is it in the city or not? You must be more precise . . . Tell us the truth, we're not children. *With returning energy*. We are men, damn it! We've proved it in tighter corners than this. When the country needed us we joined the National Guard without turning a hair. Now where's that epidemic, speak up!

VOICES. Yes, where? Speak up!

MAYOR. You don't give me a chance. It is in the city, and yet not within it—or rather not quite. Let me explain!

Murmurings.

LEADER OF MAJORITY. Why don't you listen!

MAYOR, *louder than the rest*. The epidemic is in the Navy Yard, and more particularly in the barracks of the naval gunners.

LEADER OF MAJORITY. Hear, hear!

LEADER OF OPPOSITION, *furious*. Why couldn't you say so at once! Here we are, going through agonies—not that we're afraid of epidemics. We treat them with the manly scorn they deserve. But we have families—and friends, don't you know! And the Navy Yard is *not* the city. The barracks are *not* within the city. Why, there are epidemics in those barracks every year! It's not our affair. We can't help it.

ᴀʟʟ. Of course not!

ᴅᴏᴄᴛᴏʀ. Let us be calm, gentlemen. Let us keep our heads and proceed methodically. *To the* ᴍᴀʏᴏʀ. How many deaths?

ᴍᴀʏᴏʀ. Yesterday, twelve men died; this morning, sixteen.

ᴅᴏᴄᴛᴏʀ, *nodding satisfaction*. Out of how many cases?

ᴍᴀʏᴏʀ. Right now, a hundred and thirty-five.

ᴅᴏᴄᴛᴏʀ, *as before but taking notes*. Quite normal.

ʟᴇᴀᴅᴇʀ ᴏꜰ ᴍᴀᴊᴏʀɪᴛʏ. Any officers?

ᴍᴀʏᴏʀ. No, luckily, no officers. The disease stops at the lieutenants, j.g. Only the men and the non-coms seem to get it—as usual.

ᴅᴏᴄᴛᴏʀ. Quite normal.

ʟᴇᴀᴅᴇʀ ᴏꜰ ᴍᴀᴊᴏʀɪᴛʏ. I thank the Mayor, on all our behalfs, for his straightforward and reassuring account . . .

ʟᴇᴀᴅᴇʀ ᴏꜰ ᴏᴘᴘᴏsɪᴛɪᴏɴ. But then I don't see—I don't see at all—why this meeting? This epidemic does not fall within our terms of reference—I was going to say, it lies outside our jurisdiction. It has no municipal significance.

ᴍᴀʏᴏʀ. Still, a wise government must be far-sighted. The epidemic may spread. It may rise from the Navy to the citizenry.

ʟᴇᴀᴅᴇʀ ᴏꜰ ᴏᴘᴘᴏsɪᴛɪᴏɴ. Tell it to the Marines!

ᴅᴏᴄᴛᴏʀ. We are not bound to take into account what hasn't yet happened. I know the course of these epidemics, I might go so far as to say that I am familiar with their tendency. Theirs is a spirit of discipline, of respect for hierarchy. If contrary to the dictates of science the epidemic should spread, and if any alarming symptoms occurred, we should have ample time to take the necessary precautions. As things are, we need not intervene. *Firmly*. Let the Navy take steps if it sees fit.

ᴍᴀʏᴏʀ. Just so, gentlemen! Such was my original purpose. *Confidentially*. But the Naval Commissioner is boiling mad. I saw him last night. He said that things could not go on. His view is that the barracks being filthy are the cause of the infection. *Murmurings*. That the drinking water is contaminated. *Fresh murmurs*. To make a long story short, he wants us to build new barracks. *Protests*. And connect them with the city water supply. *Howls of anger*. He further demands . . .

ʟᴇᴀᴅᴇʀ ᴏꜰ ᴏᴘᴘᴏsɪᴛɪᴏɴ, *raising his arms*. He demands! . . . He demands! . . . Colossal impudence!

ʟᴇᴀᴅᴇʀ ᴏꜰ ᴍᴀᴊᴏʀɪᴛʏ, *like the preceding*. He is mad!

ʟᴇᴀᴅᴇʀ ᴏꜰ ᴏᴘᴘᴏsɪᴛɪᴏɴ, *striking the table*. Sheer waste!

ꜰɪʀsᴛ ᴄᴏᴜɴᴄɪʟʟᴏʀ. We have no money to spend on whims. The tax rate is already crushing. And the new theatre comes first.

sᴇᴄᴏɴᴅ ᴄᴏᴜɴᴄɪʟʟᴏʀ. Don't forget the redecoration of this room. *He points*. What kind of City Hall is this? The barracks—why, these are the barracks.

ꜰɪʀsᴛ ᴄᴏᴜɴᴄɪʟʟᴏʀ. The commissioner's out of his mind, out of his mind.

LEADER OF MAJORITY. If those gunners don't like the water, let 'em drink beer.

LEADER OF OPPOSITION. If the barracks are unhealthy, let 'em camp out.

VOICES. That's the idea!

MAYOR. No doubt you are right. In principle you are right. But you know how the Commissioner is—tough, obstinate, wants his own way. He said he would move his men to another station—another town. That means trade lost to us, gentlemen—and no band concert on Sundays—a serious blow to our beloved citizens. What he said was: "I'm not going to let my men croak like rats." His very words.

LEADER OF OPPOSITION. He's trying to scare us. Don't tell me he can move a Navy Yard from place to place like a circus. A naval squadron isn't a merry-go-round.

LEADER OF MAJORITY. After all, it may be too bad, but these people, when they enlist, they expect to die, don't they?

LEADER OF OPPOSITION. That's what they're for!

LEADER OF MAJORITY. It's their duty—

VERY OLD COUNCILLOR. Their honor!

LEADER OF OPPOSITION. At a time when the country is not at war, these epidemics are schools of heroism—a wonderful training—and salutary. Where else would our men learn contempt for death and sacrifice of self?

VOICES. Hear, hear! True enough!

LEADER OF OPPOSITION, shrugging. Where would they develop the national characteristic virtue, which is courage? What the Commissioner is really asking us to do is to condone cowardice!

LEADER OF MAJORITY. He insults our troops—

LEADER OF OPPOSITION. What! Let him soil our national honor! Weaken patriotism! I say, No! Never!

General applause.

DOCTOR, rising, claiming and getting attention. I heartily concur in the noble sentiments so beautifully expressed by my honorable colleagues. I go even farther. Today a certain kind of science preaches hygiene, filtered water, death to microbes—in a word—an-ti-sep-sis. With scorn. Gentlemen, I call this a mere hypothesis, a hypothesis incubated by intellectuals, by men of letters—never verified by any crucial experiment. Tomorrow, other theories will be spawned contradicting those of today—and equally fallacious and remote from facts. This being so, must communities such as ours imperil their progressive programs by following the will o' the wisps of irresponsible theorists, whose ruinous whimsies change from week to week usurping the name of science? I rather think not! Brief applause. And yet I too am a man of science. Applause.

SECOND COUNCILLOR. Very good! He can tell them off, all right!

DOCTOR. Our fathers, gentlemen, knew nothing of hygiene, had never heard of bacilli, cultures, and serums, of inoculations, vaccinations, and bacteriology. They did not attend medical conventions and had never heard of a Mr. Pasteur. They were content with the houses and the drinking water that they had. More, they did not even take baths! Not even baths, do you understand? And yet, does history record that their health was any worse? Not at all! Just the contrary!

SECOND COUNCILLOR. That's right. That's right.

DOCTOR. They keep repeating: "What about England?" But gentlemen, we are not in England. England is England and France is—France. Each people has its peculiar genius. *Enthusiastic response.* Above all, let us remain French!

FIRST COUNCILLOR. *Vive la France!*

DOCTOR. Let us then allow this epidemic to run its natural course, its necessary ee-vo-lu-tion. Nature must never be defied. Believe me, nature, nature knows what she is about! *He sits down amid congratulatory shouts and gestures.*

MAYOR. Please allow me to add a word which may throw further light upon our discussion. Despite his rough manners, the Naval Commissioner is not an unreasonable man. I believe an understanding with him could be reached. I have the feeling that he is not so much concerned about the epidemic *as* epidemic—or at least . . . . . I mean, what bothers him is public opinion. He fears the newspapers—and possibly a question raised in Parliament. You all know that just now the Navy is under fire. Now the very thought makes our good friend go wild. Put yourself in his place.

LEADER OF OPPOSITION. Well?

MAYOR. Well, if my impression of his state of mind is correct, the Commissioner would be prepared to consider his demands satisfied if we simply passed the appropriation for the specified works. What he wants us to do is to go through the formalities. He would not press us to carry them out. All he asks is that things should look right in the eyes of the press, the public, Parliament—and the Secretary of the Navy. Isn't that, after all, perfectly reasonable—praiseworthy?

SECOND COUNCILLOR. But ticklish, risky, for us. What guaranty have we that he'll play fair, as regards the expense?

MAYOR. I will guarantee it.

SECOND COUNCILLOR. That's not enough. Have you a written agreement?

MAYOR. No.

FIRST COUNCILLOR. Have you his word of honor?

MAYOR. No. I have something better than all that: his desire for a quiet life.

SECOND COUNCILLOR. We have to be careful just the same.

MAYOR. Why? Careful about what? I assure you that once the epidemic is over, there won't be another word out of him. Next year, if necessary, we'll repeat the procedure. We'll do it annually.

SECOND COUNCILLOR. I'd be careful, just the same.

MAYOR. If we don't go along with him, what will happen? We'll have the whole city buzzing about our ears. Rows and gossip and editorials and reform movements—we'll never hear the end of it—let alone keep our constituencies. To say nothing of the fact that the women—all our wives —go out with the Naval officers and we—

VOICES. Speak for yourself! What did you say? *Laughter.*

MAYOR, *dignified.* I scorn your vulgar and unwarranted innuendos. Wher was I? Oh yes—with the Naval officers. Think it over, gentlemen. Don' let any set ideas, however sound they may seem, stand in the way of m expedient suggestion. I submit that we can vote the money. I think tha we should even be generous about the amount—since it will cost u nothing.

LEADER OF OPPOSITION. I object. It would open a serious door, I mean cr ate a dangerous precedent.

LEADER OF MAJORITY. All the barracks in the country are polluted.

LEADER OF OPPOSITION. All the water is undrinkable.

VERY OLD COUNCILLOR, *his voice shaking.* Typhoid fever is a national inst tution. Let us not lay violent hands on our national traditions.

DOCTOR, *bounding up.* No! Let us do nothing to sap the strength of ou splendid young men, to stain the honor of our forces, ever intrepid i the face of death. Let us not afford the foreigner the shameful spectac of a French army in retreat before a few problematic microbes. Th army, gentlemen, which stands for Austerlitz and Marengo does n stand for Asepsis and Sanitation. *A storm of applause. With a gestur* I know not what course other gentlemen may take, but as for me, giv me Liberty or give me—*The applause drowns him out.*

LEADER OF OPPOSITION, *much moved.* After the deathless words you hav just heard, and the enthusiasm which greeted them, I think it will b unnecessary to take a vote on the appropriation.

A VOICE. Right, right!

MAYOR. I bow to your decision.

ANOTHER VOICE. No vote!

ANOTHER. No appropriation!

LEADER OF OPPOSITION. No shilly-shallying, now, make it unanimous.

DOCTOR. The country can still boast hearts of oak. *All rise, talk and laug as the formal business is put through by the* MAYOR *and the* SECRETAR *In the midst of this, enter the* USHER, *looking upset. He delivers a lett to the* MAYOR.

MAYOR. What is it? *Taking the letter.* What's this?

USHER. I don't know, sir.

MAYOR. Who brought it?

USHER. A man in mourning.

MAYOR. A man in mourning? Ah! *He turns the letter over, looking ha at each side.* A city man?

USHER. I don't know, sir.

MAYOR. You'd never seen him before?

USHER. No, sir.

MAYOR. Ah! He left no word?

USHER, *painfully.* He did not say a word.

MAYOR, *also upset.* That's queer. I don't know why . . . I have a presen ment . . . Gentlemen, I think this letter brings bad news.

LEADER OF MAJORITY. Open it, then, open it!

MAYOR. I'm afraid to open it. *All are silent, staring at the* MAYOR. Here goes. *He opens the letter, reads a few words and turns pale as he lets out an exclamation.* Oh! God!

LEADER OF MAJORITY. Well, what is it?

General confusion.

MAYOR. God, oh God!

LEADER OF OPPOSITION, *to the others.* Be quiet! *To the* MAYOR. Tell us!

MAYOR. Gentlemen—*He cannot go on.*

LEADER OF OPPOSITION. Are you ill?

LEADER OF MAJORITY. What makes you look so—?

MAYOR. Gentlemen—

LEADER OF OPPOSITION. Why, you're shaking.

MAYOR, *mastering his emotion.* Gentlemen . . . Something terrible—unheard of—appalling!

ALL. Speak! Tell us! Out with it!

MAYOR. Gentlemen! *The letter falls to the table.* One of our citizens has died!

LEADER OF OPPOSITION. What's that you say?

MAYOR. A citizen . . . a bourgeois . . . has died—carried off—by the epidemic!

A FEW VOICES. It can't be! Impossible!

DOCTOR, *screaming.* Don't touch that letter! . . . It's surely not been disinfected! Burn it! *He dashes forward, seizes it by one corner and throws it into the fireplace. He then pulls out of his pocket an atomizer with which he sprays himself and the whole room, striding swiftly.* Disinfection, gentlemen, dis-infection!

While terror overwhelms the COUNCILLORS, *who have suddenly become motionless, holding rigid poses, the* MAYOR *continues speaking through the deathly silence, in a shaken, tearful voice.*

MAYOR. We do not know his name . . . No matter, we are intimate with his soul . . . Gentlemen, he was a venerable burgher, sleek, rosy-cheeked, blissful. His emergent stomach was the envy of the poor . . . Every day at the same hour, he took his constitutional on the esplanade, with a smiling, contented countenance. His double chin, his chubby hands were to everyone a living lesson in social welfare . . . It seemed as if he should never die, and yet he has died. A burgher has died!

LEADER OF MAJORITY, *as if chanting the Miserere.* A burgher has died!

LEADER OF OPPOSITION, *likewise.* A burgher has died!

ALL, *one after the other.* A burgher has died!

Silence. All the COUNCILLORS *stare at one another.*

MAYOR. It is not in my power, gentlemen, to render judgment on the life of the fellow-burgher whose passing we all lament, this worthiest of burghers, friend and brother to us all. Some who have a better right will accord him the supreme tribute he deserves. Gentlemen, if the citizen whose tragic and premature loss we deplore never managed to bring himself to the notice of his contemporaries in this city—this city, which, thanks to your generous trust, I have the honor to govern—if, I say, he never drew attention to himself by any act of liberality, by any recorded

benefaction, nor by any stroke of superior talent that might prove usef
to the life of the community, nevertheless I want with your permissio
to voice what I feel to be the unanimous feelings of our good peopl
and in a few words do justice to the memory of the dear departed, u
known though he still is.

A few COUNCILLORS *wipe away their tears.*

A COUNCILLOR. Yes, speak!

MAYOR, *mastering his emotion.* I see him now! But I can hardly put int
words . . . He was short and round, above spindly legs. Behind h
waistcoast he was upholstered smooth and tight. His chin lapped ov
his shirtfront in faintly yellow layers of fat, and his little eyes, sur
within puffy lids, gave off the respectably white gleam of a pair of silv
coins. He was a magnificent sight. No one more closely resembled th
beau ideal of Political Economy. He incarnated the notion which liber;
governments and democratic societies have formed of Man, that is to sa
something without personality, creativeness, or energy; something qui
dead, yet able to speak, digest, take walks and make gestures; a bein
who calculates and disburses according to rules that may be found i
the Civil Code—in short, a fundamental form of life which is called
Small Investor.

A COUNCILLOR. How true! Bravo!

MAYOR. I know I am right. Joseph. *With pride and pity mixed.* Let
call him Joseph—like his immortal ancestor, Joseph was more than
man. He was a social principle. Throughout his life he gave witho
faltering the priceless example of a thoroughly French virtue, a virtu
which makes for outstanding men and free peoples—the habit of savin
In the midst of life Joseph stood for Savings. His was the type of savi
which no disappointment can touch, which no disaster can discourag
He might be deceived, cheated, or ruined, yet he would continue
save— for the sake of future bankruptcies. At the cost of inconceivab
sacrifices he would save amounts destined never to delight, never
enrich, never to feed the passions of anyone but embezzlers. What hero
forgetfulness of self, gentlemen, what altruistic concentration, symboliz
in Joseph's woollen sock!

THIRD COUNCILLOR, *weeping.* Oh, the pity of it! The pity of it! *Sobs.*

MAYOR. It will be to Joseph's lasting credit that in times of crisis like ou
he remained faithful through thick and thin to those national traditio
of the petty bourgeois which alone can restore optimism. For as was sa
on one occasion by a great philosopher whose name escapes me, th
Habit of Saving is the Mother of Virtue and the safeguard of Law an
Order. Let us lament and venerate our Joseph.

SEVERAL COUNCILLORS. Long live Joseph!

MAYOR. Let us venerate him, for he never indulged in the slightest pleasur
Even in the time of his youth, even in the time of his prosperity,
never knew what the beggars themselves often know—an hour of enjo
ment. He always did without; he lived more deprived than the vagra
on the highway, his sole satisfaction in duty done. Never did he acce
any honors or responsibilities, fearful as he was that he might have

pay for them in the form of obligations, reciprocities, or affections; which in turn would have distracted him from his great work. The sublime lesson of his life is that the more he saved the poorer he became, and the poorer he was, the more he saved.

THIRD COUNCILLOR, *sobbing.* The pity of it! The pity of it!

MAYOR. He was a hero, gentlemen, *our* hero. A great statesman did say once that heroic times are a thing of the past, but he had forgotten the small investor. And so, Joseph, farewell!

VERY OLD COUNCILLOR. A hero, without a doubt. Silent, modest, solitary. He knew how to keep from his door any possible friends, dogs or paupers. He shrewdly managed to preserve his heart from the corruption of love and his spirit from the infection of art! He loathed—or better—he ignored all poetry and all culture. For he hated exaggeration and was in all his ways exact and regular. Although the sights of human misery never caused him disgust, his reward was that the sights of nature spared him all feelings whatever. Each morning he entrusted to his daily tabloid the task of feeling and thinking for him.

THIRD COUNCILLOR. What a pity! Oh the pity!

VERY OLD COUNCILLOR. Wherefore, gentlemen, I have the honor to put before the Council the two following resolutions: first, Be it resolved that the funeral of Joseph shall be grandly solemnized at the expense of the City. Second, Be it resolved that a statue shall be erected to the memory of Joseph on one of our principal squares.

ALL, *somewhat recovering from shock.* Yes, yes! Sure!

VERY OLD COUNCILLOR. I propose moreover that we give one of our most handsome streets Joseph's full name—as soon as we find out what it is.

A COUNCILLOR, *absent-mindedly.* A street by any other name would smell as sweet!

General approval. Cheers, rising vote.

DOCTOR. And now, gentlemen, we must not allow ourselves to be bowed down by this unexpected decease, which is highly irregular and I daresay anti-scientific—don't you see? We must resist!

ALL. Yes, you're right.

DOCTOR. Up and at 'em!

ALL. Right! You said it!

DOCTOR. In the face of adversity, we must be men!

ALL. Cheers!

DOCTOR. When evil threatens, we gird our loins!

ALL. Hurrah!

DOCTOR. Are you game for the supreme sacrifice?

LEADER OF OPPOSITION. We are!

LEADER OF MAJORITY. We are!

ALL. Of course! We are!

DOCTOR. It will take money.

LEADER OF MAJORITY. We will get it.

LEADER OF OPPOSITION. We will find it, make it.

LEADER OF MAJORITY. We'll float a loan!

LEADER OF OPPOSITION. Raise taxes!

DOCTOR. Use eminent domain!

ALL. That's it! We will!

DOCTOR. Destroy the slums, which are seedbeds of pestilence!

FIRST COUNCILLOR. We'll raze them to the ground!

DOCTOR. And then rebuild!

FIRST COUNCILLOR. We will rebuild!

ALL. We will! We will!

DOCTOR. Next, we must cut broad, clear highways.

LEADER OF MAJORITY. Make room for public gardens!

ALL. Yes, yes!

LEADER OF OPPOSITION. Plant avenues of trees!

ALL. Yes, trees! Broad avenues!

DOCTOR. Pour light into dark corners, sanitate the sewers!

LEADER OF MAJORITY. Double the area of open ground!

LEADER OF OPPOSITION. Use germicidal sprays!

DOCTOR. Relieve the congestion in schools, convents, houses of prostitution— and barracks.

ALL. Naturally, yes! We will!

DOCTOR. We shall have to tap new sources of pure water—reservoirs as big and deep as the sea.

LEADER OF OPPOSITION. The waters will spring!

DOCTOR. We shall go seek them within the virgin hearts of the ancient hills . . .

ALL. Yes, yes!

DOCTOR. . . . from as far away as the Swiss Alps!

LEADER OF OPPOSITION. The Carpathians!

DOCTOR. The Caucasus!

ALL. Yes, yes!

DOCTOR. We shall need powerful steam filters, sterilizers running twenty-four hours a day!

LEADER OF MAJORITY. A monumental apparatus!

DOCTOR. Tanks of phenol and laboratories providing chemical anti-sep-sis!

ALL. Yes, yes.

DOCTOR. We will set up a committee for Hygiene—I said Hygiene—a standing committee.

ALL. Bravo!

LEADER OF OPPOSITION. A Board of Health, with Commissioners of Prophylaxis!

LEADER OF MAJORITY. Who will attend medical conventions . . .

DOCTOR. And the Pasteur institutes . . .

LEADER OF OPPOSITION. While we ring the city round with hospitals.

ALL. The very thing! Yes, yes!

DOCTOR. Let us vote! It's for war against microbes! Down with death! Long live science!

THIRD COUNCILLOR. Joseph shall be avenged!

DOCTOR. A vote! A vote!

MAYOR. Yes, gentlemen, we are about to vote. We are about to vote unheard of things—emergency measures, I may say, revolutionary ones—to the tune of incredible amounts. But before we do so, I propose that the Council enter upon its minutes a formal censure of Isidore Theophrastus Barbaroux, whose criminal acts and contaminated meats may well have contributed to the spread of the epidemic, if not to the virulence of its contagion.

DOCTOR. Barbaroux is a scoundrel, a poisoner of wells, a murderer.

LEADER OF MAJORITY. Worse! An anarchist and a socialist!

ALL. Hang him! Down with Barbaroux!

MAYOR. And now, dear friends, to a vote!

DOCTOR. I ask for ten millions!

LEADER OF OPPOSITION, shrugging contemptuously. What can you do with ten millions? Don't be silly: twenty millions!

LEADER OF MAJORITY. Fifty!

LEADER OF OPPOSITION. All right! Seventy-five millions.

DOCTOR. A hundred, at the very least!

Deafening applause.

MAYOR. Let us settle for a round figure—one hundred millions. And if a hundred millions is found inadequate, we can always raise the ante.

ALL. Yes, a hundred, one hundred.

VERY OLD COUNCILLOR. But where will we get it?

MAYOR, scornfully. We shall find it, sir, in our patriotism . . .

ALL. Bravo! Well said!

MAYOR. . . . our heroism . . .

DOCTOR. . . . in our will and our faith.

ALL. Yes, yes.

MAYOR. To a vote, my friends, a vote!

ALL. Question! Let's vote! Here's my vote! A vote! *They scramble about the table brandishing ballots, their faces flushed, their gestures uncontrolled.*

The Marquis of Keith

BY FRANK WEDEKIND

Translated by BEATRICE GOTTLIEB

CHARACTERS

CONSUL CASIMIR, *a merchant*
HERMANN CASIMIR, *his son* (*15 years old; played by a girl*)
THE MARQUIS OF KEITH
ERNST SCHOLZ
MOLLY GRIESINGER
ANNA, COUNTESS WERDENFELS, *a widow*
SARANIEFF, *a painter*
ZAMRIAKI, *a composer*
SOMMERSBERG, *a writer*
RASPE, *a police inspector*
OSTERMEIER, *proprietor of a brewery*
KRENTZL, *a master-builder*
GRANDAUER, *a restaurateur*
FRAU OSTERMEIER
FRAU KRENTZL
BARONESS VON ROSENKRON ⎫ *divorcées*
BARONESS VON TOTLEBEN ⎬
SASHA (*played by a girl*)
SIMBA
A BUTCHER'S HELPER
A BAKERY WOMAN
A PORTER
PATRONS *of the Hofbräuhaus*

The action takes place in Munich, late summer, 1899.

ACT ONE

A study, the walls of which are hung with pictures. In the rear wall, on the right,[1] is the door to the hall; on the left is the door to a waiting room. Downstage right is a door which leads to the living room. Downstage left is a writing table on which are lying unrolled plans; on the wall near the writing table, a telephone. Downstage right, a sofa; in front of it a smallish table; in the center, partly upstage, is a larger table. Book cases full of books. Musical instruments. Sheafs of notes and documents.

The MARQUIS OF KEITH *is sitting at the writing table, engrossed in one of the plans. He is about 27 years old: medium height, slim, bony physique. His figure would be perfect if it were not for a limp in his left leg. His features are vigorous and alert, at the same time rather hard. He has piercing grey eyes, a small blond mustache; his unruly short straw-blond hair is carefully parted in the middle. He is exquisitely, but not foppishly, dressed in a finely tailored suit. He has the coarse red hands of a clown.*

MOLLY GRIESINGER *comes out of the living room and puts a tray with food on the small table in front of the sofa. She is a plain creature with brunette hair, somewhat shy and harassed-looking, wearing a plain house dress; but she has large, black, soulful eyes.*

MOLLY. Here, dear. Here's tea and caviar and cold meat. You got up at nine o'clock today.

KEITH, *without moving.* Thank you, my dear child.

MOLLY. You must be awfully hungry. Do you know yet whether the Fairyland Palace is going to be established?

KEITH. Can't you see I'm working?

MOLLY. You're always working when I come in. That's why I have to learn about you and your projects from your lady friends.

KEITH, *turning around in his chair.* I knew a woman once who covered her ears when I spoke about plans. She'd say, "Come and tell me when you've *done* something!"

MOLLY. That's my hard luck, that you've known all kinds of women. *A bell rings.* Merciful Lord, who can that be now! *She goes into the hall to open the door.*

KEITH, *to himself.* Poor little wretch!

MOLLY, *returns with a card.* A young gentleman wishes to see you. I told him you were working.

KEITH, *after reading the card.* Just the person I want to see!

MOLLY *shows* HERMANN CASIMIR *in and exits into the living room.*

HERMANN CASIMIR, *a student of fifteen, in an exquisitely tailored cycling habit.* Good morning, Herr Baron.

KEITH. What brings you here?

---

[1]Right and left are indicated from the actor's point of view.

HERMANN. The best thing is for me to come right out with it. Last night I was at the Café Luitpold with Saranieff and Zamriaki. I told them I was in desperate need of a hundred marks. Saranieff thought I might ask you.

KEITH. Everyone in Munich thinks I'm an American railroad baron!

HERMANN. Zamriaki said you always had money.

KEITH. I patronize Zamriaki because he is the greatest musical genius since Richard Wagner. But those brigands aren't fit company for you!

HERMANN. I find the brigands interesting. I made the acquaintance of these gentlemen at an anarchist meeting.

KEITH. It must be a pleasant shock to your father to find out that you go to revolutionary meetings.

HERMANN. Why doesn't my father let me leave Munich!

KEITH. Because you're too young for the great world.

HERMANN. But I find that at my age you learn infinitely more through real experience than by squirming on a school bench until you grow up.

KEITH. Real experience only strips you of your personal gifts. This is particularly true of you, the son and sole heir of the greatest financial genius in Germany. What does your father say about me?

HERMANN. My father never talks to me.

KEITH. But he talks to other people.

HERMANN. Perhaps. I'm not at home very much.

KEITH. That's not right of you. I've followed your father's financial operations since I was in America. Unfortunately, your father thinks that no one else can be as clever as he is. That's why he obstinately refuses to join my project.

HERMANN. Try as I may, I can't imagine ever finding pleasure in a life like my father's.

KEITH. Your father doesn't know how to make you interested in his work.

HERMANN. But the important thing is not just to live but to learn everything about life and the world.

KEITH. Your desire to learn everything about the world will land you in a hole. The most important thing is always to maintain an attitude of approval toward the circumstances into which you were born. It will protect you from degrading yourself so cheerfully.

HERMANN. You mean by pumping you for cash? There are things of higher value than money!

KEITH. That is bookish wisdom. Those things are called "higher" because they're built on money; they're only brought into existence by money. You, of course, are free to devote yourself to an artistic or scientific career since your father's already made a fortune. But if in doing so you ignore the world's guiding principle your legacy will drop right into the clutches of swindlers.

HERMANN. If Jesus Christ had acted according to this guiding principle...

KEITH. Don't forget that Christianity liberated two thirds of mankind from slavery. No ideas—social, scientific, or artistic—deal with anything but goods and property. That's why the anarchists are sworn enemies of ideas. And don't think the world will ever change. It's man who adjusts or perishes. *Has sat down at the writing table.* I will give you the hundred marks. But come around sometime even when you don't need money. How long is it since your mother died?

ERMANN. It will be three years this spring.

EITH, *handing him a sealed note.* You're to take this to the Countess Werdenfels, Brienner Street, number 23. Tell her I send my very best regards. I happen to have nothing in my pocket today.

ERMANN. Thank you, Herr Baron.

EITH, *shows him out; as he closes the door after him.* To be sure, the pleasure was mine. *He goes back to the writing table; rummaging among the plans.* His old man treats me like a dog catcher. I must arrange a concert as soon as possible. Then public opinion will force him to join my project. If worst comes to worst it will have to do without him. *There is a knock at the door.* Come in!

NNA, THE COUNTESS WERDENFELS, *enters. She is a voluptuous beauty of thirty. White skin, turned-up nose, pale eyes, luxuriant chestnut-brown hair.*

EITH, *goes up to her.* Well, here you are, my queen! I just sent young Casimir to you with a little request.

NNA. So that was the young Herr Casimir?

EITH, *after kissing her lightly on her mouth, which she has offered him.* He'll come again if he doesn't find you home.

NNA. He doesn't look at all like his father.

EITH. Let's forget his father. I have approached a number of people whose social ambition I think will fill them full of burning enthusiasm for my project.

NNA. But everyone says that Casimir Senior patronizes actresses and singers.

EITH, *devouring* ANNA *with his eyes.* Anna, when I see you in front of me, I become another person, as though you were the living pledge of my good fortune. But won't you have breakfast with me? There's tea and caviar and cold meat.

NNA, *sits down on the sofa and eats.* I'm having a lesson at eleven. I've come for just a moment. Madame Bianchi tells me that in a year I can be the best Wagnerian soprano in Germany.

EITH, *lights a cigarette.* Perhaps in a year you will have done so well that the best Wagnerian sopranos will go to you for patronage.

NNA. That's fine. It's hard for me, with my limited woman's intelligence, to see how I can reach the heights so soon.

EITH. I can't tell you how before it happens. I just let myself be pulled along without resisting until I reach a spot where I feel at home and then I say to myself: this is where to build!

NNA. I'll be your loyal accomplice. For some time now I've had such a desperate love of life I've thought of suicide.

EITH. Some men seize what they want by force, others get it as a gift. When I went out into the world my highest hope was to die a village schoolmaster somewhere in Upper Silesia.

NNA. You could hardly have dreamt that one day Munich would lie at your feet.

EITH. Munich was something I'd only heard about in geography class. If

Frank Wedekind playing the title role in *The Marquis of
Keith. Drawing by Baroness Lida von Wedell.*

my career hasn't been an altogether spotless one, one must not forge
the depths from which I have risen.

ANNA. Every night I fervently pray to God to transmit some of your re
markable energy to me.

KEITH. Nonsense, I have no energy.

ANNA. But you're so constituted that you have to keep running your hea
through stone walls.

KEITH. My talent is restricted by the unfortunate circumstance that I can'
breathe in a bourgeois atmosphere. If I get what I want in spite of th
restriction I can't claim any credit for it. Other men find themselve
planted on a certain level and vegetate there all their lives without eve
coming into conflict with the world.

ANNA. You, on the contrary, fell from the sky a completely individual pe
sonality.

KEITH. I am a bastard. My father was a very distinguished man in inte
lectual circles, particularly in connection with mathematics and suc
scientific matters. My mother was a gipsy.

ANNA. If only I could read the secrets in people's faces, like you! I'd grin
their noses into the ground with my foot.

KEITH. Accomplishments like that are more likely to arouse distrust tha
do you any good. Bourgeois society has been secretly afraid of me a
my life because of this gift. But I've made my fortune through th
timidity of bourgeois society, against its will. The higher I climb th
more they trust me. In fact, I expect eventually to reach the poir

where the crossing of philosopher with horse thief will be appreciated at its full value.

NNA. The whole town is talking about your Fairyland Palace.

EITH. The Fairyland Palace only serves as a rallying point for my powers. I know myself too well to expect myself to audit account books at this stage in my life.

NNA. But what's to become of me? Do you think I want to take singing lessons forever? You said yesterday that the Fairyland Palace is being built especially for me.

EITH. Yes, but not for you to spend the rest of your life dancing on your hind legs and being raked over the coals by the fools of the press. You could use a few more highpoints in your past.

NNA. Well, I have no family tree to show, like Mesdames von Rosenkron and von Totleben.

EITH. You needn't be jealous of them for that.

NNA. I should hope not! What feminine charms *should* I be jealous of them for?

EITH. Both ladies came with the concert agency as a legacy from my predecessor. As soon as I've secured my position, they may peddle radishes or write novels for a living, for all I care.

NNA. I'm more concerned about the shine on my shoes than I am about your love. Do you know why? Because you are the most inconsiderate person in the world, caring only for your own sensual gratification. If you left me I should feel nothing but pity for you. But watch out that you aren't the one that gets left!

EITH, *caressing* ANNA. I have behind me a life full of sudden changes, but now I'm thinking seriously of building a house; a house with high ceilinged rooms, with a park, and broad steps leading to the entrance. Complete with beggars decorating the driveway. I've cut myself off from my past and have no desire to go back. It was too often a life-and-death struggle, you know. I wouldn't advise a friend to take my career as a model.

NNA. But you're indestructible.

EITH. Yes, that's what I can thank for everything I've accomplished till now. Anna, I think that if we had been born in two different worlds we would have had to find each other.

NNA. I'm indestructible too.

EITH. Even if Providence hadn't shown us we were made for each other by giving us such fabulously similar tastes, we have something else in common . . .

NNA. Rugged good health.

EITH, *sits beside her and caresses her.* As far as women are concerned, I believe that cleverness, good health, sensitivity, and beauty are inseparable; any one leads automatically to the other three. If these traits are intensified in our children . . .

ASHA, *a thirteen-year-old errand boy in livery, enters from the hall and laces an armful of newspapers on the center table.*

EITH. What does Councillor Ostermeier say?

SASHA. The Herr Councillor gave me a letter. It's with the newspaper *He goes into the waiting room.*

KEITH, *has opened the letter.* I owe this to your being with me! *Read* ". . . I have been told something about your plans and am very interes ed in them. Meet me at noon today in the Café Maximilian . . ." Th puts the world right in the palm of my hand! Now I can turn my rea to old Casimir if he decides to come along. With these worthy gentl men on my side I have a position of undisputed authority.

ANNA, *has risen.* Can you give me a thousand marks?

KEITH. Are you in the red again?

ANNA. The rent is due.

KEITH. That can wait till tomorrow. Don't worry about it.

ANNA. As you think best. Count Werdenfels prophesied on his deathbe that I would learn about life's grim realities some day.

KEITH. If he had known your worth better he might still be alive.

ANNA. So far his prophecy has not been fulfilled.

KEITH. I'll send you the money tomorrow at noon.

ANNA, *as* KEITH *sees her out.* No, please don't; I'll come and get it.

The stage remains empty for a moment. Then MOLLY GRIESINGER *comes ot of the living room and clears away the tea things.* KEITH *returns from th hall.*

KEITH, *calls.* Sasha! *Takes one of the pictures off the wall.* This will hav to see me through the next two weeks.

MOLLY. Then you still hope that we can keep going like this?

SASHA, *comes out of the waiting room.* Herr Baron?

KEITH, *gives him the picture.* Go to Tannhäuser. Tell him to put th Saranieff in his window. I'll give it to him for three thousand marks.

SASHA. Very good, Herr Baron.

KEITH. I'll be there myself in five minutes. Wait! *He takes from the wri ing table a card which says "3000 M." and fastens it to the picture fram* Three thousand marks! *Goes to the writing table.* First I have to das off a newspaper article on it.

SASHA *exits with the picture.*

MOLLY. If only we ever saw the slightest bit of real accomplishment in a this big talk.

KEITH, *writing.* "The Aesthetic Ideal in the Modern Landscape."

MOLLY. If this Saranieff could paint you wouldn't have to write articl about him.

KEITH, *turning around.* I beg your pardon?

MOLLY. I know, you're working.

KEITH. What did you wish to say?

MOLLY. I got a letter from Bückeburg.

KEITH. From your mama?

MOLLY, *finds the letter in her pocket and reads.* "You are both welcom here at any time. You could have the two front rooms on the third floo Then you could wait at your leisure until your negotiations in Munic were over."

KEITH. Don't you see, my dear child, that these little letters of yours undermine my credit?

MOLLY. There's no bread for tomorrow.

KEITH. Then we'll dine at the Hotel Continental.

MOLLY. I wouldn't be able to swallow a morsel for fear the bailiff would come and attach our beds in the meantime.

KEITH. He's still in the process of thinking about it. Why is there nothing in your little head but food and drink? Your existence could be so much happier if only you looked at the brighter side of things. You cherish an incorrigible affection for misfortune.

MOLLY. I think *you* cherish an affection for misfortune! Other people have such an easy time of it; they don't ever have to worry. They live for each other, in comfortable homes where their good fortune is not threatened. But you, with all your gifts, rush about like a madman, ruining your health, and we still never have a cent in the house.

KEITH. But you've always had enough to eat! If you don't spend anything on clothes it's not my fault. As soon as I write this article I'll have three thousand marks in my hand. Take a cab and buy up anything you can think of on the spur of the moment.

MOLLY. He'll pay three thousand marks for that picture like I'll wear silk stockings thanks to you.

KEITH, *getting up involuntarily.* You're a jewel!

MOLLY, *throws her arms about him.* Have I hurt you, darling? Please forgive me! What I just told you—I'm convinced that it's the solemn truth.

KEITH. Even if the money only lasts until tomorrow night, I won't regret the sacrifice.

MOLLY, *wailing.* I know how hateful it was of me. Beat me!

KEITH. The Fairyland Palace is as good as certain.

MOLLY. At least let me kiss your hand. Please, please, let me kiss your hand.

KEITH. If I can only preserve my composure for the next few days.

MOLLY. Won't you let me? How can you be so inhuman?

KEITH, *takes his hand out of his pocket.* It's about time you took counsel with yourself. Otherwise you're in for a sudden revelation.

MOLLY, *covering his hand with kisses.* Why won't you beat me? I surely deserve it.

KEITH. You are cheating yourself of happiness with all the means that a woman has at her disposal.

MOLLY, *jumps up indignantly.* Don't imagine that I'm frightened by your flirtations! We're held together by too strong a bond. If it ever breaks I won't keep you any more. But as long as you are in misery you belong to me.

KEITH. It will be your downfall, Molly, that you fear my good fortune more than death. If my hands are free tomorrow you won't stay here another minute.

MOLLY. That's fine, as long as you're so sure.

KEITH. But I'm not in misery!

MOLLY. At least let me keep on working for you until your hands are free.

KEITH, *seats himself again at the writing table.* Very well, do what you won't let me do. You know there's nothing I dislike more than a woman . who works.

MOLLY. I will not make myself a monkey or a parrot for your sake. If I stand over a washtub instead of riding about half-naked to masquerades with you I certainly can't ruin you.

KEITH. Your obstinacy is something superhuman.

MOLLY. I'm sure it's beyond your comprehension.

KEITH. Even if I understood you it wouldn't help you.

MOLLY, *triumphantly.* I don't *have* to push it in your face, but I'll give it to you in black on white, if you want! I wouldn't be any happier if I acted different and thought I was better than God made me—*because you love me!*

KEITH. That is obvious.

MOLLY, *triumphantly.* Because you can't live without my love! Have your hands as free as you want! You'll let me stay if I let you have some love left over for other women! Let them dress themselves in finery and idolize you as much as they please; it saves me going to comedies. Oh you're a real idealist; I know all about that. But if you ever did any thing about your ideals—a fine chance there is of it!—I'd gladly let my self be buried alive.

KEITH. If you would only be pleased with what fortune offers you!

MOLLY, *tenderly.* What does it offer, my love? We had these endless fear in America too. Everything always went to pieces in the end. In Santi ago you weren't elected president and were nearly sentenced to be sho because we had no brandy on the table on the decisive evening. You remember how you shouted, "A dollar, a dollar, a republic for a dollar!"

KEITH, *jumps up furiously and goes to the sofa.* I came into the world a cripple. I do not feel I'm destined to be a slave because of it. And the fact that I was born a beggar does not prevent me from looking at the most extravagant luxury as my rightful heritage.

MOLLY. As long as you live you'll only *look at* luxury.

KEITH. Only death can change what I'm telling you. And death doesn' dare attack me, because it's afraid of making itself ridiculous. If I di without having lived, my ghost will come back.

MOLLY. You just have a swelled head.

KEITH. I know I am justified! When you ran away to America with me you were an irresponsible child of fifteen, straight out of the schoolroom. If we part now and you're left to fend for yourself, you will come to the worst end imaginable.

MOLLY, *throws her arms around his neck.* Come to Bückeburg then! My parents haven't seen their Molly in three years. They'll be so overjoyed they'll give you half their wealth. And how well we could live!

KEITH. In Bückeburg?

MOLLY. All troubles come to an end.

KEITH, *pulling away.* I'd rather collect cigar butts in the cafés.

SASHA, *returns with the picture.* Herr Tannhäuser says he can't put th picture in the window. Herr Tannhäuser says he already has a dozen pictures by Herr Saranieff.

MOLLY. I knew it all along!

KEITH. That's why I keep you with me! *Goes to the writing table and tears up the paper on which he was writing.* At least I don't have to write an article on it any more!

SASHA *puts the picture on the table and goes into the waiting room.*

MOLLY. These Saranieffs and Zamriakis, you see, are people who belong to an entirely different race from us. They know how to empty people's pockets. We're both of us too simple for the great world.

KEITH. Your kingdom is not yet come. Leave me alone. Bückeburg will have to wait.

MOLLY, *at a ring in the corridor, claps her hands maliciously.* The bailiff! *She runs to open the door.*

KEITH, *looks at his watch.* What else can be sacrificed to fortune . . . ?

MOLLY, *shows in* ERNST SCHOLZ. The gentleman won't give me his name.

ERNST SCHOLZ *is a slim man of extremely aristocratic appearance, about 27 years old; black, wavy hair; a vandyke; under powerful elongated eyebrows big watery-blue eyes which express helplessness.*

KEITH. Gaston! Where have you come from?

SCHOLZ. Your greeting is a good sign. I am so changed I thought you would hardly recognize me.

MOLLY *wishes to remove the breakfast dishes but, after a glance at* SCHOLZ, *is afraid that she will disturb them; she goes into the living room without the dishes.*

KEITH. You look a little worn out; but life is no child's play.

SCHOLZ. Certainly not for me; that's why I'm here. And it's because of you that I've come to Munich.

KEITH. Thank you; whatever I have left over from my business is yours.

SCHOLZ. I know that life is a hard struggle for you. But I want to be associated with you now on a personal basis. I would like to submit myself to your moral instruction for a time, but on one condition: you must allow me to assist you as much as you need with the money at my disposal.

KEITH. But what for? I'm about to become the director of a tremendous corporation. And you are doing well too? If I'm not mistaken the last time we saw each other was four years ago.

SCHOLZ. At the legal convention in Brussels.

KEITH. You had just passed your State examination.

SCHOLZ. You were already writing for all the daily papers. Do you recall how I reproached you for your cynicism at the ball in the Palace of Justice at Brussels?

KEITH. You had fallen in love with the daughter of the Danish ambassador, and you were furious at me when I maintained that women are by nature more materialistic than men could ever become, even after experiencing the greatest luxury.

SCHOLZ. I still find you an unscrupulous monster, as I did all through our boyhood; but—you were perfectly right.

KEITH. I've never in all my life had a more flattering compliment.

SCHOLZ. I am worn out. Although I abhor your view of life from the bottom of my heart, I entrust to you today the riddle of my existence, which I find insoluble.

KEITH. Praise God that you are at last coming out of your melancholy and turning toward the sun!

SCHOLZ. This is not a cowardly surrender. I've tried in every way to solve the riddle myself.

KEITH. So much the better, to have that behind you. During the Cuban revolution I was to be shot with twelve conspirators. At the first shot I fell down, of course, and stayed "dead" until they came to bury me. Since that day I have felt I am truly the master of my fate. *Jumping up.* We incur no obligations at birth, and we have only one life to throw away. Those who live on after death are outside the rules. In Brussels at that time you intended going into civil service?

SCHOLZ. I went into our Ministry of Railroads.

KEITH. I wondered why, with your enormous wealth, you didn't prefer to live as a great lord, following the dictates of your fancy.

SCHOLZ. I wanted to become, first, a useful member of human society. If I had been born the son of a day laborer it would have happened as a matter of course.

KEITH. In this world you can help your fellow men most when you work for your own advantage. The broader my interests, the more people I can provide with a livelihood. Whoever thinks he's accomplishing anything by merely filling his post and feeding his children is pulling the wool over his own eyes. The children would be thankful to their creator if they'd never been brought into the world, and a hundred poor devils are begging for the same post.

SCHOLZ. But I didn't see why it was necessary to be a useless drone simply because I was a rich man. I have no artistic talent, and I did not consider myself insignificant enough to think my only vocation was for marriage and having children.

KEITH. Then you've left the civil service?

SCHOLZ, *hanging his head.* Because I was responsible for a terrible disaster while I held office.

KEITH. When I came back from America, someone who had seen you the year before in Constantinople told me you had spent two years traveling but that you were at home again and about to be married.

SCHOLZ. I broke my engagement three days ago. Up to now I have been only half a man. Since I came of age I have been guided by the single conviction that I would not be able to enjoy my existence until I had justified it through honest work. Such a one-sided point of view has led me today to seek purely material gratification (through sense of duty, nothing else, as though I were doing some kind of penance). But every time I want to open out my arms to life I am paralyzed by the thought of those unfortunate people who lost their lives so horribly because of my exaggerated conscientiousness.

EITH. What happened?

CHOLZ. I changed one of the railroad regulations. There had been some danger that this regulation could not be obeyed to the letter. My fears were exaggerated, of course, but every day I seemed to see disaster come closer. I don't have the mental equilibrium that comes to people from homes where human values are respected. The first day after my new regulation was put into effect two express trains collided; nine men, three women, and two children lost their lives. I can still see the spot where the accident took place. It's not my fault that I am still alive after seeing it.

EITH. And then you went traveling?

CHOLZ. I went to England, to Italy, but I still feel cut off from all living activity. In cheerful, gay surroundings, in the midst of deafening music, I suddenly hear a piercing cry, because I have unexpectedly been reminded of the disaster again. In the Orient too I lived like a frightened owl. To be frank, since that disastrous day I have become thoroughly convinced that I can buy back the joy of living only through self-sacrifice. But I must have access to life. I hoped to get it when I became engaged last year to a very fine girl of humble origin.

EITH. You really wanted to make her the Countess Trautenau?

CHOLZ. I am no longer Count Trautenau. You can't understand that. The press played up quite effectively the contrast between my rank and name and the disaster I was responsible for. I felt it was my duty to my family to take another name. For two years my name has been Ernst Scholz. That is why my engagement could occasion no surprise; but disaster would have come from that, too. In her heart, not a spark of love; in mine, only the need to sacrifice myself; our relationship an endless chain of the most trivial misunderstandings . . . I've given the girl an ample dowry so that she will be a desirable match for anyone in her walk of life. She was so overjoyed at having her freedom again she hardly knew what to say. And now I must finally acquire the difficult art of forgetting myself. Men face death with complete awareness; but life is impossible unless one can forget oneself.

ITH, *throws himself into a chair.* My father would turn over in his grave if he knew that you—were asking for my advice.

HOLZ. That's how life contradicts bookish wisdom. Your father contributed his share to my one-sided spiritual development.

ITH. My father was as selfless and conscientious as the tutor and mentor of a Count Trautenau had to be. You were his model student, and I was the whipping boy.

HOLZ. Don't you remember, when you were at the castle, how tenderly you used to be kissed by the chambermaids, particularly when I happened to be around?! *Getting up.* I shall spend the next two or three years singly and solely . . . *With tears in his voice* . . . in training myself to be an epicurean.

ITH, *jumping up.* Let us first of all go to the dance hall at the Nymphenburg this evening! It's as unworthy of people of our sort as you can

imagine. But with all the rain and sleet descending on my head I'r
tempted to bathe in the mire again.

SCHOLZ. I don't have any great desire for market cries.

KEITH. You won't hear a single loud word, only something like the hollo
roar of the ocean uprooted from its bed. Munich is both Arcadia an
Babylon. The silent Saturnalian frenzy which overpowers the soul her
at every opportunity retains its charm even for the most blasé.

SCHOLZ. How could *I* be blasé? I have never to this day found pleasur
in anything.

KEITH. We shall have to guard ourselves against the crowd on the danc
floor! They react to my appearance in such places as flies to carrior
But I can vouch for it that you will forget yourself. You will eve
forget yourself three months from now when you think back to th
evening.

SCHOLZ. I have asked myself in all seriousness if my tremendous wealt
is the source of all my misfortune.

KEITH, *indignant*. That's blasphemy!

SCHOLZ. I'm sure you have already wondered whether I renounced n
wealth as I renounced my title. As long as I am alive, such a renunc
ation could only benefit my family. I can wait for my deathbed
dispose of my property advantageously, after it has ruined my lif
If I had had to struggle from youth, with my moral earnestness ar
my diligence I would probably be in the middle of the most brillia
career today, instead of being an outcast.

KEITH. Or else you would be revelling with some lower-class girl in th
most common sort of vulgar lovemaking, and cleaning other mer
dirty shoes.

SCHOLZ. I would take that in exchange for my lot anytime.

KEITH. Don't think that this railroad disaster is a real impediment. Yc
find satisfaction in such hideous memories only because you can't pr
vide yourself with more delicate nourishment.

SCHOLZ. You may be right. That is why I would like to entrust myse
to your spiritual guidance.

KEITH. We'll find some kind of tid-bit tonight. I'm sorry I can't a
you to have breakfast with me. I have a business appointment
twelve with a local big-wig. But I will give you a few lines to take
my friend Raspe. Spend the afternoon with him; we will meet
six at the Hofgarten Café. *He has gone to the writing table and
writing a note.*

SCHOLZ. What kind of business are you in?

KEITH. I am an art dealer. I write for the papers. I have a conce
agency—none of it worth talking about. You have come just in tir
to see the founding of a well-endowed concert hall which is bei
built exclusively for my artists.

SCHOLZ, *takes the picture from the table and examines it.* You have
nice picture gallery.

KEITH, *jumping up.* I wouldn't take ten thousand marks for that.
Saranieff. *Turns the picture around.* You have to hold it this way.

SCHOLZ. I don't know anything about art. In all my travels I never visited a single museum.

KEITH, *gives him the note.* This man is an international authority on crime; so don't be too open with him at first. A charming man. People never know whether they should keep an eye on me or whether I am here to keep an eye on them.

SCHOLZ. Thank you for your kind reception. This evening, then, at six at the Hofgarten Café.

KEITH. Then we go to the Nymphenburg. Thank you for finally having some confidence in me.

KEITH *shows* SCHOLZ *out. The stage is empty for a moment. Then* MOLLY GRIESINGER *comes out of the living room and removes the tea things from the table.* KEITH *returns immediately.*

KEITH, *calling.* Sasha! *Goes to the telephone and rings up.* Seventeen thirty-five—Inspector Raspe!

SASHA, *comes out of the waiting room.* Herr Baron!

KEITH. My hat! My overcoat!

SASHA hurries into the hall.

MOLLY. I beg you not to have anything to do with this patron! He wouldn't come if he didn't want to exploit us.

KEITH, *speaks into the telephone.* Thank God you're there! Just wait ten minutes. You'll see for yourself. *To* MOLLY, *as* SASHA *helps him on with his overcoat.* I'm rushing out to the newspaper offices.

MOLLY. What should I write to Mama?

KEITH, *to* SASHA. A carriage!

SASHA. Yes, Herr Baron. *Exit.*

KEITH. Tell her I offer her homage. *Goes to the writing table.* The plans —Ostermeier's letter—tomorrow morning Munich must know that the Fairyland Palace is going to be built!

MOLLY. Then you're not coming to Bückeburg?

KEITH, *the rolled-up plans under his arm, takes his hat from the center table and puts it on at an angle.* I can't help wondering how he's going to become an epicurean! *Exit hastily.*

ACT TWO

In the MARQUIS OF KEITH's *study the center table is laid for breakfast: champagne and a large dish of oysters. The* MARQUIS OF KEITH *is sitting on the writing table with his left foot on a stool, as* SASHA, *kneeling in front of him, buttons his shoes with a button hook.* ERNST SCHOLZ *is standing behind the sofa, trying out a guitar which he has taken from the wall.*

KEITH. What time did you get back to your hotel this morning?

SCHOLZ, *with a radiant smile.* At ten.

KEITH. Wasn't I right to leave you alone with that delightful creature?

SCHOLZ, *smiling blissfully.* After last night's conversations about art and modern literature I wonder whether I shouldn't take lessons from that girl. I was amazed when she asked if she might wait on your guests at that garden party you spoke of, which is going to set all Munich agog.

KEITH. It's quite simple: she considers it an honor! Besides, we have time to talk about the garden party. Tomorrow I'm going to Paris for a few days.

SCHOLZ. This comes at a very inconvenient time for me.

KEITH. Come along. I want one of my artistes to sing for Madame Marquesi before she makes her debut here.

SCHOLZ. Must I be reminded of the mental torments I once lived through in Paris?

KEITH. Won't last night's experience help you to face it? Very well, spend your time with Saranieff, the painter, in my absence. He'll probably turn up somewhere today.

SCHOLZ. The girl told me that Saranieff's studio is a chamber of horrors, full of the most shocking atrocities known to man. And then she chattered in the most delightful way about her childhood, how she used to spend the whole summer sitting in the cherry trees in the Tyrol and how on winter evenings she used to go sleigh riding with the village children till nightfall. How can such a girl consider it an honor to be a serving maid at your party?

KEITH. The girl considers it an honor because it gives her an opportunity to fight down the contempt with which she is regarded by bourgeois society.

SCHOLZ. But how is the contempt justified? How many hundreds of women in the best circles of society live ruined lives because the wellsprings of life are dried up in them. In her they overflow. In her excesses of joy this girl is never guilty of a sin like the deadly discord in which my parents managed to spend twenty years together!

KEITH. What is sin!!

SCHOLZ. Even yesterday it seemed to me I was sure I knew. Today I can say without despair what thousands and thousands of respectable people like me have felt: a man whose life is unfulfilled is bitterly envious of those who have strayed from the path of virtue.

KEITH. The happiness of those creatures would not be so despised if it weren't the most unprofitable business imaginable. Sin is a mythological expression meaning: bad business. Good business eventually fits itself into the existing social order! No one knows that better than I. Today all Munich is talking about me, the Marquis of Keith; yet as far as my European reputation is concerned, I am as much outside the pale of society as that girl. In fact, that's the only reason I'm giving a garden party. I'm terribly sorry that I can't receive the dear little thing as one of my guests. It will be in much better taste if she is one of the servants.

SASHA, *has risen.* Does the Herr Baron wish me to call a carriage?

KEITH. Yes.

SASHA *exit.*

EITH, *stamping his feet to get his shoes on securely.* Did you read that The Fairyland Palace Company was founded yesterday?

CHOLZ. I haven't glanced at a newspaper since yesterday, of course. *They both sit down at the breakfast table.*

EITH. The whole project rests on a brewer, a master builder, and a restaurant keeper. They are the Caryatids who support the pediment of the temple.

CHOLZ. By the way, your friend Raspe, the police official, is a charming person.

EITH. He's a scoundrel, but I like him for a different reason.

CHOLZ. He told me he was originally a theology student, but he lost his faith from studying too much, and tried to get it back the way the prodigal son did.

EITH. He sank deeper and deeper until finally the prosecuting arm of the law embraced him and restored his lost faith by keeping him under lock and key for two years.

CHOLZ. That girl absolutely could not understand why I had never learned to ride a bicycle. She thought it was very clever of me not to ride a bicycle in Asia and Africa, because of the wild animals. But I could have begun in Italy!

EITH. I warn you again, my dear friend, don't be too open with people! The truth is our most precious possession and we must be sparing with it.

CHOLZ. Is that why you've taken the name "Marquis of Keith"?

EITH. I have as much right to be called the Marquis of Keith as you have to be called Ernst Scholz. I am the adopted son of Lord Keith, who in 1863, . . .

ASHA, *enters from the hall, announcing.* Professor Saranieff!

ARANIEFF *enters. Wears a black walking coat with sleeves a little too ong, light-colored trousers—a little too short—thick shoes, and bright red loves; his somewhat long, bristling black hair is cut straight all around; n front of his eyes, which are full of promise, are pincenez on a black ribon à la Murillo; his profile is very expressive; he has a small Spanish ustache. After his greeting he hands his top hat to* SASHA.

ARANIEFF. I wish you the best of luck from the bottom of my heart, my dear friend. At last the moorings are cut and the balloon can rise!

EITH. My High Command is awaiting me; I'm sorry I can't invite you to breakfast now.

ARANIEFF, *sitting down at the table.* I release you from the obligation of issuing an invitation.

EITH. Another place, Sasha!

SASHA *has hung the hat up in the hall and goes into the living room.*

ARANIEFF. The only thing that surprises me is that the great Casimir's name is not on the membership list of the Fairyland Palace Syndicate.

EITH. That is because I don't want to give up the credit for having created my own work. *Introducing them.* Saranieff, the painter—Count Trautenau.

ARANIEFF, *takes a glass and plate and helps himself. To* SCHOLZ. Count,

I know you thoroughly, inside and out. *To* KEITH. Simba was just wit[me; she's sitting for a Boecklin this time.

KEITH, *to* SCHOLZ. Boecklin was a great painter, too, you know. *To* SAR[NIEFF. You don't have to boast about such tricks!

SARANIEFF. Make me famous, and I won't need any more tricks! I'll pa[you thirty percent for life. Zamriaki's mind is tottering like a ricket[fencepost because he insists on becoming immortal by ethical means.

KEITH. I am concerned only with his music. For the true composer a min[is an obstacle.

SCHOLZ. To want to be immortal one needs to have an extraordinary lov[of life.

SARANIEFF, *to* SCHOLZ. By the way, our Simba described you to me as a[extremely interesting person.

SCHOLZ. Yes, I can easily believe she doesn't often come across old grouche[like me.

SARANIEFF. She classed you with the Symbolists. *To* KEITH. And then sh[raved about some imminent celebration for the founding of the Fair[land Palace, with remarkable fireworks.

KEITH. You can't dazzle a dog with fireworks, but the most rational ma[feels hurt if you don't give him any. At any rate, I'm going to Paris fo[a few days first.

SARANIEFF. You've been asked to state your opinion on a mutual-aid treat[between Germany and France?

KEITH. But don't say anything about it!

SCHOLZ. I had no idea you were active in politics too!

SARANIEFF. Do you know anything in which the Marquis of Keith is no[active?

KEITH. I don't want people to say I have no concern for the age I live in[

SCHOLZ. Don't one's own affairs keep one busy enough if one takes lif[seriously?

SARANIEFF. *You* certainly take it damned seriously! Tell me, did a laun[dress in the village of Gizeh, at the foot of the pyramids, change one o[your collars by mistake?

SCHOLZ. You seem to have been thoroughly informed about me. Will yo[permit me to visit you in your studio some day?

SARANIEFF. If it suits you we can have coffee at my place right now. You'[find your Simba still there.

SCHOLZ. Simba? — Simba? — You keep talking about Simba. The girl tol[me her name was Kathi!

SARANIEFF. Her real name is Kathi; but the Marquis of Keith christene[her Simba.

SCHOLZ, *to* KEITH. No doubt because of her remarkable red hair?

KEITH. With all the goodwill in the world I can't give you any informatio[on the subject.

SARANIEFF. She's made herself comfortable on my Persian divan and i[sleeping off her hangover.

MOLLY GRIESINGER *comes out of the living room and sets a place for* SAR[NIEFF.

SARANIEFF. Heartiest thanks, my dear madam; as you can see, I have already finished eating. Forgive me, I have not yet had the opportunity of kissing your hand.

MOLLY. Save your flattery for better opportunities! *A bell rings in the corridor;* MOLLY *goes to open the door.*

KEITH, *looks at his watch and gets up.* You will have to excuse me, gentlemen. *Calls.* Sasha!

SARANIEFF, *wipes his mouth.* We're going with you, of course. *He and* SCHOLZ *get up.*

SASHA *comes from the waiting room with the coats and helps* KEITH *and* SCHOLZ *put theirs on.*

SCHOLZ, *to* KEITH. Why didn't you tell me you were married?

KEITH. Here, let me fix your tie. *He does it.* You must be more careful of your appearance.

MOLLY *comes back from the hall with* HERMANN CASIMIR.

MOLLY. Young Herr Casimir wishes to see you.

KEITH, *to* HERMANN. Did you convey my respects yesterday?

HERMANN. The countess was waiting for money from you herself!

KEITH. Wait here a moment. I'll be back at once. *To* SCHOLZ *and* SARANIEFF. Shall we, gentlemen?

SARANIEFF, *taking his hat from* SASHA. With you through thick and thin!

SASHA. The carriage is waiting, Herr Baron.

KEITH. Sit with the driver!

Exeunt SCHOLZ, SARANIEFF, KEITH, *and* SASHA.

MOLLY, *putting the breakfast dishes together.* I wonder what you're after in this madhouse! You would be much better off at home with your mama!

HERMANN, *wishes to leave at once.* My mother is not alive, madam; but I don't wish to disturb you.

MOLLY. For heaven's sake, stay! You're not in anyone's way here. But what inhuman parents, not to protect their child from associating with such ruffians! I had a happy home like yours and was no older nor wiser than you when I leaped into the bottomless pit without giving it a second thought.

HERMANN, *greatly agitated.* Heaven take pity on me—I must find a way! I'll be ruined if I stay in Munich any longer! But the Marquis will refuse to help me if he suspects what I have in mind. I beg you, madam, don't betray me!

MOLLY. If you knew the state of my feelings you wouldn't have the slightest fear I'd be concerned with your stories! I hope you don't fare worse than I did! If my mother had let me work as I work now, instead of sending me off to skate every afternoon, I would still have a lifetime of happiness ahead of me!

HERMANN. But—if you're so very unhappy and know—that you could still be happy, why—why don't you get divorced?

MOLLY. For heaven's sake, don't talk about things you don't understand! If you want a divorce you have to be married first.

HERMANN. I'm sorry, I — thought you were married.

MOLLY. God knows, I don't want to complain about anybody! But to get married anywhere in the world you need to have some papers. An that's beneath his notice, having papers! *As a bell rings in the corrido* From morning to night it's just like a post office! *Exit to the hall.*

HERMANN, *collecting himself.* How could I have made such a blunder!

MOLLY *shows in* COUNTESS WERDENFELS.

MOLLY. You may wait for my husband here. He will probably be here an minute. May I introduce you?

ANNA. Thank you. We are acquainted.

MOLLY. Certainly! Then I'm not needed. *Exit into the living room.*

ANNA, *sits down on the writing-table bench next to* HERMANN *and puts he hand on his.* Now tell me frankly, my dear young friend, why you nee so much money at school.

HERMANN. I won't tell you.

ANNA. But I want to know so badly!

HERMANN. I can believe that!

ANNA. Stubborn mule!

HERMANN, *pulls his hand away from hers.* I won't be bribed!

ANNA. Who's bribing you? Don't flatter yourself! You see, I divide mai kind into two general classes. Young blades and old maids.

HERMANN. Of course in your opinion I am an old maid.

ANNA. If you can't even say why you need all that money . . .

HERMANN. Of course I can't, I'm an old maid!

ANNA. No, I could tell at the first glance: you're a young blade!

HERMANN. Of course I am; otherwise I'd be content to stay in Munich.

ANNA. You want to go out into the world!

HERMANN. And you'd like to know where. To Paris—to London.

ANNA. Paris isn't at all fashionable any more!

HERMANN. I don't really care about going to Paris.

ANNA. Why don't you stay here in Munich? You have a father who's ro ing in wealth . . .

HERMANN. Because you don't experience anything here! I'll go to piec here in Munich, especially if I have to waste any more time at schoc An old classmate of mine writes me from Africa that when you're u happy in Africa you're ten times happier than when you're happy i Munich.

ANNA. I'll tell you something: your friend is an old maid. Don't go t Africa. Better stay here in Munich with us and experience something.

HERMANN. But that's impossible here!

MOLLY *shows in* POLICE INSPECTOR RASPE. RASPE *is in his early twenties, wearing a light-colored summer suit and a straw hat, has the innoce childlike features of an angel by Guido Reni. Short blond hair, the b ginnings of a mustache. When he thinks he is being observed he clam blue pincenez on his nose.*

MOLLY. My husband is coming soon; if you wish to wait a moment. M. I introduce . . .

RASPE. I really don't know, my dear madam, if it will do the Baron a ser ice if you introduce me.

MOLLY. Oh, all right, then! —for heaven's sake! *Exit into the living room.*

ANNA. Your precautions are quite unnecessary, of course. We are acquainted.

RASPE, *sits down on the sofa.* Hm—I shall have to recollect . . .

ANNA. When you've recollected sufficiently, by the way, I'd like to ask you not to introduce me either.

RASPE. How is it that I've never heard you mentioned here!

ANNA. Only a change of name. I was told that you spent two years in utter solitude.

RASPE. And of course you let on to no one that you knew me at the height of my glory.

ANNA. Is there anyone who hasn't had his glory!

RASPE. You're quite right. Pity is blasphemous. How could I help it! I was a sacrifice to the insane confidence everyone had in me.

ANNA. But now you're a young blade again.

RASPE. Now I use that same insane confidence for the good of my fellow men. By the way, can you tell me anything else about this epicurean?

ANNA. I'm terribly sorry; he hasn't been put through his paces for me yet.

RASPE. That's surprising. A certain Herr Scholz, who wants to train himself as an epicurean here in Munich.

ANNA. And so the Marquis of Keith has him meet a police inspector?

RASPE. A thoroughly harmless person. I hardly knew what to do with him. For the sake of his education I took him to the Hofbräuhaus. That's right next door.

MOLLY *opens the entrance door and shows in* CONSUL CASIMIR. *He is a man in his middle forties, somewhat thick-set, very well dressed; a full face with thick whiskers, a powerful mustache, bushy eyebrows, his hair carefully parted in the middle.*

MOLLY. My husband is not at home. *Exit.*

CASIMIR, *without speaking to anyone, goes up to* HERMANN. There's the door! — — I have to hunt you up in this robbers' den!

HERMANN. You wouldn't have looked for me here if you weren't afraid for your business!

CASIMIR, *threatens him.* Will you be quiet! — I'll make you move!

HERMANN, *takes out a pocket revolver.* Don't touch me, Papa! — Don't touch me! I'll shoot myself if you touch me!

CASIMIR. — I'll make you pay for this at home!

RASPE. Why should anyone let himself be pushed around like that!

CASIMIR. Must I be insulted here too . . . !

ANNA, *walks up to him.* Please, sir, or there'll be a disaster. Calm yourself first. *To* HERMANN. Be reasonable; go with your father.

HERMANN. There's nothing for me at home. He wouldn't even notice if I drank myself to distraction because I don't know what I'm living for!

ANNA. Then tell him calmly what you intend to do; but don't threaten your father with that revolver. Give me that thing.

HERMANN. A fine idea.

ANNA. You won't regret it. I'll give it back when you're calm. — Do you think I'm a liar?

HERMANN *hesitatingly gives her the revolver.*

ANNA. Now ask your father to forgive you. If you have a spark of honor in you you can't expect your father to make the first move.

HERMANN. But I will not be ruined!

ANNA. First ask his pardon. You know that your father can be reasoned with then.

HERMANN. I — I — beg you to . . . *He falls to his knees, sobbing.*

ANNA, *tries to stand him up.* For shame! Look your father in the eye!

CASIMIR. His mother's nerves!

ANNA. Prove to your father that he can have confidence in you. — Now go home, and when you have calmed down, tell your father your plans and wishes. *She leads him out.*

CASIMIR, *to* RASPE. Who is this lady?

RASPE. This is the first time I've seen her in two years. At that time she was a clerk in a shop on Perusa Street, and her name was Huber, if remember correctly. But if you want to know any more about her . .

CASIMIR. Thank you very much. At your service! *Exit.*

MOLLY *comes out of the living room to carry out the breakfast things.*

RASPE. Excuse me, madam, did the Baron really intend to come back before dinner?

MOLLY. For God's sake, please don't ask me such ridiculous things!

ANNA, *comes back from the hall, to* MOLLY. May I help you carry something?

MOLLY. You ask if you can help me . . . *Putting the serving tray back on the table.* Anyone who wants to can clear the table; I didn't sit there *Exits into the living room.*

RASPE. You were absolutely perfect with the boy.

ANNA, *sitting down at the writing table again.* How I envy the handsom carriage his old man is taking him home in.

RASPE. Tell me, what ever became of that Count Werdenfels who gave one champagne party after another two years ago?

ANNA. I bear his name.

RASPE. I should have guessed it! — Will you convey to the Count my sincerest felicitations on his choice?

ANNA. That's impossible now.

RASPE. You have separated?

ANNA. Yes, obviously. *As voices become audible in the corridor.* I'll tell you about it some other time.

KEITH *enters with* HERR OSTERMEIER, HERR KRENTZL, *and* HERR GRANDAUER *all three of them more or less big-bellied, blear-eyed Munich Philistine They are followed by* SASHA.

KEITH. What a wonderful coincidence! I can introduce you at once to one of our leading artists. — Sasha, remove this stuff!

SASHA *exit into the living room with the breakfast things.*

KEITH, *introducing them.* Herr Ostermeier, the brewery proprietor, Herr Krentzl, the master builder, and Herr Grandauer, the restaurateur, the Caryatids of the Fairyland Palace — the Countess Werdenfels. But you time is limited, gentlemen; you wish to see the plans. *Takes the plans from the writing table and unrolls them on the center table.*

STERMEIER. Take your time, my friend. Five minutes more or less won't matter.

EITH, *to* GRANDAUER. Will you please hold this. — What you see here is the large concert hall with receding ceiling and skylight, so that it may be used as an exhibition palace in the summers. Next to it is a smaller theater, which I shall make popular through the most up-to-date style of decoration — you know, something that is half dance hall and half death chamber. The most up-to-date is always cheapest and most effective.

TERMEIER. Hm — you haven't forgotten the toilets?

ITH. Here are the facilities for the cloak rooms and toilets in complete detail. — Here, Herr Krentzl, is the facade; approach, pediment, and caryatids.

RENTZL. Say, I wouldn't want to be one of them caryatids!

ITH. That's just my little joke, honored sir!

RENTZL. What would my old lady say if I let myself be hacked into a caryatid up there, 'specially on a Fairyland Palace!

ANDAUER. Remember, as owner of a restaurant, the main thing for me in this business is that I have some room.

ITH. As for the location of the restaurant, my dear Herr Grandauer, the entire ground floor is set aside for it.

ANDAUER. You can't pack in folks for food and drink like you can for art and music.

ITH. For afternoon coffee, my dear Herr Grandauer, you have here on the first floor a terrace with a magnificent view of the grounds along the Isar.

TERMEIER. I'd just like to ask you, my friend, if we could see your preliminary expense sheet.

ITH, *producing a piece of writing.* Four thousand shares at 5000 makes roughly twenty million marks. — I am going on the assumption that each of us, gentlemen, subscribes for forty shares, preferred, and pays for them at once. As you can see, the estimated profit is exceptionally low.

ENTZL. Then all we need is the city council's go-ahead.

ITH. For that reason we are going to put out, in addition to shares, a number of interest-drawing bonds, and some of these we will allot to the city to use for worthy purposes. — It is proposed that members of the board get ten per cent of the net profit before deductions for depreciation and reserves.

TERMEIER. All as it should be. Can't ask for more.

ITH. As for the Bourse, we'll have to work at that a bit. I am going to Paris for that purpose tomorrow. Two weeks from now we will have our founders' party in my villa on Brienner Street.

ANNA *starts suddenly.*

TERMEIER. If only Consul Casimir would decide to go along with us by the time of the party!

KRENTZL. That would be really shrewd. If we had Consul Casimir the ci•
council would agree to anything.

KEITH. I hope, gentlemen, that we will be able to call a general meetin•
before the party. Then we will see how I can take note of your refe•
ences to Consul Casimir.

OSTERMEIER, *shakes his hand.* Then I wish you a pleasant journey, m•
friend. Let's hear from you from Paris. *Bowing to* ANNA. Allow me •
wish you good day; my compliments.

GRANDAUER. My respects; allow me to wish you good afternoon.

KRENTZL. I'm honored; at your service!

KEITH *shows the gentlemen out.*

ANNA, *when he returns.* What in the world do you mean by arranging •
have your founders' party at my house?!

KEITH. I'm going to have a concert gown made for•you in Paris that w•
make it unnecessary for you to be able to sing. — *To* RASPE. I expe•
that at this founders' party, Inspector, you will use all the charm of yo•
personality to bewitch the consorts of the three Caryatids.

RASPE. The ladies will have nothing to complain of.

KEITH, *giving him money.* Here are three hundred marks. I'm going •
bring back fireworks from Paris the like of which Munich has never see•

RASPE, *pocketing the money.* He got this from the Epicurean.

KEITH, *to* ANNA. I use all mortals according to their talents, and I mu•
recommend caution in dealing with my dear friend, Police Inspect•
Raspe.

RASPE. When a man looks as though he has just been cut down from t•
gallows, like you, getting through life honestly is no art. I'd like to s•
where you would be today with my angelic countenance!

KEITH. With your countenance I would have married a princess.

ANNA, *to* RASPE. If I remember correctly, you were introduced to me und•
a French name.

RASPE. I no longer use French names, now that I've become a usef•
member of human society. — Permit me to pay my respects. *Exit.*

ANNA. But I'm not equipped with a staff for big suppers!

KEITH, *calls.* Sasha!

SASHA, *comes out of the waiting room.* Herr Baron?

KEITH. Will you help serve at my friend's garden party?

SASHA. The pleasure's all mine, Herr Baron. *Exit.*

KEITH. I'd like to have you meet today my oldest boyhood friend, Cou•
Trautenau.

ANNA. I have no luck with counts.

KEITH. No matter. I only ask you not to discuss my domestic arrangemen•
with him. He is a moralist through and through, by nature and conv•
tion. He has already questioned me about my household today.

ANNA. Heavens, this man really wants to become an epicurean?!

KEITH. It's a complete self-contradiction. Since I've known him he has do•
nothing but sacrifice himself, without ever being aware that he has t•
souls in his breast.

ANNA. That too! I find one is too many. — But isn't his name Scholz?

KEITH. One of his souls is named Ernst Scholz and the other is named Count Trautenau.

ANNA. Then I must decline! I won't have anything to do with people who can't come to an understanding with themselves.

KEITH. He's a paragon of understanding. The world has no more pleasures to offer him, unless he is to start again from the bottom.

ANNA. But man should always climb higher!

KEITH. What's upsetting you so?

ANNA. You want to make a match between me and this horrible monster!

KEITH. He's as gentle as a lamb.

ANNA. Thank you so much! I will not let disaster personified into my boudoir!

KEITH. You don't understand me at all. I can't do without his confidence at the moment and so don't wish to expose myself to his censure. If he doesn't meet you, so much the better for me; I will not have to be afraid of his reproaches.

ANNA. Who can ever know where your calculations will lead!

KEITH. What did you think?

ANNA. I thought you wanted me as a whore for your friend.

KEITH. You can believe that of me?!

ANNA. You said just a moment ago that you use every mortal according to his talents. And no one would doubt for a moment that I have talents as a whore.

KEITH, *taking* ANNA *in his arms*. Anna — I am going to Paris tomorrow, not to see about the Bourse or to buy fireworks, but because I must breathe fresh air, because I must stretch out my arms, if I am not to lose the careful front I've put on here in Munich. Would I take you to Paris with me, Anna, if you weren't everything to me?! — — Do you know, Anna, not a night goes by that I do not dream of you with a diadem in your hair? If you asked me to get you a star out of the firmament, I wouldn't shrink back, I'd find ways and means.

ANNA. Use me as a whore! — You'll see if I don't yield a profit!

KEITH. And at this moment I have no thought in my head but for the concert gown that I'm going to have made for you at St. Hilaire's . . .

SASHA, *enters from the hall*. A Herr Sommersberg asks if he may see you.

KEITH. Have him come in. *To* ANNA, *describing the gown*. A silvery cascade of mauve silk and paillettes from shoulder to knee, so tightly laced and cut so low in front and back that the dress will look like a glistening jewel on your slender body!

SOMMERSBERG *has entered. Late thirties, deeply lined face, hair and beard unkempt and streaked with gray. A thick winter overcoat covers his shabby clothes. He wears torn kid gloves.*

SOMMERSBERG. I am the the author of *Songs of a Happy Man*. I don't look it.

KEITH. I once looked like that too!

SOMMERSBERG. I wouldn't have found the courage to come to you except that I've hardly eaten a thing in the last two days.

KEITH. That's happened to me hundreds of times. How can I help you?

SOMMERSBERG. A little something — for lunch . . .

KEITH. You don't think I'm capable of doing any more for you?

SOMMERSBERG. I'm an invalid.

KEITH. But half your life is still ahead of you!

SOMMERSBERG. I have thrown my life away in order to come up to the ex
pectations people had of me.

KEITH. You may still find a current to take you out to the open sea. — O
are you afraid?

SOMMERSBERG. I can't swim; and here in Munich resignation isn't hard.

KEITH. Come to our founders' party on Brienner Street two weeks from
today. You may make some very valuable contacts there. *Gives him
money.* Here are a hundred marks. Keep enough in reserve to buy your
self a dress suit for that evening.

SOMMERSBERG, *hesitatingly taking the money.* I have a feeling I'm deceiving
you . . .

KEITH. Don't deceive yourself! You are doing a good turn to the next poo
devil who comes to me.

SOMMERSBERG. Thank you, Herr Baron. *Exit.*

KEITH. You're very welcome! *After he shuts the door, taking* ANNA *in h
arms.* And now, my queen, we're off to Paris!

ACT THREE

*A garden room is visible, illuminated by electric lights; a wide glass do
on the right leads into the garden. The center door in the rear wall lea
into the dining room, where a meal is under way. When the door is ope
the upper end of the table is visible. At the left, a door with a curta
leads into the game room, through which there is also access to the dinir
room. Near this door, an upright piano. Downstage right, a lady's writir
table, downstage left, a settee, chairs, tables, etc. In the corner at the upp
right is a door which leads to the entrance hall.*

In the dining room a toast is being drunk. As the glasses clink, SOMMER
BERG, *in shabby evening clothes, and* KEITH, *in a full-dress suit, enter t
salon through the center door.*

KEITH, *closing the door behind him.* You've composed the telegram?

SOMMERSBERG, *paper in hand, reads.* "The founders of The Munich Fair
land Palace Company yesterday evening entertained prominent citizens
the gay city on the Isar at a lovely garden party held at the Marquis
Keith's villa on Brienner Street. A remarkable fireworks display ente
tained residents of the neighboring streets till after midnight. To th
project, which has begun under such favorable auspices, we wish
extend . . . ?

KEITH. Excellent! — Who can go to the telegraph office . . . ?

ᴏᴍᴍᴇʀsʙᴇʀɢ. Let me take care of it. After all the champagne I've had, a little fresh air will do me good.

ᴇxit sᴏᴍᴍᴇʀsʙᴇʀɢ *to the hall; at that moment enter* ᴇʀɴsᴛ sᴄʜᴏʟᴢ; *he is wearing a full-dress suit and an overcoat.*

ᴇɪᴛʜ. You've kept us waiting a long time!

ᴄʜᴏʟᴢ. And I've only come to tell you that I can't stay.

ᴇɪᴛʜ. I'm being made a laughing stock! Old Casimir has already left me in the lurch; but at least he sent a congratulatory telegram.

ᴄʜᴏʟᴢ. I don't belong among men! You complain that you are outside society; I am outside humanity!

ᴇɪᴛʜ. Don't you now have every pleasure a man can dream of?!

ᴄʜᴏʟᴢ. What pleasures! The riot of sensations I revel in makes me indistinguishable from a barbarian. True, I have learned to appreciate Rubens and Richard Wagner. The disaster which used to arouse my pity is now almost unbearable because of its ugliness. And so I've become an enthusiastic devotee of the artistic creations of dancers and acrobats. — If I had only progressed one step after all this! Because of my money I am *treated* like a human being. As soon as I want to *be* one I run up against invisible walls!

ᴇɪᴛʜ. If you envy lucky devils who take root wherever they can and then are blown away as soon as the wind changes, don't look to me for sympathy! The world is a cursedly sly beast, and it's not easy to conquer. But once you succeed, you are proof against any misfortune.

ʜᴏʟᴢ. If such phrases give you satisfaction, I can hope to gain nothing from your company. *Is about to leave.*

ᴇɪᴛʜ, *stops him.* They are not phrases! Today no misfortune can touch me. We know each other too well, misfortune and I. For me a misfortune is an opportunity, like anything else. Any ass can suffer misfortune; it takes skill to exploit it to one's advantage.

ʜᴏʟᴢ. You cling to the world like a whore to a pimp. You can't understand that a person can become as vile as carrion to himself if he exists for himself alone.

ᴇɪᴛʜ. Then in the name of all the fiends be satisfied with your godly way of life! Once you have this purgatory of earthly vice and joy behind you, you will look down like a Church Father on this poor wretch of a sinner.

ʜᴏʟᴢ. If only I had my human birthright! Better to crawl away into the wilderness like a beast than to have to apologize for my existence every step of the way! — — I can't stay here. — I met the Countess Werdenfels yesterday. — I have no idea what I did to offend her. I suppose I unconsciously adopted the tone I've become accustomed to use with our Simba.

ᴇɪᴛʜ. I've received more slaps from women than I have hairs on my head! But no one has ever laughed at me behind my back for it!

ʜᴏʟᴢ. I am a man without breeding! — And with a woman for whom I have the highest respect!

ᴇɪᴛʜ. A man like you, whose every step from earliest youth has led to a spiritual conflict, can become the master of his times and ruler of the world long after we others have become food for worms!

SCHOLZ. And then there's little Simba, who is playing the serving-maid he tonight! — The most practiced diplomat never had to deal with such delicate situation!

KEITH. Simba doesn't know you!

SCHOLZ. I'm not afraid that Simba will be too friendly with me; I am afra of offending Simba by ignoring her for no reason.

KEITH. How could you offend Simba that way! Simba understands class d tinctions a hundred times better than you.

SCHOLZ. I've learned all about class distinctions! God knows, they are th fetters which reveal man's utter weakness in its most extreme form!

KEITH. Do you think I have no weakness to contend with? Even if n conduct is as correct as the course of the planets, even if I dress in th best clothes, it is as hard to change these plebeian hands as it is for a imbecile to become a model of intellect! With my gifts I shou have long ago enjoyed a better position in society, if not for my hand — Come, you would do better to leave your coat in the next room!

SCHOLZ. Leave me alone! I can't have a single calm word with the counte today.

KEITH. Then stay with the two divorcées; they're going through confli similar to yours.

SCHOLZ. With both of them?!

KEITH. Neither over twenty-five, perfect beauties, ancient Nordic stoc and so ultra-modern in their principles I feel like an old flintlock I comparison.

SCHOLZ. It seems to me that I too am not very far from being a moder SCHOLZ *goes into the game room;* KEITH *wishes to follow him, but at th moment* SARANIEFF *enters from the hall.*

SARANIEFF. Tell me, is there still something to eat?

KEITH. Please leave your coat outside! — I haven't eaten a thing all day.

SARANIEFF. It's not so easy to steal it in here. I have to ask you somethin very important first.

SARANIEFF *hangs his hat and ulster in the hall; meanwhile* SASHA, *in fro coat and satin breeches, comes out of the game room with a cooler full champagne and is about to go into the dining room.*

KEITH. When you set off the fireworks later, Sasha, be careful of the I mortar. It's loaded with all the fires of hell!

SASHA. I ain't afraid, Herr Baron! *Exit into the dining room, closing t door behind him.*

SARANIEFF, *comes back from the hall.* Do you have any money?

KEITH. But you just sold a picture! Why do you think I sent my friend you!

SARANIEFF. What could I do with that dried-out lemon. You've alrea stripped him to his shirt. He has to wait three days before he can p me a cent.

KEITH, *gives him a note.* Here are a thousand marks.

SIMBA *a typical Munich girl, with fresh coloring, a light step, luxuriant r hair, in a tasteful black dress with a white pinafore, comes out of the dini room with a tray of half-empty wine glasses.*

SIMBA. The Councillor'd like to propose another toast to the Herr Baron.

KEITH *takes one of the glasses from the tray and steps through the open door to the table. Exit* SIMBA *into the game room.*

KEITH. Ladies and gentlemen! Tonight's festivities mark the beginning of an era for Munich which will eclipse everything that has gone before. We are creating an art center in which all the arts of the world will find a welcome home. If our project has occasioned general astonishment, you must remember that only what is truly astounding has ever been crowned with great success. I empty my glass to the vital principle which has pre-ordained Munich a city of the arts, to Munich's good citizens and her beautiful women.

As the glasses are still clinking, SASHA *comes out of the dining room, closes the door behind him, and goes into the game room. —* SIMBA *comes out of the game room with a platter of cheese covered with a glass bell and is about to go into the dining room.*

RARANIEFF, *stopping her.* Simba! Have you been struck blind?! Can't you see, Simba, that your Epicurean is about to escape from your toils and be taken in by the countess from Perusa Street?!

SIMBA. Why are you staying out here? — Go ahead, sit down at the table with the others!

RARANIEFF. Me sit down with the Caryatids! — Simba! Do you want all the lovely money your Epicurean has in his pocket to be gobbled up by the insane Marquis of Keith?!

SIMBA. Oh, leave me be! I got to wait on table!

RARANIEFF. The Caryatids don't need any more cheese! Let them wipe their mouths and have done! *Puts the cheese platter on the table and takes* SIMBA *on his lap.* Simba! Don't you have any feelings for me any more?! Am I to beg twenty-mark pieces from the Marquis amid wailing and gnashing of teeth when you can draw thousand-mark notes fresh from their source?!

SIMBA. Thanks a lot! Never has anyone in the world plagued me like this Epicurean with his compassion, his stupid compassion! He's trying to convince me that I'm a martyr of civilization! How do you like that?! Me, a martyr of civilization! I said to him: Tell that to your society ladies, I said. They like it when you think they're martyrs of civilization because otherwise they're nothing at all! If I drink champagne and have a wonderful time, I'm supposed to be a martyr of civilization!

RARANIEFF. Simba! If I were a woman with your qualities the Epicurean would have to pay for every soulful look with an ancestral castle!

SIMBA. Well, that's how he talks! He asks me why he's a man. As if there aren't enough *spooks* in the world! Do you hear me asking people why I'm a girl?!

RARANIEFF. And you also don't ask us to toss away fifty millions on some confounded pet idea!

SIMBA. Oh my, the sad, sad millions! You know, I've seen the Epicurean smile just once in all the time I've known him. I told him, the Epicurean, that he had to learn to ride a bicycle. So he learned. So we cycled to Schleisheim, and while we were in the woods such a storm broke that

I honestly thought the world was coming to an end. So then, for the
first time since I met him, he started to laugh. Heavens, how he laughed!
Well, says I, now you're a real epicurean. At every thunderbolt he
laughed. The more it thundered and lightninged, the more he laughed
like a fool! — Hey, don't stand under the tree, says I, it'll be struck by
lightning! — No lightning will strike me, says he, and laughs and laughs.

SARANIEFF. Simba! Simba! You could have become an Imperial countess!

SIMBA. Thanks a lot! A Social Democrat, that's what I could have become!
Improving the world, humanitarianism, those are his specialties. No, I'll
tell you something, I'm not right for the Social Democrats. They're too
moralistic for me! If they ever get into power, that's the end of champagne suppers. — Tell me, have you seen my sweetheart?

SARANIEFF. Have I seen your sweetheart? *I'm* your sweetheart!

SIMBA. Anybody might claim the honor! — You know, I have to watch that
he doesn't get tipsy, or the Marquis won't hire him for the new Fairyland Palace.

      SOMMERSBERG *enters from the hall.*

SIMBA. Here he is! Where in the world have you been all this time?

SOMMERSBERG. I've sent a telegram off to the papers.

SARANIEFF. The graves are opening up! Sommersberg! Aren't you ashamed
to rise from the dead in order to become the secretary of this Fairyland
Palace?!

SOMMERSBERG, *indicating* SIMBA. This angel has restored me to the world.

SIMBA. Oh, go on, lovey! — He comes to me and asks me where he can
get money. — Oh, says I, go straight to the Marquis of Keith; if he
don't have any, you won't find a red cent in the whole city of Munich!

RASPE, *in extremely elegant evening clothes, a small chain with an Order on
his breast, comes out of the game room.* Simba, it's downright scandalous
of you to make the whole Fairyland Palace Company wait for its cheese!

SIMBA, *seizes the cheese platter.* Saints alive — I'm comin' right away!

SARANIEFF. Why don't you stay with the old hags you were hired to amuse!

SIMBA, *taking* RASPE's *arm.* Leave the lad in peace! — You'd be tickled
pink, both of you, if you was as handsome as him!

SARANIEFF. Simba — you're a born whore!

SIMBA. What am I?

SARANIEFF. You're a born whore!

SIMBA. Say that again?

SARANIEFF. You're a born whore!!

SIMBA. No, I'm not a born whore. I'm a born cheese-scoop. *Exit with*
RASPE *into the game room.*

SOMMERSBERG. I even dictate her love letters.

SARANIEFF. Then it's you I have to thank for destroying my castles in the
air!

      SASHA *comes out of the game room with a glowing lantern.*

SARANIEFF. For God's sake, are you decked out! You want to marry a
countess here too?

SASHA. I'm goin' to set off the fireworks in the garden now. When I light that big mortar, you'll see something! The Marquis says it's loaded with all the fires of hell. — *Exit into the garden.*

SARANIEFF. His master is afraid he might go up in flames if he set off the fireworks himself! — Dame Fortune is very wise not to let him get the upper hand! — Once he's in the saddle he rides anything so hard not a shred of flesh is left on its bones! — *As the center door opens and the guests leave the dining room.* Come, Sommersberg! Now we will have our Simba dish us up a Lucullan feast!

The guests stream into the salon; first, RASPE *between* FRAU COUNCILLOR OSTERMEIER *and* FRAU KRENTZL; *then* KEITH, *with* OSTERMEIER, KRENTZL, *and* GRANDAUER; *then* ZAMRIAKI *with* BARONESS VON ROSENKRON *and* BARONESS VON TOTLEBEN; *finally,* SCHOLZ *and* ANNA. — SARANIEFF *and* SOMMERSBERG *take places at the table in the dining room.*

RASPE. Will the esteemed ladies join me in a cup of exquisite coffee?

FRAU OSTERMEIER. My word, a gracious cavalier like you isn't to be found in all South Germany!

FRAU KRENTZL. Our noblemen of the Royal Horse could take an example from you!

RASPE. I give my word of honor that this is the happiest moment of my life. — *Exit with the two ladies into the game room.*

OSTERMEIER, *to* KEITH. Say, it was really nice of old Casimir to send us a congratulatory telegram. You know, my friend, old Casimir is a very cautious man!

KEITH. No matter! No matter! At the first general meeting we will have him in our midst. — Would you gentlemen care for a cup of coffee?

Exeunt OSTERMEIER, KRENTZL, *and* GRANDAUER *into the game room.*

BARONESS V. ROSENKRON, *to* KEITH, *who wishes to follow the other men.* Promise me, Marquis, that you'll let me study to be a dancer for the Fairyland Palace.

BARONESS V. TOTLEBEN. And me a trick-rider!

KEITH. I swear to you, my lovely deities, that we won't open the Fairyland Palace without you! — What's the matter with you, Zamriaki? You're as white as a corpse . . .

ZAMRIAKI, *a slender short conservatory musician with long black wavy hair, carefully parted in the middle; speaks with a Polish accent.* Day and night I am working on my symphony. — *Taking* KEITH *to one side.* Permit, Marquis, I wish to ask, please, for an advance of twenty marks on the wages of conductor of the Fairyland Palace Orchestra.

KEITH. With the greatest of pleasure. *Gives him money.* Couldn't you give us a preview of your new symphony soon at one of my Fairyland Palace concerts?

ZAMRIAKI. I will play the Scherzo. The Scherzo will have great success.

BARONESS V. ROSENKRON, *at the glass door to the garden.* My word, a sea of lights! Look, Martha! — Come, Zamriaki, escort us into the garden!

ZAMRIAKI. I come at once, ladies! At once. *Exit into the garden with* BARONESS V. ROSENKRON *and* BARONESS V. TOTLEBEN.

KEITH, *following them.* Good heavens, children, stay away from the big mortar! It's loaded with my loveliest rockets!

Exit into the garden. SIMBA *shuts the center door from the dining-room side.* — ANNA *and* SCHOLZ *remain alone in the salon.*

ANNA. I haven't the slightest idea what I could have taken amiss. Has this tactlessness of which you speak ever come over you with any other lady?

SCHOLZ. Absolutely not. But, you see, I am as happy as a person who's been in a dungeon since his earliest childhood and for the first time in his life breathes free air. That is why I'm so uncertain of myself at every step I take; I'm afraid of losing my happiness.

ANNA. I imagine it must be fascinating to live one's life in the dark, with one's eyes shut!

SCHOLZ. You see, Countess, if I could succeed in exchanging my existence for one which works for the common good, I would not be able to thank my Creator enough.

ANNA. I thought you wanted to train yourself as an epicurean here in Munich?

SCHOLZ. My training as an epicurean is only a means to the end. I give you my most earnest assurance of that! Don't think I'm a hypocrite because of that! — Oh, there's so much good left to fight for in the world! I will soon find a place for myself. As the blows rain down on me, my skin will become more precious to me, though I've found it such a burden up to now. And I am certain of one thing: If I ever succeed in placing myself at the service of my fellow men, I shall never, never claim any credit for it! Whether my path leads me up or leads me down, I want to belong to that terrible, pitiless race of men who care only for their self-preservation!

ANNA. Perhaps it's always happened that famous people became famous because they couldn't stand being with us ordinary run-of-the-mill creatures!

SCHOLZ. But you do not understand, Countess. — As soon as I have found my proper sphere, I shall be the most unassuming, gracious company. I've already begun by learning how to bicycle. I was as pleased as though I hadn't looked at the world since the earliest days of my childhood. Every tree, every bit of water, the hills, the sky — all were like a great revelation of which I once had a presentiment in another life. — May I take you cycling some day?

ANNA. Is tomorrow morning at seven all right for you? Or aren't you fond of getting up early?

SCHOLZ. Tomorrow morning at seven! I see my life spread out before me like a never-ending spring landscape!

ANNA. But don't keep me waiting!

ZAMRIAKI, BARONESS V. ROSENKRON, *and* BARONESS V. TOTLEBEN *come back from the garden.* — SIMBA *comes out of the game room.*

BARONESS V. ROSENKRON. Oh, it's cold! — Martha, we'll have to take our shawls next time we go out. Play us a cancan, Zamriaki! — *To* SCHOLZ. Can you do the cancan?

SCHOLZ. I regret that I cannot, madam.

BARONESS V. ROSENKRON, *to* BARONESS V. TOTLEBEN. Then we'll dance with each other!

ZAMRIAKI *has sat down at the piano and struck up a waltz.*

BARONESS V. ROSENKRON. Do you call that a cancan, Maestro?!

ANNA, *to* SIMBA. You can do the waltz, can't you?

SIMBA. If madam wishes . . .

ANNA. Come!

BARONESS V. ROSENKRON, BARONESS V. TOTLEBEN, ANNA, *and* SIMBA *dance a waltz.*

BARONESS V. ROSENKRON. Faster tempo, please!

KEITH *comes back from the garden and turns out all but a few of the electric lights, so that the salon is dimly lit.*

ZAMRIAKI, *breaking off his playing with annoyance.* With each beat I am coming closer to mine symphony!

BARONESS V. TOTLEBEN. Why is it dark all of a sudden?

KEITH. So that my rockets will be more impressive! — *Opens the door to the game room.* I should like to ask you, ladies and gentlemen . . .

RASPE, HERR *and* FRAU OSTERMEIER *and* HERR *and* FRAU KRENTZL *enter the salon.* — *Exit* SIMBA.

KEITH. I am pleased to be able to inform you that in the course of the next few weeks the first of our great Fairyland Palace concerts will take place. They will be excellent as advance publicity. Countess Werdenfels will introduce several songs of recent composition, while our conductor, Herr Zamriaki, will personally direct the playing of several excerpts from his symphonic poem "The Wisdom of the Brahmans."

General expressions of approval. In the garden a rocket rises hissing into the air and throws a reddish glow into the salon. KEITH *turns off all the lights and opens the glass door.*

KEITH. Into the garden, ladies and gentlemen! Into the garden, if you want to see something!

A second rocket goes up as the guests leave the salon. — KEITH, *who wishes to follow them, is held back by* ANNA. — *The stage remains dark.*

ANNA. Why did you announce that I would take part in your Fairyland Palace concert?!

KEITH. If you wait until your teacher pronounces you ready to appear in public you'll get old and gray without ever singing at all. — *Throws himself into a chair.* At last, at last, the precarious tight-rope performance is coming to an end! I had to dissipate my energy for ten years in the effort to keep my balance. — From now on the way is up!

ANNA. Where am I supposed to get the cheek to appear before the Munich public with my so-called singing?!

KEITH. Weren't you going to be the best Wagnerian soprano in Germany in two years?

ANNA. I said that as a joke.

KEITH. I couldn't know that!

ANNA. Other concerts are prepared months ahead!

KEITH. I have not denied myself thousands of times in my life in order to model myself after others. Those who don't like your singing will be intoxicated by your brilliant Paris concert gown.

ANNA. If only the others looked at me with your eyes!

KEITH. I'll make them use the right glasses!

ANNA. You see and hear fantastic day-dreams whenever you look at me. You overrate my appearance as much as you do my art.

KEITH, *jumping up.* I have never been suspected of overrating women, but I knew you for what you were at first sight! Is is any wonder, when I searched for you for ten years on two continents! You might have met me several times in the past, but you were either in the clutches of a bandit like myself, or I was reduced to such a state that there was no practical advantage to appearing in your luminous circle.

ANNA. If you are losing your mind out of love for me, is that any reason for me to heap the scorn of all Munich on myself?

KEITH. Other women have heaped worse on themselves for my sake!

ANNA. But I'm not infatuated with you!

KEITH. They all say that! Submit to your inevitable good fortune. I will inspire you with the necessary naiveté for your first appearance — even if I have to drive you on with a loaded revolver!

ANNA. If you push me around like that everything will soon be over between us!

KEITH. Place your confidence in the fact that I am a man who takes life damned seriously! Although I like to bathe in champagne, I can, unlike most people, deny myself all pleasure if necessary. No hour of my existence is bearable unless I come closer to my goal!

ANNA. It's high time you reached your goal!

KEITH. Anna, do you really think I would arrange the Fairyland Palace concert if I were not absolutely sure you would enjoy the most brilliant triumph?! — Let me tell you something: I am a man of *faith* . . .

In the garden a rocket goes up with a hissing sound.

KEITH. . . . I have an unshaken faith that we are rewarded in this world for our efforts and sacrifices!

ANNA. You need that faith, to wear yourself out as you do!

KEITH. If we aren't, our children will be!

ANNA. You haven't any yet!

KEITH. You will give them to me, Anna — children with my mind, with bodies that radiate good health, and with aristocratic hands. And I will build you a home fit for a queen, as a woman of your stamp deserves! And I will place at your side a consort who has the power to gratify every wish uttered by your great dark eyes! *He kisses her passionately. In the garden some fireworks are set off, bathing the pair in a lurid glow for a moment.*

KEITH. — — Go into the garden. The Caryatids are panting for the privilege of kneeling before our Divinity!

ANNA. Aren't you coming too?

KEITH, *turns on two of the electric lights, so that the salon is dimly lit.* I'll just write a brief newspaper notice about our concert. The notice has to appear in tomorrow morning's papers. In it I shall congratulate you in advance on your extraordinary triumph.

Exit ANNA *into the garden.* KEITH *sits down at the table and jots down a few words.* — MOLLY GRIESINGER, *a colorful shawl on her head, hurriedly enters from the hall, greatly agitated and provoked.*

MOLLY. I have to speak to you for just a minute.

KEITH. As long as you want, my dear child; you don't disturb me in the least. I told you you wouldn't be able to stick it out alone at home.

MOLLY. I pray to heaven a dreadful disaster overtakes us! It's the only thing that will save us!

KEITH. But why don't you come with me when I ask you!?

MOLLY, *shuddering.* To your friends?!

KEITH. The people here are the business we are both living on. But you can't stand it if I'm here with my thoughts and not with you.

MOLLY. Does that surprise you?! — You know, when you're with these people you're an entirely different person; you're someone I never knew, never loved, would never have followed so much as one step, let alone have given up my home, family, happiness, all. — You're so good, so wonderful, so dear! — But with these people — as far as I'm concerned — you're worse than dead!

KEITH. Go home and dress up a bit; Sasha will accompany you. You *must not* be alone tonight.

MOLLY. I'm just in the mood for getting dolled up. Your behavior upsets me; I feel as though the world were going to end tomorrow. I have the feeling I must do *something*, no matter what, to keep off the horrors in store for us.

KEITH. Since yesterday I draw a yearly salary of one hundred thousand marks. You need no longer fear that we're going to die of hunger.

MOLLY. Don't joke! You're sinning against me! I can hardly bring myself to express what I fear!

KEITH. Well, then, tell me what I can do to calm you. I'll do it at once.

MOLLY. Come with me! Come out of this murderers' den, where they are all intent on your ruin. It's true, I've complained about you to people; but I did it because I couldn't look on at your childish delusions any longer. You're so thick. Yes, you are! You let yourself be taken in by the lowest, most ordinary swindlers and you obligingly let them cut your head off!

KEITH. It is better, my child, to suffer injustice than to be unjust.

MOLLY. Oh, if you only knew! But they take care that your eyes are not opened. They flatter you by telling you that you are heaven knows what miracle of cleverness and diplomacy! Because your vanity doesn't aim at anything higher! And all the time they are calmly and cold-bloodedly putting the rope around your neck!

KEITH. What terrible thing are you afraid of?

MOLLY, *whimpering.* I can't say it! I can't put it into words!

KEITH. Please say it; then you'll laugh about it.

MOLLY. I'm afraid that . . . I'm afraid . . . *A muffled report sounds from the garden;* MOLLY *cries out and falls to her knees.*

KEITH, *helping her up.* That was the big mortar. — — You must calm yourself! — Come, have a couple of glasses of champagne; then we'll both go and watch the fireworks . . .

MOLLY. Those fireworks have been burning me up for two weeks now! — You were in Paris! — Who were you with in Paris! — I swear to you by all that's holy, I will forget how I trembled for you, I will forget how I suffered, if you come with me now!

KEITH, *kisses her.* Poor creature!

MOLLY. A crust to a beggar. — Yes, yes, I'm going now . . .

KEITH. You're staying here; what are you thinking of! — Dry your tears! Someone is coming up from the garden . . .

MOLLY, *throws her arms around him passionately and kisses him several times.* — You're so dear! — So wonderful! — So good! — *She frees herself, smiling.* It just happens that I wanted to see you once with your friends. You know I'm sometimes a little . . . *She rotates her fist in front of her forehead.*

KEITH, *wants to keep her back.* You're staying here, girl . . . !

MOLLY *bursts out through the hall door.* SCHOLZ *enters from the garden through the glass door, limping and holding his knee.*

SCHOLZ, *very pleased.* Please don't be alarmed! — Turn out the light, so that they can't see me from outside. No one has noticed it. *He drags himself to a chair, into which he lowers himself.*

KEITH. What's the matter with you?

SCHOLZ. Turn out the light first. — It's really nothing. The big mortar exploded! A piece of it hit me in the kneecap!

KEITH, *has turned out the lights; the stage is dark.* It would happen to you!

SCHOLZ, *in a blissful voice.* The pains are already beginning to subside. — Believe me, I am the most fortunate creature under the sun! I will of course not be able to keep my appointment to go cycling with the Countess Werdenfels tomorrow morning. But what does that matter! *Jubilantly.* I have vanquished the evil spirits; happiness lies before me; I belong to life! From this day forward I am another man . . .

A rocket goes off in the garden and bathes SCHOLZ's *features in a lurid glow.*

KEITH. For God's sake— I hardly recognized you just now!

SCHOLZ, *jumps up from the chair, and hops exultantly about the room on one foot while holding the other knee with both hands.* For ten years I considered myself an outcast! A man outlawed! To think that it was all my imagination! Everything was my imagination! Nothing but imagination!

ACT FOUR

In the COUNTESS WERDENFELS' *garden room a number of huge laurel wreaths are lying about on arm chairs; there is an impressive bouquet of flowers in a vase on the table.* ANNA, COUNTESS WERDENFELS, *wearing an attractive morning costume, is discovered in conversation with* POLICE INSPECTOR RASPE *and* HERMANN CASIMIR. *It is forenoon.*

ANNA, *a sheet of colored notepaper in her hand, to* HERMANN. Thank you, my young friend, for the pretty verses you composed for me last night after our first Fairyland Palace concert. And thank you for your splendid flowers. — *To* RASPE. But it's strange that you, sir, should come to me this morning with such serious rumors about your friend and benefactor.

RASPE. The Marquis of Keith is neither my friend nor my benefactor. Two years ago I asked him to testify at my trial as a psychiatric expert. He could have saved me a year and a half in prison. But instead he streaked off to America as fast as a greyhound, with a fifteen-year-old kid !

SIMBA, *wearing a tasteful maid's uniform, enters from the hall and hands* ANNA *a card.*

SIMBA. The gentleman asks if he may see you.

ANNA, *to* HERMANN. Heavens, your father!

HERMANN, *frightened, looking at* RASPE. How could my father know I was here!

RASPE. He didn't find out anything from me.

ANNA, *lifts the curtain to the game room.* Go in there. I'll send him away at once.

Exit HERMANN *into the game room.*

RASPE. Then it's best to pay my respects and leave at once.

ANNA. Yes, please do.

RASPE, *bowing.* Madam! *Exit.*

ANNA, *to* SIMBA. Ask the gentleman to come in.

SIMBA *shows in* CONSUL CASIMIR, *followed by a flunkey from whom he has taken a bouquet; exit* SIMBA.

CONSUL CASIMIR, *handing her the flowers.* Allow me, madam, to offer you my sincerest congratulations on your triumph of last evening. Your debut has taken all Munich by storm; but you cannot have made a deeper impression on any of your audience than you did on me.

ANNA. Even so, I am overwhelmed by your coming to tell me so in person.

CASIMIR. Do you have a moment? — I wish to discuss a purely practical matter.

ANNA, *offers him a seat.* I'm sure you must be on the wrong track.

CASIMIR, *after both have sat down.* We shall see in a moment. — I wanted to ask you to be my wife.

ANNA. — How am I to understand this?

CASIMIR. That is why I am here, for us to come to an understanding about it. Permit me to tell you from the outset that you would of course have to give up the attractive artistic career which you embarked on last evening.

ANNA. You've surely not given yourself time to consider this step carefully.

CASIMIR. At my age, madam, one takes no ill-considered step. Later, yes — or earlier. Will you let me know what other scruples present themselves to you.

ANNA. You know of course that I can't answer such a proposal?

CASIMIR. Of course I know. I am, however, speaking for the time, not too far off, when you will be absolutely free to make a decision about your-self and your future.

ANNA. At this moment I can't imagine the possibility of such a thing.

CASIMIR. Today, you see, I am the most respected man in Munich, but to-morrow I might be under lock and key. I would not find fault with my best friend if he doubted whether he should stick by me in such a re-versal of fortune.

ANNA. Wouldn't you find fault with your wife if she had doubts?

CASIMIR. My wife, certainly; my mistress, never. I do not wish an answer from you at present. I speak only in case you are left high and dry or circumstances arise which release you from your obligations; to be brief and to the point, in case you do not know where to turn next.

ANNA. And then you would make me your wife?

CASIMIR. I suppose it seems pretty insane to you; that is a tribute to your modesty. But in such a matter one has only one's self to hold to account. As you perhaps know, I have two small children at home, girls of three and six. And, as you can imagine, there are other considerations . . . as for you, I take all responsibility upon myself that you will not dis-appoint my expectations, — even in spite of yourself.

ANNA. I admire your self-confidence.

CASIMIR. You may depend on me completely.

ANNA. But after a success like last night! — It seemed as though an entirely new spirit had come over the Munich public.

CASIMIR. Believe me, I sincerely envy the perspicacity of the founder of the Fairyland Palace. And by the way, I must pay you a particular compli-ment on the choice of your concert gown last night. You had such an aristocratic assurance that it showed off your person with the most telling effect that I was hardly able — I admit it — to follow your song recital with the attention it deserved.

ANNA. Please don't think I overrate the applause won by my artistic per-formance.

CASIMIR. I should certainly not blame you if you did; your teacher tells me, however, that a success like yours of last night has brought misfortune to many. And, also, please do not forget one thing: Where would the most celebrated songstress today be if rich men did not hold it their moral duty to listen to her with no hope of return. No matter how brilliant the fee may be in some cases, in reality the people always live on charity.

ANNA. I was quite stunned by the favorable reception the audience gave every number.

CASIMIR, *rising.* Till that man Zamriaki's unfortunate symphony. However, I haven't the slightest doubt that in time we will come to worship the noise produced by Herr Zamriaki as a divine artistic revelation. Let us allow the world its ways, hope for the best, and be prepared for the worst. — Allow me, madam, to wish you good day. *Exit.*

ANNA *clutches her temples with both hands, goes to the game room, lifts the curtain, and steps back.*

ANNA. Didn't even shut the door!

HERMANN CASIMIR *steps out of the game room.*

HERMANN. Could I ever have dreamed a person could go through such an experience!

ANNA. Go now, so that your father will find you at home.

HERMANN, *notices the second bouquet*. The flowers are his? — I seem to have inherited that from him. — But he doesn't feel the expense as much as I do.

ANNA. How do you come to have money for such crazy purchases!

HERMANN, *significantly*. From the Marquis of Keith.

ANNA. Please go now! You look tired. Did your drinking party last very late last night?

HERMANN. I helped to save the composer Zamriaki's life.

ANNA. Do you consider that a worthy occupation for yourself?

HERMANN. What do I have to do that's any better?

ANNA. It's quite nice of you to have a heart for unfortunate people; but you don't have to sit at the same table with them. Misfortune is contagious.

HERMANN, *significantly*. That's what the Marquis of Keith says.

ANNA. Go now! I beg you.

SIMBA enters from the hall and hands ANNA a card.

SIMBA. The gentleman asks if he may see you.

ANNA, *reading the card*. "Representative of the South German Concert Agency." — Tell him to come back in two weeks.

Exit SIMBA.

HERMANN. What answer will you give my father?

ANNA. This is too much! You're becoming insolent!

HERMANN. I'm going to London — even if I have to steal the money. My father won't have me to complain about any more.

ANNA. You're the one who'll benefit most.

HERMANN, *uneasily*. I owe it to my two little sisters. *Exit.*

ANNA, *ponders a moment, then calls*. Kathi!

SIMBA comes out of the dining room.

SIMBA. Madam?

ANNA. I want to dress.

A bell rings in the corridor.

SIMBA. At once, madam. *Goes to open the door.*

Exit ANNA into the game room. — Immediately afterward SIMBA shows in ERNST SCHOLZ; he walks with the aid of an elegant walking stick, limping because of his stiff knee, and he carries a large bunch of flowers.

ERNST SCHOLZ. I have not had an opportunity, my dear child, to thank you for your tactful, sensitive conduct the other evening at the garden party.

SIMBA, *formally*. Does the Baron wish to be announced to madam?

Enter KEITH from the hall, in a light-colored overcoat, a bundle of newspapers in his hand.

KEITH, *removing his overcoat*. It's the will of Heaven that I should find you here! *To SIMBA*. What are you still doing here?

SIMBA. Madam took me into her service as housemaid.

KEITH. You see, I've made your fortune. — Announce me!

SIMBA. Very good, Herr Baron. *Exit into the game room.*

KEITH. The morning papers have the most enthusiastic reviews of yeste
day's concert! *He sits down at the little table downstage left and lea
through the newspapers.*

SCHOLZ. Have you heard where your wife is staying?

KEITH. She's with her parents in Bückeburg. You suddenly disappeare
during the banquet last night?

SCHOLZ. I had the most urgent need to be alone. How is your wife?

KEITH. Thanks; her father is about to go bankrupt.

SCHOLZ. You surely can spare enough to protect her family from that e
tremity!

KEITH. Do you know what the concert yesterday cost me?

SCHOLZ. You take these things too lightly!

KEITH. You really would like me to help you hatch the eggs of eternity?

SCHOLZ. I would consider myself fortunate if I could transfer some of th
overflow of my sense of duty to you.

KEITH. Lord protect me from that! I need all the elasticity imaginable no
to make the most of this success.

SCHOLZ, *self-confidently*. I have you to thank for the fact that today I fa
life calmly and confidently. I therefore consider it my duty to speak t
you as frankly as you spoke to me two weeks ago.

KEITH. The only difference is that I have not asked for your advice.

SCHOLZ. As far as I am concerned, that is only another reason for comple
candor. Through my exaggerated zeal for duty I was responsible for th
death of twenty people; but you behave as though one had *absolute
no duties* toward one's fellow men. What is more, you like to play wit
people's lives!

KEITH. In my case they get away with just a few scratches.

SCHOLZ, *with increasing self-confidence*. That is your personal good fortun
But you do not realize that others have exactly the same claims to th
enjoyment of life as you do. And as for *morality*, the sphere in whic
mankind's greatest accomplishments are to be seen, you haven't th
slightest understanding of it.

KEITH. You remain true to your nature. — You come to Munich with th
express purpose of training yourself as an epicurean, but through som
oversight train yourself as a moralist.

SCHOLZ. By means of the variegated life of Munich I have come to a sel
evaluation which is modest yet all the more just. In these two weeks
have experienced such tremendous inner transformations that if yo
wished to listen to me I really could speak as a moralist.

KEITH, *irritably*. My good fortune galls you!

SCHOLZ. I don't believe in your good fortune! I am so unspeakably happ
that I could embrace the whole world, and I really and sincerely wis
you the same happiness. But you will never have it as long as you co
tinue to joke about the highest values of life in your puerile way. Ti
I came to Munich I appreciated only the *spiritual* side of the relatio
ship between men and women, and thought sensual gratification som

thing vulgar. It was really the other way around. But in all your life you have never valued a woman for anything higher than sensual gratification. As long as you make no concessions to the moral order (as I had to), all your good fortune stands on clay feet!

KEITH, *seriously.* It's really quite different. I'm indebted to the last two weeks for my *material* freedom and, as a result, am at last able to enjoy my life. You are indebted to the last two weeks for your *intellectual* freedom and are at last able to enjoy *your* life.

SCHOLZ. Except that all my pleasures are connected with the idea of becoming a useful member of human society.

KEITH, *jumping up.* Why does one have to become a useful member of human society?!

SCHOLZ. Because otherwise there is no justification for one's existence!

KEITH. I need no justification for my existence! I asked no one for my existence, and I deduce from that that I'm justified in existing according to my lights.

SCHOLZ. And so with the utmost calm you give your wife over to ruin, though she has shared all your dangers and hardships for three years!

KEITH. What can I do! My expenses are so steep I don't have a single penny left for my own use. I paid up my share of the founding capital with the first payment of my salary. For a moment I thought of appropriating the money that was given me for financing the preliminary work. But I can't do that. — Or would you advise me to?

SCHOLZ. I may be able to give you ten or twenty thousand marks if you can't help yourself any other way. It happens that just today I received a note from my steward for ten thousand marks. *Removes a note from his portfolio and hands it to* KEITH.

KEITH, *tears the paper out of his hand.* But please don't come to me tomorrow and tell me you want to have the money back!

SCHOLZ. I don't need it now. The remaining ten thousand has to be sent through my banker in Breslau.

ANNA, *in elegant street clothes, comes out of the game room.*

ANNA. Forgive me for making you wait, gentlemen.

SCHOLZ, *hands her his flowers.* I could not deny myself the pleasure, madam, of wishing you luck with all my heart on the first morning of your promising artistic career.

ANNA, *puts the flowers in a vase.* Thank you. In my excitement last night I completely forgot to ask you how your injuries are coming along.

SCHOLZ. Heaven knows, they're not worth talking about. My doctor says that in a week's time I can climb mountains if I like. What pained me, however, was the loud and scornful laughter that greeted Herr Zamriaki's symphony.

KEITH, *has sat down at the writing table.* I can do no more than give people a chance to show what they can do. Those who fail to make the grade are left by the wayside. I'll find plenty of conductors in Munich.

SCHOLZ. Didn't you yourself say that he was the greatest musical genius since Richard Wagner?

KEITH. I wouldn't call my own horse a nag! I have to be responsible fo
the accuracy of my accounts at every moment. *Rising.* I've just been a
the city council with the Caryatids. The question came up whether th
Fairyland Palace is something Munich needs. It was answered unan
mously in the affirmative. A city like Munich can hardly begin to drean
of all it needs!

SCHOLZ, *to* ANNA. I suppose madam has world-embracing plans to discus
with her fortunate impressario.

ANNA. No, thank you, we have nothing to discuss with each other. Are yo
leaving us already?

SCHOLZ. You will allow me to come again some time in the next few days

ANNA. Please do; you're always welcome.

> SCHOLZ *has shaken* KEITH's *hand. Exit.*

KEITH. The morning papers have very enthusiastic notices of your pe
formance yesterday.

ANNA. Have you heard where Molly is?

KEITH. She's with her parents in Bückeburg. She's floating in an ocean c
petit-bourgeois sentimentality.

ANNA. Next time we won't let ourselves get so frightened about her! Bu
you know, she really needed to prove how completely unnecessary she
to you!

KEITH. Thank God that to you overwhelming passion is a book seale
sevenfold. If a person who is passionately in love with you can't mak
you happy she wants at least to set fire to the roof over your head!

ANNA. Nevertheless you ought to inspire more confidence in your busines
projects! It's no fun sitting on a volcano day and night!

KEITH. Why do I have to hear moral lectures from all sides today?!

ANNA. Because you always act as though you need a sedative! You neve
rest. I've found that as soon as one is uncertain about choosing to d
one thing over another it's best to do *nothing at all*. It's only doin
things that lays one open to all kinds of unpleasantness. I do
little as I possibly can and have always been happy. You can blame n
body for distrusting you if you chase after your good fortune day an
night like a starving wolf.

KEITH. I can't help being insatiable.

ANNA. Sometimes there are people with loaded rifles sitting in the sleigl
and they go bang-bang.

KEITH. I am bullet-proof. I have two Spanish bullets from Cuba in n
body. And besides, I have the most inviolable guaranty of my goo
fortune.

ANNA. This is really the limit!

KEITH. At least the limit of the herd-mentality! — It must have bee
twenty years ago that young Trautenau and I, in short trousers, we
standing at the altar of the whitewashed village church. My father w
playing the organ. The village priest handed us each a picture with
biblical verse. Since then I've hardly seen the inside of a church, b
that verse at my confirmation has been fulfilled in ways that have amaze

me. And if an obstacle is placed in my path today I always smile scornfully as I think back to it: "We know that all things work together for good to them that love God."

NNA. "Them that love God"?! — You think you're capable of that love?!

EITH. As to *whether I love God,* I've tested all existing religions and in no religion have I found any difference between love of God and love of one's own well-being. Love of God is everywhere only a concentrated, symbolic way of expressing love of oneself.

SIMBA *enters from the hall.*

MBA. Will the Marquis please to come out a moment. Sasha's here.

EITH. Why doesn't the boy come in?

Enter SASHA *with a telegram.*

ASHA. I didn't know if I should or shouldn't, because the Baron said never to deliver a telegram in company.

EITH, *opens the telegram, crumples it into a ball and throws it down.* Damn it again! — My overcoat!

NNA. From Molly?

EITH. No! — I only hope to heaven not a soul finds out!

NNA. She isn't with her parents in Bückeburg?

EITH, *as* SASHA *helps him into his overcoat.* No!

NNA. But you just said . . .

EITH. Is it my fault if she isn't in Bückeburg?! — No sooner do I have a bit of success, then something happens to gum up the works! — *Exeunt* KEITH *and* SASHA.

MBA, *picks up the telegram and gives it to* ANNA. The Marquis has forgotten his telegram.

NNA. Do you know where Sasha is from?

MBA. Sasha's from the country. His mother's a housekeeper.

NNA. But then his name surely could not be Sasha?

MBA. Originally his name was Sepperl, but the Marquis christened him Sasha.

NNA. Bring me my hat.

A bell rings in the corridor.

MBA. At once, madam. *Goes to open the door.*

NNA, *reads the telegram*: ". . . Molly not here. Please inform by return wire if you have had any signs of Molly. Await word anxiously . . ."

SIMBA *returns.*

MBA. The Baron has forgotten his gloves.

NA. Which Baron?

MBA. Oh, I meant the Epicurean.

NA, *searching hastily.* Lord, where are those gloves . . . !

Enter ERNST SCHOLZ.

HOLZ. Permit me two more words, madam.

NA. I'm about to go out. *To* SIMBA. My hat, and quickly! *Exit* SIMBA.

HOLZ. My friend's presence prevented me from expressing . . .

NA. Perhaps you'd prefer to wait for a more suitable opportunity.

HOLZ. I hoped I could wait a few more days for your decision. But my feelings overpower me, Countess! To assure you that it is your happiness alone which I seek through this offer, let me confess that I am — unutterably — I love you.

ANNA. Well? And what might your offer be?

SCHOLZ. Until you reap the fruits of uncontested recognition as an artist, many obstacles will put themselves in your path . . .

ANNA. I know that, but I don't expect to sing any more.

SCHOLZ. You don't want to sing any more? How many unfortunate artists would give half their lives for your talent!

ANNA. You have nothing else to tell me?

SCHOLZ. I've offended you again without realizing it. You expected, of course, that I would offer you my hand . . .

ANNA. Isn't that what you wanted to do?

SCHOLZ. I wanted to ask you to be my *mistress*. — I could honor you as my wife no more highly than I would esteem the mistress in you. *From this point he speaks with the rude aggressive bearing of a madman.* Whether wife or mistress, I offer you my life, I offer you everything I possess. You know that it was only after the most complete self-conquest that I reconciled myself to the moral attitudes current here in Munich. If my happiness should be dashed to pieces by the conquest made so that I could share my fellow men's happiness, it would be *a revolting farce!*

ANNA. I thought all you wanted was to become a useful member of human society!

SCHOLZ. I dreamed about improving the world as a prisoner behind iron bars dreams about the snow on the mountains! Now I hope for only one thing, to make the woman I love so unutterably happy that she will never regret her choice.

ANNA. I'm sorry to have to tell you that I'm indifferent to you.

SCHOLZ. You're indifferent to me?! I've never had more proof of inclination from any woman than I've had from you!

ANNA. That's not my fault. Your friend described you to me as a philosopher who has no concern for reality.

SCHOLZ. It was reality that tore me away from my philosophy! I am not one of those who preach against earthly vanity all their lives yet when they are deaf and lame must be bludgeoned into accepting death!

ANNA. The Marquis of Keith is helped to overcome every mishap by his confirmation verse! He considers it an infallible magic formula before which police and bailiff take flight!

SCHOLZ. I do not lower myself to the point of believing in omens! If this adventurer is right, I received at my confirmation just as infallible a magic formula for misfortune. Our priest gave me the verse: "Many are called but few are chosen." — But that doesn't bother me! Even if I had the most certain proofs that I did not belong to the chosen, it would only strengthen me in my dauntless fight against my destiny!

ANNA. Please spare me your dauntless fight!

SCHOLZ. I swear to you that I would sooner give up my reason than allow myself to be convinced by that reason that certain people are shut off from all happiness at the very outset through no fault of their own!

NNA. Complain about that to the Marquis of Keith!

CHOLZ. I'm not complaining! The longer the hard school of misfortune holds out, the more intrepid becomes the mind's power of resistance. People like me can experience an enviable transformation. *My spirit is indestructible!*

NNA. I congratulate you!

CHOLZ. That is the source of my irresistible power! The less you feel for me the greater and more powerful becomes my love for you and the sooner do I see the moment when you will say: I fought against you with all the means at my command, but I love you!

NNA. Heaven protect me from that!!

HOLZ. Heaven will not protect you from that! If a man with my strength of will, who does not allow himself to be broken by any mishap, concentrates all his thought and endeavor on *one* design, there are only two possibilities: he reaches his goal or he loses his mind.

NNA. I think you're right.

HOLZ. I will run the risk! Everything depends on which is better able to resist, your lack of feeling or my mind. I am counting on the worst outcome and cast no glance behind me before I reach my goal; for if I cannot fashion a happy life out of the bliss which fills me at this moment, there is no hope left for me. Never again will the opportunity offer itself!

NA. I thank you with all my heart for reminding me of that! *She sits down at the writing table.*

HOLZ. For the last time the world lies before me in all its splendor!

NA, *writing a note.* That applies to me too! — *Calls.* Kathi! — *To herself.* The opportunity won't offer itself again to me either.

HOLZ, *suddenly coming to himself.* Why are you apprehensive, madam?! — Why are you apprehensive? You're mistaken, Countess! — You entertain a horrible suspicion . . .

NA. Haven't you noticed that you're keeping me? — *Calls.* Kathi!

HOLZ. I can't possibly leave you like this! Give me your assurance that you have no doubts about my sanity!

Enter SIMBA *with* ANNA'S *hat.*

NA. Where have you been so long?

IBA. I was scared to come in.

IOLZ. Simba, you of all people know that I'm in command of my senses . . .

IBA, *pushing him away.* Go on, don't talk so stupid!

NA. Please leave my maid alone. *To* SIMBA. Do you know Consul Casimir's address?

IOLZ, *suddenly petrified.* — — I bear the mark of Cain on my brow . . .

ACT FIVE

In the MARQUIS OF KEITH's *study all the doors are open. As* HERMANN CASIMIR *seats himself on the center table,* KEITH *calls into the living room.*

KEITH. Sasha! *As he gets no answer, he goes to the waiting room; to* HERMANN. Excuse me. *Calls into the waiting room.* Sasha! — *Comes down stage; to* HERMANN. So you're going to London with your father's consent. I can give you excellent recommendations to take to London. *Throws himself on the sofa.* First of all I recommend that you leave your German sentimentality at home. Social Democracy and Anarchism no longer create a stir in London. Let me tell you one more thing: The only proper way to use one's fellow men to one's advantage is by appealing to the good in them. Therein lies the art of being well-liked, the art of getting what one wants. The more you defraud your fellow men the more scrupulous you have to be that they have the right on their side. Never seek your advantage at the expense of a virtuous man, but always at the expense of scoundrels and blockheads. And now I bequeath you the philosopher's stone; the most splendid business in the world is morality. I haven't got to the point of going into the business myself but I would not be the Marquis of Keith if I passed it up altogether.
A bell rings in the corridor.

KEITH, *calls.* Sasha! — *Rising.* I'll box that rascal's ears. *He goes to the hall and comes back with* COUNCILLOR OSTERMEIER. You couldn't have come at a better time, my dear Herr Ostermeier . . .

OSTERMEIER. My colleagues on the Board of Directors have commissioned me, my friend . . .

KEITH. I have a plan to discuss with you which will multiply our receipts a hundredfold.

OSTERMEIER. Do you wish me to state at our general meeting that I was again unable to examine your account books?

KEITH. You're raving, dear Herr Ostermeir! — Won't you outline the matter in hand calmly and objectively?

OSTERMEIER. The matter is your account books, my friend.

KEITH, *irritably.* I work and slave for those bleary-eyed numbskulls . . .

OSTERMEIER. So he's right after all! *Turning to go.* At your service!

KEITH, *pulling open a drawer in the writing table.* Here, have yourself a time with account books! *Turning to* OSTERMEIER. Who's right after all?

OSTERMEIER. A certain Herr Raspe, a police inspector, who bet five bottles of Pommery at the American Bar last night that you don't keep any books.

KEITH, *standing on his dignity.* It's true, I do not keep books.

OSTERMEIER. Then let me see your notebook.

KEITH. How could I have had time to set up an office since the founding of the Company!

OSTERMEIER. Let me see your notebook.

KEITH, *standing on his dignity.* I have no notebook.

OSTERMEIER. Then let me see the deposit receipts which the bank gave you.

KEITH. Did I take your money in order to put it out at interest?!

OSTERMEIER. Don't excite yourself, my friend. If you have no books you must surely make notes of your expenditures somewhere. Any errand boy does that.

KEITH, *throws his memorandum book on the table.* Here is my memorandum book.

OSTERMEIER, *opens it up and reads.* "A silvery cascade of mauve silk and paillettes from shoulder to knee — " That's all there is!

KEITH. If, after I have won success after success, you want to put rocks in my path, you can count on it with absolute certainty that you will never see your money again, either in this world or the next!

OSTERMEIER. The Fairyland Palace shares are not in such a bad position, my friend. We'll see our money again. — At your service! *Wishes to go.*

KEITH, *holding him back.* You undermine the project with your snooping! Forgive me, sir; I'm excited because I feel toward the Fairyland Palace as a father does toward his child.

OSTERMEIER. Then you needn't have any more worries about your child. The Fairyland Palace is secured and will be built.

KEITH. Without me?

OSTERMEIER. If necessary, without you, my friend!

KEITH. You can't do that!

OSTERMEIER. You, at any rate, are the last person to stop us!

KEITH. That would be a low scoundrelly trick!

OSTERMEIER. Better yet! Because we won't let ourselves be cheated by you you call us cheats!

KEITH. If you think you're being cheated you should sue me for your money!

OSTERMEIER. Very nice idea, my friend, if we didn't belong to the Board of Directors!

KEITH. What are you thinking of! You sit on the Board of Directors in order to support me in my work.

OSTERMEIER. And that's why I've come to you; but you don't seem to be working at anything.

KEITH. My dear Herr Ostermeier, you cannot expect me as a man of honor to allow myself to be treated so abominably. Take over the business end; let me be the artistic manager of the project. I admit certain failings in my running of the business, but I let them pass because I was convinced that it was the last time and that after my position had been consolidated I would never be guilty of the slightest fault.

OSTERMEIER. You could have said this yesterday when I was here with the other gentlemen; but instead you chattered our ears off. Even today I might say: Let's try again — if you had at least shown yourself to be an honest man. But if we are always to hear falsehoods . . .

KEITH, *standing on his dignity.* Tell the gentlemen: I will build the Fairyland Palace as surely as the idea for it sprang from my brain. If you build it, however, — tell this to your gentlemen! — I will see that the Fairyland Palace together with the Board of Directors *and* the stockholders are blown to bits!

OSTERMEIER. I will give an accurate report, neighbor! You know, I don't like to give offense to a man's face, let alone throw him out on his . . . At your service! *Exit.*

KEITH, *staring after him.* . . . on his behind! I thought something was up. — — *To* HERMANN. Don't leave me alone now or I'm afraid I'll go to pieces and nothing will be left of me. — — — Is it possible? — — *With tears in his eyes.* After all those fireworks! — — Shall I be an outcast again, driven from country to country?! — — No! No! — I must not let myself be pushed to the wall!! — For the last time in my life the world lies before me in all its splendor! *Standing up very straight.* No! — I'm not tottering yet. On the contrary, I'll take a leap that will astound all Munich. Then, while the town's still shaking with amazement, I'll fall on its prostrate body to the sound of drums and trumpets and tear it limb from limb. Then we'll see who can get back on his feet first!

The COUNTESS WERDENFELS *enters.*

KEITH, *hurrying to her.* My queen . . .

ANNA, *to* HERMANN. Please leave us alone for a moment.

KEITH *shows* HERMANN *into the living room.*

KEITH, *shutting the door behind him.* You look so sure of yourself?

ANNA. That's possible. Since our Fairyland Palace concert I've had half a dozen proposals of marriage every day.

KEITH. That means damned little to me!

ANNA. But not to me.

KEITH, *scornfully.* Have you fallen in love with him?

ANNA. Of whom are you speaking?

KEITH. The Epicurean!

ANNA. You're making fun of me!

KEITH. Of whom are *you* speaking?!

ANNA, *indicating the living room.* His father.

KEITH. And you wish to talk about this with me?

ANNA. No, I only wanted to ask you if you've had any sign of Molly.

KEITH. No, but what about Casimir?

ANNA. What about Molly? — — You're keeping her disappearance a secret?

KEITH, *uneasily.* To be frank, I'm less afraid that a misfortune has overtaken her than that her disappearance might knock the ground out from under me. If that seems inhuman, I've made up for it by spending the last three nights at the telegraph office. — My offense to her consists in her never having heard an angry word from me since we've known each other. She is consumed by a longing for her petit-bourgeois world, where, brow pressed against brow, people live in humiliation, drudgery — and love. No free outlook, no free breath! Nothing but love! As much as possible and of the most common sort!

ANNA. If Molly can't be found, what then?

KEITH. I confidently expect that when my house has crashed about my ears she will return with a contrite smile, and say: "I won't ever do it again." — Her goal has been reached; I can pack up.

NNA. And what will become of me?

EITH. So far you've gained most from our project and I hope you will gain much more from it. You can lose nothing, because you've invested nothing.

NNA. Are you sure?!

EITH. — — Why, what . . . ?!

NNA. Yes, yes!

EITH. — What answer did you give him?

NNA. I wrote him that I couldn't give him an answer just yet.

EITH. You wrote him that?!

NNA. I wanted to discuss it with you first.

EITH, *seizes her by the wrist and pushes her away.* If it's only a matter of discussing it with me, — marry him!!

NNA. A person who is as scornful of feelings as you are can surely discuss purely practical matters calmly!

EITH. Let's not discuss my feelings! I'm furious because you have no more family pride, to be able to sell your birthright for a mess of pottage!

NNA. Anything different from you you consider a mess of pottage!

EITH. I know my weak points; but those men are domestic animals! One of them has a weak head, another a weak spine! Do you want to bring monsters into the world, who can't see before their eighth day?! — If all is over with me, I will gladly let you have whatever glowing spirit I imbued in you for you to use in your career. But if you hide from the artist's hard lot behind a moneybag you are worth no more than the grass that will grow on your grave!

NNA. — If you only had the slightest inkling of what has become of Molly!

EITH. Don't revile me! — *Calls.* Sasha!

NNA. If you insist that we part . . .

EITH. Of course I insist.

NNA. Then give me back my letters!

EITH, *scornfully.* Do you want to write your memoirs?

NNA. No, but they might fall into the wrong hands.

EITH, *jumping up.* Sasha!!

NNA. What do you want with Sasha? — I sent Sasha on an errand.

EITH. How do you come to do that?!

NNA. Because he came to me. I've already done so a number of times. If worst comes to worst the boy knows where he can earn something.

EITH, *sinks down into the chair at the writing table.* My Sasha! *Wipes a tear from his eye.* You haven't forgotten him either! — — If you leave the room now, Anna, I'll break down like an ox in the slaughterhouse. — Give me a reprieve!

NNA. I have no time to lose.

EITH. Only until I've become accustomed to doing without you, Anna! — I need mental balance now more than ever . . .

NNA. Will you give me back my letters?

KEITH. You're horrible! — But you're doing it out of pity! Yes, I should at least be able to curse you now that you're no longer my mistress.

ANNA. As long as you live you'll never learn to judge a woman rightly!

KEITH, *holding his head up proudly.* I will not renounce my faith, even on the rack! You're going in the direction of good fortune; that's human. You are still what you were to me.

ANNA. Then give me back my letters.

KEITH. No, my child! I shall keep your letters for myself. Otherwise one day when I am on my deathbed I'll wonder whether you were a phantom of my brain. *Kissing her hand.* Good luck!

ANNA. Even without you! *Exit.*

KEITH, *alone, wrenched by heart spasms.* — Ah! — Ah! — This is death! — *He staggers to the writing table, removes a handful of letters from a drawer and rushes toward the door.* Anna! Anna!

In the open door he is met by ERNST SCHOLZ. SCHOLZ *is walking without any difficulty, without a trace of his injury.*

KEITH, *starting back.* . . . I was just going to your hotel.

SCHOLZ. There's no point to that. I am leaving.

KEITH. Then give me the twenty thousand marks you promised me yesterday!

SCHOLZ. I shall give you no more money.

KEITH. The Caryatids are crushing me! They want to take my directorship away!

SCHOLZ. That confirms me in my resolution.

KEITH. It's only a matter of overcoming a temporary crisis!

SCHOLZ. My wealth is more important than you! My wealth guarantees the members of my family a lofty and unhampered position of power for all time! But you will never reach the point where you will do any good to anyone!

KEITH. You parasite, how do you have the cheek to accuse me of being good for nothing?!

SCHOLZ. Let's not quarrel! — I am finally making the great renunciation which many a man must succumb to in this life.

KEITH. What's that?

SCHOLZ. I have freed myself of my illusions.

KEITH, *scornfully.* Are you revelling again in the love of a lower-class girl?

SCHOLZ. I have freed myself of everything. — I am going into a private sanatorium.

KEITH, *crying out.* There's nothing more infamous than betraying yourself!

SCHOLZ. Your anger is very understandable. — In the last three days I've fought the most horrifying battle that can fall to the lot of an ordinary mortal.

KEITH. In order to crawl away in the end like a coward?! — As the victor, to renounce your worth as a human being?!

SCHOLZ, *irritably.* I'm not renouncing my worth as a human being! You have no reason either to insult me or to make fun of me! — If a man allows himself to be closed in by the restraints which I put on myself *against* his will, he may lose his worth as a human being. But in that case he is relatively happy; he is preserving his illusions. — A man who settles his account with reality coldly and dispassionately as I do forfeits neither the esteem nor the sympathy of his fellow men.

KEITH, *shrugs his shoulders.* I'd take a little more time to think it over.

SCHOLZ. I have thought it over very carefully. It is the last duty my destiny requires me to fulfil.

KEITH. Once you're in it's not so easy to come out.

SCHOLZ. If I had the slightest hope of ever coming out I wouldn't go in. The burden of renunciation which I laid on myself, the self-conquest and joyful hope which I was able to wrest from my soul — I undertook all this in order to change my lot. I no longer have any doubt, for which I bewail God, that I am different from other men!

KEITH, *very proudly.* Thank God, I have never doubted that I'm different from other men!

SCHOLZ, *very calmly.* Bewail God or thank God — till now I have considered you the most cunning of scoundrels! — I've given up that illusion too. A scoundrel has fortune on his side, as surely as an honest man keeps his good conscience even in an irrevocable mishap. You are no more fortunate than I am, but you don't know it. That's the frightful danger that hangs over you!

KEITH. There's no danger hanging over me except that I will have no money tomorrow!

SCHOLZ. For as long as you live you will have no money tomorrow! — I wish I could be sure you were safe from the disastrous consequences of your delusion. That's why I'm coming to you once more. I'm firmly convinced that the best thing for you is to accompany me.

KEITH, *suspiciously.* Where?

SCHOLZ. To the sanatorium.

KEITH. Give me the thirty thousand marks and I'll come along!

SCHOLZ. If you accompany me you will not need money any more. You'll find a more comfortable home than you've perhaps ever known. We'll keep a horse and carriage, play billiards . . .

KEITH, *embracing him.* Give me the thirty thousand marks!! Do you want me to prostrate myself before you? I may be arrested on the spot!

SCHOLZ. Has it gone so far?! — *Pushing him away.* I don't give sums like that to madmen!

KEITH, *shouts.* You're the madman!

SCHOLZ, *calmly.* I have come to my senses.

KEITH, *scornfully.* — If you want to go into a lunatic asylum because you've come to your senses, — go right ahead!

SCHOLZ. You're one of those who must be taken there by force!

KEITH. — I suppose you'll resume your title in the lunatic asylum?

SCHOLZ. Haven't you gone bankrupt on two continents in every way that bourgeois life permits?!

KEITH, *with venom.* If you consider it your moral duty to free the world of your superfluous existence you can find more radical means than going for drives and playing billiards!

SCHOLZ. I tried that a long time ago.

Frank Wedekind playing the title role in *The Marquis of Keith*. *Drawing by Baroness Lida von Wedell.*

KEITH, *shouts at him.* Then what are you still doing here?!

SCHOLZ, *gloomily.* I was unsuccessful in that as in everything else.

KEITH. Through some oversight, I suppose, you shot someone else!

SCHOLZ. They removed the bullets from between my shoulders, near th spinal column. — Today is the last time in your life that you will b offered a helping hand. What sort of experiences lie ahead of you yo know.

KEITH, *throws himself on his knees in front of him and clutches his hand* Give me the forty thousand marks and I am saved!

SCHOLZ. They won't save you from the penitentiary!

KEITH, *starting up in horror.* Quiet!!

SCHOLZ, *pleading.* Come with me and you will be safe. We grew up t gether; I don't see why we should not wait for the end together. Bou geois society judges you a criminal and throws you to all kinds of i human medieval tortures . . .

KEITH, *moaning.* If you don't want to help me, go, I beg you!

SCHOLZ, *tears in his eyes.* Don't turn your back on your only refuge! know that you are as little responsible for the choice of your lamentab lot as I am for mine.

KEITH. Go! Go!

SCHOLZ. Come. Come. — You will have in me a companion as gentle as lamb. It would be a dim ray of light in the nighttime of my life if could rescue my boyhood friend from his terrible fate.

KEITH. Go! I beg you!

SCHOLZ. — — Entrust yourself to my guidance from now on, as I wanted to entrust myself to you . . .

KEITH, *calls in despair.* Sasha! Sasha!

SCHOLZ. — — — Then don't forget where you have a friend to whom you will always be welcome. *Exit.*

KEITH, *crawls about, searching.* — — Molly! — — Molly! — — It's the first time in my life I've ever cried on my knees in front of a woman! — — *Suddenly hearing a sound in the living room.* There . . . ! There . . . ! *After he has opened the living-room door.* . . . Oh, it's you?

      HERMANN CASIMIR *comes out of the living room.*

KEITH. I can't ask you to stay here any longer. I am — not quite well. I have to — first — sleep on it, to be master of the situation again. — Go with . . . with . . .

      Heavy footsteps and many voices are heard on the front stairs.

KEITH. Listen . . . That noise! The uproar! — It means something not good . . .

HERMANN. Why don't you close the door?

KEITH. I can't! — I can't — It's her . . . !

A number of patrons from the Hofbräuhaus drag in MOLLY's *lifeless body. Water drips from her body, her clothing is in tatters. Her loosened hair covers her face.*

A BUTCHER'S HELPER. Well, here's the crook! — *To himself.* Right? — Sure! *To* KEITH. Look what we fished out! Look what we're bringin' you! Look, if you have the guts!

A PORTER. We pulled her outa the sewer! From under the iron grating! She was prob'ly in the water there almost a week!

A BAKERY WOMAN. And meanwhile that filthy tramp runs around with his shameless crowd! Six weeks he hasn't paid for's bread! Lets his poor wife go begging at all the shops for somethin' to eat! It would've melted a stone to see how she looked at the end!

KEITH, *retreating to the writing table as the crowd presses around him with the body.* I beg you, please calm yourselves!

THE BUTCHER'S HELPER. Oh shut your trap, you swindler! Or you'll get a tap on the nose from me that'll knock you off your feet! — Look over here! — Is it her or ain't it her?! — Look here, I said!

KEITH, *has grasped* HERMANN's *revolver behind him on the desk, where the* COUNTESS WERDENFELS *had left it lying earlier.* Don't touch me or I'll make use of this weapon!

THE BUTCHER'S HELPER. What's the yellowbelly sayin'?! — What's he sayin'?! — Will you give me the revolver?! — Ain't you done enough harm to *her,* you dog?! — Give it here, I said . . . !

The BUTCHER'S HELPER *grapples with* KEITH, *who succeeds in reaching the outside door, through which* CONSUL CASIMIR *enters at that moment.* HERMANN CASIMIR *has meanwhile approached the body; he and the* BAKERY WOMAN *carry it to the sofa.*

KEITH, *defending himself like a desperate man, calls.* Police! — Police! *Catches sight of* CASIMIR *and clings to him.* Save me, for God's sake! I'm **being lynched!**

CONSUL CASIMIR, *to the crowd.* Now look here, if this keeps up, you'll se
another side of me! — Leave that woman on the couch there! — Now
get out! — That's where they put the door, see! *Dragging forward h*
son, who wants to leave with the crowd. Wait a minute, sonny! You'r
going to take a nice lesson with you on your trip to London!

> *The people from the Hofbräuhaus have left the room.*

CASIMIR, *to* KEITH. I was about to invite you to leave Munich within twent
four hours; but now I think it would really be best for you if you le
on the next train.

KEITH, *still holding the revolver in his left hand.* I — I am not responsib
— for this disaster . . .

CASIMIR. You can arrange that to please yourself! But you *are* responsib
for forging my signature on a congratulatory telegram at your founder
party on Brienner Street.

KEITH. I can't leave . . .

CASIMIR, *gives him a paper.* Please sign this receipt. In it you vouch f
the fact that the sum of ten thousand marks owed you by the Counte
Werdenfels has been received from me.

> KEITH *goes to the writing table and signs.*

CASIMIR, *counting the money out of his wallet.* As your successor in th
directorship of the Fairyland Palace Company I am asking you in the i
terests of our project's success not to be seen in Munich again in th
near future!

KEITH *standing at the writing table, gives* CASIMIR *the note and mechanical*
receives the money.

CASIMIR, *pocketing the note.* Pleasant journey! — *To* HERMANN. Get goin

> HERMANN *slips out shyly.* CASIMIR *follows.*

KEITH, *the revolver in his left hand, the money in his right, takes sever*
steps toward the couch but shrinks back in horror. Then he irresolute
regards the revolver and the money in turn. — As he lays the revolv
behind him on the center table, with a grin. Life is a slippery bu
ness . . .

him

BY E. E. CUMMINGS

looking forward into the past or looking
backward into the future I
walk on the highest
hills and
I laugh
about
it
all
the way
ANNE BARTON

CHARACTERS

THREE WEIRDS
DOCTOR (*alias* THIRD MIDDLE-AGED MAN, SOAP BOX ORATOR, INTRUDER, PERSONAG
    PLAINCLOTHESMAN, QUESTIONING PASSENGER, MUSSOLINI, GENTLEMAN, BARKER
HIM (*alias* INTERLOCUTOR)
ME (*alias* PRINCESS ANANKAY)
TWO MIDDLE-AGED MEN
VIRGO
PORTER
WILL
BILL
TWO BLACK FIGURES
SIX MORE BLACK FIGURES
NINE PLAYERS
FRANKIE
ENGLISHMAN
COP
PASSENGER
ETHIOPIAN
TWO CENTURIONS
FOUR FAIRIES
FASCIST
MESSENGER
MULTITUDE OF SHAPES *among whom are distinguished* FOUR *plus several oth*
    individual voices
POLICEMAN
WAITER
BLOND GONZESSE
HEADWAITER
FAIRLY YOUNG WOMAN
OLDER WOMAN
ELDERLY WOMAN
YOUTHFUL WOMAN
VESTIAIRE
WHORES
EIGHT FREAKS (NINE-FOOT GIANT, QUEEN OF SERPENTS, HUMAN NEEDLE, MISSI
    LINK, TATTOOED MAN, SIX HUNDRED POUNDS OF PASSIONATE PULCHRITUD
    KING OF BORNEO, EIGHTEEN-INCH LADY)
NEWBORN BABE

ACT ONE

SCENE ONE

ENE: *A flat surface on which is painted a* DOCTOR *anaesthetizing a* WOMAN.
▪ *this picture there are two holes corresponding to the heads of the*
'hysician and of the patient, and through these holes protrude the living
:ads of a man and of a woman.
 Facing this picture, with their backs to the audience, three withered
male FIGURES *are rocking in rocking chairs and knitting.*

RST OR MIDDLE FIGURE. We called our hippopotamus It's Toasted.

COND OR FIGURE TO THE AUDIENCE'S RIGHT. I wish my husband didn't object
to them.

IIRD. Of course it's a bother to clean the cage every day.

COND. O I wouldn't mind doing that.

RST. Be sure to get one that can sing.

IIRD. Don't they all sing?

RST. O dear no. Some of them just whistle.

COND. I've heard they're very affectionate.

RST. I find them so.

IIRD. Did it take long to tame yours?

RST. Only a few days. Now he sits on my hand and doesn't bite me.

COND. How charming.

IIRD. Is it true they imitate policemen?

RST. My dear they imitate everybody.

COND. I'm afraid my husband wouldn't like that.

RST. What do you mean my dear?

COND. If ours imitated a policeman.

IIRD. Really? Why should he object?

COND. It would make him nervous I'm afraid—the idea of the thing.

RST. Your husband is a vegetarian?

COND. On the contrary my husband is a burglar.

RST. Oh, I see. *The* WOMAN's *eyes close and her head remains in the pic-*
ture; the DOCTOR's *head disappears from the picture leaving a hole. The*
three FIGURES *continue to rock and knit. Presently the* DOCTOR *himself*
enters with HIM.

CTOR, *to* HIM. Have a cigar. *Produces two, one of which* HIM *takes. Both*
men bite off and spit out the tips of their cigars. HIM, *producing matches,*
lights the DOCTOR's *and his own cigar.* And how are the three Miss
Weirds today?

ST FIGURE, *without looking up or turning, continues knitting and rocking.*
Very well indeed, thank you doctor.

COND, *ditto.* Fine weather, isn't it?

IRD, *ditto.* One really is glad to be alive.

DOCTOR. Speaking of dust, let me introduce a distinguished foreigner. M
Anybody, press flesh with the three Weird sisters; get used to Miss Sto
Miss Look and Miss Listen. HIM *doubtfully extends his hand in tl
general direction of the unnoticing rocking and knitting* FIGURES.
FIRST FIGURE, *snobbishly, to* SECOND. I don't think I ever heard the nam
To THIRD. Did you? *All three* FIGURES *shake their heads.*
HIM. Madam, I am very noble.
DOCTOR. "Anybody" is just his nomb D. ploom you know. My friend
strictly incog.
FIRST FIGURE, *stops knitting and rocking.* How romantic!
SECOND, *ditto.* How thrilling!
THIRD, *ditto.* Do tell us his real name!
HIM. My real name, ladies, is Everyman, Marquis de la Poussière.
FIRST FIGURE, *rising, turns; revealing a maskface.* Delighted, Marquis.
SECOND, *rising, turns; revealing a maskface identical with the* FIRST'S. E
chanted.
THIRD, *rising, turns; revealing a maskface identical with the* FIRST's *and t.
second's.* Overwhelmed.
DOCTOR. Well, guess we'll blow. I got some important business to atten
to. Bye bye, girls.
ALL THREE FIGURES, *in unison.* Goodbye doctor adieu marquis. *Turnin
they resume their rocking chairs and knitting. Exeunt* DOCTOR *and* HI
SECOND FIGURE. How often do you change the water?
FIRST. I only change it once a day but Mrs. Strong changes it twice a wee
THIRD. Has Mrs. Strong a hippopotamus?
FIRST. Two, my dear. That's where I got mine—they had kittens last M;
THIRD. I wish I'd known.
SECOND. I should have made my husband steal one for me.
FIRST. What a pity. She didn't know what to do with the other six, so s
gave them to a circus.
SECOND. They're darling when they're young, aren't they?
FIRST. Perfectly darling. *The* DOCTOR's *head reappears in the picture. T
woman's eyes continue closed.*
THIRD. But I suppose it's a nuisance until the little things become hou
broken.
FIRST. O you get used to that.

                              SCENE TWO

SCENE: *A room: three visible walls and an invisible wall. Of the visi
walls one, the wall to the audience's left, is solid. In the middle wall i:
door and in the wall to the audience's right a window.
Against the solid wall is a sofa on which lies a man's brown felt h
much the worse for wear. Under the window in the opposite wall is a ta
on which reposes a large box for cigarettes; and near the table are t*

airs in the less comfortable of which HIM *sits, back to the audience, writ-*
g in a notebook.

ME *(whose head appeared in the picture, preceding scene) stands facing*
e audience just inside the invisible fourth wall. Her open eyes (which
e focussed at a point only a few inches distant) and her gestures (arrang-
g hair, smoothing eyebrows, etc.) as well as the pose of her body (which
nds slightly forward from the hips) suggest to the audience that she is
oking at her reflection in an invisible mirror which hangs on this invisible
all.

E, *to herself.* I look like the devil.

M, *absently, without looking up or turning.* Wanted: death's brother.

E, *still primping.* No but did you ever try to go to sleep, and not be able
to, and lie watching the dark and thinking about things . . . . *She cocks*
her head, surveying herself anew. Satisfied, turns; goes to the table and
stands, looking down at HIM.

M, *as before.* Did I which?

E. Nothing.

M, *looks up, smiles.* Impossible.

E, *touching his shoulder.* Look. You be nice to me—you can do THAT
any time.

M. Can I? *Pockets notebook and pencil. Gets up, faces her.*

E. It's true.

M. What's "it"?

E. "It" is, that you really don't care about . . . .

M. I'll bite the rubber angleworm: what don't I really care about?

E, *sinks into the more comfortable chair.* Anything.

M. Whereas this is what's untrue—. *Sits on the table.* Anything everything nothing and something were looking for eels in a tree, when along
came sleep pushing a wheelbarrow full of green mice.

E, *to herself.* I thought so . . . .

M. I, however, thought that it was the taller of the two umbrellas who
lit a match when they found themselves in the main street of Hocuspocus
side by each riding elephants made out of candy.

E. And you may find this sort of thing funny. But I don't.

M. May I?

E. O— suddenly I think I'd like to die.

M. I think myself that there's some thinking being done around here.
But why die now? The morn's on the thorn, the snail's on the wing, the
play's on the way; and who knows?

E. I do. I know we're absolutely different. I've tried and tried not to
know it, but what in the world is the use of trying? O, I'm so sick of
trying—

M. Me too. This business of writing a play, I mean.

E. You mean I'm no good to you and that we should have ended everything long ago; because—not being interested in all the ideas you're interested in—it's obviously silly of me to pretend.

M. To pretend? *Picking up the box, opens it and proffers cigarettes; her*
hand automatically takes one. Striking a match, he lights her cigarette

and his. He gets off the table; walks up and down, smoking. What
obviously silly of you to pretend is, that we are not in love—
ME. In love!
HIM. Precisely; otherwise we couldn't fight each other so.
ME. This may be your idea of being in love: it isn't mine. *She smok*
wearily. Pause.
HIM, *halts, facing the window.* What did you say . . . .
ME. I said, it's not my idea of love.
HIM. No; I mean when I was sitting, and you—
ME. Who cares.
HIM. —you asked me something. I have it: you couldn't go to sleep. *Wal*
to the table and stands, looking down at her. After a moment, stoopin
he kisses her hand. I'm very sorry. *Puts his arm around her.*
ME. Stop please; I don't want you to be nice to me.
HIM. But I can't help being nice to you, because I'm in love with yo
She shakes her head slowly. O yes I am. You may not be in love wi*
me, but that doesn't prevent me from being in love with you.
ME. I don't know, really . . . . O, I wish—
HIM, *releases her.* What?
ME. —because with part of you I think I'm in love. What can I do?
HIM. Well now let's see . . . here's a bright idea: you can advertise in t
Paris edition of the New York Herald for a new lover, thus—"By
freckled fragile petite brunette incapable of loneliness and cookin
wanted: a tall strong handsome blond capable of indigestion and dea
(signed) Cinderella Van Winkle."
ME, *involuntarily.* Who's she?
HIM. Don't tell me you never in your whole life heard of Cinderella V:
Winkle! The bluest blood in all Gotham my dear, directly descend
from the three wise men who went to sea in a thundermug, and gre:
great-great-GREAT-granddaughter (twice removed) of the original a
only founder of the illustrious Van Winkle family, Neverrip Van Winkl
who married a Holeproof.
ME. Being funny doesn't help.
HIM. Neither, he inadvertently answered, does being tragic.
ME. Who's being tragic?
HIM. I give it up.
ME. You mean me? I'm not being tragic, I'm being serious; because I wa
to decide something. I think you might help me instead of making f
of me.
HIM, *amorously.* There's nothing I'd rather do, my dear, than help you—
ME, *quickly.* I don't mean—.
HIM, *cheerfully.* In that case, I have a definite hunch. ME *starts.* What
the world . . . .
ME. Yes?
HIM. What's the matter?
ME, *confused.* Nothing. Go on, please; I'm listening.
HIM, *smiles.* You're also stopping and looking, which puzzles me becav
I don't see the engine.

E, *smiling.* There isn't any—go on. I was thinking.

IM. And may I ask what you were thinking?

E, *hesitantly.* Yes.

IM. Well?

E. I was thinking, when you said that . . .

IM. When I said?

E. —about having a hunch . . .

M, *sits on the arm of her chair.* Yes? *His hand caresses her hair.*

E. —about . . . a hunchback. That's all.

IM. What about a hunchback?

E. Nothing. They're good luck. Please tell me now; that is, if you'd like to.

M. "Tell" you?

E. About the play. Do you think it'll be finished soon?

M. On the contrary—that is, yes. I think it will be torn up.

E. Torn up! Why?

M. No good.

E, *earnestly.* I'm sure it's good.

M. You haven't had the misfortune to read it.

E. I'd like to—if you don't mind: can I?

M. Of course, if you wish. I tell you: it's no good.

E. I'd like to read it, anyway. Have you got it in your hump?

M, *jumps.* What?

E. —Pocket, I meant.

M. My God, have I a hump? *Rising.* Here, let me look. *Starts toward the invisible mirror.*

E, *hugging him.* Please don't be angry with me: I know I'm stupid. I can't help it.

M, *laughs.* I was just on the point of—

E. Sh.

M. —of letting our mirror decide the question. *Nods in the direction of the audience.*

E. Were you, now? I guess men are vain—but that big mirror's no good and never was any. . . .

M. Like my play.

E. Nonsense. If you really want to see yourself, I've got a little one in my—O no, I lost it.

M. A little one in your which?

E. A little mirror, stupid, in my bag. I must have dropped it in a snow-drift.

M. Not the bag?

E. No, the mirror. I can't find it anywhere.

M. Never mind: I've decided that it's safer to take your word for my looks.

E. How sweet of you. Maybe you'll let me see the play, too? Please!

M. I haven't the play with me today, unfortunately.

E. I thought you always carried notes or something around with you. *Suspiciously.* What were you writing a moment ago?

HIM. A mere trifle, as it were. A little embonpoint to the dearly beloved master of my old prepschool at Stoneacre Heights, regretting that the undersigned is unable for pressing reasons to be present at the annual grand ball and entertainment to be held forthwith on the thirteenth Friday of next Thursday beginning with last Saturday until further notice to be furnished by—

ME, *mystified*. What "master"?

HIM. I doubt if you ever heard of the fellow: his name is Bates. Haha Let us now turn to serious subjects. Assuming a zygote to result from the fusion of two gametes, the company will next attempt to visualise through halfshut optics, a semifluid semitransparent colourless substance consisting of oxygen hydrogen carbon and nitrogen—

ME, *smiles*. —were looking for eels in a tree.

HIM. Precisely; when who should come along but little Mr. Mendel, wheel ing a numerical law full of recurring inherited characteristics all wrong side up with their eyes shut on a slackwire tightrope. *Vehemently*. Damn everything but the circus! *To himself*. And here am I, patiently squeez ing fourdimensional ideas into a twodimensional stage, when all of me that's anyone or anything is in the top of a circustent . . . . *A pause*.

ME. I didn't imagine you were leading a double life—and right under my nose, too.

HIM, *unhearing, proceeds contemptuously*. The average "painter" "sculptor" "poet" "composer" "playwright" is a person who cannot leap through a hoop from the back of a galloping horse, make people laugh with a clown's mouth, orchestrate twenty lions.

ME. Indeed.

HIM, *to her*. But imagine a human being who balances three chairs, one on top of another, on a wire, eighty feet in air with no net underneath and then climbs into the top chair, sits down, and begins to swing . .

ME, *shudders*. I'm glad I never saw that—makes me dizzy just to think of it

HIM, *quietly*. I never saw that either.

ME. Because nobody can do it.

HIM. Because I am that. But in another way, it's all I ever see.

ME. What is?

HIM, *pacing up and down*. This: I feel only one thing. I have only one conviction; it sits on three chairs in Heaven. Sometimes I look at it, with terror: it is such a perfect acrobat! The three chairs are three facts— will quickly kick them out from under itself and will stand on air; and in that moment (because everyone will be disappointed) everyone will applaud. Meanwhile, some thousands of miles over everyone's head, over a billion empty faces, it rocks carefully and smilingly on three things, on three facts, on: I am an Artist, I am a Man, I am a Failure—it rocks and it swings and it smiles and it does not collapse tumble or die because it pays no attention to anything except itself. *Passionately*. I feel, I am aware—every minute, every instant, I watch this trick, I am this trick, I sway—selfish and smiling and careful—above all the people. *To himself*. And always I am repeating a simple and dark and little formula . . always myself mutters and remutters a trivial colourless microscop idiom—I breathe, and I swing; and I whisper: "An artist, a man, a failure, MUST PROCEED."

ME, *timidly, after a short pause*. This thing or person who is you, who does not pay any attention to anyone else, it will stand on air?

HIM. On air. Above the faces, lives, screams—suddenly. Easily: alone.

ME. How about the chairs?

HIM. The chairs will all fall by themselves down from the wire and be caught by anybody, by nobody; by somebody whom I don't see and who doesn't see me: perhaps by everybody.

ME. Maybe yourself—you, away up ever so high—will hear me applaud?

HIM, *looking straight at her, smiles seriously*. I shall see your eyes. I shall hear your heart move.

ME. Because I shall not be disappointed, like the others.

HIM. Women generally prefer the theatre, however.

ME. Women can't help liking the theatre any more than women can help liking men.

HIM. I don't understand.

ME. What I mean is perfectly simple. I mean, women like to pretend.

HIM, *laughs gaily*. Upon which words, our knockkneed flybitten hero executed a spontaneous inverted quintuple backsomersault, missing the nonexistent trapeze by six and seven-eighths inches.

ME, *looking away*. I'm sorry—you see it's no use trying to tell me things, because I don't understand. And I can't argue.

HIM, *walking over to her, takes her hand in his; caresses it gently*. Wrong, wrong. *Tries to look in her eyes which, drooping, evade his*. Please don't mistake him; it was meant as a compliment, he's a harmless acrobat, he was trying to show you that he feels how much finer you are than he is or has been or ever will be—you should pity him. *Stroking*. Poor clown.

ME, *withdraws her hand*. You shouldn't play up to me.

HIM. You should know better than to accuse me of playing up to you.

ME, *in disgust*. O, you can't know anything about men; they're so complicated.

HIM. MEN complicated!

ME. Women don't want so many things.

HIM. Any woman?

ME. If she's really a woman.

HIM. What does the woman who's really a woman wish?

ME, *looking at him*. That's a secret.

HIM. Really?

ME. Really a secret.

HIM. A secret is something to be guessed, isn't it?

ME, *defiantly*. You'll never guess mine.

HIM. Perhaps, but why insult—

ME. Nobody's insulting you. I simply feel that I'm this way and there's no use in my trying to be another way.

HIM, *smiles*. Speaking of secrets, here's one which I've never breathed to a single soul; sabe usted quién soy?

ME. No. Do you?

HIM. Mr. Bang, the hunter. *His voice shrinks to a whisper; he gestures mysteriously.* I hunt the gentle macrocosm with bullets made of microcosm and vice versa. *Laughs. Suddenly serious, resumes.* Yessiree—and this is a positively dead secret: I very frequently tell this to absolutely noone—. *With entire earnestness, leaning importantly toward her, enunciates distinctly and cautiously.* My gun is made of chewinggum.

ME, *quietly.* I wish I had a piece. *She struts the back of one doll-like hand across her forehead. Speaks vaguely.* Where are we? I mean, who are we; what am I doing—here?

HIM. We are married.

ME. Why do you say that?

HIM. Isn't that the way married people are supposed to feel? *Abruptly turning, walks briskly across the room; halts: halfturns, looks toward the window and mutters.* It's snowing . . . *His voice thinks to itself.* . . . showing . . . *His whisper marvels, muses.* . . . knowing. *He stands, lost in thought.*

ME, *with an effort.* Promise something.

HIM, *absently.* Yes?

ME. Promise that when the circus comes this year you'll take me.

HIM, *to her.* On one condition; that you agree to see everything.

ME. Of course.

HIM. Last year you refused to pay your respects to The Queer Folk.

ME. O. *Quickly.* But that's not the circus. And besides, whoever wants to see a lot of motheaten freaks?

HIM. I did. *Smiles to himself.* I seem to remember riding out of a circus once upon a time on somebody's shoulder; and hearing a throbbing noise, and then a coarse voice squirting a stream of bright words—and looking, and seeing a small tent with huge pictures of all sorts of queer things, and the barker spieling like a fiend, and people all about him gaping like fish. Whereupon, I began to tremble—

ME, *starting, as a drum sounds faintly.* Whatever's that?

HIM. —and begged somebody to take me in; which somebody probably did, I don't remember. . . .

ME. I hear something, don't you? *The noise nears.* That. It's ever so near now. Must be a parade, and on such a wintry day, too. Imagine.

HIM, *listening vainly.* What you hear and I don't must be either an exelevated-engineer in a silk stovepipe with a sprig of shamrock in his buttonhole riding a red white and blue tricycle like mad up 5th Avenue and waving a little green flag, or Einstein receiving the keys of the city of Coral Gables in a gondola—

ME. I'm sure it's a parade!

HIM. —or a social revolution—

ME. Will you do something?

HIM. Say it with flowers. *The noise stops.* What?

ME, *listening.* It seems to have stopped, very near—please run out and see; will you? HIM *stares, mildly astonished, as* ME *jumps up from the more comfortable chair and hurries to the sofa.* Here's your hat: and look, it's snowing; you'd better take—

HIM. To Hell with the umbrella. *Takes his crumpled hat from her.* Now in just what does your most humble and very obedient servant's mission consist?

ME. You're to take a look around the corner. Because I'm almost sure there's something.

HIM. Pardon me, Your Excellency, for remarking that I think you're crazy. *Going, he kisses her.*

ME. You don't need to tell me: I know I am. HIM *exits through door in middle wall.* ME *walks nervously up and down—pauses: goes to the invisible mirror and stands, stares, gestures, exactly as at the beginning of the scene.*

SCENE THREE

SCENE: *The picture, as at the end of Scene 1 (both heads present: WOMAN's eyes closed) and the three knitting rocking FIGURES facing the picture with their backs to the audience.*

THIRD FIGURE. I suppose so—what did you say yours was called?

FIRST. It's Toasted, but it died.

THIRD. How terrible. Did it swallow something?

FIRST. No, it fell down stairs.

SECOND. I can sympathise with you, my dear. All my children were killed in the great war.

FIRST. That's perfectly marvelous! How many did you have?

SECOND. At one time I had over eighty boys.

THIRD. Boys are the naughtiest little creatures—didn't you find them a bother?

SECOND. Not a bit, I used to keep mine out on the fireescape.

FIRST. Male or female?

SECOND. Female, so my husband says. *Enter* HIM. *The three* FIGURES *stop rocking and knitting.*

HIM, *bowing and removing his battered hat.* I beg your pardon—. *All three* FIGURES *rise and turn.* HIM *surveys their identical maskfaces doubtfully.* I . . . how do you do—? *Extends his hand to the* FIRST FIGURE, *who extends hers but instead of shaking hands twists his palm upward and studies it.*

FIRST FIGURE, *rapidly.* Yes Willie will.

HIM, *confused.* Willie—

FIRST FIGURE. Will die—

HIM, *uncomprehending.* Die?

FIRST FIGURE. One hour before midnight Daylight Saving Time February 30th.

HIM.—How?

FIRST FIGURE. At seventy kilometres an hour. Of ennui with complications. In a toilet of the train de luxe going from Fiesole to Fiesole. Next! *She whisks his hand toward the* SECOND FIGURE *who takes it and studies it.*

SECOND FIGURE, *more rapidly than the* FIRST. The key to the philosophy of Locke is John. Be careful not to swallow too much broken glass during the week and when riding a bicycle from or to work never take your feet off the handlebars even if a policeman smiles at traffic. Your favorite planet is Ringling Brothers. Horseradish will not produce consequences unless cowslips which is unlikely so be not daunted tho' affairs go badly since all will be well. The cards say and the tea leaves admit that enough is as good as a feast which will cause you some flatulence which you will not mind as long as Gipsy continues to remain a diurnal wateringpot but beware of a woman called Metope who is in the pay of Triglyph disguised as either an insurance agent or I forget which it doesn't matter and whenever a stuffed platitude hits you in the exaggerated omphalos respond with a threefisted aphorism to the precise casazza. Faretheewell n'erdoweel.—Next! *She whisks his hand toward the* THIRD FIGURE, *who takes it and studies it.*

THIRD FIGURE, *more rapidly than the* SECOND. You suffer from noble-blood-poisoning. Time is the autobiography of space. Give a woman everything and she has nothing. Life is a matter of being born. Treat a man like dirt and he will produce flowers. Art is a question of being alive. —Go in peace. *She drops his hand.* HIM *crams his hat on his head and hurries out, as the* THREE FIGURES *turn sit rock and knit.*

SCENE FOUR

SCENE: *The room of Scene 2 revolved clockwise with reference to the audience so that the fourth or invisible wall is now the window wall. The wall to the audience's right (corresponding to the window wall of Scene 2) is the door wall. The middle wall (corresponding to the door wall of Scene 2) is the solid wall, against which is the sofa. To the audience's left a new wall with a large mirror (the invisible fourth wall of Scene 2) is now visible.*

ME *is standing and gesturing before the mirror, as at the beginning and end of Scene 2; but at the point on the stage where she then stood there is now the table, near which are the two chairs.*

HIM, *coming through the doorway skims his hat at the sofa.* There wasn't anything. *Brushes snow off himself, stamps, goes to the table: sits in the less comfortable of the chairs and pulls a notebook from his pocket.*

ME, *at the mirror speaks dimly.* I thought there might be. *A pause.* I was thinking. . . .

HIM, *absently: turning leaves of notebook.* So am I.

ME, *at the mirror.* You could make ever so much money, if you wanted to.

HIM, *as before*. Hm.

ME. Writing things . . . things people want—the public. Things people would like.

HIM, *pulling out a pencil begins writing in notebook*. Uh-huh.

ME, *vaguely*. Like plays and scenarios.

HIM, *softly*. Keyring Comedies and Keyhole Farces.

ME. Not funny necessarily.

HIM, *parenthetically*. Just dull.

ME. People like serious things.

HIM, *almost inaudibly*. The Four Horses of the Apocalypse.

ME, *still primping*. Because, really, you're ever so clever . . . I know that.

HIM, *murmurs*. You made me what I am today I hope you're satisfied.

ME. No but take—

HIM, *starting up*. Aha! I see it all now: The Great American Novel (gimme a chord, professor) where for the first and only time is revealed in all its startling circularity the longlost nombrill of the Middle West. *As if quoting*. Lucy T. Wot felt That Something which is nothing like anything, and as quick as everything laying her red hot pail of blackberries down in the midafternoon moonlight, slowly raised two eyes, in both after each of which a single tear strove as it were for the mastery, to those of Henery Pudd who merely looked at her however.

ME. O well. You don't want to be serious.

HIM. Serious?—I serious? You're jesting. *Resumes writing*.

ME. I was trying to help you. *A pause*.

HIM, *reads to himself in a low voice*. "If we are dolls, It pulls the strings. If we pull strings, It is the dolls: who move." *Emerging from his thought, finds her standing beside him*. You look terribly.

ME, *breaking down*. I can't help it and I've tried so hard not to talk about it and I'm sick with worrying—. *Wrings her hands*.

HIM, *rises: drawing her into the more comfortable chair, puts his arm over her sobbing body*. Your hair is beautiful, today.

ME. Yes, I tried that first. And I even went to the dentist—but nothing works.

HIM. Since when?

ME, *shudders*. O god I don't know. And I walked miles and miles till I had to sit down in the snow or any old place: I'm sorry. *She dabs her eyes with a microscopic handkerchief*. I know I'm silly to be this way . . . I'll stop crying—really, I will. Don't be angry with me.

HIM. "Angry"?

ME. I knew you were busy and wanted to get that damned play or whatever it is done. I promised myself I wouldn't go near you or bother you. And then—I don't know . . . I couldn't. *Chokes on a sob*. O well: now I'll stop crying.

HIM, *muses*. "Angry"?

ME. Really I'll stop.

HIM, *smiling*. Our artist's conception—

ME. O, You and your "artist's conception"—. *Brushing away his arm, rises; smiles wryly*. I'm going to lie down—please go on working. *He stares*

straight before him. She takes his face in her hands. Look at me: I'm
sorry to have been so stupid. . . . *Kisses him lightly. Goes upstage to the
sofa and lies down with her back toward him and the audience.* This is
much better—I think I can go to sleep . . . good night.

HIM, *stands for a few moments looking out the invisible window, then
turns. Walks quietly to the mirror. Speaks in an almost whisper, staring
at his reflection.* If it were the first time. *Staring always into the mirror,
he passes a limp longish hand over face forehead hair.* Where's the moment—come: for an incipient dramatist you're an unearthly blockhead.
You maul the climaxes always. I'll say that as a slack wire artist you're
a heavenly plumber—you and your chairs! *Laughs silently.* "Angry"?—
on the contrary, better put everything in working order. Poor old flivver.
She coughs, she's running on one. Dirty sparkplugs. If it were the
fifteenth time, or time itself for that matter . . . Time and Space, a
softshoe turn. The wellknown writer of scenarios, properties one million
lemon pies, hero a spitball artist of the first water, much furniture everywhere broken, pity and terror incorporated, it all comes out in the wash,
happy ending, I've got the machine who's got the god? *Takes a step
forward.* Once again for luck, let's rehearse. Ars longa vita brevis. The
Est—? *Feels of his right jacket pocket.* —Yes. Are you with me? *Stares
fixedly.* You are. Good. Now I straighten up, looking my prettiest as
it were. Head, so: eyes wide open.—In a lopsided way you really are
almost handsome. We look straight ahead and we move my careful hand,
slowly, down along my jacket; to his pocket. I, slowly, put his hand into
my pocket; easily, don't you know? Or as if looking for the thirteenth
volume of the Encyclopaedia Britannica. Very good: excellent. —I should
like to see myself do this. I do this very well, really. Mistaken vocation:
should have been an actor perhaps? —And we take our hand out of this
pocket; very slowly, so as not to. *Withdraws his hand, with an automatic.* Perfect. That's the gesture—not quite slow enough, perhaps;
otherwise. . . . And lifting our, my, his, arm, in a slow easy curve, like
this; to the right temple: I do not shut my eyes. *Stares, pistol at head.
Speaks to his reflection.* Why I'm a fool, I can never get my revenge on
You. If I shut my eyes I'm not killing You. *Bitterly.* And if I don't, it's
You who kill your miserable self—quelle blague! *His hand, with the
automatic, wavers.* ME *screams. Wheeling,* HIM *pockets the pistol and
bows to her.* Morgen.

ME. —What—

HIM. It's my play: the wily villain, trapped by armies of unalterable law
and so forth, commits harrycarissima with an atomiser—ought to be a
howling success, don't you think? The Jarvanese way, you know. Sorry
to frighten—

ME. —what's—

HIM. Would you care to inspect? *He advances toward her. She cringes.*
Pistil. The female organ of a flower. But I only got a D plus in crypto-
gamic botany, when Professor Roland Thaxter was arrested for riding
his bicycle on the sidewalk. *He reaches the couch. She covers her face
with her hands, speechless, cowering.* Look. It's really very neat: in

three parts, ovary style and stigma. *He removes the magazine.* Not loaded. Don't be afraid.

ME, *peeping between her fingers.* I—thought. . . .

HIM. Stamen is what you thought, it contains the pollen. *Inserts the magazine.* Hence stamina. —Are you still unhappy?

ME, *after a short pause, touching him timidly.* Listen: did you—

HIM. You don't look unhappy. *Slowly goes to the table, on the centre of
which he carefully lays the automatic.*

ME. Did you do this—for me?

HIM. This? —I don't get you. Sorry.

ME. Because . . . I think. *Relaxing utterly, spreads herself over the sofa—
halfshut eyes smiling at the ceiling, to which she whispers.* Yes.

HIM, *half turning, looks at her; expressionless.* Ah. *Opens the box, takes a
cigarette and speaks, tapping the cigarette on his hand.* How is it with
you, lady?

ME, *quietly, to the ceiling.* It's wonderful with me.

HIM, *lights his cigarette. Sitting on the table, back to the audience, murmurs vaguely.* The king's to blame. Congratulations.

ME, *vaguely murmurs.* What . . . king.

HIM. King queen and knave, King kinkajou with his prehensile tail, King
C. Y. Didn't Gillette Meknow.

ME, *as before.* The second sounds like a nice king. . . . *Silence,* HIM *smokes.*
Are—are you busy?

HIM, *laughs.* "Busy"? Not just now.

ME. Then come over here, please.

HIM. Motive?

ME. Because I'm happy and I want you here. *He strolls upstage to the
couch. She makes room for him. As he sits down, she puts her arm
around his neck.* I guess I'll write a play myself—all about policemen
and shootings and mirrors.

HIM. Why not.

ME. I guess my play will have ever so many more scary scenes than yours
. . . nobody'll go to see your play because it won't be half so exciting.
She laughs. O—and mine will have something yours hasn't got: and all
the mothers will bring their children to see him.

HIM. Him?

ME. The elephant.

HIM. Indeed.

ME. I'll have a fullsized elephant in my play.

HIM. With a trunk and everything?

ME. Of course. *She looks at him for a moment: hugs him suddenly.* O you
darling. With its baby face—. *Sees his hat on the floor near the sofa.*
That hat's all motheaten or something: you must buy yourself a new
one. *Hugging him, whispers.* My lover.

HIM, *after a short pause.* What did you say then?

ME. "My lover." I can say that if I like, because it's true.

HIM, *gently.* Can you? —Here's something queer: I can say "that's not my
hat." *Earnestly.* And it's true.

ME. Is it, now: you mean you've given that dreadful old hat away to some-body? Not to me, I hope?

HIM, *very gently.* How could I give it away when it doesn't belong to me?

ME. You mean it's just a horrid old hat you've rented—by the year, I suppose?

HIM. Not rented. Borrowed.

ME. Well now, that's interesting: the dirty old thing—it belongs to some-body else, you mean?

HIM. It belongs . . . to a friend of ours.

ME. Of ours? That nasty old crooked disagreeable hat?

HIM. It's the Other Man's hat.

ME. What?

HIM, *gestures.* Just as these are his clothes: didn't I tell you? *Laughs.* But you knew, really. Really, you were just pretending.

ME. I knew?

HIM. —About these neckties and socks and things. *Serious.* He lets me wear them because it amuses him.

ME. What are you talking about?

HIM. Am I?

ME. I don't understand. What other man—where?

HIM. Here, of course.

ME. Really dear, you might be serious. You know I don't understand you when you're joking.

HIM. Seriously dear, I don't wish to alarm you. But there are really two men in this room—

ME. Two—?

HIM. —one of whom is jealous of the other.

ME. Are you trying to be funny or something?

HIM. I am not trying to be funny. Seriously.

ME. O; I thought you were. What are you doing?

HIM, *mysteriously.* Something extraordinarily dangerous. I am really sitting in this Other Man's cage and I am really being caressed by this Other Man's canary.

ME. Who is that?

HIM, *looking at her.* You are.

ME. "Canary"—of whom?

HIM, *slowly.* Your lover is in this room.

ME. My—. . . . *Rising.* Not any longer.

HIM. O yes he is, and I can prove it.

ME. O no. You can't.

HIM. Very easily. By showing him to you. Would you care to see him now?

ME. Now. Yes.

HIM, *rising.* This way, ladies and gentlemen—. *Guides her to the mirror, stands behind her.* —See?

ME, *puzzled.* What?

HIM. You see him, all right: why not say hello? He's looking straight at you—after all, it's no good pretending to me that you don't know this gentleman.

ME. O. Him.

HIM. Yes; therefore—. *Dropping suddenly on his knees, face to the mirror.*
—Let us pray. *Shuts his eyes and joins his hands.* O Mr. Man, if sometimes I seem to be taking your place, please don't be angry with me.
You know perfectly well that I never seriously compete with you, Mr.
Mirror Man, and I know perfectly well that you've got much too much
sense to believe what the neighbors say about her and me. Not that
she'd be to blame if there were anything really between us; but as a
matter of fact I'm innocent, too: O Man in the Mirror, I swear I'm
innocent! And since we know it's all a joke, let's speak seriously: now
as for this here young woman, I know that she's always been true to
you, and everybody knows; and, if you stop to think, you yourself
know that you're the only fellow she's ever seriously been really in love
with, or really ever seriously wanted, or seriously really ever cared about
at all. *During this speech* ME *tilts her small head sideways, inspecting
herself critically; her slender hands, having pulled at dress-hips, rise to a
cheek where their fingers automatically begin arranging stray wisps of
hair: she stares always into the mirror.* HIM *gets up. Turns to her.*
N'est-ce pas?

ME. I'm sorry. I didn't hear what you said. *With a final glance at herself, she strolls toward the invisible window.*

HIM, *picking up and putting on his battered hat, smiles suddenly.* You
aren't mad, am I?

ME, *shrugging.* I suppose it's because I'm stupid—but somehow I don't
care. . . .

HIM. Don't suppose. *Softly.* Or if you must suppose, suppose that you
are standing before a window and that continuously something happens—snow appears, covers the earth; melting, disappears—in other
words, suppose that the earth rises, reappears, moves: suppose Spring.
Or suppose that I am looking in a mirror and that my consciousness
of the surface dissolves before an image as snow may melt before rain
or as Winter melts before April and as the awake must dissolve before the asleep. . . . *Smiles to himself.* —In other words, suppose that
a part of me is talking at this moment.

ME, *standing at the table and looking out the invisible window, speaks
vaguely.* But really, everything's winter, outside.

HIM. But seriously: the nearer something is, the more outside of me it
seems. *Walks to the sofa: pulls out notebook and reads, almost inaudibly, to himself.* "These solidities and silences which we call
'things' are not separate units of experience, but are poises, self-organis-
ing collections. There are no entities, no isolations, no abstractions; but
there are departures, voyages, arrivals, contagions. I have seen an
instant of consciousness as a heap of jackstraws. This heap is not inert; it is a kinesis fatally composed of countless mutually dependent
stresses, a product-and-quotient of innumerable perfectly interrelated
tensions. Tensions (by which any portion flowing through every other
portion becomes the whole) are the technique and essence of Being:
they copulate in laughter, in your least premeditated gesture are born

myriads which die only to be incredibly reborn, they are eaten an
drunk, we breathe and excrete them under different names. I do ne
stroke edges and I do not feel music but only metaphors. Metapho
are what comfort and astonish us, which are the projected brightness (
ourselves—a million metaphors times or divided by a million metapho
constitute a moment or a coatsleeve—here is what we call smells an
flavours, the difference between this face and another, god, never, tomo
row, love, yesterday, death or whatever yourself and myself agree
entitle that minute indestructible doll which only the artist possib
may endow with a carefully passionate gesture."

ME. . . . Maybe you mean something. I don't know.

HIM, *to noone, putting the notebook in his pocket and stretching himse
wearily over the sofa.* Ah, but don't you know that there is a furth
image—which appears not so much in the window of sleep as in a sti
deeper mirror? The planes overlap sometimes and sometimes the straigl
lines seem to fall. Philosophy is a dreampistol which goes off—bang
into flowers-and-candy . . . we dissolve, you and I. Stop look and liste
to a fraction of myself. Life is a kind of lust which melts, producir
death—a child.

ME. By the way, may I be allowed to ask a question?

HIM, *absently.* You may.

ME. What's all this play of yours about?

HIM, *to himself, smiling at the ceiling.* This play of mine is all abo
mirrors.

ME. But who's the hero?

HIM, *to her.* The hero of this play of mine? *Hesitates.* A man. . . .

ME. Naturally. What sort of a man?

HIM. The sort of a man—who is writing a play about a man who is writir
a sort of a play.

ME. That's a queer hero, isn't it?

HIM. Isn't it?

ME. And what is this hero called?

HIM, *very slowly.* This hero is called "Mr. O.Him, the Man in the Mi
ror."

ME. O.Him. *Smiles.* And the heroine? *Quickly.* —Or isn't there any?

HIM. On the contrary. My heroine lives over there—. *Points to the mirro*

ME, *turning, at the invisible window.* Me?

HIM. Me, the beautiful mistress of the extraordinary Mr. O.Him.

ME. —Extraordinary because he thinks she's beautiful?

HIM. Extraordinary because I need a shave because he needs a shave.

SCENE FIVE

SCENE: *The picture, as in Scene 3 (both heads present:* WOMAN'S *ey
closed) and the three knitting rocking* FIGURES *facing the picture wi
their backs to the audience.*

SECOND FIGURE. Seesaw Margery Daw.

THIRD. Four out of five will get wedlock.

FIRST. How can I when it's Friday the 13th?

THIRD. By reading the gospel according to Saint Freud.

SECOND. Nobody would be the wiser for a glass of mercury.

FIRST. But have you ever tried standing on the third rail?

SECOND. Yes except that February has too many holidays.

FIRST. In Vino Veritas.

THIRD. Beware of pickpockets.

SECOND. Look at Napoleon: he lost the Battle of Waterloo.

THIRD. And what happened to Jesus Christ? They crucified him.

FIRST. Quite the contrary. They took after their mother.

THIRD. Immediately?

FIRST. No, with salt and pepper and of course a dash of lemon.

SECOND. But I only got beyond page six, when nothing happened and
the conductor died in my lap.

FIRST. It has wings, I think.

THIRD. That's the insidious thing about hippocampus (unpleasant breath).

SECOND. Atlantic coast from Cape Cod to Charleston.

FIRST. Greatest length seven inches.

THIRD. A Pacific Coast species grows nearly twelve inches long.

SECOND. The young are carried in a pouch by the male.

THIRD. The only fish with a grasping tail.

CURTAIN

ACT TWO

SCENE ONE

SCENE: *That amount of the actual structure of the stage etc. which lies
behind the plane of the curtain is revealed, by the curtain's rising, without
"set" of any kind.*

*The action or content of Scene 1 consists of the curtain's rising, of its
presence for one minute and of its falling. Darkness.*

VOICE OF ME. Was that an accident? Or a scene?

VOICE OF HIM. Both I trust.

VOICE OF ME. Did it really mean something?

VOICE OF HIM. It meant nothing, or rather: death.

VOICE OF ME. O, I see.

VOICE OF HIM. This is the Other Play.

VOICE OF ME. By Mr. O.Him?

VOICE OF HIM. —The Man in the Mirror.

VOICE OF ME. But tell me, what's this Other Play all about?

VOICE OF HIM: About? It's about anything you like, about nothing and
something and everything, about blood and thunder and love and

death—in fact, about as much as you can stand. (I might add that it
sure of a long run; provided, of course, we receive the proper adve
tising—you know what I mean—"Broadway is enjoying a novel trea
in one of the wittiest and most highly original products of America
genius, entitled 'How Dyuh Get That Way?' By the authors of 'Nu
Ced' . . . the subject of this rollicking farce is the 18th Amendmen
and right now we want to ask you, could anything be funnier? . .
but just to show how screamingly and even killingly funny 'How Dyu
Get That Way' is, we are going to give the assembled company
sample, taken at random; the scene is a lawn with the porch of a bu
galow to the audience's right, the time is the wee small hours").—Ar
you ready?

SCENE TWO

scene: *As previously described.*
Enter staggeringly three corpulent MIDDLE-AGED MEN, *the* THIRD *of whom*
played by the DOCTOR.
FIRST MIDDLE-AGED MAN, *heartily.* Jon playa gaim croquet.
SECOND, *irritably.* Oreye bjush wummore Ished.
THIRD, *loftily.* Sridiculous croquet lesh play tennish.
FIRST, *delightedly.* Tennish love tennish mfavorite gaim.
SECOND, *angrily.* Oreye bjush wummore Ished.
THIRD, *scornfully.* Jon ystewed.
SECOND, *fiercely.* Oreye bjush wummore.
FIRST, *rapturously.* Hoosh gota raquet.
THIRD, *witheringly.* Turrbly shtewed shdishgraysh.
FIRST, *wildly.* Hoosh gota raquet wanta play tennish.
SECOND, *furiously.* Wummore.
THIRD, *annihilatingly.* Youghta gome.
SECOND, *savagely.* Wummore.
THIRD, *abolishingly.* Gome goat bed.
FIRST, *desperately.* Shomebody mushave raquet mush play tennish wit
raquet. *Enter from the left one spinster, or* VIRGO, *with a very red nos*
clad in black pajamas and carrying a dripping candle.
VIRGO. O you big bad old men, you extraordinarily naughty husband
you typically depraved old things: aren't you just lovely?
SECOND MIDDLE-AGED MAN. Wummore.
THIRD, *to* FIRST. Shpoleashman shudup.
FIRST. Shnot poleashman shfriend mine hullo.
VIRGO. You naughty old thing: how dare you speak to me!
FIRST MIDDLE-AGED MAN. Gota tennish raquet?
SECOND. Wummore.
THIRD. Shudup.
VIRGO. O you terribly intoxicated old reprobates, you perfectly sweet o
wretches, I don't understand a word you say.

THIRD MIDDLE-AGED MAN. Officer musha pologise frien vurry drunk shdish-graysh.

SECOND. Oreye. Bjush.

FIRST, *indicating the* VIRGO *with an ample gesture.* Shoreye shfrien mine shgot tennish raquet.

VIRGO. O you lovely old rascals, aren't you simply ashamed of yourselves? What would your poor wives do if they could see you now!

FIRST MIDDLE-AGED MAN. Gimme tennish raquet oleman wanta play tennish. *He takes hold of the candle.*

VIRGO. You old wretch: don't you dare touch my candle! Just you take those naughty hands away now!

THIRD MIDDLE-AGED MAN. Doan sult thoffcer Fred.

VIRGO. O the rascal—he's got it away from me! Whatever will I do: it's pitch dark, and what a position for a woman! *Loudly.* I'm perfectly defenceless.

FIRST MIDDLE-AGED MAN. Thangsh oleman musha blige kmon Jon play tennish now gota raquet. *He makes a pass with the candle.*

VIRGO. Should I scream? —But what good would that do? O, what wicked old men you are!

SECOND MIDDLE-AGED MAN. Oreye b—

FIRST. Kmon Jon kmon George bye oletop rully musha blige tyou kmon everybody goint play tennish. *Exit.*

SECOND. Oreye. *Exit.*

THIRD. Doan mine offcer sall fun promise frien bring it rye back frien vurry drunk jush fun yknow course yunnerstan see ylater oreye goobye mush blige. *Exit.*

VIRGO, *sola.* Weren't they simply awful! Aren't men the dreadfulest wretches! And that old devil who took my candle away from me, wasn't he the limit—the poor dear thought it was a tennis raquet, can you imagine that! As for the other little man, who was simply unthinkably intoxicated, he could only say two or three words, poor dear! And then the one who spoke to me as if I were a policeman—rascally old darling! My, how I'd hate to be their wives! —I must go to bed at once before I catch my death of cold. *Utters a profound sigh.* It was really lucky they were all in such a deplorable condition, otherwise I should have felt guilty of immodesty. . . . *Sighs even more profoundly.* What a terrible thing it is to be a woman. *Enter a negro redcap Grand Central* PORTER.

PORTER, *saluting* VIRGO. Pardon me mam but is you de party asked me to find out about checkin' a pet canary?

VIRGO, *ecstatically.* My name is Gloria Quackenbush I am a dancer three years ago I had so much indigestion and constipation that I got terribly run down I was too tired and nervous to take my lessons a lady recommended yeast the constipation was relieved and I had much less trouble with gas now I am strong in every way the hydroplane in the photograph was furnished by the yeast company. *Darkness.*

VOICE OF HIM. You don't seem very enthusiastic.

VOICE OF ME. I'm not.

VOICE OF HIM. In that case, I have a bright idea. I am going to mak
a million dollars.

VOICE OF ME. You!

VOICE OF HIM. Sounds incredible, doesn't it?

VOICE OF ME. No but how?

VOICE OF HIM. I shall buy paste and labels and I shall buy boxes and
shall buy pen and ink and breadcrumbs and I shall put all of th
breadcrumbs in all of the boxes and I shall write the word RA-DI-O
LE-UM on all of the labels and I shall paste all of the labels on a
of the boxes.

VOICE OF ME. Is that all?

VOICE OF HIM. No. I shall insert, in all of the leading newspapers an
periodicals of the country, a full page advertisement.

VOICE OF ME. Saying what?

VOICE OF HIM. Saying: "WHY DIE? TRY RA-DI-O-LE-UM" . . . .

SCENE THREE

SCENE: *A streetcorner. People passing to and fro.*
A SOAP BOX ORATOR, *played by the* DOCTOR, *arrives and establishes himsel*
SOAP BOX ORATOR, *to an as yet nonexistent audience.* Ladies and gentlemen
do I look like the sort of fellow that goes around trying to drape th
universe in deep mourning? Am I one of those lopsided pessimis
that perambulate all over this beautiful world trying to persuade ever
body he runs into that sunlight costs a million dollars a quart? *Som*
body stops to look and listen. Is that the effect I make on you as
stand here today— I, that was born and raised on this very street an
worked hard all of my life in this fair city for fifty-two years and e
joyed every moment of it? *Two people stop to look and listen.* A
I a squeaking squealer or a squealing squawker or a whimpering morbi
foureyed crapehanging meanderer? I see by your faces, ladies an
gentlemen, that you don't believe so. *Three people stop to look an*
listen. All right. But let me tell you something. *Four people stop*
look and listen. Every ten men and women I see, walking or talkin
or shopping or going to the movies or riding in taxicabs busses su
ways and elevateds or doing nothing whatever or minding the chi
dren or reading the newspaper or up in the air in airoplanes, I s
to myself—five out of four will get cinderella and the other nine ha
it already. *Five people stop to look and listen.* Now let's get right dow
to fundamentals: what is cinderella? I'm here to tell you, ladies an
gentlemen, that cinderella is a newly discovered disease. *Six peop*
stop to look and listen. You will ask me—is it dangerous? —Dangerou
ladies and gentlemen? Why it's so dangerous that, compared with th
untold dangers to which cinderella subjects each and every specime
of the human race without exception in particular and mankind

general, a monthold baby cutting its milk teeth on a stick of dynamite is a picture of perfect safety. —Dangerous? Why, it's so dangerous that the three greatest elocutionists of all time—Demosthenes Daniel Webster and William Jennings Bryan—couldn't explain to you how dangerous cinderella is if they lectured steadily for six months without a glass of water. —Dangerous? Why, if I could begin to convey to your superior intelligences how dangerous this infernal and unprecedented disease known to scientists as cinderella is, I could pick strawberries in the Garden of Eden or fight the American Revolution. *Seven people stop to look and listen.* —Is it dangerous? Gracious Heavens, ladies and gentlemen, cinderella is the darkest deepest awfulest most obscure insidious hideous and perfectly fatal malady on the face of God's footstool! *Eight people stop to look and listen.* Now let me give you a little illustration, just to show you how incredibly dangerous cinderella is. —Suppose you've got cinderella (that most contagious of human diseases) or I've got cinderella, or the fellow over there's got cinderella: do we know we've got it? No, ladies and gentlemen, we don't know and we can't know! *Nine people stop to look and listen.* We may be rotting internally, our lungs intestines livers and other glands both great and small may be silently putrefying, forming invisible pockets of nauseous pus, creating microscopic sacs of virulent poison—and we don't know it! We may be neat and clean and washed and manicured outside, and inside we may be noisome squirming garbage cans breeding billions upon trillions of repulsive wormlike omnivorous germs of cinderella: that's what the scientists have just discovered! Think of it. Dream of it, ladies and gentlemen! And you ask me if this frightful disease is dangerous! Once and for all, let me tell you that cinderella is not dangerous—it is Death Itself! *Ten people stop to look and listen.* I see you're terrified, ladies and gentlemen, and I don't blame you. If you weren't afraid of death you wouldn't be human. But I'm not here primarily to give you the fright of your lives. Primarily, ladies and gentlemen, I'm here to help you. And I bring the greatest message of blessed comfort that the human soul in this day and time can possibly imagine. For—mark my words—in this little commongarden ordinary unassuming box reposes, to put it mildly, the secret of the ages. *He holds up a tin pillbox. Nine people stop to look and listen.* Now give me your close attention: when a forest fire starts, we fight the fire with fire, don't we? When a new demon of disease makes his infernal appearance on the face of this planet we turn for help to the latest discoveries of modern science, don't we? *Eight people stop to look and listen.* In this case, ladies and gentlemen, we turn with confidence to that most entirely miraculous of all miracles: Radium. *Seven people stop to look and listen.* And we find that our hopes are not unfounded. A new light breaks upon us—Radium will conquer cinderella! We are saved! Mankind, the whole human race, is saved! *Six people stop to look and listen.* Step right up, ladies and gentlemen. Feast your minds upon the unimaginable treasure which this little innocentlooking box

represents and contains. Try to picture to yourself the inherent won
derfulness of its mysterious contents. Think, or try to think, that the
medicine comprised in each of the twelve tiny threedimensional oblate
spheroids herein uselessly reposing is powerful enough to obliterate
annihilate and utterly incinerate five hundred quadrillion cinderella
bacteria! *Five people stop to look and listen.* All over the universe
ladies and gentlemen, myriads of yearning hands without exaggeration
are hopelessly reaching for the secret of life enclosed in this negligible
bit of metal. Tomorrow in this very city a hundred hearts will breathe
paeons of thankfulness for the salvation that has come to them through
this tiniest receptacle. And why? Because in this modest pillbox, ladies
and gentlemen, cinderella—the dreaded cinderella—meets its doom.
Four people stop to look and listen. —Ah, if the handful of thankful
hearts that will have sampled the delicioustasting automatically assimi
lated contents of this little box by tomorrow morning could only be a
thousand—a million—a decillion! *Three people stop to look and listen.*
But the remedy is limited, ladies and gentlemen. So infinitely precious
and prophylactic a product could not be manufactured rapidly. In time
to come we hope to be able to place this miracle on the market in large
quantities. With this end in view and no other, our fourteen model
factories at Kankakee Illinois are working night and day. We will do
our best, but we too are only human. The effort involved is incon
ceivable. As for the expense, it is simply without exaggeration fabulous.
Two people stop to look and listen. But we don't trouble ourselves on
that account: we are not here to make money, but to save our fellow
men and fellowwomen and fellowchildren from the most vomitory fate
that has ever threatened humanity in the world's entire history. *One
person stops to look and listen.* As a conclusive proof of what I say, let
me mention that we are offering the first batch of our absolutely unique
and positively guaranteed product at a dead loss—we are in fact giving
it away for less than the cost of printing the labels. Ladies and gentle
men, although my statements hitherto may have seemed unbelievable
have one yet to make which for sheer unadulterated unbelievability out
does them all—the actual expense to each and every purchaser of this
lifegiving panacea is, today here and now in this greatest and most
prosperous of cities New York, one dollar. *Nineteen people go their
nineteen ways.* Here you are: one dollar. *Seventeen people go their
seventeen ways.* Think of it! *Fifteen people go their fifteen ways.* Why
the heavily silverplated highlypolished universally useful fully guaranteed
aluminum box alone is worth a dollar. *Thirteen people go their thirteen
ways.* It lasts a lifetime! *Eleven people go their eleven ways.* Squeeze
drop shake it you can't break it, feed it to the lions roll it over Niagara
Falls shoot burn and sit down on it it's indestructible turn and twist it
at your will if it breaks we pay the bill round and over inside forward
wrongside downside upside out—ladies and gentlemen, it remains one
and the same. *Nine people go their nine ways.* Step right up! *Seven
people go their seven ways.* Each and every package positively guaranteed
to contain authentic infinitesimal amounts of the world's most precious

substance Radium, one cubic ounce of which according to painstakingly prepared strictly scientific statistics would generate sufficient dynamic energy to instigate a crop of beautiful lovely luxuriant curly chestnut hair slightly more than five miles long all over the entire surface of the terrestrial globe in six and seven-eighths seconds. *Five people go their five ways.* Step right up—here you are! *Three people go their three ways, leaving only the original somebody who stopped to look and listen.* You may not have cinderella but if you haven't it's a cinch you've got something else and no matter what it is this little box will save your life one dose alone irrevocably guaranteed to instantaneously eliminate permanently prevent and otherwise completely cure toothache sleeplessness clubfeet mumps stuttering varicoseveins youthful errors tonsilitis rheumatism lockjaw pyorrhea stomachache hernia tuberculosis nervous debility impotence halitosis and falling down stairs or your money back. *The original somebody goes his original way. Darkness.*

VOICE OF ME. That wasn't such a bright idea after all.

VOICE OF HIM. Never mind. I have another.

VOICE OF ME. Another bright idea?

VOICE OF HIM. Posolutely absitively.

VOICE OF ME. May I hear it?

VOICE OF HIM. You may. . . .

VOICE OF ME. Well?

VOICE OF HIM. . . . Well—next we have, ladies and gentlemen, Will and Bill: two partners in business who, through association, became each other. Camera!

SCENE FOUR

SCENE: *An inner office.*

At a desk is seated WILL, *a figure with a maskface which represents the real face of the* DOCTOR, *who presently enters, playing the part of an* INTRUDER.

WILL, *looking up, starts: gasps.* Who are you?

INTRUDER. You mean "Who am I."

WILL, *in a shaky voice.* Certainly: that's what I said.

INTRUDER. No. That's what I said.

WILL. Is that so. . . . *His right hand, fumbling, opens a drawer in the desk.* . . . And what did I say?

INTRUDER. "Who are you."

WILL, *covers the* INTRUDER *with a pistol.* Will you answer?

INTRUDER, *imperturbably.* Answer—?

WILL. Will you answer? —Yes or no?

INTRUDER. Which?

WILL. Which—what?

INTRUDER. Which question.

WILL. You know which question—come on now: who are you?

INTRUDER, *slowly.* I am.

WILL, *rising, ejaculates tremulously.* —I?

INTRUDER. You. *A few seconds' pause.*

WILL, *exploding in hysterical laughter, calls out.* Hey Bill!—Come in here a minute: I got something to show you. BILL, *a figure with a different maskface, hurries in.*

BILL. What's the matter Will?

WILL. Matter? —I ask this feller who he is and he says "You," did you ever hear anything like that?

INTRUDER. Not you—YOU.

BILL, *looking about him apprehensively.* Me? —Who? Which feller? —Where?

WILL, *to* INTRUDER. Shut up, YOU. —Listen Bill, this feller comes walking through the door like he owned the place or something.

BILL, *catching sight of the pistol.* What the—. Will! For Christ's sake, drop that gun—

WILL. Drop nothing. With this feller here, refusing to answer who he is? Are you crazy?

BILL. Where? What feller? —Be careful, Will, it's loaded—it might go off—

WILL. I'll shoot the sonofabitch if he don't answer me: answer, YOU—who are you?

BILL. —Will for God's sake—. *He covers his eyes with both hands.*

INTRUDER. You.

WILL. God damn you—. *He pulls the trigger: there is no explosion: he falls forward, writhes on the floor and collapses, with his maskface turned to the audience.*

BILL. Will! —O god: he's killed himself . . . what'll I do—O what'll I do. . . . *Throws himself on his knees beside the body, as Irving Berlin's "What'll I do" is heard dimly. The* INTRUDER *stealthily passes to the desk and quietly sits where* WILL *was originally seated.*

INTRUDER. Get the police to arrest you.

BILL, *vaguely, staring at nothing.* What's that . . . arrest who?

INTRUDER. You.

BILL, *as before.* . . . Me?

INTRUDER. You.

BILL, *as before.* What did I do. What for?

INTRUDER. For murdering Will, Bill.

BILL, *starts violently.* I never killed Will—

INTRUDER. Why did you kill me Bill?

BILL, *straightening, sees the* INTRUDER *for the first time—starts—his left hand with an involuntary meaningless gesture strikes the prone* WILL's *maskface, which comes off, revealing a real face to which the maskface of* BILL *corresponds.*

INTRUDER, *softly.* You shouldn't have killed me, Bill.

BILL, *to* INTRUDER *with a gasp of recognition.* —Will!

INTRUDER. Yes Bill, it's Will.

BILL. But you . . . you can't, it ain't possible—. *Cries out.* He's dead: look at him—. *His voice sinks to a wondering whisper as he stares unseeingly in the direction of the prone figure. . . . My god—. Gone! His gaze travels gradually back to the* INTRUDER'S *face.*

INTRUDER. I am Will and I am dead because you killed me, Bill.

BILL, *gradually rising from his knees.* I . . . I never . . . he killed —himself —

INTRUDER. You killed Will, Bill.

BILL. . . . So help me God—I ain't lying—if I'm lying, kill me!

INTRUDER, *sternly.* Bill killed Will and you know it.

BILL, *writhing in an agony of remorse: anguish sprouting in his body.* I'm innocent—I swear I'm innocent: kill me if I ain't—

INTRUDER, *solemnly.* You ain't, Bill.

BILL, *with a stuttering gesture of hands outstretched against some unbelievable horror, screams suddenly.* Will!

INTRUDER. Dead, Bill.

BILL, *sobbing.* Why—why did I—why did—

INTRUDER. For a woman, Bill. You killed me for a woman.

BILL, *wrapping his maskface in shivering hands.* O—. *He collapses, groveling, at the* INTRUDER'S *feet. A pause.*

INTRUDER. Bill. *No answer. He speaks gently.* Come Bill.

BILL, *upwrithing—petrified.* O—.

INTRUDER. Come with me, now. *Suddenly grabs* BILL, *who goes utterly limp in his grip: shouts, in a completely changed voice.* All right boys—I got her! *Noise of a door being broken down. Darkness.*

VOICE OF HIM. May I be so indiscreet as humbly to beg your Royal Highness's most illustrious verdict upon that deplorable scene?

VOICE OF ME. It made me feel as if I'd just swallowed a caterpillar.

VOICE OF HIM. These masks and ghosts, however, lead us into girls and dolls.

VOICE OF ME. Masks and ghosts?

VOICE OF HIM. Larva, pupa and (if we are very lucky) imago: the instantaneous futility. —You mentioned caterpillars, and so I am talking about caterpillars which I consider very interesting.

VOICE OF ME. I dare say everything is interesting if you understand it. Even angleworms are probably intensely interesting, in their way.

VOICE OF HIM. Life is a cribhouse, darling: a cribhouse with only one door: and when we step out of it—who knows but that angleworms are prodigiously and even unnecessarily interesting?

VOICE OF ME. And who cares?

VOICE OF HIM. Certainly not angleworms—eyeless and epicene which wander in ignorant darkness.

SCENE FIVE

SCENE: *The stage has become a semicircular piece of depth, at whose inmost point nine black stairs lead up to a white curtain.*

Two coalblack figures, one MALE *and one* FEMALE, *appear at opposite extremities of the semicircle's circumference* (i. e. of the foreground). *The* FEMALE *figure is holding in its arms a large boydoll at whom it looks fondly.*

MALE, *nervously.* Who you nigga?

FEMALE, *looking up, answers lazily.* Ahs de ground.

MALE, *apprehensively.* Who de ground?

FEMALE, *proudly.* Ahs de ground.

MALE, *fearfully.* Wot, you de ground?

FEMALE, *insolently.* Yas ahs de ground, ahs de ripe rich deep sweet sleek an sleepy ground, de G-R-O-U-N-D GROUND. *Strolls toward centre of semicircle.*

MALE, *faintly, pointing to the doll.* Wot you got dere.

FEMALE, *strolling, speaks angrily.* Dere? Where.

MALE, *breathlessly.* In yo arms.

FEMALE, *pausing at the centre of the semicircle, speaks sullenly.* Ah got Johnie.

MALE, *wildly.* —O Lawd! Johnie's in de arms of de ground! SIX COALBLACK FIGURES, *three male and three female, appear in succession, punctuating the circumference of the semicircle at regular intervals and in a counterclockwise direction with reference to the audience.*

FIRST, *appearing, speaks rapidly.* De ground's got a hold of Johnie.

SECOND, *appearing, speaks more rapidly.* De ground's got Johnie in her arms.

THIRD, *appearing, speaks very rapidly.* De ground won't let go.

FOURTH, *appearing, speaks very rapidly and shrilly.* Money won't make de ground let go.

FIFTH, *appearing, speaks shrilly and almost incoherently.* Love won't make de ground let go.

SIXTH, *appearing, cries hysterically.* Nothin won't make de ground let go of Johnie.

ALL SIX, *in unison, hysterically.* De ground won't let go, W O N ' T L E T G O, WON'T LET GO! *They rightface simultaneously and march around the* FEMALE *figure with its doll. Marching, they speak in succession.*

FIRST.   Look at Johnie
           was a man
           loved a woman
           like a man only can.

SECOND.   He loved her hands
           an he loved her lips
           an he loved her feet
           an he loved her hips.

THIRD.   He loved her eyes
           an he loved her breasts
           but he loved her somethin
           else the best.

FOURTH.   Now he lies
             without a sound
             lonely an small
             in de arms of de ground.

FIFTH.   Maybe he twists
             maybe he squirms
             an maybe he's full
             of lil bright worms.

SIXTH.   After workin an ashirkin
             eatin an adrinkin
             livin an alovin
             Johnie's in de ground.

*Behind the white curtain an invisible jazz band plays softly: the voices of
the players darkly sing. The* SIX FIGURES *halt, in a circle, listening.*

VOICES.   Frankie and Johnie were lovers
             sweet Christ how they could love
             they swore to be true to each other
             as true as the stars above
                         but he was a man
                         and he done her wrong

             Frankie she lived in the cribhouse
             the cribhouse had only one door
             she gave all her money to Johnie
             who spent it on a parlorhouse whore
                         he was a man
                         and he done her wrong

             Frankie went down to the corner
             to buy herself a bottle of beer
             and she said to the old bartender
             have you seen my loving Johnie in here
                         he is a man
                         and he done me wrong

             I aint agoing to tell you no secrets
             and I aint agoing to tell you no lies
             but Johnie went out just a minute ago
             with that old whore Fanny Fry
                         he is a man
                         and he done you wrong

Frankie went back to the cribhouse
this time it wasn't for fun
for under her old red kimona
she carried Johnie's .44 gun
                         she was looking for the man
                         who done her wrong

Frankie she went to the parlorhouse
she looked in the window so high
and there she saw her Johnie
just a — · — Fanny Fry
                         he was a man
                         and he done her wrong

Frankie she went to the front door
she rang the front door bell
she said stand back all you pimps and whores
or I'll blow you all to Hell
                         I want my man
                         who done me wrong

Frankie went into the parlor
Johnie commenced to run
she said don't run from the woman you love
or I'll shoot you with your own damn gun
                         you are a man
                         who done me wrong

Frankie went into the parlor
Johnie hollered Frankie don't shoot
but Frankie she out with Johnie's .44 gun
and three times rootytoottoot
                         she shot her man
                         who done her wrong

Roll me over gently
roll me over slow
roll me over on my right side
'cause my left side's hurting me so
                         you've killed your man
                         who done you wrong

Frankie she turned him on his stomach
Frankie she turned him on his side
when she turned him for the third time
he hung his head and died
                         she killed her man
                         who done her wrong

*The white curtain at the top of the nine black stairs is pulled aside sudden-
ly: the* NINE PLAYERS, *in vermillion suits, with white shirts and socks, emer-
aldgreen neckties, lemoncoloured gloves and silkhats, appear.*
NINE PLAYERS, *playing, singing and descending the nine black stairs.*

> GET OUT YOUR RUBBERTIRED CARRIAGES
> AND GET OUT YOUR DECORATED HACKS
> I'LL TAKE MY LOVING JOHNIE TO THE CEMETERY
> BUT I'LL BRING HIS—

A cadaverous PERSONAGE *with tortoiseshell spectacles spouts up out of the
third row of the audience.*
PERSONAGE, *played by the* DOCTOR. Stop! *The song ceases. The* SIX COAL-
BLACK FIGURES *slink to their original positions, as the* FEMALE *figure with
its doll rushes up the nine black stairs and vanishes behind the reappearing white curtain. The* MALE *figure advances indignantly.*

MALE. Who you.
PERSONAGE, *displays enormous badge.* John Rutter, President pro tem. of
the Society for the Contraception of Vice. *He points a cadaverous finger
at the* MALE *figure.* You were about to utter enunciate pronounce and
otherwise emit a filthy lewd indecent vile obscene lascivious disgusting
word!
MALE, *in astonishment.* O Lawd; was ah?
PERSONAGE. Don't deny it! *He climbs over the footlights and steps up to
the* MALE *figure. Producing from his inside jacket pocket a paper, he
seizes the* MALE *figure's right hand and—holding the hand aloft—reads
glibly from the paper.* I John Smith nose protruding eyes open ears
symmetrical being in my right mind do hereby swear to obstruct impede
combat hinder prevent and otherwise by every means known and unknown including extravasation knockoutdrops hypnotism and dynamite
oppose the propagation or dissemination of any immediately or ulteriorly
morally noxious or injurious or in any other way whatsoever harmful
titillation provocation or excitation complete or incomplete of the human
or inhuman mind or body or any portion of the same under no matter
what conditions or any assumption of or allusion to the existence of
such a tendency in the human species whether such allusion or assumption be oral graphic neither or both and including with the written and
spoken word the unwritten and unspoken word or any inscription sign
or mark such as has been known to occur in public places of a strictly
private character commonly or uncommonly known as comfort stations
or any other visible or invisible natural or unnatural assumption of or
inclination to assume such a tendency or any assumption of assumption
of such tendency whether comprehensible or incomprehensible inten-
tional or unintentional premeditated or spontaneous implicit or explicit
uttered or unuttered perceptible or imperceptible or any blasphemous
filthy and new idea or group of ideas such as birthcontrol bolshevism and
so forth and in general anything at all whatsoever be its origin or essence

both irrespective of and with reference to its nature or content such as in the opinion of a judge familiar with the more widely used symbols of the English and American alphabets may can must might could would or should constitute a tacit misdemeanor against the soul of a child of not less than one day and not more than one year old and I take this oath willingly and without mental reservation on my part of any kind whatsoever conscious unconscious or foreconscious so help me God one dollar please. *Releases the right hand of* MALE *figure. Pockets the paper.*

MALE, *weakly.* Ah ain got one dollar boss. *The white curtain at the top of the nine black stairs is suddenly pulled aside: a slender negress in a red kimona willows down the nine black stairs, passes the* NINE PLAYERS, *arrives behind the* PERSONAGE *and bumps him with her elbow.*

NEGRESS. Gway yoh poor whytrash.

PERSONAGE, *wheeling.* Look here, young lady, that's no way to address—

NEGRESS. Doan call me "young lady" yoh bowlegged fish: ah ain no "young lady," thang Gawd!

PERSONAGE. In that case, I should advise you to attempt by every method practicable and impracticable to conceal the fact instead of making it glaringly apparent—

NEGRESS, *drawing herself up proudly before him, speaks contemptuously.* Do yoh all know who ah am? *The* PERSONAGE *recoils.* —Ah'm Frankie!

MALE FIGURE, SIX COALBLACK FIGURES *and* NINE PLAYERS, *simultaneously* SHE'S FRANKIE!

NEGRESS, *to* PERSONAGE. Take dat! *Whisking into view something which suggests a banana in size and shape and which is carefully wrapped in a bloody napkin, points it straight at the* PERSONAGE—*who utters a scream, jumps over the footlights, rushes up the main aisle of the theatre and disappears.* FRANKIE *turns to the audience: cradling the Something in her arms, as the* GROUND *cradled her boydoll, she takes up the song where the* PERSONAGE *interrupted it.* —But I'll bring his — *The drummer taps twice.* back—

EVERYBODY, *triumphantly.*

BEST PART OF THE MAN
WHO DONE ME WRONG
Darkness.

VOICE OF ME. Tell me. . . .

VOICE OF HIM. What? *A silence.* So you're getting horribly bored with the other play.

VOICE OF ME. Why should you think I was bored?

VOICE OF HIM. I can't imagine. How did you like that fifth scene?

VOICE OF ME. Let's finish up this Other Play; then I'll be able to judge much better.

VOICE OF HIM. It's not my funeral.

VOICE OF ME. What comes next?

VOICE OF HIM. But will you promise to let me know when you've had enough?

VOICE OF ME. I promise.

VOICE OF HIM. Good. —In that case, ladies and gentlemen, the next scene is all about eels in a tree.

VOICE OF ME. I hope there are no mice in it—are there?

VOICE OF HIM. Not a mice.

SCENE SIX

SCENE: *Fifth Avenue—midnight.*

A PLAINCLOTHESMAN, *his entire being focussed on something just offstage to the audience's left, stalks this invisible something minutely. He is played by the* DOCTOR.

Enter an ENGLISHMAN *in evening clothes and a silk hat, staggering under huge trunk marked* FRAGILE—*his silk hat falls off. He looks at it ruefully, even hopelessly. Then an expression of tranquility adorns his visage, as he catches sight of the* PLAINCLOTHESMAN'S *back—he clears his throat several times—having failed to attract the* PLAINCLOTHESMAN'S *attention, he exclaims* "I say" *and* "Beg pardon" *and* "By the way"—*finally, desperate, he wheels and gently bumps the* PLAINCLOTHESMAN *with the trunk. The* PLAINCLOTHES-MAN *leaps into the air: landing with a drawn automatic, stares his innocent vis-à-vis fiercely in the eye.*

ENGLISHMAN. Ah—good evening. Excuse me. Would you mind awfully— you see, my topper just fell off.

PLAINCLOTHESMAN. Yuh wut?

ENGLISHMAN. My topper, my hat—would you be so awfully kind as to hand it to me? *The* PLAINCLOTHESMAN *contemplates the* ENGLISHMAN *from top to toe: his jowl emits a cynical leer; pocketing his automatic, and warily stooping, he picks up the silk hat and inspects it with deep suspicion.*

ENGLISHMAN, *cheerfully sticking out his head.* On my nut please, if you don't mind. *The* PLAINCLOTHESMAN *scowls ominously: places the silk hat grimly on the* ENGLISHMAN'S *head.* Glad to have met you— *He starts for the wings, right.* Cheerio!

PLAINCLOTHESMAN. HAY. *The* ENGLISHMAN *starts: staggers: turns.* Lissun. Wutchuhgut dare.

ENGLISHMAN, *apprehensively, trying to look behind himself.* There? Where?

PLAINCLOTHESMAN. On yuh back uv coarse.

ENGLISHMAN, *relieved.* O, you mean that?—*He tries to nod at what he carries.*—Don't tell me you don't know what that is.

PLAINCLOTHESMAN. Sie. Dyuh tink I doughno uh trunk wen I sees it?

ENGLISHMAN, *perplexed.* Trunk? I said nothing about a trunk.

PLAINCLOTHESMAN. Youse dough need tuh. Dyuh know wie? Becuz yuh gut one on yuh back, dat's wie.

ENGLISHMAN. Do you know I'm dreadfully sorry, old man, but I haven't the least idea what you're talking about.

PLAINCLOTHESMAN. Can dat soikus stuff. Wutchuhgut in dat— *He raps th* *trunk with his knuckles.*

ENGLISHMAN, *a light dawning.* Ah, I see. So that's what you call my trunk-

PLAINCLOTHESMAN. I calls dat uh trunk becuz dat is uh trunk, dat's wie.

ENGLISHMAN. But my dear chap, you're quite mistaken in supposing that t be a trunk.

PLAINCLOTHESMAN, *menacingly.* Dat ain uh trunk?

ENGLISHMAN. I should say not. Dear, dear no. The very idea—ha-ha-ha.

PLAINCLOTHESMAN. Wal if dat ain uh trunk, will youse kinely tell me wt dat is?

ENGLISHMAN, *to himself.* —A trunk! That's really not half bad, you knov *To the* PLAINCLOTHESMAN. But since you ask me, I don't mind tellin you.

PLAINCLOTHESMAN. Wal, wut is it?

ENGLISHMAN. Why, that's my unconscious.

PLAINCLOTHESMAN, *hand at ear.* Yuh wut?

ENGLISHMAN. My unconscious, old egg. Don't pretend you haven't heard (them in America. —Why, my dear boy, I was given to understand th; a large percentage of them originated in the States: if I'm not mistakei the one I've got is made hereabouts, in Detroit or some where like tha

PLAINCLOTHESMAN. Nevuh mine ware it wus made; wuts in it?

ENGLISHMAN. In it? *He utters a profound sigh.* Ah—if I only knew. *TI* PLAINCLOTHESMAN *recoils in amazement. The* ENGLISHMAN, *after utterir another and even more profound sigh, turns.* Well, we can't know ever thing, can we. Cheerio! *He starts out.*

PLAINCLOTHESMAN, *leaping in front of the* ENGLISHMAN, *automatic in han* HAY doan try dat stuff wid me. *The* ENGLISHMAN *pauses.* Drop dat.

ENGLISHMAN, *puzzled.* Drop? What?

PLAINCLOTHESMAN. Drop wutchugut nmake it quick get me?

ENGLISHMAN, *despairingly.* I'm afraid I don't in the least know what yc mean—

PLAINCLOTHESMAN. I mean leggo wid boat hans one after duhudder nlea duh res tuh gravity.

ENGLISHMAN. But you don't seem to understand—it's my—don't you realiz It's a part of myself—my unconscious—which you're asking me to let | of, to drop. Could anything be more impossibly ridiculous?

PLAINCLOTHESMAN. Sie lissun I doan givuh good god dam fuh youse "U con-shus." Nlemme tellyuh sumpn doan gimme no more uh youse l rI'll make uh hole in youse.

ENGLISHMAN, *agonized, wails.* But I CAN'T— *The* PLAINCLOTHESMAN *fire there is no explosion, but the* ENGLISHMAN *drops the trunk. As it lanc a terrific crash of broken glass is heard. The* ENGLISHMAN, *blinking, b gins dusting himself; speaks severely.* There—you see what you've done

PLAINCLOTHESMAN, *furiously.* Wie dinchuh tell me day wuz booze in it y\ goddam fool! *He rushes—dropping, in his haste, the automatic—at t trunk: falling on both knees, begins tearing at the lock: presently thro\ back the lid—starts—rising, recoiling, covers his eyes as if from an incc* *ceivable horror: staggers back—falls. The* ENGLISHMAN *continues to dust himself. A* COP *hurries in with a drawn revolver.*

ɔP. Hansup! *The* ENGLISHMAN *puts up his hands.* Wuts dis? Uh trunk? *He spies the* PLAINCLOTHESMAN, *who is lying on his face.* Sumun croaked —Pokes *the prostrate figure with his foot.* Wie, it's Joe! *Stooping, lifts the* PLAINCLOTHESMAN'S *left arm—releases it; the arm falls, inert.* Here's duh gun. *Picks up the* PLAINCLOTHESMAN'S *automatic; drops it in the right outside pocket of the helpless* ENGLISHMAN'S *dinner jacket, and grimly faces his prey who immediately begins explaining.*

ɴGLISHMAN. Yes you see I was carrying this when my bally topper fell off, and being quite unable to pick it up myself—the hat, that is—I asked this Joe as you call him if he'd mind awfully doing me the favour to help me.

ɔP. W-a-l.

ɴGLISHMAN. Well he very kindly obliged me. But subsequently, owing to a perfectly ridiculous misunderstanding—more or less (I believe) as to the precise character of what I was carrying—

ɔP. Youse wus carryin—wut.

ɴGLISHMAN, *pointing at the trunk.* This.

ɔP. HANSUP! *The* ENGLISHMAN'S *hand flies aloft.* Wut for.

ɴGLISHMAN. What for—O; well you see I'd heard that in the States it's practically impossible to get into a hotel with a woman without a bag.

ɔP, *puzzled.* How's dat? Say dem woids again.

ɴGLISHMAN, *raising his voice.* I say: you see it's quite commonly known that in America one simply can't get into a hotel without a woman with a bag—I mean, get into a bag—no no, get into a woman—

ɔP. Stop! Now yuh talkin doity.

ɴGLISHMAN. I mean—it's jolly difficult to express the idea—

ɔP. Nevuh mine duh idear. Gowon.

ɴGLISHMAN. —Well; and so, being as it happens extremely anxious to get into a hotel, I was for taking no chances—

ɔP. Ware's duh wummun.

ɴGLISHMAN, *in astonishment.* Woman? Did you say "woman"?

ɔP. Y-a-s.

ɴGLISHMAN. What on earth do you mean, old egg? What woman?

ɔP. Duh wummun youse wus takin tuh duh hotel—is she in duh trunk?

ɴGLISHMAN. In the trunk? —A woman? You're spoofing, old thing—

ɔP, *approaching, bores the* ENGLISHMAN'S *entrails with the muzzle of the revolver.* Kummon, wut wus youse carryin in duh trunk.

ɴGLISHMAN. But—you don't seriously suppose I'd be such a bally ass as to carry a trunk on my back with a woman inside it! —A trunk—with a woman—on my back—ha-ha-ha; that's not half bad, you know—

ɔP, *disgustedly, shoving the* ENGLISHMAN *aside.* Get ovuh dare. *He steps rapidly to the trunk—peers in; starts, gasps—recoils, dropping his revolver —and falls, lifeless, beside the trunk. Darkness.*

ɔICE OF HIM. Well?

ɔICE OF ME. I liked the Englishman. But where were the eels?

ɔICE OF HIM. The eels were in the tree.

VOICE OF ME. But I didn't see any tree.

VOICE OF HIM. There aren't any trees on 5th Avenue below 59th Street.

VOICE OF ME. Then what you said wasn't true.

VOICE OF HIM. But it wasn't untrue.

VOICE OF ME. Why not?

VOICE OF HIM. I said there weren't any mice, and there weren't. That w true, wasn't it?

VOICE OF ME. O yes—I'd forgotten about the mice.

VOICE OF HIM. And about the wheelbarrow too, I dare say? —But I hadn't

VOICE OF ME. Why should you? After all, you invented it; and the two u brellas and the tightrope and everything else. In fact, what's queer that I should have remembered those eels.

VOICE OF HIM. Allow me to remark that I consider your remembrance those eels a great and definite compliment. Next we have. . . .

SCENE SEVEN

SCENE: *A* u, *whose arms are alleys of distance and which is recognized the promenade deck of a transatlantic liner seen from the bow.*

At the end of each alley (or arm of the u*) a rotund cigarsmokir* PASSENGER, *violently attired in an outrageous cap checked stockings ar unblownnose breeches, is advancing with six balloons.*

The two PASSENGERS *meet in the foreground at the apex of the* u, *ha and converse. Each then explodes a balloon belonging to the other touching it with his cigar, rounds the apex of the* u *and continues dou the opposite side of the deck from which he emerged, until he reaches t end of his arm of the* u. *He then aboutfaces, retraverses this arm ar arrives once more at the apex where he again meets the other* PASSENGE *halts, converses, explodes a balloon and continues down the side of t deck from which he originally emerged.*

The scene comprises six meetings, six conversations and the explodi: of all the balloons. The questioning PASSENGER *is played by the* DOCTOR.

FIRST CONVERSATION. What's new? —Nothing.

   Business? —Soso.

   Happy? —Not yet.

   Solong. —Solong.

SECOND CONVERSATION. What's new? —Nothing.

   Married? —Uh-huh.

   Children? —I dunno.

   Solong. —Solong.

THIRD CONVERSATION. What's new? —Nothing.

   Happy? —Soso.

   Retired? —Not yet.

   Solong. —Solong.

OURTH CONVERSATION. What's new? —Nothing.
Divorced? —Uh-huh.
Blond? —I dunno.
Solong. —Solong.
FTH CONVERSATION. What's new? —Nothing.
Millionaire? —Soso.
Happy? —Not yet.
Solong. —Solong.
XTH CONVERSATION. What's new? —Nothing.
Married? —Uh-huh.
How long? —I dunno.
Solong. —Solong.

Darkness.

ICE OF ME. What was that about?
ICE OF HIM. Chaos—not to be confused with manifold mendacities fakes counterfeit or spurious imitations such as Cosmos or commongarden ordinary unassuming Kolynos. Cheer up: The Other Play is almost played.
ICE OF ME. What's coming now?
ICE OF HIM, *utters a profound sigh.* Ah—if I only knew.
ICE OF ME. Do you mean to say you don't know?
ICE OF HIM. Excuse me: I was quoting.—The next scene, involving all sorts of allusions to subjects of unequal importance appertaining to the past the present and the future, calls for your undivided attention. I may add that it was composed by John Dewey—the world renowned authority on education and internationally famous author of such inspiring pamphlets as: "Into a Butterfly, or The Worm Will Turn"—in collaboration with C. Petronius, the talented writer of fairytales, on a desert island in the South Pacific during the eventful summer of 3, Eastern Standard Time, and deals in a vivid way with the loves of Spurius Lartius. . . .

SCENE EIGHT

NE: *The Old Howard's conception of a luxurious Roman villa, columns everything, with a protracted glimpse of Tiber and Coliseum plus a mountains in what should be and is not the distance. Two centurions shooting craps. Enter to them, lazily and unnoticed by them, an Ethiopian slave: he stands and regards the game with accumulating interest.*
OPIAN, *finally beside himself with emotion.* Dirry me.
T CENTURION, *looking up.* Hello Sam. *Picking up the dice, he rolls.*
ND CENTURION, *also looking up.* Hello Sam. Where yuh goin? *He rolls.*
OPIAN. Hello boize. Ah ain goin nowhere.
T CENTURION. Want to come in Sam? *Rolls.*
OPIAN. Well ah doan mind if ah does. *He produces an elaborate pocketbook.* How much you boize playin for?

BOTH CENTURIONS. Two bits.

ETHIOPIAN, *producing a coin.* Yoh faded. Now len me dem dice, fellah, a feels de speerit on me— *He takes the dice from the* FIRST CENTURION *heavenwarding his eyes, kisses the dice: murmurs.* All sweet ainjills con sit on deez two babies—. *Rolls.*

SECOND CENTURION. You lose. *Enter two* FAIRIES, *in scarlet togas, with ligh ningrods. The* CENTURIONS *nudge each other—hastily pick up the di and start out.*

ETHIOPIAN, *also going, murmurs en route, glancing at the* FAIRIES. If da anything worse dan Christians, it certainly am peddyrasts.

FIRST FAIRY, *soprano.* Where IS he.

SECOND FAIRY, *calmly, alto.* I don't know my dear.

FIRST. You were with him yesterday.

SECOND. I was not, dear. I haven't seen him since day before yesterday.

FIRST. You're lying to me, Tib.

SECOND. I am not, Claud.

FIRST. O dear O dear—I could just cry. *He whimpers.*

SECOND, *consolingly.* Never mind, Claud darling.

FIRST. If he hadn't promised me; but he did—he absolutely promised i he'd be here at four o'clock sharp.

SECOND. He told ME four fifteen.

FIRST. O, so YOU'RE invited.

SECOND. Of course I'm invited. Why do you suppose I'm here, you stup creature?

FIRST. Well, really—I think he might have told me. The very idea!—But won't be treated this way, I won't stand it another instant, I won't, WON'T—

SECOND. But listen dear—he didn't tell ME. . . .

FIRST. Tell you? What? What do you mean?

SECOND, *with dignity.* That YOU would be here.

FIRST. I don't care. It's entirely different, with you. Besides, my nerves on edge and everybody knows it— *Enter a* THIRD, *portly* FAIRY.

THIRD FAIRY. Hello Tib dear. Hello Claud, what's the matter dear?

FIRST. It's just too awful.

THIRD, *severely.* Why is Claud crying, Tib? What HAVE you done?

SECOND. Now listen Con, I SWEAR I'm innocent. . . .

FIRST, *sobbing.* If—he—hadn't—promised—

THIRD. You mustn't cry this way, Claud, it ruins your complexion.

FIRST, *as before.* I—know—it does.

THIRD. Here dear, take my handkerchief—just blow your nose and brace CLAUD, *sobbing, blows his nose.* That's better, isn't it.—Now tell what's wrong between you and Tib.

SECOND. I SWEAR I'm innocent, Con, I SWEAR—

THIRD. Hush, Tib! Tell me Claud, speak right out dear and don't be afr

FIRST. It's . . . not Tib . . . it's—

SECOND. There now! Didn't I TELL you I was innocent?

THIRD, *impatiently.* Will you be still, Tibby?—What IS it Claud, tell Con

FIRST. O Con dear, I'm so nervous.

THIRD. Now don't be silly, Claud. Don't cry any more darling. I'm sure
  everything will be all right.

FIRST. He—he prom-

THIRD. Who promised?

FIRST. Suh—Caesar—

THIRD. Well, what about Caesar?

FIRST. —Pruh - promised he'd be—here at fuh - four sharp.

SECOND. He told me four fifteen. Are you invited?

THIRD. Invited? Of course. He's coming at four thirty.

FIRST. Coming! O, how w-o-n-d-e-r-f-u-l.

THIRD. There now, don't cry any more Claudie; everything will be all right.
  —By the way, have either of you girls read If Winter Comes?

SECOND. I haven't. It sounds lovely.

FIRST, *cheering up*. What a heavenly title.

THIRD. I just knew you'd want to read it, both of you—

SECOND. Have you got it on you, Con?

FIRST. Do give it to me first Con; you know I'm so nervous, I must have
  something to make me forget this horrible tragedy—

THIRD. It's Caesar's book, dear. He lent it to me yesterday to read.

SECOND. Lend it to me, Con—

FIRST. No, to me—

THIRD. I'd simply love to lend it to both of you if I had it, but I gave it
  back.

SECOND. That was horrid of you Con.

THIRD. Now Tib, I just couldn't help myself and you know I'm not to
  blame.

FIRST. But you might perfectly well have borrowed it for a long time;
  Caesar wouldn't have cared.

THIRD. Caesar will lend it to both of you girls, if you ask him nicely.—
  That's what I wanted to tell you before he arrives.

FIRST. O goody goody! I'm so nervous I just can't bear to wait another
  minute. *Enter a* FOURTH, *excited* FAIRY.

FOURTH FAIRY. Hello Con, hello Tib and Claud: listen, have all you girls
  heard the news?

FIRST. What news, Gus dear?

FOURTH. Mercy, haven't you heard! Why it's all over town—

SECOND. What is?

THIRD. Tell us quickly, Gus.

FOURTH. —EVERYONE'S talking about it.

TRIO. Tell us, tell us—

FOURTH, *archly, finger at lip*. Will you give me a big kiss, every one of you,
  if I tell—?

TRIO. Yes yes yes—. *They cover him with kisses.* What is it?

FOURTH. Guess.

THIRD. Are the baths going to be renovated?

SECOND. Is Caesar sick?

FIRST, *rapturously*. Will he whip us?

FOURTH. No. You're ALL of you wrong, every one of you.

THIRD. WHAT is it?

FIRST. O you're so exasperating.

SECOND. It's just mean of you to keep it to yourself, Gus—

FOURTH, *tantalizingly.* Shall I tell?

TRIO. Yes yes yes.

FOURTH. All right. *With enormous solemnity.* Daisy's dead.

TRIO. Dead!

SECOND. I don't believe it.

FIRST. I was with him only yesterday.

FOURTH. Well, he's dead.

THIRD. Impossible!

FIRST. How did he die?

FOURTH, *proudly, with solemnity.* Choked to death.

SECOND and THIRD. O-o.

FIRST, *rolling up his eyes and clasping his hands, murmurs rapturously.* What a b-e-a-u-t-i-f-u-l death! *Trumpets without: enter majestically the onorevole* BENITO MUSSOLINI, *more or less in the costume of Napoleon and with the traditional pose of that hero—"hands locked behind, As if to balance the prone brow Oppressive with its mind" (Browning)—but also wearing, at the end of a lightningrod, a halo, probably in token of his Christlike role in raising Italia from the dead. Changing his pose, he sticks one hand in his abdomen, à la numerous portraits of the mighty Buonaparte.*

FOUR FAIRIES, *executing, more or less together, the fascist or Roman salute.* Hail, Caesar.

MUSSOLINI, *who is played by the* DOCTOR. Hello girls, have you heard the news?

SECOND FAIRY, *repeating the fascist salute.* We have, Caesar.

FIRST, *ditto.* Gus told us, Caesar.

FOURTH, *ditto.* I told them, Caesar, about Daisy.

MUSSOLINI. Daisy be damned, shrimp.

FOUR FAIRIES, *saluting.* Aye, Caesar, aye.

MUSSOLINI. I'm talking about something important, damn it all.

THIRD FAIRY, *timidly.* If it is permitted to ask—have you lynched some more communists, Caesar?

FIRST, *ecstatically.* That would be just too wonderful!

MUSSOLINI. Lynched? I've roasted 'em alive, lozenge.

FOUR FAIRIES, *whisper.* O, w-o-n-d-e-r-f-u-l.

MUSSOLINI. Fifty today, sixty-nine yesterday, three hundred and forty-six the day before: that makes—six and nine are fifteen carry one, and four i. five, eleven, five is sixteen, one and three is four— four hundred and sixty-five exactly, not including women and children.

FOUR FAIRIES, *as before.* Div-ine.

MUSSOLINI. Nonsense, it's all a trick—anyone with brains can do it.

FOURTH FAIRY, *involuntarily.* O—no!

MUSSOLINI. I say they can, turnip! *Wheeling, shouts.* CAMERIERI! *Enter a saluting fascist.*

FASCIST. Aye Caesar.

MUSSOLINI. We know its you. —A Mussolini special. *Exit* FASCIST, *walking backwards with some difficulty and saluting at the same time.*

SECOND FAIRY, *giggling embarrassedly.* If it—if it is permit-

MUSSOLINI. Speak, thumbprint.

SECOND FAIRY, *trembling.* Can Caesar do—

MUSSOLINI. Caesar can do anything, nitwit. *Reenter* FASCIST, *bearing on a tray one liqueurglass and a fivegallon can which is labelled in huge black letters* CASTOR OIL. MUSSOLINI *takes the glass.* Pour, slave. *The* FASCIST *pours.* —Basta! *Lifting the brimming glass,* MUSSOLINI *intones.* To S.M. Il Re! MUSSOLINI *and everyone else salute:* MUSSOLINI *drains the glass at a gulp—hands it to the* FASCIST, *who exits with tray, walking backwards and saluting with his left hand at the same time.* That's better! MUSSOLINI *smacks his lips.* What was I saying, girls?

THIRD FAIRY. The news, Caesar.

MUSSOLINI. O yes; well I've forgotten now. Something of no importance—. *A terrific crash, accompanied by screams, shrieks, screechings, shouts, gasps, grunts, groans, moans and similar expressions of woe, occurs and is immediately followed by piercing yells of "POLICE!" "MURDER!" "FIRE!"—The* FOUR FAIRIES *start almost out of their skins.*

THIRD FAIRY. Whatever was that perfectly frightful noise!

SECOND. Wasn't it ghastly?

FIRST, *whimpers.* O I'm so nervous.

MUSSOLINI. CAMERIERI! *Enter saluting* FASCIST. What in Hell was that?

FASCIST, *saluting.* Rome, Caesar.

FOURTH FAIRY. I was sure something terrible had happened—

MUSSOLINI. Silence, geranium! —What about Rome, slave? What's it making that noise for?

FASCIST, *saluting.* Rome can't help it, Caesar.

MUSSOLINI. Can't help it, onion! —Whaduhyuhmean Rome can't help it!

FASCIST, *saluting.* It's burning, Caesar.

FOUR FAIRIES. —Burning!—

MUSSOLINI, *drawing himself up to his full majestic shortness roars.* SILEN-ZIO! *The* FAIRIES *cringe before him: he surveys them with utter contempt—wheeling, speaks in a businesslike tone.* Knew I'd forgotten something. —Rome, of course. *To* FASCIST. Well, what are you waiting for?

FASCIST, *saluting.* The great Caesar's orders.

MUSSOLINI. Orders, my orders—yes, naturally. *Removing his Napoleonic hat, scratches his head.* Pray to the Gods! And hurry up about it. *The* FASCIST *backs salutingly off, colliding with an entering* MESSENGER *who, disentangling himself, falls on one knee, saluting.*

MESSENGER. Hail, Caesar, reign forever.

MUSSOLINI. Cough up, snowdrop, what's on your mind?

MESSENGER. My lord, the lady Popaea craves an audience.

MUSSOLINI. I don't get yuh, kid: slip it to me easy, I'm shortwaisted.

MESSENGER. Well—. *Simpering.* She craves to see your highness.

MUSSOLINI. She ought to be ashamed of herself. Say that my highness is invisible.

MESSENGER. I have already said that, Caesar. *He laughs foolishly.* Yet she persists, forsooth.

MUSSOLINI. Try again, old dear. Tell her I've got the mumps or something. *A second frightful crash—followed by darkness.*

VOICE OF HIM. On the whole, how did that scene strike you?

VOICE OF ME. Not very favourably.

VOICE OF HIM. Really?

VOICE OF ME. You can see for yourself how silly it is to try to make a critic out of me.

VOICE OF HIM. I shall confine myself, however, to stating that your disapproval comes as a surprise; considering the allpervading atmosphere of inherent spiritual nobility—not to mention the profound, deepspread, underlying religious significance of the thing. Possibly you didn't realize that those lads in the passionate nighties were Ecce Homos: the only lineal descendants of the ancient and honourable house of Savoy?

VOICE OF ME. I hate history.

VOICE OF HIM. So do I.—Europe, Africa, Asia: continents of Give. America: the land of Keep—Keep in step Keep moving Keep young Keep your head Keep in touch with events Keep smiling Keep your shirt on Keep off the grass Keep your arms and limbs inside the car. National disease: constipation. National recreation: the movies. National heroes: Abraham Lincoln who suppressed his own smut, George Washington who bought slaves with rum and Congressman Mann who freed the slaves. National anthem: You Forgot To Remember. National advertisement: The Spirit of '76—a man with a flag a man with a fife and a drummerboy—caption: General Debility Youthful Errors and Loss of Manhood. . . . Lettergo, professor!

SCENE NINE

SCENE: *The stage as in Scene I.*

Enter two figures, the GENTLEMAN *(played by the* DOCTOR*) and the* INTERLOCUTOR *(played by* HIM*).*

INTERLOCUTOR. On the whole, how does this city strike you?

GENTLEMAN. Strike me—are you inferring that I have defective eyesight? Do you think I'm mad? Eh?

INTERLOCUTOR. I wasn't inferring that—

GENTLEMAN. Strike me! *He snorts.* How does it strike you—how does it strike anybody? *With vast contempt.* —As a dungheap!

INTERLOCUTOR. There is a great deal of misery—

GENTLEMAN. Is there. I dare say.

INTERLOCUTOR. —Among the native population, I mean.

GENTLEMAN. Let me tell you something: between you and me, after looking this place over, what seems extraordinary is that the men and women who have to spend their lives in it don't all of them commit suicide.

INTERLOCUTOR. Many of them do.

GENTLEMAN. I know I should, if I had to stay here.

INTERLOCUTOR. I take it this is your first visit—?

GENTLEMAN. Yes, and my last.

INTERLOCUTOR. Yes. And I can assure you that before the war this city was not only very gay but even beautiful.

GENTLEMAN. Damitall, that's what I always heard—and here I go out of my way to come; and what do I find? A few motheaten streets and a couple of rusty restaurants. *Philosophically.* Serves me right. That's what a fellow gets in this world when he takes anybody else's word for anything.

INTERLOCUTOR. But my dear sir, you forget the war—times have changed— you see before you the fruits of defeat—

GENTLEMAN, *vehemently.* I do forget the war. And what's more, I see no reason why everybody else shouldn't. It would be a damn good thing for some of these people if they turned over a new leaf and showed a little life! Why, look here—. *He plunges a hand into his outside jacket pocket: produces a fistful of paper money.* Look at this—

INTERLOCUTOR. Poo.

GENTLEMAN. Pooh nothing; it's no joke, let me tell you—why a fellow needs a trunk to carry a nickel's worth—

INTERLOCUTOR. You misunderstand me: I'm telling you that the unit of currency here is the poo.

GENTLEMAN. O, I see: poo—yes, of course.

INTERLOCUTOR. Do you know what the poo was equivalent to, before the war?

GENTLEMAN, *nettled.* I don't know and I don't care! It's worthless now—

INTERLOCUTOR. Worthless? No; not exactly. Do you know what a mill is?

GENTLEMAN. I'll say I do. My old man made his dough in 'em. O boy.

INTERLOCUTOR. I meant another kind—we were speaking of currency: a mill in American money is the tenth part of a cent.

GENTLEMAN. O, currency—tenth part, sure. I get you.

INTERLOCUTOR. Well: if a mill were a hundred dollars, if it WERE—you understand?

GENTLEMAN. Hundred dollars, sure.

INTERLOCUTOR. A poo, at the present rate of exchange, would be worth slightly less than half of one-eighth of the sixteenth part of one mill.

GENTLEMAN. Hm. Yas. I dare say. Terrible, isn't it.

INTERLOCUTOR. It's a great deal more terrible than you or I imagine. But speaking of the war—

GENTLEMAN, *turning on him, cries petulantly.* The war? The war's over, isn't it?

INTERLOCUTOR. Not in this part of the world, my friend. You have only to look about you to realize that—

GENTLEMAN. O well, if it isn't it ought to be, and remembering it won't do anybody any good—you'll agree to that?

INTERLOCUTOR. But one has to realize that people everywhere are hungry— that there are riots almost daily—

GENTLEMAN. Riots? What do you mean?

INTERLOCUTOR. I mean that people are rioting.

GENTLEMAN. You mean people are rioting—here are people, you and I,
neither of whom (unless I'm very much mistaken) can be said by the
most ignorant and uninformed person to be rioting.

INTERLOCUTOR. I refer to the poor. The unemployed. There are five hundred thousand of them in this city with nothing to eat, I believe.

GENTLEMAN. Do you? Let me tell you something: I believe nothing the
newspapers say.

INTERLOCUTOR. It's a fact. I saw at least ten thousand only a few days ago
—Monday, it was—demonstrating in front of the Crystal Hotel.

GENTLEMAN. Did you indeed. That happens to be my hotel.

INTERLOCUTOR. You have just moved in, perhaps?

GENTLEMAN. No, worse luck.

INTERLOCUTOR. May I ask how long you've been stopping at that hotel?

GENTLEMAN. You may. I've been there ever since I arrived. I arrived, lemme see: yes—last Saturday. I shall leave next Saturday. I should leave
this minute if there was a decent train.

INTERLOCUTOR. The demonstration which I saw in front of your hotel occurred last Monday at about eleven in the morning.

GENTLEMAN. I saw nothing unusual at eleven in the morning. In fact, if I
remember correctly, I was in bed at eleven in the morning.

INTERLOCUTOR. And you heard nothing unusual?

GENTLEMAN. I heard a mild rumpus of some sort—nothing to disturb myself
about.

INTERLOCUTOR. A few weeks ago, I believe, they smashed your hotel and
held up all the occupants, ladies included.

GENTLEMAN. I believe nothing unless I see it.—And do you believe the
occupants of my hotel gave them anything?

INTERLOCUTOR. Several billion poo and a few thousand dollars . . . of
course, the crowd may not have held up the people in bed; I don't
know about that. The wisest thing, under the circumstances, might be
to go to bed and stay there.

GENTLEMAN. My dear chap, I stay in bed when it pleases me to stay in
bed; and I get up when I like to get up; and I read all the newspapers
I can find—few enough, Heaven knows, in this godforsaken place—

INTERLOCUTOR. —And which you can understand.

GENTLEMAN. I beg your pardon?

INTERLOCUTOR. —All the newspapers in English.

GENTLEMAN. Naturally. What else should I read? —But as I was saying: I
read them all, and I believe not a word in any of them.

INTERLOCUTOR. Then may I ask why you read them?

GENTLEMAN. Because in a hole like this there's nothing else to do. Besides
which, let me tell you something: it rather amuses me to see how con-
sistently they contradict each other. *A dull booming hum is heard*: *the
noise grows, thickens—within it, noises appear and disappear.*

INTERLOCUTOR. If, as I am led to believe, you enjoy seeing things for yourself, all you need do is wait here a few minutes. Because—do you hear
that?

GENTLEMAN. I hear a noise; or if you like, I hear noises.

INTERLOCUTOR. Exactly. They're coming.

GENTLEMAN. They? Who's they?

INTERLOCUTOR. The mob.

GENTLEMAN. Well?

INTERLOCUTOR. Excuse me. I'm running along. In my experience, it's best to give these people a large berth.

GENTLEMAN. In that case, let me tell you something: I shall sit here and wait.

INTERLOCUTOR. Listen, don't be a fool: this is no laughing matter—clear out. *The noises multiply, the noise deepens.* It's damned dangerous.

GENTLEMAN. Clear out? I shall do nothing of the kind. On the contrary, I shall sit on this box and watch this mob, as you call it. *He sits down placidly on an old box.*

INTERLOCUTOR. Man! You're crazy—you don't know what you're doing. *He tugs at the* GENTLEMAN's *arm.*

GENTLEMAN. Although by your account crazy, I am sufficiently possessed of my senses to inquire why you don't go, if you don't want to stay?

INTERLOCUTOR. Idiot!— *He stands irresolute, perplexed.* Here. *He grabs out of his trouser pocket a minute gnarled loaf of coarse blackish bread. Shoves it into the* GENTLEMAN's *hands.*

GENTLEMAN. Why are you presenting me with this? *He regards it distrustfully.* What is it?

INTERLOCUTOR. Bread you ass—it may save your life. Take it.

GENTLEMAN. Thanks, I'm not hungry. *He inspects the loaf.* And if I were, I should not feel particularly inclined to eat this.

INTERLOCUTOR. You fool—throw it to them and run! *He runs for his life, as a mob—roaring, muttering, gesticulating—swarms upon the stage and curiously, gradually, fatally forms a semicircle to include the* GENTLEMAN: *beside whom, an immensely tall greenish mouldering* SHAPE *quaveringly spews itself upward.*

SHAPE. I'm hungry.

GENTLEMAN. Have you got anything to eat?

SHAPE. No.

GENTLEMAN. Then how foolish of you to be hungry—whereas, if you had something to eat, there'd be some sense in being hungry. *The greenish tall mouldering shape collapsingly sinks back into the mob: a* SECOND SHAPE, *bluish and abrupt, emerges.*

SECOND SHAPE. I have nothing to eat.

GENTLEMAN. Why don't you eat nothing then? Do you want to be hungry? *The* SECOND SHAPE *darts back into the mob. A* WOMAN *appears in its place.*

WOMAN. Give me a little piece of your bread.

GENTLEMAN, *regarding her suspiciously.* How little a piece?

WOMAN. A crumb.

GENTLEMAN. A crumb indeed. What will a crumb do?

WOMAN. It will make me live for an hour.

GENTLEMAN. Ridiculous—if what you say were true, one could, simply by eating crumbs, live forever. *Severely.* Don't forget, my dear woman, that there is such a thing as death. *The* WOMAN *disappears: an* OLD WOMAN *stands before the* GENTLEMAN.

OLD WOMAN. I'm dying.

GENTLEMAN. Are you? That's apropos of you.

OLD WOMAN. Dying yes. *She nuzzles against him.* Do you understand?

GENTLEMAN, *drawing back.* No I don't. And do you want to know why? Because, let me tell you something: I'm not dying myself. *The* OLD WOMAN *falls and is swept back into the mob, whose elements gyrate, intercreep and writhingly focus: a twisted whitish* SHAPE *spouts out.*

THIS SHAPE, *pointing.* Bread.

GENTLEMAN. Yes, that's bread. Well?

THIS SHAPE. Give.

GENTLEMAN. Give what?

THIS SHAPE. Bread.

GENTLEMAN. Why should I—what's bread for?

THIS SHAPE. Eat.

GENTLEMAN. Quite right. Bread is to eat; in giving my bread, instead of eating it, I should, therefore, be doing something quite unspeakably stupid. THIS SHAPE *spouts into the mob: a* WHORE, *hollow, delapidated, swims forward, ogling.*

WHORE, *simpers.* Give me just a tiny nibble, dearie. I'll give you something very nice for it, darling.

GENTLEMAN. Well now, that's sensible. That's talking business. You're not like the rest of them. You're businesslike, intelligent: you make me a business proposition. Well, let's hear it: just what is your proposition?

WHORE. Give me the tiniest nibble and I'll give you one deep big nice kiss.

GENTLEMAN. Your proposition interests me. Let's go on with it: what will you give me for a big nibble?

WHORE. For a big nibble I'll let you kiss me till you're tired.

GENTLEMAN, *holds up the loaf before her, speaks slowly.* And what would you do if I should give you all of this bread?

WHORE, *shrugging.* I'd give some of it away. I couldn't eat that much bread. *A* FOURTH SHAPE, *elbowing her violently aside, stands.*

GENTLEMAN, *angrily to* FOURTH SHAPE. Who are you?

FOURTH SHAPE. A human being.

GENTLEMAN, *with severity.* A being, my friend, is someone who exists; a being is someone alive. What makes you think that you're alive?

FOURTH SHAPE. I'm hungry.

GENTLEMAN. In that case, let me tell you something: what you say is sheer nonsense. Look at me—I'm not hungry. And I'm alive.

FOURTH SHAPE. No. You're not.

GENTLEMAN. What do you mean?

FOURTH SHAPE, *slowly.* You're not alive.

GENTLEMAN. Of course I'm alive. Aren't people who eat bread alive?

FOURTH SHAPE. You're. Not eating. Bread.

GENTLEMAN. Because I'm not hungry, I'm not eating it now: I prefer to save it. But I assure you I shall eat it eventually, because I'm alive and this is bread.

FOURTH SHAPE, *shakes his dark, gnarled face to left and right.* That's. Not. Bread.

GENTLEMAN. I never in all my life heard such dribble. And if it's not bread, pray what is it?

FOURTH SHAPE, *a slender mutilated finger, poking from one ragged toolong sleeve and gliding toward his filthy breast, points at his heart.* Me.

GENTLEMAN. All right then. In that case, it's more sensible that I should eat you than that you should eat yourself. *He turns away.*

FOURTH SHAPE. Dead people don't. Need to eat.

GENTLEMAN, *pettishly.* But I'm NOT dead, my dear fellow. On the contrary. I'm very much alive.

FOURTH SHAPE. Dead. You're dead, yes.

GENTLEMAN, *shrugging.* The man is crazy. Here I am sitting not two feet away from him holding a piece of bread, and he tells me I'm dead. Why, you fool, I'm no more dead than yourself, in fact much less so.

FOURTH SHAPE. I'm hungry. *His handless scarecrow sleeves gesture.* We're all hungry.

VOICES. Hungry. Yes. Eat.

GENTLEMAN, *indignantly.* And what of that? Suppose you all ARE hungry and I'm not: what the devil difference does THAT make?

FOURTH SHAPE. You're not. Hungry. Only dead people. Aren't hungry.

GENTLEMAN. This is idiotic. You don't know what you're talking about, that's the whole truth of the matter—you can't listen to reason.

FOURTH SHAPE. Listen to me. I'll make you alive.

GENTLEMAN. No thanks. My mother did that for me, some time ago.

FOURTH SHAPE. I'll be your mother. Give me your bread. I'll make you alive.

GENTLEMAN. Give you my bread, eh? What would you do with my bread if I should give it to you? —Would you eat it?

FOURTH SHAPE. Eat. Bread. Yes.

GENTLEMAN. Then by your own account you'd be dead, stupid—nobody wants to be dead.

FOURTH SHAPE. I. Want to be dead.

GENTLEMAN. O do you? Well, that's no reason why I should murder you.

FOURTH SHAPE. Yes, it's a reason.

GENTLEMAN. Now look here: I don't much fancy the idea of murdering somebody—

FOURTH SHAPE, *pointing at his heart.* Look. —Here.

GENTLEMAN. Yes, it's very dirty. —And furthermore, I see no reason why I should be a murderer against my will.

FOURTH SHAPE, *hoisting abruptly his sleeves, assumes the position of one crucified. As he does so, hands emerge.* Murder. Me. Please. *A rush of shapes around him: wallowing squirming wrestling to offer themselves—all stretching out their arms, all crying "Kill me!"*

MOTHER WITH A CHILD. Kill my baby before you kill the others; please kill my baby first.

VOICE. No, me first.

ANOTHER VOICE. Me.

GENTLEMAN, *rising, stands: trembling.—Furiously screams out.* Am I God that I should strike you all dead?

MULTITUDE OF SHAPES, *in three huge cries.* Yes. You are God. Yes.

GIRL'S VOICE, *shrill.* You are God himself.

A DARK VOICE. God is a man with a piece of bread.

GENTLEMAN. What is the—I don't—really, I don't understand you people—are you all crazy? Or am I crazy?

MULTITUDE OF SHAPES, *together.* You are dead.

GENTLEMAN, *utters a trivial brief cry.* Then damitall, kill yourselves! *He hurls the loaf. The mass of pouncing scrambling wrestling screaming yearning shapes squirmingly bulges toward the missile; revolving furiously within itself, and rumbling choking roaring, gradually disappears. Snow begins falling. The* GENTLEMAN *stands for a minute, confused—presses his hands to his head in a brittle gesture. He sits down and stares before him, with arms folded. After a minute, his hands automatically begin unbuttoning the buttons of his waistcoat. Rising, staring fixedly at the audience, he takes off his jacket—drops it to one side. Then he takes off his waistcoat and drops it on top of the jacket. Sitting down, he begins automatically unlacing one shoe. A* POLICEMAN *timidly enters.*

POLICEMAN, *saluting, speaks with the utmost respect.* Pardon me, sir. May I ask what you are doing?

GENTLEMAN, *looking up with vague eyes, does not stop unlacing.* Yes. I'm taking off my clothes.

POLICEMAN. Excuse me, sir; if I'm not mistaken it's rather cold to be undressing, isn't it? —It's snowing, sir, I believe.

GENTLEMAN, *without looking up.* I can't help it. *The snow falls more rapidly.*

POLICEMAN. Of course not, sir! But mightn't it be better to wait till you got home? *Coaxingly.* It would be warmer, sir, much warmer.

GENTLEMAN. I can't wait—I mustn't wait. *He jerks off one shoe: dropping it, begins unlacing rapidly the other.* I'm late already.

POLICEMAN. Beg pardon sir, for asking a question—if I may be so bold, why couldn't you wait? *The* GENTLEMAN, *jerking off the other shoe, holds it in both hands. His eyes lift to the* POLICEMAN'S *face. Dropping the shoe he rises suddenly; stands, staring into the embarrassed eyes before him—the* POLICEMAN *blushes.* Beg pardon; I mean (excuse me, sir, for suggesting)—it might be a trifle more decent.

GENTLEMAN, *in a low voice.* In that case, let me tell you something. *Leaning toward the* POLICEMAN, *whispers loudly.* I've. Just. Been. Born. *Hurriedly slips the suspenders from his shoulders—in another instant he steps quickly and automatically from his trousers. The* POLICEMAN *staggers. The* GENTLEMAN *drops his trousers: pauses, irresolute: after shivering doubtfully for a few seconds, he demands plaintively.* If you please what do babies wear? *The* POLICEMAN *quakes.* Very little babies? *The* POLICEMAN *totters; pulling from his left hippocket a crucifix, clamps it in fervent fists. He falls on his knees, shutting his eyes, and removes his hat into which a great deal of snow immediately falls.*

POLICEMAN, *simply.* Now I lay me down to sleep. . . .

CURTAIN

ACT THREE

SCENE ONE

SCENE: *The room of Act One, further revolved so that the fourth or invisible wall is the door wall. The wall to the audience's right (corresponding to the door wall of Act One Scene 4) is the solid wall. The middle wall is the mirror wall. The window wall is to the audience's left. HIM's hat lies on the centre of the table where the automatic was lying at the end of Act One Scene 4.*

ME and HIM are seated at opposite ends of the sofa which is against the solid wall to the audience's right.

ME. Where I am I think it must be getting dark: I feel that everything is moving and mixing, with everything else.

HIM. I feel that it's very dark.

ME. Do you—feel?

HIM. Terribly dark.

ME. Are you a little afraid of the dark?

HIM. I've always been. *The room darkens rapidly.* May I sit beside you?

ME. If you don't very much mind. *He does so.*

HIM. A hand. Accurate and incredible.

ME, *to herself.* The dark is so many corners—

HIM. Here life is, moves; faintly. A wrist. The faint throb of blood, precise, miraculous.

ME, *as before.* —so many dolls, who move—

HIM. Curve. And they talk of dying! The blood delicately descending and ascending: making an arm. Being an arm. The warm flesh, the dim slender flesh filled with life, slenderer than a miracle, frailer.

ME, *as before.* —by Themselves.

HIM. These are the shoulders through which fell the world. The dangerous shoulders of Eve, in god's entire garden newly strolling. How young they are! They are shy, shyest, birdlike. Not shoulders, but young alert birds. *The figures of ME and HIM are almost invisible.*

ME, *almost inaudibly.* Darker.

HIM. A distinct throat. Which breathes. A head: small, smaller than a flower. With eyes and with lips. Lips more slender than light; a smile how carefully and slowly made, a smile made entirely of dream. Eyes deeper than Spring. Eyes darker than Spring, more new.

ME, *to herself.* We must go very carefully . . .

HIM. These, these are the further miracles—

ME, *almost inaudibly. . . . gradually . . .*

HIM. —the breasts. Thighs. The All which is beyond comprehension—the All which is perpetually discovered, yet undiscovered: sexual, sweet. Alive!

ME, *faintly. . . . until light. Complete darkness. After a few moments her voice whispers with a sort of terror.*

VOICE OF ME. What are you saying.

VOICE OF HIM, *subdued, intense, trembling.* Not saying: praying . . . *The voice hardens. . . .* now I lay you down to not sleep—. *Silence. Then a scream: the room suddenly opens into total visibility.* ME *stands—tense erect panting—beside the sofa on which* HIM *sprawls.*

ME. No!

HIM, *slowly collecting himself rises slowly.* Are you sure? Are you terribly, wonderfully sure?

ME. Sure. Yes. *A pause. She walks upstage to the mirror. He crosses the room to the table; takes and lights a cigarette.*

HIM, *standing at the window, laughs briefly.* Mademoiselle d'Autrefois, purveyor of mental meanderings and bodily bliss to Ahsh E. M. His Imperial Majesty, the Man in the Mirror!

ME, *at the mirror.* What do you mean.

HIM. I mean—. *Twirls the match out.* —That you have been the mistress of someone.

ME. Are you terribly, wonderfully sure?

HIM. Of that? Yes. I am sure.

ME. I gave him everything, you mean?

HIM. I mean just that. Once upon a time.

ME. How extraordinary—and who were you, once upon a time?

HIM, *flicks the ash.* Why do you ask?

ME. Because—shall I tell you?

HIM. If you wish.

ME. The more I remember, the more I am sure it never happened.

HIM, *simply.* Dead.

ME, *turning from the mirror, walks toward him slowly.* And now everything changes. And I can distinguish between things. O, I begin to see things very clearly. —You are just as you were.

HIM. I understand less and less.

ME. Do you? It's clear now—can't you see?

HIM. My eyes are very bad today as the blind man said.

ME. That's what he said. *Stands before him.* And this is what you say "May I kiss you?"

HIM. I say that to whom? . . . Excuse me; will you have a cigarette?

ME, *refuses with a curt gesture.* You simply say it.

HIM. I am very dull. . . . May I kiss you?

ME. No. Because I'm not, any more—this isn't me. But somewhere me is and it would be jealous if you kissed somebody else.

HIM, *cutting a laugh in two.* "Jealous"! Why not the truth?

ME. You are making a mistake.

HIM. Probably.

ME. There's nobody else. Really: so far as I know.

HIM. I should prefer that you did not lie to me.

ME. Yes?

HIM. I should.

ME, *she looks entirely at him.* I'm not lying.

HIM, *looking intently at her.* No, you're not lying.

ME, *quietly.* The snow did it, or it was the rain—Something outside of me
    and you: and we may as well let Something alone. *She walks toward the
    sofa.*

HIM. That would be pleasant to believe.

ME, *to herself.* Which moves quietly, when everything is asleep; folding
    hands . . . I don't know. Shutting flowers I guess, putting toys away.
    She sits, in one corner of the sofa.

HIM. This is the end?

ME. Do you like to call it that?

HIM. Tell me, what is it, if it isn't the end?

ME. This might be where we begin.

HIM. To begin hurts. *A pause.* Do you think that this folding and shut-
    ting Person, who moves, can take memories away?

ME. No. *A pause. She smiles.* —I feel as if we'd never lived: everything is
    so sure, so queer. *Another pause.*

HIM. Everything will be queerer perhaps.

ME. Do you think?

HIM. When everything has stopped.

ME. Stopped?

HIM. When I and you are—so to speak—folded, with all our curves and
    gestures.

ME. In the earth?

HIM, *strolls toward the sofa.* Anywhere.

ME. Somewhere, in the Spring, you and I lying . . . together. . . .

HIM. And so exceedingly still.

ME, *smiles, shaking her head.* No: there'll be things.

HIM, *sitting opposite her.* Things?

ME. Trees pushing. And little creatures wandering busily in the ground,
    because everywhere it's Spring. *Smiles.* They will go wandering into me
    and into you, I expect—roots and creatures and things—but I shan't
    mind.

HIM. No.

ME, *in a low voice.* If I'm with you.

HIM, *in a low voice.* It will all be gone then; then it will be too late. Think.

ME. . . . I don't want to think.

HIM. Lips, which touched—at first how lightly! What were lips distinctly
    slowly coming against more than lips; mouths, firmly living upon each
    other: the focussed Ourselves (alive proud deep bewildered) approach-
    ing gradually. Nearing, exquisitely and scarcely. Touching. And then—
    heartily announced by miles, by years, of strutting light—the minute in-
    stant, the enormous Now. . . . *Pauses; smiles.* Only think, dear, of you

and of me gone, like two kites when the string breaks, positively into no
where. Shut like umbrellas. Folded like napkins.

ME, *looking at him and away, speaks softly.* Only think, dear, that you an
I have never been really in love. Think that I am not a bit the sort o
person you think. Think that you fell in love with someone you in
vented—someone who wasn't me at all. Now you are trying to fee
things; but that doesn't work, because the nicest things happen by them
selves. You can't make them happen. I can't either, but I don't wan
to. And when you try to make them happen, you don't really fool you
self and certainly you don't fool me. That's one thing about me. I'r
not clever and I don't try to make things happen. —Well, you made
mistake about me and I know that. But the fact is, you know you mad
a mistake. Everybody knows it. . . . Think what is: think that you ar
now talking very beautifully through your hat.

HIM, *his glance travels to the table and returns to her.* You are a very re
markable person—among other reasons, because you can make me afraic

ME. I'm not, and I don't want to be, remarkable. What you really thin
about me—and won't admit that you think—is true.

HIM. Don't you understand—

ME. I don't. I feel. That's my way and there's nothing remarkable abou
it: all women are like that.

HIM. Noone is like you.

ME. Pooh. I don't flatter myself—not very much. I know perfectly well it
foolish of you to waste your time with me, when there are people wh
will understand you. And I know I can't, because things were left ou
of me. —What's the use of being tragic? You know you aren't sad, rea
ly. You know what you really are, and really you're always sure of you
self: whereas I'm never sure. —If anybody were going to be tragic
ought to be me. I know that perfectly well. I've never done anythin
and I don't believe I ever will. But you can do things. Noone can mak
you unsure of yourself. You know you will go on, and all your li
you've known.

HIM, *trembling, looks at his hands.* May I tell you a great secret?

ME. A secret?

HIM. All my life I've wondered if I am any good. If my head and my hea
are made out of something firmer or more living than what I see ever
where covering itself with hats and with linen. —If all the capable an
little and disgusting minds which, somehow, are responsible for the citi
and the countries in which I exist, have not perhaps also manufacture
this thing—this bundle of wishes—which I like to call "myself." If n
arms dreams hands exist with an intensity differing from or beyond th
intensity of any other arms dreams hands. . . . You cannot imagine ho
disagreeable it is to wonder—to look about you, at the eyes and the ge
tures which promenade themselves in streets and in houses, and to l
afraid. To think: "Am I also one of these, a doll, living in a doll worl
doomed to be undressed, dressed, spanked, kissed, put to bed?" *Trem
ling, wipes carefully with his handkerchief a sweating forehead.* You car
imagine how disagreeable it is. Suppose that you spent your life buyi

a dress. Suppose that at last you found the precise and wonderful dress which you had dreamed of, and suppose that you bought it and put it on and walked in it everywhere and everywhere you saw thousands of people all of whom were wearing your dress.

1E. You mean I'm like everybody else.

1IM, *fiercely.* I mean that you have something which I supremely envy. That you are something which I supremely would like to discover: knowing that it exists in itself as I do not exist and as I never have existed. How do I know this? Because through you I have come to understand that whatever I may have been or may have done is mediocre. *Bitterly.* You have made me realize that in the course of living I have created several less or more interesting people—none of whom was myself.

1E, *with a brief gesture.* O dear. Am I like that?

IM. Like nothing.

1E. Please don't talk to me this way. I really don't understand. And I think you don't understand me, very well . . . nothing is sure.

IM, *rising, smiles.* Limbo, the without pain and joyless unworld, lady. In one act: or, my life is made of glass.

1E, *rising, moves; stands beside him.* Your—what?

IM, *carefully looking into her helpless lifted eyes, speaks carefully.* I mean a clock ticking. Words which were never written. Cries heard through a shut window. Forgotten. Winter. Flies hanging mindless to walls and ceiling around a stove. Laughter of angels. Eheu fugaces. Glass flowers. *He walks to the table and picks up his hat. Turning, makes for the invisible door.* ME *steps in front of him quickly.*

E. I have no mind. I know that. I know I'm not intelligent, and that you liked me for something else. There isn't any sense in my asking—I ask merely because I want to. I know I haven't any brains and really I don't care. I've seen women with brains and they're miserable, or anyway they look so—I don't know; it might be nice to have a mind sometimes. Please don't think I'm unhappy, because I'm not, and I'm not trying to make you unhappy. I know what I'm really like and what's more I know that you know—we're not fooling ourselves. But what you're really like I don't know; and that doesn't make me unhappy either: I don't care. I know part of you and I'm glad. As a matter of fact I'm rather proud. I think I know a great deal—for instance, if I ask you something you won't mind. And if my asking hurt you, I wouldn't care —I'm like that; it's me. I'm glad everything's over: because I've loved you very much, I'm glad there'll be nothing except memories. . . . You know what I liked best about you, what I will always like and will always remember. It's your hands—you know that and I tell you. Tell me something. Because it doesn't matter and you're going, tell me one thing. Tell me (as if I was dead and you were talking to someone else with your hands on her breasts) what there was, once, about me.

M, *after a short pause.* I hoped that I had—perhaps—told you.

E. Listen. *Earnestly, staring with entire seriousness into his eyes, almost whispers.* It's snowing: think. Just think of people everywhere and houses and rivers and trees and the mountains and oceans. Then think

of fingers—millions—out of somewhere quietly and quickly coming, hurry
ing very carefully. . . . Think of everywhere fingers touching; finger
skilfully gently everything—O think of the snow coming down beautiful
ly and beautifully frightening ourselves and turning dying and love an
the world and me and you into five toys. . . . Touch me a little. *Takin
his right wrist, she puts its hand against her dress.* It will be so pleasan
to dream of your hands. For a hundred years.

HIM, *whispers.* Dreams don't live a hundred years.

ME. Don't they? *Smiles. Lets his wrist, hand, drop.* Perhaps mine doe
*Strolling to the table, opens the box; taking, lights a cigarette; quickl
blows out the match.* It's very late, I think. *His shutting face whitens-
putting on his hat, he goes out through the invisible door; stands, facin
the audience.* ME *unsteadily crosses the room to the sofa. Darkness.*

VOICE OF ME. If I had a mind, every morning I'd jump out of bed an
hurry to a sort of secret drawer, where I kept my mind because someon
might steal it. Then I'd open the drawer with a key and find my min
safe. But to make sure, I'd take it out of the box where it lived—be
cause if I had a mind I'd be very careful of it for fear it might break
and I'd go to the window with this little mind of mine, and holding
very carefully I'd look through the window out over the roofs (wit
smoke coming up out of all the chimneys slowly and maybe a stree
where people moved carefully in the sunlight, in the morning).

SCENE TWO

SCENE: *The three rocking knitting* FIGURES, *facing the picture with the
backs to the audience. Both heads are in the picture and the* WOMAN'S *ey
are closed.*

FIRST FIGURE. I held my husband up to the light yesterday and saw throug
him.

SECOND. What did you see?

THIRD. Your Hole appearance depends upon your hair.

FIRST. I saw father eating a piece of asparagus.

SECOND. Your husband's a landscape gardener?

THIRD. It's off because it's out.

FIRST. Not exactly. He does something in the interests of science.

SECOND. Really?—What does he do?

FIRST. I'm not quite sure . . . something about guineapigs I think.

SECOND. About guineapigs? How fascinating.

THIRD. Happiness in every box.

FIRST. Yes I think he does something to them so they'll have children—

SECOND. Not really!

THIRD. A pure breath is good manners.

FIRST. —because you see he wants them to have children in the interests
science.

SECOND. How remarkable. I didn't suppose guineapigs COULD have children.

FIRST. I didn't either when I married him, but George says he doesn't see why guineapigs can't have children if children can have guineapigs.

THIRD. A clean tooth never decays.

SECOND. DO children have guineapigs?

FIRST. O yes, more's the pity. Mine often have it.

THIRD. Your nails show your refinement.

SECOND. Badly?

SCENE THREE

SCENE: *Au Père Tranquille (Les Halles). Whores asleep. Music asleep. A waiter asleep. Two customers, a* BLOND GONZESSE *and the* GENTLEMAN *of Act Two, Scene 9, sit side by each at a corner table on which are two whiskies and an ashreceiver. A bell rings violently and a* HEADWAITER *rushes into the room.*

HEADWAITER. Psst! *Exit. The whores yawn, roll off their chairs and begin dancing with one another half asleep. The pianist, starting to a sitting position, bangs out chords—the violinist, reaming his eyes, breaks into tune—the drummer, shoving back his hair, swats the cymbals. Awakened by this racket, the waiter gets up and adjusts his tie in a mirror: turning, moves glasses aimlessly here and there on tables.* TWO FEMALE VOICES *are heard in the vicinity of the doorway.*

FIRST FEMALE VOICE. Of course I know him. He's the man from whom Belasco steals his ideas.

SECOND FEMALE VOICE. Steals whose ideas?

FIRST FEMALE VOICE. Belasco's. *The owners of the voices, a* FAIRLY YOUNG WOMAN *and an* OLDER WOMAN, *enter, followed by the obsequiously ushering* HEADWAITER.

HEADWAITER, *making, unnoticed by the new arrivals, a sign of negation to music and whores.* Bon soir mesdames. Par ici mesdames? *He guides his prey to a table in the centre of the room. The whores and music cease their activities and resume their slumbers.*

OLDER. Boan swaah.

HEADWAITER, *ostentatiously presenting menus, as the new arrivals seat themselves.* Voici mesdames. *Placing himself at the* OLDER'S *elbow, he obsequiously threatens.* Qu'est-ce que c'est mesdames? *Both women pick up menus. Both study their menus attentively.*

OLDER, *absentmindedly.* Let me see. . . . *She adjusts a lorgnette.* Y-e-s. *Looking up.* Donny mwah un omb.

HEADWAITER, *feigning pleasure.* Un homme. Très bien. Et pour madame?

FAIRLY YOUNG, *flustered.* What are you having Sally?

OLDER, *laying down menu and lowering lorgnette.* An omb, dear, as usual.

FAIRLY YOUNG. That's not a bad idea. *Engagingly.* I'll have the same.

OLDER, *interpreting.* Ong kore un omb.

HEADWAITER, *as before*. Ca fait deux hommes; bien mesdames. *To* OLDER.
Et comment madame désire-t-elle son homme?

OLDER, *without hesitation*. Stewed, seal voo play.

HEADWAITER, *to* FAIRLY YOUNG. Et madame?

FAIRLY YOUNG. What does he want to know?

OLDER. He says how do you want your omb.

FAIRLY YOUNG, *puzzled and embarassed*. My, what?

OLDER. Your omb, your man.

FAIRLY YOUNG. O—my man—yes . . . how are you having yours?

OLDER. I'm having mine stewed because I like them that way, I think
they're nicest when they're stewed.

FAIRLY YOUNG, *doubtfully*. I think they're nice that way too.

OLDER. Have yours any way you like, dear.

FAIRLY YOUNG. Yes . . . let me see. *Pause*. I think I'll have mine boiled.

OLDER, *interpreting*. Voo donny ray poor mwah un omb stewed, a, poor
moan ammy, un omb boiled.

HEADWAITER, *as before*. Bien madame. Et comme boisson, madame?

OLDER. What do you want to drink, dear?

HEADWAITER, *interpolating*. Une bonne bouteille de champagne, n'est-ce pas,
madame?

FAIRLY YOUNG. I don't care.

OLDER. A voo donny ray, avek sellah, oon bootay der Ay-vyon.

HEADWAITER, *almost bursting with rage*. Merci mesdames. *Turning to the
waiting* WAITER. Bring two men immediately for these ladies and have
one of the men boiled and the other stewed.

WAITER, *saluting*. Benissimo, sehr gut. *He vanishes*.

OLDER, *produces and opens a cigarettecase: offers it*. Will you have a cigar
ette?

FAIRLY YOUNG, *hastily, producing ditto*. Try one of mine. They're camels.

OLDER. Thank you, I think I prefer lucky strikes. *Each lights her own
cigarette*. Well, dear. How do you like Paris?

FAIRLY YOUNG. I think Paris is darling. I've met so many people from New
York.

OLDER. Yes, Paris is certainly cosmopolitan.

FAIRLY YOUNG. O, very.

OLDER, *after a pause*. Have you been here long?

FAIRLY YOUNG. Only a few days. Dick and I arrived last—when was it—let
me see: today is . . . Thursday. . . .

OLDER. Today is Tuesday.

FAIRLY YOUNG. Is today really Tuesday?

OLDER. Today must be Tuesday, because Monday was yesterday. I know
because yesterday I had a fitting on a dress I bought at Poiret's. You
should see it—

FAIRLY YOUNG. O dear, then I missed an appointment at the hairdresser'
if today is Tuesday. Well, I'll go tomorrow. . . . What were we talking
about? I didn't mean to interrupt.

OLDER. Let me see . . . O I asked you if you'd been here long, that was it

FAIRLY YOUNG. O yes, of course. —Why no, Dick and I arrived . . . last

Friday, I guess it was—on the Aquitania.

OLDER. I came on the Olympic myself.

FAIRLY YOUNG. Really.

OLDER. Did you have a pleasant trip?

FAIRLY YOUNG, *enthusiastically*. Simply glorious. Dick was sick all the time.

OLDER. How silly of him. *A pause.* I suppose you've been about a great deal since you arrived?

FAIRLY YOUNG. O yes. I've seen everything there is to see.

OLDER, *dreamily*. Have you seen that old Church, such a beautiful old ruin, over somewhere to the East is it?

FAIRLY YOUNG, *promptly*. Which bank?

OLDER. I'm talking about a church, it's very famous, very old—

FAIRLY YOUNG. I meant which bank of the Sane is it on?

OLDER, *unabashed*. O, I don't know, but I think it was on the further one, if I remember rightly.

FAIRLY YOUNG. The interesting one where the students live?

OLDER. You know what I mean, the car tea a lat tan, and all that.

FAIRLY YOUNG. I think I know the one you mean.

OLDER. It's the right, isn't it? I'm always getting them mixed.

FAIRLY YOUNG. I never can keep them straight either.

OLDER. Well, anyway—it's the loveliest old thing—you must have seen it. *Pause.*

FAIRLY YOUNG. If it's very old, I must have.

OLDER. O—it's very old! *The women smoke. The whores and music snore.* *A pause.* There was something I wanted to tell you, and it's completely gone out of my head. I can't think what . . . O, yes: this dress I've just bought. It's such a LOVELY dress.

FAIRLY YOUNG, *insincerely*. I should SO like to see it.

OLDER. We'll go around there tomorrow after lunch—it's black satin, very simple, but the loveliest lines you ever saw in your life, and just oceans of real Brussels lace. *She makes an oceanic gesture.*

FAIRLY YOUNG. How wonderful. Did it cost much?

OLDER. I should say so—from Poiret, you know: terribly expensive . . . as I remember it, let me see: why I think I paid three of those very big notes; you know, the brown ones.

FAIRLY YOUNG. I thought the brown ones were fifty.

OLDER. The small brown ones are, but these were the big brown ones. *A pause.*

FAIRLY YOUNG. The yellow ones with the pictures are a hundred, aren't they?

OLDER. Yes, the pictures are a hundred, and then there's a five hundred. The ones I was thinking of are the thousand, I guess—unless there's a ten-thousand franc note. . . . I always get confused whenever I try to figure out anything which has to do with money.

FAIRLY YOUNG. So do I, here. American money is so much more sensible, I should think they'd adopt it everywhere.

OLDER. Well, I suppose it would cause some difficulties.

FAIRLY YOUNG. You'd think they'd adopt it here, though. The French are supposed to be so intelligent.

OLDER, *confidentially.* O but they're not—really. Why, only today, I tried to make a taxidriver understand where I wanted to go: it was perfectly simple, song karawnt sank roo der lay twahl, and I said it over THREE times, and even then he couldn't seem to understand—

FAIRLY YOUNG. Yes. I know.

OLDER. —so finally I had to say it in English. And then he understood!

FAIRLY YOUNG. They seem to understand English better than French nearly everywhere in Paris, now.

OLDER. Well, I suppose it's the war, don't you think so?

FAIRLY YOUNG. Dick thinks so.

OLDER. Dick—?

FAIRLY YOUNG. My husband. He was in Paris during the war.

OLDER. O. Was he.

FAIRLY YOUNG. Yes. He started in by being a major, but he soon got promoted to colonel.

OLDER. How interesting. —I wonder if you know a man named Seward.

FAIRLY YOUNG, *eagerly.* Jim Seward or Jack Seward? I know them both well I'm crazy about Jack. He came over on the boat with me.

OLDER. I think this one's name was Tom, or something like that. I can't quite remember. . . .

FAIRLY YOUNG, *as before.* Is he blond and wonderful looking?

OLDER. No, he's rather dark, and very UNattractive: in fact, quite ugly.

FAIRLY YOUNG. O. *A pause.*

OLDER. Tom Seward, yes that was his name. His father was a prominent banker or something.

FAIRLY YOUNG. I don't think I ever met him. *A pause.* Why?

OLDER. O I just wondered. *A long pause.*

FAIRLY YOUNG, *glancing about her for the first time.* It's quiet here, isn't it I expected it to be lively.

OLDER. Did you? —I thought just the opposite. The name is so quiet: Pare Trank Eel. It means Tranquil Father, you know. *A pause.*

FAIRLY YOUNG. I never heard of it. Is it well known?

OLDER. Only to those who KNOW. *A pause.*

FAIRLY YOUNG. I was just thinking it looked very exclusive. *The bell rings with terrific violence. Whores and music leap into consciousness. A* MAN'S VOICE, *cheerfully patronising, is heard in the vicinity of the doorway.*

MAN'S VOICE. Here we are! *In the doorway appear two* WOMEN, *one* ELDERLY, *one* YOUTHFUL, *attired in the last wail of fashion.*

ELDERLY, *pushing* YOUTHFUL. You go first, Alice.

YOUTHFUL, *entering with a slouchy saunter which is intended to convey the impression that she is blasé, speaks in a flat Middlewestern voice. So this is Paris. Stares about her, standing awkwardly and flatfootedly. The* ELDERLY WOMAN *follows, drawing herself up and using her lorgnette Two men, alikelooking in evening dress, block the doorway.*

OWNER OF MAN'S VOICE BEFOREMENTIONED. Go ahead, Will.

MAN ADDRESSED. You know the ropes, Bill. *He sidesteps.* BILL *bursts into the room, followed by the* HEADWAITER.

HEADWAITER. Would you like a nice table sir, over here sir—. *Salaaming, he rushes to a table in the corner opposite the* GENTLEMAN *and the* BLOND GONZESSE. *Pulls out chairs.*

BILL. This all right for ever-body?

ELDERLY WOMAN, *having completed her inspection of the room, smiles mysteriously.* I think this will be all right.

BILL. Siddown ever-body. *A* CHASSEUR *enters, taking off his cap, and approaches* WILL.

ELDERLY WOMAN. I'll sit here.

BILL. Thass right Lucy—where's Will?

YOUTHFUL WOMAN. Where do I go?

ELDERLY WOMAN. You sit here, Marjorie, where you can see everything.

WILL, *who is standing, facing the* CHASSEUR *with an expression at once vague and mistrustful.* How much do I give this feller, Bill?

YOUTHFUL WOMAN. There doesn't seem to be much to see.

BILL. Give 'im five francs. WILL, *pulling out a wad of twenty, fifty and hundred franc notes from his trouser pocket, gives a fifty to the* CHASSEUR.

CHASSEUR, *bowing briefly.* Merci msieur. *Putting on his cap he hurries out in search of new victims.*

ELDERLY WOMAN. Come here Will, and sit by me. *A* VESTIAIRE *hurries in.*

HEADWAITER, *to the* WAITER, *who has been hiding respectfully behind his superior.* Allez vite: cherchez-moi la carte. *The* WAITER *sprints to a neighboring table, grabs a menu, returning, hands it to the* HEADWAITER. *The* VESTIAIRE *comes up.*

VESTIAIRE, *insinuatingly.* Voulez-vous vous débarasser msieurs mdames?

BILL. She wants our hats 'n' coats. *He gives her his derby.*

ELDERLY WOMAN. I'll keep mine, it's rather chilly here.

BILL. Alice?

YOUTHFUL WOMAN. No thanks.

BILL, *to* VESTIAIRE. Say too. *The* VESTIAIRE *regretfully turns.* WILL *seizes her by the sleeve.*

WILL. Hay. *Whispers.* Where's thuh. *He gestures occultly, winking ponderously.*

VESTIAIRE, *removing* WILL's *derby from his hand.* Par ici, msieur. *She beckons:* WILL *follows her through the doorway.*

HEADWAITER, *bending over* BILL *and holding the menu so that* BILL *cannot quite see it, speaks caressingly.* Will you have a little soup sir, and some nice oysters—

BILL. Wait a minute. 'Re we all here? Where's—

HEADWAITER, *apologetically, in a low voice.* The gentleman'll be right in sir.

BILL. I getcha. *Loudly.* Well now, what'd you girls like to eat?

ELDERLY WOMAN. You do the ordering, Billie dear, you know we can't read it.

HEADWAITER, *suggestingly.* Oysters are very nice sir, or a nice steak—

YOUTHFUL WOMAN, *impatiently.* I'll take anything.

BILL, *importantly.* Lessee. *He takes the menu, studies it.*

HEADWAITER, *coaxingly, almost playfully.* A little soup to begin with sir—

BILL. Yas. Soup ahl un yon poor toolah mond.

HEADWAITER. Bien msieur.

ELDERLY WOMAN, *to* YOUTHFUL WOMAN. Did you see those. . . . *She nods
towards the whores.*

YOUTHFUL WOMAN. Uhhuh. *She turns her dull gaze upon the* BLOND GON-
ZESSE. *The* BLOND GONZESSE *fixes her with a glassy eye.*

BILL. 'M ordering soup for Will.

ELDERLY WOMAN, *quickly.* That's right.

HEADWAITER. Et après. . . .

BILL. Ap ray, donny mwah daze weet.

HEADWAITER, *approvingly.* Des huitres, bien msieur. Quatre douzaines,
n'est-ce pas msieur? WILL, *hands in pockets, enters vaguely.*

ELDERLY WOMAN, *beckoning anxiously.* Over here, Will!

WILL, *overhereing.* Hullo everybody.

BILL, *looks up.* Siddown Will. Thought you fell overboard.

ELDERLY WOMAN. We ordered you some soup. WILL *sits heavily beside her.*

HEADWAITER. Une douzaine chacun?

BILL. He wants to know how many—. *Desperately to* HEADWAITER. We.

HEADWAITER, *radiating approbation.* Et pour la suite msieur—un bon rumstek
—un chateau—un veau sauté—?

WILL, *ponderously, growls.* Thought I was lost out there.

ELDERLY WOMAN. Yes?

BILL. We we, kom voo voo lay. *The* HEADWAITER, *beaming, writes down a
great many things hurriedly on a pad.* Et ensuite—un peu de fromage—
un dessert—you wish strawberries?

WILL. Got some pretty slick girls out there. One of 'em tried to get my
watch.

BILL. Will you have strawberries?

YOUTHFUL WOMAN. All right, all right anything at all.

HEADWAITER. Strawberries very fresh.

BILL. Strawberries poor toola mond. Wutabout something to drink?

HEADWAITER. Il n'y a que champagne msieur.

BILL. We we, sham pain.

HEADWAITER, *tears sheet from pad and hands it to* WAITER, *who mercurially
disappears.* Bien messieurs mesdames. *Turning, beckons vehemently to
the music, which has stopped but which immediately recommences with
redoubled vigor.*

OLDER WOMAN, *to* FAIRLY YOUNG. I'll ask him. —May truh dough tell. *The*
HEADWAITER *wheels.* Seal voo play — *He comes to her table.* Voo parlay
onglay?

HEADWAITER, *irritated.* Yes, I speak English.

OLDER WOMAN, *indicating* WILL *and* BILL, *whispers.* Are those our ombs?

HEADWAITER. Yes madame. But they are not quite ready yet—a little patience, madame.

OLDER WOMAN. O, I see. All right. Thank you, may truh dough tell. *The*
HEADWAITER *hurries off. The* OLDER *whispers the news to the* FAIRLY
YOUNG, *who stares seductively at the ombs. Enter* HIM, *walking too
straight, carrying in his left hand a cabbage. He walks too straight up
to the table where the* BLOND GONZESSE *and the* GENTLEMAN *are sitting and*

bows interrogatively to the GENTLEMAN, *indicating an imaginary third place with a majestic wave of his right hand.*

HIM. Permettez, monsieur?

BLOND GONZESSE, *immediately.* Oui monsieur. *She giggles.*

GENTLEMAN. Sit down. HIM *draws up a chair. Sits, with the cabbage in his lap.* Waiter!

WAITER. Msieur?

HIM, *to* WAITER. Trois whis-ky et une assiette.

WAITER. Une assiette msieur—comment—? Une assiette anglaise?

HIM, *sternly.* Non. Une assiette nature, pour le choux.

WAITER. Ah—pour le choux. Bien msieur. *Exit.*

GENTLEMAN. I never forget faces.

HIM. Really?

GENTLEMAN. Your face is familiar.

HIM. Yes?

GENTLEMAN. I've seen you somewhere before.

HIM. Possibly. *A pause.*

GENTLEMAN. Were you ever in a city where the money is called "poo"?

HIM. I may have been.

GENTLEMAN. I think you were, and I think that's where I met you.

HIM. The world's not so big, after all. *The* BLOND GONZESSE *giggles.*

GENTLEMAN, *to* BLOND GONZESSE. Pardon—meet my friend Mr.—

HIM, *promptly.* John Brown. *Bows.*

BLOND GONZESSE. Enchantée, monsieur.

GENTLEMAN. Have a cigar. *Producing two.* The lady prefers cigarettes.

HIM, *taking one.* Thanks. *He and the* GENTLEMAN *bite off and spit out the tips of their cigars.* HIM *strikes a match: lights the* GENTLEMAN'S *cigar and his own.*

GENTLEMAN, *smoking.* Did I understand you to say you were John Brown?

HIM, *smoking.* Correct.

GENTLEMAN. In that case let me ask you something: does your body lie mouldering in the grave? *Leaning across the table.* Because mine does.

HIM. Yes?

GENTLEMAN. But that isn't all of it. *Drawing himself up, remarks smilelessly.* My soul goes marching on. HIM *inspects the cabbage gravely. The* BLOND GONZESSE *giggles.* The lady doesn't believe me. She doesn't know who I am. I just met her.

HIM. Who are you?

GENTLEMAN. I am the unpublished photograph of George Washington crossing the Susquehanna in a breechesbuoy. Who are you?

HIM. I live here.

GENTLEMAN. In that case, let me ask you something: are you one of those God, damned, artists? *The whiskies and a large plate arrive.*

WAITER, *to* HIM. Voici msieur, l'assiette nature. *The* BLOND GONZESSE *giggles.*

HIM, *carefully transferring the cabbage from his lap to the empty plate and lifting carefully his whisky, answers.* No. That is, not exactly: I earn money by taming jellyfish.

GENTLEMAN, *picking up his whisky.* The lady doesn't believe you. The lady doesn't believe anything.

HIM. The lady is a wise lady—à votre santé madame. *Gravely bows to the* BLOND GONZESSE. Ashes to ashes. *Bows gravely to the* GENTLEMAN.

GENTLEMAN. Ally upp. HIM *and the* GENTLEMAN *drink their whiskies.*

YOUTHFUL WOMAN, *angrily repulsing* BILL's *halfhearted attempt to embrace her, and gazing rapturously at* HIM *who does not see her.* Don't!

FAIRLY YOUNG WOMAN, *excitedly whispers to* OLDER, *indicating* BILL. I think mine's almost ready.

A WHORE, *yawning, to a yawning whore.* Rien à faire ce soir.

WILL, *pouring himself his fourth glass of champagne and staring fixedly at the* OLDER WOMAN. Some. Baby.

ELDERLY WOMAN, *to* WILL, *while desperately ogling the unnoticing* GENTLE-MAN. Give ME a little champagne, please.

GENTLEMAN, *to* HIM. How much.

HIM. How much what?

GENTLEMAN. How much do you make?

HIM. O—thirty cents a jellyfish.

GENTLEMAN. What do you do with them, when they're tame?

HIM. I sell them to millionaires. *He turns amorously to the* BLOND GONZESSE. Il fait chaud, n'est-ce pas, mademoiselle?

BLOND GONZESSE, *amorously.* Très chaud, monsieur.

GENTLEMAN, *to* HIM. Been over here long?

HIM. Not very. *He points to the cabbage.* I was born day before yesterday.

GENTLEMAN. In that case, you probably know a show I went to last night: foliz burshare. *The* BLOND GONZESSE *giggles.*

HIM. Never heard of them.

GENTLEMAN. The lady doesn't believe I've been. —Waiter!

WAITER, *who has just placed a third bottle of champagne on* WILL's *table and a second bottle of Evian on the* OLDER WOMAN's. Msieur.

GENTLEMAN, *to* HIM. The same? HIM *nods.* Ong kore.

WAITER. La même chose—bien msieur. *He sprints.*

OLDER WOMAN, *to* FAIRLY YOUNG, *pouring water in her glass.* I don't remember ever being so thirsty.

GENTLEMAN, *to* HIM. Are you married?

HIM. Sometimes.

GENTLEMAN. You ought to go to that show.

HIM. Good?

GENTLEMAN. Rotten. A bunch of amateurs and some handpainted scenery. They don't know how to put on a show over here. Little Old New York is the only place where the theatre's any good. *Two whiskies arrive.* One more whisky for the lady.

BLOND GONZESSE, *protestingly.* Non, merci.

HIM. The lady's got one. *Indicates an untouched glass.*

GENTLEMAN. Give the lady a drink, waiter. Ong kore.

WAITER. Encore un wis-kee—bien msieur. *Sprints.*

GENTLEMAN. As for the women, they're fat and they're clumsy and they're naked and they don't know they're alive. *He drinks his whisky.* I can hand Paris only one thing: the Scotch is sure death. What are you doing with that cabbage? Taming it?

WAITER. Un wis-kee—voici msieur. *Places another whisky on the table.*

GENTLEMAN, *to* WAITER. How much is all this?

WAITER. Ca vous fait. . . .

GENTLEMAN. Kom be an.

WAITER. Ca fait—quatre cent francs juste, msieur. *The* BLOND GONZESSE *giggles.*

GENTLEMAN. The lady doesn't think I can pay for it. *He produces a wallet and pulls out a five hundred franc note.* Sang song frong: keep the change. *He puts back the wallet.*

WAITER, *turning white with pleasure.* Merci msieur. *He and the* BLOND GONZESSE *exchange significant glances.*

BILL, *totally disregarding the anguish of the* ELDERLY WOMAN *who has been helping herself freely to champagne and is now swaying dangerously against him, lifts his glass to the* FAIRLY YOUNG WOMAN. Pyjama pyjama.

HIM, *drinking his whisky, addresses the* GENTLEMAN. Going back?

GENTLEMAN. Back?

HIM. Back to the dear old U.S.A.?

GENTLEMAN, *drunkenly shaking his head.* Can't do it.

HIM. No?

GENTLEMAN, *all of him leaning across the table speaks distinctly.* Let me tell you something: I had a son. And he's a drunkard. And I had a daughter: and she's a whore. And my son is a member of all the best clubs in New York City. And my daughter married thirteen million dollars. And I'm a member of the God, damned, bourgeoisie. *He passes out cold.*

HIM, *solemnly, to the collapsed* GENTLEMAN. Admitting that these dolls of because are dissimilar, since one goes up when the other comes down, and assuming a somewhat hypothetical sawhorse symmetrically situated with reference to the extremities of the strictly conjectural seesaw, god is the candlestick or answer. *Arising, waves majestically to the music which immediately strikes up* Yes, We have No Bananas—*turning, bows to the* BLOND GONZESSE *who has just appropriated the* GENTLEMAN's *wallet.* In that case, let me ask you something: shall we dance the I Touch? *The* ELDERLY WOMAN *vomits copiously into* BILL's *lap.*

SCENE FOUR

SCENE: *The three knitting rocking figures facing the picture with their backs to the audience.*

The DOCTOR's *head has disappeared from the picture, leaving a black hole. The* WOMAN's *head is in the picture; her eyes are closed.*

FIRST FIGURE. Terribly. Especially in summer.

SECOND. How simply frightful! All over them?

THIRD. Drowsiness rumblings sour risings heartburn waterbrash and the feeling of being stuffed.

FIRST. That depends: sometimes.

SECOND. Is it very painful?

THIRD. Ask the man who owns one.

FIRST. Not very. Like falling down stairs, and you apply the same remedy—one stick of dynamite in a tumbler of ink before meals.

THIRD. Ask dad he knows.

SECOND. I understand the dynamite but what does the ink do?

THIRD. Comes out like a ribbon lies flat on the brush.

FIRST. Why the ink dissolves the guineapigs and makes them nervous.

SECOND. And what do they do after that?

THIRD. Look for the union label on every garment.

FIRST. They? Who?

SECOND. The guineapigs.

FIRST. O! They let go of the children.

SECOND. How time flies—you never know what to expect, do you. *The* WOMAN's *head stirs in the picture: her eyes open slowly.*

FIRST. Yes life is a mystery at best.

THIRD. If it isn't an Eastman it isn't a Kodak.

SECOND. And we have so many things to be thankful for, haven't we. *The* DOCTOR's *head appears in the picture.*

FIRST. I should say so: why my husband and I were married fifty years ago come day before yesterday and we've never had a single cross word—now what do you think of that?

DOCTOR'S HEAD, *harshly, from the picture.* If you wore your garters around your neck you'd change them oftener.

SCENE FIVE

SCENE: *The room, still further revolved so that the fourth or invisible wall is the solid wall. The wall to the audience's right (corresponding to the solid wall of Scene 1) is the mirror wall. The middle wall is the window wall. The door wall is to the audience's left. On the centre of the table where* HIM's *hat was lying at the beginning of Scene 1, there is a vase of flowers.*

ME *and* HIM *sit, back to (or facing the same way as) the audience, at opposite ends of the sofa which is against the invisible wall.*

ME. I imagine, myself, it was very nice.

HIM. I remember morning. Silence. Houses in the river—April: the green Seine filled with houses, filled with windows out of which people look And everything is upside down. . . . Then there comes a least breeze And the people in the windows and the windows themselves and all the houses gradually aren't. I remember standing, thinking, in sunlight; and saying to myself "dying should be like this."

ME. Dying?

HIM. —To feel like one of the upsidedown people in one of the wrongside up windows when a breeze comes.

ME, *after a pause*. It must be a nice place, Paris, for a man.

IIM. I happened to be a dream there.

ME. But you're not any more. *Suddenly*. Tell me, do I look very old?

IIM, *smiles*. How did you get that idea?

ME. Women don't get it, they're born with it. Besides—you told me, the first time I saw you again, that I'd changed.

IIM. I don't remember saying anything.

IE. You didn't know me—which is worse.

IIM. But that's asking too much of a dream.

IE. I expect I have changed. *Shudders slightly*.

IIM. Have I?

IE. Changed? —A little.

IIM. I ask because, if you remember, you once said you had changed but that I was the same.

IE. O—yes, I remember saying that. . . .

IIM. You were right about memories.

IE. Was I?

IIM. Wonderfully right.

IE. Isn't it queer. I feel as if we'd—as if you hadn't gone. . . . Do you feel that?

IM. I can't believe that we're together.

IE. With me it's just the other way.

IIM. When one has been a dream, it takes some time to—. *He gestures smoothly*. —So to speak, renovate oneself.

IE, *almost to herself*. Let's not talk about dreams any more.

IM, *looking at her*. I shall try not to.

IE, *taking his hand, smiles*. Such a queer day, when I saw you again and you didn't recognize me—and I didn't care. *A pause*.

IM. It was raining.

IE. Terribly hard. When I saw you I was running, because I'd forgotten to take my umbrella. Then I stopped—

IM. In the rain.

IE. —in front of you.

IM. We looked at each other, probably.

IE. We never said anything.

IM, *to himself*. I seem to remember very well, looking.

IE. . . . Then you offered me your umbrella.

IM. Did I?

IE. We walked along together under your umbrella. We walked quite a distance; and most of it, people were laughing.

IM. Were people laughing?

IE. —Until we stood before the door. . . . Then I spoke to you. Do you remember what I said?—I said "it isn't raining." It hadn't been for some time and I knew; but I didn't say anything.

IM. I didn't know.

IE. You must have been a little happy?

IM. Yes.

ME. Then—do you know what you did?

HIM. No.

ME. Well, you shut the umbrella.

HIM. The key squeaked in the lock more than I expected. The floor creaked more than I remembered its creaking.

ME. Yes, I was going to use mine when you stopped me and took out yours

HIM. You had forgotten giving me that key, once upon a time.

ME. I never dreamed you'd kept it.

HIM, *to himself.* I couldn't go carefully enough.

ME. You frightened me a little when you shut the door. You shut it s very very gently. I remember how you walked to the sofa and how you sat down.

HIM. Perhaps I was afraid of breaking someone. *A pause.*

ME. We sat for a long time, where we're sitting now.

HIM. A long time?

ME. Nearly an hour, I guess. Until you got up suddenly and looked ou the window.

HIM. Outside, someone was putting away pieces of sky which looked re markably like toys.

ME, *in a low voice.* And always you stood, looking—. Your hands . . . fold ing, shutting. Finally (just as it was getting very dark) —"I think," yo said "my hands have been asleep." Very gently you said that and wen out, shutting the door carefully. I heard your feet going down the stair I sat, hearing for a long time in the rain your feet, in the dark. Wall ing. *A pause.* Tell me—when you left, without your umbrella, where di you go?

HIM. "Go?"

ME. It's silly of me to ask—I ask because I want to. Did you go to a par . . . like the big one with the animals, or the little park where th harbor is?

HIM. Harbor—how did you guess? *To himself.* Queer that I should hav done that; avoiding the animals?

ME. Ships go out sometimes; maybe you were thinking of ships.

HIM. And sometimes come in. And there I met a man with green eyes . .

ME. A man—? What was he doing?

HIM. Doing? Doing nothing, I think. Let me see: a man came and s down beside me on a bench. Because it was raining.

ME. Or because he guessed you were lonely?

HIM. . . . and a crumpled hat; who said, I remember, that he had only ju returned from Paris. O—and he didn't wear spats.

ME. Did he talk to you much?

HIM. I suppose so.

ME. What did he talk about—Paris?

HIM. Probably.

ME. Didn't you talk to him?

HIM. I don't think I did. O yes—no I didn't talk to him.

ME. Why?

HIM. Because I killed him.

ᴍᴇ, *starting violently.* —The man?

ʜɪᴍ. Himself.

ᴍᴇ. —You didn't—

ʜɪᴍ. Kill him?

ᴍᴇ. —him—

ʜɪᴍ. O, him. *Easily.* Of course I didn't. *Smiles.* —Just the other way
'round.

ᴍᴇ, *earnestly.* What do you mean?

ʜɪᴍ. It's clear now—can't you see? *Gently.* He killed me.

ᴍᴇ. Please, dear, I'm—so nervous. *Taking his other hand.* Don't.

ʜɪᴍ. —Frighten you? All right, sorry. He didn't kill me.

ᴍᴇ. Of course not!

ʜɪᴍ. On the contrary—instead, what did the wretch do?

ᴍᴇ. Never mind. Let's—

ʜɪᴍ. Why as sure as you live and as cool as you please producing from the
vicinity of his exaggerated omphalos an automatic, he asked me to shoot
himself; or perhaps I asked me to shoot himself, I can't quite remember
which. . . .

ᴍᴇ. Why are you like this?

ʜɪᴍ. Or as I said to the man in the green hat with crumpled eyes: why in
the name of Heaven should a gentleman recently returned from Paris
ask him to kill myself? And do you know what the rascal replied to that?

ᴍᴇ. I don't want to know; let's talk about something else; the play.

ʜɪᴍ. —Sir, said he, the reason I ask me to kill yourself is that a gentleman
also recently returned from Paris—

ᴍᴇ. The one you were working on when. The one, you know.

ʜɪᴍ. —from Paris, mind, has recently penetrated God's country by fast
freight with the express purpose of—

ᴍᴇ. With the negroes in it.

ʜɪᴍ. —committing the pardonable sin with my ex . . . Libido, I think was
the accurate and incredible word which he employed. *Relaxing, looks
upward.* Then the ocean, filled with trillions of nonillions of ablebodied
seamen and only-half-human mermaids and thousands upon hundreds of
whales, came up everywhere over the earth—up everywhere over the
world—and up up up to the bench where we were sitting. And the mermaids' bellies were full of little slippery fish, and the frolicking great
whales were swaying and playing upon harps of gold, and the seamen
were sailing before the mast, and the ocean . . . the ocean rose and
stood solemnly beside us, resting its chin in its hand and looking at the
recently returned gentleman from Paris. Whereupon the recently returned gentleman from Paris invited the ocean to sit down.

ᴍᴇ. You—

ᴍ. But You never said anything. You was much too busy, eyeing the
mermaids and counting the seamen and admiring the golden harps of
the most enormous of all mammals—

ᴍᴇ. —didn't—

ᴍ. —until suddenly You looked. *He smiles.* The ocean had gone: and

away off—ever so many thousands of hundreds of billions of millions o
years away—You heard a sound. It was the sound of the mermaids, witl
bellies full of gooey fish and with long hair, chasing the seamen every
where and snatching the golden harps from the hands of the resplenden
whales. And all this sound went away slowly. Finally You looked al
about You: and You was alone, holding in You's hand—. *He laughs.* —*A*
papyrus from Harun-al-Rashid inviting us all to petit déjeuner in th
most excellent Arabic at twenty-three hours on January thirty-second
seven thousand one hundred and seventeen Columbus crossed the ocean
blue. *A pause.*

ME, *quietly.* Is that all?

HIM. I put it in my pocket—the ocean green. But You didn't care a cont
nental damn.

ME. That's all?

HIM, *nodding in the direction of the table, upstage.* I see flowers.

ME. Yes, thank you. *A pause.* Do you know something?

HIM. I understand less and less.

ME. You HAVE changed.

HIM. Much?

ME. Quite a lot: your eyes . . . or maybe it's the light. Did you—

HIM. Aren't my eyes green?

ME. It's been a long time, hasn't it; since you—. *Timidly.* Please tell m
Am I different . . . very much?

HIM. "Different"?

ME. Olderlooking.

HIM, *smiles.* You seem to me a little younger, just a little younger.

ME. You're joking. I know I look older. *Shudders.*

HIM. I'm not joking, seriously. —So my eyes have changed. Probably you'r
right. Like Rip Van Winkle they've been asleep.

ME. You mean that when your eyes see me they know they've been aslee

HIM. I really mean that they don't have people like you, up there.

ME. Where?

HIM. Up in the mountains where they play a game with thunder. An
where. Nowhere. Where for a hundred years I fell asleep.

ME. O—those mountains.

HIM. Those.

ME, *after a pause.* Are you quite sure you're not sorry that you're awake

HIM. Wonderfully sure—you see, Rip's story and my story are . . . differer

ME, *laughing.* Because you haven't a beard? —O but I'm glad you haven't
beard. You know I can't stand men with beards. Or spats.

HIM. Not because I haven't a beard, but because when I woke up and can
down out of those mountains, you were younger than before.

ME. How do you know that I. Maybe I'm married, and have ever so mai
. . . didn't his?

HIM. His?

ME. Rip Van Winkle's girl; or was it his wife? I thought she'd forgotten a
about him in the meantime and married someone else.

HIM, *thoughtfully.* I only seem to remember that she was dead.

ME. O. . . .

HIM, *vaguely.* I was thinking . . . so am I. I suppose nobody, including his children, really believed him when he told them.

ME. When he told them—about the mountains?

HIM. About the mountains and about being asleep.

ME. Do you think? O dear; I'm sorry, but this is getting too complicated for me.

HIM, *earnestly.* Please be happy. Why should I talk about myself? I'd much rather talk about you.

ME. Me? *Bitterly.* There's nothing to talk about.

HIM. Isn't there? I'm very sorry. We all make mistakes.

ME, *looks at him.* I know. I make them.

HIM. You? Stop.

ME. Listen. Suppose—

HIM. Don't suppose.

ME, *bravely.* —suppose I made a mistake; and it was the mistake of my life. And suppose: O suppose—I'm making it!

HIM, *steadily.* You're wrong, quite wrong. It's the mistake of my life.

ME, *whispers.* Is it?

HIM, *quietly.* Yes.

ME, *looking at him.* It may take two people to make a really beautiful mistake.

HIM, *expressionlessly.* The nicest things happen by themselves. —Which reminds me: I had a dream only the other day. A very queer dream: may I tell it to you? *A pause.*

ME. Do you want to very much?

HIM. If you don't very much mind.

ME, *hesitantly.* If it's not too queer.

HIM. Will you promise to interrupt me if it's too queer?

ME. All right.

HIM, *leaning forward, looks at nothing.* You were with me in a sort of room. I was standing beside you and you seemed to be telling me something. But I was only tremendously glad to feel you so near. . . .

ME. Go on.

HIM. That was beautiful to me. —Then you took my left hand and you led me somewhere else in this room—and through the roomshaped dark softness I tiptoed wadingly. You paused and I stood next you: next your blood, your hair, hands, breathing. I felt that you were smiling a little. You pointed to something. And stooping carefully I could not quite see —but through this dark softness I seemed to feel—another person, lying very quietly with an entire quietness that queerly frightened me. . . . May I go on?

ME. Go on.

HIM. When I could see, this other person's eyes and my eyes were looking at each other. Hers were big and new in the darkness. They seemed to be looking at me as if we had known each other somewhere else. They were very close—so close that my breath almost touched them: so close

that my mind almost touched what looked at me from them . . . I can't
describe it—a shyness, more shy than you can ever imagine, a shyness
inhabiting very easily and very skilfully everything which is profoundly
fragile and everything which we really are and everything which we
never quite live. But—just as I almost touched this shyness—it suddenly
seemed to touch me; and, touching, to believe me and all from which
had come and into which I was changing with every least thought of
with each carefully hurrying instant. I felt a slight inexplicable gesture
—nearer than anything, nearer than my own body—an inscrutable timidity, capturing the mere present in a perfect dream or wish or Now . .
a peering frailness, perfectly curious about me; curiously and perfectly
created out of my own hope and out of my own fear. . . . I did not see
any more, then. *Pauses; smiling, resumes.* Then I stooped a little lower
and kissed her hair with my lips and with the trembling lips of my mind
I kissed her head, herself, her silence. But as I kissed her, she seemed to
me to be made out of silence by whatever is most perfectly silent; so
that, to find out if she were perhaps real, I spoke to her—and her voice
answered as if perhaps not speaking to me at all, or as if it felt embarrassed because it knew that it was doing something which it should not
do; and yet, I remember her voice was glad to feel, close by it, the unreal someone whom I had been. —Then the darkness seemed to open:
know what I saw then: it was a piece of myself, a child in a crib, lying
very quietly with her head in the middle of a biggish pillow, with her
hands out of the blankets and crossing very quietly and with a doll i
the keeping fingers of each hand. . . . So you and I together went out
of this opened darkness where a part of ourselves somehow seemed to be
lying—where something which had happened to us lay awake and in the
softness held a girl doll and a boy doll. Perhaps you closed the door
gently . . . but I remember nothing about coming into the light. *He
eyes search the face of* ME *and find a different nothing.* That is m
dream. *Rises.* —Into the mirror with it, we'll throw it away! *Strides t
the mirror, makes a quick futile gesture and stands facing the mirror. .
short pause.* ME *rises and goes to* HIM *slowly: stands, simply, sorrowfull
Turning from the mirror to* ME, HIM *speaks slowly.* Hark. That was m
dream which just fell into my soul and broke.

ME, *touches his arm pityingly, slightly.* I guess it took so long to fall b
cause it was made of nothing. *She returns to the sofa and sits down.*

HIM. You have a bright idea. *Returning to the sofa, sits opposite her.
pause.* Shall we smoke a cigarette—or two perhaps? *Fumbles in pocket
finds matches and a package of cigarettes: offers cigarettes to* ME *wh
does not see them.* Then I will; unless you—

ME. I don't mind.

HIM, *lights carefully his cigarette: pockets the matchbox. Presently remar
to himself.* But there was a dog, named something or other. *Short s
lence.*

ME. A dog.

HIM. I used to take him to bed with me. In fact we travelled everywhe
together. God spelled backwards.

ME. What sort of a dog?

HIM. The name being Gipsy. It didn't last long because it was a cloth dog. Tell me something.

ME. What.

HIM, *quietly.* Tell me you used to have a cloth dog too.

ME. I didn't . . . at least I don't think so.

HIM. Didn't you? Not ever? There was a battleship, which wound up, with invisible wheels that made it move along the floor: it was very fragile. They called it The Renown. —Did you have dolls?

ME. I guess so, I don't remember.

HIM. I perfectly remember that I had a great many dolls, but that I only loved one—a wax doll named Bellissima who melted in front of the fire. *Getting up, strolls to the table.*

ME, *half to herself.* I suppose you cried.

HIM. On the contrary, I asked for a cup of tea. *He takes from the table an imaginary cup and saucer; drops into the imaginary cup an imaginary piece of sugar.* —But you have given me symbols. Look: I see my life melting as what you call Winter. . . . The edges are fading: gradually, very gradually, it diminishes. *Takes an imaginary sip.* But notice: there is a purpose in the accident, I mean there is someone beyond and out-side what happens—someone who is thirsty and tired. Someone, to whom the disappearance of my being sweetens unbeing as, let us say, this dis-solving cube of sugar—pardon: God would like a slice of lemon. *Takes an imaginary slice.* Thank you. We are all of us just a trifle crazy, aren't we? Like Archimedes with his mirrors and like old Mr. Benjamin F. who flew kites in a thunderstorm, which reminds me—I never told you that I was flying a kite. And it pulled and rose: wonderfully reaching out and steadily climbing, climbing over the whole world until you'd never believe anything in your life could be so awfully far and bright—until you almost thought it had found some spot where Spring is all the time. . . . But suddenly my foolish hands were full of common twine string.

ME, *looking straight before her, speaks to herself after a moment.* It's snow-ing.

HIM. Gay may change, but all my thoughts are in the wash and I haven't a clean thing to put on. —After all, thoughts are like anything else you wear, they must be sent to the crazy laundry once in a while and the crazy laundry wears out more crazy thoughts than ever a crazy man did. Hypnos and Thanatos, a couple of Greek boys who made a fortune over-night, the laundry of the Awake, Incorporated: having mangled our lives with memories it rinses them in nightmare. *A drum sounds faintly.* ME *starts.* I think I hear nothing. *Puts imaginary tea carefully on table; turns, slowly walks to the middle of the room and stands facing the audi-ence.* But if I ask you something, now, will you promise to answer truth-fully? *She shakes her head.* Because you can't? —Tell me; why can't you answer me truthfully, now?

ME, *rising.* Now you want—truth?

HIM. With all my life: yes!

ME, *advancing toward him slowly.* You wanted beauty once.

HIM, *brokenly.* I believed that they were the same.

ME. You don't think so any longer?

HIM. I shall never believe that again.

ME, *pauses, standing before him.* What will you believe?

HIM, *bitterly.* That beauty has shut me from truth; that beauty has walls—is like this room, in which we are together for the last time, whose walls shut us from everything outside.

ME. If what you are looking for is not here, why don't you go where it is? *The drumsound heightens.*

HIM. In all directions I cannot move. Through you I have made a discovery: you have shown me something . . . something about which I am doubtful deep in my heart. I cannot feel that everything has been a mistake—that I have inhabited an illusion with you merely to escape from reality and the knowledge of ourselves. *To himself.* How should what is desirable shut us entirely from what is? No! That must be not quite all: I will not think that the tragedy can be so simple. There must be something else: I believe that there IS something else: and my heart tells me that unless I discover this now I will never discover it.— Am I wrong?

ME. You were talking about dolls. You see, I think sometimes.

HIM. Are you thinking, now?

ME. Now—yes. *Total darkness. The drumsound drowns in a whirling nearness of mingling voices out of which juts suddenly* ONE VOICE.

ONE VOICE. Ladies un genlmun right dis way step dis way evrybudy tuh duh Princess Anankay tuh duh Tatood Man tuh duh Huemun Needl tuh duh Missin Link tuh duh Queen uv Soipunts tuh duh Nine Foot Giun tuh duh Eighteen Inch Lady tuh duh Six Hundud Pouns uv Passionut Pullcrytood tuh duh Kink uv Borneo dut eats ee-lectrick light bulbs!

SCENE SIX

SCENE: *The stage has become a semicircular piece of depth crowded with jabbering and gesticulating people, viz.* HIM (*hatted*), *the other participant in Act 2 with the exception of those characters which were played by the* DOCTOR, *and the three Miss* WEIRDS *minus their chairs and knitting. The circumference of the semicircle is punctuated at equal intervals by nine similar platforms. The fifth platform (counting, from either extremity of the circumference, inward) supports a diminutive room or booth whose front wall is a curtain. On each of the other eight platforms sits lollingly a freak.*

Beginning with the outermost platform to the audience's left and following the circumference of the semicircle inward we have: NINE FOOT GIANT QUEEN OF SERPENTS, HUMAN NEEDLE, MISSING LINK *and the fifth or inmost platform with its mysterious booth. Continuing, outward, we have:* TATTOOE

MAN, SIX HUNDRED POUNDS OF PASSIONATE PULCHRITUDE, KING OF BORNEO *and,*
on the outermost platform to the audience's right, EIGHTEEN INCH LADY.
MISS STOP WEIRD, *to* MISS LOOK. I don't suppose he really eats them. *To*
MISS LISTEN. Do you? *All three* WEIRDS *shake their maskfaces skeptically.*
HIM, *bowing and removing his battered hat.* Excuse me, ladies—. *Indicates
the* DOCTOR, *who, disguised as a hunchback* BARKER, *has just appeared on
the platform of the* GIANT. —Who is that little creature?
MISS STOP. A harmless magician with whom we are only slightly acquainted.
MISS LOOK. A master of illusion.
MISS LISTEN. A person of no importance, his name is Nascitur.
HIM, *bows and replaces his battered hat on his head: looking about him,
speaks to himself.* Barnum, thou shouldst be Darwin at this hour.
BARKER, *beckons fervently from the platform of the rising* NINE FOOT GIANT,
toward whom the crowd swirls. Make it quick goils kummun fellurs foist
we have, Dick duh Giunt I begs tuh call duh undievieded attention uv
all lilypewshuns here presun tuh dis unparrallul phenomenun uv our
own day un time duh leas skepticul may be pardun fur nut believin wut
I states us duh in-con-tro-voitubl troot dut dis extraordinury freak uv
nachure wen standin in his stockin feet describes uh longitoodinul
trajectory uv one hundun un eight inches no more no less in duh gigantic palm uv his colussul han he easily supports his lidl frien Madame
Petite while ut duh same time consultin uh twentytwo carut gole time-
piece made tuh ordur by uh famous Swiss consoin duh diul uv wich
measures fourteen inches in dieametur un is protected by windowglass
one quartur uv un inch in tickness upun duh summit uv his ee-normous
head he wears uh specially constructed strawhat weighin five pouns un
fourteen ounces duh amount uv clawt require fur uh single pair uv dis
poisun's elephantine pants would make six blokes like youse un me two
un one half suits apiece his mammut neddur extremities fur wich num-
bur twenty-six shoes has been created bohs toiteen toes all in poific condition duh smalles biggur dun my wrist expoits have decided upun investigation dut in duh course uv one loonur day his garganchoon appetite consumes un duh average frum toitytwo tuh fortyfive ordinury beef-
steaks ur duh protein ee-quivalunt it is estimated by duh managemunt
uv dis exhibit dut twelve normul poisuns could exis fur fiftyfour hours
twentytree minutes nine un sevuneights secuns un wut dis monstur com-
munly annihilates fur breakfust alone I will merely add dut in ordur tuh
facilitate inspection uv oit's mohs vas biped uh sixteen hundud candle-
powur rubburtire telescope is placed ut duh disposition uv duh genrul
public fur wich no extruh charge will be made walk right up un bring
duh chilrun. *He steps down and disappears in the crowd. The* GIANT
*displays his watch, converses, offers photographs of himself. Many grasp
the opportunity to observe him through the telescope. The* BARKER, *reappearing on the platform of the* EIGHTEEN INCH LADY, *beckons fervently.* Dis way gents step dis way ladies—. *The crowd swirls in his direction.*
—Nex we have, Madame Suzette Yvonne Hortense Jacqueline Heloise
Petite duh eighteen inch Parisiun doll un uncompromisin opticul inspection uv dis lidl lady will prove tuh duh satisfaction uv all consoin

dut dis lidl lady is uh poificly form pocket edition uv sheek femininity born undur duh shadow uv duh Eyfl Towur in Paris were she buys all her close spiks floounly nineteen languages excloosive uv her native tongue is toityone years old in duh course uv her adventurous career has visited each un evry country uv duh civilised un uncivilise globe incloodin Soviet Russiuh were subsequunt tuh bein arrested by duh Checkur us uh spy she wus kidnapped un kep fur sevuntytwo hours widout food ur drink in duh inside ovurcoat pocket uv uh membur uv duh Secret Soivice havin escape by cuttin her way out wid uh pair uv nailscissurs she fell tuh duh frozun ground in uh dead faint in wich she wuz discovur by uh faitful moocheek who fled wid her across duh steps uv Siberiuh pursood by wolves un suckseeded in deliverin her tuh duh French consul ut duh Polish frun-teer receivin us uh reward fur his valur frum duh French guvurnmunt duh crorduhgair wid two palms un frum duh Polish ortorities duh cross uv Sain Graballsky wile duh lidl lady hoiself presented her rescoor wid un autograph photo in spite uv her wellestablish Parisiun origin Madame Petite is passionutly fond uv duh home wus in fac sevun times married tuh various internationully famous specimuns uv duh uppercrust uv duh pigmy woild such us Purfessur Tom Tumb un has divorced ur outlived all her husbans us uh mewzishun Madame is equully voisitil purfurrin especiully duh French horn trombone xylophone violin granpieannur youkuhlayly un jewshap un wich insturmunts she has had duh honur tuh purform before duh crown heads uv five nations un tree continunts duh genrul public will be gratifie tuh loin dut Madame Suzette Yvonne Hortense Jaqueline Heloise Petite has recunly completed duh only autentic story uv her life wich undur duh significunt title Minyuhchoors uv Ro-mance ur Many Abelards has already sold out four editions uv one hundud tousund copies each un is ut presun in duh process uv bein tran-slated intuh twenty languages incloodin Arabic un Eskimo Madame Petite will be glad tuh answur any un all questions un give advice tuh duh best uv her ability un all un any subjecs tuh whoever cares tuh unboidun her ur his troubles male un female step right up.

MISS LOOK WEIRD, *suspiciously.* What was she doing among the Bolsheviki?

BARKER. I will answur dut unnecessury question Madame Petite wus un uh mission uv moicy havin been delegated by duh French Red Cross tuh assis duh Salvation Army in its uplif woik among starvin Armeniun chilrun nooly rescood frum duh Toiks in West Centrul Youkraniuh.

MISS LOOK WEIRD, *satisfied.* Thank you. *The* EIGHTEEN INCH LADY *converses and offers copies of her book and photographs of herself.* THE BARKER *disappears, only to reappear on the* QUEEN OF SERPENTS' *platform.*

BARKER, *beckoning fervently to the crowd.* Dis way ladies ovur here gents—. *The crowd swirls in the direction of the* QUEEN OF SERPENTS, *who rises.—* Get uh knockdown tuh Herpo chawms duh lawges specimuns uv duh reptillyun genus each un evry one alive dis way fellurs take uh good squint ut Herpo hanuls duh deadlies becaws mohs poisunous uv all snakes duh cobruh duh capello like youse boys would hanul yur bes goil ovur here evrybudy see duh only livin boaconstrictur in captivity lengt toity-

nine feet sevun un nine toitysecunds inches swollud five indigenes ten
cartridgebelts six Winchestur rifles fortytwo rouns uv amyounition un uh
Stetson hat ut one gulp subsequunly capchoord wile fast asleep by Capn.
Frank Mac Dermot D.S.C. etceteruh un shipped F.O.B. un twelve freight-
cars fur twentyone days tuh duh mowt uv duh Amazon rivur nevur
woked up till fiftyfour hours out tuh sea wen duh en-tire crew incloodin
duh capn took toins settin un duh heavily-padlock covur uv duh fortyfive
foot bamboo box boun wid steel hoops in wich duh monstur wus tem-
purrurrilly imprisoned in spite uv wich precaution he trashed about so
much duh S.O.L. passengurs wus all seasick till duh ship reached Hamburg were sevun uv um died see duh mammut rep-tile wine hisself lov-
inly toiteen times aroun Herpo wile she drinks un icecream soduh un
smokes Virginiuh cigarettes dis way ladies un gents dis way. *Steps down
and disappears in the crowd. The* QUEEN OF SERPENTS *takes out of a box,
wraps around her and puts back in the box, four ancient and decrepit
snakes, each larger than the other.*

VIRGO OF ACT TWO, SCENE 2, *fascinated.* I hate snakes—ugh!

QUEEN OF SERPENTS, *calmly, through her gum.* Dat's because youse cawn't
chawm dum dearie. *Laughter.*

BARKER, *reappearing on the platform of the* KING OF BORNEO, *who rises.*
Evrybudy dis way—. *He gestures fervently. The crowd swirls toward the*
KING OF BORNEO. —Nex we comes tuh one uv duh principul kyouriosities
uv dis ur any epock sometimes frivolously allooded tuh by ignorun poisuns us Duh Huemun Ostrich I refois propurly speakin tuh His Impeereel
Majusty Kakos Kalos duh ex-Kink uv Borneo duh lad wid duh unpunk-
shooruble stumick speciully engaged ut ee-normous expense fur duh
benefit uv duh Great Americun Public durin uh recen revolooshun in
purhaps duh mohs primitive uv all semicivilise commyounities Kink
Kakos Kalos nut only los his trone but had duh additionul misforchoon
tuh be trode by his noomerous enemies intuh uh dun-john ur hole tuh
use duh vulgur woid approximutly ninety six feet in dept un twotoids
full uv rainwatur frum wich he wus pulled aftur fourteen days un nights
un forcibly fed nails tincans broken glass barbwire un uddur dangerous
objecs ovur uh period uv toitysix hours ut duh end uv wich time duh
revolooshunuries lef dier victim fur dead but nix kid fur tanks tuh duh
kink's younique un unparllul constitution wich us any uv youse is ut
liburty tuh ascertain can assimilut wid ease such hidertoo erroneously
considured indiegestubl substunces us carpettacks knittinneedles safety-
razorblades pins jackknives un dynamite he live tuh tell uh tale so incredible us tuh outrivul duh imaginury experiunces uv duh Barun Mun-
chchowsun hisself but whose vuracity is prove beyon duh shadow uv uh
doubt by duh fac dut it bein now five tuh five ur teatime in one two
tree four five minutes Kink Kakos Kalos may be seen by all presun in
duh intimut act uv swallurin un ee-lectrick light bulb step right up
ladies un gents Duh Huemun Ostrich is in duh tent duh Kink's waitin
fur youse KRK KRK KRK he champchomps sharp un brittle chews
bright prickly glass. *Disappears in the crowd. The* KING OF BORNEO *holds*

up a huge electric light bulb, points to it, points to his mouth and winks solemnly to the spectators.

FIRST FAIRY OF ACT TWO, SCENE 8, *soprano.* How unpleasant.

SECOND FAIRY OF DITTO, *alto.* Positively repellent.

THIRD FAIRY OF DITTO. Perfectly disgusting.

FOURTH FAIRY OF DITTO. Makes one absolutely nauseated—ugh!

KING OF BORNEO, *furiously.* Sempre abasso Savoia putana madonna viva Lenine! *He crams the electric light bulb far into his mouth—chews noisily. The* FOURTH FAIRY *faints and is carried off by the other three* FAIRIES.

BARKER, *reappearing on the platform of the* HUMAN NEEDLE. Right dis way evrybudy—. *He beckons fervently. The crowd swirls toward the* HUMAN NEEDLE, *who rises.* —Nex we have, Adamus Jones fumilyully known tuh his many friens us Duh Huemun Needl dis young man is twentytree years old un still lookin fur uh wife summuh youse ladies in duh same interestin condition bettur tink twice before toinin down his prick statistics reinforce wid copious affidavits tens tuh show dut Mr. Jones who is uh native uv Melbourne Australiuh is sevunty un tree quarters inches in height un sevun un one eight inches in widt no more no less his highly illoominatin story is us follows ut duh age uv toiteen years Mr. Jones weighed approximutly tree hundud pouns un wus un acute suffrur frum many uv duh besknown ailmunts such us noomoniuh gout acne tootache indiegestion pulmunnurry tooburcyoulosis un dut mohs obscoor uv all huemun diseases cindurulluh in considuration uv wich fact uh council made up uv mohs uv duh notuble soigeons un speciulis frum duh Younighted Kinkdumb requested duh suffrur tuh place hisself upun uh carefully selected gastrunomic program compose chiefly uv watur radishes stringbeans un wustursheer sauce upun wich he has subsisted evur since ut duh presun writin Mr. Jones tips duh beam ut precisely sixtynine pouns un says he nevur felt bettur in his life wears day un night un his left ankle chust above duh knee un ordinury size seal-ring inscribe wid duh initiuls A.J. un presunted tuh duh wearur un duh fort uv Chooleye nineteen hundud un five by duh Inturnationul An-tie-hippo-fajic Association in tribute tuh his undenieubl poisyveerunce loyulty un courage dis way evrybudy step dis way. *Disappears. The* HUMAN NEEDLE *converses, offers photographs of himself and displays his anklering.*

MISS LOOK WEIRD, *to* MISS LISTEN. Think of a man starving himself to avoid honest labour! MISS LISTEN *shakes her maskface disgustedly.*

BARKER, *from the platform of the rising* SIX HUNDRED POUNDS OF PASSIONATE PULCHRITUDE, *gestures fervently.* All right boys un goils right ovur here un make it snappy—. *The crowd swirls toward him.* —Nex we have, upun uh speciully design reinforce concrete platform wich travuls wid her werever she goes duh knee plus ultry uv affectionut obesity duh indolunt acmy uv amorous adiposity duh mountain uv libidinous ee-quilib-rium Miss Eva Smith bettur known tuh uh legiun uv admirurs us Lidl Eva built like uh big bright bunch uv B. U. tiful bulloons takes one minute un sevunteen secuns fur all uv um tuh sit down two minutes un fiftytwo secuns fur all uv um tuh stand up un frum half uh day tuh twentyfour hours fur duh on-sombul tuh rise from uh recumbunt position unassisted by duh stopwatch ladies un genlmun tuh contumplate dis climax uv frankly female corpulanse is tuh agree wid duh celubrated preachur who wus hoid tuh remark diereckly aftur makin Lidl Eva's acquaintunce dut if duh o-riginul Eve had been like her duh price uv figleaves would have tripled in duh Gawdn uv Eden step right up close evrybudy youse nevur seen nutn like Eva caws Eva doan begin un Eva doan end un Eva's chust one chin aftur unuddur dis way ladies blow yur eyes tuh uh good time wid duh livin illustration uv duh famous maxim Eat Un Grow Tin I wishes tuh announce in duh case uv Miss Smith dut duh managemunt inkois no responsubility fur feyenanciul un uddur losses occasion tuh poisuns nut already acquainted wid duh fac dut youse can lose uh five dollur bill in duh smalles wrinkle uv her eyelid step right up glimpse duh six hundud pouns of poisunully conducted pullcrytood dut makes uh billiardball look like uh cookie dis way tuh duh fort diemension. *The* SIX HUNDRED POUNDS OF PASSIONATE PULCHRITUDE *converses and offers photographs of herself as the* BARKER *disappears in the crowd.*

MISS LISTEN WEIRD, *to* MISS LOOK. You'd think people would have a little shame, wouldn't you. MISS LOOK *shakes her maskface disgustedly.*

BARKER, *from the* MISSING LINK's *platform.* Ladies un genlmun—. *The crowd swirls toward his fervent beckonings: the* MISSING LINK *does not move.* Gimme duh honur uv yur attention nex we have, Ge Ge duh mystury uv duh ages duh missin link in duh chain uv evulooshun frum prehistoric times tuh now duh huemun inturrogationpoint duh secrut uv our hairy ancesturs nut tuh be confuse wid manifole mendacities fakes counterfeit ur spyourious imitations uv duh o-riginul wich wus discovered in nineteen hundud un one in duh jungles uv Darkest Africuh by un expedition compriesin toiteen memburs uv duh Royul Darwiniun Society see It pounce upun Its meat like summuh youse fellurs seen uh swell skoit pounce on uh T. totully tran-sparunt bargain ut duh lonjuhray countur eminun speciulis frum all ovur dese Younighted States un purfessurs uv sighkology uv our foremost universities havin toroughly examine Ge Ge by evry intimut means known tuh duh corporeel un mentul sciences incloodin syntetic bloodtests telepatic waves cerebrul photogruphy postprandiul iodic injections testicullur hypnotism rhapsodic vaginul ee-lectrolysis decalcomaniuh un X ray have purnounce Him ur Her posolutely younique un absitively jenyouwine five hundud dollurs reward will be paid tuh duh man womun ur chile dut can solve Ge Ge's mystury step dis way evrybudy. *Disappears, as the* MISSING LINK *jumps about uttering uncouth cries and pointing happily to* ITSELF.

WILL *and* BILL OF ACT TWO, SCENE *4, in unison, to the* MISSING LINK. Who are you?

MISSING LINK, *interrupting Its antics, haughtily retorts in excellent English.* I am. *It resumes Its crying and jumping.*

BARKER. Right ovur herc ladies dis way gents step right up evrybudy—. *The crowd swirls toward the platform of the* TATTOOED MAN, *who rises.*

—Ladies un genlmun nex we have, A. I. Dolon duh Tatood Man born in duh city uv Boston un duh twelft day uv Augus eighteen hundud un ninetyeight shipped us cabinboy un duh skoonur Muddur Mucree chust off duh coast uv Timbucktoo duh vessul hit uh cyclone un sunk in mid-ocean all hans bein lost excep duh heroic cabinboy who swum fur sevun days un six nights landin in uh state uv complete spirichool un physicul exhustion only tuh fine hisself surrounded by uh tribe uv two hunded headhuntin maneatin canibuls all poligamous starknaked un yellin bloody moidur wus ovurpowured in spite uv un heroic defence un put in duh fatninpen fur Sunday dinnur in wich pitiful condition he nevur-duhless suckseeded in attractin duh notice uv duh favorite wife uv duh canibul kink who had him released un made uh membur uv duh tribe un condition dut his en-tire body widout exception should be adorned embellished un uddurwise ornamented wid emblums mottos pickshurs un similur insigniuh symbolic uv duh occasion prefurin decoration tuh det duh heroic seamun ak Y. essed wid duh trooly incredibul results wich fur duh fois time it is duh privilege uv duh genrul public tuh be-hold incloodin un soitn more intimut parts uv Mr. Dolan's unatumy portraits uv his tiotyfive B. U. tiful wives all between duh ages uv twelve un sixteen step right up ladies un gents.

MISS STOP WEIRD, *skeptically.* May I ask how long this person lived among the savages?

BARKER. Youse may lady fur ten years durin wich time A. I. Dolon con-voited duh en-tire tribe tuh Christianity un in addition established uh tuh speak milely flourishin branch uv duh Y.W.C.A.

MISS STOP WEIRD, *convinced.* That was very noble of him. *The* BARKER *steps down from the* TATTOOED MAN'S *platform and disappears in the crowd. The* TATTOOED MAN *revolves slowly.*

ENGLISHMAN OF ACT TWO, SCENE 6. I say old egg, you carry a bally picture-gallery on your back—what?

TATTOOED MAN, *insultedly.* Dat ain no picher gallry, buddie.

ENGLISHMAN. Indeed? I rather supposed it was.

TATTOOED MAN, *indignantly.* Soitnly not. Dat's Awt, dat is.

BARKER, *reappearing beside the fifth platform, gestures fervently and shouts.* Evrybudy dis way please—. *The crowd swirls toward the fifth platform with its mysterious curtained booth.* —Now we comes tuh duh cornbeef-uncaviare uv duh hole shibang duh boin my close I'm in Heavun duh now youse sees it un now youse tinks youse sees it duh jenyouwine P.S. duh resistunce duh undielooted o-riginul milkshake uv duh ages Princess Anankay duh woil's foist un foremohs exponunt uv yaki-hooluh-hiki-dooluh uddurwise known us duh Royul Umbilicul Bengul Cakewalk comes frum duh lan were duh goils bade in nachurl shampain tree times uh day un doan wear nutn between duh knees un duh neck evrybudy wise up tuh dis fac duh managemunt is incloodin Princess Anankay's soopurspectaclur ac widout extruh charge tuh nobudy get dat ladies un gents youse see her strut her stuff fur duh o-riginul price uv admission no more no less namely un to wit two bits two five jits five makin fiveun-twenty ur twentyfive cents duh fort part uv uh silvur dollur all youse

bohs guys bums ginks un nuts wut are treaded fur uh screw step
dis way duh Princess Anankay is about tuh perform fur duh benefit uv
duh Oreye-entul Ee-lectrickully Lighted Orphunts' Home un duh boys
in genrul uh hiddurto strickly sacred Oo-pee-lah ur Spasmwriggle diereck
frum duh temple uv You You walk right up gents duh Princess wears so
lidl youse can stick her full uv looks like she wus uh pincushion O dut
ticklish dut magnifisunt Huemun Form Divine—. *Shouts, pointing at* HIM
who stands on the outskirts of the crowd. —Crawl right up un all fives
fellur give duh Princess uh fiftyfifty chawnce wid youse kiddo she'll boost
yur splendifurous bowlegged blueeyed exterior out uv duh peagreen in-
terior uv pinkpoiple soopurconsciousness fourteen million astrul miles
intuh duh prehensile presinks uv predetoimine prehistoric preturnachurl
nutn! *With a vivid gesture, he pulls aside the curtain. A woman's figure
—completely draped in white and holding in its arms a newborn babe at
whom it looks fondly—stands, motionless, in the centre of the diminutive
room. The crowd recoils.*

THREE MISS WEIRDS, *disgustedly, in unison.* It's all done with mirrors! *The
woman's figure proudly and gradually lifts its head: revealing the face of*
ME. HIM *utters a cry of terror. Total darkness—confused ejaculations of
rage dwindle swirlingly to entire silence.*

SCENE SEVEN

SCENE: *The room as it first appeared (Act One, Scene 2), but without* HIM's
hat on the sofa and with the flowers on the table.

ME *and* HIM *occupy the same positions with respect to each other and to
the room itself as when Scene 5 of Act Three was interrupted by darkness.*

ME. I am thinking.

HIM. And may I ask what you are thinking?—Anything everything nothing
or something: which is it?

ME. The last.

HIM. Something?

ME. Something.

HIM, *after a pause.* Is it something about the window?

ME. No.

HIM. About the door?

ME. No.

HIM. About what's behind you?

ME. Not exactly. No.

HIM. But you're thinking something about this room, aren't you?

ME. Yes, I'm thinking something about this room.

HIM. I'm afraid that you'll have to tell me what you are thinking.

ME. Can't you guess? I'll give you time.

HIM. Time is the because with which some dolls are stuffed. No, I can't
guess.

ME, *quietly.* It has only three walls.

HIM, *looks about him in astonishment.* Behind you—that's a wall, isn't it?

ME. That's one.

HIM. One—and what's there? *Pointing to the door wall.*

ME. A wall.

HIM. Two—and there? *Pointing over his shoulder to the window wall behind him.*

ME. Three.

HIM. Three—and what do you see there? *Indicating the invisible wall.*

ME. People.

HIM, *starts.* What sort of people?

ME. Real people. And do you know what they're doing?

HIM, *stares at her.* What are they doing?

ME, *walking slowly upstage toward the door.* They're pretending that this room and you and I are real. *At the door, turning, faces the audience.*

HIM, *standing in the middle of the room, whispers.* I wish I could believe this.

ME, *smiles, shaking her head.* You can't.

HIM, *staring at the invisible wall.* Why?

ME. Because this is true.

CURTAIN

Venus and Adonis

BY ANDRÉ OBEY

Translated by WILLIAM BECKER

CHARACTERS

ADONIS
MARTIAL
SOSTHEME
CUPID
VENUS
ZOE
DEATH

Daybreak. Cock. Magpie. Cuckoo. Blackbird. Enter ADONIS *at the rear.*
He is in riding habit.

ADONIS, *stretches, then.* Ah! Good morning! . . . Good morning! Good
morning! . . . I've really slept! It's going to be a fine day. What's the
time? . . . *He looks at his wristwatch.* Half past four. Good! We'll get
a whole flock of nesting game. *He claps his hands.* Saddle my mare!
Hurry! Hurry! Get a move on! Tallyho! Tallyho! Has my friend Mr.
Martial arrived? *Enter* MARTIAL *downstage left.* Ah! There you are.
Good morning! You're late.

MARTIAL. It isn't my fault; it's practically impossible to get into your house
now. What are all these thickets and lawns and shrubs and arbors surrounding the house? A man doesn't know where to put his feet anymore.
Ten roses get crushed with every step. Have you taken up gardening?

ADONIS. It isn't me. It's my neighbor. Come on. Tallyho!

MARTIAL. What neighbor?

ADONIS. A lady . . . and what not . . . who came to live in the forest behind
my house and transformed it into a garden.

MARTIAL. What lady?

ADONIS. One named Venus.

MARTIAL. Venus?

ADONIS. That's her name.

MARTIAL. Really?

ADONIS. You're asking me too much about it. I read her name on a letter
that was sent to me by mistake.

MARTIAL. Is she beautiful?

ADONIS. Euh! . . .

MARTIAL. Young?

ADONIS. I haven't taken much notice of her.

MARTIAL. Now see here, one certainly knows if one has a goddess for a neighbor, the devil, man! What does she do?

DONIS. Why, my friend . . . she . . . No, I don't know. She seems to be
very fond of flowers, birds, music, and flimsy dresses.

MARTIAL. That would be right. Alas, poor Adonis!

DONIS. Don't call me that. I've told you before. I hate Adonis. It nauseates
me.

MARTIAL. My apologies. Tallyho! Donny!

DONIS. There! Tallyho!

BOTH, *uttering a war cry.* Hahouou.

       Enter middle right ZOE, VENUS' *servant.*

ZOE. You couldn't possibly make a little less noise? Madam is sleeping.

MARTIAL. Madam is making a mistake. She should have been up long ago.
Anyone who gets up after sunrise this time of year offends the gods.

ZOE. Oh! my dear young man, madam knows better than you what pleases or displeases the gods. Much better than you, believe me. Anyway, I'm not talking to you but to the young Lord Adonis.

ADONIS. Oh! Good god! . . . "Adonis" by itself is irritating, but "Lord Adonis" is frightful . . . And as for "the young Lord Adonis," euh! . . . Young woman, please, tell your mistress that we are deeply grieved to have wakened her.

ZOE. Then come and tell her yourself, your Lordship.

ADONIS. No . . . I can't. I'm in a hurry. *Turns toward the wings.* And what about my mare, is no one going to bring her to me? Hurry up, come on, hurry up! . . . *To* ZOE. Yes, I'm going hunting. As for seeing Madam Venus, I can't, you will excuse me. I am unsociable. I am afraid of new friendships. And besides, I lead my own life, a solitary life. You must understand. Put that nicely, into suitable form, style, and language; I'm in a hurry, forgive me. Come along, Martial.

Hunting horn sounds in the wings. They go out at the back.

ZOE. Either I am mistaken or Madam will have her work cut out with this young man . . . She thought she had only to appear . . . The gods are extraordinary! Because they are eternal, because they have some general ideas about human things, they think they know all about man. But there are more changes on earth in a year than there are in a century on Olympus. They haven't any younger generation where the gods live. That changes everything!

Birds singing. Enter VENUS *by the middle door.*

ZOE. Madam slept well?

VENUS. No, my good Zoe.

ZOE. I have seen the young Lord and I have spoken to him.

VENUS. Ah! dear me, what happened?

ZOE. He is very young.

VENUS. Oh! yes.

ZOE. I ask Madam's pardon, but I am new to her service. I have read quickly through the memoires which she very kindly intrusted to me. I have read them at one go: they make astonishing reading. I was able to skip the details . . . I should like to know . . . Has Madam often been resisted

VENUS. Never, my child.

ZOE. Well then—may Madam pardon me!—I very much fear that this young man is going to open the chapter of rebels.

VENUS. You're joking.

ZOE. Madam, he is a hunter, a sportsman, an athlete, a horseman, a tennis player, maybe even a boxer, but he is not a lover.

VENUS. Ha! ha!

ZOE. I don't know if there are many things in the world that interest him But I know, I felt, that there is one at least that leaves him perfectly cold

VENUS. And that, I suppose, is love.

ZOE. That, Madam, is love, yes.

VENUS. You are a charming girl, Zoe, you are pleasing, nicely built, pretty enough. But is that sufficient to assume that a man who is insensible to your looks is insensible to love?

ZOE. Madam will see.

VENUS. Madam *will* see. Now go and make my breakfast.

ZOE. Very good, Madam.

VENUS. Hurry up. I hear his voice.

ZOE *goes out middle right.* VENUS *retires a little to the left downstage. Enter at the back* ADONIS *and* MARTIAL.

ADONIS. Hello, look, Martial. There she is. Is she beautiful?

MARTIAL. She is very beautiful.

ADONIS. Swear you didn't expect her to be so beautiful.

MARTIAL. I swear.

ADONIS. How lithe she is! What nobility!

MARTIAL. A marvel.

VENUS. That good Zoe!

ADONIS. Notice her small head, and her little ears, her long straight legs, her magnificent legs!

VENUS *sighs with pleasure.*

MARTIAL. That wide eye, that beautiful neck!

ADONIS. And that broad rump!

VENUS. Broad rump?

MARTIAL. Her sleek coat.

ADONIS. Her nostrils.

VENUS. Nostrils?

MARTIAL. Her thick tail.

ADONIS. And her mane. Ah! her mane! . . . She's the most beautiful beast in the world!

VENUS. Oh! how horrible! it's the mare!

At VENUS' *cry, the young men come running.*

ADONIS. Have you hurt yourself, Madam?

VENUS. No, no, I . . . I thought I saw a snake.

ADONIS. There are no . . . There are no more snakes here. Rest assured!

VENUS. One would think you regretted it.

ADONIS. No, certainly not! I like danger, but not that danger. And I would be glad to see the end of the reptiles, if with them had not gone the wild beasts—the bears, the wolves, the foxes, and even the weasels.

VENUS. Have you had nothing in return for them?

ADONIS. Yes, yes, flowers . . . birds . . . shade . . . and a certain disgusting balminess in the air. I think the ground around here is fast becoming sick.

MARTIAL, *softly.* Careful, Donny! I do believe it's true.

VENUS. You don't like the flowers, the birds, and the trees?

ADONIS. Yes, yes, yes, they're nice. *He sighs.* I think I'm going to move.

VENUS. Ah!

ADONIS. Have you seen my horse?

VENUS. I don't like horses.

ADONIS. Obviously, we are made for each other. Good-bye, Madam, my compliments.

VENUS. We shall see each other again?

ADONIS. I should like to, but our hours coincide no more than our tastes. You sleep late, I get up early.

VENUS. We shall see each other again, yes yes! Cheerio!

Hunting horn offstage.

ADONIS. Gee up!

ADONIS *and* MARTIAL *go out left middle. The sound of the horn moves off*

VENUS. Zoe! Zoe!

ZOE, *entering right.* Madam?

VENUS. Get me the gardener.

ZOE. Yes, Madam. *She goes up again a little toward the back right, then* Madam has seen the young Lord?

VENUS. Go find me the gardener.

ZOE. Very well, Madam. *She goes out upstage right.*

VENUS *takes some steps from left to right, pensively. The whistle of an arrow is heard.* VENUS *raises her head and looks toward the right middle.*

VENUS. Ah! I've caught you at it, little one. Haven't I told you a hundred times not to shoot at the birds? Here, don't run away. Come here.

Enter right CUPID *with his bow and quiver.*

VENUS. You deserve to be punished.

CUPID. Madam, I'm in training. You told me to practice.

VENUS. I got a magnificent archery set up for you at the bottom of the garden. Shoot at trees, shoot at walls, shoot at men if you like, but do not shoot at the birds.

CUPID. Yes, Madam.

VENUS. And don't pout, don't cry . . . Ah! don't go cry . . . I warn you that at the moment I have no patience . . . There! That's finished. Show me what progress you have made . . . Stand there and aim at that cedar for me . . . There, yes . . . Body straight, your little legs firm. More flexible! The movement of the right arm more flexible! Right elbow higher! Head a little inclined. Release your arrow! . . . Good, my dear, very good! *Enter the gardener followed by* ZOE *upstage right.* Wait a second.

VENUS, *to the gardener.* Come here Sostheme, come here . . . Here. I have just taken a walk around the garden and everything I have seen is ridiculous.

SOSTHEME. Madam!

VENUS. Sh! . . . Ridiculous, yes! There is too much grass, too much greenery, too much perfume, too much shade, and too many flowers . . . Look you understand. It's a lifeless garden . . . a garden full of balminess . . . of a disgusting balminess. Do you get it?

SOSTHEME. Madam, I am your servant, your humble servant. But I have my pride: the pride of a servant. It was I, Madam, who made with my own hands, with these very hands, the garden of the Hesperides . . .

VENUS. We're talking about *this* garden, Sostheme, about this lifeless garden without vigor, full of little knicknacks like this and thingumbobs like that, and where there aren't even any snakes!

SOSTHEME. Snakes! Madam would like . . . ?!

VENUS. What has become of the wild beasts we found here when we arrived

SOSTHEME. The . . . beasts . . . ?

VENUS. Yes, the bears, the foxes . . . And the weasels, see here, the ordinary weasels, where are they, Sostheme?

SOSTHEME. But . . .

ZOE. Madam knows quite well that since she appeared . . .

VENUS. Silence, my child. Answer me, Sostheme.

SOSTHEME. I am only a humble servant, but I dare to say this to Madam: never could Madam speak so harshly to me if she had any idea of gardening, if she only suspected the . . . the . . . genius . . . yes, that was needed to graft golden apples . . .

VENUS. Cut down the roses for me! Mow the lawns! Break them up, rip them out, you hear! Throw rubble everywhere, dead leaves, poisonous moss, decayed lichen. Lovingly cultivate brushwood, thorns, brambles, thistles, and those little bare plants that tremble under the winds of the North.

SOSTHEME. Never, Madam!

VENUS. What?

SOSTHEME. Never!

VENUS. By Jupiter! *Turning towards* CUPID *who has remained at play to one side.* Here, little one.

The child runs up.

VENUS. Look, you see that old man? Practice on him.

CUPID. That's fine.

SOSTHEME. Mercy, Madam! Don't set fire to my dry old carcass! Don't heat up my blood which has been cold for so many years! I am so cold, so peaceful!

ZOE. Mercy on him, Madam!

VENUS. Do you want to play target, too?

ZOE. Ah! good god, no! I tasted love once. That satisfied me for life.

VENUS. Shoot, my little archer!

CUPID, *bends his bow and shoots.* Tzin!

SOSTHEME. Full on the heart! O good gods! There's the burning! I feel the flame leaping up from the bottom of my belly: it dries my throat, roasts my brain, scorches my nerves. Alas! *He gets up.* I shall have to start chasing women again . . . *He sighs, looks around him, sees* ZOE, *runs to her.*

ZOE. Ah! no, not me!

SOSTHEME. Yes, you! O you! How could I have lived so close to you without seeing you, o my beauty!

ZOE. Help! *She flees.*

SOSTHEME. My wonderful beauty! *He pursues her.*

Both go out upstage, right.

VENUS. *to* CUPID. My child, my child, I'm so unhappy! . . . This confusion you see me in, to think that I have so many times provoked it in others. To think that I who was so often besought, am on the verge of beseeching.

CUPID. Can I help you, Madam?

VENUS. No, my pet, alas! This boy I love has a heart of stone. Even your arrows would not pierce it.

CUPID. They have pierced harder ones.

VENUS. I don't believe it.

CUPID. *I'm* sure of it. The general's heart wasn't tissue paper.

VENUS. That's true, still . . . Still it is true that the god of war was my slave! That he laid his spear, his helmet, and his shield on my altars! That he made my arms his field of battle!

CUPID. And that he learned how to dance just to please you, Madam!

VENUS, *smiling.* Yes, just to please me he learned how to dance.

CUPID. Laugh, Madam! Look, I'll show you the general in a dancing mood. *He does a few steps of a grotesque dance.*

VENUS. Ha! ha! ha! It's really him. I can see him again . . . Poor Mars! How long ago that is!

CUPID. Come dance with me!

VENUS. No, child, that's enough. You've made me laugh. I feel much better. Go play.

CUPID. Yes, Madam. But I'll be right at hand. A sign from you and I will hunt the hunter.

VENUS. I would prefer, you understand, not to owe you the victory.

CUPID. Certainly! *Goes out right.*

VENUS. If I were ugly, foul, wrinkled with age, crooked, churlish, my eyes dim, my voice harsh, barren, lean, lacking juice . . . But I defy him to find a single wrinkle in my brow . . . My eyes are blue, bright, and quick, my flesh soft and plump. My hand tender, so tender that if it were clasped in his, it would seem to melt in his fingers. Were he to bid me speak, I would enchant his ear. Let him but say the word and, like a fairy, like some nymph with long hair, I would dance with unseen steps across the sands. This love so light, how could he think it heavy?

Upstage passing from right to left is seen ZOE *chased by* SOSTHEME *brandishing a bouquet.*

VENUS. If only he would touch my lips with his beautiful lips! Oh! if he were to look into the pupils of my eyes, he would see his beauty there! And then, when we're eyes in eyes, why not lips on lips?

Hunting horn in the distance.

VENUS. He's coming back from the hunt. O gods, inspire me! I would give all my conquests, all my triumphs, all my pleasures, all happiness that I have ever known for one tender glance from him.

The sound of the horn grows nearer. VENUS *stands aside to the right Laughter is heard in the wings. Enter* ADONIS *left middle. A few second. later the head of* ADONIS' *horse appears at the left through the bushes.*

ADONIS, *to* MARTIAL. Cheerio! Until later, then. But you're wrong not to dine with me . . . As you like, old man, as you like! . . . Bye, bye. *On entering, he catches sight of his horse.* Ah! here you are, you, my gallant good, beautiful creature. We've both run well, eh? You are beautiful, you know? You're getting more beautiful every day. *He kisses her above the nostrils.* All right! Go and eat!

The horse disappears. ADONIS *starts to run upstage.*

VENUS. Adonis! . . . ADONIS *stops.* Adonis! . . . *He comes back down. She goes toward him.* I've got to tell you: you're handsome! . . . Very handsome! . . . Too handsome! . . .

ADONIS, *surprised and shocked.* Oh! . . .

VENUS. You are more lovely than a man, fresher and more red than hyacinths or roses. Come sit down with me.

ADONIS. Madam! . . .

VENUS. Oh! sit down first. First sit down.

ADONIS. But, Madam . .

VENUS, *pushing him by the shoulders.* Sit down, I tell you. Start by sitting down. I'll listen to nothing if you remain standing.
     She pushes him harder. He falls sitting on the ground.

VENUS. There.

ADONIS. Madam, I don't understand.

VENUS, *putting her hand over his mouth.* If it's to scold, your lips will never open. Beautiful lips . . .

ADONIS, *gagged.* But . . .

VENUS. Beautiful lips, be quiet! *Takes her hand away from* ADONIS' *mouth.*

ADONIS. But . . .

VENUS, *gagging him again.* Sh! . . . *Pause. She releases him.* There . . . I'm looking at you. I'm happy. I like looking at you. You are furious. You are confused. You go from embarrassment to anger. Do I love you more when you blush or when you are pale with rage? . . .

ADONIS, *exploding.* But I haven't had lunch yet!

VENUS. All right, eat me!

ADONIS. By no means! What an idea! I have a small leg of venison . . . Look here, would you like to dine with me?

VENUS. It's you that I'm hungry for.

ADONIS. It's good, the venison, you know.

VENUS. We'll go and eat your venison if you'll grant me . . . a kiss.

ADONIS. A . . .

VENUS. . . . kiss, yes.

ADONIS. Good! . . . all right . . . quickly!

VENUS. Oh! no. Not quickly.

She opens her arms to him. ADONIS *enters them, sighing. As his lips are about to touch those of* VENUS, *he draws back.*

ADONIS. Impossible!

VENUS. Why?

ADONIS. I don't know. I can't.

VENUS. He's ashamed of a kiss. Very well, close your eyes. I'll close mine and day will become night. Let yourself go, come on . . . Relax yourself completely.

ADONIS. Madam, I beseech you.

VENUS. Quiet! Relax!

ADONIS. Madam, once again . . .

VENUS. Are you like Narcissus? Is it yourself that you love? Will you die kissing your shadow in a brook? I adore you, Adonis.

ADONIS. Fi! Fi! No more of love! The sun is burning my face. I'm thirsty.

I'm hungry. I *must* go have lunch. *He gets up again. Also* VENUS . . . *but without letting him go.*

VENUS. Are you made of stone? Are you made of marble? Can you be a woman's son, you who cannot feel what a woman is? Come, give me a kiss.

ADONIS. No, Madam.

VENUS. One little kiss!

ADONIS. No! I said.

VENUS. Oh! cold stone! Painted idol! Statue pleasing nothing but the eye! You who look like a man, yet are not a man!

She turns her back on him furiously tapping her foot on the ground. ADONIS *takes advantage of this to take several steps upstage.*

VENUS, *turning round.* Pity, I emplore you. A small favour! A shadow of tenderness.

ADONIS. No, good-bye! *He starts off upstage. But noises, cries, voices echoing in the wings, left.*

VENUS. Here! what? What's that?

Noise in the wings. Enter SOSTHEME *upstage left.*

SOSTHEME. Madam, Mr. Adonis' mare is up to her old tricks.

ADONIS. What is she doing?

SOSTHEME. She's playing the fool, Your Honour.

ADONIS *starts to dash off.* SOSTHEME *holds him back.*

SOSTHEME. No use! She's far away . . . You must understand: she saw a beautiful stallion go by. The stallion saw her. They fell for each other. Bedame! Your animal slipped her halter at one go. And there they were —gone! . . . It's beautiful to see, love!

ADONIS. Aspasia! Aspasia! *He whistles.*

SOSTHEME. She'll never hear you. And even if she did, it wouldn't matter. It's got a hold of her!

ADONIS *sits on the ground and sulks.*

SOSTHEME. Ah! it's very beautiful, love! *To* VENUS. If only Madam had seen! They have left the garden in pieces. And they threw themselves into the woods like two lunatics. To think that Madam is queen of all those passions!

VENUS. Shut up and go away!

SOSTHEME. Our queen of all lovers! . . .

VENUS. Get out!

SOSTHEME. Yes, my queen. I'm going. VENUS *makes for him. He moves away.* My most sober fires, Madam . . . My most burning devotion! . . *He goes out upstage.*

VENUS, *approaching* ADONIS. Are you angry with me?

ADONIS. Huh! of course. My horse is gone. It's your fault. Go away. I beg you, go away.

VENUS, *falling on her knees next to him.* Let me excuse your courser, gentle boy. And learn from her, I heartily beseech you, to take advantage of what joy presents itself. Learn to love. The lesson is so simple! *She takes his hand.*

ADONIS. Give me my hand.

VENUS. And you, give me my heart.

ADONIS. For shame, let me go!

VENUS. Eh! let me go yourself.

ADONIS. You're hurting me.

VENUS. If my love can make you suffer, let me die!

ADONIS, *getting up.* Oh! let's leave this idle theme! This futile chatter! Love! Love! No, I don't know Cupid. I don't want to know him!

VENUS. Take care he doesn't venge himself!

ADONIS. I'll await him unflinchingly. If he is a wild beast I will give him chase. Love, I'm told, is a life of agony, that one breath turns to tears and another to laughter. Thank you! I don't want any of that!

VENUS. What! you can talk? You know how to talk? You have a tongue!

ADONIS. Don't jeer, I beg you. Yes, I have a tongue which, like my hand, can hurl hard things, shafts which wound and draw blood. You'll see, Madam Venus.

VENUS. No, no, be quiet.

ADONIS. I will speak, by Zeus! I think it's my turn. Madam Venus, I tell you . . .

VENUS, *uttering a cry.* Ah! . . . *Swoons.*

ADONIS. Well, I like that!

Dumb show of a man very fed up. He scratches his head, goes to look for help, thinks better of it, etc. Finally he kneels and gets to work, fans VENUS' *face, pinches her nose, breathes on her eyeballs. All in vain.*

ADONIS. If I were to sing her a little song?

While slapping her hands, he intones in a false voice a sort of hunting fanfare.

ADONIS. Ta ra ta pa pi pa! Ti ri ti pi pa pi!

Enter MARTIAL *left, bewildered.*

MARTIAL. What's this?

ADONIS. Ah! old chap!

MARTIAL. What's going on?

ADONIS. I'll tell you. But first, help me. Here, take her left hand and let's get down to work.

MARTIAL. What do I do?

ADONIS. You slap like this, softly and firmly. Come on, old man, come on!

Both slap in time while singing the hunting air.

ADONIS. Ta ra ta pa pi pa. Tu ru ti pa pu . . .

MARTIAL, *while* ADONIS *sings.* Your horse has come back. Tu ru ti pi pa pu.

ADONIS, *while* MARTIAL *sings.* In good condition? Ta ra ta pi pa pa!

MARTIAL, *as before.* Yes, but her bridle is ruined. Tu ru tu . . .

ADONIS, *as before.* That's not important . . . Ta ra tave . . .

MARTIAL, *same.* All the same she's a beautiful woman . . . Ta ra tum . . .

ADONIS, *same.* I didn't say she wasn't . . . Ta ra ta-ta-ti-tere! . . . Hold on! I think she's coming to. Go away! And wait for me!

MARTIAL. All right, but not too long. Eh? I've been informed that there's a tremendous wild boar near here.

ADONIS, *standing.* A wild boar?

VENUS, *groaning.* Oh! Oh!

ADONIS. There you are! *He goes back on his knees and continues his work.*

To MARTIAL. Five minutes and I'll be there. Get everything ready.
MARTIAL. Good. *He goes left.*
ADONIS. Look here, I haven't had lunch.
MARTIAL. My grandmother told me that once there were people who lived
on love. *He goes out singing.*
Silent, sulky, concentrated, ADONIS *slaps* VENUS' *hands, the left, then the
right, then the left . . .*
VENUS. Where am I? What time is it? Oh! my hands are all red . . .
ADONIS, *mopping his brow.* Phew!
VENUS. There you are, my love. I was afraid of losing you. But it's you
There you are.
ADONIS *smiles at her uneasily.*
VENUS. What? Always as cold? . . . I dreamt just now I was in your arms . . .
I dreamt, yes, alas!
ADONIS. Fair queen, listen. If you have any love for me, measure my coldness
against the greenness of my youth. Don't seek to know me before I know
myself. Ripe fruit falls. The green sticks fast.
VENUS, *sadly.* Yes, I see. What control of yourself you have, you young
people of today. *Grows enthusiastic.* Nothing takes you out of yourselves.
Nothing puts you in a fever. There's nothing, is there, nothing in the
world? . . . *She snaps her fingers behind her back:* CUPID *enters furtively
right and looks for a good place to shoot from.*
ADONIS. Let me say good-bye and you say the same nicely.
VENUS. Ah! well, good . . . No, I can't. It tears me to pieces . . . it . .
The whistle of an arrow leaving the bow interrupts her. ADONIS *dodges
goes through the movements of catching the arrow in full flight, breaking
it in two, and throwing the bits on the ground.*
ADONIS. Missed, my little boy. Would you like me to show you?
Second arrow. ADONIS *as before.*
ADONIS. Missed again!
CUPID, *furious.* Oh!
ADONIS. What damned blunderer taught you to handle a bow?
For the third time, CUPID, *red with rage, draws his bow.*
ADONIS. What an appalling position! Are you made of wood, little one
You must work up your flexibility. But, hang it, not like that!
Third arrow. ADONIS *as before.* CUPID *prances with rage.*
ADONIS. Come now, calm down! Try again! Yes, yes, there, that's better
That's a little more like it, this time. Try it like that.
Fourth arrow. ADONIS *as before.* CUPID *bursts into tears.* ADONIS *howls with
laughter.*
VENUS, *to* CUPID. Stop, my child.
CUPID. Madam, Madam, don't scold me.
VENUS. I, scold you?! You see . . . this man is stronger than we are. Go
along, dearest. And give me a hug. You're sweet.
CUPID, *sobbing in* VENUS' *arms.* Madam, it's not my fault!
VENUS. No, my poor little archer. It's no one's fault. Go along!
CUPID. Yes . . . Madam. *He takes some steps toward the right.*
ADONIS. Would you like to hug me too?

CUPID. No!

VENUS. But yes! let us see!

ADONIS. Come then. One must be sporting. And never bear grudges against those who've beaten you. You understand that?

CUPID. Yes, Sir.

ADONIS. Come, then.

CUPID *throws himself in* ADONIS' *arms.*

ADONIS, *hugging him.* Good boy! Brave boy! One day you will be a champion. You'll see. You'll see. But don't shoot at men. Men are harmless, you know. Shoot at animals, eh? Big animals!

CUPID. Yes.

ADONIS. Yes, who?

CUPID. Yes, Donny.

ADONIS. Well done! I knew you were a good boy.

Exit CUPID *running.*

VENUS, *to* ADONIS. I ought to hate you. Ah! well, no. How funny this is: I'm not angry with you even now. You want to go off, eh? You're in a hurry to leave! What are you going to do now?

ADONIS. I'm going back to the hunt.

VENUS. Again!

ADONIS. I adore hunting!

VENUS. How you said that! Ah! if one day you could say "I adore Venus" in that same tone.

ADONIS. Madam . . .

VENUS. And what are you going to hunt? What poor innocent animal are you going to massacre?

ADONIS. A wild boar. A poor, innocent, sweet, wild boar.

VENUS, *with fear.* Wild boar? No, Adonis, not the boar! Anything you like but not that horrible monster. It's ferocious, it's . . . I don't know what . . . filthy!

ADONIS. Neither horrible nor filthy. Ferocious, yes! He is a wild animal and he defends himself. But there you have the pleasure of hunting. I've killed at least a dozen . . . But what's the matter with you?

VENUS. I've had a dream. I saw your wild boar: a kind of black pig, with his little red shining eyes, a back armed with bristly spikes, a steaming snout and two ivory tusks . . . sharply pointed . . . A horrible dream. Oh! you've brought it all back to mind.

ADONIS. You believe in dreams?

VENUS. Be quiet! I saw you overthrown under this raging beast and he gorging your side. Your blood flowed among the flowers.

VOICE OF MARTIAL, *in the wings.* Adonis! Adonis!

ADONIS. Yes, coming.

VENUS. I entreat you, not the wild boar!

ADONIS. Ah well! look here . . . it's a promise. At least . . . naturally, if he should throw himself at the legs of my horse. But I won't give chase. I swear.

VENUS. Thank you. Be very careful!

VOICE OF MARTIAL. Adonis!

ADONIS. Yes, all right! . . . *to* VENUS. Good-bye, Madam.

VENUS. Good-bye! Shall I see you tomorrow?

ADONIS. Yes, tomorrow, that's it.

VOICE OF MARTIAL. Adonis! Adonis!

ADONIS. I'm coming, old man, I'm coming! *to* VENUS. Good-bye!

VENUS. Good-bye, my love.

> ADONIS *goes out running upstage left.*

VENUS. I ought not to have let him go.

> MARTIAL *enters left downstage.*

MARTIAL. I beg your pardon, Madam. My friend isn't here?

VENUS. He left. You were calling him so desperately!

MARTIAL. I? I was calling him? But I haven't opened my mouth. I was at the kennels . . . waiting very patiently. I was looking at the new-born puppies.

VENUS, *nervously.* You weren't the one who was calling?

MARTIAL. I give you my word of honour, Madam!

VENUS. Yet it was certainly your voice . . .

MARTIAL. Really, Madam, I swear to you . . .

VENUS, *more and more nervous.* You're his friend, aren't you? Then run, and bring him back! He *mustn't* leave, you hear me? He mustn't! He's in great danger. Do you know, Martial, who was calling him? Do you know who was using your voice to call him?

MARTIAL. You don't mean . . .

VENUS. Silence! Run, Martial! Bring him back to me!

MARTIAL, *rushing left.* And then I ought to bind him hand and foot! *He goes out in haste.*

VENUS. Zeus, Zeus, saviour! All-powerful Zeus! Good and fatherly Zeus! You won't allow this, will you? Answer me. Don't act deaf. Ah! I'm not forgetting that I came down to earth against your will. But you won't have the heart to punish me so harshly. Eh? Don't do this to me, I beg you, don't do it . . .

> *Enter* ZOE *middle right.*

ZOE. Madam called for me?

VENUS. No, Zoe.

ZOE. Madam didn't call for me?

VENUS. No, no, Zoe.

ZOE. Well!

VENUS. What's the matter?

ZOE. Nothing . . . I don't know. I thought I heard someone walking at the bottom of the garden . . . a light step like yours.

VENUS. Like mine . . .

ZOE. Yes, yes, lithe, fleet . . . I went out. I saw no one . . . I heard something like a call . . .

VENUS. A call . . .

ZOE. Yes, Madam. A woman's voice calling at a distance through an extraordinary silence. *Nervous.* What's the matter, Madam?

VENUS. I don't know . . . I don't know.

> *Enter* MARTIAL *left.*

MARTIAL, *out of breath.* I haven't seen him. Nobody can tell me where
    he is. I'll get my horse. I'll bring him back. *He goes out.*

ZOE. Madam, what's the matter?

VENUS. I don't know . . .

                    Enter CUPID *downstage right.*

CUPID, *panic stricken, glancing over his shoulder.* No! no! no! no!

VENUS *and* ZOE, *crying out.* Ah!

CUPID. She! . . . She laughed to herself. She laughed to herself . . . Oh! oh!
    I am terribly afraid.

A VOICE IN THE WINGS. Adonis! Adonis!

VENUS. No, that's nothing, it's Martial's voice. Keep calm, I beg you.

VOICE OF SOSTHEME, *upstage.* Miss Zoe!

ZOE. Ah, my god!

VENUS. Easy, my child, here!

SOSTHEME, *appearing upstage.* Miss Zoe, do come this way with me and have
    a look. Something strange is happening.

ZOE. I daren't.

SOSTHEME. Oh! if it's me you're afraid of, you can rest easy. Things are
    happening here right now that take away one's desire to play at love.
    Come and see.

VENUS. *You've* nothing to fear.

ZOE *slowly joins* SOSTHEME *and goes out with him upstage. Then is heard:*

VOICE OF ZOE, *surprised and terrified.* Ah!

VOICE OF SOSTHEME. For something strange, this *is* strange, eh?

VOICE OF ZOE. Ah! Madam . . .

CUPID. What is it? What is it?

VENUS. Sh! . . . Nothing! One must be brave and, above all, not tremble. If
    one trembles! Ah! if one trembles . . . she sees you immediately . . .
    and then . . . you remember Orpheus' day? We were both hidden in the
    laurel bush, we watched him. When he saw her, he trembled, poor man.

CUPID. Orpheus' day, Madam . . . but then . . .

VENUS. Sh!

CUPID. But who is going? . . .

VENUS. Be quiet, I beg you. Ah! my god! There she is!

CUPID *escapes toward the back stifling his cry with his fists. Enter* DEATH
    *right. She is a sort of small "chatelaine," slight and well-groomed. Half-
    mask.*

VENUS. Good evening, Madam.

DEATH. Good evening, Madam, good evening. Was it your little boy who
    just ran out crying?

VENUS. He wasn't crying, Madam, he was laughing.

DEATH. Ah! very well. I'd thought . . . Please forgive me, Madam, for
    crossing your garden. I have something to do near here and I am in
    a hurry.

VENUS. You have the right of way everywhere, Madam. And I am glad to
    have the opportunity of seeing you.

DEATH. You are glad?

VENUS. The word is a little strong. But I am pleased to see you . . . Are you really in such a hurry that you can't visit my house? Wouldn't you take a cup of tea?

DEATH. Presently, Madam, presently. On my way back . . . You've grown even more beautiful since last we met.

VENUS. A thousand thanks, Madam. But I'm getting on, you know.

DEATH. Not a bit! Not a bit! You're rosy cheeked. In full bloom. You are a happy woman, Madam.

VENUS. Don't you believe it! I'm getting on, I tell you. And with age comes care.

DEATH. You need to be diverted, Madam . . . Excuse me for leaving you, but what I have to do won't wait.

VENUS. No, no, don't go away so soon. We see each other too seldom for me to let you go like this.

DEATH. Do you wish to see more of me?

VENUS. I didn't say that. *She laughs bravely.* Ha! ha! ha!

DEATH, *also laughs, unpleasantly.* Ha! ha! ha! *And begins to put on her gloves, long white gloves to the elbow.*

VENUS. No! I didn't say that, but I would like to gossip a little with you . . . No! no! don't put your gloves on already.

DEATH. They're new and hard to button.

VENUS. Euh! . . . Do you know that in this district just at the bottom of the hill we have an old man who screams out for you?

DEATH. No, I didn't know it. Where is he?

VENUS. A stone's throw from here. *She shows her.* There, down below, do you see?

DEATH. That little white house?

VENUS. That's it, Madam. A good and honest man, really. He says he has done his time and will go willingly. He suffers horribly from fevers and the maladies of old age. It would be a pity to cure him.

DEATH. That we shall see.

VENUS. People say you are cruel. They are stupid. I imagine you sometimes come into their lives like a benediction.

DEATH. That could be.

VENUS. My old man also says that to save the life of a young person who is handsome and good, he would give his own as thanks to the gods. That is great and just . . . the life of a young person. Isn't it, Madam?

DEATH. Certainly, Madam, certainly.

VENUS. Look, you take that little footpath. You have only to go down it and you'll be there in a jiffy.

DEATH. Thank you, Madam, I will go there this evening without fail.

VENUS. Why not now?

DEATH. Now I have something else to do.

VENUS. The old man also said . . .

DEATH. He is inexhaustible!

VENUS. He says he isn't afraid of you . . . that he'll laugh in your face. .

DEATH. Ha! ha!

VENUS. . . . if one can call what you have on the front of your head a face

... that's what he says, Madam ... and that he has only to lift himself up in his bed, on his hands, to send you fleeing shamefully off.

DEATH. We'll see about that, we'll see about that. Excuse me, but this time I must leave.

VENUS, *with a cry.* No! no! *Pulling herself together.* No, not before having seen ... the people who live with me.

DEATH. Is it really necessary?

VENUS. Absolutely. It will not be said that I lacked respect for a friend like you. *She calls.* Zoe! Sostheme! Little one! ... Come here, hurry up, come along! *To* DEATH. Since you don't want to come to the house, the house comes to you. ...

Enter upstage SOSTHEME *and* CUPID, *awkward and trembling.* VENUS *goes upstage toward them.*

VENUS, *quietly to* SOSTHEME. And Zoe? She's not there?

SOSTHEME, *quietly.* She's half dead with fright.

VENUS, *quietly.* Ah! *Turning to* DEATH. Here is the king of gardeners. He is sober, honest, healthy, respectable ...

SOSTHEME, *bowing to* DEATH. I made so bold as to cut some roses from the garden for Madam. *He holds them out to her.*

VENUS, *under her breath.* Brave Sostheme!

DEATH. Many, many thanks, my friend. *She takes the roses and sniffs them.*

VENUS, *pushing* CUPID *who resists in front of her.* This boy, do you recognize him?

DEATH. Come here, little one, come here ... I think I *do* recognize him! Ha! ha! ha! It's Cupid! It's Cupid! Ha! ha! ha!

CUPID, *astounded, utters a piercing shriek and runs off.*

VENUS. Forgive him, he's nervous.

DEATH. But of course, it's so natural at his age ... Well, then, I'm going off. Good-bye, Madam. *She heads off left.*

VENUS. It's a mistake to go that way, Madam.

DEATH. Why so?

VENUS. Because ... isn't it, Sostheme?

SOSTHEME. There's a hunt on over there, quite near. A boar hunt. It's dangerous.

DEATH. A hunt, really? For a boar? I love hunting. It's gay, lively! And such handsome boys are seen there. I love them, you know. Handsome boys ... careless, unfortunately ... very careless ... Good-bye, Madam. Nice to have seen you happy.

She draws out from under her cloak a long white-gloved arm and goes out left. As soon as she is gone, VENUS *collapses.*

SOSTHEME, *kneeling by her, supporting her.* My dear Lady! My little Lady! Courage! You have been so brave!

VENUS. She is going to kill him, Sostheme.

SOSTHEME. It wasn't said. It wasn't said at all! You bamboozled her! Absolutely certain. You bamboozled her! She's a nasty woman, I agree, but she ought to understand all about courage.

VENUS. She's going to kill him!

SOSTHEME. No, no, Madam. She only wanted to frighten you. *He gets up.*

Oh! filthy viper, the day you enter my room to give me the sting of death, you will find me standing, leaning on my spade. And I will certainly manage to break your back.

VENUS. Be quiet. She'll hear you.

SOSTHEME. I don't give a damn! Saving your presence, I don't give a damn. Let her come! I'm waiting.

VENUS, *getting up, anxious.* Listen a minute . . . *They prick up their ears.* No, I thought . . . Listen! Listen! . . .

SOSTHEME. I don't hear anything.

VENUS. Yes, yes, that time . . . it's the dogs. Listen, do you hear?

SOSTHEME. Yes, it sounds like . . . See here, Madam, it's only the dogs. That's nothing dreadful.

VENUS. Don't you think they are barking in a strange way?

SOSTHEME. No, no. Their bark is the same as ever.

VENUS. Hum!

Silence. Enter ZOE *and* CUPID *upstage, abashed.*

ZOE. Madam, Madam, forgive me, I have been a coward.

CUPID. Forgive me, Madam.

VENUS. I'm not angry with you. I too was in a cold fright . . . Listen! *Pause* I tell you, the dogs are howling.

SOSTHEME. We must expect that she'll loose a pack of extraordinary beasts in the young gentleman's path. But he has seen others, eh? He'll not be easily startled.

VENUS. I'm afraid.

Distant wailing of a horn.

VENUS. I'm afraid.

ZOE *and* CUPID *press close against her, one left, one right.* SOSTHEME, *fist clenched, sniffs around him like a bulldog.*

SOSTHEME, *under his breath.* Maggoty drab! . . . Ah! maggoty drab, if only I had you now.

VENUS, *quietly.* Be quiet, Sostheme, I beg you . . . *Loud voice.* Death! Death! . . . Queen of the graves. Tomb of the kings! Empress of men! I dare speak your name; I implore you. Don't strike at random! Old age is your target, not the heart of a child . . . Oh! let your ebony dart spare him whom Cupid's white arrow wouldn't wound. Pleasant Death! Sweet Death! O lovable Death!

Sound of a horn.

SOSTHEME. I hear a horse galloping. Victory, Madam, he's coming back! She heard you!

Noise in the wings, left.

VENUS. It's you? . . . Is it you? . . . Adonis! Adonis!

Enter MARTIAL, *left.*

MARTIAL. It's over, Madam, all over . . . Finished! . . . *Sob.* When I found him he was lost to us. I found him and lost him.

VENUS, *in tears.* Where is he? Take me to him.

MARTIAL. No, Madam. You cannot see him. Even I scarcely dared to look at him . . . What murder! The beast slaved at him. His poor body only a wound.

ENUS. Adonis! Adonis!

MARTIAL. He was a delightful soul, Madam. He was strong and brave and loyal. He was a marvelous friend. Ah! my poor, poor hunter.

ENUS. Take me to him, I beg you!

MARTIAL. No, Madam. We others shall go. We shall wash him, and put him in order, and bring him back to you. *To* SOSTHEME *and* ZOE. Will you come with me?

SOSTHEME *and* ZOE. We'll follow you, Sir.

ENUS. Before everything else, Zoe, gently lay this handkerchief on his wound.

ZOE. Very gently, Madam.

ALL three go out, left. VENUS *and* CUPID *remain alone on the stage.* VENUS, *standing rigid, eyes far away, distractedly stroking the little head of* CUPID *turned toward her.*

ENUS. The world is empty. There is no one else on earth. World! World, you have just lost all your wealth. What countenance remains that is worthy to be looked upon? Where now is that voice which was music? Ah! from now on no creature need wear bonnet or veil. Neither sun nor wind will seek to reach you. When Adonis lived, the wind and sun were always lurking about to tickle and caress him. He wore a helmet. How handsome he was in that helmet!

CUPID. Yes, Madam.

ENUS. But he wore it in vain. The sun peeped underneath, the wind would blow it off and then, the one after the other would play with his locks.

CUPID. Yes, Madam.

ENUS. When he beheld his shadow in the brook, the fishes spread their golden gills on it. When he passed by, under the trees, the trees would fill with birds. Do you remember that day a thrush brought him a cherry in its beak?

CUPID. Yes, yes, Madam.

ENUS. But this grim boar could not have seen him before he killed him. Or perhaps it was a mistake and thinking to kiss him inadvertently sheathed his tusk in that soft flesh . . . Ah! I too, I too, Adonis, had my teeth been as violent as my love, I should have killed you with a kiss!

She weeps. Enter left, slowly, MARTIAL, ZOE, SOSTHEME.

ENUS, *who has heard them, lifts her head, without looking at them, her sad eyes straight in front of her.* I greet you, Adonis, on the threshold of your house . . . Dear child for whom I have waited so long, how delayed is your return! How great is your sleep, you who could not remain abed, how long will be your present sleep! Red cheeked young man, with fiery blood, capering young man, come home, all white and covered with dead blood—come home on your back. *She turns her head toward the left.*

MARTIAL, *very quietly.* Madam, we have not brought him back.

ENUS. What?

SOSTHEME. It's not our fault: we were holding him firmly.

ZOE. We were bent over him . . .

MARTIAL. He dissolved . . .

ZOE. . . . vanished, like a vapour, in our hands.

SOSTHEME. In short, someone has stolen him from us.

VENUS. It's all right this way. It's better like this.

THE THREE. Yes, Madam.

ZOE. I brought you back the handkerchief tinged with his blood.

She puts one knee on the ground and gives the handkerchief to VENUS. VENU
takes the handkerchief, goes slowly upstage, followed by the others, bend
down and passes the handkerchief over the ground in front of ADONIS' *hous*

VENUS. Let no one set foot on this blood stained earth. Let none dare t
cross this threshold reddened with the purest of blood. *She comes dow*
stage a little. There! The world is weeping in silence. Let us be quiet
Let the silence of the world fall on our heads.

All are silent.

SOSTHEME, *who has remained behind.* Ah! bless us! Madam must see! Look
everywhere the handkerchief has touched are flowers!

ZOE. It's true.

MARTIAL. It's true.

SOSTHEME. Anemones.

VENUS. Anemones.

SOSTHEME. See! how beautiful and bright! Just fancy! It's a miracle!

CUPID, *delighted.* A miracle!

VENUS, ZOE, MARTIAL, *softly.* A miracle!

SOSTHEME. I beg you to trust me to take care of them.

VENUS. Adonis! Adonis! . . . Seed . . . Sap . . . Youth . . .

SOSTHEME. That's not a garden flower.

VENUS, MARTIAL, ZOE, CUPID. It isn't a garden flower.

SOSTHEME. It's a beautiful forest flower.

VENUS, MARTIAL, ZOE, CUPID. He was the flower of the forests.

SOSTHEME. All white.

THE FOUR. So white!

SOSTHEME. With one tiny red spot. . . . *He picks one. He carries it to* VEN
as the curtain falls.

CURTAIN

Electra

A PLAY IN TWO ACTS

BY JEAN GIRAUDOUX

Translated by WINIFRED SMITH

CHARACTERS

ORESTES
THE EUMENIDES *(first as three little girls, later as fifteen-year-olds)*
GARDENER
PRESIDENT OF THE COUNCIL
AGATHA, *his young wife*
AEGISTHUS
BEGGAR
CLYTEMNESTRA
ELECTRA
YOUNG MAN
CAPTAIN
NARSES' WIFE
GUESTS, SERVANTS, MAIDS, SOLDIERS

ACT ONE

SCENE ONE

*A stranger (*ORESTES*) enters, escorted by three* LITTLE GIRLS, *just as, from the opposite side, the* GARDENER *comes in dressed for a festival, and accompanied by* GUESTS *from the village.*

FIRST LITTLE GIRL. How fine the gardener looks!

SECOND LITTLE GIRL. Of course! It's his wedding day.

THIRD LITTLE GIRL. Here it is, sir, your Agamemnon's palace!

STRANGER. What a strange façade! Is is straight?

FIRST LITTLE GIRL. No. There's no right side to it. You think you see it, but that's a mirage. Like the gardener you see coming, who wants to speak to you. He's not coming. He won't be able to say a word.

SECOND LITTLE GIRL. Or he'll bray—or meow—

GARDENER. The façade is perfectly straight, stranger. Don't listen to these liars. You are confused because the right side is built of stones from Gaul which sweat at certain seasons. The people then say the palace is weeping. The left side is built of marble from Argos, which—no one knows why—will suddenly be flooded with sunshine, even at night. Then they say the palace laughs. What's happening just now is that the palace is laughing and crying at the same time.

FIRST LITTLE GIRL. So it's sure not to be mistaken.

SECOND LITTLE GIRL. It's really a widow's palace.

FIRST LITTLE GIRL. Or of childhood memories.

STRANGER. I can't remember seeing such a sensitive building anywhere.

GARDENER. Have you already visited the palace?

FIRST LITTLE GIRL. As a baby.

SECOND LITTLE GIRL. Twenty years ago.

THIRD LITTLE GIRL. He couldn't walk yet.

GARDENER. But he must remember if he saw it.

STRANGER. All I can remember of Agamemnon's palace is a mosaic. They set me down on a square of tigers when I was naughty and on a hexagon of flowers when I was good,—and I remember creeping from one to the other, going across some birds.

FIRST LITTLE GIRL. And over a beetle.

STRANGER. How do you know that, child?

GARDENER. And did your family live in Argos?

STRANGER. And I remember many, many bare feet. Not a face, faces were way up in the sky, but lots of bare feet. I tried to touch the gold rings under the edges of the skirts; some ankles were joined by chains, slaves' ankles. I remember two little feet, very white ones, the barest, the whitest. Their steps were always even, timid, measured by an invisible chain. I imagine they were Electra's. I ought to have kissed them, oughtn't I? A baby kisses everything it touches.

SECOND LITTLE GIRL. Anyway that would have been the only kiss Electra ever had.

GARDENER. It sure would!

FIRST LITTLE GIRL. Jealous, gardener?

STRANGER. Electra still lives in the palace?

SECOND LITTLE GIRL. Still. But not much longer.

STRANGER. That her window, the one with jasmine?

GARDENER. No. That's the room where Atreus, the first king of Argos, killed his brother's sons.

FIRST LITTLE GIRL. The meal at which he served up their hearts took place in the room next it. I'd love to know how they tasted.

THIRD LITTLE GIRL. Did he cut them up or cook them whole?

SECOND LITTLE GIRL. And Cassandra was strangled in the sentry-box.

THIRD LITTLE GIRL. They caught her in a net and stabbed her. She yelled like a crazy woman, through her veil. I'd love to have seen it.

FIRST LITTLE GIRL. That all happened in the laughing wing, as you see.

STRANGER. The one with roses?

GARDENER. Stranger, don't try to connect the windows with flowers. I'm the palace gardener. I plant them at random. They're just flowers.

SECOND LITTLE GIRL. Not at all. There are flowers and flowers. Phlox doesn't suit Thyestes.

THIRD LITTLE GIRL. Nor mignonette Cassandra.

GARDENER. Oh, be quiet! The window with the roses, stranger, is the one where our king, Agamemnon, coming back from the war, slipped into the pool, fell on his sword and killed himself.

FIRST LITTLE GIRL. He took his bath after his death. About two minutes after. That's the difference.

GARDENER. That's Electra's window.

STRANGER. Why is it so high up, almost on the roof?

GARDENER. Because from there she can see her father's tomb.

STRANGER. Why is she there?

GARDENER. Because it's Orestes' old room, her brother, whom her mother sent out of the country when he was two and who's not been heard of since.

SECOND LITTLE GIRL. Listen, sisters, listen! They're talking about Orestes!

GARDENER. Will you clear out! Leave us! You're just like flies.

FIRST LITTLE GIRL. We certainly won't leave. We're with this stranger.

GARDENER. Do you know these girls?

STRANGER. I met them at the door. They followed me in.

SECOND LITTLE GIRL. We followed him because we like him.

THIRD LITTLE GIRL. Because he's a lot better looking than you are, gardener.

FIRST LITTLE GIRL. No caterpillars in his beard.

SECOND LITTLE GIRL. Nor June bugs in his nose.

THIRD LITTLE GIRL. If flowers are to smell sweet, the gardener has to smell bad.

STRANGER. Be polite, children, and tell us what you do all the time.

FIRST LITTLE GIRL. What we do is, we're not polite.

SECOND LITTLE GIRL. We lie, we slander, we insult.

FIRST LITTLE GIRL. But specially, we recite.

STRANGER. And what do you recite?

FIRST LITTLE GIRL. We never know ahead of time—we invent as we go along. But we're very, very good.

SECOND LITTLE GIRL. The king of Mycenae, whose sister-in-law we insulted, said we were very, very good.

THIRD LITTLE GIRL. We say all the bad things we can think up.

GARDENER. Don't listen to them, stranger. No one knows who they are. They've been wandering about the town for two days, without friends or family. If we ask who they are, they pretend they're the little Eumenides. And the horrible thing is that they grow and get fat as you look at them. Yesterday they were years younger than today. Come here, you!

SECOND LITTLE GIRL. Is he rude, for a bridegroom!

GARDENER. Look at her! See how her eyelashes grow. Look at her bust. I understand such things, I've seen mushrooms grow. They grow fast, like an orange.

SECOND LITTLE GIRL. Poisonous things always win out.

THIRD LITTLE GIRL, *to the* FIRST LITTLE GIRL. Your bust's growing, is it?

FIRST LITTLE GIRL. Are we going to recite or not?

STRANGER. Let them recite, gardener.

FIRST LITTLE GIRL. Let's recite Clytemnestra, Electra's mother—You agree? Clytemnestra?

SECOND LITTLE GIRL. We agree.

FIRST LITTLE GIRL. Queen Clytemnestra has a bad color. She uses rouge.

SECOND LITTLE GIRL. Her color is bad because she sleeps badly.

THIRD LITTLE GIRL. She sleeps badly because she's afraid.

FIRST LITTLE GIRL. What is Queen Clytemnestra afraid of?

SECOND LITTLE GIRL. Of everything.

FIRST LITTLE GIRL. What's everything?

SECOND LITTLE GIRL. Silence. Silences.

THIRD LITTLE GIRL. Noise. Noises.

FIRST LITTLE GIRL. The idea that midnight is near. That the spider on her thread is about to pass from the time of day when she brings good luck to the time when she brings bad luck.

SECOND LITTLE GIRL. Of everything red, because blood is red.

FIRST LITTLE GIRL. Queen Clytemnestra has a bad color. She puts on blood.

GARDENER. What a silly story!

SECOND LITTLE GIRL. Good, isn't it?

FIRST LITTLE GIRL. See how the end goes back to the beginning—couldn't be more poetic!

STRANGER. Very interesting.

FIRST LITTLE GIRL. As you're interested in Electra we can recite about her. You agree, sisters? We can recite what she was like at our age.

SECOND LITTLE GIRL. We certainly do agree!

THIRD LITTLE GIRL. Even before we were born, before yesterday, we agreed.

FIRST LITTLE GIRL. Electra amuses herself by making Orestes fall out of his mother's arms.

SECOND LITTLE GIRL. Electra waxes the steps of the throne so her uncle, Aegisthus, will measure his length on the marble.

THIRD LITTLE GIRL. Electra is preparing to spit in the face of her little brother, Orestes, if he ever returns.

SECOND LITTLE GIRL. For nineteen years she's prepared poisonous spittle in her mouth.

THIRD LITTLE GIRL. She's thinking of your slugs, gardener, to make her mouth water more.

GARDENER. Now stop, you dirty little vipers!

SECOND LITTLE GIRL. Oh, ha, ha, the bridegroom gets mad!

STRANGER. He's right. Get out!

GARDENER. And don't come back!

FIRST LITTLE GIRL. We'll come back tomorrow.

GARDENER. Just try to! The palace is forbidden to girls of your age.

FIRST LITTLE GIRL. Tomorrow we'll be grown up.

SECOND LITTLE GIRL. Tomorrow will be the day after Electra's marriage to the gardener. We'll be grown up.

STRANGER. What are they saying?

FIRST LITTLE GIRL. You've not defended us, stranger. You'll be sorry for that.

GARDENER. Horrible little beasts! You'd think they were three little Fates. Dreadful to be a child Fate!

SECOND LITTLE GIRL. Fate shows you her tail, gardener. Watch out if it grows.

FIRST LITTLE GIRL. Come, sisters. Let's leave them both in front of their tainted wall.

The little EUMENIDES *go out, the* GUESTS *shrinking away from them in terror.*

SCENE TWO

The STRANGER. *The* GARDENER. *The* PRESIDENT OF THE COUNCIL *and his young wife,* AGATHA THEOCATHOCLES. VILLAGERS.

STRANGER. What did these girls say? That you are marrying Electra, gardener?

GARDENER. She'll be my wife an hour from now.

AGATHA. He'll *not* marry her. We've come to prevent that.

PRESIDENT. I'm your distant cousin, gardener, and the Vice President of the Council; so I've a double right to advise you. Run away to your radishes and squashes. Don't marry Electra.

GARDENER. Aegisthus orders me to.

STRANGER. Am I crazy? If Agamemnon were alive, Electra's wedding would be a festival for all Greece,— and Aegisthus gives her to a gardener, whose family, even, objects! Don't tell me Electra is ugly, or hunch-backed!

GARDENER. Electra is the most beautiful girl in Argos.

AGATHA. Oh, she's not too bad looking.

PRESIDENT. And she's perfectly straight. Like all flowers that grow in the shade.

STRANGER. Is she backward? Feeble-minded?

PRESIDENT. She's intelligence personified.

AGATHA. An especially good memory. Not always for the same thing, though. I don't have a good memory. Except for your birthday, darling, *that* I never forget.

STRANGER. What can she have done, or said, to be treated this way?

PRESIDENT. She does nothing, says nothing. But she's always *here*.

AGATHA. She's here.

STRANGER. She has a right to be. It's her father's palace. It's not her fault he's dead.

GARDENER. I'd never have dreamed of marrying Electra, but as Aegisthus orders me to, I don't see why I'd be afraid.

PRESIDENT. You have every reason to be afraid. She's the kind of woman that makes trouble.

AGATHA. And you're not the only one! Our family has everything to fear.

GARDENER. I don't understand you.

PRESIDENT. You will understand. Life can be pleasant, can't it!

AGATHA. Very pleasant! Immensely so!

PRESIDENT. Don't interrupt me, darling, especially just to repeat what I say. It *can* be very pleasant. Everything has a way of settling itself in life— spiritual suffering can be cured more quickly than cancer, and mourning than a sty. Take any group of human beings at random, each will have the same per cent of crime, lies, vice and adultery.

AGATHA. That's a horrid word, adultery, darling.

PRESIDENT. Don't interrupt me, especially to contradict me. How does it happen that in one group life slips by softly, conventionally. The dead are forgotten, the living get on well together, while in another there's hell to pay? It's simply that in the latter there's a woman who makes trouble.

STRANGER. That means there's a conscience in the second group.

AGATHA. I can't help thinking of your word, adultery,—such a horrid word!

PRESIDENT. Be quiet, Agatha. A conscience, you say! If criminals don't forget their sins, if the conquered don't forget their defeats, if there are curses, quarrels, hatreds, the fault is not with humanity's conscience, which always tends toward compromise and forgetfulness, but it lies with ten or fifteen women who make trouble.

STRANGER. I agree with you. Those ten or fifteen women save the world from egoism.

PRESIDENT. They've saved it from happiness! I know Electra. Let's agree that she is what you say—justice, generosity, duty. But it's by justice, generosity, duty, and not with egoism and easy going ways, that the state, individuals, and the best families are ruined.

AGATHA. Absolutely! But why, darling? You've told me, but I forget.

PRESIDENT. Because those three virtues have in common the one element fatal to humanity—implacability. Happiness is never the lot of implacable people. A happy family makes a surrender. A happy epoch demands unanimous capitulation.

STRANGER. You surrender at the first call?

PRESIDENT. Alas, no! Some one else got in first. So I'm only the vice-president.

GARDENER. Against what is Electra implacable? She goes every night to her father's tomb, is that all?

PRESIDENT. I know. I've followed her. Along the same road which my duty made me take one night, pursuing our most dangerous murderer, along the river I followed and saw the greatest innocent in Greece. A horrible walk, behind the two of them. They stopped at the same places, at the yew, at the corner of the bridge, at the thousand year old milestone, all gave the same signs to innocence and to crime. But because the murderer was there, the night was bright, peaceful, clear. He was the kernel taken out of the fruit, which, in a tart, might have broken your tooth. Electra's presence, on the contrary, confused light and darkness, even spoiled the full moon. Have you seen a fisherman, who before going out to fish, arranges his bait? All the way along the river, that was she. Every evening she spreads her net for everything that, without her, would have abandoned this pleasant, agreeable earth,—remorse, confessions, old blood stains, rust, bones of murdered men, a mass of accusations. In a short time everything will be ready, everything will move. The fisher will only have to pass by.

STRANGER. He always does come, sooner or later.

PRESIDENT. That's not so.

AGATHA, *much taken by the* STRANGER. A mistake!

PRESIDENT. This child herself sees the leak in your argument. A triple layer of earth daily piles up over our sins, our failures, our crimes, and stifles their worst effects! Forgetfulness, death, human justice. It is madness to remember these things. A horrible country, one where because of an avenger of wrongs, ghosts walk, dead men, half asleep,—where no allowance is ever made for human weakness, or perjury, where a ghost and an avenger constantly threaten. When guilty men's sleep continues to be more troubled after legal prosecution, than the sleep of the innocent, society is terribly disturbed. When I look at Electra, I'm troubled by the sins I committed in my cradle.

AGATHA. And I by my future sins. I'll never commit them, darling. You know that. Especially that adultery, which you will talk about. But those other sins already bother me.

GARDENER. I'm rather of Electra's opinion. I don't much care for wicked people. I love truth.

PRESIDENT. Do you know what truth is for our family that you proclaim it so openly? A quiet, well thought of family, rising fast. You'll not deny my assertion that you are the least important member of it. But I know by experience that it's not safe to venture on thin ice. It won't be ten days, if you marry Electra, before the discovery—I'm just inventing this— that our old aunt, when a young girl, strangled her baby so her husband wouldn't find out about it, and in order to quiet suspicion, no longer concealed attacks on her grandfather's virtue. My little Agatha, in spite of being gayety itself, can't sleep because of all this. You are the only one

who doesn't see Aegisthus' trick. He wants to pass on to the Theocathocles family everything that might some day throw a sinister light on the
Atrides.

STRANGER. And what have the Atrides to fear?

PRESIDENT. Nothing. Nothing that I know of, it's like every happy family or
couple, every satisfied person. Yet it does have to fear the most dangerous
enemy in the world, who would devour it to the bone, Electra's ally, un-
compromising justice.

GARDENER. Electra loves my garden. If she's a little nervous the flowers will
do her good.

AGATHA. But she'll not do good to the flowers.

PRESIDENT. Certainly. You'll get to know your fuchias and geraniums. You'll
see that they're not just pretty symbols. They'll show their knavery and
their ingratitude. Electra in the garden is justice and memory among the
flowers—that means hatred.

GARDENER. Electra is devout. All the dead are for her.

PRESIDENT. The dead! The murdered, half melted into the murderers, the
shades of the robbed and the tricked mixed with those of the thieves, rival
families scattered among each other, all moving about and saying "Oh,
Heavens! here's Electra! And we were so peaceful."

AGATHA. Here comes Electra!

GARDENER. No, not yet. It's Aegisthus. Leave us, stranger, Aegisthus doesn't
like strange faces.

PRESIDENT. You, too, Agatha. He's rather too fond of well-known women's
faces.

AGATHA, *with marked interest in the stranger's good looks.* Shall I show you
the way, handsome stranger?

AEGISTHUS *enters, to the hurrahs of the* GUESTS, *as* SERVANTS *set up his throne,
and place a stool beside a pillar.*

SCENE THREE

AEGISTHUS. *The* PRESIDENT. *The* GARDENER. SERVANTS.

AEGISTHUS. Why the stool? What's the stool for?

SERVANT. For the beggar, my lord.

AEGISTHUS. What beggar?

SERVANT. The god, if you prefer. This beggar has been wandering through
the city for several days. We've never seen a beggar who's so much a
beggar, so it's thought he must be a god. We let him go wherever he
likes. He's prowling around the palace now.

AEGISTHUS. Changing wheat to gold? Seducing the maids?

SERVANT. He does no harm.

AEGISTHUS. A queer god! The priests haven't found out yet whether he's a
rascal or Jupiter?

SERVANT. The priests don't want to be asked.

AEGISTHUS. Friends, shall we leave the stool here?

PRESIDENT. I think it will be better to honor a beggar than to insult a god.

AEGISTHUS. Leave the stool there. But if he comes, warn us. We'd like to be just a group of human beings for a few minutes. And don't be rude to him. Perhaps he is delegated by the gods to attend Electra's marriage. The gods invite themselves to this marriage, which the President considers an insult to his family.

PRESIDENT. My lord. . .

AEGISTHUS. Don't protest. I heard everything. The acoustics in this palace are extraordinary. The architect apparently wanted to listen to the council's discussions of his salary and bonus, so he built it full of echoing passages.

PRESIDENT. My lord. . .

AEGISTHUS. Be quiet. I know everything you're about to say on the subject of your fine honest family, your worthy sister-in-law, the baby-killer, your satirist uncle, and your nephew, the slanderer.

PRESIDENT. My lord. . .

AEGISTHUS. An officer, in a battle, to whom the King's standard is given to turn the enemy's fire on him, carries it with more enthusiasm. You're losing your time. The gardener will marry Electra.

SERVANT. Here is the beggar, my lord.

AEGISTHUS. Detain him a moment. Offer him a drink. Wine is appropriate for a beggar or a god.

SERVANT. God or beggar, he's drunk already.

AEGISTHUS. Then let him come in. He'll not understand us, though we must speak of the gods. It might even be amusing to talk about them before him. Your notion of Electra, President, is true enough, but it's peculiar, definitely middle-class. As I'm the Regent, allow me to give you more elevated, philosophical ideas. You believe in the gods, President?

PRESIDENT. Do you, my lord?

AEGISTHUS. My dear President, I've often asked myself if I believe in the gods. Asked myself because it's the only problem a statesman must decide for himself. I do believe in the gods. Or rather, I believe I believe in the gods. But I believe in them, not as great caretakers and great watchmen, but as great abstractions. Between space and time, always oscillating between gravitation and emptiness, there are the great indifferences. Those are the gods. I imagine them, not constantly concerned with that moving mould on the earth which is humanity, but as having reached the stage of serenity and universality. That is blessedness, the same thing as unconsciousness. They are unconscious at the top of the ladder of being, as the atom is at the bottom. The difference is that theirs is the unconsciousness of lightening, omniscient, thousand-faceted so that in their normal state, like diamonds, powerless and deaf, they only react to light, to omens, but without understanding them.

BEGGAR, *at last seated, feels he must applaud.* Well said! Bravo!

AEGISTHUS. Thanks. On the other hand, President, it's undeniable that sometimes there seem to be interruptions in human life so opportune and extensive that it's possible to believe in an extraordinary superhuman interest or justice. Such events have something superhuman or divine about them, in that they are like coarse work, not at all well designed. The plague breaks out in a town which has sinned by impiety or folly, but it also ravages the neighboring city, a particularly holy one. War breaks out when a nation becomes degenerate and vile, but it destroys all the just, the brave, and preserves the cowards. Or, whose ever the fault, or by whom committed, it's the same family that pays, whether innocent or guilty. I know a mother of seven children, who always spanked the same child—she was a divine mother. This fits our idea of the gods, that they are blind boxers, always satisfied by finding the same cheeks to slap, the same bottoms to spank. We might even be surprised if we understood the confusion that results from a sudden waking to beatitude, that their blows weren't given more at random. That the wife of a good man, and not a perjurer's, is brained by a shutter in a wind storm. That accidents strike down pilgrims and not troops. Always humanity suffers . . . I'm speaking generally. We see crows or deer struck down by an inexplicable epidemic—perhaps the blow intended for mankind went astray, either up or down. However it be, it's certain that the chief duty of a statesman is to watch fiercely that the gods are not shaken out of their lethargy, and to limit the harm they do to such reactions as sleepers snoring, or to thunder.

BEGGAR. Bravo! That's very clear! I understand it very well!

AEGISTHUS. Charmed, I'm sure!

BEGGAR. It's truth itself. For example, look at the people walking along the roads. Sometimes every hundred feet you'll see a dead hedgehog. They go over the roads at night by tens, male and female, and get crushed. You'll say they're fools, that they could find their mates on their side of the road. I can't explain it, but love for hedgehogs begins by crossing a road. What the devil was I trying to say? I've lost the thread . . . Go on, it'll come back to me.

AEGISTHUS. Indeed! What is he trying to say!

PRESIDENT. Shall we talk about Electra, my lord?

AEGISTHUS. What do you think we've been talking about? Our charming little Agatha? We were talking only about Electra, President, and about the need I feel to get her out of the royal family. Why, since I've been Regent, while other cities are devoured by dissension, other citizens by moral crises, are we alone satisfied with other people and with ourselves? Why are we so rich? Why in Argos alone are raw materials so dear and retail prices so low? Why, when we're exporting more cows, does butter go down in price? Why do storms pass by our vineyards, heresies our temples, animal diseases our barns? Because, in this city, I wage merciless war against all who signal to the gods.

PRESIDENT. What do you mean, signal to the gods?

BEGGAR. There! I've found it!

AEGISTHUS. Found what?

BEGGAR. My story, the thread of my story. I was speaking of the hedgehogs' deaths.

AEGISTHUS. One moment, please. We're speaking of the gods.

BEGGAR. To be sure! The gods come first, the hedgehogs later. But I won der if I'll remember.

AEGISTHUS. There are not two ways of signaling, President: it's done by separating one's self from the crowd, climbing a hill and waving a lantern or a flag. The earth is betrayed, as is a besieged city, by signals. The philosopher signals from his roof, the poet or a desperate man signal from his balcony or his swimming pool. If for ten years the gods have not meddled with our lives, it's because I've kept the heights empty and the fairgrounds full. I've ordered dreamers, painters, and chemists to marry; and because, in order to avoid racial trouble between our citizens— something that can't help marking human beings as different in the eye of the gods—I've always given great importance to misdemeanors and paid slight attention to crimes. Nothing keeps the gods so quiet as an equal value set on murder and on the theft of bread. I must say the court have supported me splendidly. Whenever I've been forced to be severe they've overlooked it. None of my decisions has been so obvious as to allow the gods to avenge it. No exile. I kill. An exile tends to climb up a steep road, just like a ladybird. I never execute in public. Our poor neighboring cities betray themselves by erecting their gallows on the top of a hill; I crucify at the bottom of a valley. Now I've said every thing about Electra.

GARDENER. What have you said?

AEGISTHUS. That there's just one person in Argos now to give a signal to the gods, and that's Electra. What's the matter?

BEGGAR *moves about among the* GUESTS.

BEGGAR. Nothing's the matter. But I'd better tell you my story now. In five minutes, at the rate you're talking, it won't have any sense. It's just to support what you say. Among those crushed hedgehogs you'll see dozens who seem to have died a hedgehog's death. Their fronts flattened by horse's hoofs, their spines broken under wheels, they're just smashed hedgehogs, nothing else. They're smashed because of the original sin of hedgehogs—which is crossing the main or side roads, on the pretext that the snail or partridge egg on the far side tastes better, but actually to make hedgehog love. That's their affair. No one prevents them. Suddenly you see a little young one, not flattened like the others, not so dirty, his little paw stretched out, his lips closed, very dignified, and you feel that he's not died a hedgehog's death, but was struck down for someone else, for you. His cold little eye is your eye. His spikes, your beard. His blood your blood. I always pick up those little ones, for they're the youngest the tenderest to eat. A year goes by, a hedgehog no longer sacrifice himself for mankind. You see I understand. The gods were mistaken they wanted to strike a perjurer, a thief, and they kill a hedgehog. A young one.

AEGISTHUS. Very well understood.

BEGGAR. And what's true of hedgehogs holds true for other species.

PRESIDENT. Of course! Of course!

BEGGAR. Why, of course? That's all wrong. Take the martin. Even though you're a President of the Council, you'll never pretend to have seen birds dying for you?

AEGISTHUS. Will you let us go on talking about Electra?

BEGGAR. Talk! Talk! But I must add when you see dead men, many seem to have died for bulls or pigs or turtles, not many for mankind. A man who seems to have died for mankind, he's hard to find, or even for himself. Are we going to see her?

AEGISTHUS. See whom?

BEGGAR. Electra. I'd like to see her before she's killed.

AEGISTHUS. Electra killed? Who says Electra's to be killed?

BEGGAR. You.

PRESIDENT. There's never been a thought of killing Electra.

BEGGAR. I have one gift. I don't understand words—I've had no education— but I do understand people. You want to kill Electra.

PRESIDENT. You don't understand at all, stranger. This man is Aegisthus, Agamemnon's cousin, and Electra's his darling niece.

BEGGAR. Are there two Electras? The one he was talking about who ruins everything, and the other one, his darling niece?

PRESIDENT. No! There's only one.

BEGGAR. Then he wants to kill her. No doubt about it. He wants to kill his darling niece.

PRESIDENT. I repeat, you don't understand in the least.

BEGGAR. Oh, I move about a lot. I knew a family, name of Narses. She was better than he. She was sick, her breathing bad. But a great deal better than he. No comparison.

GARDENER. He's drunk, a beggar, you know.

PRESIDENT. He's raving. He's a god.

BEGGAR. No. I started to tell you they had a wolf cub. It was their darling little pet. But one day around noon, wolf cubs, you know, grow up. They couldn't foretell the day. Two minutes before noon they were petting her, one minute after twelve she jumped at their throats. I didn't mind about him!

AEGISTHUS. Well?

BEGGAR. Well, I was just passing by. And I killed the wolf. She was beginning to eat Narses' cheeks, she liked them. Narses' wife got away, not too badly hurt. Thanks! You'll see her. She's coming for me pretty soon.

AEGISTHUS. What's the connection . . .?

BEGGAR. Oh, don't expect to see an Amazon queen. Varicose veins age a person.

PRESIDENT. He asked, what's the connection?

BEGGAR. The connection? It's because I think this man, as he's head of the state, must be more intelligent than Narses. No one could imagine such stupidity as Narses'. I never could teach him to smoke a cigar except by the lighted end. And what about knots? It's terribly important to know how to make knots. If you make a curlycue where you ought to have a knot, and *vice versa,* you're lost. You lose your money, you catch cold, you choke, your boat veers away or collides, you can't pull off your

shoes. I mean if you want to pull them off. And the laces? You know
Narses was a poacher.

PRESIDENT. We've asked you, what is the connection?

BEGGAR. Here's the connection. If this man distrusts his niece, if he knows
that one of these days she'll give a signal, as he said, she'll begin to bite,
to turn the city upside down, push up the price of butter, start a war, etc.,
he can't hesitate. He ought to kill her dead before she reveals herself.
When will she reveal herself?

PRESIDENT. What do you mean?

BEGGAR. What day, at what time will she reveal herself? When will she turn
into a wolf? When will she become Electra?

PRESIDENT. But nothing tells us she'll turn into a wolf?

BEGGAR, *pointing to* AEGISTHUS. Yes. He thinks so. He says so.

GARDENER. Electra is the gentlest of women.

BEGGAR. Narses' wolf cub was the gentlest of wolves.

PRESIDENT. Your expression "reveals herself" makes no sense.

BEGGAR. My expression makes no sense? You know nothing about life. The
29th of May, when you see the hills astir with thousands of little red,
yellow, and green balls flying, squawling, quarreling over every little bit
of thistle fluff, never making a mistake nor going after dandelion down
aren't the butterflies revealing themselves? And June 14th, when you
see on the river bank two reeds move without wind or wave till June 15th
and, too, without bubbles made by carp, isn't the pike revealing himself?
And judges like yourself, the first time they condemn to death, when the
condemned man appears, distraught, don't they reveal themselves by the
taste of blood on their lips? Everything in nature reveals itself. Even
the King. And the question today, if you'll believe me, is whether the
King will reveal himself as Aegisthus before Electra reveals herself a
Electra. So he has to know the day when it will happen to the girl, so
he can kill her on the eve, down in a valley, as he said, down in a little
valley, the handiest and least visible, in her bath.

PRESIDENT. Isn't he awful?

AEGISTHUS. You're forgetting the wedding, beggar.

BEGGAR. True. I am forgetting the wedding. But a wedding, if you want to
kill someone, isn't as sure as death. Especially as a girl like her, sensitive
rather backward, etc., will reveal herself the moment a man takes her in
his arms for the first time. You're marrying her?

AEGISTHUS. At once. Right here.

BEGGAR. Not to the king of a neighboring city, I hope?

AEGISTHUS. Not on your life! To this gardener.

PRESIDENT. To this gardener.

BEGGAR. She'll take him? I'd not reveal myself in the arms of a gardener
But everyone to his taste. I revealed myself in Corfu, at the fountain nea
the bakery, under the plane trees. You should have seen me that day! I
each tray of the scales I weighed a hand of the baker's wife. They neve
weighed the same. I evened them up in the right tray with flour, in the
left with oatmeal . . . Where does the gardener live?

GARDENER. Outside the walls.

BEGGAR. In a village?

GARDENER. No. My house stands alone.

BEGGAR, *to* AEGISTHUS. Bravo! I catch your idea. Not bad! It's quite easy to kill a gardener's wife. Much easier than a princess in a palace.

GARDENER. Whoever you are, I beg you . . .

BEGGAR. You'll not deny that it's easier to bury some one in compost than in marble?

GARDENER. What are you imagining? For one thing she'll not be a minute out of my sight.

BEGGAR. You'll bend down to plant a pear tree. Transplant it again because you hit a hard clod. Death has passed by.

PRESIDENT. Stranger, I fear you don't know where you are. You're in Agamemnon's palace, in his family.

BEGGAR. I see what I see, I see this man is afraid, he lives with fear, fear of Electra.

AEGISTHUS. My dear guest, let's not misunderstand each other. I'll not deny that I'm anxious about Electra. I know misfortunes and troubles will come to the family of the Atrides the day she reveals herself, as you say. And to us all, for every citizen is affected by what happens to the royal family. That's why I'm handing her over to a lowly family, unseen by the gods, where her eyes and gestures will not inflame, where the harm will be only local and in the middle class, the Theocathocles family.

BEGGAR. A good idea, a good idea! But the family ought to be especially lowly.

AEGISTHUS. It is, and I'll see that it stays so. I'll see that no Theocathocles distinguishes himself by talent or courage. As for boldness and genius, I'm not afraid they'll make their mark.

BEGGAR. Take care! This little Agatha is not exactly ugly. Beauty too can give a signal.

PRESIDENT. I beg you to leave Agatha out of our argument.

BEGGAR. Of course it's possible to rub her face with vitriol.

PRESIDENT. My lord!

AEGISTHUS. The case has been argued.

PRESIDENT. But I'm thinking of fate, Aegisthus! It's not a disease. You think it's infectious?

BEGGAR. Yes. Like hunger among the poor.

PRESIDENT. I can hardly believe that fate will be content with one obscure little clan instead of the royal family, or that it will become the fate of the Theocathocles instead of the Atrides.

BEGGAR. Don't worry. A royal cancer spreads to the middle classes.

AEGISTHUS. President, if you don't want Electra's entrance into your family to mark the disgrace of its legal members, don't add a word. In a third class zone the most implacable fate will do only third class harm. I personally am distressed, because of my great esteem for the Theocathocles family, but the dynasty, the State and the city can no longer take any risks.

BEGGAR. And perhaps she can be killed a little anyway, if an occasion arises.

AEGISTHUS. I have spoken. You may fetch Clytemnestra and Electra. They're waiting.

BEGGAR. It's not too soon. Without blaming you, I must say our talk lacks women.

AEGISTHUS. You'll have two, and talkers!

BEGGAR. And who'll argue with you a little, I hope?

AEGISTHUS. You like arguing women?

BEGGAR. Adore them. This afternoon I was in a house where a dispute was going on. Not a very high-toned discussion. Not compared to here. Not a plot of royal assassins as here. They were arguing whether they ought to serve guests chickens with or without livers. And the neck, of course. The women were furious. Had to be separated. Now I think of it, it was a fierce dispute. Blood flowed.

SCENE FOUR

The same. CLYTEMNESTRA, ELECTRA, MAIDS.

PRESIDENT. Here they both are.

CLYTEMNESTRA. Both! That's a manner of speaking. Electra is never more absent than when she's present.

ELECTRA. No. Today I'm here.

AEGISTHUS. Then let's make the most of it. You know why your mother has brought you here?

ELECTRA. It's her habit. She's already led a daughter to sacrifice.

CLYTEMNESTRA. There's Electra to the life! Never a word that's not treason or insinuation.

ELECTRA. Excuse me, mother. The allusion is quite àpropos in the family of the Atrides.

BEGGAR. What does she mean? Is she angry with her mother?

GARDENER. It would be the first time anyone has seen Electra angry.

BEGGAR. All the more interesting!

AEGISTHUS. Electra, your mother has told you of our decision. We've been anxious about you for a long time. I hardly think you realize that you're like a sleepwalker in broad daylight. In the palace and the city people speak of you only in whispers, they're so afraid you'd wake and fall if they raised their voices.

BEGGAR, *shouting.* Electra!

AEGISTHUS. What's the matter with him?

BEGGAR. Oh, I'm sorry, it's just a joke. Excuse it. But you were scared, no she. Electra's no sleepwalker.

AEGISTHUS. Please—

BEGGAR. At least the experiment has been made. You were the one who flinched. What would you have done if I'd shouted: Aegisthus?

PRESIDENT. Let our Regent speak.

BEGGAR. I'll shout Aegisthus pretty soon, when nobody expects it.

AEGISTHUS. You must get well, Electra, no matter what it costs.

ELECTRA. To cure me, that's easy. Give life to a dead man.

AEGISTHUS. You're not the only one who grieves for your father. But he'd not ask you to make your mourning an offense to the living.

ELECTRA. He's free. That's why he comes.

AEGISTHUS. Do you really think he's pleased to see you weep for him, not like a daughter but like a wife?

ELECTRA. I am my father's widow, for lack of another.

CLYTEMNESTRA. Electra!

AEGISTHUS. Widow or not, today we'll celebrate your marriage.

ELECTRA. Yes, I know your plot.

CLYTEMNESTRA. What plot? Is it a plot to marry a twenty-one year old daughter? At your age I had the two of you in my arms, you and Orestes.

ELECTRA. You carried us badly. You let Orestes fall on the marble floor.

CLYTEMNESTRA. What could I do? You pushed him.

ELECTRA. That's a lie. I never pushed him.

CLYTEMNESTRA. What do you know about it? You were only fifteen months old.

ELECTRA. I did *not* push Orestes! I remember it, far back in my memory. Oh, Orestes, wherever you are, hear me! I did not push you.

AEGISTHUS. That's enough, Electra.

BEGGAR. This time they're really going! Would be funny if the little girl revealed herself right in front of us.

ELECTRA. She lies, Orestes, she lies!

AEGISTHUS. Please, Electra!

CLYTEMNESTRA. She did push him. Obviously at her age she didn't know what she was doing. But she did push him.

ELECTRA. With all my strength I tried to hold him. By his little blue tunic. By his arm. By the end of his fingers. By his shadow. I sobbed when I saw him on the floor, with the red mark on his forehead.

CLYTEMNESTRA. You shouted with laughter. The tunic, by the way, was mauve.

ELECTRA. It was blue. I know Orestes' tunic. When it was drying you couldn't see it against the sky.

AEGISTHUS. Am I to have a chance for a word? Haven't you had time these twenty years to settle this debate?

ELECTRA. For twenty years I've waited for the chance. Now I have it.

CLYTEMNESTRA. Why can't she understand that she might be wrong, even honestly?

BEGGAR. They're both honest. That's the truth.

PRESIDENT. Princess, I beg of you! Of what interest is this question today?

CLYTEMNESTRA. Of none, I grant you.

ELECTRA. What interest? If I had pushed Orestes I'd rather die, I'd kill myself. My life would have no meaning.

AEGISTHUS. Must I force you to keep quiet? Are you as mad as she, Queen?

CLYTEMNESTRA. Electra, listen. Let's not quarrel. This is exactly what happened: He was on my right arm.

ELECTRA. On your left!

AEGISTHUS. Have you finished, yes or no, Clytemnestra?

CLYTEMNESTRA. We've finished. But a right arm is a right arm, a mauve tunic is mauve, not blue.

ELECTRA. It was blue. As blue as Orestes' forehead was red.

CLYTEMNESTRA. That is true. Very red. You touched the wound with your finger and danced around the little prone body. You laughed as you tasted the blood.

ELECTRA. I? I wanted to bruise my head on the step that hurt him. I trembled for a week.

AEGISTHUS. Silence!

ELECTRA. I'm still trembling.

BEGGAR. Narses' wife tied hers with an elastic rope that had some play. Often it was askew but he didn't fall.

AEGISTHUS. Enough. We'll soon see how Electra will carry hers. For you agree, don't you? You accept this marriage?

ELECTRA. I agree.

AEGISTHUS. I must admit not many suitors throng around you.

BEGGAR. They say . . .

AEGISTHUS. What do they say?

BEGGAR. They say you've threatened to kill the princes who might marry Electra. That's what they say in the city.

ELECTRA. Good! I don't want any prince.

CLYTEMNESTRA. You'd rather have a gardener?

ELECTRA. I know you two have decided to marry me to my father's gardener. I accept.

CLYTEMNESTRA. You shall not marry a gardener.

AEGISTHUS. Queen, we settled that. Our word is given.

CLYTEMNESTRA. I take mine back. It was a wicked word. If Electra is ill we'll care for her. I'll not give my daughter to a gardener .

ELECTRA. Too late, mother. You have given me.

CLYTEMNESTRA. Gardener, you dare to aspire to Electra?

GARDENER. I'm unworthy, Queen, but Aegisthus commands me.

AEGISTHUS. I do command you. Here are the rings. Take your wife.

CLYTEMNESTRA. If you persist, gardener, it's at the risk of your life.

BEGGAR. Then don't persist. I'd rather see soldiers die than gardeners.

CLYTEMNESTRA. What's that man saying? Marry Electra, gardener, and you die.

BEGGAR. It's your business. But go into the garden a year after the death of the gardener. You'll see something. You'll see what's happened to the endive, widowed of its gardener. It's not like kings' widows.

CLYTEMNESTRA. That garden won't suffer. Come, Electra.

GARDENER. Queen, you can deny me Electra, but it's not nice to say bad things about a garden you don't know.

CLYTEMNESTRA. I know it, empty land, with scattered plantings.

GARDENER. Empty? The best tended garden in Argos.

PRESIDENT. If he begins to talk about his garden we'll never finish.

AEGISTHUS. Spare us your descriptions!

GARDENER. The Queen provoked me, and I answer. My garden is my dowry and my honor.

AEGISTHUS. Never mind! Enough of quarrels.

GARDENER. Empty, indeed! It covers ten acres of hilly land, and six of valley. No, no, you'll not silence me! Not a sterile inch, is there, Electra? On the terraces I have garlic and tomatoes, on the slopes grape vines and peach trees. On the level land vegetables, strawberries and raspberries. A fig tree at the bottom of each slope, against the wall, which warms the figs.

AEGISTHUS. Fine! Let your figs get warm and take your wife.

CLYTEMNESTRA. You dare talk of your garden! I've seen it from the road. It's all dry, a bald skull. You shall not have Electra.

GARDENER. All dry! A brook flows between the box and the plane trees, never dry in hottest weather; from that I've dug two little trenches, one turned on the meadow, the other cut in the rock. Try to find skulls like that! And scattered plantings! In spring it's full of narcissus and jonquils. I've never seen Electra really smile but in my garden. I saw something on her face almost like a smile.

CLYTEMNESTRA. See if she's smiling now!

GARDENER. I call that Electra's smile.

CLYTEMNESTRA. Smiling at your dirty hands, your black nails. . .

ELECTRA. Dear gardener. . .

GARDENER. My black nails? Look, see if my nails are black! Don't believe it, Electra. You're unlucky today, Queen, for I spent this morning white-washing my house, so there's not a sign of mice there, and my nails came out, not black, as you say, but mooned with white.

AEGISTHUS. That's enough, gardener.

GARDENER. I know, I know it's enough. And my dirty hands! Look! Look at these dirty hands! Hands that I washed after taking down the dried mushrooms and onions, so nothing would trouble Electra's nights. I'll sleep in the outhouse, Electra; from there I'll keep guard so that nothing disturbs your sleep, whether an owl, or the open floodgate, or a fox, hunting in the hedge, with a chicken in his mouth. I've spoken.

ELECTRA. Thanks, gardener.

CLYTEMNESTRA. And that's how Electra will live, Clytemnestra's daughter, watching her husband going around his border, two pails in his hands. . . .

AEGISTHUS. There she can weep for her dead to her heart's content. Get ready your wreaths of everlasting tomorrow.

GARDENER. And there she'll escape from anxiety, torture, and perhaps tragedy. I don't understand people, Queen, but I do know the seasons. It's time, full time, to transplant misfortune from our city. The Atrides won't be grafted on our poor family, but on the seasons, the fields, the winds. I think they'll lose nothing by that.

BEGGAR. Be persuaded, Queen. Don't you see that Aegisthus hates Electra so much he'll be driven to kill her, giving her to the earth by a kind of play on words, he gives her to a garden. She gains by that, she gains life. AEGISTHUS *rises*. What? Was I wrong to say that?

AEGISTHUS, *to* ELECTRA *and the* GARDENER. Come here, both of you.

CLYTEMNESTRA. Electra, I beg you!

ELECTRA. You're the one who wanted it, mother.

CLYTEMNESTRA. I no longer want it. You see I don't want it now.

ELECTRA. Why don't you want it? Are you afraid? Too late!

CLYTEMNESTRA. How can I make you remember who I am and who you are?

ELECTRA. You'll have to tell me I didn't push Orestes.

CLYTEMNESTRA. Stupid girl!

AEGISTHUS. Are they beginning again?

BEGGAR. Yes, yes, let them begin again.

CLYTEMNESTRA. And unjust! And stubborn! I let Orestes fall! I who never break anything! Never let fall a glass or a ring! I'm so steady that birds light on my arms. It's possible to fly away from me but not to fall. That's just what I said when he lost his balance: Why, why did an ill fate bring his sister so near him?

AEGISTHUS. They're crazy!

ELECTRA. And I said to myself, as soon as I saw him slipping: if she's a true mother she'll stoop down to soften his fall, or she'll bend to make a slope and catch him on her thigh or her knees. We'll see if they'll catch him, the noble knees and thighs of my mother. I'm not sure. I'll see.

CLYTEMNESTRA. Be quiet!

ELECTRA. Or she'll bend backward, so little Orestes will slip off her like a child from a tree where he's picked off a nest, or she'll fall, so he won't, or so he'll fall on her. She knows all the ways a mother uses to catch her son, she still knows them. She can still be a curve, a shell, a motherly slope, a cradle. But she stood fixed, straight, and he fell right down from the full height of his mother.

AEGISTHUS. The case is heard. Clytemnestra, we'll leave.

CLYTEMNESTRA. Just let her remember what she saw when she was fifteen months old and what she didn't see. That's the point.

AEGISTHUS. Who except you believes her or listens to her?

ELECTRA. There are a thousand ways of preventing a fall, and she did nothing.

CLYTEMNESTRA. The slightest movement, and you would fall.

ELECTRA. Just as I said. You were a nurse, not a mother.

CLYTEMNESTRA. Dear little Electra. . .

ELECTRA. I'm not your little Electra. Your motherly feeling is tickled and awakened by your rubbing your two children against you. But it's too late.

CLYTEMNESTRA. Please—!

ELECTRA. There you are! Open your arms, see what you've done. Look, everybody. That's just what you did.

CLYTEMNESTRA. Let's go, Aegisthus. *She leaves.*

BEGGAR. I believe the mother is frightened.

AEGISTHUS, *to the* BEGGAR. What's that you say?

BEGGAR. I? I say nothing. I never say anything. When I'm hungry I talk, everyone hears me. Today I've drunk a little something.

ELECTRA, BEGGAR, GARDENER, STRANGER, AGATHA.

AGATHA. This is the right time, Aegisthus isn't here. Get out, gardener.

GARDENER. What do you mean?

AGATHA. Get out, fast. This man will take your place.

GARDENER. My place with Electra?

STRANGER. Yes, I'll marry her.

ELECTRA. Let go my hand.

STRANGER. Never.

AGATHA. Just look at him, Electra. Before you turn your back on a man, at least look at him. I'm sure you'll lose nothing by that.

ELECTRA. Gardener, help!

STRANGER. I owe you nothing, gardener. But look me in the eye. You understand species and kinds. Look at me and see the kind I am. So! Look, with your poor peasant eyes, with the gaze of humble folk, a blear-eyed mixture of devotion and fear, the sterile look of the poor, unchanged by sunshine or misfortune, see if I can give way to you. Fine! Now give me your ring. Thanks!

ELECTRA. Agatha, cousin! Help me! I swear I'll not tell about your rendezvous, your quarrels, I'll tell nothing.

AGATHA, *leading off the* GARDENER. Come, the Theocathocles are saved. Let the Atrides work it out.

BEGGAR. She runs away. Just like a wood-louse, hiding under a stone to escape from the sun.

ELECTRA, STRANGER, BEGGAR.

STRANGER. Don't struggle any more.

ELECTRA. I'll struggle till I die.

STRANGER. You think so? In a minute you'll take me in your arms.

ELECTRA. No insults!

STRANGER. In a minute you'll embrace me.

ELECTRA. Shame on you for profiting from two infamies!

STRANGER. See how I trust you. I let you go.

ELECTRA. Farewell forever!

STRANGER. No! I'll say one word to you and you'll come back to me, sweetly.

ELECTRA. What lie is this?

STRANGER. One word, and you'll be sobbing in my arms. Just one word, my name.

ELECTRA. There's only one name in the world that could draw me to anyone.
STRANGER. That's the one. My name.
ELECTRA. Are you Orestes?
ORESTES. Ungrateful sister, only recognizing me by my name!

CLYTEMNESTRA *appears.*

SCENE SEVEN

CLYTEMNESTRA. ELECTRA. ORESTES. BEGGAR.

CLYTEMNESTRA. Electra!
ELECTRA. Mother?
CLYTEMNESTRA. Come back to your place in the palace. Leave the gardener
    Come!
ELECTRA. The gardener has left, mother.
CLYTEMNESTRA. Where is he?
ELECTRA. He's given me to this man.
CLYTEMNESTRA. What man?
ELECTRA. This man. He's my husband now.
CLYTEMNESTRA. This is no time for jokes. Come!
ELECTRA. How can I come? He's holding my hand.
CLYTEMNESTRA. Hurry!
ELECTRA. You know, mother, those clogs they put on the legs of foals to pre-
    vent their running away? This man has put them on my ankles.
CLYTEMNESTRA. This time I command you. You must be in your room by
    tonight. Come!
ELECTRA. What? Leave my husband the night of my wedding?
CLYTEMNESTRA. What are you doing? Who are you?
ELECTRA. He'll not answer you. This evening my husband's mouth and all
    his words belong to me.
CLYTEMNESTRA. Where do you come from? Who is your father?
ELECTRA. If it's a misalliance it won't be a serious one.
CLYTEMNESTRA. Why do you look at me like that? Why the challenge in your
    eyes? Who was your mother?
ELECTRA. He never saw her.
CLYTEMNESTRA. She's dead?
ELECTRA. Perhaps what you see in his eyes is that he never saw his mother
    Handsome, isn't he?
CLYTEMNESTRA. Yes. He looks like you.
ELECTRA. If our first married hours make us look alike, that's a good omen.
    isn't it, mother?
CLYTEMNESTA. Who are you?
ELECTRA. What does it matter to you? There was never a man less yours.
CLYTEMNESTRA. Whatever or whoever you are, stranger, don't give in to her
    caprice. We'll see tomorrow if you're worthy of Electra. I'll win over

Aegisthus. But I've never known a less propitious night. Leave this man, Electra.

ELECTRA. Too late! His arms hold me.

CLYTEMNESTRA. You can break iron if you want to.

ELECTRA. Iron, yes, *this* iron, no!

CLYTEMNESTRA. What has he said against your mother that you accept him this way?

ELECTRA. We've had no time yet to speak of my mother or his. Go, we'll begin!

ORESTES. Electra!

ELECTRA. That's all he can say. If I take my hand from his mouth, he just says my name without stopping. You can't get anything else out of him. Oh, husband, now that your mouth is free, kiss me!

CLYTEMNESTRA. Shame! So this madness is Electra's secret!

ELECTRA. Kiss me, before my mother.

CLYTEMNESTRA. Farewell! But I didn't think you were a girl to give yourself to the first passer-by.

ELECTRA. Nor I. But I didn't know what the first kiss was like.

SCENE EIGHT

ELECTRA. ORESTES. BEGGAR.

ORESTES. Why do you hate our mother so, Electra?

ELECTRA. Don't speak of her, above all not of her! Let's imagine for a minute that we were born without a mother. Don't talk.

ORESTES. I have everything to tell you.

ELECTRA. You tell me everything just by being here. Be quiet. Close your eyes. Your words and your look touch me too poignantly, they wound me. I often wished that I'd find you in your sleep, if I ever found you. Now I can't bear to have all at once the look, the voice, the life of Orestes. I ought to have come on your image, dead at first, then coming alive little by little. But my brother was born like the sun, a golden animal at his rising. Either I'm blind or I find my brother by groping—oh, the joy of being blind, for a sister who finds her brother! For twenty years my hands have fumbled over mean or indifferent things, and now they touch a brother. A brother in whom everything is true. Some dubious or some false bits might have been in this head, this body, but by a wonderful chance, everything in Orestes is fraternal, everything is Orestes!

ORESTES. You smother me.

ELECTRA. I don't smother you. I don't kill you. I caress you. I'm calling you to life. From this brotherly shape which my dazzled eyes have scarcely seen I'm making my brother in all his features. See, how I've made my brother's hand, with its straight thumb. See how I've made my brother's chest, which I'm animating so it swells and breathes out, giving life to my brother. See how I make his ear, little, curled, transparent like a bat's wing. One last touch and the ear is finished. I make the two alike. What a success, these ears! And now I'll make my brother's mouth, gentle and dry, and fasten it on his face. Take your life from me, Orestes, not from our mother.

ORESTES. Why do you hate her? Listen. . .

ELECTRA. What's the matter with you? Are you pushing me away? That's the ingratitude of sons. They're hardly finished before they get away and escape.

ORESTES. Someone is watching us from the staircase.

ELECTRA. It's she, certainly she. From jealousy or fear. It's our mother.

BEGGAR. Yes, yes, it's she.

ELECTRA. She suspects we're here, creating ourselves, freeing ourselves from her. She thinks that my caresses will cover you, wash you clear of her, make you an orphan. Oh, brother, who else could do me such a service!

ORESTES. How can you speak so of her who bore you? I'm less hard on her, though she was so harsh to me.

ELECTRA. That's just what I can't stand about her, that she bore me. That's my shame. I feel that I came into life in a dubious way, that her motherhood is only a plot to bind us together. I love everything that comes from my father. I love the way he put off his fine wedding garment and lay down to beget me, from his thought and from his body. I love his eyes, and his surprise the day I was born; I came from him far more than from my mother's pains. I was born from his nights of deep sleep, his nine month's emaciation, the comfort he found with other women while my mother was carrying me, his fatherly smile when I was born. I hate everything about my birth that comes from my mother.

ORESTES. Why do you detest women so?

ELECTRA. I don't detest women, I detest my mother. And I don't detest men, I detest Aegisthus.

ORESTES. Why do you hate him?

ELECTRA. I don't know yet. I only know it's the same hatred. That's why it's so hard to bear, that's why I'm suffocating. Many times I've tried to find out why I hate each of them with a special hatred. Two little hatreds could be borne—like sorrows—one balances the other. I tried to think I hated my mother because she let you fall when you were a baby, and Aegisthus because he's stolen your throne. But it's not true. I really pitied this great queen, who ruled the world, yet suddenly, frightened and humble let her child fall, like a feeble grandmother. I pitied Aegisthus, that cruel tyrant, whose fate is to die miserably from your blows. All the reasons I had for hating them left me thinking them human and pitiable, but as soon as my hatred had left them clean and adorned and I found myself gentle and obedient before them, a heavy wave, charged with hate, flowed over them. I hate them with a hatred that is not really me.

ORESTES. I'm here. It will vanish.

ELECTRA. You believe that? I used to think your return would free me of this hatred. I thought my illness was because you were far away. I prepared for your return by becoming all tenderness, tenderness for everyone, for them too. I was wrong. My illness tonight is caused by your being here and all the hatred in me laughs and welcomes you, it is my love for you. It caresses you as a dog does the hand that frees him. I know that you have given me the sight, the smell of hatred. The first scent and now I follow the trail. Who's there? Is it she?

BEGGAR. No, me. You're forgetting the time. She's gone up. She's undressing.

ELECTRA. She's undressing. Before her mirror, looking long at herself, our mother, Clytemnestra, undresses. Our mother, whom I love for her beauty and pity because she's aging, whose voice and looks I admire, our mother, whom I hate.

ORESTES. Electra, sister darling, please calm yourself.

ELECTRA. Then I'm to follow the trail?

ORESTES. Calm yourself.

ELECTRA. I? I'm perfectly calm. I'm all sweetness. Sweet to my mother, very sweet. It's this hatred for her that swells up and kills me.

ORESTES. Now it's your turn not to talk. We'll think about that hatred tomorrow. This evening let me taste for an hour at least, the sweetness of this life I've never known and now return to.

ELECTRA. An hour. All right, one hour.

ORESTES. The palace is so beautiful beneath the moon. My palace. All the power of our family emanates from it at this hour. My power. In your arms let me imagine all the happiness these walls might have held for more reasonable and calmer people. Oh, Electra, how many of our family's names were originally sweet and tender, and should have been happy names!

ELECTRA. Yes, I know. Medea, Phaedra.

ORESTES. Even those, why not?

ELECTRA. Electra. Orestes.

ORESTES. Isn't there still time for them? I've come to save them.

ELECTRA. Silence! She's there.

ORESTES. Who?

ELECTRA. She with the happy name: Clytemnestra.

SCENE NINE

ELECTRA. ORESTES. CLYTEMNESTRA, *then* AEGISTHUS.

CLYTEMNESTRA. Electra?

ELECTRA. Mother?

CLYTEMNESTRA. Who is this man?

ELECTRA. Guess.

CLYTEMNESTRA. Let me see his face.

ELECTRA. If you can't see it at a distance you'd see him less well near to.

CLYTEMNESTRA. Electra, let's stop fighting. If you really want to marry this man, I'll agree. Why do you smile? Wasn't it I who wanted you to marry?

ELECTRA. Not at all. You wanted me to be a woman.

CLYTEMNESTRA. What's the difference?

ELECTRA. You wanted me in your camp. You didn't want the face of your worst enemy constantly before you.

CLYTEMNESTRA. You mean my daughter's?

ELECTRA. Chastity, rather!

ORESTES. Electra. . !

ELECTRA. Let me alone, let me alone. I've found the trail.

CLYTEMNESTRA. Chastity! This girl who's devoured by desire, talks about chastity! This girl at two years old couldn't see a boy without blushing. It was because you wanted to embrace Orestes, if you want to know, that you pulled him out of my arms.

ELECTRA. Then I was right. I'm proud of it. It was worth while.

Trumpets. Shouts. Faces in the windows. AEGISTHUS *leans down from balcony.*

AEGISTHUS. Are you there, Queen?

BEGGAR. Yes, she's here.

AEGISTHUS. Great news, Queen. Orestes is not dead. He's escaped. He's coming toward Argos.

CLYTEMNESTRA. Orestes!

AEGISTHUS. I'm sending my lifeguard to meet him. I've posted my most faithful men around the walls. You say nothing?

CLYTEMNESTRA. Orestes is coming back?

AEGISTHUS. Coming back to seize his father's throne, to prevent my being regent and you being queen. His emissaries are going around preparing a revolt. But don't worry. I'll keep order everywhere. Who's down there with you?

CLYTEMNESTRA. Electra.

AEGISTHUS. And her gardener?

BEGGAR. And her gardener.

AEGISTHUS. I hope you're not still trying to separate them? You see how well founded my fears were! You're agreed now?

CLYTEMNESTRA. No. I'm not trying any more.

AEGISTHUS. Don't let them leave the palace. They especially. I've ordered the gates closed till the soldiers return. You hear me, gardener?

ELECTRA. We'll not leave.

AEGISTHUS. Queen, come upstairs. Go back to your room. It's late and the Council is to meet at dawn. I wish you a goodnight.

ELECTRA. Thanks, Aegisthus.

AEGISTHUS. I was speaking to the queen, Electra. This is no time for irony. Come, Queen.

CLYTEMNESTRA. Good-bye, Electra.

ELECTRA. Good-bye, mother.

                    CLYTEMNESTRA *goes, then turns back.*

CLYTEMNESTRA. Good-bye, my daughter's husband.

BEGGAR. What you see in families! You really see everthing!

ELECTRA. Who spoke?

BEGGAR. No one! No one spoke. You think someone would speak at such a
time.

SCENE TEN

ELECTRA. ORESTES. BEGGAR.

ORESTES. Tell me, Electra! Tell me!

ELECTRA. Tell you what?

ORESTES. Your hatred. The reason for your hatred. You know it now,
when you were talking to Clytemnestra a moment ago you almost fainted
in my arms. It might have been from joy or horror.

ELECTRA. It was from both joy and horror. Are you strong or weak, Orestes?

ORESTES. Tell me your secret and I'll find out.

ELECTRA. I don't know my secret yet. I hold only the beginning of the
thread. Don't worry. Everything will follow. Take care! Here she is.

> CLYTEMNESTRA *appears at the back of the stage*

SCENE ELEVEN

ELECTRA. CLYTEMNESTRA. ORESTES. BEGGAR.

CLYTEMNESTRA. So it's you, Orestes?

ORESTES. Yes, mother, its I.

CLYTEMNESTRA. Is it sweet to see a mother when you're twenty?

ORESTES. A mother who sent you away? Sad and sweet.

CLYTEMNESTRA. You're looking at her from far away.

ORESTES. She's as I imagined her.

CLYTEMNESTRA. My son. Handsome, Regal. And nevertheless I draw near.

ORESTES. Not I. At a distance she's a magnificent mother.

CLYTEMNESTRA. Who tells you that near to her magnificence remains?

ORESTES. Or her motherliness? That's why I don't move.

CLYTEMNESTRA. The mirage of a mother is enough for you?

ORESTES. I've had so much less until today. At least I can tell the mirage
what I'd never tell my real mother.

CLYTEMNESTRA. If the mirage deserves it, that's all right. What will you
tell her?

ORESTES. Everything that I never tell you. Everything that would be a lie
if said to you.

CLYTEMNESTRA. That you love her?

ORESTES. Yes.

CLYTEMNESTRA. That you respect her?

ORESTES. Yes.

CLYTEMNESTRA. That you admire her?

ORESTES. That the mother and the mirage can share.

CLYTEMNESTRA. It's the opposite for me. I don't love the mirage of my son.
But when my son is actually before me, speaking, breathing, I lose my
strength.

ORESTES. Think of hurting him, you'll recover it.

CLYTEMNESTRA. Why are you so hard? You don't look cruel. Your voice
is gentle.

ORESTES. Yes, I'm exactly like the son I might have been. You too, of course.
You look so like a wonderful mother. If I weren't your son I'd be deceived.

ELECTRA. Then why are you both talking? Where does this horrible
maternal coquetry get you, mother? Since at midnight the little window
which allows a mother and son to see each other as they are not, has
opened for a minute, shut it now, the minute has passed.

CLYTEMNESTRA. Why so quickly? How do you know that one minute of
maternal love is enough for Orestes?

ELECTRA. Everything tells me that you have no right to more than a minute
of your son's love in your whole life. You've had it. And that's the end.
What a comedy you're playing! Go away. . . .

CLYTEMNESTRA. Very well. Good-bye.

A LITTLE FURY, *appearing from behind the columns.* Good-bye, truth of my
son.

ORESTES. Good-bye.

SECOND LITTLE FURY. Good-bye, mirage of my mother.

ELECTRA. You might say *au revoir.* You'll meet again.

SCENE TWELVE

ELECTRA *and* ORESTES *asleep. The little* EUMENIDES. BEGGAR. *The* EUMENIDES
now seem to be about twelve or thirteen years old.

FIRST LITTLE GIRL. They're asleep. It's our turn to play Clytemnestra and
Orestes. But not the way they played. Let's play it truly.

BEGGAR, *to himself, though out loud.* The story about the push or not push
—I'd like to know . . .

SECOND GIRL. You there, let us play. We're playing.

The three little EUMENIDES *take the positions of the actors in the preceding
scene and play it as a parody. I'd like them to wear masks.*

FIRST GIRL. So it's you, Orestes?

SECOND GIRL. Yes, it's I, mother.

FIRST GIRL. You've come to kill me and kill Aegisthus?

SECOND GIRL. News to me!

FIRST GIRL. Not to your sister. You've already killed, little Orestes?

SECOND GIRL. The things one kills when one is good! A doe. And to be little kind, I killed her fawn too, so it wouldn't be an orphan. But to kill my mother, never! That would be parricide.

FIRST GIRL. Was that the sword you used to kill with?

SECOND GIRL. Yes. It will cut iron. See, it went through the fawn so fast he felt nothing.

FIRST GIRL. I'm not suggesting anything. I don't want to influence you. But if a sword like that were to kill your sister, we'd all be at peace!

SECOND GIRL. You want me to kill my sister?

FIRST GIRL. Never! That would be fratricide. If the sword were to kill her by itself, that would be ideal. Let it come out of its scabbard, like this, and kill her by itself. I'd just quietly marry Aegisthus. We'd call you home, Aegisthus is getting old. You'd succeed him very soon. You'd be King Orestes.

SECOND GIRL. A sword doesn't kill by itself. It needs an assassin.

FIRST GIRL. Certainly! I should know! But I'm talking about the times when swords will kill by themselves. People who revenge wrongs are the curse of the world. And they get no better as they get older, I beg you to believe that. As criminals improve with age, virtuous people without exception become criminals. Surely this is a fine moment for a sword to think for itself, move of itself and kill by itself. They'd marry you to Alcmena's second daughter, the laughing one, with the fine teeth—You'd be the married Orestes.

SECOND GIRL. I don't want to kill my sister, whom I love, nor my mother, whom I detest.

FIRST GIRL. I know, I know. In a word you're weak and you have principles.

THIRD GIRL. Why are you two talking? Because the moon is rising, the nightingale singing here in the middle of this night of hatred and threats; take your hand off the hilt of your sword, Orestes, and see if it will have the intelligence to act by itself.

FIRST GIRL. That's right. Take it off . . . it's moving, friends, it's moving!

SECOND GIRL. No doubt of it! It's a thinking sword. It thinks so hard it's half out!

ORESTES, *asleep*. Electra!

BEGGAR. Off with you, screech owls! You're waking them.

ELECTRA, *asleep*. Orestes!

SCENE THIRTEEN

ELECTRA, ORESTES, BEGGAR.

BEGGAR. I'd love to get straight that story of the pushed or not pushed. For whether it's true or false it would show whether Electra is truthful or lying and whether she lies knowingly or whether her memory plays her false. I don't believe she pushed him. Look at her: two inches above the ground she's holding her sleeping brother as tight as if they were over an abyss. He's dreaming that he's falling, evidently, but that's not her

fault. Now the Queen looks like those bakers' wives who never stoop
even to pick up their money, or like those bitches who smother their
prettiest pup while they sleep. Afterward they lick it as the Queen licked
Orestes, but no one ever made a child with saliva. I can see the story as
if I'd been there. It's understandable, if you imagine the Queen had put
on a diamond pin and a white cat had passed by. She's holding Electra on
her right arm, for the girl was getting heavy, and the baby on the left,
a bit away from her so he'll not scratch himself on the brooch or drive
it into him. It's a queen's pin, not a nurse's. And the child sees the white
cat, a magnificent creature—a white life, white hair—his eyes follow it,
he rocks himself, and she's an egotistical woman. Anyway, seeing the child
capsizing, in order to hold him she need only free her arm of little Electra,
throw little Electra off on the marble floor, get rid of little Electra. Let
little Electra break her neck so the son of the king of kings be unhurt.
But she's an egotist. For her a woman is as good as a man, she's a
woman; the womb as good as the phallus, and she's a womb; she wouldn't
dream for a second of destroying her daughter to save her son, so she
keeps Electra. Now look at Electra. She's revealed herself in her
brother's arms, and she's right. She couldn't wish for a better moment.
Fraternity is the mark of human beings. Beasts know only love . . .
cats, parrots, etc.; they only recognize fraternity by the hair. To find
brothers they have to love men, to turn to men. . . . What does the
duckling do when he gets away from the other ducks and with his
tender little eye shining on his slanting duck's cheek, he looks at us
humans, eating and playing games, because he knows men and women are
his brothers? I've taken little ducks in my hands, and could have wrung
their necks, because they came to me so fraternally, trying to understand
what I was doing, I, their brother, cutting my bread and cheese and
adding an onion to it. Brother of ducks, that's our real title, for when
they raise the little heads they've plunged into the water and look at
a man, they're all neatness, intelligence and tenderness—not eatable except for their brains. I could teach those little duck heads to weep! . .
So Electra didn't push Orestes! That makes everything she says legitimate, everything she undertakes irrefutable. She's unadulterated truth,
a lamp without a wick. So if she kills, as looks likely, all happiness and
peace around her, it's because she's right. It's as if the soul of a girl, in
bright sunlight, felt a moment of anguish, as if she sniffs escaping gas
in the midst of splendid festivals, and she has to go after it, for the young
girl is the guardian of truth, she has to go after it whether or not the
world bursts and cracks down to its foundations, whether innocents die
the death of innocents to let the guilty live their guilty lives. Look at
those two innocents! What will be the fruit of their marriage? To bring
to life for the world and for ages to come a crime already forgotten, the
punishment of which will be a worse crime? How right they are to
sleep this hour that is still theirs! Leave them. I'm going for a walk. I'll
wake them. I always sneeze three times when the moon is full, and
sneezing in these hands means taking a frightful risk. But all you who

remain here, be quiet, now. This is Electra's first rest and the last rest of
Orestes.

CURTAIN.

INTERLUDE: THE GARDENER'S LAMENT

I'm no longer in the running. That's why I'm free to come and tell you
what the play can't tell you. In stories like this the people won't stop killing
and biting each other in order to tell you that the one aim of life is to love.
It would be awkward to see the parricide stop, with his dagger raised and
make a speech praising love. That would seem artificial. A lot of people
wouldn't believe him. But I really don't see what else I can do here in this
confusion and desolation. And I speak impartially. I'll never marry anyone
but Electra, and I'll never have her. I was made to live with a woman day
and night, but I'll always live alone. I was meant to give myself fully and
yet I have to keep myself to myself. This is my wedding night that I'm
living through, all alone—but thank you for being here—and the orangeade
I'd prepared for Electra, I had to drink up myself; there's not a drop left,
and this was a long wedding night. Now who will doubt my word? The
trouble is that I always say the contrary of what I mean, and that would
be miserable today when my heart is so heavy and my mouth so bitter—
oranges are really bitter—and if I forgot for an instant that I must speak
to you of joy. Yes, joy and love. I come to tell you they're preferable to
bitterness and hate. That's a motto to carve on a porch or to put on a
handkerchief, or better, in dwarf begonias in a clump. Of course life is a
failure, yet it's very, very good. Of course nothing ever goes right, never is
well planned, yet you must confess, sometimes everything comes out splendidly, is splendidly planned. . . . Not for me . . . or perhaps just for me. . . .
If I can judge from my wish to love everything and everyone, which is the
result of the greatest misfortune in my life; what will happen to people who've
had less bad luck? How much love must men feel who marry wives they
don't love, what joy those feel who leave a wife they adore after having had
her in their home an hour? And the people whose children are ugly? Of
course, tonight in my garden I wasn't very happy. As a little festival it
didn't come off. I pretended sometimes that Electra was near me, I talked to
her and said: "Come in, Electra! Are you cold, Electra?" But nobody was
deceived, not even the dog, not to say myself. The dog thought: "He
promised us a bride, and he only gives us a word. My master has married
a word; he put on his white garment, the one my paws soil, which keeps
me from caressing him, just to marry a word! He gives his orangeade to a
word. He scolds me for barking at shadows, real shadows which aren't alive,
yet he tries to embrace a word."
    And I didn't lie down: to sleep with a word was impossible. I can
speak with a word, that's all! But if you were sitting like me in this garden,
where everything is confused at night, where the moon is shining on the
sundial and the blind owl tries to drink at the cement walk instead of at

the brook, you'd understand what I've understood: the truth! You'd understand that the day your parents died, that day your parents were born; the day you were ruined, that you were rich; when your child was ungrateful, that he was gratitude itself; when you were abandoned, that the whole world was coming to you in rapture and tenderness. That was exactly what happened to me in this empty, silent suburb. All these stony trees, these immovable hills, rushed toward me. This all applies to our play. To be sure, we can't say Electra is all love for Clytemnestra. But note the difference, she tries to find a mother and would see one in the first comer. She was marrying me because I was absolutely the only man who could be a kind of mother to her, though I'm not really the only one. There are men who'd be glad to carry a child nine months, if they had to, just to have daughters. All men, actually. Nine months are rather long, but to carry a week, or a day, any man would be proud. Perhaps to find a mother in her mother she'll have to cut open her breast, though with royalty that's rather theoretical. Among kings you have experiences that are never found among humble folk, pure hatred, for instance, and pure wrath. Always purity. That's tragedy, with its incests and parricides: purity, meaning innocence. I don't know if you're like me, but to me in Tragedy, Pharoah's daughter killing herself, means hope, the treasonous Marshall means faith, the Duke—assassin speaks of tenderness. Cruelty is a deed of love—excuse me, I mean Tragedy. That's why I'm sure this morning, that if I asked, Heaven would approve me, would give a sign that a miracle is near, which would show you that joy and love are written in Heaven, and that they echo my motto, though I'm abandoned and alone. If you wish, I'll ask. I'm as sure as I'm here that a voice from on high would answer me, that loud speakers and amplifiers and God's thunder are all prepared by God himself to shout, if I ask: "joy and love." But I'd rather you didn't ask. First it would be indecent. It's not the gardener's role to demand of God a storm, even one of tenderness. Moreover it would be useless. We know so well that at this moment, and yesterday and tomorrow and always, they're all up there, as many as there are, or perhaps only one, or even if that one is absent, they're all ready to shout: joy and love. It's much better for a man to take the gods at their word—that's a euphemism—without forcing them to underline it, or to be held by it, or to create among themselves obligations of creditor and debtor. I'm always convinced by silences. Yes, I've begged them, haven't I? not to shout joy and love. But let them shout it if they really want to. Yet I'd rather conjure them, I do conjure you, God, as a proof of your affection, of your voice and your shouts, to keep silent, silent for one second. . . . That's much more convincing. . . . Listen. . . . Thanks!

ACT TWO

SCENE ONE

The same setting, shortly before dawn.

ELECTRA, *seated, holding* ORESTES, *asleep.* BEGGAR. *A cock. Sound of a trumpet in the distance.*

BEGGAR. It won't be long now, eh, Electra?

ELECTRA. Yes. It's not far away.

BEGGAR. I said it, I meant the day.

ELECTRA. I meant the light.

BEGGAR. It's not enough for you that liars' faces are shining in the sun? That the adulterers and murderers move about freely? That's what the day brings—not too bad.

ELECTRA. No. But I want their faces to look blank at noon, and their hands red. That's what light brings out. I want their eyes to be rotten, their mouths diseased.

BEGGAR. As you say, you can't ask too much!

ELECTRA. There's the cock . . . shall I wake him?

BEGGAR. Wake him if you wish, but if I were you, I'd give him another five minutes.

ELECTRA. Five minutes of nothingness! A poor gift!

BEGGAR. You never know. I believe there's an insect that lives only five minutes. In five minutes he's young, adult, noisy; he runs through childhood and adolescence, to the time of lame knees and cataract, and legitimate and morganatic unions. While I'm speaking he must be having measles and growing into puberty.

ELECTRA. Let's wait till he dies. That's all I'll agree to.

BEGGAR. Our brother sleeps well.

ELECTRA. He went to sleep right away. He escaped from me. He slipped into sleep as though that were his real life.

BEGGAR. He's smiling there. It *is* his real life.

ELECTRA. Tell me anything you like, beggar, except that Orestes' real life is a smile.

BEGGAR. Loud laughter, love, fine clothes, happiness. I guessed that as soon as I saw him. Orestes would be gay as a lark, if life were good to him.

ELECTRA. He has bad luck.

BEGGAR. Yes, he's not very lucky. All the more reason for not hurrying him.

ELECTRA. Good! As he was made to laugh, to dress well, as he's a lark, I'll give Orestes five minutes, for he'll wake to a life time of horror.

BEGGAR. In your place, as you can choose, I'd see to it that this morning the light and truth depart at the same time. That doesn't mean much, but it would be a young girl's role and would please me. Man's truth is part of his habits, it leaves him somehow, whether at nine o'clock in the

morning when workers strike, or at six in the evening, when women
confess, etc.; these are always bad things, always unclear. Now I'm used
to animals. They know when to leave. A rabbit's first jump in the
heather, the very second the sun rises, the plover's first flight, the young
bear's first run from his rock, these, I can tell you, go toward the truth
If they don't get there, that's just because they don't have to. A mere
nothing distracts them, a gudgeon, a bee. But do as they do, Electra, go
toward the dawn.

ELECTRA. A fine kingdom where gudgeons and bees are liars! But your
animals are already moving!

BEGGAR. No. Those are the night creatures who are turning in. Owls, Rats
The night's truth turning in. Hush! Listen to the last two, the nightingales
of course: the nightingales' truth.

SCENE TWO

The same. AGATHA. *A* YOUNG MAN.

AGATHA. Oh, my dear love, you do understand, don't you?

YOUNG MAN. Yes, I'll have an answer for everything.

AGATHA. If he sees you on the stairs?

YOUNG MAN. I'll have come to see the doctor who lives up there.

AGATHA. You already forget! He's a veterinary. Buy a dog. . . . If he find
me in your arms?

YOUNG MAN. I've picked you up in the street, you've sprained your ankle.

AGATHA. If it's in our kitchen?

YOUNG MAN. I'll pretend to be drunk—I don't know where I am. I'll break
the glasses.

AGATHA. One will be enough, darling, a small one, the large ones are
crystal. If it's in our room and we're dressed?

YOUNG MAN. That I'm looking for him, to talk politics. That I had to go
there to find him.

AGATHA. If it's in our room and we're undressed?

YOUNG MAN. That I entered unexpectedly, that you're resisting me, that
you are perfidy itself, that you treat as a thief someone who's pursued you
for six months. . . . You're a fool!

AGATHA. Oh, my love!

YOUNG MAN. A real fool!

AGATHA. I understand. Darling, it's almost day and I've hardly had you for
an hour, and how many more times do you think he'll believe I walk in
my sleep, and that it's less dangerous to let me stroll in the grove than on
the roof? Oh, my love, do you think it would be a lie that would let me
have you in our bed at night, me between you two, and that it would seem
quite natural to him?

YOUNG MAN. Look! You'll invent something.

AGATHA. A lie that would let you two talk about your elections and the races, over the body of your Agatha. So he'd not suspect anything? That's what we need,—just that.

YOUNG MAN. Just that!

AGATHA. Alas! Why is he so vain? Why is his sleep so light? Why does he adore me?

YOUNG MAN. The eternal litany! Why did you marry him? Why did you love him? —

AGATHA. I? Liar! I never loved anyone but you!

YOUNG MAN. Than I? Remember in whose arms I found you day before yesterday!

AGATHA. That was only because I'd sprained my ankle. The man you mention was picking me up.

YOUNG MAN. I knew about that sprain a moment ago.

AGATHA. You know nothing. You understand nothing. You don't realize that that accident gave me an idea for us to use.

YOUNG MAN. When I meet him on the stairs he has no dogs, I can tell you, and no cats.

AGATHA. He rides horseback. You can't take a horse to the doctor up the stairs.

YOUNG MAN. And he's always leaving your room.

AGATHA. Why do you force me to betray a state secret? He comes to consult my husband. They're afraid of a plot in the city. Please don't tell anyone, that would mean his dismissal. You'd bring me to the stake.

YOUNG MAN. One evening he was hurrying, his scarf not fastened, his tunic half unbuttoned. .

AGATHA. Of course, that was the day he tried to kiss me. I fixed him!

YOUNG MAN. You didn't let him kiss you, and he so powerful? I was waiting downstairs. He stayed two hours. .

AGATHA. He did stay two hours but I didn't let him kiss me.

YOUNG MAN. Then he kissed you without your leave. Confess, Agatha, or I'll go away.

AGATHA. Force me to confess! That's a fine reward for my frankness. Yes, he did kiss me . . once . . on my forehead.

YOUNG MAN. And that seems dreadful to you?

AGATHA. Dreadful? Frightful!

YOUNG MAN. And you don't suffer for it?

AGATHA. Not at all! . . . Ah, do I suffer? It's killing me, killing me! Kiss me, darling. Now you know everything, and I'm glad of it. Aren't you happy that everything is cleared up between us?

YOUNG MAN. Yes. Anything is better than a lie.

AGATHA. What a nice way you have of saying you prefer me to everything else, my love!

SCENE THREE

ELECTRA, ORESTES. BEGGAR. *Then the little* EUMENIDES. *They are taller thar before, and seem fifteen years old.*

BEGGAR. A dawn song, at the dawn of such a day! It's always like this.

ELECTRA. The insect is dead, beggar?

BEGGAR. Dispersed in the universe. His great grand-children are now fight ing gout.

ELECTRA. Orestes!

BEGGAR. You see he's no longer asleep. His eyes are open.

ELECTRA. Where are you, Orestes? What are you thinking about?

FIRST FURY. Orestes, there's just time. Don't listen to your sister.

SECOND FURY. Don't listen to her. We have learned what life holds for you it's wonderful!

THIRD FURY. Just by chance. As we grew up during the night.

SECOND FURY. We're not saying anything about love to you, does that seen strange?

FIRST FURY. She's going to spoil everything with her poison.

THIRD FURY. Her poison of *truth,* the only one that has no antidote.

FIRST FURY. You're right. We know what you're thinking. Royalty is magni ficent, Orestes! Young girls in the royal parks, feeding bread to th swans, King Orestes' miniature hanging on their blouses; they kiss i secretly. Soldiers going to war, the women on the roofs, the sky like veil over them, a white horse prancing to music. The return from wa the king's face looking like the face of a god, just because he's chilly o hungry or a little frightened, or pitying his people. If the truth is going t spoil all that, let it perish!

SECOND FURY. You're right. And love is magnificent. Orestes! Lovers, seems, will never part. They're never separated that they don't rus back to each other, to clasp hands. Or if they go away, they find eac other face to face again immediately. The earth is round for the sak of lovers. Everywhere I run into him I love, though he's not yet alive. A this is what Electra wants to take from you, and from us too, with he *Truth.* We want to love. Flee from Electra!

ELECTRA. Orestes!

ORESTES. I'm awake, sister.

ELECTRA. Wake up from your awakening. Don't listen to these girls.

ORESTES. Oh, Electra, are you sure they aren't right? Are you sure that it not the worst kind of arrogance for a human being to try to go back o his path? Why not take the first road and go forward, at random? Tru yourself to me. At this moment I can see so clearly the track of th game called happiness.

ELECTRA. Alas! That's not what we're hunting today.

ORESTES. The only thing that's important is not to leave each other. Le go to Thessaly. You'll see my house, covered with roses and jasmin.

ELECTRA. Darling Orestes, you've saved me from the gardener. That wasn't to give me to flowers.

ORESTES. Be persuaded! Let's slip out of this trap which will soon catch us! Let's rejoice that we woke up before it did! Come!

FIRST FURY. It's awake! Look at its eyes!

THIRD FURY. You're right. The spring is wonderful, Orestes. When you can see over the hedges only the moving backs of the animals browsing in the new grass, and the donkey's head looking at you over them. That donkey's head would look funny to you if you murdered your uncle. Pretty funny, a donkey looking at you when your hands are red with your uncle's blood—

ORESTES. What's she saying?

THIRD FURY. Talk on about the spring! The buttery mould that floats on the watercress in the brooks—you'll see what a comfort that will be for a man who kills his mother. Spread your butter on your bread that day with a knife, even if it's not the knife that killed your mother, and you'll see.

ORESTES. Help, Electra!

ELECTRA. So! You're like all men, Orestes! The least little flattery relaxes them, the slightest breath captivates them. Help you? I know what you'd like me to say.

ORESTES. Then say it to me.

ELECTRA. That on the whole human beings are good, that life, too, after all, is good.

ORESTES. Isn't that true?

ELECTRA. That it's not a bad fate to be young, handsome and a prince. To have a young sister who's a princess. That it's enough to leave men alone in their mean, vain business, not lancing human ulcers, but living for the beauty of the earth.

ORESTES. Isn't that what you're telling me?

ELECTRA. No! I'm telling you our mother has a lover.

ORESTES. You lie! That's impossible.

FIRST FURY. She's a widow. She's quite right.

ELECTRA. I'm telling you our father was murdered.

ORESTES. Agamemnon! Murdered!

ELECTRA. Stabbed, by assassins.

SECOND FURY. Seven years ago. It's ancient history.

ORESTES. You knew that and let me sleep all night!

ELECTRA. I didn't know it. It's the night's gift to me. These truths were tossed to me by the night. Now I know how prophetesses work. They hold their brother close to their heart all through one night.

ORESTES. Our father killed! Who told you?

ELECTRA. He himself.

ORESTES. He spoke to you before he died?

ELECTRA. Dead, he spoke to me. The very day of his death, but it's taken seven years for his word to reach me.

ORESTES. He appeared to you?

ELECTRA. No. His corpse appeared to me last night, looking like him the

day he was murdered, but illuminated; I just had to read: There was a
fold of his garment which said, I'm not a fold of death but of murder.
And on his shoe there was a buckle which repeated, I'm not an acci-
dental buckle but a criminal buckle. And on his eyelid there was a
wrinkle which said, I didn't see death, I saw regicides.

ORESTES. And about our mother, who told you that?

ELECTRA. She herself. Herself again.

ORESTES. She confessed?

ELECTRA. No. I saw her dead. Her body betrayed her. There's no doubt
possible. Her eyebrow was the eyebrow of a dead woman who'd had
a lover.

ORESTES. Who is this lover? Who is this murderer?

ELECTRA. I've waked you so you can find out. Let's hope they're both the
same, then you'll have to strike just one blow.

ORESTES. Girls, I think you'll have to clear out. My sister presents me as
I wake with a harlot queen and a murdered king . . . my parents.

FIRST FURY. That's not too bad. Add nothing more.

ELECTRA. Forgive me, Orestes.

SECOND FURY. Now she's excusing herself.

THIRD FURY. I'm killing you, but excuse it, please.

BEGGAR. She's wrong to excuse herself. This is the kind of awakening we
generally reserve for our wives and sisters. They seem to be made for that.

ELECTRA. They are made just for that. Wives, sisters-in-law, mothers-in-law,
they're the ones to shake up the men who, barely awake, see nothing but
purple and gold, till the women give them, with their coffee and hot
water, the hatred of injustice and the scorn of small joys.

ORESTES. Forgive me, Electra!

SECOND FURY. It's his turn to beg pardon. Aren't they polite in this family!

FIRST FURY. They take off their heads and bow to each other.

ELECTRA. And they watch for their waking. For men put on the armor of
happiness if they sleep no more than five minutes: and with it satisfaction, indifference, generosity, appetite. And a spot of sunlight reconciles
them to all blood spots. And a bird song to all lies. But the women are
there, all of them, worn by insomnia, with jealousy, envy, love, memory
and truth.   Are you awake, Orestes?

FIRST FURY. And we'll be as old as he in an hour! Let's hope heaven makes
us different!

ORESTES. I believe I'm waking up.

BEGGAR. Here comes your mother, children.

ORESTES. Where's my sword?

ELECTRA. Bravo! That's what I call a good awakening. Take up your sword.
Take up your hatred. Take up your strength.

SCENE FOUR

The same. CLYTEMNESTRA.

CLYTEMNESTRA. Their mother appears. And they turn into statues.

ELECTRA. Orphans, rather.

CLYTEMNESTRA. I'm not going to listen any longer to an insolent daughter.

ELECTRA. Listen to your son.

ORESTES. Who is it, mother? Confess.

CLYTEMNESTRA. What kind of children are you, turning our meeting into a melodrama? Leave me, or I'll call.

ELECTRA. Whom will you call? Him?

ORESTES. You struggle too much, mother.

BEGGAR. Be careful, Orestes. An innocent creature struggles as much as a guilty.

CLYTEMNESTRA. Creature? What kind of creature am I for my children? Speak, Orestes, speak!

ORESTES. I don't dare.

CLYTEMNESTRA. Electra then. She'll dare.

ELECTRA. Who is it, mother?

CLYTEMNESTRA. Of whom, of what are you speaking?

ORESTES. Mother, is it true you have . . . ?

ELECTRA. Don't specify, Orestes. Just ask who it is. There's a name somewhere in her. However you ask your question, the name will come out.

ORESTES. Mother, is it true you have a lover?

CLYTEMNESTRA. That's your question too, Electra?

ELECTRA. It might be put that way.

CLYTEMNESTRA. My son and daughter ask if I have a lover?

ELECTRA. Your husband can't ask it now.

CLYTEMNESTRA. The gods would blush to hear you.

ELECTRA. That would surprise me. For some time they've not blushed much.

CLYTEMNESTRA. I have no lover. But watch your step. All the evil in the world is caused by the so-called pure people trying to dig up secrets and bring them to light.

ELECTRA. Rottenness is born from sunshine, I grant that.

CLYTEMNESTRA. I have no lover. I couldn't have a lover if I wanted one. But take care. Curious people have had no luck in our family: they tracked down a theft and found a sacrilege; they carried on a love affair and ran into an incest. You'll not find out I have a lover because I haven't one, but you'll stumble on a stone which will be fatal for your sisters and yourselves.

ELECTRA. Who is your lover?

ORESTES. Electra, at least listen to her.

CLYTEMNESTRA. I have no lover. But who would call it a crime if I had one?

ORESTES. Oh, mother, you're a queen.

CLYTEMNESTRA. The world is not old and day is just dawning. But it would take us at least till twilight to recite the list of queens who've had lovers.

ORESTES. Mother, please! Fight on this way. Convince us. If this struggle gives us back a queen, it's blessed, everything is given back to us.

ELECTRA. Don't you see you're giving her weapons, Orestes?

CLYTEMNESTRA. That's enough. Orestes, leave me alone with Electra, will you?

ORESTES. Must I, sister?

ELECTRA. Yes, yes. Wait there, under the arch. And run back to me as soon as I call, Orestes. Run as fast as you can. It will mean I know everything.

SCENE FIVE

CLYTEMNESTRA. ELECTRA. THE BEGGAR.

CLYTEMNESTRA. Help me, Electra!

ELECTRA. Help you to what? To tell the truth or to lie?

CLYTEMNESTRA. Protect me.

ELECTRA. That's the first time you stoop to your daughter, mother. You must be afraid.

CLYTEMNESTRA. I'm afraid of Orestes.

ELECTRA. You lie. You're not the least afraid of Orestes. You see what he is, passionate, changeable, weak. He's still dreaming of an idyl in the Atrides' family. It's I you're afraid of, it's for me you're playing this game, the meaning of which still escapes me. You have a lover, haven't you? Who is he?

CLYTEMNESTRA. He knows nothing. There's no question of him.

ELECTRA. He doesn't know he's your lover?

CLYTEMNESTRA. Stop acting like a judge, Electra. Stop your pursuit. After all, you're my daughter.

ELECTRA. After all! Exactly, after all! For that reason I'm questioning you.

CLYTEMNESTRA. Then stop being my daughter. Stop hating me. Just be what I look for in you, a woman. Take up my cause, it's yours. Defend yourself by defending me.

ELECTRA. I'm not a member of the Women's Association. Some one other than you will have to recruit me.

CLYTEMNESTRA. You're wrong. If you betray your equal in body, in misfortune, you're the first one Orestes will loathe. Scandal always strikes back at people who start it. What good does it do you to bespatter all women by bespattering me? You'll sully in Orestes' eyes all the qualities you get from me.

ELECTRA. I'm not like you in anything. I never look in my mirror except to be certain of that luck. All the shiny marble, all the fountains of the palace have cried out to me, your own face cries it: Electra's nose is not the least like Clytemnestra's nose. My forehead is my own. My mouth's my own. And I have no lover.

CLYTEMNESTRA. Listen! I have no lover. I'm in love.

ELECTRA. Don't try that trick. You throw love at me the way drivers pursued by wolves throw them a dog. Dog is not my food.

CLYTEMNESTRA. We're women, Electra. We have a right to love.

ELECTRA. I know there are many rights in the sisterhood of women. If you pay the entrance fee, which is steep, which means admission only for weak, lying, base women, you have a right to be weak, lying and base. Unfortunately women are strong, loyal and noble, so you're wrong. You had the right to love only my father. Did you love him? On your wedding night, did you love him?

CLYTEMNESTRA. What are you driving at? Do you want me to say that your birth owes nothing to love, that you were conceived in indifference? Be satisfied. Not everyone can be like your Aunt Leda, and lay eggs. You never spoke in me. We were indifferent to each other from the first. You didn't even cause me pain at your birth. You were small and withdrawn, your lips tight. When you were a year old, your lips were sealed so "mother" wouldn't be your first word. Neither of us cried that day. We've never wept together.

ELECTRA. Weeping parties don't interest me.

CLYTEMNESTRA. You'll surely weep soon, perhaps over me.

ELECTRA. Eyes can weep by themselves. They're there for that.

CLYTEMNESTRA. Yes, even yours, which look like two stones. Some day tears will drown them.

ELECTRA. I hope that day comes! But why are you trying to hold me by such cold words instead of by love?

CLYTEMNESTRA. So you'll understand I have a right to love. So you'll know that my whole life has been as hard as my daughter from her very first day. Since my marriage I've never been alone, never at peace. I never went to the forest except for festivals. No rest, even for my body. That was covered every day by golden robes and at night by a king. Always mistrust, even of things, animals, plants. I often said to myself, as I looked at cross, silent lindens, smelling like a wet nurse: "They're like Electra's head, the day she was born." No queen has ever suffered so deeply the fate of queens, a husband's absence, a son's suspicions, a daughter's hatred. What had I left?

ELECTRA. What the others had left: waiting.

CLYTEMNESTRA. Waiting, for what? Waiting is horrible.

ELECTRA. For her who has caught you today, perhaps.

CLYTEMNESTRA. Can you tell me what you're waiting for?

ELECTRA. I no longer wait for anything. For ten years I've waited for my father. Waiting is the only happiness in the world.

CLYTEMNESTRA. A virgin's happiness, a solitary happiness.

ELECTRA. You think so? Except for you and the men, everything in the palace waited for my father with me, everything was party to my waiting. Mother, that began in the morning with my early walk under the lindens which hate you, which waited for my father with an eagerness they tried in vain to repress; they were sorry to live by the year and not by the decade, ashamed every spring that they couldn't hold back their flowers and perfume, that they grew weak with me over his absence. That went on till noon time when I went to the brook that was the luckiest of us all, for it waited for my father as it ran to the river that ran to the sea. And in the evening, when I wasn't strong enough to wait near his dogs and his horses, poor short lived beasts, who couldn't wait for centuries, I took refuge with the columns and the statues. I modeled myself on them. I waited in the moonlight for hours, motionless like them, without thought, lifeless. I waited for him with a stony heart—marble, alabaster, onyx—though it was beating, shattering my breast. Where would I be if there weren't still hours to wait, to wait for the past, wait for him still!

CLYTEMNESTRA. I'm not waiting, I love.

ELECTRA. So everything goes well with you now?

CLYTEMNESTRA. Very well.

ELECTRA. Flowers obey you? Birds talk to you?

CLYTEMNESTRA. Yes, your lindens signal to me.

ELECTRA. Quite likely. You've robbed me of everything in life.

CLYTEMNESTRA. Fall in love. We'll share.

ELECTRA. Share love with you?! Are you offering to share your lover with me? Who is he?

CLYTEMNESTRA. Oh, Electra, have some pity! I'll tell you his name, though it will make you blush. But wait a few days. What good will a scandal do you? Think of your brother. Can you imagine the Argives letting Orestes succeed an unworthy mother?

ELECTRA. An unworthy mother? What are you getting at with this confession? What time do you want to gain? What trap are you setting for me? What brood are you hoping to save, limping off, like a partridge, toward love and unworthiness?

CLYTEMNESTRA. Spare me public disgrace! Why do you force me to confess love someone below me in rank?

ELECTRA. Some little nameless lieutenant?

CLYTEMNESTRA. Yes.

ELECTRA. You're lying. If your lover were some little nameless inglorious officer, or a bathhouse servant or a groom, you'd love him. But you're not in love, you've never loved. Who is it? Why do you refuse to name him as you'd refuse a key? What piece of furniture are you afraid of opening with that name?

CLYTEMNESTRA. Something of my own, my love.

ELECTRA. Tell me the name of your lover, mother, and I'll tell you if you love. And we'll keep it to ourselves forever.

CLYTEMNESTRA. Never!

ELECTRA. You see! It's not your lover but your secret that you're hiding from me. You're afraid his name would give me the one proof I'm lacking in my pursuit.

CLYTEMNESTRA. What proof? You're mad.

ELECTRA. The proof of the crime. Everything tells me, mother, that you committed it. But what I don't yet see, what you must tell me, is why you committed it. I've tried all the keys, as you say. Not one opens it yet. No

love. You love nothing. Not ambition. You scoff at queenship. Not anger.
You're deliberate, calculating. But your lover's name would clear up
everything, tell us everything, wouldn't it? Whom do you love? Who is he?

SCENE SIX

The same. AGATHA, *pursued by the* PRESIDENT.

PRESIDENT. Who is he? Whom do you love?

AGATHA. I hate you.

PRESIDENT. Who is it?

AGATHA. I tell you that's enough. Enough lies. Electra's right. I'm on her
side. Thanks, Electra, you give me life.

PRESIDENT. What is this song?

AGATHA. Wives' song. You'll soon know it.

PRESIDENT. So, she's going to sing!

AGATHA. Yes, we're all here, with our unsatisfactory husbands or our widow-
hood. And we all kill ourselves, trying to make life and death pleasant.
And if they eat cooked lettuce they have to have salt and a smile with it.
And if they smoke we have to light their horrid cigars with the flame of
our hearts.

PRESIDENT. Whom are you talking about? I never ate cooked lettuce.

AGATHA. Sorrel, if you prefer.

PRESIDENT. Your lover doesn't eat sorrel or smoke cigars?

AGATHA. The sorrel my lover eats turns into ambrosia, and I lick up what's
left. And everything soiled by my husband's touch is purified by his hands
or lips. I myself! God knows!

ELECTRA. I've found out, mother, I've found out!

PRESIDENT. Collect yourself, Agatha.

AGATHA. Precisely. I've done just that. Twenty-four hours a day we kill ourselves to please someone whose displeasure is our only joy, for a husband
whose absence is our only delight, for the vanity of the only man who
humiliates us daily by showing us his toes and his shirt tails. And see how
he dares reproach us for stealing from him one hour a week of this hell!
But, sure enough, he's right. When this wonderful hour comes, we don't
greet it with a dead hand!

PRESIDENT. Electra, this is your work. This very morning she kissed me!

AGATHA. I'm pretty and he's ugly. I'm young and he's old. I'm bright and
he's stupid. I have a soul and he hasn't. Yet he has everything. At least
he has me. And I have nothing. Though I have him! Until this morning, I gave everything and had to seem grateful. Why? I black his shoes.
Why? I brush off his dandruff. Why? I make his coffee. Why? The truth
might be that I'm poisoning him, rubbing his collar with pitch and ashes.
Of course you can understand about the shoes. I spit on them. I spit on
you. But it's all over, finished. Welcome, truth! Electra has given me her
courage. I'm through. I'd as soon die.

BEGGAR. Don't these wives sing well!

PRESIDENT. Who's that?

ELECTRA. Listen, mother! Listen to yourself. It's you talking.

AGATHA. Who's that? All husbands think it's just one person.

PRESIDENT. Lovers? You have lovers?

AGATHA. They think we deceive them only with lovers. Of course we have lovers, too. But we deceive you with everything. When I wake and my hand slips along the wooden bedstead, that's my first adultery. Let's for once use your word, adultery. How often, when I'm wakeful, I've caressed that wood—olive wood, so soft! What a pretty name! I start when I hear an olive tree mentioned in the street—I hear my lover's name! And my second adultery is when I open my eyes and see daylight through the blinds. And my third, when my foot touches the bathwater and when I jump in. I betray you with my fingers, with my eyes, with the soles of my feet. When I look at you, I deceive you. When I listen to you and pretend to admire you in court, I'm deceiving you. Kill the olive trees, the pigeons, the five year old children, boys and girls, and water and earth and fire! Kill this beggar. You're betrayed by all of them.

BEGGAR. Thanks!

PRESIDENT. And yesterday this woman was still pouring my tea! And finding it too cool! Having the water boiled again! You're all pleased, aren't you? This little scandal within a great one can't displease you!

BEGGAR. No. It's like the squirrel in a big wheel. It gives the right rhythm.

PRESIDENT. And this scene before the queen herself! You'll pardon it?

ELECTRA. The queen envies Agatha. The queen would give her life to have the chance Agatha has today. Who is it, mother?

BEGGAR. Sure! Don't let anything distract you, President. It's almost a minute since you asked her who it is.

PRESIDENT. Who is it?

AGATHA. I've told you. Everybody. Everything.

PRESIDENT. This is enough to drive me to suicide, to make me bash my head against the wall.

AGATHA. Don't stop on my account. The Mycenean wall is solid.

PRESIDENT. Is he young? Or old?

AGATHA. A lover's age—between 16 and 80.

PRESIDENT. And she thinks she's disgracing me by insulting me! Your insults only hurt yourself, abandoned woman!

AGATHA. I know. I know. Outrage is called majesty. In the streets the most respectable people slip on dung.

PRESIDENT. At last you'll find out who I am! Whoever your lovers are, I'll kill the first one I find here.

AGATHA. The first one you find here? You choose the place badly. You couldn't even face him.

PRESIDENT. I'll make him kneel down and kiss and lick the marble.

AGATHA. You'll see how he'll kiss and lick the marble when he comes into this court in a minute and sits down on the throne.

PRESIDENT. Wretch, what are you saying?

AGATHA. I'm saying that at present I have two lovers and one is Aegisthus.

CLYTEMNESTRA. Liar!

AGATHA. What! She too!

ELECTRA. You too, mother?

BEGGAR. That's funny. I'd have thought that if Aegisthus had a liking, it was for Electra.

PAGE, *announcing.* Aegisthus!

ELECTRA. At last!

THE FURIES. Aegisthus!

AEGISTHUS *comes in. Much more majestic and calm than in the first act. Far above him, a bird hovers in the air.*

SCENE SEVEN

The same. AEGISTHUS. *A* CAPTAIN. SOLDIERS.

AEGISTHUS. Electra is here. . . . Thanks, Electra! I'll stop here, Captain. Headquarters are here.

CLYTEMNESTRA. I, too, am here.

AEGISTHUS. I'm glad. Welcome, Queen!

PRESIDENT. I too, Aegisthus!

AEGISTHUS. Good, President. I need your help.

PRESIDENT. And now he insults us!

AEGISTHUS. What's the matter with you all, that you stare at me so?

BEGGAR. What's the matter is that the queen is waiting for a perjurer, Electra for an infidel, Agatha for a faithless lover. He's more humble, he's waiting for the man who seduced his wife. They're all waiting for you, but it's not you who have come!

AEGISTHUS. They have no luck, have they, Beggar.

BEGGAR. No, they have no luck. Waiting for a rascal, they see a king enter! I don't care about the others, but for our little Electra, the situation is complicated.

AEGISTHUS. You think so? I think not.

BEGGAR. I knew it would happen. I told you so yesterday. I knew the king would reveal himself in you. He has your strength and your years. He finds the right moment. Electra is near. That might have involved a bloody act. But you've revealed yourself. Fine for Greece! But not so gay for the family.

CLYTEMNESTRA. What do these riddles mean? What are you talking about?

BEGGAR. Lucky for us, too! Since there has to be some kind of meeting better let Electra meet with nobility than with wickedness. How did you get this way, Aegisthus?

AEGISTHUS, *looking at* ELECTRA. Electra is here! I knew I'd find her looking this way, her statuesque head, her eyes, which see only when the lids are closed, deaf to human speech.

CLYTEMNESTRA. Listen to me, Aegisthus!

PRESIDENT. How well you choose your lovers, Agatha! What impudence!

CAPTAIN. Aegisthus, there's no time!

AEGISTHUS. Your ears are ornaments, aren't they, Electra? Mere ornaments. . . . The gods said, we gave her hands so she'd not touch, eyes so she'd be seen, we can't let her head be without ears! People would soon discover that she hears only us. . . . Tell me what you hear when an ear leans toward them! What a roaring! What does it come from?

CLYTEMNESTRA. Are you mad? Take care! Electra's ears do hear you.

PRESIDENT. They blush for it.

AEGISTHUS. They hear me. I'm sure of that. Since what happened to me just now in the outskirts of Argos, my words come from beyond myself. And I know she sees me too, she's the only one who does see me. The only one to guess what I've become since that moment.

CLYTEMNESTRA. You're talking to your worst enemy, Aegisthus!

AEGISTHUS. She knows why I galloped toward the city from the mountains, Electra, you'd have thought my horse understood. He was beautiful, that light chestnut, charging toward Electra, followed by the thunder of the squadron, in which the knowledge of rushing toward Electra grew less from the white stallions of the trumpeters to the piebald mares of the rear guard. Don't be surprised if my horse sticks his head between the pillars neighing to you. He knew that I was strangling, with your name in my mouth like a golden stopper. I had to shout your name, and to you—shall I shout it, Electra?

CLYTEMNESTRA. Stop this outrageous behavior, Aegisthus.

CAPTAIN. Aegisthus! The city is in danger!

AEGISTHUS. True! Pardon me! Where are they now, Captain?

CAPTAIN. You can see their lances coming over the hills. I've never seen harvest grow so fast. Nor so thick. There are thousands of them.

AEGISTHUS. The cavalry's no use against them?

CAPTAIN. Repulsed, prisoners taken.

CLYTEMNESTRA. What's happening, Aegisthus?

CAPTAIN. The Corinthians are surrounding us, no declaration of war, no reason for it. Their regiments entered our territory last night. The suburbs are already on fire.

AEGISTHUS. What do the prisoners say?

CAPTAIN. Their orders are to leave no stone standing in Argos.

CLYTEMNESTRA. Show yourself, Aegisthus, and they'll flee!

AEGISTHUS. I fear, Queen, that wouldn't be enough.

CAPTAIN. They have friends in the city. The reserves of pitch have been stolen, so the bourgeois quarters can be burned. Gangs of beggars are gathering around the markets ready to pillage.

CLYTEMNESTRA. If the guard is loyal, what is there to fear?

CAPTAIN. The guard is ready to fight. But it's muttering. You know, they've never willingly obeyed a woman. The city's the same way. They both demand a king, a man.

AEGISTHUS. They're right. They shall have one.

PRESIDENT. Whoever wants to be king of Argos, Aegisthus, will have to kill Clytemnestra first.

BEGGAR. Or simply marry her.

PRESIDENT. Never!

AEGISTHUS. Why, never? The queen can't deny that's the only way to save Argos. I don't doubt she'll consent. Captain, tell the guard the wedding has this moment taken place. Keep me informed of events. I'll wait here for your bulletins. And do you, President, go meet the rioters and tell them this news most enthusiastically.

PRESIDENT. Never! I must first speak to you, man to man, no matter what happens.

AEGISTHUS. No matter if Argos falls, if war comes? You're outrageous.

PRESIDENT. My honor, the honor of all Greek judges, is at stake.

BEGGAR. If Greek justice lies in Agatha's lap, that's just what it deserves. Don't hinder us at such a time. Look at Agatha, see if she cares for the honor of Greek judges, with her nose in the air.

PRESIDENT. Her nose in the air! Agatha is your nose in the air?

AGATHA. My nose is in the air. I'm looking at that bird hovering over Aegisthus.

PRESIDENT. Lower it!

AEGISTHUS. Queen, I'm waiting for your reply.

CLYTEMNESTRA. A bird? What is that bird? Get from under that bird, Aegisthus.

AEGISTHUS. Why? He's not left me since sunrise. He must have his reasons. My horse noticed him first. He kicked without any provocation. I looked all around and then up there. He was kicking at that bird, and plunging and rearing. It's exactly above me, isn't it, beggar?

BEGGAR. Exactly above. If you were a thousand feet tall, your head would be there.

AEGISTHUS. Like a mark on a page, isn't it? A black mark.

BEGGAR. Yes, at the moment you're the most marked man in Greece. We'll have to find out whether the mark is over the word "human" or the word "mortal."

CLYTEMNESTRA. I don't like this hovering bird. What is it? A kite or an eagle?

BEGGAR. He's too high up. I might recognize him by his shadow, but so high up we can't see it, it's lost.

CAPTAIN, returning. The guard is delighted, Aegisthus. It's joyfully getting ready to fight. It's just waiting for you to appear on the balcony with the queen, so it can cheer you.

AEGISTHUS. My oath, and I'll go.

PRESIDENT. Electra, help me! Why should this rake teach us courage?

BEGGAR. Why? Listen! . . .

AEGISTHUS. Oh, Heavenly Powers, since I must pray to you on the eve of battle, I thank you for the gift of this hill which overlooks Argos the moment the fog evaporates. I dismounted, weary from the night patrol, I leant against the battlement, and I suddenly saw Argos as I had never before seen it—new, rebuilt by me, and you have given it to me. You've given it all to me, its towers, its bridges, the smoke from its farm machines, the flying pigeons, its first movements, the grinding of its locks, its first

cry. Everything in your gift has equal value, Electra, the sunrise ove
Argos, the last lantern in the city, the temple, the ruins, the lake, the tan
neries. And the gift is forever! This morning I was given my city fo
eternity, as a mother her child, and in agony I asked myself if the gift wer
not even greater, if you hadn't given me far more than Argos. In th
morning God never counts his gifts: he might even have given me th
whole world. That would have been dreadful. I should have felt a despai
like that of a man who expects a diamond on his birthday and is given th
sun. Electra, you see my anxiety! I anxiously stretched my foot and m
thoughts beyond Argos. What joy! I had not been given the Orient, i
plagues, earthquakes, famines: I realized that with a smile. My thirst wa
not like that of those who quench it in the great, warm rivers flowin
through the desert, but, I discovered, I could quench it at an icy sprin
And nothing in Africa is mine! Negresses can pound millet at the doo
of their huts, the jaguar drive his claws into the crocodile's flank, not
drop of their soup or their blood is mine. I'm as happy over the gifts n
given me as over the gift of Argos. In a fit of generosity the Gods hav
not given me Athens or Olympia or Mycenae. What joy! They have give
me the Argive cattle markets, not the treasures of Corinth, the short nos
of the Argive girls, not the nose of Athena; the wrinkled prune of Argo
not the golden fig of Thebes! That's what they gave me this morning; m
the wastrel, the parasite, the knave, a country where I feel myself pur
strong, perfect; a fatherland; a country where, instead of being a slave,
am king, where I swear to live and die—you hear me, judge, and to save

PRESIDENT. I rely on you only, Electra!

ELECTRA. Rely on me. No one should save his fatherland with impure hand

BEGGAR. A coronation purifies everything.

ELECTRA. Who crowned you? Who witnessed your coronation?

BEGGAR. Can't you guess? Just what he begged of you. For the first time h
sees you in your truth and power. The thought has suddenly dawned o
him that Electra is included in this gift of Argos.

AEGISTHUS. Everything on my way consecrated me, Electra. As I galloped
heard the trees, the children, the streams shout to me that I was king. B
the holy oil was lacking. I was a coward yesterday. A rabbit, whose trem
ling ears showed over a furrow, gave me courage. I was a hypocrite. A f
crossed the road, his eye crafty, and I became frank. And a couple of ma
pies gave me independence, an ant hill, generosity. And if I hastened ba
to you, Electra, it was because you are the only creature who can give n
her very being.

ELECTRA. And that is—?

AEGISTHUS. I think it is rather like duty.

ELECTRA. My duty is certainly the mortal enemy of yours. You shall not mar
Clytemnestra.

PRESIDENT. You shall not marry her.

CLYTEMNESTRA. And why shan't we marry? Why should we sacrifice our liv
to ungrateful children? Yes, I love Aegisthus. For ten years I've love
Aegisthus. For ten years I've postponed this marriage for your sake, Ele
tra, and in memory of your father. Now you force us to it. Thanks! B

not under that bird. That bird annoys me. As soon as the bird flies away, I consent.

AEGISTHUS. Don't worry, Queen. I'm not marrying you in order to create new lies. I don't know if I still love you, and the whole city doubts that you ever loved me. For ten years our liaison has dragged along between indifference and neglect. But our marriage is the only way to cast a little truth over our past lies, and it will safeguard Argos. It must take place, this very hour.

ELECTRA. I don't believe it will take place.

PRESIDENT. Bravo!

AEGISTHUS. Will you be quiet? Who are you in Argos? A deceived husband or the chief justice?

PRESIDENT. Both, certainly.

AEGISTHUS. Then choose. I have no choice. Choose between duty and prison. Time is short.

RESIDENT. You took Agatha from me.

AEGISTHUS. I'm not the one who took Agatha.

RESIDENT. Weren't you given all the deceived husbands in Argos this morning?

BEGGAR. Yes. But he's not the one who cheated them.

RESIDENT. I understand. The new king forgets the outrages he committed as regent.

BEGGAR. Agatha looks like a rose. Outrages make her rosy?

AEGISTHUS. A king begs you to pardon today the insult a rake inflicted on you yesterday. That must satisfy you. Listen to my orders. Go quickly to your courtroom, try the rebels and be severe with them.

AGATHA. Be severe. I have a little lover among them.

PRESIDENT. Will you stop looking at that bird? You irritate me.

AGATHA. I'm sorry. It's the only thing in the world that interests me.

PRESIDENT. Idiot! What will you do when it goes away?

AGATHA. That's what I'm wondering.

AEGISTHUS. Are you disobeying me, President? Don't you hear those shouts?

PRESIDENT. I'll not go. I'll help Electra prevent your marriage.

ELECTRA. I don't need your help, President. Your role ended when Agatha gave me the key to everything. Thanks, Agatha!

CLYTEMNESTRA. What key?

AEGISTHUS. Come, Queen.

CLYTEMNESTRA. What key did she give you? What new quarrel are you trying to start?

ELECTRA. You hated my father! Oh, everything is clear in the light of Agatha's lamp.

CLYTEMNESTRA. There she goes again! Protect me, Aegisthus!

ELECTRA. How you envied Agatha just now! What joy to shout out your hatred to the husband you hate! That joy was not allowed you, mother. Never in your life will you have it. Till the day of his death he believed you admired and adored him. At banquets and festivals I've often seen your face harden, your lips move soundlessly, because you wanted to cry out you hated him. You wanted passers-by, guests, the servant pouring wine, the detective guarding the silver, to hear you, didn't you? Poor mother, you could never go to the country alone to cry out to the bushes. All the bushes say you adored him!

CLYTEMNESTRA. Listen, Electra!

ELECTRA. That's right, mother, cry it out to me! Though he's not here, I'm his substitute. Cry to me! That will do you as much good as to say it to him. You're not going to die without letting him know you hated him.

CLYTEMNESTRA. Come, Aegisthus! Never mind the bird!

ELECTRA. If you take one step, mother, I'll call.

AEGISTHUS. Whom will you call, Electra? Is there anyone in the world who can take from us the right to save our city?

ELECTRA. Save our city from hypocrisy, from corruption? There are thousands. The purest, the handsomest, the youngest is here, in this courtyard. If Clytemnestra takes a step, I'll call.

CLYTEMNESTRA. Come, Aegisthus!

ELECTRA. Orestes! Orestes!

The EUMENIDES *appear and bar the way.*

FIRST FURY. Poor girl! You're too naive! Do you think we'll let Orestes move around us, sword in hand? Accidents happen too quickly in this palace. We've gagged him and chained him up.

ELECTRA. That's not true! Orestes! Orestes!

SECOND FURY. You, too, it will happen to you.

AEGISTHUS. Electra, dear Electra, listen to me. I want to persuade you.

CLYTEMNESTRA. You're losing precious time, Aegisthus.

AEGISTHUS. I'm coming! Electra, I know you're the only one who understands what I am today. Help me! Let me tell you why you must help me!

CLYTEMNESTRA. What is this craze to explain, to argue? There are cocks in this courtyard, not human beings. Do we have to go on explaining till our eyes are gouged out? Must the three of us be carried off by force to separate us?

PRESIDENT. I think that's the only way, Queen.

CAPTAIN. I beseech you, Aegisthus! Hurry!

BEGGAR. Don't you understand? Aegisthus must settle once and for all the business about Agamemnon—Clytemnestra—Electra. Then he'll come.

CAPTAIN. In five minutes it will be too late.

BEGGAR. We'll all do our bit. It will be settled in five minutes.

AEGISTHUS. Take away this man.

Guards take out the PRESIDENT. *All the spectators leave. Silence.*

AEGISTHUS. Now, Electra, what do you want?

SCENE EIGHT

ELECTRA. CLYTEMNESTRA. AEGISTHUS. BEGGAR.

ELECTRA. She's not late, Aegisthus. She just won't come.

AEGISTHUS. Of whom are you speaking?

ELECTRA. Of her you're waiting for. The messenger of the gods. If divine justice absolves Aegisthus because he loves his city, and is marrying Clytemnestra because he despises lies and wants to save the middle class and the rich, this is the moment for her to appear before you two, bearing her diplomas and her laurels. But she'll not come.

AEGISTHUS. You know she has come. This morning's sunbeam on my head was she.

ELECTRA. That was a morning beam. Every scurfy child thinks he's a king when a morning sunbeam touches him.

AEGISTHUS. Do you doubt my sincerity?

ELECTRA. Alas! I don't doubt that, but in your sincerity I recognize the hypocrisy and malice of the gods. They change a parasite into a just man, an adulterer into a husband, a usurper into a king. They thought my task not painful enough, so they made a figure of honor out of you, whom I despise! But there's one change they can't carry through! They can't transform a criminal into an innocent man. They bow to me there.

AEGISTHUS. I've no idea what you mean.

ELECTRA. You have a little idea. Listen to the small voice beneath your heroic soul. You'll understand.

AEGISTHUS. Who can explain what you're talking about?

CLYTEMNESTRA. Of whom can she talk? What has she always talked about during her whole life! Of what she knows nothing. Of a father she never knew.

ELECTRA. I? I never knew my father?

CLYTEMNESTRA. You touched a corpse, ice that had been your father. But *not* your father.

AEGISTHUS. Please, Clytemnestra! How can you quarrel at such a moment!

CLYTEMNESTRA. Everyone must have a turn in this debate. It's my turn now.

ELECTRA. For once you're right. We've come to the core of the debate. If I'd not touched my living father, from whom would I have drawn my strength, my truth?

CLYTEMNESTRA. Precisely. But now you're talking wildly. I wonder if you ever kissed him. I watched that he didn't lick my children.

ELECTRA. I never kissed my father!

CLYTEMNESTRA. Your father's dead body, perhaps, not your father.

AEGISTHUS. I beg you . . !

ELECTRA. Ah, now I see why you're so firm as you face me. You thought me unarmed, you thought I'd never touched my father. What a mistake!

CLYTEMNESTRA. You're lying.

ELECTRA. The day my father came home you two waited for him just a minute too long on the palace stairs, didn't you?

CLYTEMNESTRA. How do you know? You weren't there!

ELECTRA. I was holding him back. I was in his arms.

AEGISTHUS. Now listen, Electra . . .

ELECTRA. I'd waited in the crowd, mother. I rushed toward him. His escorts were frightened, they feared an attempt on his life. But he recognized me, smiled at me. He understood Electra's attempt, and, brave father, he met it fully. And I did touch him.

CLYTEMNESTRA. You may have touched his leg armor, his horse,—leather and hair!

ELECTRA. He got down, mother. I touched his hands with these fingers, his lips with these lips. I touched a skin you'd never touched, purified from you by ten years of absence.

AEGISTHUS. That's enough. She believes you!

ELECTRA. My cheek on his, I felt my father's warmth. Sometimes in summer the whole world is exactly as warm as my father. I faint from it. And I did hug him in these arms. I thought I was taking the measure of my love,—it was also that of my vengeance. He freed himself, mounted his horse, more agile, more shining than before. Electra's "attempt" was over. He was more alive, more golden because of it. And I ran to the palace to see him again, but I was really running not toward him, but toward you, his murderers.

AEGISTHUS. Pull yourself together, Electra!

ELECTRA. Perhaps I am out of breath. I've reached my goal.

CLYTEMNESTRA. Rid us of this girl, Aegisthus. Give her back to the gardener. Or turn her over to her brother.

AEGISTHUS. Stop, Electra! Why, at the very moment that I see you, that I love you, when I'm at the point of understanding you—your scorn for abuses, your courage, your disinterestedness,—why do you persist in fighting?

ELECTRA. I have only this moment.

AEGISTHUS. Don't you know Argos is in danger?

ELECTRA. We don't see the same dangers.

AEGISTHUS. Don't you know that if I marry Clytemnestra, the city will quiet down, the Atrides will be saved? If not, riots, conflagrations?

ELECTRA. Perhaps.

AEGISTHUS. Don't you know that I alone can defend the city against the Corinthians who are already at the city gates? If not, there'll be pillage, massacre.

ELECTRA. Yes. You'd be victor.

AEGISTHUS. Yet you are obstinate! And you ruin my work. And you sacrifice your family and your country to a dream!

ELECTRA. You're mocking me, Aegisthus! You pretend to know me yet think I'm the kind to whom you can say: "If you lie and let other people lie, you'll have a prosperous country. If you hide your crimes your country will be victorious." What is this poor country that you're all of a sudden putting between us and truth?

AEGISTHUS. Your country—Argos.

ELECTRA. You're wrong, Aegisthus. This morning, at the very hour you were given Argos, I also received a gift. I expected it, it had been promised me, but I still didn't know just what it would be. I had already been given a thousand gifts, which seemed incomplete, I couldn't see their appropriateness, but this night, near Orestes as he slept, I saw they were all one and the same gift. I'd been given the back of a truck driver, the smile of a laundress, suddenly stopped in her work, watching the river. I'd been given a fat, naked little child, running across the street, as his mother and the neighbors shouted to him, and the cry of a caged bird

set free, and that of a mason I one day saw fall from a scaffold, his legs
sprawling. I was given the water plant, resisting the current, fighting
and dying; the sick young man, coughing, smiling and coughing; and my
maid's red cheeks, puffed up each winter morning as she blows on the
ashes of the fire. I too thought I was given Argos, everything in Argos
that is modest, tender, beautiful and wretched, but just now I found out
that it's not so. I knew I'd been given all the servants' cheeks as they
blow on wood or coal, all the laundresses' eyes, whether round or almond-
shaped, all the falling masons, all the water plants which seem lost and
grow again in streams or the sea. But Argos is only a speck in this universe, my country only a village in that country. All the light and the
cries in sad faces, all the wrinkles and shadows on joyful faces, all the
desires and despair on indifferent faces,—these are my new country. And
this morning, at dawn, when you were given Argos and its narrow
borders, I also saw it as tremendous, and I heard its name, which is not
to be spoken, but which is both tenderness and justice.

CLYTEMNESTRA. So that's Electra's motto! Tenderness! That's enough. Let's
go.

AEGISTHUS. And you dare call this justice, which makes you burn your city,
damn your family, you dare call this the justice of the gods?

ELECTRA. Far from it! In this country of mine care for justice is not the gods'
business. The gods are only artists. A beautiful light from a conflagration,
beautiful grass on a battle field, such is their justice. A magnificent repentance for a crime is the gods' verdict on your case. I don't accept it.

AEGISTHUS. Electra's justice consists in re-examining every sin, making every
act irreparable?

ELECTRA. Oh, no! Some years frost is justice for the trees, other times its
injustice. There are criminals we love, murderers we embrace. But when
the crime is an assault on human dignity, infects a nation, corrupts its
loyalty, then no pardon is possible.

AEGISTHUS. Have you any idea of what a nation is, Electra?

ELECTRA. When you see a huge face fill the horizon and you look straight at
it with pure, brave eyes, that's a nation.

AEGISTHUS. You talk like a young girl, not like a king. There's also a huge
body to rule and to nourish.

ELECTRA. I speak like a woman. There's a bright look to sift, to gild. And
the only gold is truth. Those great eyes of truth, they're so beautiful, when
you think of the real nations of the world.

AEGISTHUS. There are truths that kill nations, Electra.

ELECTRA. Some dead nations shine forever. Pray Heaven that will be the
fate of Argos! But since my father's death, since our people's happiness is
founded on injustice and crime, since everyone has become a cowardly
accomplice in murder and lies, since the city can prosper, sing, dance, conquer, heaven may shine on it, but it will be nothing but a cellar where
eyes are unnecessary. The newborn nurse blindly.

AEGISTHUS. A scandal can only destroy it.

ELECTRA. Possibly. But I can no longer endure the dim, lustreless look in
its eyes.

AEGISTHUS. That will cost thousands of glazed, dead eyes.

ELECTRA. That's the price. It's not too high.

AEGISTHUS. I must have this day. Give it to me. Your truth, if there is such a thing, will find a way to be revealed at a time more suitable for it.

ELECTRA. The revolt shows this day is made for it.

AEGISTHUS. I beseech you! Wait till tomorrow.

ELECTRA. No. This is the day for it. I've seen too many truths fade away because they were a day too late. I know young girls who waited a second before saying no to an ugly, vile thing, and who could then say nothing but yes, yes. The beautiful and cruel thing about truth is that she is eternal, but is also like a flash of lightning.

AEGISTHUS. I must save the city and Greece.

ELECTRA. That's a small duty. I'm saving their face. . . . You did kill him, didn't you?

CLYTEMNESTRA. How dare you say that, daughter? Everyone knows your father slipped on the tiles.

ELECTRA. Everyone knows it because you've said so.

CLYTEMNESTRA. Crazy girl, he slipped and fell.

ELECTRA. He did not slip. For one obvious reason. Because my father never slipped.

CLYTEMNESTRA. How do you know?

ELECTRA. For eight years I've been asking the grooms, the maids, his escort in rain and hail. He *never* slipped.

CLYTEMNESTRA. The war came since then.

ELECTRA. I've asked his fellow soldiers. He crossed Scamander without slipping. He took the battlements by assault without slipping. He never slipped, in water or in blood.

CLYTEMNESTRA. He was in haste that day.

ELECTRA. I'm the guilty one, am I not? That's Clytemnestra's kind of truth. Your opinion, too, Aegisthus? Electra murdered Agamemnon!

CLYTEMNESTRA. The maids had soaped the tiles too well. I know. I almost slipped myself.

ELECTRA. Ah, you were in the bathroom, too, mother? Who held you up?

CLYTEMNESTRA. What's wrong in my being there?

ELECTRA. With Aegisthus, of course?

CLYTEMNESTRA. With Aegisthus. And we weren't alone. Leo, my counsellor, was there, wasn't he, Aegisthus?

ELECTRA. Leo, who died the next day?

CLYTEMNESTRA. Did he die the next day?

ELECTRA. Yes. Leo slipped, too. He lay down on his bed and in the morning was found dead. He'd found a way to slip into death, while he slept, without slipping. You had him killed, didn't you?

CLYTEMNESTRA. Aegisthus, defend me. I'm calling for help.

ELECTRA. He can do nothing for you. You've come to the place where you must defend yourself.

CLYTEMNESTRA. Oh, God! Have I come to this? A mother! A queen!

ELECTRA. Where is "this"? Tell us where you've come.

CLYTEMNESTRA. Brought by this heartless, joyless daughter! Ah, fortunately, my little Chrysothemis loves flowers.

ELECTRA. Don't I love flowers?

CLYTEMNESTRA. To come to this! Through this idiotic journey called life, to come to this! I, who when a young girl loved quiet, tending my pets, laughing at meal time, sewing! . . . I was so gentle, Aegisthus, I swear I was the gentlest. . . There are still old men in my birthplace who call gentleness Clytemnestra.

ELECTRA. If they die today they needn't change their symbol. If they die this morning!

CLYTEMNESTRA. To come to this! What injustice! Aegisthus, I spent my days in the meadows behind the palace. There were so many flowers I didn't have to stoop to pick them, I sat down. My dogs lay at my feet, the one who barked when Agamemnon came to take me away. I teased him with flowers and he ate them to please me. If I only had him! Anywhere else, if my husband had been a Persian, or an Egyptian, I'd now be good, careless, gay! When I was young I had a voice, I trained birds! I might have been an Egyptian queen, singing gaily; I'd have had an Egyptian aviary! And we've come to this! What has this family, what have these walls done to us!

ELECTRA. Murderers! . . . These are wicked walls.

MESSENGER. My lord, they've forced an entrance. The postern gate gave way.

ELECTRA. All right. Let the walls crumble.

AEGISTHUS. Electra, heed my final word. I forgive everything,—your foolish fancies, your insults. But can't you see your country is dying?

ELECTRA. And I don't love flowers! Do you imagine flowers for a father's grave are picked sitting down?

CLYTEMNESTRA. Well, let this father return! Let him stop being dead! What nonsense, this absence, this silence! Let him come back, in his pomp, his vanity, his beard! That beard must have grown in the grave—a good thing, too!

ELECTRA. What are you saying?

AEGISTHUS. Electra, I promise that tomorrow, as soon as Argos is saved, the guilty, if there are any, shall disappear, for good and all. But don't be stubborn. You're gentle, Electra, in your heart you're gentle. Listen! The city will perish.

ELECTRA. Let it! I can already feel my love for a burnt and conquered Argos! No! My mother has begun to insult my father, let her finish!

CLYTEMNESTRA. Why are you talking about the guilty! What do you mean, Aegisthus?

ELECTRA. He's just told me in a word all that you deny!

CLYTEMNESTRA. And what do I deny?

ELECTRA. He's told me that you let Orestes fall, that I love flowers and that my father didn't slip.

CLYTEMNESTRA. He did slip. I swear he slipped. If there's a truth in the world, let lightning from heaven show it to us. You'll see it revealed with all its burdens.

AEGISTHUS. Electra, you're in my power. Your brother too. I can kill you.

Yesterday I should have killed you. Instead of that I promise, as soon as the enemy is repulsed, to step down from the throne and establish Orestes on it.

ELECTRA. That's no longer the question, Aegisthus. If the gods for once change their methods, if they make you wise and just in order to ruin you, that's their affair. The question now is: will she dare tell us why she hated my father!

CLYTEMNESTRA. Oh, you want to know that?

ELECTRA. But you'll not dare tell.

AEGISTHUS. Electra, tomorrow, before the altar where we celebrate our victory, the guilty man shall stand, for there is only one guilty man, in a parricide's coat. He'll confess his crime publicly and determine his punishment himself. First let me save the city.

ELECTRA. You've "saved" yourselves today, Aegisthus, and in my presence. That's enough. Now I want her to finish!

CLYTEMNESTRA. So, you want me to finish!

ELECTRA. I dare you to!

MESSENGER. They're entering the court yards, Aegisthus!

AEGISTHUS. Come, Queen!

CLYTEMNESTRA. Yes, I hated him. Yes, you shall know what this fine father was like. Yes, after twenty years I'll have the joy that Agatha had today. A woman might belong to anyone, but there was just one man in the world to whom I couldn't belong. That man was the king of kings, father of fathers! I hated him from the first day he came to wrench me from my home, with his curly beard and the hand with the little finger always sticking up. He raised it when he drank, when he drove, when he held his sceptre . . . and when he held me close I felt on my back only four fingers. It drove me wild, and the morning he sacrificed your sister, Iphigenia,—horrible,—I saw the little fingers of both his hands sticking out, dark against the sun—king of kings! What nonsense! He was pompous, indecisive, stupid. He was the fop of fops, the most credulous creature. The king of kings was never anything more than that little finger and the beard that nothing could soften. The bathwater in which I soaked his head didn't soften it, nor did the nights of false love when I pulled and tangled it, nor the storm at Delphi which turned the dancers' hair into manes; it came out in gold ringlets from water, bed, and rain. He would beckon me with his little finger and I would go, smiling. . . . Why? He would tell me to kiss his mouth in that fleece and I would run to kiss it . . . . Why? And when I woke and was unfaithful to him, like Agatha, with the wooden bedstead—a royal bed— and he bade me talk to him, though I knew he was vain, empty, tiresome, I told him he was modest, strange, even splendid. . . . Why? And if he persisted, stammering, pathetic, I swore to him he was a god. King of kings! The only excuse for that title is that it justifies a hatred of hatreds. Do you know what I did, Electra, the day of his departure, when his ship was still in sight? I sacrificed the curliest ram I could find and toward midnight I stole into the throne room quite alone, and took the

sceptre in my hands! Now you know everything. You wanted a hymn
to truth, and here's a beautiful one.

ELECTRA. Oh, father, forgive!

AEGISTHUS. Come, Queen.

CLYTEMNESTRA. Take this girl first and chain her up.

ELECTRA. Father, will you ever forgive me for having listened to her?
Aegisthus, shouldn't she die?

AEGISTHUS. Farewell, Electra.

ELECTRA. Kill her, Aegisthus. And I'll forgive you.

CLYTEMNESTRA. Don't let her go free, Aegisthus. They'll stab you in the back.

AEGISTHUS. We'll see about that. Leave Electra alone. . . . Unbind Orestes.

AEGISTHUS and CLYTEMNESTRA *go out.*

ELECTRA. The bird is coming down, beggar, the bird is coming down.

BEGGAR. Look, it's a vulture!

SCENE NINE

ELECTRA. NARSES' WIFE. BEGGAR. *Then* ORESTES.

BEGGAR. You here, Narses' wife?

NARSES' WIFE. All of us beggars, the lame, the halt and the blind, have
come to save Electra and her brother.

BEGGAR. Justice, eh?

NARSES' WIFE. There they are, untying Orestes.

A crowd of BEGGARS *enter, a few at a time.*

BEGGAR. This is how they killed, listen, woman. This is the way everything
happened, I never invent anything. It was the queen who had the steps
soaped that go down to the bath; the two of them did it. While all the
housewives in Argos scrubbed their thresholds, the queen and her lover
soaped the door-sill to his death. Think how clean their hands were
when they greeted Agamemnon at his entrance! And your father slipped,
Electra, as he reached out his arms to her. You were right except on
this one point. He slipped on the steps, and the noise of his fall, because
of his golden cuirass and helmet, was that of a king falling. And she
threw herself on him, he thought, to raise him up, but she held him
down. He didn't understand why his darling wife was holding him down,
he wondered if it was a love transport, but then why did Aegisthus stay?
Young Aegisthus was awkward and indiscreet. (We'll consider his promotion.) The ruler of the world, the conqueror of Troy, who had just
reviewed the army and navy parade, must have been humiliated, to fall
like that, on his back and in his noisy armor, even if his beard was untouched, in the presence of his loving wife and the young ensign. All
the more annoyed because this might be a bad omen. The fall might
mean he'd die in a year, or in five years. And he was surprised that his
beloved wife caught his wrists and threw herself on him to hold him
down, as the fisherwomen do with the big stranded turtles on the shore.
She was wrong, and not so beautiful, her face flushed, her neck wrinkled.

Not like young Aegisthus, who was trying to extricate his sword for fear he'd hurt himself, apparently, he looked handsomer every minute. What was strange, though, was that the two of them were silent. He said "Dear wife, how strong you are!" "Young man," he said, "Pull out the sword by its handle!" But they said nothing, no one had told him that the queen and the squires had become mutes in the last ten years. They were as mute as travellers are who hurry to pack a trunk when time is short. They had to do something quickly, before anyone else came in. What was it? Suddenly Aegisthus kicked his helmet as a dying man kicks his dog, and the truth was plain. And he cried, "Wife, let me go. Wife, what are you doing?" She took care not to answer, she couldn't say aloud, "I'm killing you, murdering you!" But she said to herself, "I'm killing you because there's not one gray hair in your beard, because it's the only way to murder that little finger."

She undid the laces of his cuirass with her teeth and the gold turned scarlet, and Aegisthus,—beautiful with the beauty of Achilles killing Hector, of Ulysses killing Dolon,—approached, with drawn sword. Then the king of kings kicked Clytemnestra's back, so she shook all over, her silent hand shook, and he shouted so loud Aegisthus had to roar with laughter to cover the noise. Then he drove in the sword. And the king of kings was no longer the mass of bronze and iron he'd thought himself, he was just soft flesh, as easy to pierce as a lamb, and the sword cut so deep it split the marble. The murderers were wrong to hurt the marble, for it's revenged itself. I found out about the crime from that split tile.

So he stopped struggling, let himself go, between the woman, who became uglier every moment, and the man, who was handsomer and handsomer. One good thing about death is that you can trust yourself to her, death is your only friend in an ambush, she has a familiar look, he recognized that and called on his children, first the boy, Orestes, then the girl, Electra, to thank them for revenging him in future, lending their hands to death. Clytemnestra, foam on her lips, did not let go of him, and Agamemnon was willing to die but not to have this woman spit in his face, on his beard. She didn't spit because she was walking around the corpse, trying not to get blood on her sandals, her red dress looked to the dying man like the sun. Then the shadow fell, because each of them took an arm and turned him over on the floor. On his right hand four fingers were already stiff. Then, as Aegisthus had pulled out the sword without thinking, they turned him over again and put it gently, deliberately, back in the wound. Aegisthus was grateful to the dead man for having let himself be killed so very easily. Dozens of kings of kings could be killed like that, if murder was so easy.

But Clytemnestra's hatred of the man who had struggled so fiercely, so stupidly, grew as she foresaw how every night she would dream of this murder. That's just what happened. It's seven years since she killed, so she's killed three thousand times.

ORESTES *has come in during this speech.*

NARSES' WIFE. Here's the young man! Isn't he handsome?

BEGGAR. As beautiful as Aegisthus when young.

ORESTES. Where are they, Electra?

ELECTRA. Darling Orestes!

NARSES' WIFE. In the southern courtyard.

ORESTES. I'll see you soon, Electra, and we'll never part.

ELECTRA. Go, my lover.

ORESTES. Don't stop, beggar. Go on, tell them about the death of Clytemnestra and Aegisthus.

He goes out, sword in hand.

NARSES' WIFE. Tell us, beggar.

BEGGAR. In two minutes. Give him time to get there.

ELECTRA. He has his sword?

NARSES' WIFE. Yes, daughter.

BEGGAR. Are you crazy? Calling the princess your daughter!

NARSES' WIFE. I call her daughter, I don't say she's my daughter. I've often
seen her father, though. Heavens, what a fine man!

ELECTRA. He had a beard, hadn't he?

NARSES' WIFE. Not a beard, a sun. A wavy, curly sun, a sun just rising from
the sea. He stroked it with his hand. The most beautiful hand in the
world.

ELECTRA. Call me your daughter, Narses' wife! I am your daughter. . . .
I heard a cry!

NARSES' WIFE. No, my daughter.

ELECTRA. You're sure he had his sword? He didn't go to them without a
sword?

NARSES' WIFE. You saw him going. He had a thousand swords. Be calm,
be calm!

ELECTRA. What a long minute, mother, you waited at the edge of the bath!

NARSES' WIFE. Why don't you tell us? Everything will be over before we
know about it.

BEGGAR. One minute! He's looking for them. Now! He's found them.

NARSES' WIFE. Oh, I can wait. Little Electra is soft to touch. I had only
boys, gangsters. Mothers who have only girls are happy.

ELECTRA. Yes . . . happy . . . This time I do hear a cry.

NARSES' WIFE. Yes, my daughter.

BEGGAR. So, here's the end. Narses' wife and the beggars untied Orestes. He
rushed across the court. He didn't even touch or embrace Electra. He
was wrong, for he'll never touch her again. He found the murderers on
the marble balcony, calming the rioters. As Aegisthus leaned down to
tell the leaders that everything was going well, he heard behind him
the cry of a wounded beast. But it wasn't a beast crying, it was Clytemnestra. She was bleeding. Her son had stabbed her. He struck at the
couple blindly, his eyes closed. A mother, though, even when unworthy,
is sensitive and human. She didn't call on Electra or Orestes but on her
youngest daughter, Chrysothemis, so Orestes thought he had killed
another and an innocent mother. She clung to Aegisthus' arm; she was
right, that gave her a last chance to stand up. But she prevented Aegisthus
from drawing his sword. He shook her, to free his arm. She was too

heavy to serve as a shield. And that bird was beating his head with its
wings and attacking him with its beak, so he struggled. Just with his
unarmed left arm, the dead queen, loaded with necklace and pendants,
on his right arm. He was in despair over dying like a criminal, when he
had become pure and holy; to be fighting because of a crime which was
no longer his; to find himself, though loyal and innocent, infamous
before this parricide. He struggled with one hand, which the sword was
cutting little by little, but the lacing of his cuirass caught on a brooch of
Clytemnestra and it opened. Then he no longer resisted; he only shook
his right arm to rid himself of the queen, not only to fight but to die
alone, to lie in death far from Clytemnestra. But he didn't succeed. For
ever Clytemnestra and Aegisthus will be coupled. He died, calling out
a name I'll not repeat.

AEGISTHUS' *voice off stage.* Electra!

BEGGAR. I talked too fast. He caught up with me.

SCENE TEN

ELECTRA. BEGGAR. NARSES' WIFE. *The* EUMENIDES, *who are exactly the same
height and figure as* ELECTRA.

SERVANT. Flee, everybody, the palace is on fire!

FIRST FURY. That's the light Electra wanted. Three, with this fire, the day
light and truth!

SECOND FURY. You satisfied, Electra? The city's dying .

ELECTRA. I'm satisfied. I knew a minute ago that it will be born again.

THIRD FURY. And the people killing each other in the streets, will they be
born again? The Corinthians started the attack and they're murdering.

FIRST FURY. Your pride has brought you to this, Electra. You have nothing
left, nothing.

ELECTRA. I have my conscience, I have Orestes, I have justice, I have every
thing.

SECOND FURY. Your conscience! Will you listen to your conscience in the
early mornings to come? For seven years you've not slept because of a
crime other people committed. Now you're the guilty one.

ELECTRA. I have Orestes. I have justice. I have everything.

THIRD FURY. Orestes! You'll never see Orestes again. We're leaving you to
pursue him. We've taken on your age and your shape so as to pursue
him. Good-bye! We'll not leave him until he's been driven to madness
or suicide, cursing his sister.

ELECTRA. I have justice. I have everything.

NARSES' WIFE. What are they saying? They're back. What have we come
to, my poor Electra, what have we come to?

ELECTRA. What have we come to?

NARSES' WIFE. Yes, tell me. I'm not very quick to understand. I know some thing's happened but I don't know just what. How can you explain it, when a day dawns, like today, and everything's ruined, and pillaged; though we're still breathing, we've lost everything, the city's burning, innocent people are killing each other, the guilty are dying, too,—and the sun still rises?

ELECTRA. Ask the beggar. He knows.

BEGGAR. It all has a beautiful name, Narses' wife, it's called the dawn.

CURTAIN

The King and the Duke

A MELODRAMATIC FARCE FROM *HUCKLEBERRY FINN*

BY FRANCIS FERGUSSON

"That corpse you planted last year in your garden — —
Has it begun to sprout?"

CHARACTERS

HUCKLEBERRY FINN

NIGGER JIM

THE KING

THE DUKE

MARY JANE

SUSANNA   } *Nieces of Peter Wilks, deceased*

JOANNA, *a harelip*

Townspeople of Piperville:

DEACON LOT HOVEY, *Undertaker, Caller and Auctioneer*

BEN RUCKER

DOCTOR ROBINSON

LAFE BUCKNER   }

HANK BUCKNER   } *Town Loafers*

THE WIDOW BARTLEY

MRS. HOVEY, MRS. RUCKER, *and other townspeople who do not speak.*

The townspeople from time to time form a chorus, in the style of the old-time minstrel show, for their "walk-arounds," their patter songs, and their "play-party" dances.

REVEREND HARVEY WILKS   }

WILLIAM WILKS, *deaf and dumb* } *Brothers of Peter Wilks, from England*

The action of the play takes place in Piperville, a little "cracker" town on the Mississippi, in the summer of 1845.

The stage is set in the style of the Minstrel Show, in order to suggest the period and also the Mississippi River, as we learn of it in song and story. There is a painted backdrop of the River, with lush trees and perhaps a steamboat; and baroque cutout wings, like those of a provincial opera house, representing foliage or architecture. There is an act-curtain painted to represent the ramshackle village of Piperville, and certain scenes are played before this curtain. But there are no naturalistic settings, and for most of the scenes there is a semicircle of chairs on stage for the Piperville crowd, like the chairs used by the Minstrel Chorus.

The music is played by a countrified band.

ACT ONE

Overture

SCENE ONE

The Walkaround: "Waitin by the River"
"Walkaround Music" as the curtain opens, revealing the Piperville curtain,
and the people of Piperville lined up in a flat arc, like the traditional minstrel
chorus, before it. The men are on one side, and the women on the other,
as at the beginning of a country dance; and DEACON LOT HOVEY, *master of*
ceremonies, is in the center. He is gaudily dressed à la 1850, but his tall
hat is decorated with funereal crepe. The people are all shuffling slightly in
time to the music: atmosphere of high jinks, and a big night coming.
LOT, *patter.*

Ladies and Gentlemen, this is Piperville here:
We're as good as the next one and a dern sight better.
                    Calling.
Honor your corner! Honor your partner!
            All bow to their neighbors and across the stage.
We're just waitin here and gettin ready,
Waitin for what's to come floatin down the river.
CHORUS, *singing.*

Waitin by the River, O starry sky!
Waitin by the River, O shiny night!
Waitin by the River for the boat on the River.
LOT.

Where's that floatin palace with a gilt saloon
Makin sparks in the sky and a streak on the water?
CHORUS, *trudging like a side-wheeler.*

Hoo-hoo! Boat on the River.
LOT.

In the darkness of the night she's lit up like noon — —
CHORUS.

When she comes floatin, floatin down the River.
LOT.

The Queen o'Sheba come afloatin that way,
When she and her thousand gals made Solomon shiver.
MEN.

Now nothin 'pears to int'rest him an' me all day
But what comes floatin, floatin down the River.
CHORUS.

Waitin by the River, O starry sky!
Waitin by the River, O shiny night!
Waitin by the River for the boat on the River.

BEN RUCKER, *stepping out from the line.*
> Lot, tell the folks what we're doin out here.
>> *To audience.*
> Mr. Lot Hovey here calls for our dances
> Hollers goin goin gone at all our auctions
> And when we're dead he sees we git buried right.
>> *To LOT.*
> Tell em, Lot.

LOT, *wheeling the corpse of Peter Wilks out from the wings on a light two wheeled cart.*
> We're waitin.
> It's our duty to wait with pore Peter here.
> He died before his brothers could come from England
> And he hadn't seen em in forty year.
> But we reckon they'll see *him* — — if they git here soon.

BEN.
> Lot, how long do you reckon pore Peter'll last?

LOT.
> Four more days I reckon. Five if it's cool.

WIDOW BARTLEY, *ushering the three GIRLS forward.*
> These is Peter's orphan nieces an they're waitin too.
> Their dear uncles from England is long overdue.

LOT.
> And we're *helpin* em wait, as it's our duty to do.

GALS.
> We're Peter Wilks's lonesome nieces, we can't hardly wait!
> Oh, uncles, dear uncles, ain't you comin *ever*?

They do a delicate "right-hand star," looking longingly over their left shoulders: back in place.
> Uncle Peter's gettin mouldy an you'll be too late too late!
> Floatin . . . floatin . . . floatin down the River.

CHORUS.
> Waitin by the River, O starry sky!
> Waitin by the River, O shiny night!
> Waitin by the River for the boat on the River.

DOCTOR ABE ROBINSON, *stepping forward pugnaciously.*
> But them English won't fool us in Piperville here!
> Every man's a king on the Mississippi River!

LOT.
> Honor your corner! Honor your partner!
>> *They bow right and left with ominous and oafish formality.*

DOC.
> I reckon we know when it's our cue to fight!
> We're as good as the next one and a dern sight better!

MEN.
> We could whip our weight in wildcats if we had a mind!
> We don't feed on nothin but jest wildcat liver.
> Hey, hey!

The men lumber dangerously across the stage to the women, swing them around a few times, then suddenly drop them and slink disconsolately back to their places.

But nothin 'pears to int'rest us in Piperville all night
But what's to come floatin, floatin down the River.

The GALS *fly sobbing to* MIZ BARTLEY'S *arms. Music stops, and the crowd stops shuffling.*

WIDOW. *Now* see what you done, Abe Robinson! You made them pore gals cry!

DOC, *embarrassed.* All right, all right.

WIDOW. *Tain't* all right!

LOT. Why, Miz Bartley, Doc and the boys don't mean nothin by it! They're just as anxious for the gals' uncles to come as you are.

WIDOW. Huhh. Nice *welcome* they'll give em! Trouble with you, Abe Robinson, you sawbones think you kin cure anything. But they's some things you *can't* cure.

Pause. All eye PETER.

BEN, *solemnly.* Abe . . . I reckon she's right.

WIDOW. You can't he'p them orphans, nor bury Peter, nor ship him safe to glory.

DOC. I ain't said nothin! I wash my hands of the matter! *Folds his arms.*

WIDOW. As for you, Lafe and Hank, you don't know *what* to do with strangers, if you don't fight 'em or lynch 'em. Dear, o *dear!* What will them English *think* of us!

LOT. Now, Miz Bartley — — The boys is a little savage, but their *hearts* is right.

BEN, *softly.*
Tell em, Lot.

LOT, *coming forward as the music begins softly; confidentially to audience.*
Ladies and Gentlemen, as you'll see tonight
We're ringtailed roarers, best not interfere;
Half hoss, half alligator in Piperville here.
We're a *little* savage but our *hearts* is right,
Waitin, waitin by the River here.

CHORUS.
Waitin by the River, O starry sky!
Waitin by the River, O shiny night!
Waitin by the River for the boat on the River.

LOT, *as all peer forward.*
Oh, what do you see when you look up the River?

CHORUS, *softly; patter.*
Just the pure air of freedom for a thousan mile.

LOT.
Sh — — what do you hear? You can't hear the River?

MARY JANE.
A little bird complainin in the virgin wild.

WOMEN.
>O pure air of freedom! Oh, broken heart!
>O, pure air of freedom! Oh, long lost child!

CHORUS.
>Waitin by the River, O starry sky!
>Waitin by the River, O shiny night!
>Waitin by the River for the boat on the River.

LOT, *calling.*
>Swing your partner like a boat on the River!
>>*As they swing, cries.*
>Queen o' Sheba I could cry for joy!
>Floatin palace I could cry for joy!
>Furrin heirs from England I could cry for joy
>If you would only come afloatin, floatin —
>Floatin down the River . . . . .
>>*They sink back to their places. Silence.*

BEN. Don't see nothin yet.

LOT. No—but the River Queen's due tomorrow night. I reckon they'll be on her, sure.

"River Music" as the Piperville Curtain opens slowly, and the people wheeling Peter, disappear into the wings.

SCENE TWO

The Raft on the River

As the Piperville Curtain slowly opens, "River Music," and the tune of JIM's *song. The stage is set to indicate a "shiny night" on the River: cut-out wings, in the style of the provincial opera house, representing trees and foliage, and a large painted backdrop showing the Mississippi. In the center of the stage a small raft, with a little pile of packing cases on it, and beyond that, the peak of an improvised tent. Downstage, on the end of the raft,* HUCKLEBERRY FINN *and* NIGGER JIM *are taking their ease.*

JIM. Mighty peaceful out heah on de ribber.

HUCK, *lazily.* Mmm. Mighty still — like all the stars was out just for us.

JIM. But Huck . . . Whar *is* we?

HUCK. I've lost track . . . What did that galoot say? You heard him holler across the water?

JIM. Next little town's Piperville, he say.

HUCK. Don't worry, Jim.

JIM. But Huck, Ise afraid we's floatin *South*. Dat's dangerous country for me. Slave country, Huck.

HUCK. Don't worry about it, Jim. It's better not to.

JIM. Is it, honey?

HUCK. Ain't nothin better than a raft, is there, Jim? The days and night slide by so smooth and lovely . . . if you don't *worry*.

JIM, *sighs.* Jest as you say. *Sings softly.*
  O Lawd, Ise a-listenin'
  Oh! Lawd!
  O Lawd, Ise a-listenin'
  To find my way.

  A-float in de night-time
  Lost my way
  A-float in de starlight
  Lost my way . . .
                 Silence. They both listen.

HUCK. Listen.

JIM. I hears it . . . Hounds. Pooty far away. But Ise glad we's way out heah on de water.
    Distant barking of hounds giving tongue; faint echoing halloo.

JIM, *in terror.* What dat, Huck? Dey after us?

HUCK. How could they see us? We ain't got a lantern.

JIM. Mought make out a black streak, de Ribber's so shiny tonight.
         Barking nearer. A cry for help.

JIM. Dey's gwine ketch us! Dey's got a rowboat!

HUCK. Sh . . . One of em hollered help.

JIM. Must be de dogs was after dem!

HUCK. Sh . . . Sh!

JIM. How kin we git away?

HUCK. We can't.

JIM. Huck . . . Ise scared.

HUCK. *Sh* — don't *act* scared. They don't have to know you're a runaway nigger, do they? — whoever they are. And I won't say.

HUCK *goes upstage, disappearing behind the tent and pile of crates in the middle of the raft.* JIM *follows. Sound of oarlocks approaching.*

KING, *still far away.* Kin we git aboard, gentlemen?

HUCK, *calling.* I reckon.

Sounds of boat, splash, etc. KING *and* DUKE *come down stage, followed by* HUCK *and* JIM. *The* KING *is an old man, with a white beard and bald pate; the* DUKE *in his thirties — a type of hick barnstorming Shakespearean actor. Both dressed like tramps and carrying fat carpetbags.*

KING. You've saved our lives, gentlemen—them crackers was after us. —

DUKE. But we hadn't done a thing —

KING. But they was chasin us for it —

DUKE. Men and dogs — hear em?

Pause. All listen. Barking and yelping grows fainter, as though the hunt were moving away in the distance.

KING. They're at the swamp. Hehe! That'll puzzle em.

DUKE. Yeah, they've lost our trail . . . *Sighs.* But who . . . *Peers first at* HUCK *and then at* JIM. Why, there ain't nobody here but a nigger and a boy!

KING, *softly.* Derned if it ain't so . . . what's your name, my boy?

HUCK. Huckleberry Finn.

KING. And why are you floatin down at night, this-a-way?

HUCK. Well, you see—

DUKE. He's a runaway nigger, ain't he?

HUCK. Who, *Jim?* Goodness sakes! Would a runaway nigger run South?

DUKE, *cagey.* No—I reckon he wouldn't.

HUCK, *pathetically.* My folks all died off but me—warn't nothin left but sixteen dollars, the raft, and our nigger Jim here. I'm tryin to git down to Orleans, to my uncle. But we can't run daytimes cause folks tries to take my Jim away—*they* think he's a runaway too, you see. So we run *nights,* you see.

KING. Oh. I see . . . *Suspicious glance at the* DUKE. Say . . . what was it got you into trouble?

DUKE. Well, I'd been selling an article to take the tartar off the teeth—and it does take it off, too, and generly the enamel along with it—but I stayed about one night longer than I ought to . . . That's the whole yarn. What's yourn?

KING. I had a little act called The Royal Nonesuch — Ladies and Children not Admitted. Mostly it's just me without no close on, jest painted up in stripes. It makes them flatheads laff to see me caper that-a-way, with my white whiskers and bald pate . . . But when they got to thinkin it over they felt *sold.* A nigger rousted me out this afternoon and told me the people was gatherin on the quiet with their dogs, and if they caught me they'd tar and feather me and ride me on a rail sure. I didn't wait for no supper — I warn' hungry . . . .

HUCK, *softly.* They don't *know* each other, Jim!

KING, *who has been peering at the* DUKE. What's your line—mainly?

DUKE. I do a little in patent medicines; theatre-actor—tragedy, you know; take a turn to mesmerism and phrenology when there's a chance; teach singing geography school fer a change—most anything comes handy, so it ain't work . . . What's *your* lay?

KING. I've done considerable in the doctorin way in my time. Layin on o' hands is my best holt—fer cancer and paralysis and such things. Preachin's my line too, and workin camp-meetins, and missionaryin' around . . . . *Sighs.*

HUCK. Won't you set down?

KING, *sitting down.* What's the *beds* like?

HUCK. Well, me and Jim has two *corn-shuck* beds.

DUKE, *darkly.* Corn-shuck beds . . .

KING. Don't apologize — I reckon it's the best you kin do.

DUKE. Alas. *He drops his carpetbag with a thump, walks to the edge of the raft, and sinks on a box in a pose of Hamlet-like gloom.* Alas!

JIM, *whispers.* Huck, what's *he* gwine do?

KING, *truculently, to* DUKE. What you alassin' bout?

DUKE, *to himself.* Cornshuck beds. *Aloud and tragically.* To think I should have lived to be degraded down to such company!

KING, *after shocked pause.* Dern your skin! Ain't the company good enough fer you?

DUKE, *tearfully, to* KING. Yes, it *is* good enough for me: as good as I deserve!

Turns away again. But some day I'll lie down and forgit it all, and then my poor broken heart will be at rest.

KING. Drot your pore broken heart! What are you heavin' it at *me* for?

DUKE. I ain't. *I* don't make no moan . . . The secret of my birth —

KING, *crossing to seize his hand.* The secret of your *birth!* — You mean to say —

DUKE, *pulling* KING *down beside him.* Sir: I will reveal it to you. I feel I *can.* By rights I am a duke!

KING. No! You can't mean it?

DUKE. Yes. My great grandfather, oldest son of the Duke of Bridgewater, fled to this country about the end of the last century to breathe the pure air of freedom. He married here and died, leaving a son. I am the lineal descendant of that infant—I am the rightful Duke of Bridgewater—and here I am, forlorn, lost in the vast wilderness—torn from my high estate, hunted of men, heartbroken—and now degraded down to the companionship of felons on a raft! *Sobs.* And cornshuck beds.

KING. . . . Hm. *Moves across the raft, and turning his back, sits moping on another box.*

JIM, *to* DUKE. Don't you fret, honey, we'll take keer of you. You get *used* to de beds.

HUCK. Don't cry, Duke; if there's anything we kin do —

DUKE. No. I thank you. Just call me your grace and bow when you speak to me, that's all.

HUCK *and* JIM, *bowing.* Yes, your grace.

DUKE. And wait on me at dinner and get me any little thing I need.

HUCK *and* JIM, *bowing.* Yes, your grace.

DUKE, *turning away.* I thank you — thanks . . .

KING, *tragically, from his box.* Looky here, Bilgewater, I'm nation sorry for you, but you ain't the only person that's had troubles like that!

DUKE, *coldly.* No?

KING, *tears rising.* No, you *ain't! You* ain't the only person that's been snaked down wrongfully out'n a high place!

DUKE. Alas.

KING. And you ain't the only person that's had a secret to his birth! *Blubbers.*

JIM. Look at *dat,* Huck!

HUCK. Sh . . .

DUKE. Hold! What do you mean?

KING. Bilgewater, kin I trust you?

DUKE. To the bitter death! Speak.

KING. Bilgewater, I am the late Dauphin!

DUKE. You are what?

KING. Yes, my friend, it's too true. Your eyes is lookin at this moment on the pore disappeared Dauphin, Looy 17, son of Looy 16 and Marry Antonette!

DUKE. You! At *your* age! No — you must be the late Charlemagne. You must be six or seven hundred years old at the very *least.*

KING. Trouble has done it, Bilgewater, trouble has brung these grey hairs and this premature balditude. Yes, sir, you see before you in blue jeans

and misery the wanderin exiled trampled on sufferin rightful King of
France! *Bellows.*

DUKE, *in disgust.* Aaaaaa . . . .

JIM. Huck, what we gwine do?

HUCK. Don't take on so, King. Ain't there anything we kin do?

KING. No, t'ain't no use: but wait. I *have* noticed it makes me feel a little
better if people treats me accordin to my rights.

DUKE. Your rights. *Aaaaaaa!*

HUCK. How would that be?

KING. Wait on me first at meals, and don't set down till I ask you, and get
down on one knee when you speak to me, and say "your majesty."

HUCK *and* JIM, *kneeling.* Yes, your majesty.

JIM. Does yo majesty feel better?

KING. A little. I thank you . . . Rise. HUCK *and* JIM *get up, and they all watch
the* DUKE. Looky here, Bilgewater, tain't my fault I was born a King, and
tain't your fault you was born a Duke.

DUKE. No, it *ain't.*

KING, *dramatically crossing to him.* Give me your hand, Duke! *They clasp
hands.* And don't blame them two, neither. They'll do what they kin
to make it up to us — fer all we done and suffered, Bilgy.

JIM. Yes indeedy.

DUKE. Yes — let it pass.

KING, *looking around at* HUCK *and* JIM. Aii now we kin *all* be friends, eh?

JIM. Yes *indeedy.*

HUCK. Jim and I sure are mighty glad to see it. You don't want any un-
comfortableness on a raft, so far out, this-a-way.

KING. Mmm. Jest like *I* always say. *Thoughfully sits.*

They all sit down quietly, looking out into the dark. JIM *begins to sing
softly.*

JIM.

O Lawd. Ise a-listenin'
Oh! Lawd!
O Lawd Ise a-listenin'
To find my way.

Oh, de night-time Ribber —
                    All sing the next stanza.
Oh, de night-time Ribber
Mighty still
A-floatin de sinner
Whar it will.

                    Silence.

KING. Gentlemen: whar *is* we?

HUCK. 'Bout twenty mile above Piperville, I reckon.

JIM. Lawdy, Lawdy.

HUCK. Shh . . .

KING. I have a reason for askin. *Pointing skyward.* Thar she is! Providence;
watchin over us!

DUKE. Eh?

KING. Listen, Bilgy, I'll tell you a little story 'bout a rich man died there, day before yestiday. I us mighty sorry to hear it.

DUKE. Alas.

KING. Leavin 6000 dollars, and I don't know *how* much prop'ty.

DUKE. We'll *all* come to it.

KING. Willed everything to his three lovely nieces, and his two brothers — but the brothers is in England — he hadn't seen em in forty year. The brothers is expected, any day, but they ain't *come*. And the folks can't bear to settle the estate, or bury Peter, till they *do* come.

DUKE. Well! — But then, we're *all* mortal, ain't we? George Washington, gone, Hanibal, gone. Great Caesar's ghost, *gone!*

KING. Jest what *I* say. I got all the facts from a young greenhorn I met — he was waitin fer the Orleans boat.

Imitating.

"Ain't nobody left, now, but the three gals, Mary Jane, Susanner and the Harelip Joanner," sez he.

"Poor things!" sez I, "to be left alone in the cold world so!"

"Well, they could be worse off, ole Peter had friends," sez he. "Deacon Lot Hovey and Ben Rucker, and Doc Robinson, and all their wives— and the Widow Bartley," sez he. I could jest see that-thar cracker town, with its jimson weeds, in my mind's eye.

"But I recken them poor souls *need* the brothers?" sez I.

"Most desperately," he sez, fer he was polite and well-spoken, fer a green-horn. "Older one's named Harvey, a dissenterin preacher: younger one is William, an William's deef and dumb," sez he.

Pause.

DUKE, *sings softly.*

O Lawd, Ise a-listenin'
Oh! Lawd!
O Lawd Ise a-listenin'
To find my way.

The KING *and the* DUKE *get up with one accord.*

KING. We're goin to see the beds. Mind you stay at this end o' the raft. It might be that me and his grace will have somethin private to say.

They disappear quickly.

JIM. Don't seem so peaceful out heah no mo!

HUCK. No.

JIM. But what do you reckon dey's up to *now,* Huck?

HUCK. I don't know, Jim.

JIM, *after a pause.* Don't it s'prise you de way dem Kings acts, Huck?

HUCK. No, it don't. I reckon they're all like these two.

JIM. Sho 'nuff, Huck?

HUCK. Yes. Take Henry the Eight, and Louis Fourteenth, and Richard Second, and forty more.

JIM. But dis one do smell so lak de nation, Huck.

HUCK. Yes . . . But the Duke ain't so bad.

JIM. No, take de Duke, he's a tol'able likely man, en some ways.

JIM *starts crawling off on his hands and knees.*

HUCK. Where you going?

JIM. Ise gwine *see. He disappears.*

HUCK. Warn't no use to tell Jim they ain't really Kings and Dukes, but right-down red-eyed rapscallions, and dangerous, too, I'm afeared. As long as we've got em on the raft, and they're fixin to stay, it wouldn't a done no good to mention it. It would just worry Jim. Say nothin. It's the best way.

He sighs. JIM *silently appears.*

HUCK. What are they up to, Jim?

JIM. I doesn't know.

HUCK. What are they *doin?*

JIM. Dey's gettin out dere store close, an puttin em on . . . . De King he sho do look starchy in de starlight. He look dat grand, an good, an pious, he mighta stepped right outa de Ark. He might be ole Levitious himself, Huck. *Softly.* Ise skeered.

HUCK. Come on, set down, Jim . . . It's quiet here.

JIM *sits beside* HUCK. *Both look silently forward. The Piperville Curtain closes slowly, as* JIM *sings.*

JIM.

Oh, de night-time Ribber
Mighty still
A-floatin de sinner
Whar it will —
A-floatin de sinner
Whar it will.

CURTAIN

SCENE THREE

"United at Last."

The light comes up quickly on the Piperville Curtain. Distant boat-whistle. The CHORUS *is heard singing a rousing refrain offstage.*

Safe to Glory! Safe to Glory!
O we'll ship pore Peter safe to Glory
When his boat comes in.

BEN RUCKER *runs across the stage. In a moment he runs back again. Boat-whistle is much closer.*

The refrain is sung again offstage, while LOT *crosses, with dignity, but in a hurry.*

In a moment LOT *reappears, ceremoniously bowing in the* KING *and the* DUKE. *They are now in respectable black, their arms over each other's shoulders, weeping into big white handkerchiefs.* HUCK, *also slicked up, follows, loaded down with the baggage.*

LOT *solemnly points them the way, and in the manner of the discreet* *country undertaker, tiptoes ahead of them. The little procession follows* *him to stage center, where the* DUKE *suddenly halts the* KING.

KING, *in stage whisper.* What is it?

DUKE, *scared.* Did you hear them voices?

KING. Whole town, I reckon.

DUKE. But why ain't they here?

KING. Timid, pore things. Ain't never seed an Englishman, most likely.

DUKE. Got them names?

KING. Susanner, Joanner . . . Yeah.

DUKE. Let's *run.*

KING. What? Cold *feet? Tearfully.* After all we aim to do fer em? Why, them pore gals is orphans, Duke! S'pose their uncles don't *never* come? Who'd bury Peter then, eh? — er ship him safe to Glory? *Suddenly seizes* DUKE's *throat.* Say nothin—do you hear? Say nothin, and *watch me.*

DUKE. Well, if it's our *duty* —

KING, *letting go and sobbing.* Come!

The KING *puts his arm over the* DUKE's *shoulder, and weeping once more into their handkerchiefs, they march off.* HUCK *follows, solemn, laboring with the baggage.*

The curtain opens in silence, revealing the entire town, except for DOC *ROBINSON, watching intently. The open coffin is in the center, with* LOT *on one side and* WIDOW BARTLEY *and the three* GIRLS *on the other.*

The little procession enters from the wings, and for a moment the crowd and the KING *and* DUKE *eye each other.*

KING, *stage whisper aside to* DUKE. Take yer cue from *me.*

LOT, *in low, genteel voice, giving her the cue.* Miz Bartley . . .

WIDOW BARTLEY, *pushing* GIRLS *forward.* Mary Jane . . . Susanner . . . Joanner!

The GIRLS *fly by one by one to hug and kiss their "uncles," then back to their places.*

WIDOW, *aside to audience, softly.* I could cry for joy to see them meet at last and have *sech* good times!

The KING *sharply nudges* DUKE, *indicating coffin. They advance upon it; bow their heads, their backs shaking with sobs.* KING *turns, holds up his hand for attention.*

KING. You dear lovely people, that I reckon I know already from my pore brother's letters, me and William jist wants to say it's a sore trial for us to lose the diseased, and to miss seein diseased alive after our long journey of 4000 miles, but it's a trial that's sweetened and sanctified to us by this dear sympathy an' these holy tears; an' so I thank you out of my heart and out o' William's heart, case out of our mouths we can't, mere words bein too weak an' cold. Amen.

CROWD, *sings lustily.*

Safe to Glory! Safe to Glory!

O we'll ship pore Peter safe to Glory

When his boat comes in.

A-a-a-a-*men.*

Brief awkward pause. WIDOW *makes signals to* MARY JANE.

MARY JANE, *handing* KING *a letter.* There, Uncle Harvey . . . I reckon that's for you.

KING. What's this, Mary Jane? It's not . . . It's not . . .?

MARY JANE, *sobbing.* Yes. It's from *Uncle Peter—*to you and Uncle William. It's the last word he left behind, and I guess it's a kind of a *will,* too, Uncle. It was the only kind of a will they could get him to write.

KING. Will? *Wipes his eye.* Pore Peter . . . A-hem. Let me say right off that me and William here is mighty glad all you friends of the diseased is with us for the readin'. It's only fitten you should hear what Peter said, and how he fixed for these dear gals; for I'm sure he *did,* and I hope he didn't give William an' me nothin of theirs. *Slowly breaks seal and unfolds letter.*

WIDOW. Ain't that jest *like* the dear soul!

BEN, *to "boys."* Now we'll see who calc'lated right 'bout his savins.

WIDOW. Sh.

KING, *deeply moved, reads.* "My dear brothers, I'm writin this to you because Dr. Robinson says I mightn't last to see you. *Glance at corpse.* I give the dwellin house and three thousand dollars gold to my beloved nieces and the tanyard along with my prop'ty down by the river, that Levi Bell knows about, and three thousand dollars gold, to you, Harvey and William. There's six thousand cash all together, and it's hid out back under some old boards. If you get this letter I'll be gone without seein you in forty year, but I reckon to last ten days longer. It's all I ask. Your lovin brother Peter."

KING, DUKE *and* GIRLS *embrace in tears; men begin discussing the will.*

BEN. 6000 Cash!

LOT. All Gold too.

LAFE. Gee whillikins I'd like to see that!

WIDOW. Sh!

LOT. No, but it must be a mighty fine sight, all them yallerboys!

BEN. Did *you* know he had that in gold, Lot?

LOT. Why, Ben, I was tellin you only yesterday—

KING, *emerging from the embrace: loudly.* An' now . . . *They quiet down.* An' now, me and William begs you all to excuse us a minute; we aims to git the gold counted and out' the way . . . Not fer you, not fer *me,* not fer William—not fer him, thar, *he* don't need it; but fer these here pore orphans he left behind . . . An' then we kin plan fer *him.* Adolphus!

HUCK *jumps; he and* KING *and* DUKE *start off downstage.*

LOT, *takes charge; solemnly.* All together, folks.

CHORUS, *sings softly.*

Safe to Glory, Safe to Glory!
O we'll ship pore Peter safe to Glory
When his boat comes in.

The Piperville Curtain closes on the crowd, and in a moment KING *and* DUKE *enter downstage, with heavy bags of gold, followed by* HUCK *with a lantern. The curtain is now lighted to indicate night. They dump the gold on the floor and begin counting it.*

KING. Oh, this ain't bully nor nothin! Oh, no. I reckon not! Why, Bilgy,

it ain't no use talkin; being brothers to a rich dead man and representatives of furrin heirs that's got left is the line fer you an me, Bilge. Thish
yere comes of trustin to *Providence*. It's the best way, in the long run.
I've tried em all, and there ain't no better way.

DUKE. 5585

KING, *after pause.* Yeah—5585.

Both hunt frantically for the missing money.

KING. Dern him, I woner what he done with that 15 dollars?

DUKE. Well, he was a pretty sick man, and likely he made a mistake. I reckon
that's the way of it. The best way's to let it go, and keep still about it.
We can spare it.

KING. Oh shucks, yes, we can *spare* it. I don't kyer nothing 'bout that. But
they'll want to tetch it, they'll want to paw it . . . They might even
count it.

DUKE. A-oh. They *might.*

Pause; both listen.

KING. They're a-purrin now, and I don't never want to hear em roar.

DUKE. Ugh.

KING. I don't never want to see their *teeth.* When a dead man says there's
6000 dollars, you know, we don't want to—

DUKE. Hold on! Le's make up the deficit. *Pulls money from his pocket.*

KING. It's a most amazin idea, Duke—you have got a rattlin clever head on
you! *Pulls out his money.* Hehe! jest a little investment, you might say—

DUKE. Say, I got another idea. Let's go back, and show em all this money,
and then take and GIVE IT TO THE GIRLS!

KING. Good Lan', Duke! Lemme hug you! It's the most dazzlin idea at
ever a man struck. You have certainly got the most astonishin head I
ever see. Oh, this is the boss dodge, there ain't no mistake *bout* it! Let
em fetch along their suspicions now, if they want to—this'll finish em,
this'll lay em out—hehe—like Peter thar.

They stuff the money into the bags and hurry off, motioning HUCK *ahead of
hem with the lantern. The Piperville Curtain opens in silence, revealing
he crowd in one long, intent, speechless line across the stage. In a moment*
ING, DUKE, *and* HUCK *sidle in, backs to audience, facing the crowd.* DOC ROB-
NSON *has come, and stands apart, arms folded, lowering at the* KING. KING *sees*
OC *and stops short.*

KING, *aside to* DUKE. Good lan'! Who's *that?*

They advance to the center. KING *really worried under his solemnity.*

KING. Friends all: My pore brother that lays yonder has done generous by
them that's left behind in the vale of sorrors. He has done generous by
these yer pore little lambs that he loved and sheltered, and that's left
fatherless and motherless. Yes—and we that knowed him knows that he
would a done more generous by em if he hadn't been afeared o' wounding
his dear William an me. Now, *wouldn't* he? There ain't no question
bout it in *my mind.* Well, then, what kind a brothers would it be that'd
stand in his way at sech a time? And what kind a uncles would it be
that'd rob, yes *rob,* sech pore sweet lambs as these, 'at he loved so, at
sech a time? Well, then—*this here money ain't rightfully ours at all!*

Gasp in the crowd. KING *turns slowly to* DUKE. And if I know William—and I *think* I do—he'll—well, I'll just ask him.

He makes signs to DUKE, *who bobs joyfully in answer, hugs* KING.

KING, *tearfully and triumphant.* I knowed it; I reckon that'll convince anybody the way *he* feels about it. Here, Mary Jane, Susanner, Joanner. *Pointing to the gold.* Take the money, take it *all.* It's the gift of him that lays yonder, cold but joyful.

The GIRLS *embrace their "uncles"; the crowd is much affected.*

BEN, *shaking hands with* LOT. That was mighty fine, Lot. Mighty fine. Three cheers for Reverend Wilks!

CROWD. Hooray! Hooray! Hooray!

WIDOW, *leaning toward* BEN, *indicating* DOC, *who has not joined in the cheering.* Now how do you s'pose he feels?

All eye DOC.

DOC, *stepping pugnaciously forward.* Did you count the money?

KING. Yes, friend.

DOC. How much was it?

KING. 6000 dollars gold.

DOC. Is it all there?

CROWD, *shocked; ad lib.* Why, Doctor! Why, jest think! What do you mean! What the . . . *etc.*

KING. Yes, friend. You kin count it if you wish. *Suddenly loud and hearty* Enough o' this dreary *money!* Me and William and my nieces and him that lays yonder — we wants you all to take supper with us here tonight

MARY JANE. Oh yes, Uncle.

KING, *his confidence growing as he rattles on.* For it would be *his* wish; and I knows who he would name, if he could, for they was names that wa. very dear to him, and mentioned often in his letters, and I will now name them as follows, to wit, namely: Deacon Lot Hovey, and Mr. Ben Rucker and Mr. Abner Shackleford, and Lafe and Hank o' *course* the Widow Bartley! *Pause, staring at* DOC. And if anybody else has come in I hope they speaks up. DOC *stares back, saying nothing.* And that ain't all Tomorrer we want you all for the Orgies! He liked everybody, he respected everybody, and its fittin his funeral Orgies should be public!

BEN. Eh?

DOC. What?

DUKE. *in stage whisper, without moving.* Obsequies, you old fool.

KING, *in terror.* Eh? Haha. Pore William. Afflicted as he is, his *heart's* allu right! — Asks me to invite everybody to come to the Orgies — wants me to make em *all* welcome. But he needn't a worried, it was jist what was *at.* How could I do any different? The Orgies doesn't belong to me They don't belong to William, the Orgies belongs to the whole of Pipe County, and to the dear remainders laying there an keeping so mum. say ORGIES, not because it's the common term, because it *ain't* — ob sequies bein the common term — — but because orgies is the *right* term Obsequies ain't used in England no more now — — it's gone out. W say orgies now in England. Orgies is better because it means the thin you're after more exact. It's a word that's made up out'n the Greek org outside, open, abroad; and the Hebrew Jeesum, to plant, cover up; hence, *inter.*

DOC, *steps forward and laughs insultingly in* KING's *face.* Hahaha!

WIDOW. Doctor!

KING. Er . . . *Gets the idea from the* WIDOW; *shoots forth his hand. Is* it dear my dear brother's good friend and Physician! I —

DOC. Keep your hands off me! I guessed something was queer, and now I *see!* Orgo, eh? Jeesem, eh? It don't sound like an Englishman to *me!*

HANK. Jest a minute. *Advances ominously on* DOC. Me and Lafe aims to get this straight. Do you say what's a good enough Englishman for Piperville ain't good enough for *you?* Eh? Do you say you know more than me?

LAFE. Pin back his ears.

WIDOW. Quiet. It ain't your *cue* to fight! *In "private" tones to* DOC. Ain't you ashamed to be sleepin that-a-way? Ain't you heard the *news?* This is *Harvey Wilks.* He knows all the names, and what they done for the last twenty *year,* and the names of the very *dogs,* an what *they* done!

DOC. Bah! *Who's* sleepin? . . . Lot! What do *you* say?

LOT, *mysteriously.* Aaa! . . Doc . . Mary Jane! What do you say? You can't be dreaming like these galoots here — — you've got some spirit! Do you really want to take in them tramps — — them *thin frauds?* If you'll let *me* handle em — —

MARY JANE. Here is my answer . . . . After the generous thing *he* done, I can do not other! *Plumps the gold in the* KING's *arms.* Take this 6000 dollars gold, and invest it for me and my sisters any way you want to, and don't give us no receipt for it, either!

Triumphant tableau: KING, DUKE, GIRLS *and Gold.*

CROWD. Hooray! Hooray for Mary Jane! Hooray!

They stamp and whistle.

DOC, *yelling.* All right, all right! Go to it! Make a night of it! But mark my words — you'll feel mighty sick before you git through.

KING. Sick, did you say, Doctor? Then we'll try to git em to send for you!

Loud laughter.

MEN. It's a prime good hit! A prime good hit!

DOC *goes off. Crowd begins to shuffle in slight embarrassment.*

BEN. He's gone.

LAFE, *to audience.* Any other gentleman want to interfere?

Laughter.

KING. Can't *nobody* interfere!

CROWD. Hooray!

KING, *solemnly.* Not with *Piperville,* they can't. I hope you folks won't mind my sayin it—for it ain't flattery. In all my travels I ain't never seed sech a town as Piperville is, *right here!*

CROWD. Hooray! Hooray!

KING, *holds up his hand for silence.* But remember who deserves the credit. *Impressively.* Fer it was a kind of *miracle* we all got acquainted so nice, now warn't it? *Slowly raises his hand and points aloft.* It was the Hand O' Providence brung us together.

Pause.

LOT. The Reverend has said it. The Hand of Providence brung us together. *Suddenly changing his tone.* Now! Pick your partners to march to supper!

As LOT *takes charge, rousing music starts for the Supper Walkaround. The people, with a few preliminary capers, shuffle into place, two by two, with the corpse in the center: and* LOT *advances to the audience.*

LOT, *patter.*

> Ladies and Gentlemen, this is Piperville here!
> We may be savage, but our hearts is right!
> — And we won't let nothin interfere,
> For our hearts is set on Big Times Tonight!
> > *Calling.*
> Honor your partner! Honor the Reverend!
> > *All bow with the music.*

KING, *bows to the people, then advances to audience; patter.*

> The dear remainders and William and me
> Wants you *all* for the orgies tonight!

WIDOW, *bobbing out and interrupting; in ecstacy.*

> For the Hand of *Providence* brung us together!

FULL CHORUS, *singing.*

> Waitin by the River, O starry sky!
> Waitin by the River, O shiny night!
> The River Boat's come in for us all tonight!

LOT, *calling.* Reverend Wilks, you lead the way!

The KING *capers up to* MARY JANE, *while the whole procession, including the corpse, begins to move.*

MARY JANE. Just a minute, Mr. Hovey.
> > *Procession stops, music continues.*

LOT. What is it, Mary Jane?

MARY JANE, *crosses in time to the music to* HUCK, *who has been watching solemnly from the downstage corner. She takes his hand.* I can't a-bear to see *him* lookin blue.

HUCK, *overcome.* Why, Miss Mary Jane, why I —

CROWD. Hooray for Mary Jane! Hooray for Mary Jane!

LOT, *singing.*

> Queen o'Sheba, I could cry for joy!

MARY JANE *leads* HUCK *to the head of the procession, as* CHORUS *sings and the couples whirl.*

CHORUS.

> Queen o'Sheba, I could cry for joy!
> Floatin palace I could cry for joy!
> Furrin heirs from England I could cry for joy!
> The River Boat's come for us all tonight!

The WIDOW *has the* KING, SUSANNA *and* JOANNA, *the* DUKE; *and the whole procession now moves off, with its calfish majesty, while the* CHORUS *sings lustily.*

Waitin by the River, O starry sky!
Waitin by the River, O shiny night!
The River Boat's come in for us all tonight!
                    Piperville Curtain closes

SCENE FOUR

                    "Did you ever see the King?"

HUCK *enters slowly before the Piperville Curtain. Night. He is thoughtfully gnawing a chicken leg.*

HUCK. Music *is* a good thing—sounds so honest and bully . . . after that hog-wash. *Eyes his chicken.* Well—I never *et* such a supper! *Softly.* And when Miss Mary Jane come for me there—red as fire, and her eyes all shiny. Maybe the King is *right.* Yes, I judge he *is* right. Bein furrin heirs long lost in England is the life. It *suits* me . . . But who —
                    JOANNA, *the Harelip, enters.*
HUCK, *disappointed.* Oh. It's *you.*
HARE. Yes, it's me. *Not* Mary Jane . . . Mary Jane, *she's* got it all straight about *you.* But *I* ain't. There's things *I* need to *know.*
HUCK. There is, is there? Well, fire away.
HARE, *taking impudent stance.* Did you ever see the King?
HUCK. Who? William Fourth? Well, I bet I have. He goes to our church.
HARE. What, regular?
HUCK. Yes, regular. His pew's right over opposite ourn—on t'other side the pulpit.
HARE. I thought he lived in London.
HUCK. Well, he does. Where *would* he live?
HARE. I thought *you* lived in Sheffield?
                    He chokes on the bone.
HUCK. I mean he goes to our church regular when he's in Sheffield. That's only the summer time, when he comes there to take the sea-baths.
HARE. Why, how you talk—Sheffield ain't on the sea.
HUCK. Well, who said it *was?*
HARE. Why, you did.
HUCK. I *didn't* nuther.
HARE. You did.
HUCK. I didn't.
HARE. You did!
HUCK. I never said nothing of the kind.
HARE. Well, what did you say then?
HUCK. Said he comes to take the sea *baths,* that's what I said.
HARE. Well, then, how's he going to take the sea baths if it ain't on the sea?
HUCK. Looky here, did you ever see any Congress-water?
HARE. Yes.

HUCK. Well, did you have to go to Congress to get it?

HARE. Why, no.

HUCK. Well, neither does William Fourth have to go to sea to get a sea bath.

HARE. How does he get it then?

HUCK. Gets it the way people here gets Congress-water—in barrels. There in the palace at Sheffield they've got furnaces, and he wants his water hot. They can't bile that amount of water away off there at the sea. They haven't got no conveniences for it.

HARE. Oh, I see now. You might have said that in the first place and saved time. Mary Jane, now, I s'pose she would a *known* . . . . Do you go to church too?

HUCK. Yes, regular.

HARE. Where do you set?

HUCK. Why, in our pew.

HARE. *Whose* pew?

HUCK. Why, *ourn*—your Uncle Harvey's.

HARE. His'n? What does *he* want with a pew?

HUCK. Wants it to set in. What did you *reckon* he wanted with it?

HARE. Why, I thought he'd be in the pulpit.

He chokes on the bone again.

HUCK. Blame it, do you suppose there ain't but one preacher to a church?

HARE. Why, what do they want with *more?*

HUCK. What! To preach before a King? I never did see such a girl as you. They don't have no less than seventeen.

HARE. Seventeen! My Land! I wouldn't set out such a string as that, not if I *never* go to glory! It must take em a week . . Tain't no use! I jest can't *believe* it!

She trails off, seeing MARY JANE *and* SUSANNA, *who have come in and are watching her disapprovingly.*

MARY JANE. What's that you won't do to get to Glory?

HARE. I won't swaller the whoppers he's been tellin me. I *can't.* I . . .

MARY JANE. I s'pose you know what's a whopper, don't you — about England? But one thing you *don't* know. You don't know what's right and kind to a *stranger.*

SU. 4000 mile from home and his own people! And you won't believe him!

HARE. I don't *understand* you, Ma'm! Sailin in to help him—why he ain't hurt! He—

SU. How would you like it if you was far, faraway, and they said they didn't *believe* you?

HARE. Why, he said —

MARY JANE. Don't make no difference what he said.

SU. He's our *guest,* Jo.

HARE. But I wouldn't —

SU. *You'd* feel pretty mean! Now, wouldn't you?

HARE, *in tears.* Let up, can't you? I—I'm downright sorry, Adolphus . . . But what kin I *do?* . . . Now you're all against me! *Runs out.*

Embarrassed pause.

MARY JANE. It's just her way, you see . . . Don't hold it against her.

HUCK, *overcome.* Why, Miss Mary Jane, I—why—

SU. She's too young to understand — — and too brash. Can't make out True Love that counts not the cost . . . True Love stumps her. *Runs out.*

JIM's *song played softly, offstage.*

MARY JANE, *after a pause—embarrassed.* Silly ain't they? . . . I reckon they're a little flustered, bein left alone, you know—and our new uncles a little strange to em yet . . .

HUCK. Oh, Oh.

MARY JANE. I reckon they just wanted to say they wanted everybody to feel right and kind to each other . . . I feel that way, too, don't you? I can't a-bear to see anybody in trouble, can you?

HUCK. I—No—Miss Mary — — Most always I can't.

MARY JANE. I—I wanted you to know.

> *She runs out. Pause. Offstage music continues, very faintly.*

HUCK. Oh, Oh, Oh, . . . And these are the gals I'm lettin that old reptile rob, and make fools of, and *betray!*

> JIM *starts singing very softly offstage.* "O Lawd, Ise a-listenin'."

HUCK. Jim? . . . must be scared. *Calls softly.* Jim! Jim!

JIM, *coming stealthily out of the wings.* Is you all right, honey? I sho is glad to see you! I uz afraid, wid dem store close—I uz afraid you'd be *strange.*

HUCK, *looking at the floor.* You shouldn't-a come, Jim. You know that. S'pose you're seen?

JIM. I knows. But I got worried. Is everythin' all right?

HUCK, *with gloomy vehemence. All right?* Why, the folks took them two to their hearts like long-lost brothers, and me too! Piperville ain't seen such times in years, I reckon. Chicken an all. It's a regular love-feast. You heard the singin'.

JIM. Yes. I uz sho glad to hear it . . . But Huck, whar's dat *gold?* 'Case I got to thinkin, de gold don't belong to *dem,* do it? Den what dey doin wid it, Huck?

HUCK. They give it back to the gals.

JIM. Dey *did?* Well — — dat's nice, anyway.

HUCK. Then the gals took an give it back to *them.*

JIM. Sho *nuff?* Why? Didn't they need it?

HUCK. It seemed right at the time, Jim, and mighty fine and generous, too, I reckon you wouldn't understand it.

JIM, *sighs.* Don't seem so, do it? . . . Come on back wid me, Huck. Back to de ole raff! We'll slip away in de dark — — by mawning we'll be clean away!

HUCK. I can't.

JIM, *scared.* Why?

HUCK. I might as well make a clean breast of it. Things *ain't* all right, and they're movin too fast for me. I reckon you knew all along: when you first heard em holler across the water. We should a got away then, just like you said.

JIM, *after pause.* But now *dat* gold keeps you. I guessed it! . . . I knowed it'd make mischief . . . What is it, honey?

HUCK. The King hid it in the straw tick of his bed.

JIM. Lawdy, Lawdy, Youse gwine try an steal it, for de orphans. Ain't you? . . . But *ef you gits caught* — —

HUCK. I know. It wouldn't be healthy. For you *or* me.

JIM. Oh! Oh! Dat King an dat Duke!

HUCK. Listen, Jim. You've got to get back to the raft, and what's more, not let so much as a dog see you. It's lucky the people is all so busy! I'll come as quick as I can . . . . And I won't never let on about you, no matter what happens. And I won't never leave you, Jim.

JIM. I knows dat, honey.

HUCK. Hurry. Jest lie quiet, and wait for me.

JIM. Dat King and dat Duke! You say all dem Kings is like — —

HUCK. Shh—go along, Jim.

JIM. I'm jest goin. Lawdy, Lawdy! *He steals out.*

HUCK. Well, there you are. First Mary Jane shows me up, trustin me that-a-way, and then Jim . . . . But I see what I have to do, and before dawn too. I have to steal that gold for Miss Mary Jane, leave her a note to say where it's hid, and get away. That way nobody will need to know how low-down and ornery and mean I am—and Miss Mary Jane won't ever know I'm hidin a runaway nigger. I couldn't a-bear for her to know about me . . . She's the only perfect girl I ever see. *He steals quickly out.*

SCENE FIVE

Watching the Ashes

After HUCK's *exit, the Piperville Curtain opens in silence. The stage is dimly lighted, and set with the minstrel circle of chairs, Peter in the middle in his coffin, and a candle burning.* LOT *and* BEN *are dozing uncomfortably on two of the chairs.*

BEN, *shifting his position.* It's mighty quiet after all thet humbug talky-talk at supper . . . I et plenty.

LOT. Me too. Never et better. *Sighs.*

BEN. Must be nigh dawn. *Yawns rigidly.* It's so *blame* quiet, I believe I could snatch forty winks.

LOT. *He* won't bother you none.

BEN. Sh.

LOT. Ain't nothin dumber than the clay.

BEN. Don't *talk* so, Lot.

LOT. I find it gets right down understandin and companionable, along about the middle of the night . . . when you get *used* to him.

Pause. BEN *begins to snore.*

LOT. That's right . . . *that's* right. He don't ask for no conversation. Mum's the word for him . . . solemn an mum . . . solemn an . . . mum.

LOT *begins to snore. In a moment* HUCK *tiptoes on, a heavy bag of Gold in each hand. Watches them for a moment without moving.*

HUCK, *softly.* Asleep. . . . wisht I was asleep, and dead to the world! . . . *He slowly approaches the coffin.* I couldn't think of any place to hide it but one—where nobody'd care to look for it. *Stretches his neck and peers at Peter.* Bet the dead belly's mighty *cold. Shivers, shuts his eyes, and extends both bags of gold.* Maybe, if I shut my eyes—*He hears something.* What's that?

He runs downstage and hides in the wings. KING *stealthily pulls on* DUKE.

KING, *softly. He* won't hear us—couldn't *be* more private.

DUKE. But—do you reckon *they're* really asleep?

KING. After that supper?—don't be afeard. Now, what is it?

DUKE. I ain't easy, King. I ain't comfortable. We ought to glide out o' this —and before it gets light!

KING. Why, what do you mean, Bilgewater?

DUKE. I reckon having that money given back to us—instead of our havin to *steal* it back—was a kind of a sign, King. A sign for us to go and no hard feelins! Why, we can't get any *more!* I'm for lightin out with what we've got!

KING. What! And not sell out the rest o' the prop'ty? March off like a passel of fools leavin 8 or 9 thousand dollars worth o' prop'ty layin around jest sufferin to be scooped in? House, niggers, furniture—and all good saleable stuff, too.

DUKE. Your majesty's too *greedy!* Why, how could we git all that so quick? Your eyes is bigger than your *belly!*

KING. Whar's your head, Duke? Why, we kin bill the house and the niggers and all the prop'ty for auction straight off—right after the funeral. Why, I even aim to sell the niggers *before* the funeral—reasonable, for three-day drafts, you know. I've enquired for a nigger trader to do business with early this mornin.

> LOT *snorts and groans in his sleep. Both jump. Pause.*

KING. Jest dreamin.

DUKE. Mm—but he *won't* be, in the mornin. And what do you s'pose the folks will say when they wake up, and hear about this auction? *Mighty quick,* they'll say!

KING. Not at all, I'll spread it around town that I gotta git back to the preachin—the folks back in Sheffield can't wait, they need me back so bad. *They'll* understand. *They'll* see.

DUKE. The Doctor, too? Don't the *doctor* lay on your mind?

KING. Cuss the Doctor. *Chuckles.* Hehe—he can't get a *word in!* After we give the gold to the gals, what kin *he* say? The folks kin listen to *him* after we're gone. Meantime, they're gettin their satisfaction, ain't they? And tomorrer—why, you know how them crackers loves an auction! It's most as good as burglary, fer pawing over the neighbor's things. . . . *He changes to a pathetic tone.* As fer the dear gals, they're goin to England with us, of course, so *they* won't need their prop'ty. That-a-way we kin pick the leavins *clean.*

DUKE, *appalled.* But I don't *want* to go no deeper! Alas, them pore gals! Do you want to rob a lot of orphans of *everything* they have?

KING. Why, how you do talk! We shan't rob em of nothin at all but jest this here money. The people that *buys* the property is the sufferers, cause the sale won't be valid — and after we've slid it'll all go back to the estate.

DUKE, *weakly*. Will it now?

KING. O' course. *Tearfully*. These here orphans'll git their house back again, and that's enough for *them*—they're young and spry and c'n easy earn a livin. *They* ain't a goin to suffer. Why, jest think, there's thousands that ain't nigh so well off. Bless you, *they* ain't got nothin to complain of.

DUKE. Yes—yes, if you think of it *that* way . . . if you think they don't really *need* it—

KING. No question bout it—not like you an me.

DUKE. Alas — — no.

KING. Besides, we can't go before the funeral. We owe it to the gals to bury him thar . . . . *Both look over their shoulders at the corpse.* We're all mortal, ain't we?

DUKE, *shining*. Oh, Oh! What a fate! Your majesty has talked me *blind!* *Strikes tragic pose.* "And all our yesterdays have lighted fools the way to dusty death. Out, out brief candle!"

KING. Mm—I ain't ever seed much Shakespeare. Too young when pappy used to have em at the palace. An besides I've been in this country so long, and seed so much trouble, I've most forgot it! Come on!

He takes the DUKE's *arm and they glide out.*

HUCK, *emerging with gold; appalled.* I never see anything *like* it! Old one and young one both. Makes a body scared—ashamed of the human race. *They* never rest . . . *Eyeing sleepers* . . . while them greenhorns snores. But when they wake up—! Will they see how unmerciful they're *had?* Or will the King give em so much mischief to get into that he'll git clean away? *Shivers, looking around him and away.* Wisht I was well out of it—back on the River, with Jim. Stars beginnin to pale, out there. And nary a sound but the birds. *Hears soft music.* But what—?

Music. He backs slowly into the wings. Music stops. Enter MARY JANE, *a la Juliet, in a white nightgown, her hair down, holding a candle over her head. She pauses, rather frightened.*

MARY JANE. Oh . . . I'd most forgot he was so *still* . . . . Nary a word . . . . But why should I be afraid? — — "Love knows not fear."

Music. She sings.

Nary a word, poor heart! ask nary a word.
Love is still. Be still and know
That Love goes with you where you go.

The night in its going
Won't say,
Nor the stars paling
For break of day!

Approaches coffin and looks at Uncle.

Nary a word, poor heart! ask nary a word.
Love is still. Be still and know
That Love goes with you where you go.

Hides her eyes with her handkerchief a moment. Raises her head and listens.
　　Whistle of thrushes
　　Now and then
　　In the dark bushes
　　Can't tell, can't tell—

　　Nor the wide River,
　　Poor child—
　　Nor the woods-wilderness
　　Nor virgin Wild!

　　The night in its going
　　Won't say
　　Nor the stars paling
　　For break of day!
　　　　　　　　　She walks slowly out.
　　Nary a word, poor heart! ask nary a word.
　　Love is still. Be still and know
　　That Love goes with you where you go.
HUCK, *creeps out, watching where she disappeared.* She's done it again. Now
there ain't no help fer it—I've *got* to go through with it. *Closes his eyes and
thrusts the gold under the coffinlid along the belly.* For you, Mary Jane,
from me!
　　　　　He runs off as the curtain slowly closes.

A C T   T W O

Overture

SCENE ONE

The Funeral. "Orgies is better — — it's what you're after more exact."
*The overture to this act has a funereal theme based on the majestic tolling
of a bell. As it ends, the curtain opens on the Piperville Curtain. The*
CHORUS *is entering, the men and women in separate groups. All have crepe
on their hats. The style of this "walkaround" is that of the old-fashioned
backwoods revival; shuddering, bending to weep, raising clasped hands to
heaven—and all the while singing, now weepily, now uproariously. The men
have a jug which they pass back and forth, but the women are still prim and
longsuffering.*
CHORUS, *singing.*
　　Come, Sinner! Come, Sinner!
　　Beyond the last black deep dark River
　　You'll—Be—Free! You'll—Be—Free!

WOMEN, *drearily.*
> Come sister! Come Brother!
> To that bright land beyond the River

MEN, *rousingly.*
> Hooray! Hooray!
> We sinners all shall meet in Glory
> In—That—Day! In—That—Day!

Enter LOT, *with his professional manner, a long thin spade over his shoulder*
The music stops.

LOT, *in lowered tones.* The chairs is all set out. He looks real peaceful. I'll be in presently.

CHORUS, *singing as they march in with a few "shakes," but with discreetly lowered eyes.*
> The chilly clay, the chilly clay
> Shall be pretty and fresh in that sweet day
> I'm—Goin'—Home! I'm—Goin'—Home!

                                        Silence.

LOT, *reassuringly to audience.* We'll be all right soon's we git to the parlor. Won't be long, I figger.

                        Enter BEN RUCKER.

BEN. Reverend Wilks come yet?

LOT, *looking at his watch.* No.

BEN. S'prised he *ain't.*

LOT. Mm. Never see nothin *like* him, fer speed. Lots of Peter's things is sold off already—and he wants the auction right after the buryin, you know. Niggers is *gone.* Nigger trader took em this mornin.

BEN. And did they holler! I heard em. It was real dreary.

LOT. He needs the money.

BEN. Poor soul! Well—I ain't seed Piperville turn out so strong only twice before: the day the circus come to town, and the night we lynched that dude from Cincinnati, two years ago last Fourth of July.

LOT. Sh—here comes Widow Bartley, now. *She enters solemnly.* Is the family ready?

WIDOW, *in sickroom voice.* Yes. But I don't want the pore things to have to wait.

LOT. It's most time now. I did the best I could with Peter. Only thing, he's commencin to grin. Show his teeth a little, you know.

WIDOW. Mm. It's a mercy we don't have to wait no longer . . . I ain't told the gals the niggers is gone.

LOT. Didn't they hear em carryin on?

WIDOW. I made an excuse, and got em out o' the house; I don't see how I'm goin to face Mary Jane with it! She won't *never* see why they had to go so sudden. But I'll have to tell her — — after the buryin.

LOT. We'll be mighty busy, all of us, after the buryin.

BEN, *sighs.* Don't seem like I can face *him* again. Why is funerals so long? He's quiet, but he's mighty stubborn.

WIDOW. Sh—here's Reverend Harvey now. Think what *he's* had to bear! *Sobs.* Lean on that dear soul—git your strength from him!

LOT *puts his finger to his lips and motions them to go. All three tiptoe discreetly out. The* KING *and the* DUKE *cross the stage after them. They are in their mourning pose; arms over each other's shoulders, and "dripping" into big white handkerchiefs. Enter* HUCK, *as they go out.*

HUCK. They wouldn't be in sech a sweat to git him shovelled in if they knowed the gold was going with him. . . That is, the gold will go if they don't find it when they come to screw down the lid! It warn't a good place to hide it — — I see that now . . . Soon as I find out, I'll try for a getaway. *Sighs.* This is most as dreary as a real funeral—but o'course I know it ain't—can't be—the old buzzard ain't no real preacher. *He sighs again, deeply, and goes off.*

The Piperville Curtain slowly opens. The chairs are arranged, with their backs to the audience, in two groups on either side of the stage, leaving a very wide aisle down the center, at the end of which Peter reposes in his open coffin. LOT *is behind him, his finger tips together, his head on one side. He sees something amiss on Peter's face; and wetting a finger delicately brushes it away. As though this were a signal, the congregation starts filing by for a last look at Peter.* LOT *shakes each one by the hand, and ushers him quickly on his way. There is no sound but the shuffling of the feet and a few repressed sniffles. When the people are all standing by their chairs, there is a brief pause, and the chief mourners enter: The* WIDOW *and the* GIRLS, *then the* KING *and the* DUKE. *All shake hands with* LOT *and take their places behind the people near the coffin.*

LOT, *very softly.* Gentlemen . . . be seated.

They all sit. The KING *solemnly takes* LOT's *place behind the coffin. Bows his head in silent prayer. He then opens a huge Bible, and lifting his head and raising his eyes to heaven, opens his jaws very wide to intone "O Lawd."*

Violent barking of a small dog offstage. The KING, *caught with his mouth open, slowly closes it, lowers his eyes and head, waits. The people shift slightly in their seats. Barking stops suddenly.*

The KING *again slowly opens up to speak, as the people relax with a faint sigh.*

Barking again, more vicious that before. KING *slowly descends and waits again, as all the people's backs are seen leaning to the left as they extend their ears to hear. Barking stops.*

KING *starts again.*

Barking starts again. It sounds as though it were reaching some sort of desperate climax, and though it now and then breaks down into strangled growls, it immediately mounts up again. By the stretching of all the rigid backs we see that the people are near the breaking point. The KING, *in dismay, his Bible shaking in his hand, looks wildly about for help.*

LOT *rises in the back, and tiptoes with set face all the way around behind the people, and out, to the accompaniment of yapping and panting. Offstage we hear a couple of sharp slaps, followed by a string of agonized yelps, diminishing rapidly in the distance. Silence.* LOT *tiptoes back. Stops down stage center. All the backs lean center.*

LOT, *in stage whisper to* KING. He had a rat!

KING, *slowly closing his book.* Aaamen.

CHORUS, *with a sigh, as they sink back.* Aaa-men.

KING, *signalling* LOT. Amen. *Sharply.* Amen!

LOT *draws forth a screwdriver, points it and advances upon the coffin with*
deliberate stealth. As he goes, HUCK *comes in from the wings on his hands*
and knees, half raises up to watch. LOT *slides the coffinlid lovingly over the*
face, hunches his shoulders, and whistling with the effort, securely tightens
down the screws. HUCK *sinks, but stays to watch.*

KING, *sharply, to* LOT. Git him up!

      LOT *can't believe it's over; doesn't understand.*

KING, *shouting in revival style.* GLO-RY, Glory Be! Come! Oh, Come to
    Mourn!

CHORUS, *reviving.* Amen!

KING, *to* LOT. *Git him up!* I can't bear no more! *Git him up! Shouting*
    Come, Black with sin! Oh, Come to Mourn!

CHORUS, *shouting.* AAAAA-*Men!*

LOT *gets the idea, and beckons frantically to* LAFE *and* HANK *who run out*

KING. Come, lame and halt and blind! (Amen!) Come pore and needy
    sunk in shame! (Amen!) Come *all!* Come all to *Mourn!*

The CHORUS *is now bellowing with a will it's "Amens."* LAFE *and* HANK *trot*
in with Peter's little rubber-tired cart, and they and LOT *begin struggling*
with the coffin to move it on the cart.

KING. On your feet! Music thar! GLORY! Glory-Hallelujah! On your feet
    to sing!

      CHORUS *rises. Rumble of their feet on the floor. Music.*

KING, *singing loudly.*

    Don't shake, don't shiver!

CHORUS, *shaking and shivering.*

    Don't shake, don't shiver!
    We sinners all shall meet in glory
    In that Day! In that Day!

The KING *starts parading around the stage in a shuffle, shivering and shaking*
and raising clasped hands. CHORUS *falls in behind him. Singing, and cries*
of "Glory!" "Hallelujah!" etc. The procession begins to move off; the
Piperville Curtain swishes shut. The KING *shuffles and shakes in downstage*
followed by the people.

CHORUS.

    The chilly clay, the chilly clay (Hallelujah!)
    Beyond the last black deep dark River (Hooray!)
    Don't you shake and don't you shiver
    Shall be pretty and fresh in that sweet day (Hallelujah!)
    In that sweet day! In that sweet day!

LOT *trots across downstage, wheeling Peter at great speed to his buryin. Behind*
him come the DUKE, *and the* WIDOW *with the* GIRLS *firmly grasped by the*
hand, all nearly running to keep up. The KING *and* CHORUS *fall in quick*
behind them, still shivering, weeping, yelling, and singing lustily. The racket
dies quickly offstage.

SCENE TWO

"Is something Gone Wrong?"
When the noise of the "Buryin'" has died out offstage, DOCTOR ROBINSON
comes on with long, still strides; pauses abruptly, listens a moment.
DOC, *to audience, as though to say, "I told you so."* Mighty still, *ain't* it?
Whole town closed up tight—like fer *any* plague. Well, the galloping
heebeejeebies ain't nothing like it. *Taps a packet of letters he has in his
hand sharply.* But now I reckon I'se ready to *operate. Several crashes are
heard offstage.* What the—Oh. That'll be the boys heavin' Peter's things
out in the street. I got out just in time. They must've sprinted — — can
they have him buried *already? Peers offstage. Must* be!
He hides quickly downstage in the wings. HUCK *hurries across. Not far
behind him, in pursuit, come the* KING *and the* DUKE; *they are still in their
pose of grief, and trying to look dignified, but nearly trotting.* DOCTOR
emerges slowly.
DOC. *Something* hit em, sure! *Looks offstage again.* And *them!*
He hides again. MARY JANE *hurries across sobbing. She is followed at a
little distance by the* WIDOW, *dragging the other* GIRLS *by the hand.*
WIDOW, *trying to call soothingly.* Now, now! There, there! Now, Mary Jane!
They disappear. DOC *emerges again.*
DOC. Go it Mary Jane, go it Widow! Put salt on her tail—if you *can. Looks
after them a moment, meditating.* I reckon Lot's my man. If anybody's
still cool enough to listen, he'll be—he's half dead already, you might say.
He goes out. The KING *and the* DUKE *return with* HUCK. *They each hold him
by an ear.*
KING. Where was you goin in sich a hurry?
HUCK. Nowhere, your majesty.
KING. Was you in my room last night?
HUCK. No, your majesty.
KING. Was you in there early this morning?
HUCK. No, your majesty.
KING. Honor bright, now—no lies.
HUCK. Honor bright, your majesty. I'm telling you the truth. I ain't been
a-near your room since Miss Mary Jane took you and the Duke and
showed it to you.
DUKE. Have you seen anybody else go in there?
HUCK. No, your grace, not as I remember I believe.
DUKE. Stop and think.
HUCK. Well . . . I see the niggers go in there several times.
They drop his ear.
DUKE. What, *all* of them?
HUCK. No . . . leastways not all at once—that is, I don't think I ever see
them all come *out* at once . . . but jest one time.

DUKE. Hello! When was that?

HUCK. It was just before the nigger-trader came and took em away . . . Musta been, because I'd been getting dressed for the funeral . . . and I see them.

DUKE. Well, go on, *go* on! What did they do? How'd they act?

HUCK. They didn't do nothing. And they didn't act any way, much, as fur as I see. They tiptoed away . . .

Pause. KING *and* DUKE *suddenly sick and scared.*

DUKE. U-hu. No *wonder* it warn't there. We've given *them* the 6000 dollars gold.

KING. Great guns . . . This *is* a go.

HUCK, *innocently.* Is something gone wrong?

KING, *beside himself.* None o' your business! You keep your hed shet! Long as you're in this town don't you forgit that, you hear?

HUCK *backs slowly away, then stops to listen.*

KING, *to* DUKE. We got to jest swaller it.

DUKE. Mmm—if *you* ain't swallered it, already.

KING. What does your grace mean by *that*?

DUKE. Quick sales *and* small profits—for me.

KING. Why, you—! I'll learn ye to blame me!

KING *grips the* DUKE *by the throat and starts to strangle him. Short struggle. The* DUKE *disengages the* KING's *hands, and grips him by the throat.*

DUKE. You *will*? You're to take the blame, see? *Shakes him.* Say Uncle! *Relaxes his grip a bit.*

KING. Uncle . . . Uncle. *Tearfully.* Don't you *trust* me, Bilgy?

DUKE, *solemnly brushing off his hands.* Like rat pizon—unto death. First the ORGIES. Then that there *rat.*

KING. After nigh a week—was it *my* fault he smelled him?

DUKE. It's your fault if them people smelled *you.* You're at your pizenest with a corpse, old man. Oh, oh! It's degrading. Did your majesty think you was running a revival meetin'? Is that why you was brayin' like a jackass, jawin' and bawlin' the few wits out o' that bald pate—cryin' fer greed and pity?

KING. But ain't they *all* mortal, Duke? They *likes* to cry! You heard the Deacon: they may be savage, but their *hearts* is right.

DUKE. Their hearts—ugh. It's their *teeth* I'm skeered of.

KING, *in terror.* Eh?

DUKE. Remember what you said, yesterday?

KING, *quietly, in terror.* What shall we do?

DUKE. That's just it. What kin we do? Somebody's got the gold — — niggers or somebody. Then somebody knows, don't they? Leavin *us*, like fools in the dark. After the tears we shed with em, after the good times we had together, and all we done—all lies, all treachery! That's what we get! Yes, crush cold world this breakin' heart! . . . But there's only one chance to get away with anything, even our skins, and *its* mighty slim: brazen it out. Brazen it out! if you *kin*!

KING, *clasping the* DUKE's *hand.* True till death, ain't you, Bilgy?

DUKE, *pushing him away. Whose* death? *Dramatically.* Here I am— misunder

stood, deef, dum—and tied to you like a hound-dog to a garbage pail!
. . . Brazen it out! but if I give you the sign to slide out, *slide*, slide fer
your life, see?

KING, *weakly*. Good ole Bilgy . . .

DUKE. Come on!

He takes the KING *by the arm and hustles him off. Distant bell, and cry, offstage:* "Going, going, Gone!"

HUCK, *left alone*. This would be the time for me to go—after them two let
me off so lucky. I could leave the letter about the gold for Mary Jane,
and go. *Offstage:* "Going, going, gone!" Listen at them people, gatherin for
the auction — — I reckon the King is right — *they're* on a *spree*. And the
auction will tell the end of the story. Why should I *care?* Why do I feel
so blue?

The HARELIP *comes in, in her usual scornful sidling way, and stands impu-
dently gazing at* HUCK.

HUCK, *noticing her; sadly*. Oh—it's you.

HARE. Yes, it's only *me*. Don't look so glad and s'prised to see me. I reckon
you forgot I'll be on the boat with you this evenin'—and in England, too.

HUCK. England? . . . Oh.

HARE. I aim to see the King for myself, the minute I get there — — and them
sea-baths that's so far from the sea. But Mary Jane, she don't *want* to
go. Says it's the niggers. I reckon *somethin'* ails her — wantin' to see *you*
so bad. She can't even wait till this evenin'.

HUCK. *What?*

HARE. Are you deef? She wants you — right off.

HUCK. Me?

HARE. Don't look so flabbergasted; she sent me to tell you. I said I'd come,
just to put her out of her misery. There ain't no doubt, *somethin'* ails
her. Niggers, pollagra—or True *Love*, maybe! Hehehehe! *She runs out
laughing shrilly.*

HUCK, *inspired*. Wants to see me! And if it hadn't been for them two frauds.
and all my lies, I never would-a seen her—never seen Mary Jane! . . .
Well, it's most over, *now,* lies, sea-baths, Mary Jane—and all. It'll all come
out—except about Jim: I can't never tell *that. Sadly*. But the rest, I
reckon, she 'most guesses already—and it's best, that way, for *her. Sighs*.
Yes, things is so bad, blest if it don't look like the truth is better, and
actually safer, than a lie! . . . for *Mary Jane.*

HUCK *goes off. The ringing of the auction bell is heard approaching from the
wings. It is* LOT, *who enters swinging it. He still has his spade over his
shoulder, but now a red flag labelled* "Auction This Day" *has been tied to
the end of it.* LOT *comes to a disconsolate stop. The* DOCTOR, *with his packet
of letters, comes on from the other side.*

DOC. Who hung *that* on you?

LOT *only glowers.*

DOC. Looks like all the folks is took *bad,* and in a hurry. *Comes close to* LOT;
with ominous formality. Lot, I want a word with you. Private. And before the folks gets here.

LOT. All right. *Carefully lays by the spade, flag and bell. Takes wary boxer's stance.* I'm your man. What shall it be? No holts barred? Stompin' and gougin?

DOC. All in good time. I'm ready to oblige any man thinks he needs it. But I reckon we've got other business first, and it can't wait. The folks is rarin' to go.

LOT. What is it?

DOC. Hold your hosses, and I'll tell you quick as I can.

LOT, *places his finger tips together and inclines his ear.* I'm listenin'.

DOC. Lot, you smell somethin's *wrong,* don't you?

LOT. Was with the buryin'. The old man was in such a sweat, he wouldn' let me take time to plant him right—not for eternity. I ought to dig him up and start over. T'aint fair to the *clay.*

DOC. All *right.* Now listen. While you was buryin', I was busy, thar in the house. These is letters Reverend Wilks wrote to Peter—I wanted to see what the handwritin' was like — — and they'll come in handy. But thi is it: *This* letter I found hadn't ever been opened. Must've come jest when Peter died, and so they forgot about it. But what it says is mighty *queer* It says Harvey and William Wilks is comin' on the River Queen, du tonight.

LOT. Eh? *Tonight?*

DOC. That's what it said.

LOT, *slowly.* If I was thinkin' what *you're* thinkin — —

DOC. You'd know what to do, eh?

LOT. I reckon.

DOC. We all would.

LOT, *eyeing* DOC *coldly.* And you'd git your way. Soon as it's dark . . . "W know what we are, but we know not what we *may* be . . ." It ain't n proof—yet. Not till tonight.

DOC. I know it ain't. All in good time.

        CHORUS *chant heard offstage.* "Going, going, gone!"

LOT. What do you aim to do?

DOC. I can't tell the boys yet—wouldn't be healthy. Stands to reason the won't like it any more than *you* do, bein took in that way! Had, you ma say . . . I'll have to watch my chance at the Auction, and corner them two mighty slow, and sure, and *fair* — — for all to see. Ain't that the righ way?

LOT, *gloomy.* Mmm.

DOC. The gang's comin. Won't be denied . . . Easy does it, eh? Say nothin!

LOT, *ominously.* I won't bother you none. Mum's the word for me. Cool an mum. *Calling suddenly.* Going, going, gone! Going, going, *gone!*

        CHORUS *answers offstage* "Going, going, gone!" *as* DOC *sneaks off.*

LOT. I don't *feel* like sayin nothin. It's got to come, if he's right. But it ain no cure for what ails *me.*

Rings his bell, as the "gang" comes swaying in, in lock-step, hands on each other's shoulders, chanting its childish refrain. They are a little tousell the women's mourning hats over one eye; and a jug is in evidence. Th form a semicircle to "josh" LOT.

BEN. Well, here we are, Lot!

WIDOW. I declare, I'm so sore-tired, and ravelled-out, and tired, and distracted, I can't be responsible no more! I don't *care!* — not when I think what the Reverend done: the bucketfuls o'tears he shed, kissin the gals to make em happy, and the house upset, and the niggers hollerin—and all the time in a sweat to get Peter buried and safe to Glory, and the gals sold out, and safe across the ocean for *their* good times! *Sniffles.* —"in that bright land beyond the River!"—I reckon they're most packed *now* . . . What do *you* say, Lot.

LOT. Nothin.

BEN, *passing jug to* WIDOW. Jest a sip, Miz Bartley.

WIDOW. I reckon I need it. *Drinks.*

LOT, *softly.* Going, going, *gone.*

BEN. No, but it's pitiful, partin so soon, this-a-way. At the Auction I'm gonna git me that green bird Peter had to remember the Reverend by: the stuffed one, you know, with glass eyes like real. We deserve some o' the nice things, *cheap,* the Reverend says. Lot: what do *you* say?

LOT. Nothin.

WIDOW. Well, I say it's the *least* we deserve — — and the Reverend says the same. In all his travels he never see such tireless, bright, longsufferin folks as us right here in Piperville!

LAFE. *That* ain't no lie. Why, Hank and me had Peter shovelled in thar before he knew what *hit* him. And then we was back so quick, he warn't hardly wheeled out of his house, seemed like, before we was dumpin his things in the street. Three cheers for Reverend Wilks!

CHORUS. Hooray! Hooray! Hooray!

LAFE, *to* LOT. Now what do you say?

LOT. What *kin* I say—to the likes of you? You're half hoss, half alligator, ain't you? —and kin see in the dark. Here's what I say. *Ringing bell.* Going, going, gone!

Loud laughter.

LAFE. Three cheers for Lot.

CHORUS. Hooray! Hooray! Hooray!

They gang up again and march out shouting their cheers, as LOT *leads the way ringing his bell. Offstage, in the distance, the cheers change to the hant* "Going, going, gone!" *Silence.*

SCENE THREE

"No Uncles at all."

The Piperville Curtain opens to reveal the minstrel circle of chairs, now empty. The place in the center where Peter used to be is now occupied by an open trunk, with a few clothes trailing out of it. MARY JANE *sits beside it, her face in her hands,* HUCK *enters very slowly.*

HUCK. Miss Mary Jane . . . *She raises her head.* You can't a-bear to see people
in trouble. You said that to me, once . . . And *I* can't, most always. What
is it?

MARY JANE. The beautiful trip to England is most spoiled for me. And I
don't know why . . . unless it's the niggers.

HUCK. I just expected it.

MARY JANE. To think they ain't ever going to see each other any more! *Sob*

HUCK, *shaking his head slowly.* No, that ain't it, Miss Mary Jane. *They'll see*
each other, and soon.

MARY JANE. What! *She jumps up and hugs him.* Say it *again!* Say it *again!*
As he says nothing she slowly draws back and looks at him. But—look here:
what do you mean?

HUCK. I'm a-going to tell you, Miss Mary Jane. There ain't no other way.
But first—is there any place out of town where you could go for tonight?

MARY JANE. Yes,— there's Lothrop's. . . . Why?

HUCK. Never mind why, yet. If I tell you about the niggers, and the rest,
which is much worse, you've got to promise me to go off to Lothrop's
mighty quiet, and spend tonight there. Will you?

MARY JANE. *Tonight?* I'll spend a *year!*

HUCK. All right. I don't want nothin more out of *you* than just your word.
Sighs; in low voice. The Auction's goin on—you can't hear it from here.
Them people have got hold of all your things—in a regular fever they
are; but they don't know why, no more than you . . . Well, this is why
those uncles o' yourn ain't no uncles at all: that Doctor guessed right.
They're dead-beats: frauds . . . . There. Now we're over the worst. You
can stand the rest middlin' easy.

MARY JANE, *jumps to her feet.* Why it can't be—why—why I

HUCK. *softly.* It hurts. I couldn't help it.

MARY JANE, *seizing his arms.* Oh, oh, oh. You've got to tell me! You've got
to explain!

HUCK. I want to. But you must be quiet, Miss Mary Jane. You said you
would.

MARY JANE, *sitting down.* I will. I will.

HUCK. That doctor was right. Two days before the funeral that old bea
happened to meet a young greenhorn goin up to take the steamboat fo
Orleans; and he pumped all the names and facts right out of him. Then
we stopped up the River two miles and boarded the River Queen; she
landed us in style . . . . Well, you know the rest. As soon as the Widov
Bartley give the word, you jumped for 'em and kissed 'em sixteen o
seventeen times, and — — —

MARY JANE, *jumps up in a fury.* The brute! Come! What are we waitin for
Don't waste a minute—not a second—tar em and feather em — — fling en
in the River!

HUCK. Yes. Yes *indeed.* But do you mean *before* you go to Lothrop's, or -

MARY JANE. Oh, what am I *thinking* about—after I promised you! *Takes hi*
hand. Don't mind what I said. Please don't. You won't now, will you?

HUCK, *his eyes on her hand.* I'd die first.

MARY JANE. I was so stirred up, I—I never thought. *Withdraws her hand an sits down.* Can't see my way no more! *You* tell me what to do. And whatever you say, I'll do it.

HUCK. As long as you go along now, like I said, and lay low till the worst is over, there ain't much you *can* do, now. You see, the niggers will be back in a few days, 'cause the sale ain't valid. The Auction has got to go on, but it won't count either, and you'll get your things back again . . . . Why, tomorrow you'll say, it warn't nothin, after all!

MARY JANE, *sadly.* Oh . . . But why can't we get em *now?*

HUCK, *after short pause.* I don't dare to, Miss Mary Jane. And I can't tell you just why . . . . They're a rough gang, those two. And there's another person would be in awful trouble if I blew on em now; that's all I can say. I'd tell you if I could, Miss Mary Jane—but I reckon you'll just have to believe me.

MARY JANE. I do, I do! . . . But to think it would all turn out this way! I'm to blame. *Softly.* Kissin' . . . *Shivers.* No wonder I couldn't sleep last night, when it was all quiet. Must be I nearly knew.

HUCK, *very low.* I know.

MARY JANE. Like somethin' was tryin' to tell me . . . What *shall* I do?

HUCK, *gently.* Go along to Lothrop's, Miss Mary Jane. There ain't no other way.

MARY JANE. And then?

HUCK. Lay low till nine or half past, then get them to fetch you home again. Put a candle in your window, when you get home. I'll see it, and know what it means. . . . Wait till eleven, and then, if I don't turn up, you can tell the Doctor — and — well, let it come.

MARY JANE. Where will *you* be?

HUCK, *hesitates a moment.* If it just happens I get took up along with them, you must up and say I told you the whole thing beforehand, and you must stand by me all you can.

MARY JANE. Stand by you! Indeed I will! They shan't touch a hair of your head! . . . Oh, oh.

HUCK. Don't grieve.

MARY JANE. Must I go — — *now?*

HUCK. Quicker than that. Why did you reckon I wanted you to go at all?

MARY JANE. Why?

HUCK. Because you ain't one of these leatherface people. I don't want no better book than what your face is, to read what you feel. *Sighs.* Do you reckon you could kiss them tramps again, and never —

MARY JANE. There, there, don't. I'll go—I'll be glad to. *Gets up.*

HUCK. There's just one more thing. Those bags of money.

MARY JANE. Makes me feel pretty silly to think how they got it.

HUCK. They hain't got it.

MARY JANE. Why—who has?

HUCK. I wished I knowed, but I don't. I had it, because I stole it. And I stole it to give to you—and I hid it for you. But it warn't a good place . . . I'm awful sorry, Miss Mary Jane, I'm just as sorry as I can be, but I done the best I could, I did honest.

MARY JANE. I know you did. It wasn't your fault! . . . Where'd you hide it?

HUCK, *after painful pause.* I'd ruther not tell you, Miss Mary Jane. If you don't mind lettin' me off; but I'll write it out for you on a piece of paper, and you can read it along the road to Lothrop's. Do you reckon that'll do?

MARY JANE. Yes.

HUCK, *turns away, downstage, produces pencil stub and paper, and writes, painfully pronouncing each word.* I put it . . . in the coffin . . . I was in there . . . when you was cryin' there . . . away in the night . . . I was behind the door . . . And I was mighty . . . sorry for you, Miss Mary Jane. *He slowly folds the paper and hands it to her.*

MARY JANE, *puts it in her breast: overcome.* Good-bye . . . I'm goin to do everything just like you told me, and put out my candle for you to see . . . And—in case I don't ever see you again, I shan't ever forget you. And I'll think of you a many and many a time. *Sob* . . . And I'll pray for you too! *She runs out.*

HUCK, *choking.* Pray for me! I reckon if she knowed me she'd take a job more nearer her size. . . . You may say what you want to, but in my opinion, she has more sand in her than any girl I ever see. And when it comes to beauty—and goodness, too—she lays over them all — — — — I couldn't a-bear to tell her I won't ever see her no more. I couldn't ever say I'll *think* of her — a many and many a million times—goin' out tha door.

He comes slowly downstage, wiping his eye. The Piperville Curtain close behind him. In a moment HARELIP *and* SUSANNA *run brightly on, hatted and gloved for the trip, their shiny bags in their hands. When they see him the stop, appalled.*

HARE. My land! What hit *him? To* HUCK. Is she dyin'?

HUCK. No. . .

HARE. Then what's the matter with her?

HUCK. Nothin. *With sudden violence.* There's *nothin* wrong with Miss Mary Jane, and don't you forget it! Do you hear?

HARE. All *right,* all *right.* I—

HUCK, *recovering.* But, er . . . *Ominously.* What's the name of them people across the River —

SU. Proctors?

HUCK. That's the name, I most forgot it. Well, she's gone over there in dreadful hurry—one of em's bad off.

SU. Which one?

HUCK. I don't know—but I *think* it's—

SU. Sakes alive, I hope it ain't *Hanner?*

HUCK. I'm sorry to say it, but Hanner's the very one.

SU. My goodness, and she so well only last week! Is she took *bad?*

HUCK. It ain't no name for it. They set up with her all night, Miss Mary Jane says, and they don't think she'll last many hours.

SU. Only think of that, now! What's she *got?*

HUCK. Er — Mumps.

HARE. *Mumps!* Yer granny! They don't set up with people that's got mumps

HUCK. They don't, don't they? Well, they do with *these* mumps. It's new kind.

HARE. How's it a new kind?

HUCK. Mixed up with other things.

HARE. *What* other things?

HUCK. Well, measles and whooping cough and erysipelas and consumption, and yaller janders, and brain fever, and I don't know *what* all.

HARE. My land! And they call it the *mumps?*

HUCK. That's what Miss Mary Jane said.

HARE. Well what in the nation do they call it the mumps for?

HUCK. Because it *is* the mumps—that's what it starts with.

HARE, *in despair.* There ain't no sense to it! A body might just as well stump his toe and take pizen and fall down a well and break his neck—and somebody ask what killed him, and a numskull like you up and say he stumped his toe—. Is it ketching?

HUCK. *Ketching?* Is a *harrow* ketching, in the *dark?* We're lucky if the whole town ain't caught with it, and burnin up, right now.

SU. It's *awful, I* think! I'm goin straight to Uncle Harvey—

HUCK. Yes, do! Don't lose no time.

HARE. Well, why wouldn't you?

HUCK. What would he be obleeged to say? Why, he'll say, it's a great pity about the preachin thar in Sheffield, and the trip to England, but my niece has been exposed to the dreadful Pluribus Unum Mumps! It's my bounden duty to set down here and wait the three months it'll take to show on her, if she's got it. Yes, come to think, you better tell him!

HARE. And stay foolin around here when we could all be having good times in England? You talk like a Muggins. You do beat all for natural stupidness! *In stage whisper to* SUSANNA. There ain't no way, if it's a plague, but just to not tell anybody at *all.*

SU. But I reckon we better tell Uncle Harvey she's gone out a while? So he won't be uneasy about her. It's most time to go!

HUCK. She'll be back soon. When you see em, give em *her* love and kisses, too!

SU. All right!

HARE. Come on, let's clear out, and lay for our uncles, and give em the love and kisses, and the whole message!

> *They pick up their bags and hurry out.*

HUCK. And plan for them good times—thar in England. *He goes off, thoughtfully, the other way.*

SCENE FOUR

"Dig Him Up And See."

Piperville *Curtain opens in silence on the empty stage with the circle of chairs, and a table in the center. Very distant boat whistle. Enter* KING, DUKE, *and* LOT.

LOT. Thar she blows . . . way up by the bend. The River Queen! What does the Poet say? -- "and everything is set—for England."

KING. Yeh . . . Yeah. Mighty nigh time. I look for Mary Jane back any minute, now, to go. Me and William and the gals is all packed.

LOT. And do you aim to clean up *everything* before you go?

KING. Got to. Need to, bad. . . whar *is* everybody?

LOT. Watchin for *her*, I reckon. They like to see her when she rounds the bend. *Sighs.* Ain't much left, you know, to bring em — — nothin but a little old triflin lot in the graveyard . . . You might save time — — and go.

DUKE *begins shaking, goo-gooing and making signs to* KING.

LOT. Why — what's the matter with him?

KING. Nothin at *all*. Ague takes him that-a-way sometimes, impatient to be gone. But he don't mean nothin by it. *Whispers to* DUKE, *who freezes up.* Sell it, I tell you! I need what I kin git.

LOT *rings bell.*

The little procession moves off. Boat whistle a bit nearer. It is echoed off-stage by LAFE, *who calls "Hoo-hoo! Hoo-hoo!" Music. Enter the crowd. With* LAFE *as caller, they are making a sort of play-party game with bits of loot from the house, which they carry on their heads or coquettishly before their faces. The women have a spread fan, a baby's dress, a mirror, a daguerreotype in an oval frame: the men a stovepipe hat too big for the wearer, a stuffed bird, a grandfather clock, a tiny crib, an axe. They enter in step and in silence.*

LAFE.

Hoo-hoo! Hoo-hoo!

HANK.

The River Queen is leavin
The niggers is sold —

LAFE.

Swing, swing, scarecrow in the wind!
They swing with their fetishes.
The pretty bird is sold — honor your partner!
All bow.
The little crib is sold — honor your partner!
All bow.
The dainty fan is sold — etc., etc.
— And honor your corner if you ain't too late!
They bob their fetishes rapidly to right and left.

HANK.

Hahaha! Hahaha!
The axe is sold
The dainty fan is sold
The lovely ladies leavin and Peter cold—

Boat whistle much nearer. Enter LOT *carrying a small headstone on his shoulder, carved with a weeping willow a la 1830, and inscribed "HERE LIES—" He is followed by* KING, DUKE, *and* HUCK.

LOT, *as music stops.* Gentlemen, be seated.

They sit in the circle of chairs, in silence, their bits of loot before their faces. LOT, KING *and* DUKE *take their places by the table in the center, where* LOT *places the headstone.*

LOT, *knocking with his hammer.* Going! Going! Who'll start the biddin? — there's just one thing left; who'll get the little lot in the graveyard?
Silence.

KING, *piously eyeing heaven.* It's small, but it's a nest for the loved ones that's passed away. It'll last till judgment, folks.

LOT, *knocking.* Going, going—do I hear *gone*? What am I offered for the graveyard lot?

KING. Jest a quiet place for the dear ones' bones. Fer grannie's bones, er Mannie's bones when she's gone too. We're mortal, folks, all mortal, don't forgit that . . . .

Boat whistle much nearer. All the people's faces come out from behind their fetishes to listen. LAFE *and* HANK *sneak out.*

KING. Well. *Aside to* LOT. Where are *they* going?

LOT. See the River Queen. They can't wait.
HUCK starts to sneak off.

KING. Hey! HUCK *stops, caught in the act.* Did you want to sneak off?

HUCK. No, your majesty — er — Oh, no, Reverend Wilks, I jest —

KING. Set down.

HUCK *goes back to his place and sits. We become aware of chanting offstage, gradually make out a savage and rapidly growing rhythmic refrain:* "You pays your money and you takes your choice!"

KING, *scared.* What's that?

LOT. The River Queen is docked . . . . Something she dropped, must be . . .
Enter LAFE *and* HANK, *escorting the true* WILKS BROTHERS.

LOT *and* HANK, *delighted.* You pays your money and takes your choice!

LOT, *gloomily, in the sudden silence.* Who are you?

HARVEY. Er — this is William Wilks . . . WILLIAM *bows* . . . and I am his brother the Reverend Harvey Wilks.

MOB. AaaaaaH!

HARVEY. Haha—this *is* a surprise, I must confess! . . . And the trouble is, I can't prove anything. Your American manners are a little *strange* to us yet, and then we've had misfortunes, you know. My brother broke his arm; and then our luggage, by some *queer* mistake, was put off the River Queen last night instead of here today. So we haven't our luggage, you see, and we cawn't get the papers we need. . . . *Looks about in gentle bewilderment at the tense faces.* Er — well! If one of you gentlemen will be good enough to show us to a hotel, we shall simply have to wait until we can prove our identity. But we are who we say we are, of *course.*

KING, *loud hollow laugh.* Haha. Broke his arm—*very* likely, *ain't* it? and very convenient, too, for a fraud that's got to make signs and ain't learned how. Lost their baggage! That's *mighty* good — — and mighty ingenious — under the *circumstances!* Hahaha.

MOB, *coldly.* Hahaha.

BEN, *contemplating his stuffed bird.* I don't care for you, no more, . . . There! *Slams it into the wings.*

MOB, *pitching the loot offstage*. There! There! THERE! THERE!
They whirl back and eye the KING, *as the* DOCTOR *enters and stands with folded arms*.

LAFE. Say! I jest thought! *To* KING. Looky here. If you're Harvey Wilks, when'd you come to town?

KING. The day before the funeral, friend.

LAFE. But what *time* o' day?

KING. In the evenin'—'bout an hour er two before sundown.

LAFE. How'd you come?

KING. On the River Queen—comin' *down* the river.

LAFE, *yelling in triumph*. Then how'd you come to be up at the Pint in the *mornin?*

KING, *slowly*. I warn't up at the Pint in the mornin.

LAFE. It's a lie! Hines *saw* him up thar—him and the boy!
                 All turn to HUCK *who gets to his feet*.

HUCK. I — er —

LAFE. Set down! *To crowd*. Preacher be hanged! He's a fraud and a liar!

LOT. Hold on there, Lafe. I *saw* em git off the River Queen. Bout sundown, like he says.

LAFE. EH? Well I'll be —

Crowd starts whispering: "What's going on? Do you believe him? Do you reckon Lafe's seein double?" *etc., etc.*

DOC, *advancing into the arena with raised hand*. Ladies! Gentlemen!

MOB. The *Doc!*
                 DOC *bows; they quiet*.

DOC. It *is* mighty queer, as this one says. But there's one thing sure: if we ain't sold already, we stand to be. I think I mentioned something of the kind before. SOLD: do you hear?

BEN. Sold, eh?

MOB, *yelling*. Sold! Sold!

DOC. Gentlemen! Ladies! *They quiet*. I reckon we've *paid* our money — and jest see what we got for it — double value! We've got it, and we'll find out *somethin* before we're through — open the package an see what's *inside*. eh?

MOB. HOORAY!

DOC. But we'll go slow, this time, till we really *know*, eh? We'll hold em right here if it takes all night — an affront the two couples! I reckon it's our right and our bounden duty! Fetch lights to see by! Everybody stay to judge.

MOB. Hey! Hey! Hey! We'll judge! *"Chase Music" starts*. You pays your money and takes your choice! You pays your money and you takes your choice!

The two couples are placed in the center with ironic formality, while the chant goes on.

DOC. Now . . . *Silence*. Now *if* these two are frauds — if they are — we need to know whar that gold is, don't we? To pertect it for the pore orphans. Now if they *ain't* frauds they won't object to sendin fer it and lettin us keep it till they prove they're all right — ain't that so?

MOB. Send for it! Send for it!

KING. Gentlemen, I wish the money *was* thar, for I ain't got no disposition to throw anything in the way of a fair open out and out investigation of this miserable business: but, alas, the money *ain't* thar; you k'n send and see, if you want to.

DOC. Where *is* it then?

KING. Well, when my niece give it to me to keep for her I took and hid it inside the straw tick o' my bed, not wishin to bank it for the few days I'd be here. The niggers stole it the very next mornin before the funeral; and when I sold em I hadn't missed the money yet, so they got clean away with it. My servant here k'n tell you 'bout it, gentlemen.

MOB, *turning to* HUCK. Mmmmm?

DOC. Are *you* English, too?

HUCK. Yes.

DOC. Haha! Set down!

Laughter which dies out quickly.

LAFE, *to* DOC. Well? . . . Go it, Doc! Go it Preacher!

Titters.

DOC. I'll corner him. All in good time — he can't git away. *Draws forth pencil and paper, which he extends to* HARVEY. You jest write me a line if you please and sign your name.

HARVEY writes. DOC *offers the paper to the* KING.

LAFE. What's he doin?

WIDOW. Shhh! You'll see.

DOC. Now *you.*

KING, *pale and dry-lipped, slowly and with difficulty writes. Also the* DUKE. DOC *pulls the packet of letters out of his pocket and compares the three specimens.*

DOC. You see, these here is old letters that Harvey Wilks writ to pore Peter. Found em this mornin, and thought they might come in handy! . . . Now here's some writin by *these* two . . . *He looks again.* Well, well!

MOB. What *is* it?

DOC. Anybody can see *they* didn't write em. *Pointing to* KING *and* DUKE. But here's *his* writin . . . *Pointing to* HARVEY . . . and anybody can tell *he* didn't write em either! . . . Well. I thought I had it clinched, I thought I —

HARVEY. Pardon me. My hand is illegible, as you can see. My brother writes all my letters *for* me. It's *his* hand you have there in those letters, not mine, of *course.*

DOC. Well, then, why don't *he* write a line?

HARVEY. But he *cawn't* you know! He broke his arm, you see.

DOC. EH? I'll be jiggered! I'd clean forgot! *Titters in the crowd.* But wait! *Whirls on the* KING. One thing's proved! *They* didn't write em! *They* ain't Wilkses — whatever they *are.*

KING, *in terror.* Tain't no fair test! Haha! My brother William's the cussedest joker in the world! — why he ain't *tried* to write. I see, the minute he put pen to paper, he was figurin to play one of his jokes! Haha! Why, he—

LAFE, *yelling.* You pays your money and you takes your choice!

MOB, *savagely.* You pays your money and you takes your choice! **Pays your money and takes your choice!**

HARVEY, *holding up his hand.* Er . . . *Sudden silence. Pardon* me. Perhaps I can help you. Is there anyone here who helped to lay out my brother—who helped to lay out the late Peter Wilks — — fer burying?

LOT *and* BEN *advance.*

LOT *and* BEN, *sepulchral.* Yes. We done it. We're here.

HARVEY. Oh — good. So you know the — er — *body.* Now will this gentle-man please tell us all what was tattooed on the breast?

KING, *after tense pause.* Mf. It's a *very* tough question, ain't it? Yes, sir, I kin tell you what's tattooed on his breast. It's jest a small, thin, blue arrow—that's what it is. And if you don't look clost, you can't see it on account o' the hair. *Now* what do you say — Heh?

HARVEY. There. You've heard what he said. Now what *did* you see on the breast?

BEN *and* LOT. No — Such — Mark.

HARVEY. Quite. But what you did see was a small, dim P and a B — an initial he dropped many years ago — and a W — separated by dashes, so . . . *Makes sign in the air.* Didn't you? Eh?

BEN *and* LOT. NO. We — Never — Seed — Any — Mark — at — *All.*

BEN. And there ain't much *hair.*

MOB, *with rhythmic stamping and "Chase Music."* The whole *bilin'* of em's frauds! Duck em! Drown em! Ride em on a rail! Duck em! Drown em! Ride em on a rail!

LOT. Gentlemen, *Gentlemen! Sudden silence.* And Ladies. There's just one way to know, just one way to be sure: I knowed you'd come to it — you all do, in the end. Back to the graveyard; and the clay. You'll have to dig him up again . . . you'll have to dig him up to *see!*

MOB. Hooray! Hooray!

DOC. Hold on! Don't lose em in the dark! Collar all four men and the boy!

MOB. Hooray! *They sweep forward.* Dig him up! Dig him up and see! Dig him up! Dig him up and see!

"Chase Music." The scene washes out in confusion, the act curtain closes quickly; and almost at once the race to the graveyard passes across down-stage: LOT *nimbly ushering the* KING *and the* DUKE *with ceremonious gestures;* LAFE *and* HANK *with dangerous tools like rakes and axes; the real* WILKSES, *hustled and bewildered;* HUCK; *and the rest of the men and women nearly running to keep up. The racket diminishes slightly as the procession disap-pears, the act curtain opens on a dark and empty stage. The procession crosses again about stage center, faster than before — and no sooner has it disappeared than we see it again far upstage against the river backdrop, sprinting now in single file, the women with their petticoats hiked up, the men with long houndlike strides. The racket fades out quickly... Moment of silence,* MARY JANE *enters, hurrying, pausing, listening, with a lantern.*

MARY JANE. I'm back— I came just like you told me to . . . Am I too late? . . . I had so much to say, and now there's nothing to say it with, for ever and ever, but only just this little light!

Music. MARY JANE *sings.*

Away in the night, hope he sees my light!
Mighty dark. Oh, oh. Hope he sees my light
Away in the night.

Listens, distant thunder.

Crying in the dark, I raised up Cain!
Too late. Oh. Oh, I raised up Cain
Crying in the dark.

Starts off.

Hiding in the dark, hope he sees my candle!
Mighty little. Oh. Oh. Hope he sees my candle
Hiding in the dark.

She disappears. Thunder. The stage, nearly dark, is filling with people. They are in the graveyard, hunting and groping for the right grave. Distant cries: "Fetch spa-ades! He-ey! Fetch la-nterns!" *We hear the clink of stones, and muttering:* "Now whar do you s'pose — This it? — Can't see a blame thing — That you?" *And then when they find it;* "Here! — This way! Here!" *Grunts, sounds of digging.* "All together now — heave! Uh. Heave! Uh. Prize him out." *Screams of nails priod out of wood. Sudden tableau as* LOT *raises a lantern aloft: the diggers around the ripped-open grave.*

LOT. Gentlemen: The *clay.*

BEN. By the livin jingo, here's the gold on his chest!

DOC. So *they're* the ones that done it!

LAFE, *diving for the money.* Here — — gimme that!

MOB. No, me, *me!* Ouch! etc.

The lantern is doused, and we hear struggling, yelling and "Chase Music" in the dark. In a moment the KING *and the* DUKE *are seen downstage, sneaking quickly away.*

DOC, *in the dark.* After them frauds! Git em! Git em!

MOB. Git em! Git em!

They stream off at the double quick. "Chase Music." The voice of the mob sounds like the yelping of hounds about to catch a quarry. It fades quickly. Silence.

HUCK, *upstage, dimly seen.* They're on the river road . . . .They took the wrong turnin; cornered *now* . . . Ugh . . . they forgot *me. He comes downstage, trotting, stopping, panting a little; searching; peers out into the audience.* Our house . . . I aimed my eye for *it. In deep disappointment.* No light there. All dark . . . *His face is gradually and slightly lighted. There!* In Mary Jane's window . . . *Sobs.* I'll never see *her* no more, in this *world!* Good-bye! Good-bye, Mary Jane! Good-bye! . . . She was the best girl I ever see, and had the most sand.

He turns away and runs off. Music starts, at first faintly: it is the savage, strongly rhythmic beat of the last appearance of the crowd: a dance-pantomime which marks the ceremonious end of the KING *and the* DUKE: *The men on one side and the women on the other enter with a rocking shuffle, like an Indian dance, facing upstage, backs to audience.*

Then the black-and-white starchy clothes of the KING *and the* DUKE *are brought in far upstage, as though walking in the air. They are draped over*

very tall pitchforks, and keep time to the music.
DOC, *low.* Go it, boys.
The fluttering coats and shirts of the KING *and the* DUKE *are swooped to the ground in the center, and the mob leaps in for the "kill." Alternate tearing of the clothes and violent whirling in couples.*

Then the crowd grows tired, and the music more sentimental, with echoes of earlier tunes. The whole dance moves downstage, and the act curtain closes behind it. The women, one after the other, are swung high in the air with a flutter of skirts and petticoats.

Silence. The people file out, drunk, exhausted, like a beast after a kill.
JIM, *sings softly offstage.*

Oh, de night-time Ribber
Mighty still
A-floatin de sinner
Whar it will —
A-floatin de sinner
Whar it will.

SCENE FIVE

"O Lawd, Ise a-listenin' "
The Piperville Curtain opens on the raft, the river back-drop, the night lighting, and HUCK *and* JIM *alone, as in Act One, Scene One.*
JIM, *after a short pause.* Den how did you git away, honey?
HUCK. Hank dropped my arm when they found the gold, and I lit out and shinnied for the road in the dark.
JIM. Dat sho was mighty lucky . . . I wonder what happened to de po ole King, an de **Duke.**
HUCK. I don't want to think of it.
JIM. Does you *know?*
HUCK. Them people rushed on past me with torches, and an awful whoopin' and yellin', while I was hidin' in the dark. I see they had 'em a-straddle of a rail. They didn't look like nothin' in the world that's human. I reckon the mob had its good times with *them,* when it caught 'em . . . . That's why I ain't feelin' so brash.
JIM. Why, Huck, *you* ain't to blame.
HUCK, *after a short pause.* And I've got to tell you, Jim: those two warn't no Kings at all nor fallen grandeur, nor furrin heirs — — but just poor pitiful rascals wantin' what they couldn't have, and didn't deserve . . . like you an me.
JIM, *softly.* Sho 'nuff, Huck?
HUCK. But I reckon it's all right now. I reckon we won't see 'em no more, now . . . . Nor Mary Jane, for ever and ever.
JIM. Mary Jane?

HUCK. But I saw her light. Like she promised. In her window, to let me know. Just like she said . . . Mary Jane.

JIM, *sings very low.*

O Lawd Ise a-listenin'
Oh! Lawd!
O Lawd Ise a-listenin'
To find my way.

CURTAIN

The Dark Tower

A RADIO PARABLE PLAY

BY LOUIS MACNEICE

*Reprinted from THE DARK TOWER AND OTHER BROADCAST PLAYS
by permission of Faber and Faber Ltd.*

CHARACTERS

SERGEANT-TRUMPETER
GAVIN
ROLAND
MOTHER
TUTOR
SYLVIE
BLIND PETER
SOAK
STEWARD
NEAERA
SHIP'S OFFICER
PRIEST
ROLAND'S FATHER
PARROT
RAVEN
CLOCK VOICE

OPENING ANNOUNCEMENT

*The Dark Tower. The programme which follows is a parable play—suggested
by Robert Browning's poem "Childe Roland to the Dark Tower came." The
theme is the ancient but ever-green theme of the Quest—the dedicated ad
venture; the manner of presentation is that of a dream—but a dream that i
full of meaning. Browning's poem ends with a challenge blown on a trumpet*
                            And yet
   Dauntless the slughorn to my lips I set
   And blew. "Childe Roland to the Dark Tower came."
*Note well the words "And yet." Roland did not have to—he did not wish
to—and yet in the end he came to: The Dark Tower.*

A trumpet plays through the Challenge Call.

SERGEANT-TRUMPETER.
There now, that's the challege. And mark this:
Always hold the note at the end.

GAVIN.
Yes, Sergeant-Trumpeter, yes.

ROLAND, *as a boy.*
Why need Gavin hold the note at the end?

SERGEANT-TRUMPETER.
Ach, ye're too young to know. It's all tradition.

ROLAND.
What's tradition, Sergeant-Trumpeter?

GAVIN.
Ask Mother that one. *With a half-laugh.* She knows.

SERGEANT-TRUMPETER.
Aye, *she* knows.
But run along, sonny. Leave your brother to practise.
          The trumpet begins—but breaks off.

SERGEANT-TRUMPETER.
No. Again.
          The trumpet re-begins—breaks off.

SERGEANT-TRUMPETER.
Again.
          The trumpet re-begins and is sustained.

SERGEANT-TRUMPETER.
That's it now. But hold that last note—hold it!
          On the long last note the trumpet fades into the distance.

ROLAND.
Mother! What's tradition?

MOTHER.
Hand me that album. No—the black one.

ROLAND.
Not the locked one!

MOTHER.
Yes, the locked one. I have the key.
Now, Roland, sit here by me on the sofa.
We'll look at them backwards.

ROLAND.
Why must we look at them backwards?
MOTHER.
Because then you may recognise—
Now! You know who this is?
ROLAND.
Why, that's my brother Michael.
And here's my brother Henry!
Michael and Henry and Denis and Roger and John!
> *He speaks with the bright callousness of children.*
Do you keep this album locked because they're dead?
MOTHER.
No . . . not exactly.
Now—can you guess who this is?
ROLAND.
That's someone I saw in a dream once.
MOTHER.
It must have been in a dream.
He left this house three months before you were born.
ROLAND.
Is it . . . is it my father?
MOTHER.
Yes. And this is your grandfather. And this is *his* father—
For the time being you needn't look at the rest;
This book goes back through seven long generations
As far as George the founder of the family.
ROLAND.
And did they all die the same way?
MOTHER.
They did, Roland. And now I've answered your question.
ROLAND, *already forgetting.*
What question, Mother?
> *The trumpet call is heard in the distance.*
ROLAND.
Ah, there's Gavin practising.
He's got it right at last.
> *The Call ends and* GAVIN *appears.*
GAVIN, *excited.*
Mother! I know the challenge. When can I leave?
Tomorrow?
MOTHER.
Why not today, Gavin?
GAVIN.
Today! But I haven't yet checked my equipment;
I mean—for such a long journey I—
MOTHER.
You will travel light, my son.

GAVIN.

Well, yes . . . of course . . . today then.

ROLAND.

Where are you going, Gavin?

GAVIN.

Why, surely you know; I'm—

MOTHER.

Hsh!

ROLAND.

I know where he's going. Across the sea like Michael.

GAVIN.

That's right, Roland. Across the big, bad sea.

Like Michael and Henry and Denis and Roger and John.

And after that through the Forest.

And after that through the Desert—

ROLAND.

What's the Desert made of?

GAVIN.

Well . . . I've never been there.

Some deserts are made of sand and some are made of grit but—

MOTHER, *as if to herself.*

This one is made of doubts and dried-up hopes.

ROLAND, *still bright.*

And what do you find at the other end of the desert?

GAVIN.

Well, I . . . well . . .

MOTHER.

You can tell him.

GAVIN.

I find the Dark Tower.

The Dark Tower theme gives a musical transition to the schoolroom.

TUTOR.

Now, Master Roland, as this is our first day of lessons

I trust I shall find you as willing a pupil

As your six brothers before you.

ROLAND.

Did you like teaching my brothers?

TUTOR.

Like it? It was an honour.

It was teaching to some purpose.

ROLAND.

When's my brother Gavin coming back?

TUTOR.

What!

ROLAND.

Gavin. When's he coming back?

TUTOR.

Roland! . . .

I see I must start from the beginning.

I thought your mother'd have told you but maybe being the youngest—

ROLAND.

What would my mother have told me?

TUTOR.

You ask when your brother Gavin is coming back?

You must get this straight from the start:

Your family never come back.

ROLAND *begins to interrupt.*

TUTOR.

Now, now, now, don't let me scare you.

Sit down on that stool and I'll try to explain.

Now, Roland—

I said that to teach your brothers was an honour.

Before your mother engaged me to tutor John

I was an usher in a great city,

I taught two dozen lads in a class—

The sons of careerists—salesmen, middlemen, half-men,

Governed by greed and caution; it was my job

To teach them enough—and only enough—

To fit them for making money. Means to a means.

But with your family it is a means to an end.

ROLAND, *naïvely puzzled.*

My family don't make money?

TUTOR.

They make history.

ROLAND.

And what do you mean by an end?

TUTOR.

I mean—surely they told you?

I mean: the Dark Tower.

ROLAND.

Will *I* ever go to the Dark Tower?

TUTOR.

Of course you will. That is why I am here.

ROLAND, *gaily.*

Oh well! That's different!

TUTOR.

It is.

ROLAND.

And that means I'll fight the Dragon?

TUTOR.

Yes—but let me tell you:

We call it the Dragon for short, it is a nameless force

Hard to define—for no one who has seen it,

Apart from those who have seen its handiwork,

Has returned to give an account of it.
All that we know is there is something there
Which makes the Dark Tower dark and is the source
Of evil through the world. It is immortal
But men must try to kill it—and keep on trying
So long as we would be human.

ROLAND.

What would happen
If we just let it alone?

TUTOR.

Well . . . some of us would live longer; all of us
Would lead a degraded life, for the Dragon would be supreme
Over our minds as well as our bodies, Gavin—
And Michael and Henry and Denis and Roger and John—
Might still be here—perhaps your father too,
He would be seventy-five—but mark this well:
They would not be themselves. Do you understand?

ROLAND.

I'm not quite sure, I . . .

TUTOR.

You are still small. We'll talk of the Dragon later.
Now come to the blackboard and we'll try some Latin.
You see this sentence?

ROLAND.

Per ardúa . . .

TUTOR.

Per ardua ad astra.

ROLAND.

What does it mean?

TUTOR.

It does not go very well in a modern language.
We had a word "honour"—but it is obsolete.
Try the word "duty"; and there's another word—
"Necessity."

ROLAND.

Necessity! That's a bit hard to spell.

TUTOR.

You'll have to spell it, I fear. Repeat this after me:
N—

ROLAND.

N—

TUTOR.

E—

ROLAND.

E—

As they spell it through, their voices dwindle away and a tolling bell grows up out of the distance.

SERGEANT-TRUMPETER.

    Ah God, there's the bell for Gavin.

    He had the greatest power to his lungs of the lot of them.

    And now he's another name in the roll of honour

    Where Michael's is still new gold. Five years it is—

    Or would it be more like six—since we tolled for Michael?

    Bells and trumpets, trumpets and bells,

    I'll have to be learning the young one next;

    Then he'll be away too and my lady will have no more.

MOTHER, *coldly; she has come up behind him.*

    No more children, Sergeant-Trumpeter?

SERGEANT-TRUMPETER.

    Ach, I beg your pardon. I didn't see you.

MOTHER.

    No matter. But know this:

    I have one more child to bear.

    No, I'm not mad; you needn't stare at me, Sergeant.

    This is a child of stone.

SERGEANT-TRUMPETER.

    A child of . . . ?

MOTHER.

    Stone. To be born on my death-bed.

    No matter. I'm speaking in metaphor.

SERGEANT-TRUMPETER, *relieved to change the subject.*

    That's all right then. How's young Roland

    Making out at his lessons?

MOTHER.

    I don't know. Roland lacks concentration; he's not

      like my other sons,

    He's almost flippant, he's always asking questions—

SERGEANT-TRUMPETER.

    Ach, he's young yet.

MOTHER.

    Gavin was his age once.

    So were Michael and Henry and Denis and Roger and John.

    They never forgot what they learnt. And they asked no questions.

SERGEANT-TRUMPETER.

    Ah well—by the time that Roland comes to me

    When he's had his fill of theory and is all set for action,

    In another half dozen years when he comes to learn the trumpet call—

MOTHER.

    Hsh, don't talk of it now.

                As if to herself.

    Let one bell toll at a time.

The bell recedes into nothing, covering a passage of years. ROLAND *is now grown up.*

TUTOR.

    So ends our course on ethics. Thank you, Roland;
    After all these years our syllabus is concluded.
    You have a brain; what remains to be tried is your will.
    Remember our point today: the sensitive man
    Is the more exposed to seduction. In six years
    I have come to know you; you have a warm heart—
    It is perhaps too warm for a man with your commission,
    Therefore be careful. Keep to your one resolve,
    Your single code of conduct, listen to no one
    Who doubts your values—and above all, Roland,
    Never fall in love— That is not for you.
    If ever a hint of love should enter your heart,
    You must arise and go . . . . That's it: Go!
    Yes, Roland my son. Go quickly.
          His last words fade slightly and SYLVIE's *voice fades in.*

SYLVIE.

    But why must you go so quickly? Now that the sun's come out.

ROLAND.

    I have my lesson to learn.

SYLVIE.

    You're always learning lessons!
    I'll begin to think you prefer your books to me.

ROLAND.

    Oh, but Sylvie, this isn't books any more.

SYLVIE.

    Not books? Then—

ROLAND.

    I'm learning to play the trumpet.

SYLVIE, *irritated.*

    Whatever for? Roland, you make me laugh.
    Is this another idea of your mother's?
    I needn't ask. What's all this leading to?

ROLAND, *quietly.*

    I could tell you, darling. But not today.
    Today is a thing in itself—apart from the future.
    Whatever follows, I will remember this tree
    With this dazzle of sun and shadow—and I will remember
    The mayflies jigging above us in the delight
    Of the dying instant—and I'll remember *you*
    With the bronze lights in your hair.

SYLVIE.

    Yes, darling; but why so sad?
    There will be other trees and—

ROLAND.

    Each tree is itself, each moment is itself,
    Inviolable gifts of time . . . of God—
    But you cannot take them with you.

SYLVIE.

Take them with you where?

ROLAND.

Kiss me, Sylvie. I'm keeping my teacher waiting.
                    The Challenge Call is played through once.

SERGEANT-TRUMPETER.

Nicely blown! Nicely blown!
You've graduated, my lad.
But remember—when I'm not here—hold the note at the end.

ROLAND, *a shade bitter.*

You mean when *I'm* not here.

SERGEANT-TRUMPETER.

Aye, you're right. But you are my last pupil,
I'll be shutting up shop, I want you to do me credit.
When you've crossed the sea and the desert and come
    to the place itself
I want you to do me credit when you unsling that horn.

ROLAND.

I hope I will.
                    He pauses; then slightly embarrassed.

ROLAND.

Sergeant?

SERGEANT-TRUMPETER.

Eh?

ROLAND.

Do you believe in all this?

SERGEANT-TRUMPETER.

All what?

ROLAND.

Do you think that there really is any dragon to fight?

SERGEANT-TRUMPETER.

What are you saying! What was it killed Gavin?
And Michael and Henry and Denis and Roger and John,
And your father himself and his father before him and
    all of them back to George!

ROLAND.

I don't know but . . . nobody's *seen* this dragon.

SERGEANT-TRUMPETER.

Seen him? They've seen what he's done!
Have you never talked to Blind Peter?
I thought not. Cooped up here in the castle—
Inside this big black ring of smothering yew-trees—
You never mixed with the folk.
But before you leave—if you want a reason for leaving—
I recommend that you pay a call on Peter.
And his house is low; mind your head as you enter.
                    Another verbal transition.

BLIND PETER, *old and broken*.
> That's right, sir; mind your head as you enter.
> Now take that chair, it's the only one with springs,
> I saved it from my hey-day. Well now, sir,
> It's kind of you to visit me. I can tell
> By your voice alone that you're your father's son;
> Your handshake's not so strong though.

ROLAND.
> Why, was my father—

BLIND PETER.
> He had a grip of iron.
> And what's more, sir, he had a will of iron.
> And what's still more again, he had a conscience—
> Which is something we all need. *I* should know!

ROLAND.
> Why?

BLIND PETER.
> Why what?

ROLAND.
> Why do you sound so sad when you talk about having a conscience?

BLIND PETER.
> Because his conscience is something a man can lose.
> It's cold in here, I'll make a long story short.
> Fifty years ago when I had my sight—
> But the Dragon was loose at the time—
> I had a job and a wife and a new-born child
> And I believed in God. Until one day—
> I told you the Dragon was loose at the time,
> No one had challenged him lately; so he came out
>   from his den—
> What some people call the Tower—and creeping
>   around
> He got to our part of the world; nobody saw him of course,
> There was just like a kind of a bad smell in the air
> And everything went sour; people's mouths and eyes
> Changed their look overnight—and the government changed too—
> And as for me I woke up feeling different
> And when I looked in the mirror that first morning
> The mirror said "Informer"!

ROLAND, *startled*.
> Informer?

BLIND PETER.
> Yes, sir. My new rôle.
> They passed a pack of laws forbidding this and that
> And anyone breaking 'em—the penalty was death.
> I grew quite rich sending men to their death.
> The last I sent was my wife's father.

ROLAND.

But . . . but did you believe in these laws?

BLIND PETER.

Believe? Aha! Did I believe in anything?
God had gone round the corner. I was acquiring riches.
But to make a long story short—
When they hanged my wife's father my wife took poison,
So I was left with the child. Then the child took ill—
Scared me stiff—so I sent for all the doctors,
I could afford 'em then—but they couldn't discover
Anything wrong in its body, it was more as if its soul
Was set on quitting—and indeed why not?
To be a human being, people agree, is difficult.

ROLAND.

Then the child . . . ?

BLIND PETER.

Quit.
Yes; she quit—but slowly.
I watched it happen. That's why now I'm blind.

ROLAND.

Why? You don't mean you yourself—

BLIND PETER.

When you've seen certain things, you don't want to see no more.
Tell me, sir. Are people's faces nowadays
As ugly as they were? You know what I mean: evil?

ROLAND.

No, not most of them. *Some,* I suppose—

BLIND PETER.

Those ones belong to the Dragon.

ROLAND, *exasperated.*

Why put the blame of everything on the Dragon?
Men have free choice, haven't they?
Free choice of good or evil—

BLIND PETER.

That's just it—
And the evil choice is the Dragon!
But I needn't explain it to you, sir; *you've* made up your mind,
You're like your father—one of the dedicated
Whose life is a quest, whose death is a victory.
Yes! God bless you! *You've* made up your mind!

ROLAND, *slowly and contemplatively.*

But have I, Peter? Have I?

Verbal transition.

SYLVIE.

Have you, Roland dearest? Really made up your mind?

ROLAND, *without expression.*

I go away today.

SYLVIE.
  That's no answer.
  You go away because they tell you to.
  Because your mother's brought you up on nothing
  But out of date beliefs and mock heroics.
  It's easy enough for her—

ROLAND, *indignantly.*
  Easy for her?
  Who's given her flesh and blood—and I'm the seventh son!

SYLVIE.
  I've heard all that. They call it sacrifice
  But each new death is a stone in a necklace to her.
  Your mother, Roland, is mad.

ROLAND, *with quiet conviction.*
  The world is mad.

SYLVIE.
  Not all of it, my love. Those who have power
  Are mad enough but there *are* people, Roland,
  Who keep themselves to themselves or rather to each other,
  Living a sane and gentle life in a forest nook or a hill pocket,
  Perpetuating their kind and their kindness, keeping
  Their hands clean and their eyes keen, at one with
  Themselves, each other and nature. I had thought
  That you and I perhaps—

ROLAND.
                    There is no perhaps
  In my tradition, Sylvie.

SYLVIE.
  You mean in your family's.
  Isn't it time you saw that you were different?
  You're no knight errant, Roland.

ROLAND.
  No, I'm not.
  But there is a word "Necessity"—

SYLVIE.
  Necessity? You mean your mother's orders.

ROLAND, *controlled.*
  Not quite. But apart from that,
  I saw a man today—they call him Blind Peter—

SYLVIE.
  Leave the blind to mislead the blind. That Peter
  Is where he is because of his own weakness;
  You can't help him, Roland.

ROLAND.
  Maybe not—
                 With sudden insight.
  But maybe I can do something to prevent
  A recurrence of Blind Peters.

SYLVIE.
Imagination!
ROLAND.
Imagination? . . . That things can be bettered?
That action can be worth-while? That there are ends
Which, even if not reached, are worth approaching?
Imagination? Yes, I wish I had it—
I have a little— You should support that little
And not support my doubts.

A drum-roll is heard.

ROLAND.
Listen; there is the drum.
They are waiting for me at the gate.
Sylvie, I—
SYLVIE.
Kiss me at least.

Pause, while the drum changes rhythm.

ROLAND.
I shall never—
SYLVIE.
See me again?
You will, Roland, you will.
I know you. You will set out but you won't go on,
Your common sense will triumph, you'll come back.
And your love for me will triumph and in the end—
ROLAND.
This is the end. Good-bye.

The drum swells and ends on a peak. This is the Scene of Departure.

TUTOR.
To you, Roland, my last message:
For seven years I have been your tutor.
You have worked hard on the whole but whether really
You have grasped the point of it all remains to be seen.
A man lives on a sliding staircase—
Sliding downwards, remember; to be a man
He has to climb against it, keeping level
Or even ascending slightly; he will not reach
The top—if there is a top—and when he dies
He will slump and go down regardless. All the same
While he lives he must climb. Remember that.
And I thank you for your attention. Good-bye, Roland.
SERGEANT-TRUMPETER.
To you, Roland, my last message:
You are off now on the Quest like your brothers before you
To take a slap at the Evil that never dies.
Well, here's this trumpet; sling it around your waist
And keep it bright and clean till the time comes
When you have to sound the challenge—the first and the last time—

And I trust you will do your old instructor credit
And put the fear of God—or of Man—into that Dragon.
That's all now. God bless you. But remember—
Hold that note at the end.

MOTHER.

To you, Roland, my last message:
Here is a ring with a blood-red stone. So long as
This stone retains its colour, it means that I
Retain my purpose in sending you on the Quest.
I put it now on your finger.

ROLAND.

Mother! It burns.

MOTHER.

That is the heat in the stone. So long as the stone is red
The ring will burn and that small circle of fire
Around your little finger will be also
The circle of my will around your mind.
I gave a ring like this to your father, Roland,
And to John and Roger and Denis and Henry and Michael
And to Gavin the last before you. My will was around and behind them.
Should ever you doubt or waver, look at this ring—
And feel it burn—and go on.

ROLAND.

Mother! Before I go—

MOTHER.

No more words. Go!
Turn your face to the sea. *Raising her voice.* Open the gates there!
Aside.
The March of Departure, Sergeant.
Let my son go out—my last. And make the music gay!
The March begins at full volume, then gradually dwindles as ROLAND *and
the listener move away. By the time the music has vanished* ROLAND *has
reached the Port, where he addresses a stranger.*

ROLAND.

Forgive me stopping you, sir—

SOAK, *old, alcoholic, leering.*

Forgive you? Certainly not.
I'm on my way to the Tavern.

ROLAND.

I'm on my way to the quays. Is it this turning or next?

SOAK.

Any turning you like. Look down these stinking streets—
There's sea at the end of each of 'em.
Yes, young man, but what's at the end of the sea?
Never believe what they said when you booked your passage.

ROLAND.

But I haven't booked it yet.

SOAK.

Not booked your passage yet! Why, then there's no need to hurry.
You come with me to the Tavern; it's only a step.

ROLAND.

I cannot spare a step.

SOAK.

All right, all right;
If you won't come to the Tavern, the Tavern must come to you.
Ho there, music!

The orchestra strikes up raggedly—continuing while he speaks.

SOAK.

That's the idea. Music does wonders, young man.
Music can build a palace, let alone a pub.
Come on, you masons of the Muses, swing it,
Fling me up four walls. Now, now, don't drop your tempo;
Easy with those hods. All right; four walls.
Now benches—tables—No! No doors or windows.
What drunk wants daylight? But you've left out the bar.
Come on—Cellos! Percussion! All of you! A bar!
That's right. Dismiss!

The music ends.

SOAK.

Barmaid.

BARMAID.

Yes, sir?

SOAK.

Give us whatever you have and make it triple.

ROLAND.

Just a small one for me, please.

SOAK.

Oh don't be so objective. One would think,
Looking at your long face, that there's a war on.

ROLAND.

But—

SOAK.

There is no war on—and you have no face.
Drink up. Don't be objective.

ROLAND.

What in the name of—

BARMAID.

Look, dearie; don't mind *him*.
He always talks like that. You take my tip;
You're new here and this town is a sea-port,
The tone is rather . . . . You go somewhere inland.

ROLAND.

But how can I?
I have to go to sea.

BARMAID, *seriously*.
> The sea out there leads nowhere.

SOAK.
> Come, sweetheart, the same again.

BARMAID.
> Nowhere, I've warned you. *In a whisper*. As for our friend here,
> Don't stay too long in his company.

SOAK.
> What's that? Don't stay too long in my what?

BARMAID.
> Company was the word.

SOAK.
> Company? I have none. Why, how could I?
> There's never anyone around where I am.
> I exist for myself and all the rest is projection.
> Come on, projection, drink! Dance on your strings and drink!

BARMAID.
> Oblige him, dearie, oblige him.

SOAK.
> There! My projection drinks.
> I wrote this farce before I was born, you know—
> This puppet play. In my mother's womb, dear boy—
> I have never abdicated the life of the womb.
> Watch, Mabel: my new puppet drinks again—
> A pretty boy but I've given him no more lines.
> Have I, young man?

> Pause.

> You see, he cannot speak.
> All he can do henceforward is to drink—
> Look! A pull on the wire—the elbow lifts.
> Give him the same again.

BARMAID.
> Well . . .

SOAK.
> There is no well about it. Except the well
> That has no bottom and that fills the world.
> Triplets, I said. Where are those damned musicians?
> Buck up, you puppets! Play!
> *The orchestra strikes up a lullaby, continued behind his speech.*

SOAK, *sleepily*.
> Good. Serenade me now till I fall asleep
> And all the notes are one—and all the sounds are silence.
> Unity, Mabel, unity is my motto.
> The end of drink is a whole without any parts—
> A great black sponge of night that fills the world
> And when you squeeze it, Mabel, it drips inwards.
> D'you want me to squeeze it? Right. Piano there.
> Piano—I must sleep. Didn't you hear me?

Piano, puppets. All right, pianissimo.
Nissimo . . . nissimo . . . issimo . . . .
> *The music ends and only his snoring is heard.*

ROLAND.

A puppet? . . . A projection? . . . How he lies!
And yet I've sometimes thought the same, you know—
The same but the other way round.
There is no evidence for anything
Except my own existence—he says his.
But he's wrong anyway—look at him snoring there.
If I were something existing in his mind
How could I go on now that he's asleep?

SOAK, *muffled.*

Because I'm dreaming you.

ROLAND.

Dreaming?

BARMAID.

Yes, sir.
He does have curious dreams.

SOAK.

Yes, and the curious thing about my dreams
Is that they always have an unhappy ending
For all except the dreamer. Thus at the moment
You'd never guess, young man, what rôle I've cast you for—

ROLAND.

What the—

BARMAID.

Never mind, dear.
Tomorrow he'll wake up.

ROLAND.

Tomorrow *he'll* wake up?
And I—Shall I wake up? Perhaps to find
That this whole Quest is a dream. Perhaps I'm still at home
In my bed by the window looking across the valley
Between the yew-trees to where Sylvie lives
Not among yews but apples—

He is interrupted by a terrific voice crashing in on the "Bar" from the outer world.

STENTOR.

All Aboard!

ROLAND.

What's that?

STENTOR.

All Aboard!

SOAK.

You'd never guess
What happens in my dream . . . .

STENTOR.

> All Aboard! All Aboard!
>
> Come along there, young man—unless you want to be left.
>
> All Aboard for the Further Side of the Sea,
>
> For the Dead End of the World and the Bourne of No Return!
>
> *The noise of a crowd materialises, increasing.*

STENTOR.

> All Aboard, ladies and gents, knaves and fools, babes and sucklings,
>
> Philistines, pharisees, parasites, pimps,
>
> Nymphos and dipsos—All Aboard!
>
> Lost souls and broken bodies; make it snappy.
>
> That's right, folks. Mind your feet on the gangway.

Through the racket of gadarening passengers is heard the mechanical voice of the TICKET COLLECTOR.

TICKET COLLECTOR.

> Ticket? Thank you . . . Ticket? Thank you . . .
>
> Ticket? Thank you . . . Ticket? Thank you . . .
>
> *The crowd noises fade out;* ROLAND *is now below decks.*

STEWARD, *with an "off-straight" accent.*

> This way, sir. Let me show you your stateroom.
>
> Hot and cold and a blue light over the bed.
>
> Ring once for a drink, twice for an aspirin.
>
> Now if you want anything else—a manicure, for example—

ROLAND.

> No, steward. A sleeping draught.

STEWARD, *archly.*

> Sir! In the morning?

ROLAND.

> Morning be damned. My head aches.

STEWARD.

> Drinking last night, sir?

ROLAND.

> Thinking.

STEWARD, *rattling it off.*

> Thinking? That's too bad, sir.
>
> But you'll soon get over that, sir.
>
> In this ship nobody thinks, sir.
>
> Why should they? They're at sea, sir . . .
>
> And if your brain's at sea, sir—

ROLAND, *angrily.*

> Listen! I want a sleeping draught.
>
> How many times do I have to ring for that?

STEWARD, *unperturbed.*

> As many times as you like, sir.
>
> *If* you can keep awake, sir.
>
> > Pimpishly.
>
> But talking of sleeping draughts, sir,
>
> Do you hear that lady playing the fiddle?

ROLAND.

Fiddle? No. I don't.

STEWARD.

Ah, that's because she plays it in her head.
But she's a very nice lady, sir.
Her name, sir, is Neaera.

ROLAND.

Why should I care what her name is?
I tell you, steward—

STEWARD.

Of course if you'd rather play tombola—

ROLAND.

Tombola?

STEWARD, *throwing it away*.

Game of chance, sir. They call out numbers.
Kills the time, sir. Rather like life, sir.
You can buy your tickets now in the lounge.
The ship's started, you know, sir.

ROLAND.

Oh, so the ship's started?

>   *Worried*.

But I can't hear the engines.

STEWARD.

Can't you, sir? I was right then.

ROLAND.

Right? What do you mean?

STEWARD.

I thought so the moment I saw you.
You don't, sir; of course you don't.

ROLAND.

Don't what, damn you? Don't what?

STEWARD.

You don't know where you're going, sir.

The ship's engines are heard on the orchestra; from them emerges the
chatter of the lounge with the banal laughter of tombola players.

OFFICER.

Clickety-click; sixty-six . . . .
Kelly's Eye: Number One . . .
And we—

CROWD, *raggedly*.

Shake the Bag!

>   *The orchestral engines give place to a solo violin.*

NEAERA, *to herself, velvety*.

. . . Andantino . . . rallentando . . . adagio—

>   *Her violin-playing breaks off.*

NEAERA, *foreign accent*.

Mon Dieu! You startled me.

ROLAND.

    I'm sorry, I—

NEAERA, *cooingly.*

    Do sit down. So you're going Nowhere too?

ROLAND.

    On the contrary, Madam—

NEAERA.

    Call me Neaera.

ROLAND.

    But—

NEAERA.

    And I'll call you Roland.

ROLAND.

    How do you know my name?

NEAERA.

    A little bird told me. A swan, if you want to know;
He sang your name and he died.
That's right, sit down. I've seen your dossier too.

ROLAND.

    Seen my—

NEAERA.

    Oh yes, chéri. In the Captain's cabin.

ROLAND.

    But how can I have a dossier? I've done nothing.

NEAERA.

    That's just it. It's dull.
But the future part amuses me.
Oh yes, my dear, this dossier includes the future—
And you don't come out of it well.

ROLAND.

    What do you mean?

NEAERA.

    You never believed in this Quest of yours, you see—
The Dark Tower—the Dragon—all this blague.
That's why you were so easy to seduce
In the idle days at sea—the days that are just beginning.

*Her violin begins again, then gives way to the lounge chatter, covering
a passage of time.*

OFFICER.

    Key of the Door: Twenty-One!
Eleventh Hour: Eleven!
Ten Commandments: Nine!
Kelly's Eye: Number One!
And we—

CROWD.

    Shake the Bag!

The violin re-emerges.

NEAERA.
> . . . Lento . . . accelerando . . . presto . . . calando . . . morendo. . . .

The violin fades away: it is meant to have established an affaire between
ROLAND *and* NEAERA.

STEWARD, *slyly.*
> Well, sir? So the lady is still practising.
> Golden days, sir, golden days.
> At sea, sir, have you noticed
> One doesn't notice time?
> You probably feel you just came on board yesterday
> And yet you got your sea-legs weeks ago, sir.

ROLAND.
> Sea-legs? Why, this trip has been so calm
> I've never felt—

STEWARD.
> That's right, sir; never feel.
> There's nothing in life but profit and pleasure.
> Allegro assai—some people plump for pleasure
> But I now fancy the profit—
>> *Receiving a tip.*
> Ah thank you, sir, thank you.
> The sea today in the sun, sir, looks like what shall I say, sir?

ROLAND.
> The sea today? A dance of golden sovereigns.

NEAERA.
> The sea today is adagios of doves.

ROLAND.
> The sea today is gulls and dolphins.

NEAERA.
> The sea today is noughts and crosses.

OFFICER, *cutting in rapidly.*
> And we—

CROWD.
> Shake the Bag!

NEAERA.
> The sea today, Roland, is crystal.

ROLAND.
> The sea today Neaera, is timeless.

NEAERA.
> The sea today is drums and fifes.

ROLAND.
> The sea today is broken bottles.

NEAERA.
> The sea today is snakes and ladders.

OFFICER, *as before.*
> Especially snakes!

CROWD.
> Especially snakes!

NEAERA, *wheedling.*

Roland, what's that ring? I've never seen one like it.

ROLAND.

There is no other ring like it.

NEAERA.

A strange ring for a man . . .
My colour, you know—that red . . .
Why do you twitch your finger?

ROLAND.

Because it burns.

NEAERA.

It burns?
Like tingling ears perhaps? Someone is thinking of you.

ROLAND, *startled—and suddenly depressed.*

What? . . . I hope not.

Changing the subject.

Come, darling, let's have a drink.

OFFICER.

And we—

CROWD.

Shake the Bag!

ROLAND.

The sea today is drunken marble.

NEAERA.

The sea today is silver stallions.

ROLAND.

The sea today is—Tell me, steward:
Where's all this floating seaweed come from?

STEWARD.

I imagine, sir—forgive me mentioning it—
That we are approaching land.

ROLAND.

Land?

STEWARD.

Yes, sir—but *you* won't be landing of course.
The best people never land, sir.

ROLAND.

No? . . . *To himself, fatalistically.* I suppose not.

NEAERA's violin is heard again.

NEAERA, *to herself.*

. . . piu sonoro . . . con forza . . . accelerando . . . crescendo . . . .
*The orchestra is added for a final crashing chord and at once we hear the
hubbub of a crowd.*

STENTOR.

Anyone more for the shore? Anyone more for the shore?
Line up there on the forward deck
All what wants to chance their neck!
Anyone more for the shore?

TICKET COLLECTOR.

This way: thank you— This way: thank you—
This way: thank you— This way: thank you.

STENTOR.

Anyone more? Hurry up please!
But remember this: Once you're off
You can't come back not ever on board.
We leave at once. At once!

TICKET COLLECTOR.

This way: thank you— This way: thank you—
This way: thank you— This way: thank you.

1ST PASSENGER, *cockney.*

Here, here, who're you shoving? What's the blinkin' hurry?

HIS WIFE.

That's right.

1ST PASSENGER.

Some people seem very keen to land in the future.
Can't use their eyes—if you ask me!

HIS WIFE.

That's right. Look at them vicious rocks.

1ST PASSENGER.

And that tumble-down shack what thinks it's a Customs House.

HIS WIFE.

And them horrible mountains behind it.

2ND PASSENGER, *northern.*

You'd think this country was uninhabited.

TICKET COLLECTOR.

This way: thank you— This way: thank you— *With finality.* This
way: thank *you!*

Wearily.

O.K., sir. That's the lot.

STENTOR.

Gangway up! Gangway up!
Clear away there. Mind your heads!

NEAERA.

What are you staring at, Roland?
Come away, chéri; the show's over.
There goes the gangway; we're moving out now.
What *are* you staring at, darling?

ROLAND, *to himself.*

Was that . . . was that . . . I couldn't see in the face of the sun but—
Steward, you've sharp eyes.
Did you see over there on the quay, sitting on a rusty bollard—

STEWARD.

Hsh, sir, Neaera will hear you.
Yes, sir; a very nice piece.
She was looking at you, sir, too—staring in fact, one might say.
Seems to be staring still—but what's she doing now?

Climbing up on the bollard?
Good Lord, sir, that's bad form; she's making gestures.

SYLVIE, *distant cry.*

Roland! . . . Roland! . . .

ROLAND.

Sylvie!
I knew it. Out of my way there!

STENTOR.

Here, here, here! Stop him!
Man gone mad there! Don't let him jump!

General commotion.

NEAERA.

Roland! Come back!

A loud splash from the orchestra.

STENTOR.

Man overboard! Man overboard!

The CROWD *reacts excitedly.*

STENTOR.

Lifebuoy! Where's the lifebuoy?

VOICE.

Garn! This here ship don't carry no lifebuoys.
Nor he won't need one. Look! He's climbing up on the quay.

The orchestral engines start up again.

OFFICER, *triumphantly.*

And we—

CROWD.

Shake the Bag!

NEAERA, *now revealing her hardness.*

Well, James . . . That's that.

STEWARD.

Yes, madam.

NEAERA.

You can drop the madam now.

STEWARD.

Yes, Neaera—my sweetie-pie.

NEAERA, *matter-of-fact.*

That's more like it, James, my great big he-man.
Come to my cabin now; we'll count the takings.

The fading engines take the liner to sea; ROLAND *is left on the Shore, with* SYLVIE *sobbing.*

ROLAND, *dead-pan.*

There she goes now.

SYLVIE, *echoing him.*

There she goes now . . .

Then bursting out.

Roland, you are a hypocrite!

ROLAND, *quietly—but ashamed.*

    No, Sylvie; merely a sleep-walker.

    Ugh! *He shivers.*

SYLVIE, *calm again.*

    The sea must have been cold. Come, let's walk.

ROLAND.

    How did you get here, Sylvie?

SYLVIE, *a shade bitter.*

    I followed you—but not on a luxury liner.

    Mine was a cargo boat, its limit was seven knots.

ROLAND.

    And yet you got here first.

    And now I suppose you regret it.

    Are you going to leave me, Sylvie?

SYLVIE.

    How can I? We're marooned here.

    This is a desolate land. *With forced control.* I suggest we keep together.

ROLAND.

    You have the gift of forgiveness.

SYLVIE.

    I have the gift of common sense.

    As you're bound to be seduced from your so-called Quest,

    In future, Roland, leave the seducing to me.

    Or can't I, perhaps, compete with your ladies of pleasure?

ROLAND.

    Pleasure? That was not pleasure.

SYLVIE.

    It was. But it was not happiness.

ROLAND.

    And *you* offer me happiness?

SYLVIE.

    You doubt that I have it to offer?

ROLAND.

    No, I don't doubt that. But my tutor always said

    Happiness cannot be taken as a present.

SYLVIE.

    Forget your tutor. This is a foreign land

    Where no one will interfere with us.

ROLAND.

    No one? No *man* perhaps.

SYLVIE.

    What do you mean by that?

ROLAND.

    Look round you, Sylvie. See the deserted port,

    The ruined shacks, the slag-heaps covered with lichen

    And behind it all the frown and fear of the forest.

    This is the Dragon's demesne.

SYLVIE.
Roland, how childish you are.

ROLAND.
You think so? Look at this notice
That flaps here on the hoarding—
And this one and this one and this one.

SYLVIE, *reading.*
"Wanted for Murder" . . . "Wanted for Murder" . . . "Wanted"—

ROLAND.
You're reading the words wrong. Not "for," Sylvie; "to"!

SYLVIE.
"Wanted to Murder." You're right.
But what does it mean?

ROLAND.
It means we are on a soil where murder pays.

SYLVIE.
It pays in many places.

ROLAND.
Yes, but here
The paymaster is the government—and pay-day
Is every day of the week.
The Dragon's doing, I tell you.

SYLVIE.
Well, if it is, *you* cannot cure it.
At the best you can cure yourself—
                              Tentatively.
And that only through love.

ROLAND.
Love?

SYLVIE, *stronger.*
Through me, Roland, through me.
                              Pause.

ROLAND, *quietly, as if solving a problem.*
Yes, I think you're right.
                    Then with sudden decisiveness.
Sylvie, take this ring; I cannot wear it now,
I have failed this ring—but this ring will not fail you.

SYLVIE.
You mean . . . ?

ROLAND.
Yes. Let me put it on your finger.

SYLVIE.
Not yet, Roland. That must be done in a church.

ROLAND.
And where can we find a church round here?

SYLVIE, *half abstracted.*
What a strange colour. Like the blood of a child.

ROLAND.

    I repeat! Where can we find a church or a chapel here?
          The TOUT *pops up. He speaks in broken English.*

TOUT.

    'Scusa. Lady and gentleman want guide to chapel?

ROLAND.

    God! Where did this come from?

TOUT.

    Me? Me come from sewer.
    Me accredited guide—very good, very funny.
    Lady and gentleman see chapel today?

ROLAND.

    Where is this chapel of yours?

TOUT.

    Chapel not mine, chapel belong to God.
    Me take you there up this road, see.
    Me tell you history, very much history, cheap.
          A distant bell is heard, which continues as they speak.

TOUT.

    That chapel bell, tee-hee!
    Ting-a-ling for the wedding!

ROLAND.

    What wedding?

TOUT.

    Me not know. No, sir, nobody know.
    Happy pair not come yet.

SYLVIE.

    Roland, this is a sign.
    Tell him to show us the way.

TOUT.

    Me show you the way sure,
    Beautiful lady put best foot first.
    Chapel up there in forest.

ROLAND.

    In the forest?

TOUT.

    Sure, boss, Chapel old.
    Chapel in forest before forest grew.
    But needs repairs now bad.
    Haunted too—tee-hee!

ROLAND.

    Haunted!

TOUT.

    Sure, boss.
    Plenty ghosts—tu-whit, tu-whoo.
    Me need bonus for them ghosts.

ROLAND.

You'll have your bonus. Only get us there quick.

Sylvie, we will exorcise these ghosts.

You know how, my dearest?

SYLVIE, *heart-felt.*

I know how.

*The bell continues but is gradually submerged by orchestral chapel music.
The latter swells to a definite close, leaving* ROLAND *and* SYLVIE *in the
Haunted Chapel. The voices echo in the emptiness.*

PRIEST, *old and tired but kindly.*

You have the ring? Good.

Before I complete this ceremony making you man and wife

I must deliver a warning.

The original sin is doubt.

And in these days of contempt for the individual

It is also the topical sin.

So if either of you has doubts of the holiness of marriage

Or if either of you has doubts of the other

And can conceive a time when he or she

Will think again and wish this thing undone,

Now is your time to speak.

Pause.

Good. So you have no doubts. There is one other formality.

Although there is no congregation present,

Although apart from ourselves and a few sparrows and field-mice

This chapel is now empty, I must still put the question:

If anyone here know just cause or impediment—

He is interrupted by voices with a strange acoustic.

BLIND PETER'S VOICE.

I do!

GAVIN'S VOICE.

I do!

FATHER'S VOICE.

I do!

BLIND PETER'S VOICE.

This young man who's come to you to get married

Promised me when he left, a week before I died,

As he would avenge my blindness and bring it about

How no one should go the way I went in future.

Well, has he done it? No, and he'll never do it—

Not if you splice him up to that poor simple girl

Who only dreams how he and she will be happy.

GAVIN'S VOICE.

No, Roland, my brother; Blind Peter is right.

Forget your dreams of a home. You can never be happy

If you forsake the Quest. And if you could—

Happiness is not all. You must go on—

Turn your back on this chapel, go on through the forest,
Alone, always alone, and then across the desert,
And at the other end of that desert—

FATHER'S VOICE, *very deep.*

You will find what I found, Roland.

ROLAND.

You?

FATHER'S VOICE.

You should know my voice though you never heard it.
Though you had not seen me, you knew my portrait.

ROLAND.

My father?

FATHER'S VOICE.

I am still waiting to be your father.
While you malinger, you are no son of mine.

ROLAND, *shattered.*

Sylvie . . . .

SYLVIE.

I know what you want . . . Your ring.
        She tries to retain self-control in making her renunciation.
There . . . Back on your finger.
Look how it glows in this darkness.

ROLAND, *bitterly.*

Glows? It will burn me up.

SYLVIE.

Roland, before we part—

PRIEST.

This chapel is now closed. I am sorry.
Good-bye, my daughter; your way lies back,
Back by the road you came over the hopeless sea,
Back to your little house and your apple orchard
And there must you marry one of your own kind
And spray the trees in spring and raise the ladders in autumn
And spread the shining crop on the spare-room floor and—

ROLAND.

Sylvie, before we part—

PRIEST.

This chapel is now closed. I am sorry.
Good-bye, my son; your way lies forward,
Forward through the gibbering guile of the forest,
Forward through the silent doubt of the desert.
And here let me warn you: if in the forest
You hear any voices call from the trees,
Pay no attention, Roland, pay no attention . . . .

*His voice fades as forest music grows up; out of its tangle come the voices
of the* BIRDS, *harsh and mechanical, speaking in a heavily stressed sing-song
rhythm.*

PARROT.
> Pretty Polly! Pretty Polly!
> Who's this coming now!

RAVEN.
> Caw-caw! Caw-caw!
> Who's a-walkin' in *my* forest?

PARROT.
> Pretty Polly! The leaves have fallen.

RAVEN.
> Caw-caw! He's walking late.

PARROT.
> Pretty Polly! He's looking pale.

RAVEN.
> Caw-caw! His bones will be paler.

PARROT.
> Pretty Polly! Here he comes.

RAVEN.
> Caw-caw! Greet him!

PARROT, *sneeringly.*
> Where are you going, Roland, so fast?

RAVEN.
> Roland, running away from your past?

BOTH.
> You can't do *that!* You can't do *that!*

PARROT.
> Still on the road? Still on the Quest?

RAVEN.
> None achieve it but the best.

BOTH.
> You're not the sort. You're not the sort.

PARROT.
> Why not stop, my dear young man?

RAVEN.
> Let heroes die as heroes can.

BOTH.
> *You* must *live!* *You* must *live!*
>> *The forest music swells up as* ROLAND *passes.*

PARROT.
> Pretty Polly! He's passed us by.

RAVEN.
> Caw-caw! The devil take him.

PARROT.
> Pretty Polly! The devil will.

The forest music gives place to desert music and ROLAND *is heard soliloquising.*

ROLAND, *very tired.*
> Oh this desert!
> The forest was bad enough but this beats all.
> When my tutor described it to me, it sounded strange

But now I am here, with the grit of it filling my shoes,
I find that the worst thing about it is this:
The desert is something familiar.
And with no end—no end.

> *The music ends. A mechanical* VOICE *creeps in.*

CLOCK VOICE.

Tick Tock, Tick Tock,
Sand and grit, bones and waste,
A million hours—all the same,
A million minutes—each an hour,
And nothing stops for nothing starts
But the hands move, the dead hands move,
The desert is the only clock—
Tick Tock, Tick Tock,
Tick Tock, Tick Tock. . . .

The CLOCK VOICE *recedes but can just be heard ticking as* ROLAND *speaks, with the Desert registering again musically.*

ROLAND.

Flat—No shape—No colour—Only here and there
A mirage of the past—something I've met before—
Figures arising from dust, repeating themselves,
Telling me things that I have no wish to remember.
Mirage . . . mirage . . . mirage . . . .

> *The music ends and the* CLOCK *comes near again.*

CLOCK VOICE.

Tick Tock, Tick Tock,
Tick Tock, Tick Tock. . . .

> *Continuing in the background as the first mirage is heard.*

SOAK.

A pretty boy—but I've given him no more lines.
He'd never guess what happens in my dream.
Look—a pull on the wire, his feet move forward.
Left Right, Left Right . . . .

He synchronises with the CLOCK VOICE *as it comes again into the foreground.*

CLOCK VOICE *and* SOAK.

Tick Tock, etc.
Left Right, etc.

> *They withdraw to the background as the second mirage appears.*

STEWARD.

Golden days, sir, golden days.
In the desert, sir, have you noticed
One doesn't notice time?
But I thought so the moment I saw you:
You don't know where you're going.
Golden days, golden days . . . .

He synchronises with the CLOCK VOICE *and* SOAK—*the same procedure.*

CLOCK VOICE, SOAK, *and* STEWARD.
>Tick Tock, etc.
>Left Right, etc.
>Golden days, etc.

NEAERA.
>. . . adagio . . . rallentando . . .
>This dossier includes your future—
>You don't come out of it well.
>But kiss me, Roland, kiss me.
>Kiss me, kiss me . . . .

Synchronises.

CLOCK VOICE, SOAK, STEWARD, *and* NEAERA.
>Tick Tock, etc.
>Left Right, etc.
>Golden days, etc.
>Kiss me, etc.

SYLVIE.
>But why must you go so quickly?
>Now that the sun's come out.
>You, Roland—you're no knight errant.
>Your love for me will triumph, you'll come back,
>Then you and I, you and I . . . .

Synchronises.

CLOCK VOICE, SOAK, STEWARD, NEAERA, *and* SYLVIE.
>Tick Tock, etc.
>Left Right, etc.
>Golden days, etc.
>Kiss me, etc.
>You and I, etc.

The five voices swell in the foreground, driving as it were at the camera, till
ROLAND *can bear it no longer.*

ROLAND, *screaming.*
>NO!

The voices break off as if cut with a knife.

ROLAND.
>Shapes of dust and fancy! Unreal voices!
>But where is the voice that launched me on my road?
>Where is the shape the first that I remember?
>Why doesn't *she* appear—even in fancy?
>It is the least she could—Mother, where are you?
>Yes, you; I'm calling you—my mother who sent me forth—
>It was all your doing. But for you
>I who had no beliefs of my own,
>I who had no will of my own,
>Should not be here today pursuing
>A dark tower that is only dark
>Because it does not exist. And Mother!
>It is only your will that drives me still

As signified in the blood-red stone
I wear on my finger under my glove
That burns me like a living weal.
                    Suddenly puzzled.
. . . Burns me? . . . Burns me? . . . It, always has—
But have I gone numb? I can feel nothing.
Off with this glove! I *can't* believe that—
                    A chord from the orchestra.

ROLAND.

The ring! The ring!
The colour is gone; the blood has gone out of it.
But that must mean . . . that means . . . .

MOTHER'S VOICE, *in a different acoustic, whispering.*

It means, my son, that I want you back.

ROLAND.

And the Quest then?

MOTHER.

Lapses.
On my deathbed I have changed my mind;
I am bearing now a child of stone.
He can go on the Quest. But you, Roland—come back!
        A pause while ROLAND *takes in the implications.*

ROLAND.

The ring . . . is always right.
Recall! Reprieve! A thousand years of sunshine!
And the apples will be in bloom round Sylvie's house.
Was that my mother's voice? Look at the ring.
It is as pale as death, there is no more breach of duty,
Her will is not behind me. Breach of duty?
If she is dying, *there* is the breach of duty—
Not to be there. Mother, you sent me out
And I went out. Now that you call me back
I will come back! The desert take this ring—
It serves no further purpose!
            An orchestral clink as he throws away the ring.

ROLAND, *startled.*

What was that?
It must have struck something hard. That's the first
Sound I've heard in the desert. Where did I throw that ring?
A stone? But a carved stone! Looks like a milestone.
As if the desert had any use for milestones!
            With a hysterical half-laugh.
How many miles to Babylon? Let's see now;
These letters are choked with sand, "To Those . . .
    To Those . . . "
            He deciphers the inscription, reading it aloud slowly.
"To Those Who Did Not Go Back—
Whose Bones being Nowhere, their signature is for All Men—

Who went to their Death of their Own Free Will
Bequeathing Free Will to Others."
         The BIRD VOICES *cut in, in a different acoustic, jeering.*

PARROT.
   Pretty Polly! A tall story!

RAVEN.
   Caw-caw! And not so new!

PARROT.
   Pretty Polly! Unknown warriors!

RAVEN.
   Caw-caw! Nobody cares!

PARROT.
   "Who went to their death!"—Pretty Polly!

RAVEN.
   "Of their own free will!"—Caw-caw!

ROLAND.
   Of their own free will? It wasn't like that with me.
   It was my mother pushed me to this point
   And now she pulls me back. Let's see this ring—
   Where's it fallen? Hm. Yes, there's no mistake,
   Red no longer: my mother wants me back
   And indeed it is high time; this desert has no end
   Nor even any contour, the blank horizon
   Retreats and yet retreats; without either rise or fall
   Repeats, retreats, defeats; there is no sign of a tower—
   You could see a tower for miles; there is not even a knoll,
   Flatness is all—and nothing. Own free will?
              He has been speaking quietly but now bursts out.
   As if I Roland had ever . . . . Tutors, trumpeters, women,
   Old soaks and crooked stewards, everyone I have met
   Has played his music on me. Own free will!
   Three words not one of which I understand!
   All right, Mother dear, I'm coming.
                            Pause.
   Now . . . Where are my footsteps? Better follow them back.
   Back to the forest and through it and so to the shore of the sea.
   Are these my footsteps? But how small they look!
   Well, you're a small man, Roland—Better admit it—
   You'll be still smaller now . . . But are these my footsteps?
   They are so near together—and I thought
   I was walking with great strides! O Roland, Roland,
   You thought yourself a hero—and you walked
   With little steps like that! Now you must watch
   These niggling footprints all your return journey
   To underline your shame. What's shame to me
   Who never had free will? . . . "their own free will
   Bequeathing free will to others." Others indeed!
   I begin to think my drunken friend was right

In his subjective tavern; there are no others
Apart from the projections of my mind
And, once that mind is empty, man's a desert.

Losing his temper.

Others! Who are these others? Where can I find 'em?

CHILD'S VOICE, *out of the blue.*

Nowhere, Roland. Nowhere.

ROLAND.

There! What did I say? There *are* no—

CHILD'S VOICE.

You will never find us if you go forward—
For you will be dead before we are born.
You will never find us if you go back—
For you will have killed us in the womb.

ROLAND.

What! So I'm an infanticide now?

CHILD'S VOICE.

Not yet. But if you go back . . .

ROLAND.

Who said I was going back?

CHILD'S VOICE.

I thought you had made up your mind.

ROLAND.

I never make up my mind!
Didn't I say that my mother—Look, I'll leave it to chance;
Chance is as good an arbiter as any.
Watch me, you unborn children. See this tiny cactus?
I will strip it leaf by leaf—let that decide—
This Year, Next Year, Eena-Meena—*you* know the game,
       you unborn children.
Now.

*He counts in regular time, but with growing tension, as he picks off the
leaves.*

Forward—back; forward—back; forward—back—forward;
Back—forward; back—forward; back—forward—back;
Forward—back; forward—back; forward—back—forward;
Back—forward; back—forward; back—forward—BACK.
There! The voice of chance. The oracle of the cactus.
Back! Back! That's what the cactus says.
But *I'm* . . .

He holds the suspense, then with decision.

. . . going forward, children!
Did you think that I'd let a cactus dictate to me?
Mother, don't pull on the string; you must die alone.
Forgive me, dear, but—I tell you I'm going forward.
Forward, Roland . . . into the empty desert,
Where all is flat and colourless and silent.

He pauses; the orchestra creeps in with a heart-beat rhythm.

Silent? . . . Then what's this?
Something new! A *sound*! But a sound of what?
Don't say that it's my heart! Why, Roland you poor fool,
Who would think you had one? You must be afraid;
It is fear reveals the heart.

Heart-beat louder.

ROLAND.

Aha, you piece of clockwork—
Trying to have your little say while you can!
Before your wheels run down here in the empty desert.

Sudden chord; the heart-beat continues.

Empty? . . . Where have those mountains come from?
Closing round in a ring. Hump-backed horrors
That want to be in at the death. And where's the horizon?
A moment ago this was level. What's the game?
A confidence trick? A trap! I am cooped in.
A circle of ugly cliffs—a lobster-pot of rock!
Silence, my stupid heart! This looks like . . . looks like what?
This looks like the great circus in Ancient Rome,
Only there is no audience—and no lions.

Suddenly noticing.

No audience?

Chord; heart-beat behind—and steadily increasing.

No audience! Why, that's Gavin on top of that peak!
And Michael and Denis and Henry and Roger and John!
And men that I've never seen—in outlandish clothes,
Some of them even in armour. And there's Blind Peter—
With sight in his eyes, for he's pointing—
And my father too—I remember him from the album—
And my tutor—he must be dead—looking graver than ever
And—well to the front of course—my dear old Sergeant-Trumpeter.

Figure in the music; the succeeding voices, other than ROLAND's *own, sound
as if coming from somewhere far-off and above.*

SERGEANT-TRUMPETER.

Roland, hold the note at the end.

GAVIN.

Be ready, old boy. This is it!

BLIND PETER.

Strike a good blow to avenge Blind Peter.

FATHER.

Your heritage, my son. You were born to fight and—

ROLAND.

Fight? Fight whom? This circus has no lions.

TUTOR.

No lions, Roland? Have you forgotten your lessons?
I never mentioned lions; it was a dragon—
And only that for lack of a better name.

ROLAND.

> Yes, yes, dragon of course—but you told me, my good tutor,
> The Dragon would not appear until I came to the Tower
> And until I had blown my blast—Well, there is no tower!

GAVIN.

> That fooled *me*, Roland my brother.

FATHER.

> Look over there, Roland my son.

ROLAND.

> Where? . . . Oh *that* little thing?
> Like a wart coming out of the ground!

FATHER.

> It's growing, Roland, it's growing.

TUTOR.

> You should recognise it from my lectures.

BLIND PETER.

> That's the joker all right.

> *Figure in the music.*

GAVIN.

> The tower! The Dark Tower!

SERGEANT-TRUMPETER.

> Quick now, my lad. Unsling your trumpet.

ROLAND.

> But—

FATHER.

> It's growing, my son; waste no time.

ROLAND.

> It's growing; yes, it's growing.

CHILD'S VOICE.

> Growing; Ooh! Look at it.
> Strike a good blow for us unborn children.

MOTHER, *closer than the rest.*

> And strike a blow for all dead mothers.

GAVIN.

> Jump to it, Roland.

FATHER.

> Waste no time.

SERGEANT-TRUMPETER.

> Remember that challenge call.
> Blow it the way I taught you.

ROLAND, *beginning quiet but resolute and building.*

> Yes, dear friends, I will blow it the way you taught me.
> I Roland, the black sheep, the unbeliever—
> Who never did anything of his own free will—
> Will do this now to bequeath free will to others.

> *Full out.*

> Ahoy there, tower, Dark Tower, you're getting big,
> Your shadow is cold upon me. What of that?

And you, you Dragon or whatever you are
Who make men beasts, come out—here is a man;
Come out and do your worst.

The heart-beat, having reached its crescendo, ends clean.

ROLAND, *restrained, in the sudden silence.*

Wrist be steady
As I raise the trumpet so—now fill my lungs—

The Challenge Call rings out; the SERGEANT-TRUMPETER *speaks as the last long note is reached.*

SERGEANT-TRUMPETER.

Good lad, Roland. Hold that note at the end.

The trumpet holds it, enriched and endorsed by the orchestra. They come to a full close and that is THE END.

Galileo
BY BERTOLT BRECHT
Translated by CHARLES LAUGHTON

Sketch by Robert Davison of his stage setting for Galileo.

It is my opinion that the earth is very noble and admirable by reason of so many and so different alterations and generations which are incessantly made therein.

—GALILEO GALILEI

CHARACTERS

GALILEO GALILEI
ANDREA SARTI *(two actors: boy and man)*
MRS. SARTI
LUDOVICO MARSILI
PRIULI, THE CURATOR
SAGREDO, *Galileo's friend*
VIRGINIA GALILEI
TWO SENATORS
MATTI, *an iron founder*
PHILOSOPHER *(later, Rector of the University)*
ELDERLY LADY
YOUNG LADY
FEDERZONI, *assistant to Galileo*
MATHEMATICIAN
LORD CHAMBERLAIN
FAT PRELATE
TWO SCHOLARS
TWO MONKS
INFURIATED MONK
OLD CARDINAL
ATTENDANT MONK
CHRISTOPHER CLAVIUS
LITTLE MONK
TWO SECRETARIES
CARDINAL BELLARMIN
CARDINAL BARBERINI
CARDINAL INQUISITOR
YOUNG GIRL
HER FRIEND
GIUSEPPE
STREET SINGER
HIS WIFE
REVELLER
A LOUD VOICE
INFORMER
TOWN CRIER
OFFICIAL
PEASANT
CUSTOMS OFFICER
BOY
SENATORS, OFFICIALS, PROFESSORS, LADIES, GUESTS, CHILDREN

There are two wordless roles: The DOGE *in Scene Two and* PRINCE COSMO DI MEDICI *in Scene Four. The ballad of Scene Nine is filled out by a pantomime: among the individuals in the pantomimic crowd are three extras (including the "*KING OF HUNGARY*"),* COBBLER'S BOY, THREE CHILDREN, PEASANT WOMAN, MONK, RICH COUPLE, DWARF, BEGGAR, *and* GIRL.

SCENE ONE

In the year sixteen hundred and nine
Science' light began to shine.
At Padua City, in a modest house
Galileo Galilei set out to prove
The sun is still, the earth is on the move.

GALILEO'S *scantily furnished study. Morning.* GALILEO *is washing himself.*
A bare-footed boy, ANDREA, *son of his housekeeper,* MRS. SARTI, *enters with*
a big astronomical model.

GALILEO. Where did you get that thing?

ANDREA. The coachman brought it.

GALILEO. Who sent it?

ANDREA. It said "From the Court of Naples" on the box.

GALILEO. I don't want their stupid presents. Illuminated manuscripts, a
statue of Hercules the size of an elephant—they never send money.

ANDREA. But isn't this an astronomical instrument, Mr. Galilei?

GALILEO. That is an antique too. An expensive toy.

ANDREA. What's it for?

The drawings for Galileo *were made by John Hubley to help Brecht and*
Laughton prepare their production. Fifteen of the original twenty-seven are
reproduced here by permission of T. Edward Hambleton.

GALILEO. It's a map of the sky according to the wise men of ancient Greece. Bosh! We'll try and sell it to the university. They still teach it there.

ANDREA. How does it work, Mr. Galilei?

GALILEO. It's complicated.

ANDREA. I think I could understand it.

GALILEO, *interested.* Maybe. Let's begin at the beginning. Description!

ANDREA. There are metal rings, a lot of them.

GALILEO. How many?

ANDREA. Eight.

GALILEO. Correct. And?

ANDREA. There are words painted on the bands.

GALILEO. What words?

ANDREA. The names of stars.

GALILEO. Such as?

ANDREA. Here is a band with the sun on it and on the inside band is the moon.

GALILEO. Those metal bands represent crystal globes, eight of them.

ANDREA. Crystal?

GALILEO. Like huge soap bubbles one inside the other and the stars are supposed to be tacked on to them. Spin the band with the sun on it. ANDREA *does.* You see the fixed ball in the middle?

ANDREA. Yes.

GALILEO. That's the earth. For two thousand years man has chosen to believe that the sun and all the host of stars revolve about him. Well. The Pope, the Cardinals, the princes, the scholars, captains, merchants, housewives, have pictured themselves squatting in the middle of an affair like that.

ANDREA. Locked up inside?

GALILEO, *triumphant.* Ah!

ANDREA. It's like a cage.

GALILEO. So you sensed that. *Against the model.* I like to think the ships began it.

ANDREA. Why?

GALILEO. They used to hug the coasts and then all of a sudden they left the coasts and spread over the oceans. A new age was coming. I was on to it years ago. I was a young man, in Siena. There was a group of masons arguing. They had to raise a block of granite. It was hot. To help matters, one of them wanted to try a new arrangement of ropes. After five minutes' discussion, out went a method which had been employed for a thousand years. The millenium of faith is ended, said I, this is the millenium of doubt. And we are pulling out of that contraption. The sayings of the wise men won't wash anymore. Everybody, at last, is getting nosey. I predict that in our time astronomy will become the gossip of the market place and the sons of fishwives will pack the schools.

ANDREA. You're off again, Mr. Galilei. Give me the towel. *He wipes some soap from* GALILEO's *back.*

GALILEO. By that time, with any luck, they will be learning that the earth rolls round the sun, and that their mothers, the captains, the scholars, the princes and the Pope are rolling with it.

ANDREA. That turning-round-business is no good. I can see with my own eyes that the sun comes up in one place in the morning and goes down in a different place in the evening. It doesn't stand still, I can see it move.

GALILEO. You see nothing, all you do is gawk. Gawking is not seeing. *He puts the iron washstand in the middle of the room.* Now: that's the sun. Sit down. ANDREA *sits on a chair.* GALILEO *stands behind him.* Where is the sun, on your right or on your left?

ANDREA. Left.

GALILEO. And how will it get to the right?

ANDREA. By your putting it there, of course.

GALILEO. Of course? *He picks* ANDREA *up, chair and all, and carries him round to the other side of the washstand. Now* where is the sun?

ANDREA. On the right.

GALILEO. And did it move?

ANDREA. I did.

GALILEO. Wrong. Stupid! The chair moved.

ANDREA. But I was on it.

GALILEO. Of course. The chair is the earth, and you're sitting on it.

MRS. SARTI, *who has come in with a glass of milk and a roll, has been watching.*

MRS. SARTI. What are you doing with my son, Mr. Galilei?

ANDREA. Now, mother, you don't understand.

MRS. SARTI. You understand, don't you? Last night he tried to tell me that the earth goes round the sun. You'll soon have him saying that two times two is five.

GALILEO, *eating his breakfast.* Apparently we are on the threshold of a new era, Mrs. Sarti.

MRS. SARTI. Well, I hope we can pay the milkman in this new era. A young gentleman is here to take private lessons and he is well-dressed and don't you frighten him away like you did the others. Wasting your time with Andrea! *To* ANDREA. How many times have I told you not to wheedle free lessons out of Mr. Galilei? MRS. SARTI *goes.*

GALILEO. So you thought enough of the turning-round-business to tell your mother about it.

ANDREA. Just to surprise her.

GALILEO. Andrea, I wouldn't talk about our ideas outside.

ANDREA. Why not?

GALILEO. Certain of the authorities won't like it.

ANDREA. Why not, if it's the truth?

GALILEO, *laughs.* Because we are like the worms who are little and have dim eyes and can hardly see the stars at all, and the new astronomy is a framework of guesses or very little more—yet.

MRS. SARTI *shows in* LUDOVICO MARSILI, *a presentable young man.*

GALILEO. This house is like a marketplace. *Pointing to the model.* Move that out of the way! Put it down there!

LUDOVICO *does.*

LUDOVICO. Good morning, sir. My name is Ludovico Marsili.

GALILEO, *reading a letter of recommendation he has brought.* You came by way of Holland and your family lives in the Campagna? Private lessons, thirty scudi a month.

LUDOVICO. That's all right, of course, sir.

GALILEO. What is your subject?

LUDOVICO. Horses.

GALILEO. Aha.

LUDOVICO. I don't understand science, sir.

GALILEO. Aha.

LUDOVICO. They showed me an instrument like that in Amsterdam. You'll pardon me, sir, but it didn't make sense to me at all.

GALILEO. It's out of date now.

ANDREA *goes.*

LUDOVICO. You'll have to be patient with me, sir. Nothing in science makes sense to me.

GALILEO. Aha.

LUDOVICO. I saw a brand new instrument in Amsterdam. A tube affair. "See things five times as large as life!" It had two lenses, one at each end, one lens bulged and the other was like that. *Gesture.* Any normal person would think that different lenses cancel each other out. They didn't! I just stood and looked a fool.

GALILEO. I don't quite follow you. What does one see enlarged?

LUDOVICO. Church steeples, pigeons, boats. Anything at a distance.

GALILEO. Did you yourself—see things enlarged?

LUDOVICO. Yes, sir.

GALILEO. And the tube had two lenses? Was it like this? *He has been making a sketch.*

LUDOVICO *nods.*

GALILEO. A recent invention?

LUDOVICO. It must be. They only started peddling it on the streets a few days before I left Holland.

GALILEO, *starts to scribble calculations on the sketch; almost friendly.* Why do you bother your head with science? Why don't you just breed horses?

Enter MRS. SARTI. GALILEO *doesn't see her. She listens to the following.*

LUDOVICO. My mother is set on the idea that science is necessary nowadays for conversation.

GALILEO. Aha. You'll find Latin or philosophy easier. MRS. SARTI *catches his eye.* I'll see you on Tuesday afternoon.

LUDOVICO. I shall look forward to it, sir.

GALILEO. Good morning. *He goes to the window and shouts into the street.* Andrea! Hey, Redhead, Redhead!

MRS. SARTI. The curator of the museum is here to see you.

GALILEO. Don't look at me like that. I took him, didn't I?

MRS. SARTI. I caught your eye in time.

GALILEO. Show the curator in.

She goes. He scribbles something on a new sheet of paper. THE CURATOR *comes in.*

CURATOR. Good morning, Mr. Galilei.

GALILEO. Lend me a scudo. *He takes it and goes to the window, wrapping the coin in the paper on which he has been scribbling.* Redhead, run to the spectacle-maker and bring me two lenses; here are the measurements. *He throws the paper out of the window. During the following scene* GALILEO *studies his sketch of the lenses.*

CURATOR. Mr. Galilei, I have come to return your petition for an honorarium. Unfortunately I am unable to recommend your request.

GALILEO. My good sir, how can I make ends meet on five hundred scudi?

CURATOR. What about your private students?

GALILEO. If I spend all my time with students, when am I to study? My particular science is on the threshold of important discoveries. *He throws a manuscript on the table.* Here are my findings on the laws of falling bodies. That should be worth 200 scudi.

CURATOR. I am sure that any paper of yours is of infinite worth, Mr. Galilei. . . .

GALILEO. I was limiting it to 200 scudi.

CURATOR, *cool.* Mr. Galilei, if you want money and leisure, go to Florence. I have no doubt Prince Cosmo de Medici will be glad to subsidize you, but eventually you will be forbidden to think—in the name of the Inquisition. GALILEO *says nothing.* Now let us not make a mountain out of a molehill. You are happy here in the Republic of Venice but you need money. Well, that's human, Mr. Galilei, may I suggest a simple solution? You remember that chart you made for the army to extract cube roots without any knowledge of mathematics? Now that was practical!

GALILEO. Bosh!

CURATOR. Don't say bosh about something that astounded the Chamber of Commerce. Our city elders are businessmen. Why don't you invent something useful that will bring them a little profit?

GALILEO, *playing with the sketch of the lenses; suddenly.* I see. Mr. Priuli, I may have something for you.

CURATOR. You don't say so.

GALILEO. It's not quite there yet, but . . .

CURATOR. You've never let me down yet, Galilei.

GALILEO. You are always an inspiration to me, Priuli.

CURATOR. You are a great man: a discontented man, but I've always said you are a great man.

GALILEO, *tartly.* My discontent, Priuli, is for the most part with myself. I am forty-six years of age and have achieved nothing which satisfies me.

CURATOR. I won't disturb you any further.

GALILEO. Thank you. Good morning.

CURATOR. Good morning. And thank you.

    He goes. GALILEO *sighs.* ANDREA *returns, bringing lenses.*

ANDREA. One scudo was not enough. I had to leave my cap with him before he'd let me take them away.

GALILEO. We'll get it back some day. Give them to me. *He takes the lenses over to the window, holding them in the relation they would have in a telescope.*

ANDREA. What are those for?

GALILEO. Something for the senate. With any luck, they will rake in 200 scudi. Take a look!

ANDREA. My, things look close! I can read the copper letters on the bell in the Campanile. And the washerwomen by the river, I can see their washboards!

GALILEO. Get out of the way. *Looking through the lenses himself.* Aha!

SCENE TWO

> *No one's virtue is complete:*
> *Great Galileo liked to eat.*
> *You will not resent, we hope,*
> *The truth about his telescope.*

The great arsenal of Venice, overlooking the harbor full of ships. SENATORS *and* OFFICIALS *on one side,* GALILEO, *his daughter* VIRGINIA *and his friend* SAGREDO, *on the other side. They are dressed in formal, festive clothes.* VIRGINIA *is fourteen and charming. She carries a velvet cushion on which lies a brand new telescope. Behind* GALILEO *are some* ARTISANS *from the arsenal. There are onlookers,* LUDOVICO *amongst them.*

CURATOR, *announcing.* Senators, Artisans of the Great Arsenal of Venice; Mr. Galileo Galilei, professor of mathematics at your University of Padua.

GALILEO *steps forward and starts to speak.*

GALILEO. Members of the High Senate! Gentlemen: I have great pleasure, as director of this institute, in presenting for your approval and acceptance an entirely new instrument originating from this our great arsenal of the Republic of Venice. As professor of mathematics at your University of Padua, your obedient servant has always counted it his privilege to offer you such discoveries and inventions as might prove lucrative to the manufacturers and merchants of our Venetian Republic. Thus, in all humility, I tender you this, my optical tube, or telescope, constructed, I assure you, on the most scientific and Christian principles, the product of seventeen years patient research at your University of Padua.

GALILEO *steps back. The* SENATORS *applaud.*

SAGREDO, *aside to* GALILEO. Now you will be able to pay your bills.

GALILEO. Yes. It will make money for them. But you realize that it is more than a money-making gadget? — I turned it on the moon last night . . .

CURATOR, *in his best chamber-of-commerce manner.* Gentlemen: Our Republic is to be congratulated not only because this new acquisition will be one more feather in the cap of Venetian culture, . . . *Polite applause* . . . not only because our own Mr. Galilei has generously handed this fresh product of his teeming brain entirely over to you, allowing you to manufacture as many of these highly saleable articles as you please. . . . *Considerable applause.* But Gentlemen of the Senate, has it occurred to you that—

with the help of this remarkable new instrument—the battlefleet of the enemy will be visible to us a full two hours before we are visible to him? *Tremendous applause.*

GALILEO, *aside to* SAGREDO. We have been held up three generations for lack of a thing like this. I want to go home.

SAGREDO. What about the moon?

GALILEO. Well, for one thing, it doesn't give off its own light.

CURATOR, *continuing his oration.* And now, Your Excellency, and Members of the Senate, Mr. Galilei entreats you to accept the instrument from the hands of his charming daughter Virginia.

Polite applause. He beckons to VIRGINIA *who steps forward and presents the telescope to the* DOGE.

CURATOR, *during this.* Mr. Galilei gives his invention entirely into your hands, Gentlemen, enjoining you to construct as many of these instruments as you may please.

More applause. The SENATORS *gather round the telescope, examining it, and looking through it.*

DO YOU KNOW WHAT THE MILKY WAY IS MADE UP OF?

GALILEO, *aside to* SAGREDO. Do you know what the Milky Way is made of?

SAGREDO. No.

GALILEO. I do.

CURATOR, *interrupting.* Congratulations, Mr. Galilei. Your extra five hundred scudi a year are safe.

GALILEO. Pardon? What? Of course, the five hundred scudi! Yes!

A prosperous man is standing beside the CURATOR.

CURATOR. Mr. Galilei, Mr. Matti of Florence.

MATTI. You're opening new fields, Mr. Galilei. We could do with you at Florence.

CURATOR. Now, Mr. Matti, leave something to us poor Venetians.

MATTI. It is a pity that a great republic has to seek an excuse to pay its great men their right and proper dues.

CURATOR. Even a great man has to have an incentive. *He joins the* SENATORS *at the telescope.*

MATTI. I am an iron founder.

GALILEO. Iron founder!

MATTI. With factories at Pisa and Florence. I wanted to talk to you about a machine you designed for a friend of mine in Padua.

GALILEO. I'll put you on to someone to copy it for you, I am not going to have the time. — How are things in Florence?

They wander away.

FIRST SENATOR, *peering.* Extraordinary! They're having their lunch on that frigate. Lobsters! I'm hungry!

Laughter.

SECOND SENATOR. Oh, good heavens, look at her! I must tell my wife to stop bathing on the roof. When can I buy one of these things?

Laughter. VIRGINIA *has spotted* LUDOVICO *among the onlookers and drags him to* GALILEO.

VIRGINIA, *to* LUDOVICO. Did I do it nicely?

LUDOVICO. I thought so.

VIRGINIA. Here's Ludovico to congratulate you, father.

LUDOVICO, *embarrassed.* Congratulations, sir.

GALILEO. I improved it.

LUDOVICO. Yes, sir. I am beginning to understand science.

GALILEO *is surrounded.*

VIRGINIA. Isn't father a great man?

LUDOVICO. Yes.

VIRGINIA. Isn't that new thing father made pretty?

LUDOVICO. Yes, a pretty red. Where I saw it first it was covered in green.

VIRGINIA. What was?

LUDOVICO. Never mind. *A short pause.* Have you ever been to Holland?

They go. All Venice is congratulating GALILEO, *who wants to go home.*

SCENE THREE

January ten, sixteen ten:
Galileo Galilei abolishes heaven.

GALILEO's *study at Padua. It is night.* GALILEO *and* SAGREDO *at a telescope.*

SAGREDO, *softly.* The edge of the crescent is jagged. All along the dark part near the shiny crescent, bright particles of light keep coming up, one after the other and growing larger and merging with the bright crescent.

GALILEO. How do you explain those spots of light?

SAGREDO. It can't be true . . .

GALILEO. It *is* true: they are high mountains.

SAGREDO. On a star?

GALILEO. Yes. The shining particles are mountain peaks catching the first rays of the rising sun while the slopes of the mountains are still dark, and what you see is the sunlight moving down from the peaks into the valleys

AGREDO. But this gives the lie to all the astronomy that's been taught for the last two thousand years.

GALILEO. Yes. What you are seeing now has been seen by no other man beside myself.

AGREDO. But the moon can't be an earth with mountains and valleys like our own any more than the earth can be a star.

GALILEO. The moon *is* an earth with mountains and valleys, — and the earth *is* a star. As the moon appears to us, so we appear to the moon. From the moon, the earth looks something like a crescent, sometimes like a half-globe, sometimes a full-globe, and sometimes it is not visible at all.

AGREDO. Galileo, this is frightening.

An urgent knocking on the door.

GALILEO. I've discovered something else, something even more astonishing.

More knocking. GALILEO *opens the door and the* CURATOR *comes in.*

CURATOR. There it is—your "miraculous optical tube." Do you know that this invention he so picturesquely termed "the fruit of seventeen years research" will be on sale tomorrow for two scudi apiece at every street corner in Venice? A shipload of them has just arrived from Holland.

AGREDO. Oh, dear!

GALILEO *turns his back and adjusts the telescope.*

CURATOR. When I think of the poor gentlemen of the senate who believed they were getting an invention they could monopolize for their own profit. . . . Why, when they took their first look through the glass, it was only by the merest chance that they didn't see a peddler, seven times enlarged, selling tubes exactly like it at the corner of the street.

AGREDO. Mr. Priuli, with the help of this instrument, Mr. Galilei has made discoveries that will revolutionize our concept of the universe.

CURATOR. Mr. Galilei provided the city with a first rate water pump and the irrigation works he designed function splendidly. How was I to expect this?

GALILEO, *still at the telescope.* Not so fast, Priuli. I may be on the track of a very large gadget. Certain of the stars appear to have regular movements. If there were a clock in the sky, it could be seen from anywhere. That might be useful for your shipowners.

CURATOR. I won't listen to you. I listened to you before, and as a reward for my friendship you have made me the laughingstock of the town. You can laugh—you got your money. But let me tell you this: you've destroyed my faith in a lot of things, Mr. Galilei. I'm disgusted with the world. That's all I have to say. *He storms out.*

GALILEO, *embarrassed.* Businessmen bore me, they suffer so. Did you see the frightened look in his eyes when he caught sight of a world not created solely for the purpose of doing business?

AGREDO. Did you know that telescopes had been made in Holland?

GALILEO. I'd heard about it. But the one I made for the Senators was twice as good as any Dutchman's. Besides, I needed the money. How can I work, with the tax collector on the doorstep? And my poor daughter will never acquire a husband unless she has a dowry, she's not too bright. And I like to buy books—all kinds of books. Why not? And what about

my appetite? I don't think well unless I eat well. Can I help it if I ge
my best ideas over a good meal and a bottle of wine? They don't pa
me as much as they pay the butcher's boy. If only I could have five year
to do nothing but research! Come on. I am going to show you some
thing else.

SAGREDO. I don't know that I want to look again.

GALILEO. This is one of the brighter nebulae of the Milky Way. What d
you see?

SAGREDO. But it's made up of stars—countless stars.

GALILEO. Countless worlds.

SAGREDO, *hesitating*. What about the theory that the earth revolves roun
the sun? Have you run across anything about that?

GALILEO. No. But I noticed something on Tuesday that might prove a ste
towards even that. Where's Jupiter? There are four lesser stars nea
Jupiter. I happened on them on Monday but didn't take any particula
note of their position. On Tuesday I looked again. I could have swor
they had moved. They have changed again. Tell me what you see.

SAGREDO. I only see three.

GALILEO. Where's the fourth? Let's get the charts and settle down to worl
They work and the lights dim. The lights go up again. It is near dawn.

GALILEO. The only place the fourth can be is round at the back of th
larger star where we cannot see it. This means there are small stars r
volving around a big star. Where are the crystal shells now that the sta
are supposed to be fixed to?

SAGREDO. Jupiter can't be attached to anything: there are other stars r
volving round it.

THERE IS NO SUPPORT IN THE HEAVENS

GALILEO. There is no support in the heavens. SAGREDO *laughs awkwardl*
Don't stand there looking at me as if it weren't true.

SAGREDO. I suppose it is true. I'm afraid.

GALILEO. Why?

SAGREDO. What do you think is going to happen to you for saying that ther
is another sun around which other earths revolve? And that there ar
only stars and no difference between earth and heaven? Where is Go
then?

GALILEO. What do you mean?

SAGREDO. God? Where is God?

GALILEO, *angrily.* Not there! Any more than he'd be here—if creatures from the moon came down to look for him!

AGREDO. Then where is He?

GALILEO. I'm not a theologian: I'm a mathematician.

AGREDO. You are a human being! *Almost shouting.* Where is God in your system of the universe?

ALILEO. Within ourselves. Or—nowhere.

AGREDO. Ten years ago a man was burned at the stake for saying that.

ALILEO. Giordano Bruno was an idiot: he spoke too soon. He would never have been condemned if he could have backed up what he said with proof.

AGREDO, *incredulously.* Do you really believe proof will make any difference?

ALILEO. I believe in the human race. The only people that can't be reasoned with are the dead. Human beings are intelligent.

AGREDO. Intelligent—or merely shrewd?

ALILEO. I know they call a donkey a horse when they want to sell it, and a horse a donkey when they want to buy it. But is that the whole story? Aren't they susceptible to truth as well? *He fishes a small pebble out of his pocket.* If anybody were to drop a stone . . . *Drops the pebble* . . . and tell them that it didn't fall, do you think they would keep quiet? The evidence of your own eyes is a very seductive thing. Sooner or later everybody must succumb to it.

AGREDO. Galileo, I am helpless when you talk.

church bell has been ringing for some time, calling people to mass. Enter RGINIA, muffled up for mass, carrying a candle, protected from the wind by globe.

RGINIA. Oh, father, you promised to go to bed tonight, and it's five o'clock again.

ALILEO. Why are you up at this hour?

RGINIA. I'm going to mass with Mrs. Sarti. Ludovico is going too. How was the night, father?

ALILEO. Bright.

RGINIA. What did you find through the tube?

ALILEO. Only some little specks by the side of a star. I must draw attention to them somehow. I think I'll name them after the Prince of Florence. Why not call them the Medicean planets? By the way, we may move to Florence. I've written to His Highness, asking if he can use me as Court Mathematician.

RGINIA. Oh, father, we'll be at the court!

GREDO, *amazed.* Galileo!

LILEO. My dear Sagredo, I must have leisure. My only worry is that His Highness after all may not take me. I'm not accustomed to writing formal letters to great personages. Here, do you think this is the right sort of thing?

GREDO, *reads and quotes.* "Whose sole desire is to reside in Your Highness' presence—the rising sun of our great age." Cosmo de Medici is a boy of nine.

GALILEO. The only way a man like me can land a good job is by crawling on his stomach. Your father, my dear, is going to take his share of the pleasures of life in exchange for all his hard work, and about time too. I have no patience, Sagredo, with a man who doesn't use his brains to fill his belly. Run along to mass now.

VIRGINIA *goes.*

SAGREDO. Galileo, do not go to Florence.

GALILEO. Why not?

SAGREDO. The monks are in power there.

GALILEO. Going to mass is a small price to pay for a full belly. And there are many famous scholars at the court of Florence.

SAGREDO. Court monkeys.

GALILEO. I shall enjoy taking them by the scruff of the neck and making them look through the telescope.

SAGREDO. Galileo, you are traveling the road to disaster. You are suspicious and skeptical in science, but in politics you are as naive as your daughter. How can people in power leave a man at large who tells the truth, even if it be the truth about the distant stars? Can you see the Pope scribbling a note in his diary: "10th of January, 1610, Heaven abolished?" A moment ago, when you were at the telescope, I saw you tied to the stake, and when you said you believed in proof, I smelt burning flesh!

GALILEO. I am going to Florence.

Before the next scene a curtain with the following legend on it is lowered
By setting the name of Medici in the sky, I am bestowing immortality upon the stars. I commend myself to you as your most faithful and devoted servant, whose sole desire is to reside in Your Highness' presence, the rising sun of our great age.

—GALILEO GALIL..

SCENE   FOUR

GALILEO'S *house at Florence. Well-appointed.* GALILEO *is demonstrating h.. telescope to* PRINCE COSMO DI MEDICI, *a boy of nine, accompanied by his LO.. CHAMBERLAIN, LADIES and* GENTLEMEN *of the Court and an assortment of un.. versity* PROFESSORS. *With* GALILEO *are* ANDREA *and* FEDERZONI, *the new assista.. (an old man).* MRS. SARTI *stands by. Before the scene opens the voice of t.. PHILOSOPHER *can be heard.*

VOICE OF THE PHILOSOPHER. Quaedam miracula universi. Orbes mystice ca.. orae, arcus crystallini, circulatio corporum coelestium. Cyclorum epi.. clorumque intoxicatio, integritas tabulae chordarum et architectura ela.. globorum coelestium.

.. *shall we speak in everyday language?*

GALILEO. Shall we speak in everyday language? My colleague Mr. Federzoni does not understand Latin.

PHILOSOPHER. Is it necessary that he should?

GALILEO. Yes.

PHILOSOPHER. Forgive me. I thought he was your mechanic.

ANDREA. Mr. Federzoni is a mechanic and a scholar.

PHILOSOPHER. Thank you, young man. If Mr. Federzoni insists . . .

GALILEO. I insist.

PHILOSOPHER. It will not be as clear, but it's your house. Your Highness . . . THE PRINCE *is ineffectually trying to establish contact with* ANDREA. I was about to recall to Mr. Galilei some of the wonders of the universe as they are set down for us in the Divine Classics. THE LADIES *"ah."* Remind him of the "mystically musical spheres, the crystal arches, the circulation of the heavenly bodies—"

ELDERLY LADY. Perfect poise!

PHILOSOPHER. "—the intoxication of the cycles and epicycles, the integrity of the tables of chords and the enraptured architecture of the celestial globes."

ELDERLY LADY. What diction!

PHILOSOPHER. May I pose the question: Why should we go out of our way to look for things that can only strike a discord in this ineffable harmony? *The* LADIES *applaud.*

FEDERZONI. Take a look through here—you'll be interested.

ANDREA. Sit down here, please. *The* PROFESSORS *laugh.*

MATHEMATICIAN. Mr. Galilei, nobody doubts that your brain child—or is it your adopted brain child?—is brilliantly contrived.

GALILEO. Your Highness, one can see the four stars as large as life, you know. *The* PRINCE *looks to the* ELDERLY LADY *for guidance.*

MATHEMATICIAN. Ah. But has it occurred to you that an eyeglass through which one sees such phenomena might not be a too reliable eyeglass?

GALILEO. How is that?

MATHEMATICIAN. If one could be sure you would keep your temper, Mr. Galilei, I could suggest that what one sees in the eyeglass and what is in the heavens are two entirely different things.

GALILEO, *quietly.* You are suggesting fraud?

MATHEMATICIAN. No! How could I, in the presence of His Highness?

ELDERLY LADY. The gentlemen are just wondering if Your Highness' stars are really, really there!

Pause.

YOUNG LADY, *trying to be helpful.* Can one see the claws on the Great Bear?

GALILEO. And everything on Taurus the Bull.

FEDERZONI. Are you going to look through it or not?

MATHEMATICIAN. With the greatest of pleasure.

Pause. Nobody goes near the telescope. All of a sudden the boy ANDREA *turns and marches pale and erect past them through the whole length of the room. The* GUESTS *follow with their eyes.*

MRS. SARTI, *as he passes her.* What is the matter with you?

ANDREA, *shocked.* They are wicked.

PHILOSOPHER. Your Highness, it is a delicate matter and I had no intention of bringing it up, but Mr. Galilei was about to demonstrate the impossible. His new stars would have broken the outer crystal sphere—which we know of on the authority of Aristotle. I am sorry.

MATHEMATICIAN. The last word.

FEDERZONI. He had no telescope.

MATHEMATICIAN. Quite.

GALILEO, *keeping his temper.* "Truth is the daughter of Time, not of Authority." Gentlemen, the sum of our knowledge is pitiful. It has been my singular good fortune to find a new instrument which brings a small patch of the universe a little bit closer. It is at your disposal.

PHILOSOPHER. Where is all this leading?

GALILEO. Are we, as scholars, concerned with where the truth might lead us?

PHILOSOPHER. Mr. Galilei, the truth might lead us anywhere!

GALILEO. I can only beg you to look through my eyeglass.

MATHEMATICIAN, *wild.* If I understand Mr. Galilei correctly, he is asking us to discard the teachings of two thousand years.

GALILEO. For two thousand years we have been looking at the sky and didn't see the four moons of Jupiter, and there they were all the time. Why defend shaken teachings? You should be doing the shaking. *The* PRINCE *is sleepy.* Your Highness! My work in the Great Arsenal of Venice brought me in daily contact with sailors, carpenters, and so on. These men are unread. They depend on the evidence of their senses. But they taught me many new ways of doing things. The question is whether these gentlemen here want to be found out as fools by men who might not have had the advantages of a classical education but who are not afraid to use their eyes. I tell you that our dockyards are stirring with that same high curiosity which was the true glory of Ancient Greece.

Pause.

PHILOSOPHER. I have no doubt Mr. Galilei's theories will arouse the enthusiasm of the dockyards.

CHAMBERLAIN. Your Highness, I find to my amazement that this highly in-
formative discussion has exceeded the time we had allowed for it. May I
remind Your Highness that the State Ball begins in three-quarters of an
hour?

The COURT *bows low.*

ELDERLY LADY. We would really have liked to look through your eyeglass,
Mr. Galilei, wouldn't we, Your Highness?

The PRINCE *bows politely and is led to the door.* GALILEO *follows the* PRINCE,
CHAMBERLAIN *and* LADIES *towards the exit. The* PROFESSORS *remain at the
telescope.*

GALILEO, *almost servile.* All anybody has to do is look through the telescope,
Your Highness.

MRS. SARTI *takes a plate with candies to the* PRINCE *as he is walking out.*

MRS. SARTI. A piece of homemade candy, Your Highness?

EDERLY LADY. Not now. Thank you. It is too soon before His Highness'
supper.

PHILOSOPHER. Wouldn't I like to take that thing to pieces.

MATHEMATICIAN. Ingenious contraption. It must be quite difficult to keep
clean. *He rubs the lens with his handkerchief and looks at the handkerchief.*

FEDERZONI. We did not paint the Medicean stars on the lens.

ELDERLY LADY, *to the* PRINCE, *who has whispered something to her.* No, no,
no, there is nothing the matter with your stars!

CHAMBERLAIN, *across the stage to* GALILEO. His Highness will of course seek
the opinion of the greatest living authority: Christopher Clavius, Chief
Astronomer to the Papal College in Rome.

SCENE FIVE

> *Things take indeed a wondrous turn*
> *When learned men do stoop to learn.*
> *Clavius, we are pleased to say,*
> *Upheld Galileo Galilei.*

*A burst of laughter is heard and the curtains reveal a hall in the Collegium
Romanum.* HIGH CHURCHMEN, MONKS *and* SCHOLARS *standing about talking
and laughing.* GALILEO *by himself in a corner.*

FAT PRELATE, *shaking with laughter.* Hopeless! Hopeless! Hopeless! Will you
tell me something people won't believe?

A SCHOLAR. Yes, that you don't love your stomach!

FAT PRELATE. They'd believe that. They only do not believe what's good for
them. They doubt the devil, but fill them up with some fiddle-de-dee
about the earth rolling like a marble in the gutter and they swallow it
hook, line, and sinker. Sancta simplicitas!

He laughs until the tears run down his cheeks. The others laugh with him.

A group has formed whose members boisterously begin to pretend they are standing on a rolling globe.

A MONK. It's rolling fast, I'm dizzy. May I hold on to you, Professor? *He sways dizzily and clings to one of the scholars for support.*

THE SCHOLAR. Old Mother Earth's been at the bottle again. Whoa!

MONK. Hey! Hey! We're slipping off! Help!

SECOND SCHOLAR. Look! There's Venus! Hold me, lads. Whee!

SECOND MONK. Don't, don't hurl us off on to the moon. There are nasty sharp mountain peaks on the moon, brethren!

VARIOUSLY. Hold tight! Hold tight! Don't look down! Hold tight! It'll make you giddy!

FAT PRELATE. And we cannot have giddy people in Holy Rome.

They rock with laughter. An INFURIATED MONK *comes out from a large door at the rear holding a bible in his hand and pointing out a page with his finger.*

INFURIATED MONK. What does the bible say—"Sun, stand thou still on Gideon and thou, moon, in the valley of Ajalon." Can the sun come to a standstill if it doesn't ever move? Does the bible lie?

FAT PRELATE. How did Christopher Clavius, the greatest astronomer we have, get mixed up in an investigation of this kind?

INFURIATED MONK. He's in there with his eye glued to that diabolical instrument.

FAT PRELATE, *to* GALILEO, *who has been playing with his pebble and has dropped it.* Mr. Galilei, something dropped down.

GALILEO. Monsignor, are you sure it didn't drop up?

INFURIATED MONK. As astronomers we are aware that there are phenomena which are beyond us, but man can't expect to understand everything! *Enter a very old* CARDINAL *leaning on a* MONK *for support. Others move aside.*

OLD CARDINAL. Aren't they out yet? Can't they reach a decision on that paltry matter? Christopher Clavius ought to know his astronomy after all these years. I am informed that Mr. Galilei transfers mankind from the center of the universe to somewhere on the outskirts. Mr. Galilei is therefore an enemy of mankind and must be dealt with as such. Is it conceivable that God would trust this most precious fruit of His labor to a minor frolicking star? Would He have sent His Son to such a place? How can there be people with such twisted minds that they believe what they're told by the slave of a multiplication table?

FAT PRELATE, *quietly to* CARDINAL. The gentleman is over there.

OLD CARDINAL. So you are the man. You know my eyes are not what they were, but I can see you bear a striking resemblance to the man we burned. What was his name?

MONK. Your Eminence must avoid excitement the doctor said . . .

OLD CARDINAL, *disregarding him.* So you have degraded the earth despite the fact that you live by her and receive everything from her. I won't have it! I won't have it! I won't be a nobody on an inconsequential star briefly twirling hither and thither. I tread the earth, and the earth is firm beneath my feet, and there is no motion to the earth, and the earth is the center of all things, and I am the center of the earth, and the eye of the creator is upon me. About me revolve, affixed to their crystal shells, the lesser lights of the stars and the great light of the sun, created to give light upon me that God might see me—Man, God's greatest effort, the center of creation. "In the image of God created He him." Immortal . . . *His strength fails him and he catches for the* MONK *for support.*

MONK. You mustn't overtax your strength, Your Eminence.

At this moment the door at the rear opens and CHRISTOPHER CLAVIUS *enters followed by his* ASTRONOMERS. *He strides hastily across the hall, looking neither to right nor left. As he goes by we hear him say—*

CLAVIUS. He is right.

Deadly silence. All turn to GALILEO.

OLD CARDINAL. What is it? Have they reached a decision?

No one speaks.

MONK. It is time that Your Eminence went home.

The hall is emptying fast. One little MONK *who had entered with* CLAVIUS *speaks to* GALILEO.

LITTLE MONK. Mr. Galilei, I heard Father Clavius say: "Now it's for the theologians to set the heavens right again." You have won.

Before the next scene a curtain with the following legend on it is lowered:
. . . . . . As these new astronomical charts enable us to determine

longitudes at sea and so make it possible to reach the new continents by the shortest routes, we would beseech Your Excellency to aid us in reaching Mr. Galilei, mathematician to the Court of Florence, who is now in Rome . . . . . .

> —From a letter written by a member of the Genoa Chamber of Commerce and Navigation to the Papal Legation.

SCENE SIX

When Galileo was in Rome
A Cardinal asked him to his home
He wined and dined him as his guest
And only made one small request.

CARDINAL BELLARMIN'S *house in Rome. Music is heard and the chatter of many guests. Two* SECRETARIES *are at the rear of the stage at a desk.* GALILEO, *his daughter* VIRGINIA, *now 21, and* LUDOVICO MARSILI, *who has become her fiancé, are just arriving. A few* GUESTS, *standing near the entrance with masks in their hands, nudge each other and are suddenly silent.* GALILEO *looks at them. They applaud him politely and bow.*

VIRGINIA. O father! I'm so happy. I won't dance with anyone but you, Ludovico.

GALILEO, *to a* SECRETARY. I was to wait here for His Eminence.

FIRST SECRETARY. His Eminence will be with you in a few minutes.

VIRGINIA. Do I look proper?

LUDOVICO. You are showing some lace.

GALILEO *puts his arms around their shoulders.*

GALILEO, *quoting mischievously.*
Fret not, daughter, if perchance
You attract a wanton glance.
The eyes that catch a trembling lace
Will guess the heartbeat's quickened pace.
Lovely woman still may be
Careless with felicity.

VIRGINIA, *to* GALILEO. Feel my heart.

GALILEO, *to* LUDOVICO. It's thumping.

VIRGINIA. I hope I always say the right thing.

LUDOVICO. She's afraid she's going to let us down.

VIRGINIA. Oh, I want to look beautiful.

GALILEO. You'd better. If you don't they'll start saying all over again that the earth doesn't turn.

LUDOVICO, *laughing.* It *doesn't* turn, sir.

GALILEO *laughs.*

GALILEO. Go and enjoy yourselves. *He speaks to one of the* SECRETARIES. A large fête?

FIRST SECRETARY. Two hundred and fifty guests, Mr. Galilei. We have represented here this evening most of the great families of Italy, the Orsinis, the Villanis, the Nuccolis, the Soldanieris, the Canes, the Lecchis, the Estensis, the Colombinis, the . . . .

VIRGINIA comes running back.

VIRGINIA. Oh father, I didn't tell you: you're famous.

GALILEO. Why?

VIRGINIA. The hairdresser in the Via Vittorio kept four other ladies waiting and took me first. *Exit.*

GALILEO, *at the stairway, leaning over the well.* Rome!

Enter CARDINAL BELLARMIN, *wearing the mask of a lamb, and* CARDINAL BARBERINI, *wearing the mask of a dove.*

SECRETARIES. Their Eminences, Cardinals Bellarmin and Barberini.

The CARDINALS lower their masks.

GALILEO, *to* BELLARMIN. Your Eminence.

BELLARMIN. Mr. Galilei, Cardinal Barberini.

GALILEO. Your Eminence.

BARBERINI. So you are the father of that lovely child!

BELLARMIN. Who is inordinately proud of being her father's daughter.

They laugh.

BARBERINI, *points his finger at* GALILEO. "The sun riseth and setteth and returneth to its place," saith the bible. What saith Galilei?

GALILEO. Appearances are notoriously deceptive, Your Eminence. Once when I was so high, I was standing on a ship that was pulling away from the shore and I shouted, "The shore is moving!" I know now that it was the ship which was moving.

BARBERINI, *laughs.* You can't catch that man. I tell you, Bellarmin, his

moons around Jupiter are hard nuts to crack. Unfortunately for me I happened to glance at a few papers on astronomy once. It is harder to get rid of than the itch.

BELLARMIN. Let's move with the times. If it makes navigation easier for sailors to use new charts based on a new hypothesis let them have them. We only have to scotch doctrines that contradict Holy Writ.

He leans over the balustrade of the well and acknowledges various GUESTS.

BARBERINI. But Bellarmin, you haven't caught on to this fellow. The scriptures don't satisfy him. Copernicus does.

GALILEO. Copernicus? "He that withholdeth corn the people shall curse him." Book of Proverbs.

BARBERINI. "A prudent man concealeth knowledge." Also Book of Proverbs.

GALILEO. "Where no oxen are, the stable is clean, but much increase is by the strength of the ox."

BARBERINI. "He that ruleth his spirit is better than he that taketh a city."

GALILEO. "But a broken spirit drieth up the bones." *Pause.* "Doth not wisdom cry?"

BARBERINI. "Can one walk on hot coals and his feet not be scorched?" — Welcome to Rome, Friend Galileo. You recall the legend of our city's origin? Two small boys found sustenance and refuge with a she-wolf and from that day we have paid the price for the she-wolf's milk. But the place is not bad. We have everything for your pleasure—from a scholarly dispute with Bellarmin to ladies of high degree. Look at that woman flaunting herself. No? He wants a weighty discussion! All right! *To* GALILEO. You people speak in terms of circles and ellipses and regular velocities—simple movements that the human mind can grasp—very convenient—but suppose Almighty God had taken it into his head to make the stars move like that . . . *He describes an irregular motion with his fingers through the air* . . . then where would you be?

GALILEO. My good man—the Almighty would have endowed us with brains like that . . . *Repeats the movement* . . . so that we could grasp the movements . . . *Repeats the movement* . . . like that. I believe in the brain.

BARBERINI. I consider the brain inadequate. He doesn't answer. He is too polite to tell me he considers *my* brain inadequate. What is one to do with him? Butter wouldn't melt in his mouth. All he wants to do is to prove that God made a few boners in astronomy. God didn't study his astronomy hard enough before he composed Holy Writ. *To the* SECRETARIES. Don't take anything down. This is a scientific discussion among friends.

BELLARMIN, *to* GALILEO. Does it not appear more probable—even to you— that the Creator knows more about his work than the created?

GALILEO. In his blindness man is liable to misread not only the sky but also the bible.

BELLARMIN. The interpretation of the bible is a matter for the ministers of God. GALILEO *remains silent.* At last you are quiet. *He gestures to the* SECRETARIES. *They start writing.* Tonight the Holy Office has decided that the theory according to which the earth goes around the sun is foolish, absurd, and a heresy. I am charged, Mr. Galilei, with cautioning you to abandon these teachings. *To the* FIRST SECRETARY. Would you repeat that?

FIRST SECRETARY, *reading.* "His Eminence, Cardinal Bellarmin, to the aforesaid Galilei: The Holy Office has resolved that the theory according to which the earth goes around the sun is foolish, absurd, and a heresy. I am charged, Mr. Galilei, with cautioning you to abandon these teachings."

GALILEO, *rocking on his base.* But the facts!

BARBERINI, *consoling.* Your findings have been ratified by the Papal Observatory, Galilei. That should be most flattering to you. . .

BELLARMIN, *cutting in.* The Holy Office formulated the decree without going into details.

GALILEO, *to* BARBERINI. Do you realize, the future of all scientific research is . . .

BELLARMIN, *cutting in.* Completely assured, Mr. Galilei. It is not given to man to know the truth: it is granted to him to seek after the truth. Science is the legitimate and beloved daughter of the Church. She must have confidence in the Church.

GALILEO, *infuriated.* I would not try confidence by whistling her too often.

BARBERINI, *quickly.* Be careful what you're doing—you'll be throwing out the baby with the bath water, friend Galilei. *Serious.* We need you more than you need us.

BELLARMIN. Well, it is time we introduced our distinguished friend to our guests. The whole country talks of him!

BARBERINI. Let us replace our masks, Bellarmin. Poor Galilei hasn't got one.

He laughs. They take GALILEO *out.*

FIRST SECRETARY. Did you get his last sentence?

SECOND SECRETARY. Yes. Do you have what he said about believing in the brain?

Another cardinal—the INQUISITOR— *enters.*

INQUISITOR. Did the conference take place?

The FIRST SECRETARY *hands him the papers and the* INQUISITOR *dismisses the* SECRETARIES. *They go. The* INQUISITOR *sits down and starts to read the transcription. Two or three* YOUNG LADIES *skitter across the stage; they see the* INQUISITOR *and curtsy as they go.*

YOUNG GIRL. Who was that?

HER FRIEND. The Cardinal Inquisitor.

They giggle and go. Enter VIRGINIA. *She curtsies as she goes. The* INQUISITOR *stops her.*

INQUISITOR. Good evening, my child. Beautiful night. May I congratulate you on your betrothal? Your young man comes from a fine family. Are you staying with us here in Rome?

VIRGINIA. Not now, Your Eminence. I must go home to prepare for the wedding.

INQUISITOR. Ah. You are accompanying your father to Florence. That should please him. Science must be cold comfort in a home. Your youth and warmth will keep him down to earth. It is easy to get lost up there. *He gestures to the sky.*

VIRGINIA. He doesn't talk to me about the stars, Your Eminence.

INQUISITOR. No. *He laughs.* They don't eat fish in the fisherman's house. I can tell you something about astronomy. My child, it seems that God has blessed our modern astronomers with imaginations. It is quite alarming! Do you know that the earth—which we old fogies supposed to be so large—has shrunk to something no bigger than a walnut, and the new universe has grown so vast that prelates—and even cardinals—look like ants. Why, God Almighty might lose sight of a Pope! I wonder if I know your Father Confessor.

VIRGINIA. Father Christopherus, from Saint Ursula's at Florence, Your Eminence.

INQUISITOR. My dear child, your father will need you. Not so much now perhaps, but one of these days. You are pure, and there is strength in purity. Greatness is sometimes, indeed often, too heavy a burden for those to whom God has granted it. What man is so great that he has no place in a prayer? But I am keeping you, my dear. Your fiancé will be jealous of me, and I am afraid your father will never forgive me for holding forth on astronomy. Go to your dancing and remember me to Father Christopherus.

VIRGINIA *kisses his ring and runs off. The* INQUISITOR *resumes his reading.*

S C E N E   S E V E N

> *Galileo, feeling grim,*
> *A young monk came to visit him.*
> *The monk was born of common folk.*
> *It was of science that they spoke.*

Garden of the Florentine AMBASSADOR *in Rome. Distant hum of a great city.*
GALILEO *and the* LITTLE MONK *of Scene Five are talking.*

GALILEO. Let's hear it. That robe you're wearing gives you the right to say whatever you want to say. Let's hear it.

LITTLE MONK. I have studied physics, Mr. Galilei.

GALILEO. That might help us if it enabled you to admit that two and two are four.

LITTLE MONK. Mr. Galilei, I have spent four sleepless nights trying to reconcile the decree that I have read with the moons of Jupiter that I have seen. This morning I decided to come to see you after I had said Mass.

GALILEO. To tell me that Jupiter has no moons?

LITTLE MONK. No, I found out that I think the decree a wise decree. It has shocked me into realizing that free research has its dangers. I have had to decide to give up astronomy. However, I felt the impulse to confide in you some of the motives which have impelled even a passionate physicist to abandon his work.

GALILEO. Your motives are familiar to me.

LITTLE MONK. You mean, of course, the special powers invested in certain
commissions of the Holy Office? But there is something else. I would
like to talk to you about my family. I do not come from the great city.
My parents are peasants in the Campagna, who know about the cultiva-
tion of the olive tree, and not much about anything else. Too often these
days when I am trying to concentrate on tracking down the moons of
Jupiter, I see my parents. I see them sitting by the fire with my sister, eating their curded cheese. I see the beams of the ceiling above them, which
the smoke of centuries has blackened, and I can see the veins stand out
on their toil-worn hands, and the little spoons in their hands. They scrape
a living, and underlying their poverty there is a sort of order. There
are routines. The routine of scrubbing the floors, the routine of the
seasons in the olive orchard, the routine of paying taxes. The troubles that
come to them are recurrent troubles. My father did not get his poor
bent back all at once, but little by little, year by year, in the olive orchard;
just as year after year, with unfailing regularity, childbirth has made my
mother more and more sexless. They draw the strength they need to sweat
with their loaded baskets up the stony paths, to bear children, even to
eat, from the sight of the trees greening each year anew, from the re-
proachful face of the soil, which is never satisfied, and from the little
church and bible texts they hear there on Sunday. They have been told
that God relies upon them and that the pageant of the world has been
written around them that they may be tested in the important or unimportant parts handed out to them. How could they take it, were I to tell
them that they are on a lump of stone ceaselessly spinning in empty space,
circling around a second-rate star? What, then, would be the use of their
patience, their acceptance of misery? What comfort, then, the Holy
Scriptures, which have mercifully explained their crucifixion? The Holy
Scriptures would then be proved full of mistakes. No, I see them begin
to look frightened. I see them slowly put their spoons down on the table.
They would feel cheated. "There is no eye watching over us, after all,"
they would say. "We have to start out on our own, at our time of life.
Nobody has planned a part for us beyond this wretched one on a worthless star. There is no meaning in our misery. Hunger is just not having
eaten. It is no test of strength. Effort is just stooping and carrying. It is
not a virtue." Can you understand that I read into the decree of the
Holy Office a noble motherly pity and a great goodness of the soul?

GALILEO, *embarrassed.* Hm, well at least you have found out that it is not
a question of the satellites of Jupiter, but of the peasants of the Campagna! And don't try to break me down by the halo of beauty that
radiates from old age. How does a pearl develop in an oyster? A jagged
grain of sand makes its way into the oyster's shell and makes its life
unbearable. The oyster exudes slime to cover the grain of sand and the
slime eventually hardens into a pearl. The oyster nearly dies in the process. To hell with the pearl, give me the healthy oyster! And virtues
are not exclusive to misery. If your parents were prosperous and happy,
they might develop the virtues of happiness and prosperity. Today the

virtues of exhaustion are caused by the exhausted land. For that my new water pumps could work more wonders than their ridiculous superhuman efforts. Be fruitful and multiply: for war will cut down the population, and our fields are barren! *A pause.* Shall I lie to your people?

LITTLE MONK. We must be silent from the highest of motives: the inward peace of less fortunate souls.

GALILEO. My dear man, as a bonus for not meddling with your parents' peace, the authorities are tendering me, on a silver platter, persecution-free, my share of the fat sweated from your parents, who, as you know, were made in God's image. Should I condone this decree, my motives might not be disinterested: easy life, no persecution and so on.

LITTLE MONK. Mr. Galilei, I am a priest.

GALILEO. You are also a physicist. How can new machinery be evolved to domesticate the river water if we physicists are forbidden to study, discuss, and pool our findings about the greatest machinery of all, the machinery of the heavenly bodies? Can I reconcile my findings on the paths of falling bodies with the current belief in the tracks of witches on broom sticks? *A pause.* I am sorry—I shouldn't have said that.

LITTLE MONK. You don't think that the truth, if it is the truth, would make its way without us?

GALILEO. No! No! No! As much of the truth gets through as we push through. You talk about the Campagna peasants as if they were the moss on their huts. Naturally, if they don't get a move on and learn to think for themselves, the most efficient of irrigation systems cannot help them. I can see their divine patience, but where is their divine fury?

LITTLE MONK, *helpless.* They are old!

GALILEO *stands for a moment, beaten; he cannot meet the* LITTLE MONK's *eyes.*

He takes a manuscript from the table and throws it violently on the ground.

LITTLE MONK. What is that?

GALILEO. Here is writ what draws the ocean when it ebbs and flows. Let it lie there. Thou shalt not read. LITTLE MONK *has picked up the manuscript.* Already! An apple of the tree of knowledge, he can't wait, he wolfs it down. He will rot in hell for all eternity. Look at him, where are his manners?—Sometimes I think I would let them imprison me in a place a thousand feet beneath the earth where no light could reach me, if in exchange I could find out what stuff that is: "Light." The bad thing is that, when I find something, I have to boast about it like a lover or a drunkard or a traitor. That is a hopeless vice and leads to the abyss. I wonder how long I shall be content to discuss it with my dog!

LITTLE MONK, *immersed in the manuscript.* I don't understand this sentence.

GALILEO. I'll explain it to you, I'll explain it to you.

They are sitting on the floor.

SCENE EIGHT

Eight long years with tongue in cheek
Of what he knew he did not speak.
Then temptation grew too great
And Galileo challenged fate.

GALILEO's *house in Florence again.* GALILEO *is supervising his Assistants* ANDREA, FEDERZONI, *and the* LITTLE MONK *who are about to prepare an experiment.* MRS. SARTI *and* VIRGINIA *are at a long table sewing bridal linen. There is a new telescope, larger than the old one. At the moment it is covered with a cloth.*

ANDREA, *looking up a schedule.* Thursday. Afternoon. Floating bodies again. Ice, bowl of water, scales, and it says here an iron needle. Aristotle.

VIRGINIA. Ludovico likes to entertain. We must take care to be neat. His mother notices every stitch. She doesn't approve of father's books.

MRS. SARTI. That's all a thing of the past. He hasn't published a book for years.

VIRGINIA. That's true. Oh Sarti, it's fun sewing a trousseau.

MRS. SARTI. Virginia, I want to talk to you. You are very young, and you have no mother, and your father is putting those pieces of ice in water, and marriage is too serious a business to go into blind. Now you should go to see a real astronomer from the university and have him cast your horoscope so you know where you stand. VIRGINIA *giggles.* What's the matter?

VIRGINIA. I've been already.

MRS. SARTI. Tell Sarti.

VIRGINIA. I have to be careful for three months now because the sun is in

Capricorn, but after that I get a favorable ascendant, and I can under-
take a journey if I am careful of Uranus, as I'm a Scorpion.

MRS. SARDI. What about Ludovico?

VIRGINIA. He's a Leo, the astronomer said. Leos are sensual. *Giggles.*

There is a knock at the door, it opens. Enter the RECTOR OF THE UNIVERSITY,
the philosopher of Scene Four, bringing a book.

RECTOR, *to* VIRGINIA. This is about the burning issue of the moment. He may
want to glance over it. My faculty would appreciate his comments. No,
don't disturb him now, my dear. Every minute one takes of your father's
time is stolen from Italy. *He goes.*

VIRGINIA. Federzoni! The rector of the university brought this.

　　　　　　　　　　FEDERZONI *takes it.*

GALILEO. What's it about?

FEDERZONI, *spelling.* DE MACULIS IN SOLE.

ANDREA. Oh, it's on the sun spots!

ANDREA *comes one side, and the* LITTLE MONK *the other, to look at the book.*

ANDREA. A new one!

FEDERZONI *resentfully puts the book into their hands and continues with the
preparation of the experiment.*

ANDREA. Listen to this dedication. *Quotes.* "To the greatest living authority
on physics, Galileo Galilei."—I read Fabricius' paper the other day. Fabricius says the spots are clusters of planets between us and the sun.

LITTLE MONK. Doubtful.

GALILEO, *noncommittal.* Yes?

ANDREA. Paris and Prague hold that they are vapors from the sun. Federzoni
doubts that.

FEDERZONI. Me? You leave me out. I said "hm," that was all. And don't discuss new things before me. I can't read the material, it's in Latin. *He
drops the scales and stands trembling with fury.* Tell me, can I doubt
anything?

　　　　　　GALILEO *walks over and picks up the scales silently. Pause.*

LITTLE MONK. There is happiness in doubting, I wonder why.

ANDREA. Aren't we going to take this up?

GALILEO. At the moment we are investigating floating bodies.

ANDREA. Mother has baskets full of letters from all over Europe asking his
opinion.

FEDERZONI. The question is whether you can afford to remain silent.

GALILEO. I cannot afford to be smoked on a wood fire like a ham.

ANDREA, *surprised.* Ah. You think the sun spots may have something to do
with that again? GALILEO *does not answer.*

ANDREA. Well, we stick to fiddling about with bits of ice in water. That
can't hurt you.

GALILEO. Correct.—Our thesis!

ANDREA. All things that are lighter than water float, and all things that are
heavier sink.

GALILEO. Aristotle says—

LITTLE MONK, *reading out of a book, translating.* "A broad and flat disk of ice, although heavier than water, still floats, because it is unable to divide the water."

GALILEO. Well. Now I push the ice below the surface. I take away the pressure of my hands. What happens?
Pause.
LITTLE MONK. It rises to the surface.
GALILEO. Correct. It seems to be able to divide the water as it's coming up, doesn't it?
LITTLE MONK. Could it be lighter than water after all?
GALILEO. Aha!
ANDREA. Then all things that are lighter than water float, and all things that are heavier sink. Q. e. d.
GALILEO. Not at all. Hand me that iron needle. Heavier than water? *They all nod.* A piece of paper. *He places the needle on a piece of paper and floats it on the surface of the water. Pause.* Do not be hasty with your conclusion. *Pause.* What happens?
FEDERZONI. The paper has sunk, the needle is floating.
VIRGINIA. What's the matter?
MRS. SARTI. Every time I hear them laugh it sends shivers down my spine.
There is a knocking at the outer door.
MRS. SARTI. Who's that at the door?
Enter LUDOVICO. VIRGINIA *runs to him. They embrace.* LUDOVICO *is followed by a servant with baggage.*
MRS. SARTI. Well!
VIRGINIA. Oh! Why didn't you write that you were coming?
LUDOVICO. I decided on the spur of the moment. I was over inspecting our vineyards at Bucciole. I couldn't keep away.
GALILEO. Who's that?
LITTLE MONK. Miss Virginia's intended. What's the matter with your eyes?
GALILEO, *blinking.* Oh yes, it's Ludovico, so it is. Well! Sarti, get a jug of that Sicilian wine, the old kind. We celebrate.
Everybody sits down. MRS. SARTI *has left, followed by* LUDOVICO'S SERVANT.
GALILEO. Well, Ludovico, old man. How are the horses?
LUDOVICO. The horses are fine.
GALILEO. Fine.
LUDOVICO. But those vineyards need a firm hand. *To* VIRGINIA. You look pale. Country life will suit you. Mother's planning on September.
VIRGINIA. I suppose I oughtn't, but stay here, I've got something to show you.
LUDOVICO. What?
VIRGINIA. Never mind. I won't be ten minutes. *She runs out.*
LUDOVICO. How's life these days, sir?
GALILEO. Dull. —How was the journey?
LUDOVICO. Dull. — Before I forget, mother sends her congratulations on your admirable tact over the latest rumblings of science.
GALILEO. Thank her from me.
LUDOVICO. Christopher Clavius had all Rome on its ears. He said he was afraid that the turning around business might crop up again on account of these spots on the sun.

ANDREA. Clavius is on the same track! *To* LUDOVICO. My mother's baskets are full of letters from all over Europe asking Mr. Galilei's opinion.

GALILEO. I am engaged in investigating the habits of floating bodies. Any harm in that?

MRS. SARTI *re-enters, followed by the* SERVANT. *They bring wine and glasses on a tray.*

GALILEO, *hands out the wine.* What news from the Holy City, apart from the prospect of my sins?

LUDOVICO. The Holy Father is on his death bed. Hadn't you heard?

LITTLE MONK. My goodness! What about the succession?

LUDOVICO. All the talk is of Barberini.

GALILEO. Barberini?

ANDREA. Mr. Galilei knows Barberini.

LITTLE MONK. Cardinal Barberini is a mathematician.

FEDERZONI. A scientist in the chair of Peter!

Pause.

GALILEO, *cheering up enormously.* This means change. We might live to see the day, Federzoni, when we don't have to whisper that two and two are four. *To* LUDOVICO. I like this wine. Don't you, Ludovico?

LUDOVICO. I like it.

GALILEO. I know the hill where it is grown. The slope is steep and stony, the grape almost blue. I am fond of this wine.

LUDOVICO. Yes, sir.

GALILEO. There are shadows in this wine. It is almost sweet but just stops short. — Andrea, clear that stuff away, ice, bowl and needle. — I cherish the consolations of the flesh. I have no patience with cowards who call them weaknesses. I say there is a certain achievement in enjoying things.

The PUPILS *get up and go to the experiment table.*

LITTLE MONK. What are we to do?

FEDERZONI. He is starting on the sun.

They begin with clearing up.

ANDREA, *singing in a low voice.*
The bible proves the earth stands still,
The Pope, he swears with tears:
The earth stands still. To prove it so
He takes it by the ears.

LUDOVICO. What's the excitement?

MRS. SARTI. You're not going to start those hellish goings-on again, Mr. Galilei?

ANDREA.
And gentlefolk, they say so too.
Each learned doctor proves,
(If you grease his palm) : The earth stands still.
And yet—and yet it moves.

GALILEO. Barberini is in the ascendant, so your mother is uneasy, and you're sent to investigate me. Correct me if I am wrong, Ludovico. Clavius is right: these spots on the sun interest me.

ANDREA. We might find out that the sun also revolves. How would you like that, Ludovico?

GALILEO. Do you like my wine, Ludovico?

LUDOVICO. I told you I did, sir.

GALILEO. You really like it?

LUDOVICO. I like it.

GALILEO. Tell me, Ludovico, would you consider going so far as to accept a man's wine or his daughter without insisting that he drop his profession? I have no wish to intrude, but have the moons of Jupiter affected Virginia's bottom?

MRS. SARTI. That isn't funny, it's just vulgar. I am going for Virginia.

LUDOVICO, *keeps her back.* Marriages in families such as mine are not arranged on a basis of sexual attraction alone.

GALILEO. Did they keep you back from marrying my daughter for eight years because I was on probation?

LUDOVICO. My future wife must take her place in the family pew.

GALILEO. You mean, if the daughter of a bad man sat in your family pew, your peasants might stop paying the rent?

LUDOVICO. In a sort of way.

GALILEO. When I was your age, the only person I allowed to rap me on the knuckles was my girl.

LUDOVICO. My mother was assured that you had undertaken not to get mixed up in this turning around business again, sir.

GALILEO. We had a conservative Pope then.

MRS. SARTI. Had! His Holiness is not dead yet!

GALILEO, *with relish.* Pretty nearly.

MRS. SARTI. That man will weigh a chip of ice fifty times, but when it comes to something that's convenient, he believes it blindly. "Is His Holiness dead?" — "Pretty nearly!"

LUDOVICO. You will find, sir, if His Holiness passes away, the new Pope, whoever he turns out to be, will respect the convictions held by the solid families of the country.

GALILEO, *to* ANDREA. That remains to be seen. — Andrea, get out the screen. We'll throw the image of the sun on our screen to save our eyes.

LITTLE MONK. I thought you'd been working at it. Do you know when I guessed it? When you didn't recognize Mr. Marsili.

MRS. SARTI. If my son has to go to hell for sticking to you, that's my affair, but you have no right to trample on your daughter's happiness.

LUDOVICO, *to his* SERVANT. Giuseppe, take my baggage back to the coach, will you?

MRS. SARTI. This will kill her. *She runs out, still clutching the jug.*

LUDOVICO, *politely.* Mr. Galilei, if we Marsilis were to countenance teachings frowned on by the church, it would unsettle our peasants. Bear in mind: these poor people in their brute state get everything upside down. They are nothing but animals. They will never comprehend the finer points of astronomy. Why, two months ago a rumor went around, an apple had been found on a pear tree, and they left their work in the fields to discuss it.

GALILEO, *interested.* Did they?

LUDOVICO. I have seen the day when my poor mother has had to have a dog whipped before their eyes to remind them to keep their place. Oh, you may have seen the waving corn from the window of your comfortable coach. You have, no doubt, nibbled our olives, and absentmindedly eaten our cheese, but you can have no idea how much responsibility that sort of thing entails.

GALILEO. Young man, I do not eat my cheese absentmindedly. *To* ANDREA. Are we ready?

ANDREA. Yes, sir.

GALILEO, *leaves* LUDOVICO *and adjusts the mirror.* You would not confine your whippings to dogs to remind your peasants to keep their places, would you, Marsili?

LUDOVICO, *after a pause.* Mr. Galilei, you have a wonderful brain, it's a pity.

LITTLE MONK, *astonished.* He threatened you.

GALILEO. Yes. And he threatened you too. We might unsettle his peasants. Your sister, Fulganzio, who works the lever of the olive press, might laugh out loud if she heard the sun is not a gilded coat of arms but a lever too. The earth turns because the sun turns it.

ANDREA. That could interest his steward too and even his money lender — and the seaport towns. . . . .

FEDERZONI. None of them speak Latin.

GALILEO. I might write in plain language. The work we do is exacting. Who would go through the strain for less than the population at large!

LUDOVICO. I see you have made your decision. It was inevitable. You will always be a slave of your passions. Excuse me to Virginia, I think it's as well I don't see her now.

GALILEO. The dowry is at your disposal at any time.

LUDOVICO. Good afternoon. *He goes followed by the* SERVANT.

ANDREA. Exit Ludovico. To hell with all Marsilis, Villanis, Orsinis, Canes, Nuccolis, Soldanieris. . . .

FEDERZONI. . . . who ordered the earth stand still because their castles might be shaken loose if it revolves . . .

LITTLE MONK. . . . and who only kiss the Pope's feet as long as he uses them to trample on the people. God made the physical world, God made the human brain. God will allow physics.

ANDREA. They will try to stop us.

GALILEO. Thus we enter the observation of these spots on the sun in which we are interested, at our own risk, not counting on protection from a problematical new Pope. . .

ANDREA. . . . but with great likelihood of dispelling Fabrizius' vapors, and the shadows of Paris and Prague, and of establishing the rotation of the sun. . .

GALILEO. . . . and with *some* likelihood of establishing the rotation of the sun. My intention is not to prove that I was right but to find out *whether* I was right. "Abandon hope all ye who enter—an observation." Before assuming these phenomena are spots, which would suit us, let us first set about proving that they are not—fried fish. We crawl by inches.

What we find today we will wipe from the blackboard tomorrow and reject it—unless it shows up again the day after tomorrow. And if we find anything which would suit us, that thing we will eye with particular distrust. In fact, we will approach this observing of the sun with the implacable determination to prove that the earth stands still and only if hopelessly defeated in this pious undertaking can we allow ourselves to wonder if we may not have been right all the time: the earth revolves. Take the cloth off the telescope and turn it on the sun.

Quietly they start work. When the corruscating image of the sun is focused on the screen, VIRGINIA *enters hurriedly, her wedding dress on, her hair disheveled,* MRS. SARTI *with her, carrying her wedding veil. The two women realize what has happened.* VIRGINIA *faints.* ANDREA, LITTLE MONK *and* GALILEO *rush to her.* FEDERZONI *continues working.*

SCENE NINE

> *On April Fool's Day, thirty two,*
> *Of science there was much ado.*
> *People had learned from Galilei:*
> *They used his teaching in their way.*

Around the corner from the market place a STREET SINGER *and his* WIFE, *who is costumed to represent the earth in a skeleton globe made of thin bands of brass, are holding the attention of a sprinkling of representative citizens, some in masquerade who were on their way to see the carnival procession. From the market place the noise of an impatient crowd.*

BALLAD SINGER, *accompanied by his* WIFE *on the guitar.*
When the Almighty made the universe
He made the earth and then he made the sun.
Then round the earth he bade the sun to turn—
That's in the bible, Genesis, Chapter One.
And from that time all beings here below
Were in obedient circles meant to go:
>   Around the pope the cardinals
>   Around the cardinals the bishops
>   Around the bishops the secretaries
>   Around the secretaries the aldermen
>   Around the aldermen the craftsmen
>   Around the craftsmen the servants
>   Around the servants the dogs, the chickens, and the beggars.

A conspicuous reveller—henceforth called the SPINNER—*has slowly caught on and is exhibiting his idea of spinning around. He does not lose dignity, he faints with mock grace.*

BALLAD SINGER.
Up stood the learned Galileo
Glanced briefly at the sun
And said: "Almighty God was wrong
In Genesis, Chapter One!"
>   Now that was rash, my friends, it is no matter small
>   For heresy will spread today like foul diseases.
>   Change Holy Writ, forsooth? What will be left at all?
>   Why: each of us would say and do just what he pleases!

Three wretched EXTRAS, *employed by the chamber of commerce, enter. Two of them, in ragged costumes, moodily bear a litter with a mock throne. The third sits on the throne. He wears sacking, a false beard, a prop crown, he carries a prop orb and sceptre, and around his chest the inscription "*THE KING OF HUNGARY.*" The litter has a card with "No. 4" written on it. The litter bearers dump him down and listen to the* BALLAD SINGER.

BALLAD SINGER.
Good people, what will come to pass
If Galileo's teachings spread?
No altar boy will serve the mass
No servant girl will make the bed.
>   Now that is grave, my friends, it is no matter small:
>   For independent spirit spreads like foul diseases!
>   (Yet life is sweet and man is weak and after all—
>   How nice it is, for a little change, to do just as one pleases!)

The BALLAD SINGER *takes over the guitar. His* WIFE *dances around him, illustrating the motion of the earth. A* COBBLER'S BOY *with a pair of resplendent lacquered boots hung over his shoulder has been jumping up and down in mock excitement. There are three more children, dressed as grownups among the spectators, two together and a single one with mother. The* COBBLER'S BOY *takes the three* CHILDREN *in hand, forms a chain and leads it, moving to the music, in and out among the spectators, "whipping" the chain so that the last child bumps into people. On the way past a* PEASANT WOMAN, *he steals an egg from her basket. She gestures to him to return it. As he passes her again he quietly breaks the egg over her head. The* KING OF HUNGARY *ceremoniously hands his orb to one of his bearers, marches down with mock dignity, and chastises the* COBBLER'S BOY. *The parents remove the three* CHILDREN. *The unseemliness subsides.*

BALLAD SINGER.

> The carpenters take wood and build
> Their houses—not the church's pews.
> And members of the cobblers' guild
> Now boldly walk the streets—in shoes.
> The tenant kicks the noble lord
> Quite off the land he owned—like that!
> The milk his wife once gave the priest
> Now makes (at last!) her children fat.
>> Ts, ts, ts, ts, my friends, this is no matter small
>> For independent spirit spreads like foul diseases
>> People must keep their place, some down and some on top!
>> (Though it is nice, for a little change, to do just as one pleases!)

The COBBLER'S BOY *has put on the lacquered boots he was carrying. He struts off. The* BALLAD SINGER *takes over the guitar again. His* WIFE *dances around him in increased tempo. A* MONK *has been standing near a rich* COUPLE, *who are in subdued costly clothes, without masks: shocked at the song, he now leaves. A* DWARF *in the costume of an astronomer turns his telescope on the departing* MONK, *thus drawing attention to the rich* COUPLE. *In imitation of the* COBBLER'S BOY, *the* SPINNER *forms a chain of grownups. They move to the music, in and out, and between the rich* COUPLE. *The* SPINNER *changes the* GENTLEMAN'S *bonnet for the ragged hat of a* BEGGAR. *The* GENTLEMAN *decides to take this in good part, and a* GIRL *is emboldened to take his dagger. The* GENTLEMAN *is miffed, throws the* BEGGAR'S *hat back. The* BEGGAR *discards the* GENTLEMAN'S *bonnet and drops it on the ground. The* KING OF HUNGARY *has walked from his throne, taken an egg from the* PEASANT WOMAN, *and paid for it. He now ceremoniously breaks it over the* GENTLEMAN'S *head as he is bending down to pick up his bonnet. The* GENTLEMAN *conducts the* LADY *away from the scene. The* KING OF HUNGARY, *about to resume his throne, finds one of the* CHILDREN *sitting on it. The* GENTLEMAN *returns to retrieve his dagger. Merriment. The* BALLAD SINGER *wanders off. This is part of his routine. His* WIFE *sings to the* SPINNER.

WIFE.

> Now speaking for myself I feel
> That I could also do with a change.
> You know, for me . . . *Turning to a reveller* . . . *you* have appeal
> Maybe tonight we could arrange. . .

The DWARF-ASTRONOMER *has been amusing the people by focusing his telescope on her legs. The* BALLAD SINGER *has returned.*

BALLAD SINGER.

No, no, no, no, no, stop, Galileo, stop!
For independent spirit spreads like foul diseases
People must keep their place, some down and some on top!
(Though it is nice, for a little change, to do just as one pleases!)
    The SPECTATORS *stand embarrassed. A* GIRL *laughs loudly.*

BALLAD SINGER *and his* WIFE.

Good people who have trouble here below
In serving cruel lords and gentle Jesus
Who bids you turn the other cheek just so . . . *With mimicry.*
While they prepare to strike the second blow:
Obedience will never cure your woe
So each of you wake up and do just as he pleases!

The BALLAD SINGER *and his* WIFE *hurriedly start to try to sell pamphlets to the spectators.*

BALLAD SINGER. Read all about the earth going round the sun, two centesimi only. As proved by the great Galileo. Two centesimi only. Written by a local scholar. Understandable to one and all. Buy one for your friends, your children and your aunty Rosa, two centesimi only. Abbrevi-

ated but complete. Fully illustrated with pictures of the planets, including Venus, two centesimi only.

During the speech of the BALLAD SINGER *we hear the carnival procession approaching followed by laughter. A* REVELLER *rushes in.*

REVELLER. The procession!

The litter bearers speedily joggle out the KING OF HUNGARY. *The* SPECTATORS *turn and look at the first float of the procession, which now makes its appearance. It bears a gigantic figure of* GALILEO, *holding in one hand an open*

bible with the pages crossed out. The other hand points to the bible, and the
head mechanically turns from side to side as if to say "No! No!"
A LOUD VOICE. Galileo, the bible killer!
The laughter from the market place becomes uproarious. The MONK *comes*
flying from the market place followed by delighted CHILDREN.

SCENE TEN

> *The depths are hot, the heights are chill*
> *The streets are loud, the court is still.*

Ante-Chamber and staircase in the Medicean palace in Florence. GALILEO,
with a book under his arm, waits with his DAUGHTER *to be admitted to the*
presence of the PRINCE.

VIRGINIA. They are a long time.

GALILEO. Yes.

VIRGINIA. Who is that funny looking man? *She indicates the* INFORMER *who*
has entered casually and seated himself in the background, taking no ap-
parent notice of GALILEO.

GALILEO. I don't know.

VIRGINIA. It's not the first time I have seen him around. He gives me the
creeps.

GALILEO. Nonsense. We're in Florence, not among robbers in the mountains
of Corsica.

VIRGINIA. Here comes the Rector.
The RECTOR *comes down the stairs.*

GALILEO. Gaffone is a bore. He attaches himself to you.
The RECTOR *passes, scarcely nodding.*

GALILEO. My eyes are bad today. Did he acknowledge us?

VIRGINIA. Barely. *Pause.* What's in your book? Will they say it's heretical?

GALILEO. You hang around church too much. And getting up at dawn and
scurrying to mass is ruining your skin. You pray for me, don't you?
A MAN *comes down the stairs.*

VIRGINIA. Here's Mr. Matti. You designed a machine for his Iron Foundries.

MATTI. How were the squabs, Mr. Galilei? *Low.* My brother and I had
a good laugh the other day. He picked up a racy pamphlet against the
bible somewhere. It quoted you.

GALILEO. The squabs, Matti, were wonderful, thank you again. Pamphlets
I know nothing about. The bible and Homer are my favorite reading.

MATTI. No necessity to be cautious with me, Mr. Galilei. I am on your side.
I am not a man who knows about the motions of the stars, but you have
championed the freedom to teach new things. Take that mechanical
cultivator they have in Germany which you described to me. I can tell
you, it will never be used in this country. The same circles that are

hampering you now will forbid the physicians at Bologna to cut up corpses for research. Do you know, they have such things as money markets in Amsterdam and in London? Schools for business, too. Regular papers with news. Here we are not even free to make money. I have a stake in your career. They are against iron foundries because they say the gathering of so many workers in one place fosters immorality! If they ever try anything, Mr. Galilei, remember you have friends in all walks of life including an iron founder. Good luck to you. *He goes.*

..HIS VOICE CARRIES

GALILEO. Good man, but need he be so affectionate in public? His voice carries. They will always claim me as their spiritual leader particularly in places where it doesn't help me at all. I have written a book about the mechanics of the firmament, that is all. What they do or don't do with it is not my concern.

VIRGINIA, *loud.* If people only knew how you disagreed with those goings-on all over the country last All Fools day.

GALILEO. Yes. Offer honey to a bear, and lose your arm if the beast is hungry.

VIRGINIA, *low.* Did the prince ask you to come here today?

GALILEO. I sent word I was coming. He will want the book, he has paid for it. My health hasn't been any too good lately. I may accept Sagredo's invitation to stay with him in Padua for a few weeks.

VIRGINIA. You couldn't manage without your books.

GALILEO. Sagredo has an excellent library.

VIRGINIA. We haven't had this month's salary yet—

GALILEO. Yes. *The* CARDINAL INQUISITOR *passes down the staircase. He bows deeply in answer to* GALILEO's *bow.* What is he doing in Florence? If they try to do anything to me, the new Pope will meet them with an iron NO. And the Prince is my pupil, he would never have me extradited.

VIRGINIA. Psst. The Lord Chamberlain.

The LORD CHAMBERLAIN *comes down the stairs.*

LORD CHAMBERLAIN. His Highness had hoped to find time for you, Mr. Galilei. Unfortunately, he has to leave immediately to judge the parade at the Riding Academy. On what business did you wish to see His Highness?

GALILEO. I wanted to present my book to His Highness.

LORD CHAMBERLAIN. How are your eyes today?

GALILEO. So, so. With His Highness' permission, I am dedicating the book . . .

LORD CHAMBERLAIN. Your eyes are a matter of great concern to His Highness. Could it be that you have been looking too long and too often through your marvelous tube? *He leaves without accepting the book.*

VIRGINIA, *greatly agitated.* Father, I am afraid.

GALILEO. He didn't take the book, did he? *Low and resolute.* Keep a straight face. We are not going home, but to the house of the lens-grinder. There is a coach and horses in his backyard. Keep your eyes to the front, don't look back at that man.

They start. The LORD CHAMBERLAIN *comes back.*

LORD CHAMBERLAIN. Oh, Mr. Galilei, His Highness has just charged me to inform you that the Florentine Court is no longer in a position to oppose the request of the Holy Inquisition to interrogate you in Rome.

SCENE ELEVEN

The Pope

A chamber in the Vatican. The POPE, URBAN VIII—*formerly Cardinal* BARBERINI —*is giving audience to the* CARDINAL INQUISITOR. *The trampling and shuffling of many feet is heard throughout the scene from the adjoining corridors. During the scene the* POPE *is being robed for the conclave he is about to attend: at the beginning of the scene he is plainly* BARBERINI, *but as the scene proceeds he is more and more obscured by grandiose vestments.*

no! no' no!

POPE. No! No! No!

INQUISITOR, *referring to the owners of the shuffling feet.* Doctors of all chairs from the universities, representatives of the special orders of the Church, representatives of the clergy as a whole who have come believing with child-like faith in the word of God as set forth in the Scriptures, who have come to hear Your Holiness confirm their faith: and Your Holiness is really going to tell them that the bible can no longer be regarded as the alphabet of truth?

POPE. I will not set myself up against the multiplication table. No!

INQUISITOR. Ah, that is what these people say, that it is the multiplication table. Their cry is, "The figures compel us," but where do these figures come from? Plainly they come from doubt. These men doubt everything. Can society stand on doubt and not on faith? "Thou art my master, but I doubt whether it is for the best." "This is my neighbor's house and my neighbor's wife, but why shouldn't they belong to me?" After the plague, after the new war, after the unparalleled disaster of the Reformation, your dwindling flock look to their shepherd, and now the mathematicians turn their tubes on the sky and announce to the world that you have not the best advice about the heavens either—up to now your only uncontested sphere of influence. This Galilei started meddling in machines at an early age. Now that men in ships are venturing on the great oceans—I am not against that of course—they are putting their faith in a brass-bowl they call a compass and not in Almighty God.

POPE. This man is the greatest physicist of our time. He is the light of Italy, and not just any muddle-head.

INQUISITOR. Would we have had to arrest him otherwise? This bad man knows what he is doing, not writing his books in Latin, but in the jargon of the market place.

POPE, *occupied with the shuffling feet.* That was not in the best of taste. *A pause.* These shuffling feet are making me nervous.

INQUISITOR. May they be more telling than my words, Your Holiness. Shall all these go from you with doubt in their hearts?

POPE. This man has friends. What about Versailles? What about the Viennese court? They will call Holy Church a cesspool for defunct ideas. Keep your hands off him.

INQUISITOR. In practice it will never get far. He is a man of the flesh. He would soften at once.

POPE. He has more enjoyment in him than any man I ever saw. He loves eating and drinking and thinking. To excess. He indulges in thinking-bouts! He cannot say no to an old wine or a new thought. *Furious.* I do not want a condemnation of physical facts. I do not want to hear battle cries: Church, church, church! Reason, reason, reason! *Pause.* These shuffling feet are intolerable. Has the whole world come to my door?

INQUISITOR. Not the whole world, Your Holiness. A select gathering of the faithful.

Pause.

POPE, *exhausted*. It is clearly understood: he is not to be tortured. *Pause.*
   At the very most, he may be shown the instruments.
INQUISITOR. That will be adequate, Your Holiness. Mr. Galilei understands
   machinery.
The eyes of BARBERINI *look helplessly at the* CARDINAL INQUISITOR *from under
the completely assembled panoply of* POPE URBAN VIII.

SCENE TWELVE

> *June twenty second, sixteen thirty three,*
> *A momentous date for you and me.*
> *Of all the days that was the one*
> *An age of reason could have begun.*

Again the garden of the Florentine AMBASSADOR *at Rome, where* GALILEO'S
assistants wait the news of the trial. The LITTLE MONK *and* FEDERZONI *are
attempting to concentrate on a game of chess.* VIRGINIA *kneels in a corner,
praying and counting her beads.*

LITTLE MONK. The Pope didn't even grant him an audience.
FEDERZONI. No more scientific discussions.
ANDREA. The "Discorsi" will never be finished. The sum of his findings.
   They will kill him.

FEDERZONI, *stealing a glance at him*. Do you really think so?

ANDREA. He will never recant.

Silence.

LITTLE MONK. You know when you lie awake at night how your mind fastens
on to something irrelevant. Last night I kept thinking: if only they would
let him take his little stone in with him, the appeal-to-reason-pebble that
he always carries in his pocket.

FEDERZONI. In the room *they'll* take him to, he won't have a pocket.

ANDREA. But he will not recant.

LITTLE MONK. How can they beat the truth out of a man who gave his sight
in order to see?

FEDERZONI. Maybe they can't.

Silence.

ANDREA, *speaking about* VIRGINIA. She is praying that he will recant.

FEDERZONI. Leave her alone. She doesn't know whether she's on her head
or on her heels since they got hold of her. They brought her Father Confessor from Florence.

The INFORMER *of Scene Ten enters.*

INFORMER. Mr. Galilei will be here soon. He may need a bed.

FEDERZONI. Have they let him out?

INFORMER. Mr. Galilei is expected to recant at five o'clock. The big bell of
Saint Marcus will be rung and the complete text of his recantation publicly announced.

ANDREA. I don't believe it.

INFORMER. Mr. Galilei will be brought to the garden gate at the back of the
house, to avoid the crowds collecting in the streets. *He goes.*

Silence.

ANDREA. The moon is an earth because the light of the moon is not her
own. Jupiter is a fixed star, and four moons turn around Jupiter, therefore we are not shut in by crystal shells. The sun is the pivot of our
world, therefore the earth is not the center. The earth moves, spinning
about the sun. And he showed us. You can't make a man unsee what
he has seen.

Silence.

FEDERZONI. Five o'clock is one minute.

VIRGINIA *prays louder.*

ANDREA. Listen all of you, they are murdering the truth.

He stops up his ears with his fingers. The two other pupils do the same.
FEDERZONI *goes over to the* LITTLE MONK, *and all of them stand absolutely still
in cramped positions. Nothing happens. No bell sounds. After a silence,
filled with the murmur of* VIRGINIA'S *prayers,* FEDERZONI *runs to the wall to
look at the clock. He turns around, his expression changed. He shakes his
head. They drop their hands.*

FEDERZONI. No. No bell. It is three minutes after.

LITTLE MONK. He hasn't.

ANDREA. He held true. It is all right, it is all right.

LITTLE MONK. He did not recant.

FEDERZONI. No.

They embrace each other, they are delirious with joy.

ANDREA. So force cannot accomplish everything. What has been seen can't be unseen. Man is constant in the face of death.

FEDERZONI. June 22, 1633: dawn of the age of reason. I wouldn't have wanted to go on living if he had recanted.

LITTLE MONK. I didn't say anything, but I was in agony. Oh, ye of little faith!

ANDREA. I was sure.

FEDERZONI. It would have turned our morning to night.

ANDREA. It would have been as if the mountain had turned to water.

LITTLE MONK, *kneeling down, crying.* Oh God, I thank Thee.

ANDREA. Beaten humanity can lift its head. A man has stood up and said "no." *At this moment the bell of Saint Marcus begins to toll. They stand like statues.* VIRGINIA *stands up.*

VIRGINIA. The bell of Saint Marcus. He is not damned.

From the street one hears the TOWN CRIER *reading* GALILEO's *recantation.*

TOWN CRIER. I, Galileo Galilei, Teacher of Mathematics and Physics, do hereby publicly renounce my teaching that the earth moves. I foreswear this teaching with a sincere heart and unfeigned faith and detest and curse this and all other errors and heresies repugnant to the Holy Scriptures.

The lights dim; when they come up again the bell of Saint Marcus is petering out. VIRGINIA *has gone but the* SCHOLARS *are still there waiting.*

SO THE MOUNTAIN TURNED TO WATER!

ANDREA, *loud.* The mountain did turn to water.

GALILEO *has entered quietly and unnoticed. He is changed, almost unrecognizable. He has heard* ANDREA. *He waits some seconds by the door for somebody to greet him. Nobody does. They retreat from him. He goes slowly and, because of his bad sight, uncertainly, to the front of the stage where he finds a chair, and sits down.*

ANDREA. I can't look at him. Tell him to go away.

FEDERZONI. Steady.

ANDREA, *hysterically.* He saved his big gut.

FEDERZONI. Get him a glass of water.

The LITTLE MONK *fetches a glass of water for* ANDREA. *Nobody acknowledges the presence of* GALILEO, *who sits silently on his chair listening to the voice of the* TOWN CRIER, *now in another street.*

ANDREA. I can walk. Just help me a bit.

> *They help him to the door.*

ANDREA, *in the door.* "Unhappy is the land that breeds no hero."

GALILEO. No, Andrea: "Unhappy is the land that needs a hero."

Before the next scene a curtain with the following legend on it is lowered:
> You can plainly see that if a horse were to fall from a height of three or four feet, it could break its bones, whereas a dog would not suffer injury. The same applies to a cat from a height of as much as eight or ten feet, to a grasshopper from the top of a tower, and to an ant falling down from the moon. Nature could not allow a horse to become as big as twenty horses nor a giant as big as ten men, unless she were to change the proportions of all its members, particularly the bones. Thus the common assumption that great and small structures are equally tough is obviously wrong.

> —From the Discorsi

SCENE THIRTEEN

1633-1642.
Galileo Galilei remains a prisoner
of the Inquisition until his death.

A country house near Florence. A large room simply furnished. There is a huge table, a leather chair, a globe of the world on a stand, and a narrow bed. A portion of the adjoining anteroom is visible, and the front door which opens into it.

An OFFICIAL OF THE INQUISITION *sits on guard in the anteroom.*

In the large room, GALILEO *is quietly experimenting with a bent wooden rail and a small ball of wood. He is still vigorous but almost blind.*

After a while there is a knocking at the outside door. The OFFICIAL *opens it to a* PEASANT *who brings a plucked goose.* VIRGINIA *comes from the kitchen. She is past forty.*

PEASANT, *handing the goose to* VIRGINIA. I was told to deliver this here.

VIRGINIA. I didn't order a goose.

PEASANT. I was told to say it's from someone who was passing through.

VIRGINIA *takes the goose, surprised. The* OFFICIAL *takes it from her and examines it suspiciously. Then, reassured, he hands it back to her. The* PEASANT *goes.* VIRGINIA *brings the goose in to* GALILEO.

VIRGINIA. Somebody who was passing through sent you something.

GALILEO. What is it?

VIRGINIA. Can't you see it?

GALILEO. No. *He walks over.* A goose. Any name?

VIRGINIA. No.

GALILEO, *weighing the goose.* Solid.

VIRGINIA, *cautiously.* Will you eat the liver, if I have it cooked with a little apple?

GALILEO. I had my dinner. Are you under orders to finish me off with food?

VIRGINIA. It's not rich. And what is wrong with your eyes again? You should be able to see it.

GALILEO. You were standing in the light.

VIRGINIA. I was not. — You haven't been writing again?

GALILEO, *sneering.* What do you think?

VIRGINIA *takes the goose out into the anteroom and speaks to the* OFFICIAL.

VIRGINIA. You had better ask Monsignore Carpula to send the doctor. Father couldn't see this goose across the room. — Don't look at me like that. He has not been writing. He dictates everything to me, as you know.

OFFICIAL. Yes?

VIRGINIA. He abides by the rules. My father's repentance is sincere. I keep an eye on him. *She hands him the goose.* Tell the cook to fry the liver with an apple and an onion. *She goes back into the large room.* And you have no business to be doing that with those eyes of yours, father.

GALILEO. You may read me some Horace.

VIRGINIA. We should go on with your weekly letter to the Archbishop. Monsignor Carpula to whom we owe so much was all smiles the other day because the Archbishop had expressed his pleasure at your collaboration.

GALILEO. Where were we?

VIRGINIA, *sits down to take his dictation.* Paragraph four.

GALILEO. Read what you have.

VIRGINIA. "The position of the Church in the matter of the unrest at Genoa. I agree with Cardinal Spoletti in the matter of the unrest among the Venetian ropemakers . . ."

GALILEO. Yes. *Dictates.* I agree with Cardinal Spoletti in the matter of the unrest among the Venetian ropemakers: it is better to distribute good nourishing food in the name of charity than to pay them more for their bellropes. It being surely better to strengthen their faith than to encourage their acquisitiveness. St. Paul says: Charity never faileth. — How is that?

VIRGINIA. It's beautiful, father.

GALILEO. It couldn't be taken as irony?

VIRGINIA. No. The Archbishop will like it. It's so practical.

GALILEO. I trust your judgment. Read it over slowly.

VIRGINIA. "The position of the Church in the matter of the unrest. . . ."

There is a knocking at the outside door. VIRGINIA *goes into the anteroom.*

The OFFICIAL *opens the door. It is* ANDREA.

ANDREA. Good evening. I am sorry to call so late, I'm on my way to Holland. I was asked to look him up. Can I go in?

VIRGINIA. I don't know whether he will see you. You never came.

ANDREA. Ask him.

GALILEO *recognizes the voice. He sits motionless.* VIRGINIA *comes in to* GALILEO.

GALILEO. Is that Andrea?

VIRGINIA. Yes. *Pause.* I will send him away.

GALILEO. Show him in.

      VIRGINIA *shows* ANDREA *in.* VIRGINIA *sits,* ANDREA *remains standing.*

ANDREA, *cool.* Have you been keeping well, Mr. Galilei?

GALILEO. Sit down. What are you doing these days? What are you working on? I heard it was something about hydraulics in Milan.

ANDREA. As he knew I was passing through, Fabricius of Amsterdam asked me to visit you and inquire about your health.

      Pause.

GALILEO. I am very well.

ANDREA, *formally.* I am glad I can report you are in good health.

GALILEO. Fabricius will be glad to hear it. And you might inform him that, on account of the depth of my repentance, I live in comparative comfort.

ANDREA. Yes, we understand that the church is more than pleased with you. Your complete acceptance has had its effect. Not one paper expounding a new thesis has made its appearance in Italy since your submission.

      Pause.

GALILEO. Unfortunately there are countries not under the wing of the church. Would you not say the erroneous condemned theories are still taught — there?

ANDREA, *relentless.* Things are almost at a standstill.

GALILEO. Are they? *Pause.* Nothing from Descartes in Paris?

ANDREA. Yes. On receiving the news of your recantation, he shelved his treatise on the nature of light.

GALILEO. I sometimes worry about my assistants whom I led into error. Have they benefited by my example?

ANDREA. In order to work I have to go to Holland.

GALILEO. Yes.

ANDREA. Federzoni is grinding lenses again, back in some shop.

GALILEO. He can't read the books.

ANDREA. Fulganzio, our little monk, has abandoned research and is resting in peace in the church.

GALILEO. So. *Pause.* My superiors are looking forward to my spiritual recovery. I am progressing as well as can be expected.

VIRGINIA. You are doing well, father.

GALILEO. Virginia, leave the room.

      VIRGINIA *rises uncertainly and goes out.*

VIRGINIA, *to the* OFFICIAL. He was his pupil, so now he is his enemy. — Help me in the kitchen.

      She leaves the anteroom with the OFFICIAL.

ANDREA. May I go now, sir?

GALILEO. I do not know why you came, Sarti. To unsettle me? I have to be prudent.

ANDREA. I'll be on my way.

GALILEO. As it is, I have relapses. I completed the "Discorsi."

ANDREA. You completed what?

GALILEO. My "Discorsi."

ANDREA. How?

GALILEO. I am allowed pen and paper. My superiors are intelligent men. They know the habits of a lifetime cannot be broken abruptly. But they protect me from any unpleasant consequences: they lock my pages away as I dictate them. And I should know better than to risk my comfort. I wrote the Discorsi out again during the night. The manuscript is in the globe. My vanity has up to now prevented me from destroying it. If you consider taking it, you will shoulder the entire risk. You will say it was pirated from the original in the hands of the Holy Office.

ANDREA, *as in a trance, has gone to the globe. He lifts the upper half and gets the book. He turns the pages as if wanting to devour them. In the background the opening sentences of the "Discorsi" appear:*
MY PURPOSE IS TO SET FORTH A VERY NEW
SCIENCE DEALING WITH A VERY ANCIENT
SUBJECT — MOTION. . . . AND I HAVE
DISCOVERED BY EXPERIMENT SOME PROPERTIES
OF IT WHICH ARE WORTH KNOWING. . . .

GALILEO. I had to employ my time somehow.
The text disappears.

ANDREA. Two new sciences! This will be the foundation stone of a new physics.

GALILEO. Yes. Put it under your coat.

ANDREA. And we thought you had deserted. *In a low voice.* Mr. Galilei, how can I begin to express my shame. Mine has been the loudest voice against you.

GALILEO. That would seem to have been proper. I taught you science and I decried the truth.

ANDREA. Did you? I think not. Everything is changed!

GALILEO. What is changed?

ANDREA. You shielded the truth from the oppressor. Now I see! In your dealings with the Inquisition you used the same superb common sense you brought to physics.

GALILEO. Oh!

ANDREA. We lost our heads. With the crowd at the street corners we said: "He will die, he will never surrender!" You came back: "I surrendered but I am alive." We cried: "Your hands are stained!" You say: "Better stained than empty."

GALILEO. "Better stained than empty." — It sounds realistic. Sounds like me.

ANDREA. And I of all people should have known. I was twelve when you sold another man's telescope to the Venetian Senate, and saw you put it to immortal use. Your friends were baffled when you bowed to the Prince

of Florence: Science gained a wider audience. You always laughed at
heroics. "People who suffer bore me," you said. "Misfortunes are due
mainly to miscalculations." And: "If there are obstacles, the shortest line
between two points may be the crooked line."

GALILEO. It makes a picture.

ANDREA. And when you stooped to recant in 1633, I should have understood
that you were again about your business.

GALILEO. My business being?

ANDREA. Science. The study of the properties of motion, mother of the
machines which will themselves change the ugly face of the earth.

GALILEO. Aha!

ANDREA. You gained time to write a book that only you could write. Had
you burned at the stake in a blaze of glory they would have won.

GALILEO. They have won. And there is no such thing as a scientific work
that only one man can write.

ANDREA. Then why did you recant, tell me that!

GALILEO. I recanted because I was afraid of physical pain.

ANDREA. No!

GALILEO. They showed me the instruments.

ANDREA. It was not a plan?

GALILEO. It was not.

                              Pause.

ANDREA. But you have contributed. Science has only one commandment:
contribution. And you have contributed more than any man for a hundred years.

GALILEO. Have I? Then welcome to my gutter, dear colleague in science
and brother in treason: I sold out, you are a buyer. The first sight of the
book! His mouth watered and his scoldings were drowned. Blessed be
our bargaining, whitewashing, deathfearing community!

ANDREA. The fear of death is human.

GALILEO. Even the church will teach you that to be weak is not human. It
is just evil.

ANDREA. The church, yes! But science is not concerned with our weaknesses.

GALILEO. No? My dear Sarti, in spite of my present convictions, I may be able
to give you a few pointers as to the concerns of your chosen profession.

                    Enter VIRGINIA *with a platter.*

In my spare time, I happen to have gone over this case. I have spare
time.—Even a man who sells wool, however good he is at buying wool
cheap and selling it dear, must be concerned with the standing of the
wool trade. The practice of science would seem to call for valor. She
trades in knowledge, which is the product of doubt. And this new art of
doubt has enchanted the public. The plight of the multitude is old as
the rocks, and is believed to be basic as the rocks. But now they have
learned to doubt. They snatched the telescopes out of our hands and had
them trained on their tormentors: prince, official, public moralist. The
mechanism of the heavens was clearer, the mechanism of their courts was
still murky. The battle to measure the heavens is won by doubt; by cre-

dulity the Roman housewife's battle for milk will always be lost. Word is passed down that this is of no concern to the scientist who is told he will only release such of his findings as do not disturb the peace, that is, the peace of mind of the well-to-do. Threats and bribes fill the air. Can the scientist hold out on the numbers?—For what reason do you labor? I take it the intent of science is to ease human existence. If you give way to coercion, science can be crippled, and your new machines may simply suggest new drudgeries. Should you then, in time, discover all there is to be discovered, your progress must then become a progress away from the bulk of humanity. The gulf might even grow so wide that the sound of your cheering at some new achievement would be echoed by a universal howl of horror.—As a scientist I had an almost unique opportunity. In my day astronomy emerged into the market place. At that particular time, had one man put up a fight, it could have had wide repercussions. I have come to believe that I was never in real danger; for some years I was as strong as the authorities, and I surrendered my knowledge to the powers that be, to use it, no, not *use* it, *abuse* it, as it suits their ends. I have betrayed my profession. Any man who does what I have done must not be tolerated in the ranks of science.

VIRGINIA, *who has stood motionless, puts the platter on the table.*

VIRGINIA. You are accepted in the ranks of the faithful, father.

GALILEO, *sees her.* Correct. *He goes over to the table.* I have to eat now.

VIRGINIA. We lock up at eight.

ANDREA. I am glad I came. *He extends his hand.* GALILEO *ignores it and goes over to his meal.*

GALILEO, *examining the plate; to* ANDREA. Somebody who knows me sent me a goose. I still enjoy eating.

ANDREA. And your opinion is now that the "new age" was an illusion?

GALILEO. Well. — This age of ours turned out to be a whore, spattered with blood. Maybe, new ages look like blood-spattered whores. Take care of yourself.

ANDREA. Yes. *Unable to go.* With reference to your evaluation of the author in question—I do not know the answer. But I cannot think that your savage analysis is the last word.

GALILEO. Thank you, sir.

OFFICIAL *knocks at the door.*

VIRGINIA, *showing* ANDREA *out.* I don't like visitors from the past, they excite him.

She lets him out. The OFFICIAL *closes the iron door.* VIRGINIA *returns.*

GALILEO, *eating.* Did you try and think who sent the goose?

VIRGINIA. Not Andrea.

GALILEO. Maybe not. I gave Redhead his first lesson; when he held out his hand, I had to remind myself he is teaching now. — How is the sky tonight?

VIRGINIA, *at the window.* Bright.

GALILEO *continues eating.*

*may you now guard science' light
Kindle it and use it right
Lest it be a flame to fall
Downward to consume us all*

See note four in Notes to *Galileo*

SCENE FOURTEEN

*The great book o'er the border went
And, good folk, that was the end.
But we hope you'll keep in mind
You and I were left behind.*

Before a little Italian customs house early in the morning. ANDREA *sits upon one of his traveling trunks at the barrier and reads* GALILEO's *book. The window of a small house is still lit, and a big grotesque shadow, like an old witch and her cauldron, falls upon the house wall beyond. Barefoot* CHILDREN *in rags see it and point to the little house.*

CHILDREN, *singing.*

One, two, three, four, five, six,
Old Marina is a witch.
At night, on a broomstick she sits
And on the church steeple she spits.

CUSTOMS OFFICER, *to* ANDREA. Why are you making this journey?

ANDREA. I am a scholar.

CUSTOMS OFFICER, *to his* CLERK. Put down under "reason for leaving the country": Scholar. *He points to the baggage.* Books! Anything dangerous in these books?

ANDREA. What is dangerous?

CUSTOMS OFFICER. Religion. Politics.

ANDREA. These are nothing but mathematical formulas.

CUSTOMS OFFICER. What's that?

ANDREA. Figures.

CUSTOMS OFFICER. Oh, figures. No harm in figures. Just wait a minute, sir, we will soon have your papers stamped. *He exits with* CLERK.

Meanwhile, a little council of war among the CHILDREN *has taken place.* ANDREA *quietly watches. One of the* BOYS, *pushed forward by the others, creeps up to the little house from which the shadow comes, and takes the jug of milk on the doorstep.*

ANDREA, *quietly.* What are you doing with that milk?

BOY, *stopping in mid-movement.* She is a witch.

The other CHILDREN *run away behind the Custom House. One of them shouts,* "Run, Paolo!"

ANDREA. Hmm! — — And because she is a witch she mustn't have milk. Is that the idea?

BOY. Yes.

ANDREA. And how do you know she is a witch?

BOY, *points to shadow on house wall.* Look!

ANDREA. Oh! I see.

BOY. And she rides on a broomstick at night—and she bewitches the coachman's horses. My cousin Luigi looked through the hole in the stable roof, that the snow storm made, and heard the horses coughing something terrible.

ANDREA. Oh! — How big was the hole in the stable roof?

BOY. Luigi didn't tell. Why?

ANDREA. I was asking because maybe the horses got sick because it was cold in the stable. You had better ask Luigi how big that hole is.

BOY. You are not going to say Old Marina isn't a witch, because you can't.

ANDREA. No, I can't say she isn't a witch. I haven't looked into it. A man can't know about a thing he hasn't looked into, or can he?

BOY. No! — But THAT! *He points to the shadow.* She is stirring hell-broth.

ANDREA. Let's see. Do you want to take a look? I can lift you up.

BOY. You lift me to the window, mister! *He takes a sling shot out of his pocket.* I can really bash her from there.

ANDREA. Hadn't we better make sure she is a witch before we shoot? I'll hold that.

The BOY *puts the milk jug down and follows him reluctantly to the window.* ANDREA *lifts the boy up so that he can look in.*

ANDREA. What do you see?

BOY, *slowly.* Just an old girl cooking porridge.

ANDREA. Oh! Nothing to it then. Now look at her shadow, Paolo.

The BOY *looks over his shoulder and back and compares the reality and the shadow.*

BOY. The big thing is a soup ladle.

ANDREA. Ah! A ladle! You see, I would have taken it for a broomstick, but I haven't looked into the matter as you have, Paolo. Here is your sling.

CUSTOMS OFFICER, *returning with the* CLERK *and handing* ANDREA *his papers.*
All present and correct. Good luck, sir.

ANDREA *goes, reading* GALILEO's *book. The* CLERK *starts to bring his baggage after him. The barrier rises.* ANDREA *passes through, still reading the book. The* BOY *kicks over the milk jug.*

BOY, *shouting after* ANDREA. She *is* a witch! She *is* a witch!

ANDREA. You saw with your own eyes: think it over!

> *The* BOY *joins the others. They sing.*

One, two, three, four, five, six,
Old Marina is a witch.
At night, on a broomstick she sits
And on the church steeple she spits.

> *The* CUSTOMS OFFICERS *laugh.* ANDREA *goes.*

Notes

In Series One, I wrote most of the notes myself. This time they have been written by my authors and translators—except in the cases of cummings and Brecht. cummings won't write about his work at all, and Brecht has written about his so much that I prefer to give bibliographical references. The aim of the notes remains the same: not to fill in the background but to illuminate the foreground of the subject. Individual temperament, conviction, and ability have determined how each annotator went about it.   [E.B.]

JEST, SATIRE, IRONY AND DEEPER SIGNIFICANCE (1827)

Grabbe insisted upon several occasions that the comedy in *Jest* was at root the laughter of despair—jest, satire, and irony being but the outer forms of the problem with which he was wrestling. The deeper significance of that problem was nothing less than the basic paradox of existence which Grabbe saw and formulated with such frightening foresight on the threshold of his manhood. He voiced what in various forms is one of the foremost philosophical questions of our time—and all this before Kierkegaard, Nietzsche, and Kafka. It is not for nothing that early in *Das Unbehagen in der Kultur* Freud quotes from the next-to-the-last work of Grabbe's, *Hannibal*. The words are Hannibal's before the death he himself has chosen: "Yes, we do not drop out of this world. We are in it once and for all."

It is difficult to show how profoundly Grabbe realized man's situation without quoting abundantly from *Herzog Theodor von Gothland* or such later plays as *Don Juan und Faust* and the aforementioned *Hannibal*, none of which, alas, has been translated. Yet it is possible to see through the devastating and scalding kaleidoscope of jest, satire, and irony in his one comedy much of that "deeper significance."

It is an irony in itself that, commenting upon this comedy, one becomes almost as dead serious as Grabbe probably was writing it. For when he pokes fun at the world, he means it: the barbs are none too subtle. Even the long discourse between Ratpoison and the Devil (Act Two, Scene Two) is not exactly obscure regardless whether or not specific references register. Indeed, by the end of the play the laceration has reached such a point that all ordinary worldly relationships are destroyed, the *modus vivendi* of that time drastically challenged, the fortresses of Romanticism demolished, and finally the ego ("das Ich") itself dethroned. With most of the Romanticists the "Ich" remains the "Castle" from which they cast mocking aspersions out on the world. Not so Grabbe. He does not spare even himself—and that is the deeper significance of the curious ending where all's well with the world, or so it seems, until the author himself steps into the play, coming through the woods with a lantern, and called every name imaginable by the furiously jealous Schoolmaster who does not want to let him in. But he is already "in"!

Grabbe scoffs, but with bluntness and grotesquery; he spits scorn, bitterness, anger, and unreason (for example, the speeches of the Baron). From this onslaught there can be no healing, such play leads to nihilism, contempt for all standards, ethics, religion. Even philosophy and science are by no means spared in *Jest* (note the dark tribute to Aristotle and Kant in Act Two, Scene Two and the take-off on the "Natural Scientists" in Act One, Scenes Two and Three). In *Gothland* all that is left to believe in is time. And in *Jest* that too is challenged (witness the Schoolmaster's premonition of relativity in the first scene of the play when he discusses the running time of a horse—or his throwback to Zeno, if you will!). As Grabbe says in *Gothland:*

I, even I, despise myself and,
Accordingly, also that which is still outside and beyond me.

If all this is beyond good and evil, it is also beyond fiction. Grabbe was far too true to himself as as artist to belie his actual being in his works. A letter to Kettembeil in 1827, the year of publication of both *Jest* and *Gothland,* when the writer was but twenty-six, reveals to what depths he in his pessimism had plunged:

My yearlong experiment of pouring reason like nitric acid over
my feeling seems to be nearing its end: Intellect has poured itself
out and Intuition is shattered. . . My soul is dead. . . .

It wasn't quite so, of course, for Grabbe had seven to eight years of spasmodic productivity left. But how much of his Reason was drowned in drink, and how much of his Intuition shattered by self-pity, squandered in illusions of grandeur, and wrapped away in remorse and the unhealthy despair and poverty of the remaining years of his life, we shall never know. Let it suffice to note that the bounce and bitter wit with which *Jest* abounds never returned except here and there, in certain scenes of his interesting dramatization of *Cinderella,* for example, or in some of the plebeian scenes of the historical dramas.

Grabbe's one comedy is still a comedy, and the "deeper significance" when it does not actually heighten its humor neither defeats nor damages the fun of it—any more than the banter between Don Juan and Leporello lessens the tragedy of *Don Juan und Faust.* Grabbe's Don Juan says: "Formerly man led calves and sheep to the altar to be slaughtered, now young girls to be married—nothing new under the sun."

Our delight today derives as much from the underlying critical pessimism in *Jest* as from its amazing freshness of repartee and boldness of wit, and that in spite of not infrequent lapses of taste. It is the constant interplay of paradox which is the real action of the play, not the fairly obvious though pleasantly convenient plot. We are amused at Little Gottlieb being treated as though he were a genius, and it is startling to hear the Schoolmaster discuss current events and "relativity" with the peasant Tobias. Devils usually don't appear in the dog-day heat of August; and people who wear fur coats at that time of year don't ordinarily freeze—though devils, of course, may. The Devil's transgressions on the laws of physics are calmly noted down by the near-sighted Natural Scientists who don't leave until they're thrown out, and not, to be sure, by the Baron, their host, but by the Devil, a fellow guest. The Devil weeps over a noble deed; ugly Mollfels tickles the fancy of lovely Liddy; the Schoolmaster becomes a man of action after an all-night drinking bout; and so forth. Paradox caps paradox. Good triumphs over evil; but evil is a farce. Nothing is spared, and that ultimately is the deepest meaning one is to draw from this at first sight so muddled potpourri of a puppet play.

Actually when one takes the *Jest* apart one finds there is little that does not fit into the whole: the paradoxes dovetail, each scene creating a logic of its own which in turn advances the argument of the preceding one. Yet, all this notwithstanding, the "deeper significance" is probably not always there. Grabbe was too unsure a person and too uneven a writer to achieve in terms of art the total scepticism he professed. Indeed were such an effect in a comedy of this sort possible, it would be no doubt intolerable. Grabbe balked before the pit as did Hume before him.

Consciously or unconsciously, therefore, the author avoids this dilemma by giving the play a happy ending and endowing it with a certain surface optimism. To all intents and purposes Liddy and Mollfels are quite positive people, she in particular being completely at odds with Grabbe's vaunted nihilism. And the Baron, much as we dislike him in his dogged conservatism, certainly copes with reality in a way that is also hard to reconcile with the philosophy of despair. In fact all the characters, including the bloody Count Murdax, are justified by their vitality, and it is remarkable how alive even the most grossly exaggerated of them become. A study could be made in terms of the ratio of reality to grotesquery in each character, and the significance that bears on the philosophy-action of the play as a whole. For even the most stable of these people is something of a contradiction, especially in terms of the society and literature the author here wishes to ridicule— overly modest Mollfels most obviously so in that, physically, he is the antithesis of the hero of his period. And Liddy, however real and sympathetic she may be to us, is unreal to her society precisely because she is so sensible and lovable: she is exactly what no other Romantic heroine in the German literature of that time dared to be. She is a paradox too, as George Meredith might say, in that she has both wit and charm: a rare combination. As far as the Baron is concerned, he is a contradiction in that he lets all this happen!

But the play is to be read—better yet, played—and enjoyed. It is both critic-proof and easily attacked: again a paradox. Heine, with every reason to hate the anti-Semitic Grabbe who once pinned him to the wall, praised the piece. Though most contemporaries called it unplayable, time, Grabbe's God, has proved otherwise.

[M. E.]

EASY MONEY (1870)

Ostrovsky is generally considered the greatest representative of the Russian realistic drama. Stanislavsky praises his grand epic serenity, but the Russian playgoer has chosen him as one of his most favorite dramatists for the simpler reason that he is a master of stage technique and an inexhaustible fount of entertainment.

The author of an anonymous review of Ostrovsky's plays in the July number of the *Edinburgh Review* for the year 1868, one of the most comprehensive appreciations of Ostrovsky yet published in English, remarked on the strange fact that Ostrovsky was completely unknown in England and that "we have never seen or heard of a translation of his plays into English." Since that time only five of Ostrovky's fifty plays (from his merchant cycle) have been published in an English translation, one of them, the tragedy *The Storm,* in England and four in the United States.[1]

These translations have done nothing to make Ostrovsky known to the English-speaking world and much less to make him popular on the English and American stage. This is only partly due to the fact that the five plays deal exclusively with the life of the Russian merchant class in the middle years of the last century, whose traditions, patriarchal customs and dark superstitions are unintelligible outside Russia. For even this great difficulty could have been overcome (after all the customs and superstitions of ancient Greece are no more intelligible to a modern audience) if there were not other, even greater difficulties. One of these is the marvelous vitality and colour of the language. . . . Ostrovsky . . . wrote exclusively for the stage and, being a supreme master of stage technique, his dramatic prose is the speech of living men and women and not the artificial prose of literature. [*Easy Money* has] been translated primarily with an eye to the English stage and an attempt has been made to overcome the many difficulties of Ostrovsky's style by a recasting and remoulding of his prose rather than a direct translation of it. The main difficulty of translating so vital a playwright as Ostrovsky consists in conveying to the English reader and playgoer the emotional tension which he produces. An English audience reacts to certain emotional moments differently from a Russian audience. The words used by Ostrovsky to produce this emotional atmosphere would, therefore, be either too strong or too inadequate. The dialogue has therefore also been re-created in such a way that the emotional under-current may at once be perceived and responded to by an English audience. This was done by occasionally compressing the dialogue or, more rarely, by expanding it somewhat.

[In his later plays, of which *Easy Money* is one,] Ostrovsky's realism assumes a wider and deeper significance. Ostrovsky never really submitted to the romantic conventions of the theatre according to which crime must find its fit punishment before the final curtain. . . . Right does not triumph over wrong or virtue over vice. . . . In *Easy Money* the rake Telyatev remains both unconverted and unimpressed by the triumph of Vassilkov, the only really honest character . . . and the taming of Lydia leaves the reader

---

[1] Mr. Magarshack's acquaintance with U. S. publications is evidently incomplete. Not only the four plays in *Plays,* as published by Scribners in 1917, but another twelve titles are listed in I. T. E. Firkins' *Index to Plays, 1800-1926* and the 1935 *Supplement. Easy Money* itself appeared in *Poet Lore,* Volume 40, Spring 1929, under the title *Fairy Gold.*   [E. B.]

and playgoer very much in doubt whether her change of heart is either real or permanent. . . .

It would seem that in a drama where realism is allowed to go to such lengths there is little that could appeal to the innate decency and sense of fair play of the average playgoer and even less to rouse his pity and indignation. Actually, the opposite is true. With such mastery are the secret places of the hearts of the characters exposed, so comic are the situations in which their folly lands them, so witty is the dialogue and so supremely alive is every character, that the moral effect . . . is much deeper than the one produced by . . . more conventional plays. . . .

Ostrovsky translated Shakespeare's *The Taming of the Shrew* in 1865. Five years later his brilliant version of Shakespeare's comedy was published. The problem of transplanting Katharine and Petruchio to Russia and giving them a modern setting was not an easy one, but by solving it in such a masterly fashion Ostrovsky has created one of the finest comedies in the world repertory of plays. What attracted Ostrovsky to *The Taming of the Shrew* was the fact that it was a comedy that dealt with the intimate details of family life, a *genre* which Ostrovsky made his own. But, as a modern Russian critic points out, Ostrovsky was also interested in the two protagonists of the Shakespearean comedy as human types and in the psychological problems which the clashing of interests of two strong-willed individuals exert upon each other. Vassilkov and Lydia, however, are not copies of Petruchio and Katharine. Quite the contrary, as individuals they differ from Shakespeare's hero and heroine almost as much as the Moscow of Ostrovsky differed from Shakespeare's Padua.

A comparison between the two plays . . . reveals a number of highly interesting facts. . . . To begin with, both Petruchio and Lydia are animated by the same desire of marrying for money. Petruchio tells Hortensio—

I come to wive it wealthily in Padua
If wealthily then happily in Padua.

And Petruchio's servant Grumio underscores his master's intentions:

Nay, look you sir, he tells you flatly what his mind is: why, give him gold enough and marry him to a puppet or an aglet-baby or an old trot with ne'er a tooth in her head though she has as many diseases as two and fifty horses: why, nothing comes amiss so money comes withal.

These are exactly Lydia's sentiments in marrying Vassilkov.

Glumov's intrigue to spread the rumour that Vassilkov owns goldmines and so entice Lydia and her mother into casting their net for a desirable husband seems also to be an echo from Shakespeare's comedy. Hortensio tells Petruchio that Katharine is so "intolerably curst and shrewd and froward"

That, were my state far worser than it is
I would not wed her for a mine of gold.

This reference to a mine of gold quite possibly suggested to Ostrovsky a minor but essential part of the plot of his play.

Less evident, though far from improbable, is the likelihood that a reference by Grumio to Petruchio's method of taming Katharine by throwing "a figure in her face and so disfigure her with it that she shall have no more eyes to see withal than a cat" has led Ostrovsky to invent the scene with the bills in Act Three. What Vassilkov actually does is to "throw a figure" at Lydia's face and force her complete, if only temporary, submission to his will.

Again, Petruchio's declaration to Katharine:

Now, Kate, I am a husband for your turn;
For, by this light, whereby I see thy beauty,
Thy beauty that doth make me like thee well,
Thou must be married to no man but me.

is re-echoed almost in the same words by Vassilkov to Telyatev and, later on, to Kuchumov and Glumov as well in the closing scene of Act One. Also Petruchio's assertion

O! the kindest Kate!
She hung about my neck, and kiss on kiss
She vied so fast, protesting oath on oath

describes exactly Lydia's behavior to Vassilkov.

Of the other characters in Ostrovsky's comedy, Kuchumov seems to be the only one whom Ostrovsky found in Shakespeare's comedy. Grumio is the Elizabethan counterpart of Ostrovsky's aged philanderer. Like Kuchumov, Grumio promises

Myself am struck in years, I must confess:
And if I die tomorrow, this is hers.
If whilst I live she will be only mine.

Finally, to complete this textual comparison of the two plays, Petruchio's words

And as the sun breaks through the darkest clouds,
So honour peereth in the meanest habit.

are re-echoed, though with a purely satirical intent, by Telyatev's "virtue shines through even the meanest rags."

. . . it is noteworthy that in no other play by Ostrovsky are there so many references to England. . . . Vassily, Vassilkov's valet, who so admires the English worker that he insists on dressing like one is, besides, the closest approach to a Shakespearean clown to be found in Ostrovsky's plays.

Glumov, the hero of [another Ostrovsky play]—*Even a Wise Man Stumbles*[2] —plays here only a subsidiary role. His career is rather left hanging in the air in the first comedy and is wound up here by Ostrovsky who . . . makes Glumov a *secrétaire intime* or gigolo to a rich woman.

[D. M.]

THE EPIDEMIC (1898)

Since this one-act extravaganza shows us a French city council in session, it is worth remembering that parliamentary manners on the Continent differ from those of the English-speaking world. Mirbeau is in fact parodying the French national parliament by giving us its provincial imitation.

---

[2]Recently republished as *Diary of a Scoundrel* (London, 1938), adapted by Rodney Ackland.

Accordingly, the play should be acted in the true tradition of farce, that is to say, with the utmost seriousness and solemnity, and *not* as a self-conscious burlesque. Played straight, the lesser shafts of satire will strike automatically—for instance the doctor's mad eloquence—and the councillors' sudden drops from pomposity to billingsgate will double in comic force.

It is perhaps unnecessary to point out that the Mayor and the Doctor are men of different calibre from the rest; the Mayor possessing self-respect and legitimate pretensions to good breeding, and the Doctor trading on his professional superiority in order to lecture patronizingly at his willing neighbors. As against these genuine characters, the Leader of the Majority and the Leader of the Opposition must behave like types in a morality play—Mirbeau's collection of shorter plays is aptly called *Farces et Moralités*. The dialogue between these puppets sometimes resembles the stichomythia in a Greek play, and it should be given suitable artificiality—its configuration is that of a ballet, rhythmic and symmetrical. The performance as a whole must pass without modulation from folly to reality and back again, for the work is, as I said before, an extravaganza. We can see its derivation in part from Victor Hugo's *Théâtre en Liberté* and in part from Ibsen's *Enemy of the People*, but we get nothing quite like it until Wedekind, Cocteau, and the Surrealists.

I should add that in translating *L'Epidémie*, I have changed or omitted three or four topical references (such as the name of the contemporary Secretary of the Navy), and given equivalents in place of direct translation for a few oratorical allusions accessible only to a French audience: that is how Patrick Henry comes to be quoted—and Shakespeare.

The reader may also like to be reminded that the satire was written at a tense moment in the history of the Third Republic. The Dreyfus Affair was a roaring conflagration, of which the Army and the self-styled patriots were taking advantage. To a shocked and bewildered public opinion, the Parliamentary scandals, administrative incompetence, and demagogic wordiness could still be denounced as characteristic solely of representative governments, and so it was in the reactionary press. But like a good satirist, Mirbeau hits equally at the "patriots" and at the politicians, and he caricatures the bourgeois philistine no less than the scientific know-it-all, from the vantage point of the poet and intellectual.

[J. B.]

THE MARQUIS OF KEITH (1900)

The Marquis of Keith, though based on an intricate five-act structure, is essentially a collection of comparisons and contrasts. The central action—Keith's attempt and failure to get status—touches off a chain of personal crises. From Scholz to Simba, the characters face the question of how to live the good life (the subject matter of ethics) and, more particularly, what kind of good life is possible in a modern bourgeois world which, according to Wedekind, resembles man's unfair conception of the jungle.

Keith and Scholz are obviously the most important pair of contrasting characters. Scholz starts out as a wealthy aristocrat; then, beset with feelings of guilt, drops his title. Keith, on the other hand, gives himself a bogus title, would do anything for the money which Scholz despises, but is also beset with feelings of guilt, though of a different kind. These two men, both outcasts in their way, are enabled to see quite clearly what the world about them is like, although neither can ever become a part of it. Both are "supermen"; that is, they have superior gifts and they feel they are lifted above the common mass. Each feels superior to the other, yet they are really trying to change places with each other. Though they seem diametrically opposed in every way, their careers are strangely parallel; they share a similar pattern of trying to buck fate, of wandering from country to country, of making attempts to become "established." In the teeth of the evidence, Keith remains an optimist: "All things work together for good to them that love God." It is inevitable that Scholz should assume that he is *not* one of the few who will be chosen just as it is inevitable that Keith should assume he is one of them that love God. Both are really fated to remain what they are.

The celebrated Wedekind cynicism is revealed in the play's scheme of successes and failures. The outstanding failures, Scholz and Molly, are those who cite traditional morality. The "spongers"—Saranieff, Simba, Sommersberg—are not only happy but attractive. For Anna, of course, the critical ethical question is perhaps most acute; *her* answer, free of guilty torment, is to go along with those who are on top at the moment. Raspe, who like Scholz speaks about "the good of my fellowmen," works not for their good but unscrupulously for his own good by putting himself at the service of those in power. Casimir, the ultimate "victor," is obviously Keith's model. But he has Keith's ability without Keith's romanticism. He seems to "belong" as Keith does not. And far from mocking the bleary-eyed Philistines he is practically one of them himself.

In this panorama of successes and failures the supreme irony is that the activity centers on *art*. The life-and-death struggle of bourgeois life is depicted in terms of its so-called artistic life. Here art is a commodity. These artists *bargain* for recognition. They are not the artists of romantic literature. For all we know they may be charlatans. As Molly dies though her motives are respectable so Zamriaki fails as an artist though he wants to become immortal "by ethical means." Wedekind never informs us whether Anna can really sing or Saranieff really paint or Zamriaki really compose. The issue is how they *make use of* their art.

Perhaps more interesting to us today than the social comment is Wedekind's psychological subtlety. This is less a matter of theme than of technique, though it is clear that Scholz's conflicts, his desperate attempt to "live," and his final retreat into unreality—an epitome of the neurotic pattern—are central to the play. It was called *The Epicurean* in an earlier version. As for Keith, the ambivalent attitude toward him which the spectator has to adopt is the result of deep insight. Keith's understanding of the surface realities give him an advantage over Scholz but he is hardly successful since he thinks he can ignore a tremendous chunk of reality like Casimir; one can see Keith's life stretching out before him and behind him as a succession of five-act plays like this one. Wedekind's psychological skill, however, is most impressive in his handling of dialogue, in the structure of the miniature dramas whose cumulative effect makes the play. There is a certain patness in the contrast between Keith and Scholz, and there is a lurking temptation to over-formularize the ethical idea of the play into a statement like "a middle ground between Scholz's conscience and Keith's cynicism is the answer." The impression of patness can make little headway, however, because of the wonderful sinewy realism of Wedekind's dialogue. (At times we are reminded of Hemingway.) Conversations seem disjointed, seemingly irrel-evant topics are introduced, passions flare up without apparent warning. Yet there are always reasons for the sudden transitions; what the characters *say* is sometimes meaningless, but there is always meaning in their *behavior*. Particularly impressive are the scenes between Keith and Molly. (See, for example, the dialogue on page 131.) Such a glimpse into a relationship has the authenticity of the exciting, puzzling, revealing bits of conversation overheard at the next table or in the adjoining hotel room.

[B. G.]

HIM (1927)

1.

The Provincetown Playhouse has recorded the scandal which the first appear-ance of *him* aroused in 1928 and Jacques Barzun has told how much fun it all was.[1] I first saw the play at the Provincetown in 1948. The performance opened my eyes to the vast vitality of the second act and made me wonder if one couldn't make more of the first and third. Having organized an inter-national festival for young professional actors in Salzburg (1950), I under-took to direct *him* with the British contingent.

I wonder if I am the only person who has ever seen *him* in its entirety? Up to late rehearsals, I left the play quite uncut. Only at the very end had I to admit that our performance could not hold up longer than a normal playing-time and that large excisions must therefore be made. I cut out the Paris scene entirely (Act Three, Scene Three). Many Him and Me speeches were streamlined. And in the penultimate scene the Barker was left with only a line or two for each of nine exhibits. (Though presumably the figure 9 here refers to the nine months of pregnancy I could never discover that there was much development from one speech or exhibit to the next; therefore cutting seemed in order.)

The circumstances of the production were primitive. I borrowed lighting equipment from the local movie studios and was happy to be limited to their hard white light. The studios lent me also the large wooden panels on which canvas was stretched for the use of our painter-designer, Kurt Moldovan. Four of these panels made up the four walls of our room, three in use at a time, in rotation from scene to scene as cummings prescribes.

---

[1] See the anonymous booklet *him AND the CRITICS* (with an introduction by Gilbert Seldes, no date, no publisher but evidently published by the Provincetown Playhouse) and the cummings issue of *WAKE* (Spring, 1946) respectively.

Act Three, Scene Six

The drawings for him *are impressions of Eric Bentley's Salzburg production (1950) by its designer Kurt Moldovan.*

Since they were less deep and less wide than the setting, they did not meet
at the corners. There were gaps. In Act Two the settings consisted of one
panel, centrally placed, for each scene. Such a panel might be likened to
the old-fashioned backdrop except that it indicated not only the locale but
also the subject (as seen by cummings—Moldovan). It's being less big than
the back of the stage meant that it had the back of the stage as a frame and
thus gained in emphasis. A panel was also used for the "flat surface" mentioned in cummings' first stage direction. (It was left on stage the whole
time, standing diagonally to the audience at one side of the "proscenium"
while the Three Weirds sat and knitted at the other.) All the panels were
painted in brilliant colors.

Since we did not have actors for the eight freaks, each was represented by
a painted portrait on a smaller panel. Because this scene must go straight
into the next without pause I staged it in front of the curtain (it was a
small inner curtain made of shower-curtain-material) and had the freaks
carted in through the audience.

2.

While the fun and fantasy and lyricism of this play impose themselves
on the audience without difficulty, it would be an unusual spectator who
said he could follow it all. Diversity of comment has led to the conclusion
that the play means nothing or (which is the same thing) that all inter-

pretations are correct. And the author upholds the view that the work itself says what it means, is its own explanation.

Author. Well?

Public. What is *him* about?

Author. Why ask me? Did I or didn't I make the play?

Public. But you surely know what you're making . . .

Author. Beg pardon, Mr. Public. I surely make what I'm knowing.

Public. So far as I'm concerned, my very dear sir, nonsense isn't everything in life.

Author. And so far as you're concerned "life" is a verb of two voices—active, to do, and passive, to dream. Others believe doing to be only a kind of dreaming. Still others have discovered (in a mirror surrounded with mirrors) something harder than silence but softer than falling: the third voice of "life," which believes itself and which cannot mean because it is.

Public. Bravo, but are such persons good for anything in particular?

Author. They are good for nothing except walking upright in the cordial revelation of the fatal reflexive.

Public. And your play is all about one of these persons, Mr. Author?

Author. Perhaps. But (let me tell you a secret) I rather hope my play is one of these persons.

But surely, by such an "Imaginary Dialogue between an Author and a Public," cummings brings comfort to the scoffers and promotes mystification? In Salzburg, at any rate, before a German-speaking audience, I could not avoid trying to make the play slightly less puzzling by a program note. I know there are many obscurities it does not clear up. Even when I came to know the whole text almost by heart I still was not sure of the sequence of events in Him and Me's relationship: there is attraction, intimacy, estrangement, departure, return, but in what order, with what results?[2] It is a fair subject for discussion whether the plot of a play has any right to be as obscure as this.

The following, translated into German, went into our program: *"him* is about a young American couple and their quest for reality. The action is seen through the eyes of Me who is lying under an anaesthetic awaiting the birth of a child.

"In Act One, Scene One, Me sees the three Parcae—or are they the witches out of MACBETH—or the wives of three rotarians? At all events, since they preside over the birth of Me's child, it is possible that their remarks are coloured, in Me's memory, with thoughts of phalluses, parturition, and unnatural monsters. You will think it only natural that the Doctor who is presiding over the birth of Me's child should introduce Him, who is the child's father, to the Parcae.

"In Act One, Scene Two, Me begins to look back on her life with Him. Since Him is an artist, and much more intellectual than Me, you will not blame Me if his words come back to Me in a distorted not to say fantastic form. Me didn't understand Him. Him's reality was not Me's reality.

---

[2] For a fine attempt to unravel the tangled skein, see below pages 493-494.

Act One, Scene One

Me's was external and commonsensical. Him's was internal and fanciful. Him felt that Me could not accompany Him through the dangerous acrobatics of the imagination—that Me could not help Him to discover Himself.

"Act One, Scene Three. The Parcae, as intimated, seem to Me preoccupied with sex and children, birth and death. You will forgive Me if their voices mingle with those of the fortune teller and the advertising man. There is wisdom after all in their observation that life is a matter of being born and that art is a question of being alive.

"Act One, Scene Four. Him's attempt—or intention—to kill Himself was a horrible moment and it comes to Me confused by the imagery of her present interesting condition. Another confusing fact is that there were two of Him: there was his real self and there was the part of Him Me knew, the part Him could see in the mirror. This second self—the Other Man, otherwise known as O. Him or the Man in the Mirror—was the self Me loved (at least Him said so). This was the self Me hoped would write a popular play; what his real self wanted to write is exemplified by the philosophical passage Him reads to Me in this scene.

"Act One, Scene Five. The conversation of the Parcae—or Weird Sisters—continues, as usual, precisely where it left off. It is nothing if not phallic.

"Act Two. In this act, Me's vision or dream is of Him showing Me scenes from the popular play Me hoped Him would write. There is one for each month of Me's pregnancy. It is not unnatural that a certain amount of Him's intellectuality and something of his satiric attitude to modern life should have crept into Me's fantasy. This succession of night-club skits is also a commentary on the Jazz Age.

1. Prologue.
2. Three Drunks and a Virgo. (Gentlemen of the Jazz Age and a shocked

Act Two, Scene Two

but fascinated female. Introduced in my production by elaborate pantomime of croquet and tennis.)
3. The Soap-Box Salesman. (The modern world would like to abolish
death and listens to every cheapskate who proposes a method. Style:
popular American oratory. Models: to be heard on Union Square or
where have you.)
4. Will and Bill. (The question of identity. Him's intellectuality again.
Who am I, who are You, who is Him? Style: vaudeville skit and
gangster film. Model for latter: *Scarface*—though later than cummings'
play.)
5. Frankie and Johnie. (Love and death in a world pestered by leagues
of decency. The phallic symbolism of Act One and of Act Two, Scene
Two continues. Style: minstrel show, floorshow, valudeville comedian.)
6. The Englishman in New York. (Transatlantic comedy, the old world and
the new: the Englishman blithely carrying his Unconscious, the Americans first refusing to acknowledge its existence and then not strong
enough to face it. Chief device: contrast of accents. Technique: the
skit.)
7. Americans crossing the Ocean. (Transatlantic theme again—not of
course irrelevant to Him and Me story—Him's visit to Paris depicted
in Act Three—but main theme here: rotarians abroad. The booboisee.
Emptiness of modern bourgeois life rendered by mechanical symmetry
of a gag.)
8. Mussolini and the Fairies. (The age of fascism as seen by the American
tourist in Italy. Mussolini cries "Camerieri!"—i.e., "Waiters!" instead of

Act Two, Scene Five

"Camerati!" i.e., "Comrades!" Model: ancient Rome as presented at the Old Howard burlesque theatre in Boston.)

9. The American Businessman in Ruined Europe. (American incomprehension of European misery. This version of post-1918 again most topical on post-1945 continent: in the days of the Marshall Plan, displaced persons, and bombed-out cities. This the only scene in Act Two where cummings is noticeably influenced by "highbrow" drama, notably, European expressionism. Mob episodes call for handling like that of Toller's *Masse-Mensch:* stylised grouping, ecstatic choral appeals, etc.)

"Act Three, Scene One. Me does some more thinking about her life with Him: the distance between Me and Him grew until Me refused to be Him's mistress any more and Him said: "This is the end?" and Me said "This might be where we begin." The odd thing was that, at this late date, Me began to be less diffident. Me began to understand things. That is, *some* things.

"Act Three, Scene Two. The first and second Weirds continue their almost gynecological discussion. The third spouts the wisdom of the ages—or rather of the modern age—in the form of advertising slogans.

"Act Three, Scene Three. Me dreams of Him's visit to Paris, and doubtless her dreams are subject to the distortions of dreams in general: part

Act Two, Scene Six

of her dream is realistic enough—here are Me's countrymen in Paris—but part
has to do with Me's interesting condition. Two American ladies are on a
diet of Homme (stewed or boiled) and as for Him, Me fears that he may
have had a girl friend in this gay city and conjures her up in the form of a
Choux.

"Act Three, Scene Four. The Weirds continue exactly where they left off
in Scene Two until interrupted by the Doctor who suggests that they'd
have cleaner minds if they had fewer repressions.

"Act Three, Scene Five. Me thinks of the time when Him returned from
the Paris trip. At first meeting, Him didn't recognize Me, and Me didn't
care: it was all over already. It is gratifying that Him managed to make a
little headway in life: had in fact killed both his former selves—his real self
and the Other Man. Him was now ready to emerge from the artist's world
of beauty into the real world of truth. Him was *ready:* whether Him was
able was of course another matter. As for Me, Me had at last to gain entrance
to Him's circus world of the imagination. Was a new beginning possible?
Me thought Me might bring Him to a new beginning through a single
agency—

"Act Three, Scene Six. —namely, her child. In this scene Me succeeds
in entering the circus and there confronts the Queer Folk. Me is indeed one
of them, Me with a child in her arms. In this vision of Me's, Him does not
accept the child. On the contrary. So Me returns to the room where—

"Act Three, Scene Seven. —Me finds that Him is still unable to accept

Act Two, Scene Eight

reality. Him, can see the three walls of the room-stage (the world of art),
but cannot see that the fourth wall is missing and that the public (the
world of reality) is out there watching this play.

"You must judge for yourselves whether Me's meditation amounts to
anything like a drama. There is development, up to a point: Me may claim
to have made some improvement as a human being and Him has been
brought to a couple of realizations—even while remaining a failure and
not knowing what the 'something else' is that has to be learnt.

"You might like to read Me's meditation as having to do with the birth
process itself: the nine scenes of Act Two and the nine freaks of Act Three,
like the nine months of pregnancy, end with an Unto Us a Child is Born.

"Truth and Beauty, Reality and Illusion, Seriousness and Joke, Philosophy and Vaudeville weave themselves in and out of Me. Contemplating
the apparent lawlessness of Me's imagination—its disregard of Time-Sequence,
for example—one recalls some words of the first mrs. e. e. cummings:
'Looking forward into the past or looking backward into the future I walk
on the highest hills and I laugh about it all the way.'"

mr. cummings' comment on this program note was: "The note strikes me
as extremely interesting; so much so that I am taking the liberty of enclosing
a copy of 'An Imaginary Dialogue between an Author and a Public'...."

3.

One of my Salzburg colleagues, Theodore Hoffman, contributes the following interpretation. It adds a great deal to my own note without, I think, being incompatible with it:

"If *him* wasn't inspired by F. M. Cornford's *The Origin of Attic Comedy* the book at least suggests startling parallels.

"Cornford traces old Greek comedy to a fertility rite involving a procession, sacrifice, feast and phallic hymn, a rite based on seasonal change, the death and rebirth of a god. He examines religious ritual, puppet plays, mummers' plays, and festivals in order to isolate the ritual elements that form Aristophanic comedy. A fight or quarrel between the principal characters is followed by the Agon, a rhetorical argument between the hero and an adversary, restating the quarrel in larger political terms. Preparations for a sacrifice, cooking, and a feast are interrupted by various boastful and insolent imposters, who represent the hero's bad characteristics. The hero repels them by playing the ironic buffoon, but is sometimes either defeated and revived or banished and recalled. At the feast a new god is born, frequently the hero, who marries (usually a silent courtesan). A joyous marriage procession or Komos concludes the play. Cornford further identifies the imposters as the stock masks of comedy: the aggressive Buffoon; the Doctor as Cook, Magician, or Medicine Man; the Doctor as Pedant or learned Lawyer; the boastful Soldier; the father-miser Old Man; the lascivious Old Woman; the pair of Comic Slaves; the courtesan Young Woman. The Doctor's original role, seen most clearly in the mummers' plays, was that of the Magician/Priest who restores the dead hero/combatant to life.

"The relevance of this to *him* is readily noted. cummings, like Eliot whose "Sweeney Agonistes" was inspired by Cornford's book,[3] looks for survivals of the rite in our own sterile civilization. He finds its imagery in the Circus and Burlesque,[4] its ritual in psychoanalysis, which is itself a dramatized re-enactment and resolution of a basic conflict. *him* might be read as follows:

"The Weirds, chanting phallic songs, stop to observe the ritual. Him, the playwright, representing male creativity or Art, has quarreled with Me, the mother, representing female creativity or Life. Him is psychoanalyzed by the Doctor because he has attempted to kill his other self, Mr. O. Him, by suicide. Him's resistance to analysis takes the form of projecting his false pride and insolence onto the Doctor in the Agon, the theme of which is Prohibition vs. Freedom (in the individual and in the polity). The impostor-Doctor appears to prevent the sacrifice (i.e., liberating analysis, social welfare) in various guises of fake power: as the Buffoon/Drunk (with the

[3]The text of *Sweeney* is in *From the Modern Repertoire*, Series One. A sequel to it, along with Mr. Eliot's acknowledgment of Cornford as a source, is to be found in Hallie Flanagan's book *Dynamo*. [E. B.]

[4]"Enlightened scholars have doubtless written learned treatises on the relation of burlesque to the satyr choruses, to *The Frogs* and *The Birds*, to Roman comedy, to Punchinello and Brighella, to the 'afterpieces' of the minstrel show . . . . Ive seen . . . a lot of burlesque shows . . . . "—e. e. cummings in "Burlesque, I Love It" in *Stage*, March, 1936. Incidentally, cummings' article also contains a description of the Old Howard theatre. [E.B.]

Virgo/Old Woman) ; the Medicine Man/Soap-Box Salesman; Lawyer/Pedant/Personage; Comic Slave/Intruder; Swaggerer/Plainclothesman; Old Man/Babbitt; Buffoon/Swaggerer/Mussolini; Miser/Old Man/Gentleman. Him, as author, exposes the falsehoods by presenting them in terms of ironic buffoonery. A sacrifice is effected when the bread is devoured by the crowd; but Him is also defeated; he has not mastered O. Him and is refused by Me. Expatriated to Paris (dying) for the Cooking/Feast scene, he is reborn, symbolically takes the Blond Gonzesse courtesan, and returns to New York where he discovers that he is rid of O. Him. Dream clues—a doll named Gypsy, a toy battleship (Renown), a dog (God) —reveal Him's traumatic experience at a sideshow (hinted at in Act One). The recapturing of this experience with the help of the Doctor/Priest/Hunchback, whose long spiel and freaks signify the union of the sexual organs, reunites Him with Me who, as the Princess Anankay (Fate), has given birth. The sacred marriage of Art and Life ends emotional and artistic sterility. The contestants have been reconciled. But the epilogue (Act Three, Scene Seven) can be read as a statement of the limitations of Art.[5] In ritual and childbirth the fourth wall is not missing; the participants are themselves the play. The ultimate victory lies with Me. Me is the true author of *him*."

[E. B.]

VENUS AND ADONIS (1932)

No one can read this little play without noticing how urgently it demands to be acted. And in this can be found the whole key to Obey's dramatic method. *Venus and Adonis* is, above all, an action, neatly and firmly tailored for the stage. Obey reveals himself as a painstaking craftsman, but one whose craftsmanship (unlike the craftsmanship apparent in so many "well-made plays") is built on his awareness not of what makes theatre "effective" but of what makes it rich. If *Venus and Adonis* at first seems slight to the reader, it is because the literary virtues of the play are only partial: they need to be sustained and furbished by the full mimetic means of the actor. And this means that the reader must match Obey's acute understanding of the actor's craft and enter into an imaginative visualization of the action—see the play, that is, with its theatrical togs on. The ease with which it is possible for the willing reader to grasp this theatrical perspective in *Venus and Adonis* is one measure of the play's success. (It also constitutes a rewarding lesson in how to read plays generally.) For Obey writes out of a deep sense of the possibilities not only of verbal language but of physical language too. There is constantly present in this play a kind of joy in making actors do what they *can* do, in forcing the language their acting speaks to be as poetic and entrancing as their words. It is thus that even within the severe limitations of brevity and a certain poverty of theme, *Venus and Adonis* achieves a fullness that is rare among modern literary plays.

Of course Obey was more fortunate than most modern writers for the stage in having—in the Compagnie des XV—a near-perfect instrument to

---

[5]Anticipated, for that matter, in the freak scene where Him receives the "sacred marriage" with horror. [E. B.]

write for. He tells us that these actors, highly skilled and trained by Jacques Copeau, were a constant source of inspiration; and that, in consequence, he wrote his plays "not only on command, but to measure." In Obey's conception of theatre, this *donnée* is primary.

To see how tenaciously Obey has kept his actors in mind and how thoroughly they determine his method, one has only to examine the text. Consider, first, the way the play is put together. The effects are laddered, the larger action being built on a series of distinct smaller actions, each with its own little climax, yet each dovetailing carefully into the next. The charm of these little actions depends precisely on their being *actions*: comic or dramatic situations in the grand tradition. Each involves the characters in a different combination; and, for the most part, they are taken in pairs. In this way, every character holds the stage at one point or another; each is, as it were, showcased in turn, and for this reason there are no unrewarding parts. The result is, on the one hand, economy, precision, concentration; and on the other, the richness that comes of keeping *all* the characters constantly in full fig. To write in this way means knowing what one's actors can do and seeing to it that they are kept doing it.

Next consider the lines themselves. They reveal an even deeper sense of theatrical know-how. We need to note how much physical movement and gesture are implicit merely in the way the words are assembled. Take, for example, the opening speeches of Adonis: the bouncing vitality of their rhythm is so easily translated by the mind's eye into physical action that we get at once not only an idea of the sort of person Adonis is, but a moving image of his presence. The same is true of any of the scenes between Venus and Cupid. How much the actor is *given* by speeches like these! And the director, too; for *Venus and Adonis* has in great degree—and built in, as it were—that quality dear to the modern director's heart: "speed." For all its suggestiveness, the speech is economical, almost sparse; it serves the action and (with the exception of two or three of Venus' *speeches*) no more.

We need to note, too, how much actual mime finds its way into this short play: Cupid with his bow, Sostheme chasing Zoe, or Adonis' "dumb show of a man very fed up." Nothing is done with speech that could better be done with mime or vice-versa. Nor does this use of non-verbal art ever seem intrusive. The business of the play is not tacked on; it is all carefully welded into or counterpoised with the speech. And the business that suggests itself in this way is amazingly complete. Next to nothing is left to be invented by the imagination of the director or supplied at random by the whims of the actors.

This sense of counterpoint is what gives the comic scenes their more or less classical character. And perhaps, in fact, the essential quality of *Venus and Adonis* can actually be expressed in another way—in terms of the peculiarly French tradition to which it belongs. In building his play on a series of small actions, Obey is following the spirit of the French tradition which changes the scene every time a character enters or leaves the stage. In choosing the story of Venus and Adonis, he is implying a long line of older women and younger men in the theatre, going about the business of their relations in what we think of as a uniquely "French" manner. Even the kind of glamorous, sentimental, extremely gifted actress that is required for the part of Venus tends to be pretty much a French product.

So, too, with the comedy, which most often depends on traditional comic devices of the kind described by Bergson, and scarcely ever on speeches that are witty in themselves. Note, for instance, the scene in which Venus understands Adonis' praises of the mare to refer to her, or Adonis' hand-slapping attempt to revive the fainted Venus. Again and again, the comedy takes the traditional form of speech counterfoiled by movement, or of movement underlined by speech. Obey's is thoroughly the comedy of Molière; never that of Wilde or Shaw. But in *Venus and Adonis,* Obey actually does what Molière often seems on the point of doing: he resolves the comic situation by disaster and pathos. His classical manner of construction makes this possible. In the small action involving Death, the grim note introduced into the comic play effects a complete redirection of tone, such that we are fully prepared for the violent climax and, afterwards, the wistful ending.

Venus and Adonis is, in fact, a mixture of the kind that theatre in its fullest sense is equipped to deal with: a mixture of comedy and pathos, of realism and fantasy, of prose and poetry. The cohesive force behind this mixture is simply the rich life of the imagination. "The drama," wrote Synge, "is made serious—in the French sense of the word—not by the degree in which it is taken up with problems that are serious in themselves, but by the degree in which it gives the nourishment, not very easy to define, on which our imaginations live." *Venus and Adonis* is serious in this way. After all that has been made of the Venus and Adonis myth by modern mytho-psychology, one might expect to find a modern playwright exploiting the finer implications of the play's fertility theme, and grappling with problems that are serious in themselves. Perhaps a *great* contemporary playwright (if we had one) would have done so. Instead, Obey has given us a spry little tragi-comedy. In the French, his play bears the sub-title, "A Play in One Act after Shakespeare's Poem"; and the speeches of Venus are dotted with more or less literal renderings of Shakespeare's English. (It is of course impossible to reinsert Shakespeare's words in the English version without destroying the modernity which Obey scrupulously maintains: hence the omission of the sub-title.) Thus Obey challenges us to ask him not what he has made of the myth, but what he has made of Shakespeare's poem. And the answer he gives us is simple: *theatre.* His inventions are therefore mainly technical, but technical inventions which spring from so rich and ingenious an imagination cease to be *merely* technical. Obey's play has seven characters, Shakespeare's poem has only two; but which of the five people Obey has introduced can be said not to have an essential *dramatic* function? Which of them is not incisively, suggestively, entertainingly drawn? Which of them is not an exciting example of the nourishment Synge demands?

Of an earlier play, Obey wrote:

> No more in this play than in any of those that came after was I disturbed by theses or symbols, by ideas or by lessons: the stage, that's enough! It is the teaching of Copeau, it was the rule of the XV, it is my whole theory that the play is a *thing* of theatre, so

rigorously (although so freely) invented for the stage, constructed, designed, developed on it, subjected so completely to it, that the drama has its life, its existence, its rhythm, through and above the words that express it; *before* them, would I dare to say. A language, by all means, but not of literature.

Perhaps it is unfair to find this passage smacking of that anti-intellectualism which so much of modern French literature inherits from the symbolists; it would certainly be kinder, and no less justified, to see it as a certain highly conscious pre-intellectualism. In any case, this passage does explain both the virtues and the limitations of *Venus and Adonis*. In our highly rational age, the limitations—the lack of "significance" or conceptual meaning—will be only too clear. Yet we need to beware of taking *Venus and Adonis* for something that it is not and does not try to be; and we need to keep alert to the possibilities it shows us. For even if it has no great significance, it does have wit, charm, and intelligence. It interests and moves us. It does not insult us. And it is written with a consummate understanding of what the histrionic sensibility can mean, that could prove rewarding study for any young playwright or serious theatre-goer. Like Shakespeare's poem, it is an extremely deft piece of successful *minor* art; and its virtues, if simple and unpretentious, are important because they embody serious values which no modern repertoire, in the present state of things, can afford to neglect.

[W. B.]

ELECTRA (1937)

"If the theatre today has significance it is in its turning toward spiritual rather than material values; words are more important than plot, the text than the spectacle; the dramatic conventions are now made from poetry, grace and nobility."

These words of Jouvet, the actor, explain his partnership with Jean Giraudoux, whose plays admirably express the spirit there defined.

Giraudoux was a complex and learned artist, for a time a teacher and government official, who began his literary career with novel writing and only started to write plays in 1928 with *Siegfried,* his attempt to show how Germany and France might learn to live together. Such optimism did not last, however, for in *La Guerre de Troie n'aura pas lieu* (1935), a tragedy based on the history of the Trojan War, he expressed his little hope that intelligence and reason could bring about peace, which is constantly at the mercy of human passions and stupidity.

His plays, even such light comedies as *Amphitryon* (1929), show a wide knowledge of the classics, Greek, Elizabethan and French, and a strong interest in psychology and in myth, as well as alert thought on the life of his times. His pamphlet, *Pleins Pouvoirs,* is a plea for more power to be put into the hands of the intellectuals, and a challenge to them to come out of their ivory towers and to act in the interest of humanity as a whole. In his last play, *La Folle de Chaillot* (printed 1945), he drew a fanciful picture of how this might be done by a far-seeing and courageous woman, believed mad by her contemporaries and actually the least mad of any of them.

But this play is only a flash of hope in a mind on the whole too perceptive of human weakness to see a quick and easy solution to human tragedies. In his two masterpieces, *Electra,* beautifully staged and acted by Jouvet and his troupe at the Athénée in 1937, and published by Grasset the same year, and in *La Guerre de Troie n'aura pas lieu,* both the ancient fables are thoroughly reinterpreted by a keen modern mind, aware that man's fate today does not differ much from what it was in the times of Homer and Sophocles. The wisdom of Ulysses and Hector in Troy, Electra's love of justice in Argos, cannot prevent the war and destruction brought on their countries by human passions. Electra, of course, thinks she sees beyond the destruction to the dawn of a world where justice will prevail, even as today the creators of the United Nations hopefully take the long view, beyond contemporary cataclysms.

But Giraudoux casts an ironic eye on all such hopes. The Beggar-God in *Electra,* gifted with one retrospective and one prophetic eye, apparently voices the author's cynical appraisal of human idealism. Electra is as hard as she is truthful, she hates her mother and Aegisthus as much as she loves her just found brother. It is women like her, *"femmes à histoires,"* implacable, relentless, who, according to the President, make hell on earth, destroying families and nations in their pursuit of abstract values. The Eumenides are never far from such heroines, as is shown by the three sinister little girls in Act One, who grow to full stature in the course of the tragedy and who at the end point out her lonely future to Electra, leaving her only the consolation of knowing justice has been done to the criminals who slew her father. She is still sure that a fatherland can only be saved by pure hands, like hers, not by bloodstained ones, like those of Aegisthus and Clytemnestra, and in that belief she finds some comfort.

Such an ending is characteristic of most of Giraudoux' plays. Like Shakespeare, he does not invent his main plots, but unlike Shakespeare he rather dehumanizes his characters, many of whom have been compared by French critics to Platonic Forms, each representative of an idea. Certainly he is no sentimental romanticist; in spite of his often poetic atmosphere and his striving for beauty of description and of musical phrase that have caused him to be called the *"Prince des Précieux,"* he is not without deep feeling. The desolation that surrounds Electra as we see her, alone at last, in the light of her burning city, the slow opening of the great doors of Troy as all hope of peace vanishes there, are symbols of human tragedy that are not merely the ironic expression of "preciosity" but that picture unforgettably the contradiction between human aspiration and the chaos brought about by our murderous, revengeful drives toward destruction. Giraudoux had not read Sophocles, Shakespeare and Racine without sharing their emotion as they watch the antics of "this quintessence of dust." Pity and terror are never far below the surface of his irony.

[W. S.]

THE KING AND THE DUKE (1939)

I suppose that *Huckleberry Finn* makes its most intimate appeal to those who read it in childhood, especially if their childhood was passed not too far from Huck's country. It seems to assume that the reader has south-western rhythms of speech in his ears, and has always known a wide river, bordered with cottonwoods, placid-looking in summer, dangerous, swift and muddy at high-water. It is one of those natural products of the poetic imag-ination, like *Don Quixote,* which is part of the inner life of a people and their country.

But such works have more to offer than nostalgia, they have a legendary quality which grows upon one with age. The story of the King and the Duke, simple though it is, seems to carry a great weight of American experience. If those greedy tramps can get an audience for "the balcony scene from *Romeo and Juliet,*" if they can persuade Piperville that they are foreign heirs, and "saw the King," it is because they appeal to the early-republican appetite for royalty and all its trappings. But this appetite for ancestral dreams of glory in the pure and empty air of the new continent is still with us, together with the feeling that it is doomed to disappointment on this side of the ocean. We still marvel at Russian princes in exile, British novelists who can call the great by their first names; and part of the fun is in the irony with which we enjoy them. The fakery, the venality, and the deep pathos of this complex theme is realized, once and for all, in the story of the King and the Duke.

In the book the King and the Duke are of course part of Huck's adven-tures along the river, and it would be impossible to separate their story from that of Huck and Jim. Suffice it to say that Huck's fellow-feeling for them is connected with his remote idealization of Mary Jane, with his lonely and subtle conscience, and with his fear of treachery and violence. Huck never gets beyond childhood, and his pilgrimage is confined to the dimensionless world of the Mississippi River and the little towns spaced far apart along its banks. But who shall say that his adventure with fake royalty is less rich in meaning than Milly Theale's, or Maggie Verver's, when with their childish purity they invade the wider stage of Europe?

The story of the King and the Duke seems to me to invite such specula-tions as these, and perhaps that is why I tried to put it on the stage. But I have tried to leave all interpretation to the audience, and to stick as closely as possible to the story itself, as one should do with a legend, or a story which children like. I have made no attempt to appeal to a highbrow audience, or, on the other hand, to fit the show into the taste and the con-ventions of contemporary musical comedy. Most of the dialogue is straight from the book; and I have tried for a theatrical style which should be as close as possible to Mark Twain's narrative.

The Stage itself is based on that of the Minstrel Show, which was in its prime when Mark Twain was writing *Huckleberry Finn.* I have in mind baroque cut-out wings, like those of the provincial opera-houses of the period; a painted back-drop of a scene along the Mississippi River, and a semi-circle of chairs (perhaps gilded) for the Piperville crowd, which forms a Minstrel-like chorus from time to time. I attempt to present the story in a Minstrel style also, rather than as a naturalistic play, or, on the other hand, as a Broadway Musical. The Minstrel Show, it is true, never developed very far toward drama, but its popular ballad style seemed to me a theatrical approximation to the style of the story as I see it. The Minstrel Show consisted of songs and dances by the chorus, interspersed with jokes and brief dialogue-interludes by the Interlocutor and the End Men. In this play the episodes of the story correspond to the interludes, and the musical and danced parts develop from the funeral and the auction, as celebrated by the Piperville crowd.

The main change in Mark Twain's story which I was obliged to make in order to stage it in this Minstrel style was in increasing the role of Deacon Lot Hovey. I have made him the town auctioneer, and the caller for the town's play-parties, as well as the undertaker. When he takes charge of the celebrations, he plays the role of the Interlocutor, and the crowd becomes a Minstrel chorus.

As for the lyrics, for which I am responsible, they are based upon Minstrel songs, play-party games, and hymns. When we experimented with an early version of this show in Bennington in the ill-fated summer of 1939, Mr. Gregory Tucker provided the music, based upon the tunes of the period. His musical setting, which had both the humor and the nostalgia which was required, proved to be at least as important as the staging itself. The music, if it is right, suggests the popular inner life of the period from which the whole action springs.

The only real excuse for trying to put the King and the Duke, Huck and Jim and Mary Jane on the stage is that one is fond of their story, and wishes to celebrate it publicly. The show is intended for those who are also fond of the story, and like to mull it over. "Poetry of the theatre," says M. Cocteau, "is a drop of poetry under a microscope." My intention in making this show was to use the theatre in this way—as a means of revealing, and then celebrating, a drop of poetry from *Huckleberry Finn*.

[F. F.]

THE DARK TOWER (1946)

Having in my Introduction to *Christopher Columbus* essayed a general exposition of radio-dramatic writing, I will not labour again those main points which I still consider valid, e.g., that "the first virtue of a radio script is construction." But I would like in some respects to correct myself. That the radio writer "must move on a more or less primitive plane" is, I think now, an overstatement or at least misleadingly expressed. What the radio writer must do, if he hopes to win the freedom of the air, is to appeal *on one plane*—whatever he may be doing on the others—to the more primitive listener and to the more primitive elements in anyone; i.e., he must give them (what Shakespeare gave them) entertainment.[1]

[1]The reception of *The Dark Tower* supports this. Many listeners said that they enjoyed it, found it "beautiful," "exciting," etc.—but had "no idea what it was about." In fact they were caught by the "story" but I flatter myself that, in passing, the story "slipped over" some meaning on them.

In the same Introduction I wrote: "As compared with most contemporary literature, the objective elements will preponderate over the subjective, statement over allusion, synthesis over analysis." This again I want to qualify; the comparison with contemporary *literature* may have misled me. The "psychological" novel, concerned chiefly with "subjective" experiences, deals largely in *oratio obliqua;* even that kind of *oratio recta* used to represent "the stream of consciousness" is usually not much more than a shorthand for the page. But when no character can be presented except through spoken words, whether in dialogue or soliloquy, that very *spokenness* makes this distinction between subjective and objective futile. A character in a radio play, as in a stage play, may say things that actually he never would or could say—the author may be making him utter what is only known to his unconscious—but once he has said them, there they are! As objective as Ben Jonson's Humours are objective. To take an extreme example, Virginia Woolf's novel *The Waves* is often quoted as subjective writing *par excellence;* the characters, thinking in the first person, say things they never could have formulated, being even as small children endowed with the brilliant introspection and the sad philosophy of their creator. I am confident that this method, though probably not this application of it, would be feasible on the air. Listeners might not accept Virginia Woolf's longwindedness, her preciousness, the sameness of her characters, the lack of a "story"—but that in no way proves them "allergic" to subjectivity. Once your characters speak speakable lines—once, to use a horrible piece of jargon, the subjective is objectified—you can get away with anything *so long as you entertain.*

Similarly, the distinctions made in my quotation between statement and allusion and between synthesis and analysis are perhaps equally worthless. It would have been safer to say that in radio dialogue we need a number of things which *sound like* statements—but in spoken dialogue that goes without saying; no two people can keep up a conversation which is one hundred per cent surrealist. As for allusion, not only is it difficult in any context to make any statement which is not also an allusion, i.e., suggestive of something beyond its own definitive meaning, but in all *dramatic* writing a word, let alone a phrase, pulls more than its dictionary weight; the pun is only the crudest example of a procedure familiar to, though not of course formulated by, everyone. In characterisation equally, Mr. X, who may appear to be talking at random and naturalistically, can really be talking succinctly and also symbolically, revealing himself—or whatever else is meant to be revealed—by a process of implicit logic. "Implicit" is here, as in other creative writing, a key-word. Even in the psychological novel, if it is a good one, the psychology is implicit; for explicit psychology we go to the textbooks. This is all I meant in subordinating analysis to synthesis— but this too could have gone without saying or at least I ought so to have expressed it as not to preclude "psychological" characterisation from the sphere of radio drama.

But criticism comes after the event; it is no good talking about radio until you have experienced it. It may therefore be instructive if, dropping generalities, I make a short confession of my own experiences as listener, script-writer, and producer. Before I joined the B. B. C. I was, like most of the intelligentsia, prejudiced not only against that institution but against broadcasting in general; I rarely listened to anything except concerts and running commentaries on sports events. These latter, which gave me a pleasure distinct from that which lies in *seeing* a game or race, should have provided a hint of radio's possibilities; my prejudice, however, prevented me from exploring the possible pleasures in wireless plays and features. Since then I have listened to many examples of both and must confess that often they give me no pleasure at all—but this proves nothing; we have all met the same disappointment with books, plays, and films. What does prove a point to me is that *some* plays and features have excited, amused, moved me. So the wireless *can* be worth listening to. But next: is it worth writing for?

Many writers are deterred from radio drama by fear of the middlemen and by dislike of actors. They expect their work to be doctored from the start and travestied in the presentation (which has of course sometimes happened—as it has happened both on the stage and page). But while no production will ever seem perfect to the author, the questions are whether one can gamble on a reasonably good production and whether such a production is better than none. Your answers depend on whether you really have an itch for drama; if you have, you must want sooner or later to write dialogue to be spoken somewhere—and it is no more likely to be spoken badly on the air than anywhere else (the wireless lacks the body of the stage—but also some of its impurities). If *you* provide a good script, the odds are that it will gain by being broadcast; in fact, if it loses, while it may be the fault of the production, the more likely inference is that your script was not radiogenic (a handy word, though jargon). The predominance of adapted stageplays in B.B.C. programmes has probably discouraged a number of writers, for many of these plays do lose on the air (at least as compared with the stage); few of them are radiogenic. Transposition from one medium to another is usually unfair to both. Which is why we must remember that the script-writer is a peculiar species.

The all-important difference between visual and non-visual drama, while discouraging some, may encourage others towards radio, for here and here alone can one listen to calculated speech divorced from all visual supports or interferences—even from a printed page. It would be a great pity if television were ever completely to supersede sound broadcasting as the talkies superseded the silent films. That cinema revolution was inevitable but through it we lost the unique pleasure of watching a story told visually, dispensing with people's voices. But sound alone is for most people more potent, more pregnant, more subtle, than pictures alone and for that reason— regardless of the material pros and cons of television—I hope that sound broadcasting will survive, dispensing with people's faces. As with many other media its narrow limits are also its virtue, while within those limits it can give us something unobtainable from print (though print of course will always retain its proper autonomy). When I first heard a piece, which I had written for broadcasting, broadcast, I was irritated by details of presentation but excited and delighted by the total effect (there was more to my script, I felt, than I myself had realised). The mere fact that one's words issue from other people's mouths, while gratifying no doubt to an author's vanity, is also a welcome release from his involuntary egotism. Most novelists and poets, I think, envy the playwright that specious present and that feeling of *sharedness* which are given to a play by every fresh production, just as they envy the painter as composer-executant the excitement of his manual craftsmanship and the immediate impact of his completed work (which also can be shared by several people at once). When you have written for the page, you do not see your readers reading you; which is just as well as you could never tell if in their heads they were "hearing" you properly. But in broadcasting you can, given the right speakers, force your listeners at least to hear the words as they should. The point is that here we have a means by which written lines can emulate the impact of a stage or of a painting and give the writer that excitement of a sensuous experience simultaneously shared with many which is one of the joys of life. This pleasure in a thing-being-performed-and-shared, while obtainable in all sports and some of the arts, is sadly lacking in the world of literature today. It is a pleasure I have often received, though mixed at times with mortification, when hearing my own scripts broadcast. It is succeeded, as I said before, by a feeling of frustration—because it is "over"; but in that it is not of course unusual.

I have stressed this fact of pleasure because some people assume that writing for the wireless must be hackwork. It often is—for the salaried script-writer because he must turn his hand to many things, some of them dull, for the occasional writer (less forgivably) when he deals with an uncongenial subject for money or writes badly because he is merely writing for money. But it often is not. Broadcasting is plastic; while it can ape the Press, it can also emulate the arts. Yes, people will say, that is theoretically true but in practice you will never get art—or anything like it—out of a large public institution, encumbered with administrators, which by its nature must play for safety and to the gallery. This is not the place to dispute this at length but I would maintain that in this country such an institution cannot be really authoritarian; with ingenuity and a little luck a creative person can persuade (or fool) at least some of the administrators some of the time.[2] And, thinking of the vexed question of commercial broadcasting, I would add that many of the more original programmes by my friends and myself (including *The Dark Tower*) would have been no more acceptable to sponsored radio than to the biggest and vulgarest profit-making film company. For its acceptance of such experiments I am very grateful to the **B.B.C.**

In this age of irreconcilable idioms I have often heard writers hankering for some sort of group life, a desire doomed to disappointment; the modern writer—at any rate the modern poet—is *ipso facto* a spiritual isolationist who will lose far more than he will gain by trying to pool his mentality with those of his colleagues. Thus of the several dozen poets whom I know there are very few with whom I would wish to discuss poetry and only, I think, one from whom I would often accept criticism. This solitude (which incidentally

---

[2] I am not suggesting that, as things are, all our administrators need persuading or fooling.

has nothing to do with the Ivory Tower; there are Group Towers too, remember) is *in our time* salutary—but here again we cannot but envy playwrights, actors or musical executants. And here again I for one have found this missing group experience, in a valid form, in radio. Radio writers and producers *can* talk shop together because their shop is not, as with poets, a complex of spiritual intimacies but a matter of craftsmanship. Though the poet of course is also—or should be—a craftsman, the lyrical poet's technique is—or should be—closely wedded to his unique personality and there is no more point in defending your own personality than in impugning your friend's. But radio craftsmanship, like stage craftsmanship, is something much less private; we are fully entitled to discuss whether dialogue rings true, whether the dramatic climax is dramatic, how well the whole thing works. This is refreshing for a writer.

The popular assumption that all radio professionals resemble civil servants (resting on that other assumption that civil servants are automata) is flatly untrue. The department to which, at the date of writing, I belong in the B.B.C. would compare very well for intelligence with almost any contemporary salon of literati; my radio colleagues would be found on the whole quicker-witted, more versatile, less egocentric, less conventional, more humane. But, apart from these relishes to discussion, the reason why we can work together enjoyably and effectively is that in every case our work must go through the same mill, i.e., into a microphone and out at the other end through a wireless set. This very simple physical fact is such a bond of union as is rare among creative writers, playwrights again excepted. For we share the excitements and anxieties of *the performance*. This is especially so if we are our own executants, i.e., writer-producers. There are obvious drawbacks to this combination of functions—Mr. A as writer may see so clearly what he means that Mr. A as producer will fail to notice when the meaning is not coming over—but it does put a writer more closely in touch with his work-in-performance that he can be anywhere else unless he is Mr. Noel Coward. We know what happens to a film script when the multitude of "experts" gets hold of it. On the stage there is no such multitude but there still is considerable interference and few writers have the chance, the time, the knowledge, or the capacity, to become stage-producers. But radio production being comparatively simple, not a few writers can learn to handle it—at any rate well enough to gain more than they lose (this especially applies to "experimental" scripts where the pioneer, though an amateur, has an advantage over the professional geographer).

The script itself, after all, is only half the battle and the writer who merely sends in a script and does not go near the studios is working largely in the dark; whereas a writer who produces his own scripts will cut his coat according to his cloth. Since I have been producing my own programmes, I find that I both avail myself of facilities which I previously overlooked and avoid awkwardnesses which I previously imposed on my producer. Similarly, as regards both music and actors, the writer-producer has the advantage of being able to decide at an early stage who is going to do what. Thus, when he has a composer to write special music, he can not only get this music to fit the script but adjust his script on occasion to fit the music.

He also has the say in casting, which is especially important in broadcasting both because of the shortness of rehearsals and because of the microphone's transparency to anything ham or unintelligent. In writing my more recent scripts I have always had an eye on the kinds of actor available and so avoided demanding the impossible and, when I could, the improbable; sometimes I have, from its conception, written a part for a particular actor.

The preceding paragraph was intended to amplify my point about work-in-performance. While it is obviously not normally feasible for "outside writers" to produce their own work, it is desirable, if not necessary, that they should be studio-minded; then they can explain to their producer what they want done without being embarrassing or nonsensical. I would like finally, since the chief object of this was to disprove the assumption that broadcasting is "inhuman," to inform my readers that every transmission of a play or feature, however unimportant the programme, should have—and usually has—the feeling of a First Night; it is something *being made* by a team of people. . . .

The Dark Tower is a parable play, belonging to that wide class of writings which includes *Everyman*, *The Faerie Queene* and *The Pilgrim's Progress*. Though under the name of allegory this kind of writing is sometimes dismissed as outmoded, the clothed as distinct from the naked allegory is in fact very much alive. Obvious examples are *Peer Gynt* and the stories of Kafka but also in such books as *The Magic Mountain* by Thomas Mann, where the disguise of "realism" is maintained and nothing happens that is quite inconceivable in life, it is still the symbolic core which makes the work important. My own impression is that pure "realism" is in our time almost played out, though most works of fiction of course will remain realistic *on the surface*. The single-track mind and the single-plane novel or play are almost bound to falsify the world in which we live. The fact that there is method in madness and the fact that there is fact in fantasy (and equally fantasy in "fact") have been brought home to us not only by Freud and other psychologists but by events themselves. This being so, reportage can no longer masquerade as art. So the novelist, abandoning the "straight" method of photography, is likely to resort once more not only to the twist of plot but to all kinds of other twists which may help him to do justice to the world's complexity. Some element of parable therefore, far from making a work thinner and more abstract, ought to make it more concrete. Man does after all live by symbols.

The dual-plane work will not normally be allegory in the algebraic sense; i.e., it will not be desirable or even possible to equate each of the outward and visible signs with a precise or rational inner meaning. Thus *The Dark Tower* was suggested to me by Browning's poem "Childe Roland to the Dark Tower came," a work which does not admit of a completely rational analysis and still less adds up to any clear moral or message. This poem has the solidity of a dream; the writer of such a poem, though he may be aware of the "meanings" implicit in his dream, must not take the dream to pieces, must present his characters concretely, must allow the story to persist as a story and not dwindle into a diagram. While I could therefore have offered here an explicit summary of those implicit "meanings" in *The Dark*

Tower of which I myself was conscious, I am not doing so, because it might impair the impact of the play. I would merely say—for the benefit of people like the *Daily Worker's* radio critic, who found the programme pointless and depressing—that in my opinion it is neither. *The Faerie Queene, The Pilgrim's Progress, Piers Plowman* and the early Moralities could not have been written by men without any beliefs. In an age which precludes the simple and militant faith of a Bunyan, belief (whether consciously formulated or not) still remains a *sine qua non* of the creative writer. I have my beliefs and they permeate *The Dark Tower*. But do not ask me what Ism it illustrates or what Solution it offers. You do not normally ask for such things in the single-plane work; why should they be forced upon something much more complex? "Why, look you now, how unworthy a thing you make of me!" What is life *useful* for anyway?

Comments on points of detail will be found at the end of this article. The best in this kind are but shadows—and in print they are shadows of shadows. To help the reader to *hear* this piece, I will therefore add this: in production I got the actors to play their parts "straight," i.e., like flesh and blood (in dreams the characters are usually like flesh and blood too). Out of an excellent cast I am particularly grateful to Cyril Cusack for his most sensitive rendering of "Roland." And Benjamin Britten provided this programme with music which is, I think, the best I have heard in a radio play. Without his music *The Dark Tower* lacks a dimension.

Page 387. *Roland as a boy* was, in the broadcast, brilliantly doubled by Cyril Cusack.

Page 391. *The tolling bell,* instead of being done by percussion alone, was reinforced and made ultra-suggestive by strings. Apart from percussion and one trumpet (reserved for the Challenge Call) Benjamin Britten confined himself in this programme to an orchestra of twenty-six strings from which he got the most varied and astonishing effects.

Page 392. *The Child of Stone* puzzled many listeners. The Mother in bearing so many children only to send them to their death can be thought of as thereby bearing a series of deaths. So her logical last child is stone—her own death. This motif has an echo in the stone in the ring.

Page 393. *The Verbal Transition* from one scene to another is controlled from the panel and need not seem either abrupt or confusing. It not only makes a change from the musical transition but has certain positive advantages; e.g., as here, irony.

Page 399. *The Soak* I should have called Solipsist if that word were known to the public. His alcoholism is an effect rather than a cause. Robert Farquharson wonderfully achieved the right leer in the voice and the dream-like sinister undertones.

Page 402. *"I'm dreaming you"* is a famous stumper for reason. Compare *Alice Through the Looking Glass,* the episode of Tweedledee and the Red King:

"'And if he left off dreaming about you, where do you suppose you'd be?'
'Where I am now, of course,' said Alice.
'Not you!' Tweedledee retorted contemptuously. 'You'd be nowhere. Why, you're only a sort of thing in his dream!'"

Page 402. *The Stentorian Voice* butting in here changes the scene with the speed of a dream. Radio, like dreams, having no set stage, can disregard spatial conventions.

Page 407. *"The sea today"*: this covers a number of days. The developing false idyl of Roland and Neaera is intercut with the voices of people playing tombola—always the same again. The idyl also is merely killing time.

Page 416. *The Mirage Sequence* needed a great deal of rehearsal but the stunt came off.

Page 420. *The Final Decision* may, I think, be too abrupt for a listener—though in life such a complex psychological conflict can, of course, resolve itself abruptly.

Page 421. *The Last Scene* is naturally the nearest to Browning. Compare:

> "Not see? because of night perhaps?—why day
> Came back again for that! before it left,
> The dying sunset kindled through a cleft:
> The hills, like giants at a hunting, lay,
> Chin upon hand, to see the game at bay,—
> 'Now stab and end the creature—to the heft!'

> Not hear? when noise was everywhere! it tolled
> Increasing like a bell. Names in my ears
> Of all the lost adventurers my peers. . . ."
>
> [L. M.]

GALILEO (1937, 1947)

1. This version of *Galileo* was used in the Coronet Theatre, Los Angeles, 1947, and in the Maxine Elliott Theatre, New York, 1947, both times with Charles Laughton in the title role.

2. The script was made by Mr. Brecht and Mr. Laughton working in close collaboration. New elements were introduced which will be taken over into the German text. (The first German version—as of 1937—has been faithfully rendered into English by Desmond Vesey.)

3. The quatrains preceding each scene were written in English by Mr. Brecht (who, by the way, describes them as "doggerel"). They were sung by three choir boys to music by Hanns Eisler.

4. Scene fourteen was omitted in performance. The trio sang the quatrain which precedes the omitted scene, plus this one:

> May you now guard Science' light
> Kindle it and use it right
> Lest it be a flame to fall
> Downward to consume us all.

5. Producers who have not the facilities for much music can omit the sung doggerel and substitute the following titles, which may be projected or painted on a curtain or screen.

Scene One. GALILEO GALILEI, PROFESSOR OF PHYSICS AT THE

UNIVERSITY OF PADUA, STRUGGLES TO ESTABLISH THAT THE EARTH MOVES ROUND THE SUN.

Scene Two. AUGUST 24, 1609. GALILEO PRESENTS A NEW INVENTION TO THE REPUBLIC OF VENICE.

Scene Three. JANUARY 10, 1610. GALILEO ABOLISHES HEAVEN.

Scene Four. GALILEO HAS MOVED FROM THE REPUBLIC OF VENICE TO THE FLORENTINE COURT.

Scene Five. CHRISTOPHER CLAVIUS OF THE PAPAL COLLEGE IN ROME UPHOLDS GALILEO'S DISCOVERIES.

Scene Six. FEBRUARY 19, 1616. CARDINAL BELLARMIN ENTERTAINS.

Scene Seven. THE PEOPLE.

Scene Eight. 1623. GALILEO HEARS ENCOURAGING NEWS FROM ROME.

Scene Nine. ALL FOOL'S DAY 1632. THE CHAMBER OF COMMERCE OF THE TOWNSHIP OF RAPALLO HAS CHOSEN ASTRONOMY AS THE THEME OF THIS YEAR'S CARNIVAL PROCESSION.

Scene Ten. THE INQUISITION SUMMONS GALILEO TO ROME.

Scene Eleven. THE POPE.

Scene Twelve. JUNE 22, 1633. GALILEO RECANTS.

Scene Thirteen. 1633-1642. GALILEO REMAINS A PRISONER OF THE INQUISITION UNTIL HIS DEATH.

Scene Fourteen. 1637. GALILEO'S GREAT BOOK The Discorsi LEAVES ITALY.

6. Scene Nine as described in the present version (with characters suggested by Breughel) proved too complex to use in the 1947 productions. The song was used as printed in the text but the stage-directions were as follows:

A ballad singer, carrying a drum, and his wife, carrying a suckling babe and a big bundle, enter the market place of an Italian town. Another child walks at their side. A small crowd, partly in masquerade, is waiting for the carnival procession. After a brief introduction ("Ladies and gentlemen, while we are awaiting the carnival procession I should like to present to you the sensational new ballad OF THE DISCOVERIES OF GALILEO GALILEI THE COURT MATHEMATICIAN OF FLORENCE otherwise known as FOREBODINGS OF THE FUTURE") the ballad singer sings his ballad. At the conclusion of his song, he says "Ladies and Gentlemen, see Galileo Galilei's great phenomenon: the earth turning round the sun." He pounds the drum. His wife and child step forward. The wife holds a crude image of the sun. The child circles round the wife holding up a pumpkin, image of the earth. The ballad singer points at the child as though it were performing a *salto mortale* at each step (there is a drum tap for each step). Drums backstage. A deep voice cries: "The procession!" Enter two men in rags drawing a litter with a mock throne on it. On the throne a figure with a mock crown, clad in sackcloth, and looking through a telescope. Above the throne a signboard: THE DUKE OF FLORENCE LOOKING FOR TROUBLE! Four masked men march in, carrying a large blanket. They stop and toss a dummy into the air; it is the effigy of a bishop. A dwarf bears a signboard: THE

NEW AGE. In the crowd a crippled beggar raises himself on his crutches and beats the ground in time with the four masked men (they toss the dummy rhythmically) till he falls with a crash. Enter a gigantic effigy of Galileo, bowing to the public. Ahead of the effigy a child in a sack bears an enormous bible with the two visible pages crossed out in black crayon. The ballad singer cries: "Galileo, the bible killer!" A respectable-looking man in the crowd steps forward and quietly lifts the robe of a monk who is bending down to help the beggar. Laughter.

The 1937 version is even simpler. Here is Desmond Vesey's translation:

A street in an Italian city. A Street Singer and his wife sing a song to the accompaniment of a hurdy-gurdy. At the windows people listen and laugh.
STREET SINGER. Beautiful ladies and noble gentlemen. We will now sing the latest Florentine song, which is to be heard all over upper Italy and which we have brought here at great expense. The song is entitled
THE BALLAD OF THE TERRIBLE TEACHINGS OF GALILEO GALILEI

The great Galilei once said to the sun
Unto the sun said he:
As a light to the earth your work is done
So turn no more round me.
Oh hey! Oh hey!
So the earth began to turn round itself
Instead of round Galilei.

And from that day on, when no more the sun
Did serve us for a light,
Not a man did behind his master run
Nor squire behind his knight.
Hey oh! Hey oh!
For each man prefers to turn round himself
And pick out the way he shall go.

The builder who builds a new house, I see,
Now takes it for his own.
And the wood-cutter who cuts down the tree
He burns the wood at home.
Oh hey! Oh hey!
For the woodman he said to his wife, said he,
The weather is cooler today.

The ladies I saw at the fishwife's stand,
Can it be true, ah me?
The wife had a loaf of bread in her hand
And she ate her fish, did she.
Hey oh! Hey oh!
For now the fishwife would eat her own fish
And no one can say to her NO.

The maids stay seated, alongside the men,
When Master passes by.
They'll never revolve round him again,
And that's the reason why.
Oh hey! Oh hey!
The maids and the men have enough to do
With themselves all the livelong day!

(WOMAN *only*) And when I was dancing the whole night through
Unto my man, said I:
"Things that are done to me by you
Other fixed stars can try!"
Hey oh! Hey oh!
(MAN *only*) And I lived in the hope that you, my wife,
Were content to be fixed so low!

The princes must polish their boots with grace
The kings must bake their own bread.
The soldiers are strolling around the place.
Commands are disobeyed.
Oh hey! Oh hey!
Too many hands were too busy at once
But now they will rest all the day.

(*Softly and confidentially*)
The cardinals stood in Saint Peter's Square
The Pope Himself passed by.
But the cardinals never knew he was there
And never turned an eye!
Oh hey! Oh hey!
The priests are all kissing their own feet now.
For that you can blame Galilei.

Three archangels came down to earth to chide:
Hosannahs must louder be!
But the earth replied: "There are more earths beside,
So why must it be me?"
Oh hey! Oh hey!
There's more than one earth in the universe,
Let other worlds have their say!"

(During the last verse a Jesuit enters the street. Hearing the song, he dodges and slinks off like a wet cat. The people laugh and throw coins down into the street.)

7. In the original American productions, within the permanent setting by Robert Davison, projections based on drawings by Michelangelo, Leonardo, Callot, Galileo and other masters were used.

8. The general theory of Epic Theatre (exemplified in practice by *Galileo*) has been set forth by Brecht in his notes to *The Threepenny Opera* (see *From the Modern Repertoire,* Series One) and in the essay *A Little Organum for the Theatre* (see *Accent: a Quarterly of New Literature,* Winter, 1951). Among his articles on particular aspects of Epic Theatre are: "A New Technique of Acting," in *Theatre Arts* (New York), January, 1949, and *New Theatre* (London), March, 1949 (also reprinted in the anthology *Actors on Acting,* ed. Cole and Chinoy, New York, 1949); "A Model for Epic Theatre," *The Sewanee Review,* Summer, 1949; and "Chinese Acting," *Furioso,* Autumn, 1949.

[E. B.]

N. B. In Series One were listed the standard, major modern authors who are excluded from this anthology on principle (Ibsen, Strindberg, Chekhov, Pirandello, and Shaw) along with a list of the cheapest editions of their works. This list is already partly out of date. The Luce edition of Strindberg is no longer available but Scribners has issued *Eight Famous Plays.* Dodd, Mead & Co. has published a *Selected Plays* of Shaw in three volumes, while Penguin Books have put a large number of Shaw plays on the market separately, especially in England. The Modern Library has re-issued its Ibsen in the College Editions (with an introduction by Eric Bentley). E. P. Dutton has printed an American Everyman's Library volume of Pirandello (introduction and notes by Eric Bentley).